Desktop Computers

THE JOHNS HOPKINS UNIVERSITY

Applied Physics Laboratory Series in Science and Engineering

SERIES EDITOR: John Apel

William H. Avery and Chin Wu. *Ocean Thermal Energy Conversion* (in press)

Bruce I. Blum. *Software Engineering: A Holistic View*

Richard A. Henle and Boris W. Kuvshinoff. *Desktop Computers: In Perspective*

Vincent L. Pisacane and Robert C. Moore (eds.). *Space Systems*

Desktop Computers
In Perspective

RICHARD A. HENLE
BORIS W. KUVSHINOFF
Applied Physics Laboratory
Johns Hopkins University

EDITOR
C. M. Kuvshinoff

ILLUSTRATOR
A. L. Kundratic

PROGRAMMER
R. D. Bucy

New York   Oxford
OXFORD UNIVERSITY PRESS
1992

Oxford University Press

Oxford   New York   Toronto
Delhi   Bombay   Calcutta   Madras   Karachi
Kuala Lumpur   Singapore   Hong Kong   Tokyo
Nairobi   Dar es Salaam   Cape Town
Melbourne   Auckland

and associated companies in
Berlin   Ibadan

Library of Congress Cataloging-in-Publication Data
Henle, Richard A.
Desktop computers: in perspective / Richard A. Henle, Boris W.
Kuvshinoff; editor, C.M. Kuvshinoff; illustrator, A.L. Kundratic.
p. cm.   (The Johns Hopkins University/Applied Physics
Laboratory series in science and engineering)
Includes index.   ISBN-0-19-507031-3
I. Microcomputers.   2. Microcomputer workstations.
I. Kuvshinoff, Boris W.   II. Kuvshinoff, C.M.   III. Title.
IV. Series.
QA76.5.H4587   1992
004.16—dc20   91–45410

9 8 7 6 5 4 3

Printed in the United States of America
on acid-free paper

To Linda Henle
and
to Hrisa Kuvshinoff

Preface

Desktop computers are now commodity items – bought, sold, and traded much like cameras are now and whiffletrees once were – and yet they remain shrouded in mystery, sometimes enigmatic even to those who use them regularly. Newcomers to computing are obliged to master a new universe of concepts and terminology; even computer veterans can be quite perplexed by the amazing desktop box with the glass eye that is now commonplace wherever people gather to work, do business, or conduct their other affairs.

This book is intended to help you increase your technical literacy across a broad range of topics in the area of DtC.

NOTE

Here and elsewhere *DtC* stands for *desktop computer,* commonly known as *personal computer,* or *PC.* We prefer DtC to PC for at least three reasons: One is that IBM has a product called the *IBM PC,* and we'd like to avoid ambiguity between specifics and generics. Two, personal computers are becoming less personal as they become increasingly integrated into the fabric of the workplace, whether it be an office, a business, a manufacturing concern, or other enterprise. Even at home the desktop computer is becoming a shared necessity, more communal than personal. And three, personal computers are beginning to compete with engineering workstations and are starting to encroach on the once sovereign domain of mainframes, particularly through networking, so that the catchword "personal" no longer applies. The original small, fuzzy, huggable puppy is now a great big grown working dog.

The content should give you sufficient background to begin making the right decisions when selecting DtC workstation hardware and software. After reading this book you may well have more questions than answers. But this is an important step: to be able to ask meaningful questions of individuals who know the answers through personal experience or who at least can guide you around unsuspected pitfalls.

Most importantly, however, this book lays a foundation for technical comprehension of often misunderstood issues that are critical to successful exploitation of DtC technology.

Trademarks and Products:

Product names in this book are trademarks or registered trademarks of their respective developers or manufacturers. Mention of products in text should not be construed as endorsement. What is said about products simply reflects our personal experience with them.

Acknowledgements

The material in this book was gathered from many sources: individuals, organizations, and current literature, blending hands-on user experience and industry-wide know-how.

First, we wish to acknowledge the Janney Fellowship awarded to us by The Johns Hopkins University, Applied Physics Laboratory (APL), for the purpose of revising the manuscript and making it ready for publication. We especially thank Kenneth A. Potocki, Gary L. Smith, and Vincent L. Pisacane for securing that assistance for us. For giving us the necessary flexibility to carry out the work, we would like to thank D. Gilbert Lee, Jr., Duncan P. Crawford, and Harry K. Charles, Jr., all of the APL Engineering and Fabrication Branch of the Technical Services Department, and Waldo T. Renich and Dolores E. Fallon, User Services Center, APL Business and Information Services Department. Without the support of these individuals we would not have been able to complete the manuscript.

Second, we are pleased to acknowledge several outstanding individuals who encouraged us, gave us valuable advice, and served as wellsprings of important information. Notable among these are Robert P. Rich, a colleague who struggled without complaint through two drafts and helped to round out the text with wise and unerring advice; John R. Apel, who negotiated publishing arrangements and gave us some useful "how to" and "what to" pointers; and Doug Crouch, Dale Elkiss, and John Griffin, all seasoned hands in computing, who helped us in their respective fields of expertise.

We would like to thank APL Technical Publications Group staff members Raymond J. Nosko, Jr. and Vanessa M. Grey for assistance in preparing the camera-ready copy, and Diane J. Dorsey and George O. Gill for assistance in preparing graphics. We are indebted to Rodger Bucy, of the APL Business Information Systems Group, who orchestrated the SCRIPT-to-PostScript conversion and diligently worked out a smooth procedure.

We must mention the efforts of many students who developed interesting viewpoints and discussions through class projects and term papers researched for the courses, "Small Computer Operating Systems and Applications" and "Small Computer Architecture and Interfacing," taught at The JHU Whiting School of Engineering from 1981 to the present. Special thanks go to the Summer '91 term students Beverly Irons, Roger Ratliff, and Mark Glavach, who performed prepublication technical reviews and updates in their subject areas of expertise. In particular, thanks to Isaac Berlin, who reviewed the manuscript, for correcting many errors and sharing his valuable insight. Sincere thanks also go to several colleagues and individuals at large who contributed ideas and material and reviewed parts of the manuscript. Specifically, we would like to recognize David Heldenbrand, Tracy C. Herriotts, Eugene F. Kiley, and Donald W. Reichle. Thanks also to Monica Suchoski, who proofread parts of the manuscript.

We are especially grateful to Allen L. Kundratic, Staff Artist of the APL Technical Publications Group, who worked his magic on the figures and other illustrations that make the text more readily understandable; and to C. M. Kuvshinoff, our editor, who shepherded the book through manuscript preparation and printing.

RAH/BWK

Table of Contents

List of Illustrations

List of Tables

INTRODUCTION

A few years ago computing was characterized by mainframe applications that were relatively inflexible with regard to individual user's needs. More recently, a huge market was discovered for DtCs and their almost infinite variety of accoutrements designed for small, individualized tasks. DtCs freed users from the mainframe in the same way that personal cars freed people from dependence on public transportation.

The early, relatively slow personal computers of the 80s have evolved into something we can no longer call personal computers. When first introduced, personal computers were considered a lot better than paper and pencil, some better than an electric typewriter, but little more. Good for simple stuff, you know.

The status of personal computers has been greatly elevated as we cross the threshold of the 90s. Many microcomputer users now refer to their IBMs, Apple Macintoshes, and Commodore Amigas as workstations, a term previously reserved for engineering workstations. The term 'workstation' is coming into favor because microcomputers are beginning to dominate the workplace; literally taking over from the minicomputer and the mainframe. What then is the difference between a personal computer, an engineering workstation, a minicomputer, a mainframe, and a super computer? An unequivocal answer is impossible because of the overlaps that have developed between these hardware categories.

The personal computer now can resemble each of these depending on how it is configured and networked. Spectacular advances in hardware capability and software performance have transmuted yesterday's personal computer into today's DtC workstation.

Appeal of Desktop Computing

The attraction of desktop computing to small-scale users, as it matured to its present state, is fourfold. The first and perhaps most important is that DtC technology, though modest in performance, allowed DtCs to drop into the price range of the general public; the second is the increasing availability of off-the-shelf software packages that can be used by nonprogrammers to handle almost any computing problem of interest to them; third is the realization that a lot of simple problems can be solved very well with low-level computer assistance; and the fourth is being able to personally define the system and completely control the computing environment, usage rules, and peripheral configuration for the application.

Factors that you most likely will need to control include:

- **Peripheral configurations** – Hard disk alternatives, graphics interfaces and display modes, memory expansion, printer operational modes, and interface types; e.g., parallel, serial, bus.
- **Operating system configurations** – Hard drive partitioning and buffering, I/O redirection, widowing and multitasking setup, system initialization modes, and installation of a multitude of special enhancement software.
- **Applications software products** – Selection of software products to find the best match to the required application.
- **Utility programs** – Choices involve thousands of commercial and public domain programs that can enhance or customize both operating system and applications program performance.

But this smorgasbord is by no means a free lunch. With these marvelous capabilities comes the responsibility of learning a great deal about the system you own, what it is, how to care for it, and how to use it properly.

Thumbnail History of Personal Computing

In 1981, IBM entered the personal computer marketplace and popularized the machine. In 1984, Apple Macintosh popularized public use of the 68000 microprocessor in a friendly environment. Since then, sophisticated DtC applications packages have become available. As expansion hardware edged personal computers toward architecturally imposed limits, software became available that exploited the enhanced capabilities. Further significant advances have been made lately in hardware and software to make desktop computers not only more versatile and powerful, but also easier to use.

The chronology that follows this Introduction marks a few of the more significant events and advances in microcomputing since 1972 and includes a glimpse through the mist of the immediate future.

During the same time period equally far-reaching advances occurred for software. Software innovations include:

- Debut of the spreadsheet, which popularized microcomputers.
- Availability of word processors for the masses.
- New approaches to information management.
- Improvements in user interfaces (sliding bar and pop-up menus, context-sensitive user help, and program tutorials).
- Effective use of system resources (print spooling and disk caching).
- Seamless integration of multiple software functions such as form letters, combined text/graphics systems (desktop publishing), and integration of database, graphics, and word processing functions (integrated software).
- Innovative approaches to numerical processing and engineering/scientific analysis.
- Local area network shared software applications.
- Graphical user interfaces available for all popular DtCs.
- OOP (Object Oriented Programming) software.
- Birth of data visualization software.
- Practical applications of artificial intelligence on DtCs.

The Synergy of DtC and Mainframe Computing

Until recently, mainframe computer applications were much more sophisticated than DtC applications. DtC versions of selected mainframe programs were available, but they were generally limited-feature versions of the mainframe original.

Now, the positions have reversed in many applications areas. One major area is word processing, where we find efforts to produce a mainframe word processing package as suitable for individual users as the DtC packages that are already available. Striking developments in flexible and interactive database management systems, spreadsheets, and other information processing software have created entirely new categories of software.

The appearance in the marketplace of personal computers with third generation mainframe capabilities is now a reality and software developers may be expected to offer products on the DtC market first, with mainframe versions to follow. This turnabout has occurred because of the:

- interactive nature of the DtC.
- sheer number of DtC users with appropriate applications development tools.
- variety and flexibility of applications development tools and the large user base – more individuals are motivated to create DtC applications.
- vendor's ability to respond more quickly, make adjustments during development, and get new products to market faster.
- more powerful DtCs (CPU, graphics, mass store, coprocessors).

As prices continue to fall, each user can have his own dedicated computer without paying overhead for a shared CPU and related resources. Although a complete DtC is much more expensive than a mainframe terminal, the overall advantage in most circumstances far outweighs the difference in cost. Response times for relatively small DtC applications are quite tolerable compared to those encountered when sharing mainframe resources. Still, processing tasks such as large scale simulations and querying large databases continue to be more appropriate on mainframe computers. Now evolving are multitasking DtC operating systems that allow users to perform many tasks at once. Multiusing is not a limitation when each user can easily afford his own dedicated system. Local area networks now provide the necessary communications between DtC workstations and mainframes for data and resource sharing. Since computing nodes now have considerable intelligence, communications capabilities are being manifested in ways we are only beginning to understand. Some day, tasks may be shared transparently between the DtC and mainframe, as well as between individual DtCs, with the user oblivious to which box is doing what.

We can speculate with a measure of confidence that whatever functions that can be, will be accommodated by networks of DtCs supported by expert staffs. Forces that once acted strongly to centralize computing services are now favoring the dispersal of computing equipment and resources to points where data are generated and used. This trend, moreover, is accelerating because more and more application areas are being discovered and the DtC cost/performance ratio is improving continuously in all important respects.

The DtC has become the hub of the computing universe. Dedicated to the individual, it can be custom configured for each specific need, as shown in the figure. The three major classes of such applications are:

1. **Dedicated applications** – Those that are more suitable for individually owned desktop computing systems. Local performance can compete with or exceed that of the mainframe due to dedicated processing power, interactivity, and custom

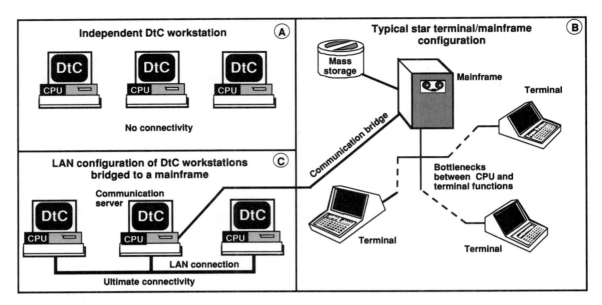

Connecting the DtC

interfaces. These applications will often be smaller than their mainframe counter-parts due to various DtC system limitations.

2. **DtC/mainframe applications** – Those that use programs and data which have processing elements on a mainframe and on DtCs. In fact, the DtC has a distinct advantage in the mainframe world as a highly flexible and versatile remote data entry terminal. Sometimes user-unfriendly mainframe applications can be made practically automatic using DtC custom data entry systems, distributed data networks, and various other data collection and pre-processing schemes. The DtC can be a powerful interface between the specific needs of users and the more general data processing capabilities of mainframe computers. Customizing can take many forms, including personalized user interfacing.

3. **LAN-based applications** – Those that use DtCs in *local area networks*. These applications may share peripherals that are connected to other DtCs in the network and share data between DtC workstations and other computers on the network. These applications are in their infancy, but are the most versatile and powerful ones for meeting the most diversified needs.

One can think of the DtC as a capacious chest of wonderous tools that can work with fine detail on small, dedicated jobs or hack away at large mainframe-type applications. Among the tools you will find

- *Writing tools* – Configurable editors, word processors, and desktop publishers.
- *Information management tools* – Flexible DBM systems, spreadsheets, project management software.
- *Communications tools* – Flexible communications locally and worldwide.
- *Language tools* – Hundreds of general-purpose and application-specific languages to solve any problem.

- **Object-oriented tools** – Intuitive and powerful software to elevate the developer above the details of algorithms and concentrate on teh data that is being manipulated.
- **CAD/CAE and display graphic tools** – Today's DtCs have the processing punch to perform graphics-intensive applications.
- **Engineering and scientific software tools** – Easing the drudgery of complex analytical tasks and providing a range of interactive analysis tools never imagined previously.
- **Experimental tools** – Preprogrammed systems for simulating neural networks, playing with chaos and fractals, and experimenting even with fuzzy logic.
- **Hardware add-ons** – An almost infinite array of special hardware add-ons from environmental control to optical character recognition.

And, all of the tools above can be operated from an intuitive graphical user interface. When DtCs and mainframe computers complement one another in this manner, benefits are amplified: the sum of computing capability becomes greater than its parts.

Microcomputing Milestones

YEAR	MILESTONE

1971 – ▪ First 4-bit microprocessor, dedicated ROM, no operating system.

1973 – ▪ ALTO computer introduces icon and mouse environment.

1975 – ▪ Microcomputers using 8-bit 8080 processor under CP/M operating system accommodate programs up to 48K.

▪ Beginning of the personal computer concept.

1977 – ▪ Apple introduces 8-bit 6502-based Apple II with 48K program sizes, novel graphics, and popularizes personal computing.

▪ Radio Shack popularizes personal computers with Z80 based TRS-80.

▪ Commodore introduces Commodore PET personal computer.

1978 – ▪ Corvus network for Apple II.

1979 – ▪ Large workstations based on 16-bit Motorola 68000. Most run under the Unix operating system, which supports the 16 MB addressability of the 68000.

1981 – ▪ IBM introduces 16-bit 8088 personal computer with 640K program/data areas.

▪ Personal computers become accepted business tools.

▪ Other manufacturers begin work on IBM-like MS-DOS computers.

▪ Pac Man becomes enormously popular video game.

▪ Over half a million units sold.

▪ First general-purpose network hardware for PCs from 3COM and Orchid.

1982 – ▪ Compaq Corporation produces first IBM clone and first portable PC. The spreadsheet arrives: Lotus introduces 1-2-3, a popular favorite even today.

▪ 3COM and Novell network operating systems.

1983 – ▪ Commodore releases the C-64, which becomes the most popular home computer of the day. PC sales top 1.5 million units.

1984 – ▪ Apple introduces the Macintosh computer, based on the 68000, popularizing public use of the Motorola 68000 microprocessor. Apple sets the standard for the graphical user interface. The system is affordable and runs the Apple proprietary operating system. Programs generally limited to 512K. AppleTalk is introduced.

▪ IBM introduces the AT based on the 16-bit Intel 80286 microprocessor. The AT becomes a business standard. Addresses 16 MB but MS-DOS limits program and data space to approximately 1 MB. Most previous 640K programs converted to use the MS-DOS supported 1 MB addressability.

▪ PC sales exceed 2.6 million units.

1986 – ▪ Various methodologies evolve for limited use of >1 MB memory models on MS-DOS computers, but no popular OS support.

▪ Laser printers by Apple, Hewlett-Packard, and others appear, making desktop publishing a reality.

▪ Sales reach almost 3.3 million units.

1987 – ▪ Apple introduces Mac II based on 32-bit 68020 microprocessor.

- Attempts to popularize more advanced 68020 applications. Advanced workstations using the 68030 microprocessor and custom RISC machines exceed rates of 15 MIPS.
- Several vendors introduce 80386-based MS-DOS computers implementing an improved AT bus.
- IBM discontinues the PC and begins the Personal System 2 line with an advanced bus structure based on the 32-bit 80386 microprocessor.
- IBM introduces OS/2, an operating system that solves the weaknesses of MS-DOS and is intended to replace MS-DOS. System still limited to 1 MB memory model due to lack of OS support.
- Sun introduces SPARC (Scalable Processor Architecture) CPU in its engineering workstation.
- Total microcomputer sales top 4 million units.

1988 –
- Advanced workstations using 32-bit 68030 and 80386 and RISC microprocessors run under improved Unix versions supporting graphics and windowing compatibility among different system units.
- Major workstation vendors provide MS/DOS backfit capability.
- LAN manager provides centralized network support.
- IBM OS/2 operating system becomes available; supports 16 MB memory models.
- Apple Macintosh IIx supports 68030 microprocessor.

1989 –
- 80386- and 68030-based systems become popular in the public domain.
- Graphics User Interfaces (GUI) appear on all major workstations.
- Operating systems support >16 MB memory and most software categories have products supporting programs of several MB.
- Introduction of Intel 80486 and Motorola 68040 microprocessors in desktop workstations.
- Total microcomputer sales top 5 million.

1990 –
- NeXT computer, NextStep graphic interface development software.
- New 80486-based systems introduced and 80860 processors become available on plug-in boards.
- Intel 586-, 686-, and 786-based systems become discussion topics in current literature.

1991 –
- Microsoft Windows enjoys phenomenal success; up to 4 million copies sold.
- IBM and Apple become partners in software company that is to produce operating systems and applications software.

PART

I

Part I. The World of DtCs

The DtC is a multifaceted tool. At one time it can be a personal editor and check your spelling; at another it can control experiments, technical information, personnel, and stock or parts on hand. Knowing its basic components and how they relate to software, knowing its history, and learning from others' mistakes are essential if you expect to reap benefits from this incredible tool.

The material that follows will give you a broad perspective on relevant issues in desktop computing and is a necessary foundation for the more detailed technical discussions of hardware, operating systems, networks, and peripherals found in the remainder of this book.

The major discussion areas:

Characterize the DtC: Emphasize DtC features that make it a unique interactive computing tool. The focus is on major DtC hardware components, how they differ from their mainframe counterparts, and how they work together. Basic guidelines are given for component selection.

Highlight microcomputer evolution: Tell the story of where DtCs came from and their hereditary links to mainframes and minicomputers.

Compare the principal systems: Place home/business, engineering/production workstations, and entertainment/education DtCs in their appropriate environments and compare their respective roles.

Make the hardware/software connection: Relate hardware and software to performance levels. Once performance levels have been established, hardware and software components can be properly matched to the application that is to be performed. Surprisingly often DtCs are acquired with little attention paid to the software that is to be used.

Treat data transfer and format compatibility: Consider the complicated business of moving data between different platforms and applications programs.

Present operational considerations: Review the factors that must be weighed when preparing to buy a DtC. Also treated are the interdependent relationships between hardware and software, managerial bridges that must be crossed, preventive maintenance tips, system setup recommendations, useful information sources, personnel training needs, and future trends.

MS-DOS Computer Nomenclature

Microcomputer nomenclature can be a jungle of confusion. A few explanatory notes on IBM PCs and their spinoffs are offered to establish a common understanding. MS-DOS computers are based on the Intel 80xxx series of microprocessors (8088, 8086, 80186, 80286, 80386, or 80486) and run the Microsoft Disk Operating System. These microcomputers date to 1981, to the introduction into the market of the IBM PC. Currently, there are more MS-DOS DtCs than any other type.

Original IBM PCs: The first series of microcomputers included the PC (Personal Computer), the XT (eXtended Technology), and the AT (Advanced Technology). The IBM PC was the first of this line.

XT-Style Compatible: Computers manufactured by others that are similar to the original IBM PCs and XTs.

AT-Style Compatible: Computers made by other manufacturers that are similar to the original IBM AT. These machines are based on the 80286 or 80386 microprocessor and IBM's AT bus. Since AT-style computers have 80386 microprocessors, they can in fact differ considerably from IBM's original AT, which supported only the 80286. The common thread is that AT-style computers have the same ISA bus as the original IBM AT with the exception of a few 32-bit slots. This bus is referred to as the AT-bus or ISA (Industry Standard Architecture) bus.

Personal System/2: An IBM line of microcomputers that features the Micro Channel bus.

MCA-Style: Other manufacturers' computers that are similar to the IBM PS/2. MCA refers to the IBM Micro Channel bus. Computers that use this bus, both IBM and others, are called MCA-style computers.

MS-DOS Computers: A general reference to a class of machines that runs the Microsoft Disk Operating System. All of the computers mentioned above may be called MS-DOS types because they all can satisfy this condition. Most MS-DOS computers are closely related in architecture. Close is an arguable point. How close must the copy be? Since many computer manufacturers improve on IBM's features, it is usually misleading to call them clones, a name that implies exact replicas.

1.0 Characterizing the DtC

■ Hardware Components
■ Operating System
■ Applications Software
■ Selection Guidelines

What is it about a DtC that makes it so flexible and so potentially useful in so many different applications? A DtC isn't just a cut-down mainframe computer. There are important differences.

When you select DtCs and peripherals, it helps to view the system unit as an arbiter of the processing power contained in the connected peripherals. A better understanding of where and how processing occurs within a DtC system can help prevent acquisition of mismatched components and peripherals.

A typical set of building blocks required to make up a microcomputer system includes:

- CPU and support circuitry
- Memory
- Mass store
- Printer
- Keyboard
- Serial interface
- Parallel interface
- Monitor and display interface
- Special-purpose peripherals
- Operating system
- Software applications and utilities

You may be sure that some form of each of these components is present in every working microcomputer system. In each case a wide selection of items is available that differs in size, capacity, power, facility, versatility, and cost. When you purchase a DtC, you should have an application in mind. Think of the items shown in Figure 1 as column headings on a Chinese menu: Pick a CPU power range from column A, memory style and size from column B, and so on until you have a DtC configuration that matches your application requirements. Both hardware and software have definable performance levels and characteristics that can be matched. These characteristics are listed later to assist you in performing this difficult match.

First-time purchasers of home computers may opt to visit a retail computer store where DtCs are sold as prepackaged systems with standard options, while the more seasoned buyer might opt to visit a computer show where computer components can be purchased directly from dealers and pieced together. Purchasers of high-end workstations undergo a more formal ritual as they meet with vendor representatives who often demonstrate complete systems and software on-site. Selection can be fraught with difficulty if purchasers don't know their way around the basic attributes of hardware and software. You must be sure that the hardware package you select

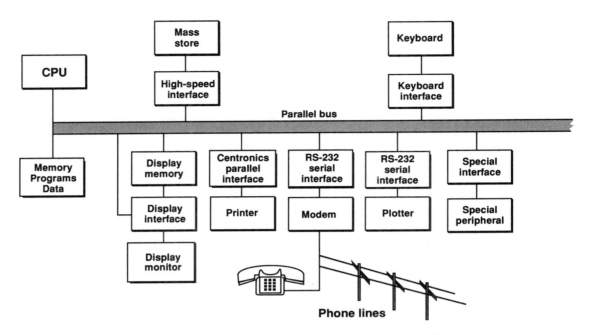

Figure 1. DtC system components: Today's DtC is a complete computing environment that can easily be extended to serve almost any need.

contains the proper components for your application needs. The vendor may recommend supplementing your application with software for word processing, spreadsheets, and other applications, and perhaps a programming language as well.

A DtC can often be assembled using the standard options and software offered by a vendor. The configuration may even seem close to optimum. Be advised, however, that optimality in the DtC environment is difficult to maintain. Conditions that were near ideal at time of purchase may change shortly thereafter. Further, off-the-shelf software tends to be general purpose, while custom applications-software is usually unique in some way. There is also a variety of compatibility constraints that can affect the performance of any system.

And, while the DtC environment offers freedom from certain outside operational restrictions and independence from the mainframe, there is a price to pay. You, the DtC user, may have to assume the direct cost and responsibility for the hardware and its operation, the software, and the media, including maintenance, upgrading, consumable supplies, as well as associated housekeeping and safekeeping chores.

Nevertheless, with good planning and a logical configuration of a DtC system and associated software, you can achieve a sensible balance between system performance requirements and the limitations imposed by an organization's policies or your personal pocketbook. Some of the more common problems encountered in DtC acquisition and usage are easily avoided by simple procedures and common sense.

The brief descriptions given below identify the principal DtC components and indicate in a general way how they fit into a system. Refer to Figure 1 to see how the components interrelate.

1.1   Central Processing Unit (CPU)

Today's DtC systems start with an appropriately powered CPU, which manages most of the system hardware. Specialized tasks are performed by add-on interfaces and coprocessors that are intended to work with the base-unit CPU. We will discuss them later.

The CPU, also known as the microprocessor, is the heart of a microcomputer. Its components are shown in Figure 2. It functions as a decision maker, a mathematician, and a traffic cop. It resides on a very large scale integrated (VLSI) chip, which also holds other electronics including a control unit and an arithmetic logic unit. Its performance is determined by *word size, clock rate, instruction set,* and *memory addressing capability.* These parameters and their significance need not concern us here; they are discussed in detail elsewhere.

The important thing to remember is that when you choose a particular DtC model, for all practical purposes you also choose that model's CPU. You probably will not sort through all available CPUs and choose a specific one because of its particular capability. The CPU inside the box you joyfully bring home and set up on your desktop may have little in common with the CPU you would have selected if you had had perfect knowledge and perfect freedom of choice. More likely your CPU choice will be made for you because it comes with the DtC that you selected for perhaps quite different reasons.

While you can wriggle out of this commitment by, for example, adding a card with a different CPU, such an alternative is generally not recommended. Most DtCs are designed around the vendor's specific microprocessor line, so a CPU substitution may simply rearrange good and bad attributes and fail to produce any overall improvement; it may in fact disable some functions you had with the old chip.

Most DtCs incorporate Intel, Motorola, or specialized RISC microprocessors. Motorola 68xxx-based DtCs, such as the Macintosh and most engineering workstations, usually start with the 68020 processor because of its 32-bit capability. MS-DOS computers use the Intel 80xxx chip, starting with the 80286. The 80286 is an attractive choice because it meets most of the speed requirements of MS-DOS software and is the minimum Intel CPU that supports extended memory required by many programs and IBM's OS/2 operating system. Most of today's users buy into the Motorola 68030 or Intel 80386 technology because these microprocessors provide superior memory management and higher speed. Premier DtCs use Motorola 68040 and Intel 80486 chips because of their even higher performance. These and other still more powerful CPUs are discussed later.

The decision to buy an MS-DOS computer may rest largely on the fact that there are many models to choose from and because there is a wealth of software products at whatever price you choose to pay – a lot of it virtually free. While the model and software attraction is unarguably true, many computer purchases occur without the buyer properly assessing the CPU's performance level, let alone understanding what makes one CPU different from another.

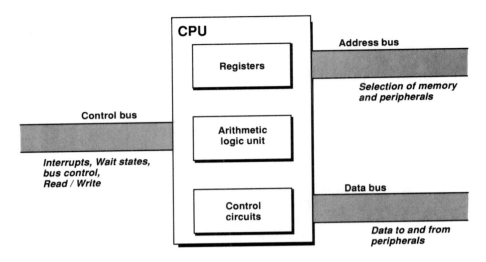

Figure 2. **CPU basic functions:** *Address bus width* determines how many devices can be directly accessed by the CPU. *Data bus width* determines how much information can be transmitted at one time, as a unit.

Apple Macintosh purchases are often stimulated by advertisements that tout simplicity of operation and promise high levels of productivity. The fact that a Motorola 68xxx CPU is under the hood is immaterial as long as it does the job. Engineering workstation buyers may have a similar mind set. They could find a high performance Intel, Motorola, or RISC processor under the hood. But as long as the workstation operates under Unix and runs their CAD software, they are content.

Generally, your system unit choice will be driven by the nature of the applications-software base supported and even by how many of your friends own the same unit and their positive experience with it. Enthusiastic recommendations can be overwhelmingly persuasive.

CPU Performance

Although the microprocessor is not the sole determinant of system performance, it is easily the single most important factor. Other things, including hard drive performance, presence of coprocessors, CPU memory size, and use of intelligent peripherals can certainly lighten its load, but the CPU is at the hub of everything taking place in the system and its importance cannot be overstated. Table 1 lists IBM, Apple, and other popular desktop computer microprocessors arranged according to their processing power levels.

Throughout this book references are made to systems equipped with these microprocessors. Systems will have respectively larger memories and hard drive capacities commensurate with the increasing capabilities of the microprocessors. As you advance from low to medium to high systems, you can expect throughput improvements of two to five times at each step, depending, of course, on how well you supplement the CPU.

Processing Power	Microprocessor		Representative Microcomputer Systems
	Type	Vendor	
Low	8080/Z80	Intel, Zilog	Early CP/M microcomputers, Radio Shack TRS-80
	6502 Family	MOS Technology	Apple II, +, IIc, IIe, early Commodore/Atari DtCs
	8088/8086	Intel	IBM PC, XT, PS/2 Model 30, XT-style MS-DOS computers
Medium	80286	Intel	IBM AT, PS/2 Model 30E series 50, 60, AT-style MS-DOS computers
	68000	Motorola	Early Apple Macintosh and Mac Classic, early engineering workstations, Commodore/Atari DtCs
High	68020	Motorola	Early Macintosh IIs, Sun, Apollo Workstations
	68030	Motorola	Modular Macs and Macintosh IIfx, Sun, Apollo Workstation, other workstations, NeXT computer
	80386	Intel	IBM PS/2 Models 70, 80, AT- and MCA-style MS-DOS computers, Sun 386I
	80486	Intel	Most vendors providing high-end MS/DOS computers, IBM Models 90/95
	68040	Motorola	High-end engineering workstations, NeXT computer

Table 1. Microprocessor and system processing power levels

Two examples of applications running with insufficient CPU power underscore the time problem in terms of how long it takes to redraw or rewrite a screen:

1. ***Desktop publishing*** – Screen redraws of a desktop publishing program could take close to a minute on low-power CPUs, while the higher-power CPUs, the Intel 80486 or Motorola 68040, could reduce this time to less than a second. Improved display controllers will also reduce the CPU's burden. However, the overall management of the display will be up to the CPU because much of the material originates in main memory.

2. ***Display scrolling*** – Spreadsheet users and document processors sometimes need to scroll through their material. Display scrolling is sluggish and choppy on lower-power CPUs. As with the desktop publishing example, display interface data width and on-board processing power could alleviate some of the problem. Much of the material being browsed, however, will reside in main memory, and therefore the CPU will continue to be responsible for manipulating it.

3. ***Database browsing*** – Browsing large datasets with filters, which narrow what you see, require CPU power. Updating many database indexes in a responsive manner also demands a lot from the CPU.

Don't blame all of your speed problems on your CPU. The fastest CPU can be held back by a slow hard disk. For example, you need to sort several thousand entries in a database that is much greater than your CPU's memory size. This process will involve extraordinarily large quantities of data being shuffled between main memory and hard disk. A speedy hard disk with cache memory could easily cut wait time in half. Comparisons such as those made above are merely guidelines; CPU selections must also take into account other system features and enhancements, described next.

CPU Selection Guidelines

Do not base your choice of CPU solely on its self-contained performance. Remember that CPU performance may be enhanced in various ways. Several devices can lighten the load on the CPU:

- *DMA controllers* – Direct memory access devices almost always transfer data independently of the CPU. Such transfers usually involve hard drives and local area network boards. Today's DtCs have more sophisticated DMA devices that have a greater number of concurrent channels available for data transfer and greater bus bandwidth to handle increased data traffic.

- *Math coprocessors* – Specialized devices that perform general math operations concurrently with normal CPU instructions.

- *Graphics coprocessors* – Devices that help the CPU by managing pixels and complex graphics transformations. Many of these coprocessing devices can perform their functions in parallel with other CPU functions.

- *Communications processors* – Devices that ease the CPU burden of communications with external devices/computers. Functions include multiple session management, protocols, data compression, and error checking. Communication can often be performed in parallel while you work on a spreadsheet or edit the text of a document.

- *Caching* – High speed memory for data that is processed most frequently.

Traditionally, strength in these areas was found only on minicomputers and on the more expensive engineering workstations. Today's lower cost MS-DOS and Apple computers either come with or can be fitted with such devices.

The typical buyer is not aware of the factors listed above. It is true that some motherboards are faster than others that have equivalent CPUs and auxiliary processing devices. Many hidden factors determine how enhancements will integrate into a CPU. Differences such as auxiliary timing frequencies, caching methodology, memory speeds, and interface types will affect processing power.

CPU performance can be increased directly by speeding up its clock. Adjustments for revving up the CPU motor are not generally built into the DtC board design and are not easy to make as an afterthought. In other words, if you want your CPU to run at a higher clock speed, you should obtain DtC equipment designed initially to run at the higher frequency. Various other system factors are affected when you boost CPU clock frequency, including RAM (read/write CPU memory), interface boards and their memories, DMA, and interrupt controller chips.

You may want to choose a CPU with more addressable memory. However, more addressable memory may not be realized for several reasons:

- Software may not be written to use all of addressable memory.
- The operating system may not support all of addressable memory.
- The DtC system box design may be limited in how much memory can be added.

Bus layout constraints may not allow you to achieve the transfer rates that best match the CPU's data width. For instance, IBM ATs have 8-bit and 16-bit slots.

The 8-bit interfaces do not take advantage of 16-bit data transfer rates possible with the 80286 microprocessor. The 80386- and 80486-based systems have additional 32-bit slots, which may be unusable to many peripheral interface cards.

1.2   Memory

■

As in larger computers, random access memory is where programs execute and where temporary data reside. Mass storage or sequential memory, described later, is where programs and data are stored pending execution. Random access memory is divided into two forms:

RAM (Read/Write Memory):   RAM is where variable programs and data are executed by the CPU when loaded from the mass store. This memory supports the various applications: word processors, spreadsheets, databases, etc. On today's DtCs, RAM size is anywhere from 256K to 32 MB. Memory performance is measured in access time.

ROM (Read Only Memory):   ROM is where permanent programs are executed and unchanging data are contained. Here too are the operating system fundamental input/output routines and unchanging system parameter data. Macintosh, Commodore, Amiga, and Atari computers place considerable graphics support in ROM; earlier units stored BASIC in ROM. On today's DtCs, ROM storage capacity is between 8K and 512K.

Memory storage possibilities are shown in Figure 3. Memory options for DtC users may be confusing because different memory models are implemented by different microprocessors and operating system support may be limited. Unlike mainframe users, you, as a DtC user, will be critically aware of these differences. Even if you are not technically cognizant of your memory status, you will eventually be confronted with not enough memory messages that never seem to go away. So many options exist for increasing memory that even experts may be stumped about which to choose.

Memory Uses

Although the parameters for selecting the size and type of memory are complex, system memory must accommodate the following (all values in bytes, of course):

Operating system requirements	50K – 4 MB
Applications program size	64K – Several MB
Size of active data areas	64K – Several MB
Size of resident enhancement utilities	64K – 400K
Memory requirements for disk/keyboard/video buffer areas, DOS drivers, interrupt tables	64K – 256K
Add-in software products	50K – 300K
LAN drivers and buffer areas	40K – 200K
RAM disks and cache memory	30K – 8 MB
Multitasking shells	50K – 300K

Memory Selection Guidelines

Memory access speed can affect the rate at which the CPU operates. Slow memory will generally require wait states that retard the CPU to keep it in step with the memory.

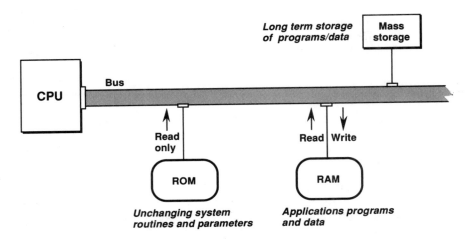

Figure 3. CPU memory and mass storage: RAM and ROM memory are directly executable by the CPU while the mass storage can be thought of as a secondary source of programs and data.

When selecting a memory upgrade, you must determine whether the operating system can support it. This may not be obvious if you consider only the claims made for the particular operating systems you are evaluating. Many manufacturers provide operating system fixes that can beef-up memory usage. But keep in mind that a fix is only a patch; while it may get you over a rough spot, it may fail you over the long haul. MS-DOS computer users should be aware of the different applications for *extended* and *expanded* memory.

Be aware that most newer DtC system units accept memory into the motherboard through special SIMMs (Single In-Line Memory Modules). The SIMM slots differ from those in the usual add-on boards. Older system units accept DRAM (dynamic RAM) chips that plug into add-on boards, which in turn plug into ordinary slots. SIMMs provide for memory expansion without using up add-on board slots. SIMMs are more reliable and are generally more intimately interfaced to the CPU, enabling higher speed configurations.

1.3   Mass Storage

Unlike mainframe users, DtC users have complete control over the mass storage process unless mass storage is shared on a local area network. Through flexible operating system configurations one may choose from a variety of mass storage options including high-density floppies, removable Bernoulli cartridges, tape back-ups, and now, laser disks. For 2.8 MB floppies, the cost of storage, not including initial cost of drives, is about $0.50 per MB. Newer magnetic tape and optical storage devices can reduce the cost to less than a penny per MB.

Hard Drives

Hard drive capacity and speed cost money, but frugality in this area may be even more expensive. It is easy to underestimate hard disk storage needs, especially if you have limited experience with large files or many small ones. Consider how

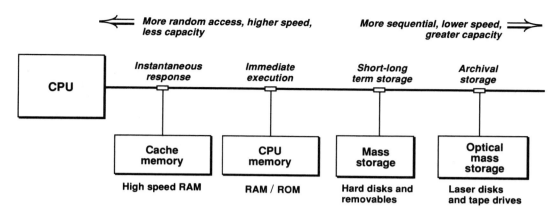

Figure 4.   Memory hierarchy: A well-designed mass storage system contains means for short- and long-term data storage. The optical drive would have 20 to 50 times the capacity of the hard drive, the hard drive would have 20 to 50 times the capacity of the CPU memory, and the CPU memory would have 20 to 50 times the capacity of the cache memory.

many applications you need online at one time and their data requirements. Be aware that a hard disk can be supplemented with more specialized storage systems such as removable cartridges, RAM disks, cache memory, optical disks, or even tape drive systems. If your hard drive is not big enough, unless you are on a network, you will be overflowing onto floppies. Repetitive loading of software onto a DtC that has insufficient mass storage can be extremely annoying. The general guideline for hard disk storage is to have at least 20 times the supported CPU memory.

In a DtC environment you are free to make and keep as many copies of programs and data as you like, except for copy-protected materials, and to manage them in any way you see fit. Your method for backup is entirely up to you. Be aware that even with conscientious care data losses will occur, so adequate backup is essential. A hierarchical system of storage devices may include large capacity, highly sequential tape storage; smaller capacity, more random access hard drives; smaller CPU memory; and even smaller cache memory (see Figure 4). Through appropriate interfaces and applications software, these four types of storage and back-up systems *can* be highly integrated.

Floppy Disks and Drives

Floppy disks are very popular in home and business DtCs. They are particularly favored in home use, where there is no interconnection to other DtCs. Engineering workstations have less need for floppy disk drives because data is exchanged over networks. In place of floppies, software will be installed on large tape drives, warranted by the size of the software. It is a good idea to configure your desktop system with at least the highest density disk drive available, making sure it is well supported. Popular MS-DOS computer recording densities are:

High Density	Low Density
3½" 1.44 MB, 2.8 MB	3½" 720K
5¼" 1.2 MB	5¼" 360K

Current Macintosh, Commodore, and Atari DtCs generally support the 3½" floppy disks as do MS-DOS computers, but the 5¼" size is still popular on the AT-style MS-DOS computers. One of the most far-reaching benefits of a DtC is that it allows one to work at home. Many users now carry a box of floppies instead of a briefcase full of paper. If you find it convenient to lend disks and borrow them from others, you may want to configure a second disk drive for copying purposes and to ensure compatibility with other DtCs, especially between the one at home and the one at work.

Mass Storage Selection Guidelines

When running your application expect to spend a fair amount of time managing files, moving information, and storing data. Consider your mass storage options at the outset to avoid problems later:

- *File intensity of application* – How much of the mass store does the application use for temporary storage?
- *Backup costs* – Relative costs and performance of removable random access media and the more sequential, but higher capacity, tape backup systems.
- *Speed and capacity features* – Relative performance speeds and capacity of hard drives, and how these systems can be emulated in memory through RAM disks and cache memory.
- *Disk compatibility* – Floppy disk and removable disk configurations for compatibility with different DtC models.
- *Hard drive performance* – Reliability of various hard drives and hard drive performance enhancement software.

1.4   Printers

Applications software and printer selection are closely bound and compatibility problems will arise if you try to use a printer that is not supported by the software package. The best time to choose a printer is when you choose applications software. Then it is a straightforward matter to choose the printer that works with the software to be run. If you attempt to operate an unsupported printer, you could experience problems with graphics and text formats and control code compatibility.

DtC printers are no longer text mode sequential character stream devices driven over the traditional serial or parallel interface. DtC laser printers usually require specialized software and can support high data rate hardware, with data rates of 1 MB to 10 MB per second becoming common. High levels of interactivity between DtC applications (desktop publishing, CAD systems) and their outputs (laser printers, plotters) increasingly demand individual output devices at each workstation. If individual devices cannot fit in the budget, then networked printers and plotters must be made foolproof and user friendly. Often you will have to weigh the direct cost advantage of common output devices against the loss of productivity that inevitably occurs when multiple users wish to share a single device.

Local Printers

Each user should have at least a dot matrix printer for local draft printouts. A low-cost dot matrix printer is an important adjunct at many workstations, fulfilling on-the-spot output needs. Most DtCs already contain the necessary interface and the printers cost only $200 to $400. Uses for low-cost printers include:

- Screen dumps
- Short notes and memos
- Printouts of network messages
- Small spreadsheets and database dumps
- Graphics and diagram printouts
- Directories, labels, and other auxiliary office necessities

Printer Support

Certain applications will require more expensive high resolution and even high volume printers, making printer sharing necessary because of the high cost.

Printer compatibility questions can leave you uncertain as manufacturers rush to market a parade of slightly better printers. Companies are quick to advertise special features of their devices but neglect to describe the incompatibilities that the improvements may bring about. As a rule, choose printers that are popular and widely supported by applications within their usage category.

As printer prices decline, their cost in proportion to total workstation cost will allow many individuals to have their own high quality output devices. Of course, personal responsibility – for installation, operation, and maintenance – will become even more demanding.

Be aware that printers require a variety of support. Expendables such as inks, toner cartridges, and paper and short lifetime items such as ribbons, print heads, and electrostatic drums will have to be stocked. If you choose a printer that is not supplied by the office stock room, you, as the DtC owner, may have to procure expendables and other items independently. Also, since printers are complex mechanical devices, they will require routine maintenance and periodic adjustment.

Printer Selection Guidelines

The printer is your outside link to the work you do on your DtC. Think about what you want to see when you look at hard copy, and don't ignore the nitty-gritty details such as:

- Size of printer carriage or paper size capability.
- Choice of different fonts, type faces, and character sizes.
- Quality/consistency of printed output.
- Rate of throughput.
- Graphics capability and ability to combine text with graphics.
- Resolution or dot size.
- PostScript capability.
- Ability to emulate plotters.
- Paper handling capability: paper size, sprocket feed, labels, sheet feed, cardstock.
- Type of DtC interface required.
- Office space available for printer.
- Repeatability (for forms).
- Color capability, type of paper required.

- Application support of specific "quirks."
- Handling of text and graphics.
- Ease of paper, ribbon, and toner installation.
- Mechanical reliability.
- Will the duty cycle support continuous printing?
- How much memory can be added to the printer?

Matching what the printer can do with the hard copy needs of your application is critically important. Low-cost dot matrix printers are adequate for draft program and data printouts. Low-end text editing and program development may be served equally well by such printers. The more sophisticated word processors and, particularly, desktop publishing software require higher resolution laser printers as well as more complex interface and support software. CAD packages generally require plotters for final output because plotters can present detailed drawings with higher precision, in larger sizes, and in more colors than conventional printers provide.

1.5   Keyboards

The importance of a good keyboard centers on the fact that most of your data may very well originate there. You will become quite attached to your keyboard and your efficiency with it will make the difference between writing novels and scratching notes. The importance of formal typing training in conjunction with a good keyboard cannot be overemphasized if you will be inputting large quantities of text.

Much of your DtC information entry activities are related to choosing items from menus, pointing to desired options, and moving objects around on your DtC's screen. For this reason mice, graphics tablets, track balls, and display pointers may be considerably more effective than a keyboard. Being restricted to a keyboard – using arrows, page ups, ends, homes, and other keyboard functions for elementary positioning of input to your software – can be frustrating. Software products such as Microsoft Windows put great pressure on you to use a mouse. In fact, many vendors bundle mice with Windows or Windows with their mice.

The more advanced CAD applications are driven from graphics tablets that have complicated selection menus wrapped around them. The center part of the tablet is used for graphics inputs. Graphics tablets provide the high precision required for positioning information while a mouse can easily perform the less demanding moves required by many drawing graphics applications.

Keyboard Alternatives

The power and versatility of a good CPU, operating system, and programmable keyboard allow effective local modifications and thus highly productive configurations. Microprocessors in DtC keyboards, intimately linked to and controlled by the local DtC CPU, provide high levels of programmable functions right in the keyboard. For example, by adjusting operating system drivers and hooking up such hardware as eyeball trackers or voice recognizers, the handicapped are given access to the computer. This access can be made transparent to the existing software base. As Figure 5 shows, new drivers can route information to your programs while isolating those programs from the particular type of input. This way, a handicapped person could operate a sophisticated word processor with eye movements, requiring no modification of the word processor software.

All users can benefit through keyboard enhancement software that can customize keyboard functions to suit virtually any data entry preference. Keyboard customizations can be related to the type of program you are operating. For example, keyboarding may be made easier by programming a given key to enter repetitive text.

Keyboard Selection Guidelines

Don't assume that all keyboards are alike. Spend time practicing on prospective keyboards and think through keyboard options and capabilities to facilitate your work. Investigate the following:

- *Key placement and arrangement* – Where and how conveniently are vital keys (shift, carriage return, escape, alt, function keys) positioned?
- *Keyboard familiarity* – Will it be a serious problem if the same operators have to use keyboards that have different layouts?
- *Keyboard feel* – Do you like a "mushy" or a "clicky" keyboard? Most touch typists prefer the "clicky" type, but noise may be undesirable.
- *Keyboard power features* – Is a typematic character repetition built in? Is it programmable?
- *Keyboard compatibility* – Is the keyboard compatible with the system? Different DtC models do not support identical keyboards.
- *Keyboard function keys* – How many function keys are on the keyboard? Many mainframe applications require 12.
- *Keystroke storage* – Can the keyboard store keystroke sequences?
- *Keyboard portability* – Do you use different DtCs at different locations? Being able to unplug, carry, and replug your favorite keyboard into another DtC could be a real benefit.

1.6   Interfaces

Today's DtCs must connect to a wide variety of peripherals, many of which require specialized interfaces. Most peripheral interface needs will be met by the standard interface, the RS-232C serial and the Centronics parallel printer interface. Many DtCs, especially the portables, have these interfaces built into their motherboards. Printer interfaces should be included in any DtC purchase.

Serial Interfaces

The serial interface has long been used to connect low data rate peripherals to their hosts over long distances. Since so many popular lower data rate peripherals are interfaced serially, you may find yourself with more peripherals than there are serial ports on your workstation. Serial ports may be shared using any of several methods, explained elsewhere. Problems in the RS-232C standard that defines signal lines, values, and connectors can frustrate the use of the serial interface. But, take heart, there are workarounds.

Popular Peripherals

Peripherals often connected through the serial interface include:

- *Mice* – For "WIMP" (Windows, Icon, Menu, Point) graphic interface software.

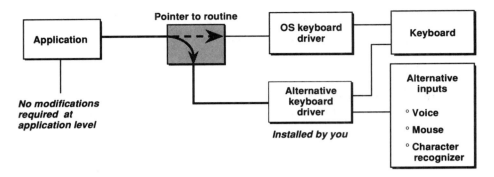

Figure 5. **Keyboard alternatives and enhancements:** To install alternative I/O device drivers, simply move the pointer to a new routine.

- *Plotters* – Most DtC plotters do not require higher than RS-232 serial transfer rates because they use efficient high-level plotting languages.

- *Impact printers* – Most of the older daisy wheel printers do not require and cannot handle high transmission rates.

- *Modem* – Modems convert RS-232 serial interface digital signals to analog signals suitable for the telephone system. The serial interface is a natural place to obtain digital data to drive a modem. The serial interface is designed to handle low-speed two-way single channel communications between computing equipment. While external modems connect to the serial interface, some internal modems can by-pass the serial interface and connect directly to the DtC's resources.

- *Other computing equipment* – The serial interface is often used as a general-purpose interface between different types of computing equipment. Also, low-cost LANs between DtCs can be implemented by the serial interface.

- *Data acquisition and process control* – Often, the serial interface is used as a data conduit between data to be collected and the DtC. Hardware at the data site collects the data in parallel and converts it to RS-232 compatible data channels. Likewise, remote processes may be controlled over serial links and even by modems for long distance control.

Primary Usage Considerations

- *Bit rate* – Can the serial interface support the bit rate of the peripheral? Serial interfaces can be programmed to operate from 75 bits to 120 Kbits per second on MS-DOS computers and up to 250 Kbits per second on Macs.

- *ACIA chip implementation* – Is the chip compatible? There have been problems – particularly noted in MS-DOS compatibles – between serial interface add-on boards manufactured in the Far East and the stock IBM serial interfaces.

- *Connector pinouts* – Are the connectors the same? Often, different connectors are used for different models. For example, the MS-DOS XT compatibles implement a 25-pin D connector while the newer AT-style compatibles implement a 9-pin D connector. Apple computers also have a similar difference in serial interface connectors between their early and late models. Mostly, you'll find the serial interface implemented by a 25-pin D connector. Adapters are readily available.

- **Number of serial ports** – Do you have have enough serial ports to accommodate your serial peripherals? Various methods including switches and LANs can be used to share these interfaces. DtCs normally come with at least one serial interface for a mouse, modem, or plotter, and one parallel interface for a printer (see Figure 6). While most add-on boards with as many as eight built-in serial interfaces are widely available for certain process control applications or just for lots of serially interfaced peripherals. Larger numbers of interfaces and sharing of single interfaces will be governed by the specific application. Serial interfaces are often included on display graphic interfaces, memory expansion boards, and even hard disk interfaces.

Parallel Printer Interfaces

The parallel printer interface included in most DtCs handles higher data rates than the previously discussed serial interface. The parallel printer interfaces moves data one byte at a time between the CPU and the printer while the previously discussed serial interface moves only one bit at a time. A Centronics standard defines pinouts and connections between the interface and the printer. Most APA matrix and laser printers connect to this interface.

Laser printers that output high resolution text and APA graphics require the higher data rates that are possible with a parallel printer interface. Although PostScript printers reduce the CPU load, the encapsulated PostScript data stream between DtC and printer is just as dense as APA streams of the earlier dot matrix and laser printers. Therefore, PostScript printers will also require the higher-than-serial speed of the parallel printer interface or even faster shared memory interfaces.

NOTE

APA stands for All Points Addressable. Any point on a field or page can be specified. This is in contrast to printers that read an ASCII code and print an entire text character as a matrix of dots. Internally, the character is formed by the printer without much user control.

1.7   Graphics Display Monitors/Interfaces

Personal computers now have display options that rival modern engineering workstations. Many factors are to be considered when selecting a display interface including color resolution, color palettes, on-board dithering, on-board graphics coprocessors, system memory usage and conflicts, display modes, software compatibility modes, refresh speed, scanning method, type of monitor supported, bus width supported, compatibility with other video display interfaces, and requisite operating system support. Obtaining the correct graphics display and monitor combination should not be undertaken without an expert's advice.

The display interface provides the necessary link between DtC and monitor, providing memory to store displayed text and graphics, scanning that memory, sweeping characters from it to the video screen, and providing synchronization signals, color and hue, and conversion of digital code to analog monitor functions.

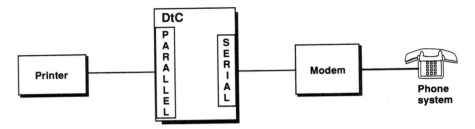

Figure 6. Standard serial and parallel printer interfaces: Most DtCs come equipped with the generic serial and parallel interfaces.

The intelligent interfaces also provide higher-level graphics drawing and manipulation to assist the CPU.

The smarter, more advanced video display systems require special software support. Operating system graphics support for MS-DOS computers has been offered only recently with OS/2 Presentation Manager, and has been renovated in the Macintosh 32-bit QuikDraw routines. Do not buy video display systems that function *only* with specific graphics programs and are not suitable for the more common spreadsheet, database, and word processor applications. Most of the more sophisticated graphics controllers are compatible with your DtC's existing video interfaces for text operations; however, you ought to check this carefully.

Data Rates

The characters and graphics displayed on your video screen are stored in your CPU's program/data memory or in a graphics controller's memory, both of which are directly accessible to the CPU, as Figure 7 shows.

Direct memory access facilitates high data rates and, therefore, high interaction levels are possible between the software and what you see on the monitor screen. Such high rates are not yet economically feasible over remote communications channels between mainframe computers and their terminals. The application and its visual output have the advantage of an intimate relationship when operators have complete control over the CPU, running dedicated DtC applications without sharing resources with other users.

Perhaps more than any other consideration, virtual independence from outside constraints is the reason that DtC applications are becoming more interactive and therefore more user friendly. At the same time networking is becoming prevalent throughout the workplace. In this environment large quantities of data must be transferred back and forth quickly. High data rate optical fiber LANs and appropriate operating system support provide the necessary interaction between multiple DtC workstations.

Video Selection Guidelines

Factors to consider when selecting graphics display monitors/interfaces are:

- *Display color* – Is the display monochrome or color? If you are not accustomed to color, you may think that monochrome is fine. But color is an excellent productivity enhancer. The newer DtC applications take particular advantage of color in

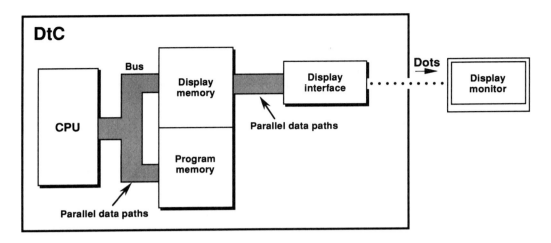

Figure 7.   Video interface, memory, and CPU: The relationship between the CPU and video display is intimate in a DtC. Both display interface and CPU talk to the same memory.

menuing, user prompting, plotting, charting, etc. Users report that proper use of color is less tiring to the eyes.

- **Resolution** – Is screen resolution adequate? Is the application primarily text or will text *and* graphics be required? Monitor/interface requirements for desktop publishing are completely different from those for simple text editing. How fine must graphic images appear?

- **Flexibility** – Will it serve your changing needs? Many DtC monitors can serve a variety of functions and are compatible with a variety of video interfaces.

- **Size** – How big is the screen? Desktop publishing requires a large monitor so that page layouts can be displayed in their entirety, close to actual size. You must be able to see a whole layout to ensure balance and proportion, and to do justice to your design. Working with a small monitor forces you to hop repeatedly from one part of your layout to another, with part of your page always obscured; it is frustrating and time consuming when you have a deadline to meet. Buying full page and dual page monitors is not the complete solution. You also need a sufficiently powerful and matched display interface.

- **Application compatibility** – What monitors and interfaces does your software require? Support?

- **Monitor/interface match** – Do the graphics display interface and monitor match? The availability of so many different monitors, displays, and interfaces, particularly in the home and business domain, makes finding an optimum match between interface and monitor a cumbersome problem. Interfaces to monitor cable pinouts, analog or digital interfaces or monitors, vertical and horizontal scanning frequencies, type of V(ertical) and H(orizontal) synchronizing signals, frequency response and pixel density of monitor vs. output resolution of the interface, and the availability of supporting drivers are among the many considerations that have to be resolved.

- *Dumb vs. intelligent display interfaces* – Is the display interface appropriate for your application? Most MS-DOS and Macintosh computers still use dumb video display interfaces that monopolize the DtC's CPU when they manipulate display memories. In a Macintosh DtC, this memory can be as large as 2 MB for the 24-bit color cards. Many DtC applications, such as desktop publishing, can be hopelessly mired by such interfaces. If you have a graphics-intensive application that requires quick response you may find that increasing the capability of the CPU has only a linear effect on graphics processing times, whereas the specialized capabilities of the smarter graphics controller-based video interfaces can provide a dramatic time improvement.

1.8   Special-Purpose Peripherals

Special-purpose peripherals can increase the functionality of a DtC beyond what is possible with larger, general-purpose mainframe computers.

Performance Enhancement

If you are doing statistical analysis on problems such as population growth, image enhancement, or resolving submarine tracks out of ocean noise, you will need to perform logical operations on millions of data items many times per second. This level of activity could be a horrendous computational job even for a supercomputer. Hardware designed to perform any computational job, no matter how specialized, can be optained and plugged into a DtC to yield performance levels exceeding those of the more generalized super computer.

On almost any DtC you shouldn't be surprised to find such peripherals as character and voice recognizers; data acquisition and process control add-ons; and DVI (digital video interactive) boards that process live video images, combined with computer graphics, if you wish, in real time. With enhanced capabilities, however, come more complex operational and configuration control problems.

Special-Purpose Peripherals Selection Guidelines

Consider the following when selecting special-purpose peripherals:

- *DtC hardware match* – Is DtC hardware suitably matched to peripheral requirements for your system's resources? The CPU must be able to get data to and from the peripheral, the bus will have to carry the data, and the mass storage device may have to store the processed data in real time.

- *Software support* – What supporting software (drivers, language extensions, etc.) are provided with the peripherals?

- *System resource contention problems* – Will your add-ons compete for interrupts, memory, and DMA channels? Newer DtCs boards alleviate contention problems through efficient management of these vital resources. For example, IDs are implanted in the peripheral interface cards of the IBM PS/2 and Macintosh II and are used by the operating systems of these DtCs to assign resources.

- *User base* – How many individuals have similar systems? How successful and efficient are they? What type of vendor or other support is available for them?

1.9   *Operating System*

Traditionally, an important function of a microcomputer operating system has been to isolate the user and the applications software from hardware details. By isolating the software from specific I/O details, the operating system allows software developers to write applications software without having to know much about the insides of a particular system. Figure 8 illustrates this basic principle.

As we will discover later, the concept of isolation becomes quite complex and philosophical with the wide range of developers and hardware affecting the software. Operating system provisions for hardware isolation are often short circuited for various reasons, particularly in the quest for speed. Today's DtC operating systems can perform functions not found even on mainframe computers. Multitasking and virtual memory support, windowing, graphic user interfaces, and automatic data sharing are some of the features that can be both a blessing and a curse to DtC software developers and users.

Today's DtC users have justifiable concerns with respect to operating systems. Can one:

- modify, add, or reroute I/O routines to allow alternative or enhanced peripheral operation?
- place graphic shells around the operating system to enhance or customize its interface to the operator?
- experiment to learn and teach system concepts?

Since each DtC system has its own complete operating system, you can have the specific performance and peripheral configurations necessary to do your specific

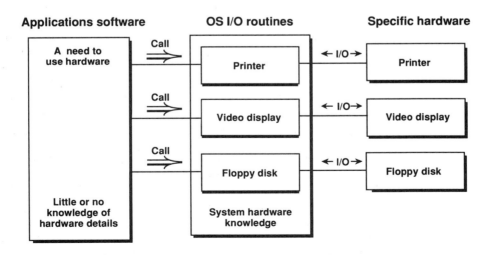

Figure 8.   OS isolates software from hardware: The operating system provides centralized support for the hardware that the software programs use, freeing them for more important matters.

job. The extent to which you control operating system factors can have profound effects on your productivity.

Fiddling with the operating system gives you the ultimate power to define and characterize your DtC's performance, a luxury seldom enjoyed by mainframe users. Along with luxury comes responsibility. When making operating system changes you will need to know much more about your system than simply how to operate the software. Misunderstood considerations such as special peripheral driver installations, LAN connections, and other system configurations can result in days of lost time, catastrophic data loss, and system crashes.

Hardware Support

Does the operating system really support the features of the CPU, multitasking and virtual memory, for example, or must your applications software base fend for itself? Later we shall see that the problem of inadequate CPU support plagues the home and business DtC category. If system acquisition is based on CPU capacity, the expectation must be moderated by what the operating system can support. How well does the operating system support the I/O requirements of your peripherals.

> **EXAMPLE**
>
> Current MS-DOS versions are only beginning to exploit the capability of the 80286 microprocessor, already well supported by OS/2. OS/2, in turn, is beginning to take advantage of the powerful modes of the 80386 microprocessor. Apple's System 7.0 supports the virtual memory capability of the Motorola 68030 Microprocessor, whereas previous versions did not.

Software Support

What is the supported software base? Does it include the particular software that you will be operating most? You don't purchase software in a vacuum. You purchase software designed to operate in a particular operating system environment. How well does the OS permit programs to work together, share data, screen display, and peripherals? Often, the software can perform its own functions without the help of the operating system. Self-sufficient programs will be more efficient than those that use operating system functions, but they will be less transportable across different system architectures and less cooperative with other software programs.

> **EXAMPLE**
>
> You may be productive with your favorite word processor, yet when it runs under Windows, it won't import, much less display, graphics images from the Windows-compliant CorelDRAW. Microsoft Word, however, will let you cut and paste from CorelDRAW.

Often, you will need to trade product familiarity with product compatibility, unless you start with compatible products in the first place. Product compatibility, however, will most likely evolve with the help of a particular operating system. How popular the software is industry wide as well as in your own organization is important. Product stability, commonality, and help availability all stem from popularity, which could well be the single most important factor.

1.10   DtC Software

Unlike mainframe users, who have little or no control over software selection, installation, and configuration, DtC users have literally thousands of software packages to choose from. Most of these programs cost less than $400 each. With many good packages between $20 and $60, much of the available software is well within reach of the average consumer. It is therefore simply a matter of choosing the right package for the job. The purpose of the hardware/software connection discussion in this book is to categorize the software and alert you to its varied nature and complex support requirements. Be aware, however, that only rough categorizations of a sampling of the multitude of software products are mentioned. Figure 9 highlights some of the more common application areas of today's software.

Software Dimensions

When you select DtC software you will face a software base of confusing dimensions that relate to how the software is developed and used. With some of the newer software systems, the distinction between software developer and software user is quite blurred. The following examples should clear away some of the confusion.

Medium-level languages, also known as third generation languages, are general-purpose languages that include C, Pascal, BASIC, and Fortran. The base languages are becoming enhanced with application-specific libraries. Also, through user friendly development environments, which include object-oriented programming (OOP) techniques, novice developers sometimes have an edge over seasoned developers of traditional software. Borland's Object Vision, for example, lets you set up information systems by flow charting on screen. Powerful links to the developmental language of the Paradox database management system give you power and flexibility when you need it. Microsoft's Visual BASIC makes programming fun and breathes life into BASIC. Programs are set up with forms, flow charts, and data objects.

The simplest and quickest way to define object-oriented programming is to contrast it with the traditional procedural programming techniques. The traditional methods view the top level as a procedural structure of control logic into which one must dig to find the data elements that are interrelated by the control logic. In object-oriented programming, however, the top level view is of the collection of objects, which correspond to the data elements in the traditional model. To discover the procedural details, one must delve into each of the objects and investigate the methods by which each is implemented. This concept can be expanded so that objects can include items not normally thought of as being data elements, such as tasks, I/O devices, and users.

OOP is not just a choice of programming styles; it is a select paradigm – a whole new way of seeing things – and it extends far beyond the traditional programming elements. The notion of object first and operation second is fundamental to OOP.

Application-Specific Programming Languages

A host of high-level languages, oriented toward particular applications, can place greater power into the developer's hands. The tradeoff is generally between more powerful commands and greater distance from the hardware. For example, a pow-

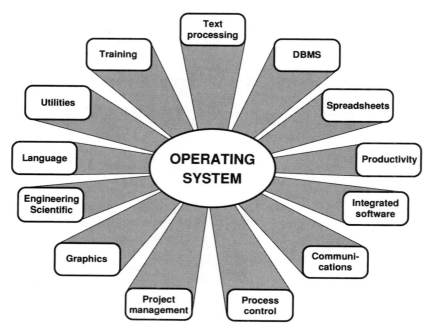

Figure 9.   Common DtC software categories

erful X-base command could index a database, or relate many databases, or create a database from scratch. If, however, you need a graphic from outside the particular supported database management application, you may need to drop down to a medium-level language subroutine, if that is allowed, or worse, down to assembly language. OOP techniques are being used more and more in application-specific programming languages.

> **NOTE**
>
> X-base is a set of powerful fourth generation database programming languages that are similar to the popular dBASE database programming language. This is analogous to the way MS-DOS compatibles are similar to IBM PCs.

Menu-driven development environments are to be found everywhere in today's DtC software products. While oriented toward particular applications, not all software products are ready to run straight from the box. The product must be customized for your particular purpose. However, you may not need to write a single line of code. Most of the products of interest are oriented toward some form of information management.

Products such as DataEase International's DataEase and Borland's Paradox can be used to develop very powerful customized database management applications simply by selecting a number of specific menued configurations. When programming is required, powerful built-in languages are provided for you to use. DataEase, for example, provides the developer with the DDL reporting language when highly customized reports beyond those obtainable by the menus are required.

Paradox provides the PAL programming language. The DataEase and Paradox systems are quite object oriented, and if you have plans for database management applications you should consider these products. Although the software mentioned operates on MS-DOS computers, you can find similar software on Macs and increasingly on EP computers.

Macro-Driven Systems

Most of today's word processors, spreadsheets, and drawing graphics programs can run immediately upon loading. You can, however, automate their functions to a higher level with a built-in application-specific programming language. Often programs designed with these languages are erroneously called *macros,* in view of their extraordinary capabilities.

The programmed macros often include recursion, subroutine capability, DO WHILE clauses, and other structured programing constructs. One can use these languages to realize some rather unexpected windfalls with, say, a word processor. A word processor or spreadsheet could be programmed with macros to be a form-driven data entry front end for a DBMS.

Turnkey Products

An endless variety of specialized software products can do everything from balancing a checkbook to tracking a farm's milk production. In the MS-DOS computer world, thousands, perhaps tens of thousands, of public domain software utility programs can give your DtC the ability to do almost anything. When purchasing turnkey software, be sure it is conformable to your needs. Because of unique data formats, turnkey software products do not, as a rule, communicate with other software products. Also, because of limited configurability, you may not be able to change the program's behavior easily.

> **NOTE**
>
> To avoid costly mistakes, a good understanding of software dimensions is essential. Some of the most sophisticated software systems can be developed by users with little or no software background. And although other systems claim that they are simple because they use, for instance, OOP, they could require extraordinary talents to set up.

Selection Guidelines

When choosing DtC applications software, the most important considerations are:

- ***Type of software*** – Do you need preprogrammed software with limited flexibility? Do you need a mid-level language or an application-specific language or OOP system to develop your own application? Answers to these questions may depend on the availability of qualified application support personnel.
- ***Software performance/usability*** – Do you need low-, medium-, or high-power capability? Can you trade usability for performance?
- ***Hardware compatibility*** – Is your software compatible with the peripherals you will need?
- ***Integration*** – How well are internal functions integrated and does the product share data easily with other DtC applications or mainframe applications?
- ***Network support*** – Can the product be networked?

- **Special hardware requirements** – Does the software require special DtC capabilities such as math coprocessors, expanded memory, special input devices, or plotters?
- **Documentation** – What is the extent of available documentation? Are tutorials, demo disks, or outside publications easily acquired from a library or bookstore? As an example, at least a hundred books have been published on the dBASE database management system.
- **Software compatibility** – Will the software operate with other applications software and resident utilities?

2.0   Microcomputer Evolution

- Microcontrollers
- Birth of Microprocessors
- Personal Computers
- Engineering Workstations
- Minicomputers
- Microcomputers

Thousands upon thousands of microcomputers have been built to function as such diverse computational devices as calculators, space shuttle flight controllers, and desktop computers used to prepare income tax returns. What is a microcomputer? Where did it come from? What is it made of? Such questions are addressed next.

In the world of computing, systems queue up in a hierarchy that, from the top down, is populated by supercomputers, mainframes, superminis, minicomputers, supermicros, and microcomputers. This hierarchy is steadily rising with respect to power. At the high end, designers dreaming of large computers foresee power so vast that invention is becoming the mother of need rather than the other way around. The question of how to make bigger and better computers is no longer as pressing as: "to what end is this enormous power to be put?"

In the midrange, today's minicomputers are more than a match for yesterday's mainframes. At the low end, microcomputers are rapidly filling the void left by minis, which are moving upscale into formerly mainframe neighborhoods. Starter micros, low-cost, low-end models that many owners cut their teeth on, are being replaced in step with the appearance on the market of more and more powerful chips – the 286, 386, 486, on up to the 786 scheduled for the turn of the century. A snapshot of DtC history is shown in Figure 10.

> **NOTE**
>
> **Basic Definitions**
> To begin, a *microprocessor* is a CPU on a semiconductor chip, usually composed of silicon but lately also of gallium arsenide, that through *very large scale integration* technology is able to hold huge numbers of tiny electronic circuits. These microcircuits provide the means for executing instructions that control the operation of a computer. A *microcomputer* is a device that uses a microprocessor as a CPU. Of course, it also needs memory, data storage facilities, and means for input and output to perform its work. The relationship of a microprocessor to other components in a microcomputer is shown in Figure 11.

2.1   Related Advances in Technology

The history of the desktop computer is particularly noteworthy when we consider how far it has come in the past twenty years. Some important highlights in microcomputer and related technologies are:

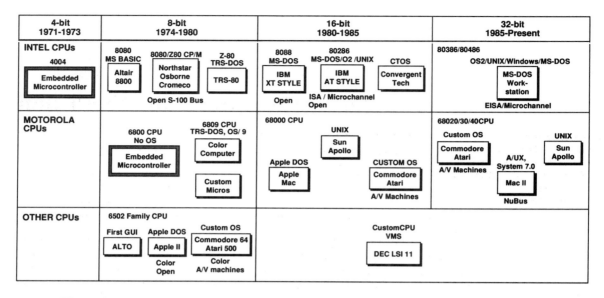

Figure 10.   The procession of microcomputer milestones: The major events that have occurred in the microcomputer evolution. Each microcomputer is tagged with its CPU and operating system, if any. The bus or other primary feature is shown below each microcomputer.

- *Mass storage* – From a rarity advanced to 200 MB drives that cost about the same as a good TV set and has progressed to erasable optical disk technology. Floppy disks starting at around 80K now boast of 2 to 8 MB densities. A Bernoulli cartridge, actually a floppy read by floating heads, has up to 90 MB capacity.
- *User interface* – The original front panel switches and LEDs have undergone a metamorphosis to become complex graphical user interfaces.
- *Memory* – 256-bit memory components have grown to 4 Mbit components.
- *Video displays* – Began with none or 40 column monochrome character displays and now have high resolution intelligent color graphics subsystems capable of displaying multiple pages of text and colorful high resolution graphics.
- *Communications* – Simple asynchronous communications have been replaced by high speed optical local and wide area networks.
- *Software* – Tedious hand assemblers, inputting programs by front panel switches was the precursor to object-oriented programming environments.
- *CPUs* – 64K addressability is now 64 terabyte virtual capability. Data width expanded from 4 bits to 32 and 64 bits. Clock speed increased from 1 MHz to 100 MHz.
- *Procurement* – What were once available only as mail order kits are now in every department store. Many households now own two or more DtCs.
- *Chip technology* – 1000 devices per chip have increased to 100 million per chip. Optical and electromechanical chips are now being prototyped and single electron switching devices is currently a hot research area.
- *Peripheral technology* – Has advanced from ASR 33 teletypewriters to color laser printers, and character recognition hardware using neural network technology.
- *Microcomputer users* – They have evolved from youthful hobbyists and hackers to high-level managers of Fortune 500 companies.
- *Operating systems* – Have developed from dedicated in-ROM systems to multi-tasking virtual memory capability.

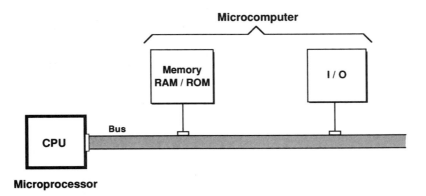

Microcomputer

Memory
RAM / ROM

I / O

CPU

Bus

Microprocessor

Figure 11. **Microprocessor in a microcomputer:** Relationship of the microprocessor to other components in a microcomputer.

2.2 The Microcontroller

The technology that spawned the microcomputer was the early four-bit microprocessor that appeared in the late '60s. Devices based on these microprocessors were known as microcontrollers. The first 4-bit microprocessors looked a lot like CPUs, but they were designed to act as complex controllers.

Controllers are complicated logic circuits that are required to operate equipments that have many different inputs and must accomplish functions that are related in a complex way to the inputs. Among their varied functions these devices controlled traffic lights according to traffic flows, elevators according to calls placed on different floors and time of day, and missiles according to position and detected targets. Rather than design the complicated circuits by complex logic, why not encapsulate the specific logical information into a general-purpose programmable logical control device? Then adjustments could be made systematically, in organized fashion.

> **NOTE**
>
> A controller is a complex of logic that takes in many inputs and creates an output that is a function of the inputs. The logic is often called random logic because the internal circuits that could involve simple logic functions (NAND, NOR, NOT), time delays, and storage functions appear as a haystack of components, relays, transistors, and circuitry. Usually the logic is highly specialized to a specific task and good at performing it, but not easily adaptable to a different functional task.

Figure 12 contrasts the complex, specialized controller with programmable logic. With programmable logic the microprocessor is at the center of activity. The logic of the general-purpose microprocessor does *not* change; the logical programming of the memory *can* change.

Thus was the microcontroller born. It could, through its I/O ports, read in various controlling inputs, make decisions according to a program in memory rather than by random combinatorial logic, and then perform a control function. The big dif-

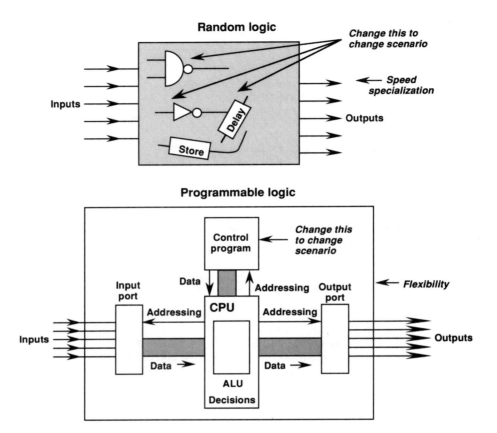

Figure 12. **Random vs. programmable logic:** Random logic is great for specialized jobs, but might resist change. General-purpose programmable logic may be less efficient, but it can be easily reprogrammed.

ference between this and the complex controller logic is that programmable logic can yield completely different logical behaviors just by modifying locations in a well-organized sequential memory chip, rather than in a conglomeration of electronic circuits. As with other things, there is a tradeoff. Specialization and parallel operation enables random combinatorial logic to function quickly; a CPU executing sequential memory will be slower. In a given application, much of the general-purpose capability of the microprocessor's instructions won't be used, and the generality will adversely affect performance. But the payoff, programmability, is worthwhile. The tradeoff between speed and programmability occurs often in the world of process control.

> **NOTE**
>
> An I/O port, like a single memory byte, is an addressable device to the CPU. I/O ports differ from memory locations in that permanent data and control information is passed in from and out to the outside world through the I/O ports. This data can be used to control elevators or to store personnel information. In contrast, memory locations store immediate programs and data.

If you program a microcontroller to run an elevator, the task includes determining how to respond to passengers waiting on different floors. What are the priorities? Who should be picked up first? When should directions be reversed? All of these complicated activities must be decided in advance, before any buttons are pressed on different floors. If you had to change the elevator's behavior without microcontroller logic, you would have to rewire the random logic, which could be a challenging logistical feat.

The early microcontrollers generally consisted of:

- **CPU** – A 4-bit microprocessor that could address 64K of memory.
- **Memory** – A 16K to 48K of ROM, also known as firmware, for storage of dedicated process control algorithms, which we now call software. 1K to 16K of RAM for storage of control program variables and scratch pad registers.
- **I/O** – A few I/O ports for transducer inputs and controlling outputs.
- **A/D converters** – These convert analog transducer signals to digital signals read in through the I/O ports.

Today's microcontrollers include most of these items in a single dedicated chip. These microprocessors are somewhat different from the CPU in your DtC because they are specialized for process control applications. Later we will look at a combined system that uses both a dedicated microcontroller and DtC in a synergistic combination.

Since programs and some data were usually burned into ROM, the early microcontrollers were simply turned on, whereupon they began performing their specific tasks. If a new process scenario was required, new ROMs were plugged in. The concept of programmable logic meant that you could change the behavior of these tiny microcomputer wonders merely by plugging in a different ROM chip, thus avoiding redesign of relay logic.

If you wanted an elevator based on programmable logic to return automatically to the ground floor every so often, you would need only to plug a different ROM into the elevator microcontroller. Early microcontrollers had no keyboards or video display monitors because there was no need to input new data or view the results.

2.3 Birth of the Microprocessor

It wasn't more than a year or two later that the 4-bit logic replacement device, the microprocessor, became widely regarded as a conventional CPU. Indeed, the little 4-bitter did have all the basic attributes of a CPU: an arithmetic logic unit (ALU), internal registers, and it ran programs stored in an external memory. This realization, coupled with the introduction of the 8-bit microprocessor, lit the fuse that touched off the desktop computer explosion.■

Since the microprocessor had grown up to look more like a CPU, it is fair to call it a microcomputer. At the time, very fast and large minicomputers based on MSI (medium scale integration) and even discrete logic were popular with those who could afford them. With the microprocessor affordable computers could be built. They were not as fast as their minicomputer cousins, nor did they have sophisticated operating systems – but time would fix that. The microcomputer was reasonable in cost because the main component, the CPU, was a single inexpensive chip.

When it found the capability of processing characters, the eight-bit microprocessor not only excelled in microcontrollers, but it also entered the public domain for general-purpose applications, and so became the microcomputer.

Figure 13 is the early microcomputer that preceded the one shown in block diagram form in Figure 14. Notice the differences in configuration. These differeces are in:

1. **CPU** – The early microcontrollers and the general-purpose microcomputers of the period often used the same 8-bit microprocessors. The Intel 8080 was quite popular. Today's DtCs, however, use the general-purpose CPUs from Intel and Motorola, while dedicated process control systems use a variety of customized CPUs from National Semiconductor, NEC, as well as Intel and Motorola, which include on-board analog/digital converters and I/O ports (discussed above).

2. **Memory** – Today's DtC has additional mass storage requirements for programs and data that the earlier microcontroller did not have. Also, in each there are different purposes for ROM and RAM memories. In the microcontroller, ROM is used to store the dedicated control program, while ROM in today's DtC is used for fundamental operating system functions. Early microcontrollers had no operating sys-

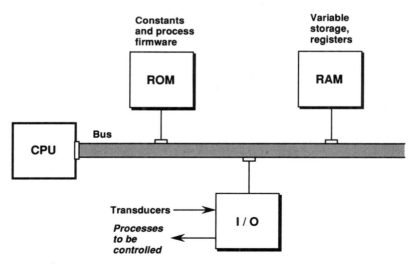

Figure 13.   Early microcontroller: The early microcontroller was quite similar to the early microcomputers except that the microcomputers had more RAM memory and peripheral interfaces.

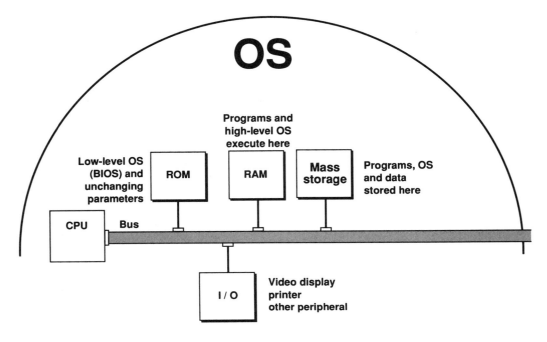

OS

Programs and
high-level OS
execute here

Low-level OS
(BIOS) and
unchanging
parameters

ROM   RAM   Mass
storage

Programs, OS
and data
stored here

CPU   Bus

I / O

Video display
printer
other peripheral

Figure 14. Today's DtC microcomputer: The microcomputer we now have is a far cry from the early microcomputers. Even with fast CPUs and hard disks and improved operating systems today's DtC has barely reached puberty. A lot of growing up remains.

tems, and were dedicated to single functions. In contrast, the DtC loads and executes a variety of different programs together with relevant data.
3. *I/O* – The microcontroller I/O required transducers and control signals, while the DtC needs a keyboard, video display, printer, and other peripherals.

As we see in Figure 14, memory comes in two major forms: random access (for execution), and sequential (for mass storage). The main difference between the early microcomputers and those we have today is that the former lacked mass storage.

2.4   The Microcomputer

The general-purpose microcomputer, later to be called *personal computer*, and finally *desktop computer* (DtC), experienced some perilous adventures in its growing up years.

The 8-bit Juggernauts

Some of the earlier general-purpose microcomputers, circa 1970, were packaged with the entire computer on a single board. They had a 20-key keyboard, for data entry only in hex. What else would you enter? There were no high-level languages, word processors, or the like for these models. You could do some work with assembly language, flash a few numbers to the displays, maybe build a clock, or control a temperature sensor. The printer was similar to the one found on calculators. It was built into the motherboard. The display was produced by 10 to 20 LEDs (light emitting diodes) soldered directly into the motherboard. These LEDs were more than enough for entering and displaying hex digits. One such model, rather popular at the time, was Rockwell's 8-bit AIM 65.

The more advanced early 8-bit microprocessors found their way into a variety of awkward-looking switch-laden microcomputer boxes. Enthusiasts could enter programs into RAM memories through the front panel switches. First, you would put the computer in a front-panel mode. Then, you would set the 16 address switches, the 8 data switches, and finally, you would hit a write switch. All of this had to be done to load *one* memory byte. If the program you were trying to load caused a system crash, you would have to enter the whole thing again. There were no floppy disks or hard drives. Lucky programs were seldom more than one thousand bytes. A program's output was generally a sequence of flashing lights. In all, not the sort of rig you would want to use to keep track of your checking account.

Later, crude operating systems consisted of a small ROM-based monitor and assembler programs in conjunction with the terminal and keyboard. Using assemblers, users could now develop and operate their machine language programs in a more civilized manner. The monitor permitted the user to enter machine language programs and data from a terminal keyboard instead of switches and view the results on a terminal's display instead of watching flashing LEDs. The terminals were connected by RS-232 interfaces. Soon, however, microcomputers implemented their own parallel keyboard interfaces and built-in memory mapped video interfaces.

One of the first advanced models of the 8-bit microcomputer was the 1974 Altair 8800, from MITS (Micro Instrumentation and Telemetry Systems), which used Intel's 8080 microprocessor. The unit was sold with MBASIC, Microsoft's BASIC interpreter written by Bill Gates (now Chairman and CEO of Microsoft). Soon, hundreds of vendors began packaging the 8080 and the newer Z80 into systems that would operate under Digital Research's standard CP/M operating system.

CP/M

The CP/M systems had built-in video interfaces, so you could connect large black and white monitors directly to the microcomputer with a simple cable. The built-in video interface yielded significantly faster display drawing times because it had a built-in display memory and did not have to communicate over a slow serial interface to a slow terminal. This increased interactivity would someday impress mainframe users. Color was not considered seriously because no one knew what to do with color, and besides, CP/M did not support color. Also, CP/M computers popularized the floppy disk as a mass storage medium, incorporating 8" floppies on massive disk drives that could stop a speeding truck.

Many early CP/M systems were expandable, using a hundred-pin bus known as the S-100, standardized by the IEEE. Because of their expandability and capability of operating under CP/M, many of these systems found happy homes in scientific laboratories and in process control environments as well as in a variety of business support areas.

Systems that were able to run under a standard operating system like CP/M
quickly gathered a following. Software operating under CP/M was desensitized to
architectural dependence. This proved to be a pivotal factor that drew hundreds of
vendors together. As we will see later, it is not easy to separate architecture and
operating systems when discussing important system features in the realms of
MS-DOS, OS/2, and Unix.

The ALTO

In 1973, as if blessed by a glimpse of the future, Xerox, at its Palo Alto Research
Center (PARC), developed the ALTO microcomputer. The ALTO, a legend in its
own time, had a removable hard drive, a 600 by 800 pixel monochrome page display, and a pioneering mouse/icon operating environment similar to that found on
most of today's GUIs. The ALTO preceded Xerox's popular Star Workstation,
which was introduced in 1981. The impact of this early research on today's DtCs
now resides in the look and feel of Apple's point and shoot menus and in MIT's
X Windows operating environment.

2.5   Personal Computers Arrive

As packaged microcomputers became prevalent in research labs and basements,
experimenters continued to develop more complex applications. Soon assemblers
and debuggers were replaced by higher-level languages, often BASIC or Pascal, and
other turnkey software applications such as word processors, spreadsheets, and small
information management programs. Vendors soon realized that there was something
to be said for having one's own computer and the metallic, unaesthetic microcomputer was repackaged more attractively in plastic, which was less expensive than
metal.

The early Commodore PET combined everything – a keyboard, monitor, and
motherboard – into a single rather forward-looking unit. The PET was mass

produced, marketed to the general public, and became quite popular for a variety of applications. Interestingly, the first Commodore PET computers were shipped with a single page of documentation. The PET allowed you to use your audio cassette player for low-cost mass storage. It was still more of a hacker's microcomputer than a desktop computer.

If we were to look for a significant date marking the arrival of the desktop computer on the public scene, the most likely candidate would be 1977, when Apple introduced the Apple II. Shortly thereafter Radio Shack came out with its TRS-80. In addition, Radio Shack introduced its color computer, based on the Motorola 6809, the most powerful 8-bit microprocessor at the time. Most of these low-cost DtCs ran disk or cartridge software, were reasonably priced, operated in-ROM BASIC, and were excellent machines for the home enthusiast and experimenter.

Atari introduced its first computer based on MOS Technology's 6502 microprocessor, the same one found in the Apple II. Commodore introduced its improved VIC20 followed by the Commodore 64 line. The Commodore computers were based on another 65xx family member, the 6510. The Commodore 64 merits special attention because it was an incredible hacker tool. The documentation was excellent and both user and vendor were able to write programs that used the add-on Commodore floppy disk drives and special features. The manual for the computer was a complete guide to its built-in BASIC, memory management (bank switching), chip timing diagrams, use of 65xx zero page memory, and a host of other information that let you delve into the machine.

While the Commodore and Atari computers concentrated on special effects for entertainment, sound chips and animation-oriented video displays, the Apple and TRS-80 computers focused on the ordinary but lucrative business uses: word processing, spreadsheets, and database applications. This traditional distinction continues, as we shall see, if we replace 8080-based CP/M machines with MS-DOS and Apple computers and then compare them with Commodores and Ataris.

At the height of their popularity, the Apple II and Radio Shack TRS-80 computers were thought to be considerably different. In retrospect, we know they were quite similar. Unlike their predecessors, which ran under the standard CP/M operating system, the Apple II and TRS-80 each ran under its own unique operating system. The Apple II and TRS-80 both flourished as the result of aggressive marketing. Apple undertook a massive effort to establish itself in the educational field. That effort continues to this day, and Apples can be seen in elementary, middle, and high schools throughout the country. Both systems ran a variety of turnkey products such as spreadsheets and word processors. Also, both systems supported built-in ROM-based BASIC, believed at the time to be an essential feature of any microcomputer.

Early Mass Storage

Many early 8-bit DtCs, the Apple II, Radio Shack TRS-80, Commodore 64, Atari 400, and IBM's original PC used audio cassette players as their mass storage medium. In many cases the tape players were commercial audio units. Using a recording method similar to that of hard disk (MFM), a data stream was placed on the audio tape. The typical data rate was 300 to 1000 bits per second. A long program (20K was considered long) could easily take many minutes to load.

Ordinary cassette tapes were used. The shorter ones, 30 and 45 minutes of recording time, were more reliable than longer tapes. Longer tapes tended to stretch. Programs and data were recorded with headers so that the operating system, at that time simply a function in BASIC, could search the tape for the header and then read in the specified file. The problem was that the searching mode was no faster than the playing mode, so you could search for a half hour just to find a desired file. Successful users learned to label their tapes with tape counter numbers, leaving a small gap between programs.

> 10 - 200 – Android Nim
> 210 - 940 – Game of Life
> 950 - 1400 – Forth Interpreter

To find a desired program, you would zero the counter, fast forward to a point just short of the program, and press PLAY. If the program failed to read in successfully, you got an error message and had to rewind the tape and try again.

Certain brands of tape worked better than others as did some cassette players. Exchanging tapes was a continuing problem because different tape players had different counter resolutions, audio characteristics, or wow and flutter characteristics. A variety of paraphernalia existed for copying cassette tapes, generally involving circuitry that would recondition the recorded audio pulses from original tape to copy tape.

The first Commodore floppy disk drive implemented a serial interface similar to the RS-232. Copying a 170K single sided floppy disk took 40 minutes. Today's hard drives and floppies bear little resemblance to their predecessors, and happily the audio cassette tape mass storage has practically disappeared.

Microcomputers Come of Age

An important attribute of the early desktop computers, the personal computers, was their well documented plug-in expandability. Both Apple and the MS-DOS computers are particularly suited for plugging in a variety of enhancement boards that combine synergistically with the main computer unit. A host of powerful add-ons are described in Part V. Figure 15 gives you a glimpse of the fun in store for experimenters who dip into the fascinating world of system add-on hardware.

The MS-DOS phenomenon was rooted in 1981, when IBM introduced the PC, using the Intel 80xxx line of microprocessors. The microcomputer industry was thenceforth and forever changed. Although IBMs original PCs were modest in performance, they were thoroughly documented and widely cloned by other manufacturers. As we shall see, widespread manufacturing led to their extraordinary popularity, so that today the MS-DOS computer is a market commodity and sometimes the IBM heritage is forgotten.

Except for relics from the past, personal computers have been replaced by desktop computers. Desktop computers of all makes and models are now being used for creative design, engineering, and business applications. They work in unison with other computers in complex networks, but you can disconnect them from the network to run them independently whenever you wish. Since the microcomputer has proved itself in so many different categories of activity, the term desktop computer is used for all machines in all types of desktop applications. The crucial point is that you own the whole computer; everything you need is in or can be accessed from a stack of boxes on your desk.

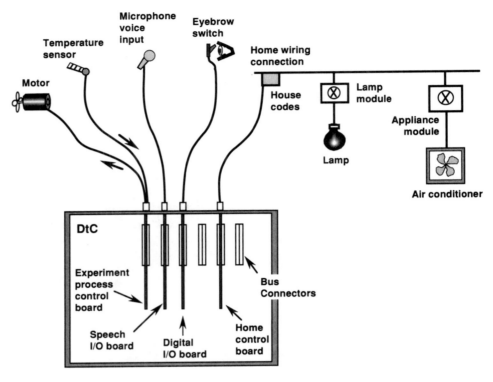

Figure 15. **Expanding the microcomputer:** Half the fun was hooking up neat gadgets to your DtC.

2.6 Arrival of Engineering Workstations

The microprocessor-based engineering workstation emerged in the late '70s, thanks mainly to the introduction of the Motorola 68000 microprocessor. The 68000 was the most powerful microprocessor at that time. Masscomp, HP Apollo, and Sun Microsystems are familiar names of vendors who jumped on the 68000 bandwagon. Later, we will see that a more powerful CPU is only one of the factors that separate engineering workstations from desktop computers. The Unix operating system was quickly adopted for these workstations, which helped to popularize them and thereby produced a perceptible impact on computing in general. In 1984, Apple built a cut-down 68000 microcomputer and called it a Macintosh, which later evolved into the Mac II line that would compete with engineering workstations. Currently Apple is introducing a combination Apple/Unix-based operating system called A/UX.

2.7   Minicomputers vs. Microcomputers

Since it is possible to describe the microcomputer as a descendant of the minicomputer, it is important to understand the key differences between the two.

1. Minicomputers are larger in size and capacity.
2. Minicomputers support multiple users.

A minicomputer is generally smaller and less powerful than a mainframe computer, yet it is not a microcomputer. Why not? Because the microprocessor, a CPU on a chip, had not yet been invented when minicomputers were born. Indeed, the CPUs of early minicomputers consisted of thousands of discrete transistors, or at best MSI (medium scale integration) chips, which made the minis quite large. Also, peripherals associated with minicomputers, particularly mass storage devices, had to be rather capacious in order to support multiple users.

Any history of microcomputers ought not to ignore Digital Equipment Corporation's Programmed Data Processor. The PDP systems were priced at $100,000 and up. In the late 1960s and early 1970s, DEC minicomputers fell in price to about $20,000, which did much to legitimize the notion of *minicomputer*. The DEC 16-bit PDP 11/70 was extremely popular and was used extensively for real time digital signal processing applications as well as for solving a variety of engineering problems. The PDP 11 minicomputers have since been replaced, beginning in the late '70s, by DEC's 32-bit VAX (Virtual Address Extended) line of minicomputers running under DEC VMS (Virtual Memory System) operating system.◨

◨ Only the most recent DtC operating systems support virtual memory.

DEC's MicroVax, which incorporates most of its big brother's better features, is less expensive and uses the popular cut back "Q" bus. Since the MicroVax implements several microprocessor CPUs we call it a microcomputer even though it performs like a minicomputer. Much of DEC's popularity derives from its solid operating system and high levels of compatibility between models. Other important minicomputers during that period were Data General Corporation's (formed by DEC employees) Nova and Eclipse.

DEC's other important contribution in the microcomputer arena in the late '70s was the 16-bit LSI (large scale integration) 11. The LSI 11's CPU was based on four proprietary VLSI chips, and therefore we call it a microcomputer. What is significant is that it ran DEC's operating system and much of its popular software base.

Soon, however, the scientific community would have an alternative to DEC's LSI 11 for low-cost microcomputing. New offerings appeared as performance advances were made in Intel and Motorola microprocessors. During the early '70s it was easy to distinguish mainframes, minicomputers, and microcomputers. Size was one criterion. Mainframes filled rooms, minis filled walls, and micros were little, bench-top, single-process computers used mostly for process control or experimentation. Microcomputers were single user; minicomputers served five to ten users; and mainframes could serve one hundred or more users. Even today, the multiuser distinction continues. Desktop microcomputers are highly specialized for serving a single user's many needs; minicomputers are often used by small groups; and mainframe usage continues for activities requiring secure, corporate-wide activities.

During the '70s mainframe computers were being redesigned to occupy smaller cubes by using MSI and later VLSI technologies. The smaller mainframes were called minicomputers. Throughout the '70s minis were distinguished from microcomputers by:

- *High speed technologies* –Minicomputers used MSI and bipolar, single transistor component technologies, which were high speed compared to the early microprocessor's VLSI technology. Minicomputers of the '70s were thus quite a bit faster than microcomputers at that time.

- *Custom computing equipment* – Minicomputers could be customized to perform specific computational tasks since one did not have to commit the entire CPU to a single VLSI chip. A minicomputer might have several quite different CPUs and other powerful I/O processing capabilities distributed throughout the system. Microcomputers implemented more general-purpose microprocessors.

- *Multitasking operating system* – Minicomputer descendants of mainframe computers had multitasking operating systems that were capable of implementing virtual memory. Access to virtual memory offered support to multiple users who had large memory requirements. Microcomputers of the period were single CPU, single tasking computers with minimal memory support and simple operating systems, if any.

- *Large backplanes* – Minicomputers generally supported large plug-in boards, each capable of its own special tasks. Large disk drives, strong I/O capability, and large memory models were implemented by plug-ins to the backplanes. Although some early microcomputers did have backplanes, they were restricted by sluggish buses and unreliable designs.

During the '80s and now into the '90s all of this has changed. We now find multiple microprocessors in minicomputers and high clock speed microprocessors and multitasking operating systems in desktop computers. Controversy over the differences between minicomputers and microcomputers is raging quietly in many quarters, especially now that many distinctions have all but vanished.

3.0   DtC Comparisons

Choosing a DtC system is somewhat like choosing a car. Different lines and models serve different purposes. There are common passenger vehicles, then special-purpose rigs like jeeps, and finally the workhorse trucks and vans. You choose a given type of vehicle based on how you plan to use it. Once you determine the type you need, you then look at details: horsepower, drive ratios, transmission types, as well as many accessories and options. The same shopping scenario holds for a DtC.

DtCs can be divided conveniently into three significantly different categories, depending on their respective evolutions and features such as performance, compatibility, applications that they run, and respective operating systems. Tables of DtC units are provided to point out the major features and differences. You will not be an expert on how many googleflops are in Apple's latest computer creation, but you will learn more about what various computer manufacturers offer that appeals to their respective audiences.

You need to be familiar with the various microprocessor lines, buses, interfaces, and microcomputer operating systems to get the maximum benefit from DtC comparisons.

Categorizing DtCs is like categorizing the fancies of youth. One week kids are into skateboards, the next week it's dirt bikes. It's the same with microcomputers. Some say that things change so fast in this industry, computing magazine articles are outdated before the ink dries. The categories defined here admittedly are in constant motion, but we can nevertheless take appropriate snapshots to freeze them for examination.

1. ***Home and business*** – Dominating the activities of the workaday world are the MS-DOS and Apple computers that now boast, almost flaunt, an incredibly wide variety of useful software for home, business, and lately, technical applications. A few years ago, we would have had to use the term personal to describe this category. However, more and more we find home/business computers in the work place, in networks, and performing higher end engineering and scientific applications.

2. ***Engineering and production*** – Dominating the technical and scientific fields are the powerhouse engineering workstations from such vendors as DEC and Sun Microsystems. Lately, MS-DOS, Apple, and the entertainment class of DtCs have begun to make inroads into this market.

3. ***Entertainment and education*** – Dominating the fun-and-games and educational arenas are the Commodore, Atari, and other computers that have spectacular visual and audio effects. These effects are no less important than the intuitive operational features that allow young and old alike to do surprisingly complicated things

with little or no introduction to the program. Software found only in the home/business category is beginning to show up in the entertainment category. This trend is expected to accelerate when special features such as sound and animation are added to otherwise bland applications.

Let's look at these DtC categories from a technical perspective and consider their important architectural characteristics.

3.1   Home and Business (HB) DtCs

Currently, the most popular suite of desktop computers is in the category we call *home and business DtCs* or HBs for short. By business we mean the DtCs used at work for day to day activities. Most large business applications continue to be hosted by minicomputers; however, there is increasing use of HB computers for database management, for document preparation, and for many network activities. Smaller group-level databases and other office applications are well suited for the HB computer. Small businesses such as doctor's offices are operated entirely by HB computers while larger organizations such as auto parts jobbers and videocassette retailers use HB computers in individual stores to serve local data to central mainframes or minicomputers. MS-DOS and Apple have penetrated almost every corner of the workaday world.

The characteristics common to the most popular DtCs are:

■ Open systems are well documented and relatively easy to expand or enhance with hardware as well as software.

- They are heavily marketed by their manufacturers.
- They are open systems.■
- They have abundant software, readily available, across the board of applications.

We begin with the most popular MS-DOS computers, spend some time discussing the Apple line, and finish with a comparisons chart of both lines.

The MS-DOS Phenomenon

MS-DOS computers are available from hundreds of different vendors, so users benefit in two ways: they can choose anything from a Tonka-toy model at one end to a machine that behaves like a real-life giant earth mover at the other, and all, relatively speaking, are competitively priced. Thanks to thorough documentation they may be studied at any depth one cares to probe. CP/M computers won popularity largely because they ran under a common CP/M operating system. The same holds true for MS-DOS computers – they too run under a common operating system.

The MS-DOS computer arrived in 1981, when IBM introduced the 8088-based PC. The 8088 microprocessor was a weakling compared to Motorola's robust 16-bit 68000. But no matter; the 8088 was sufficiently powerful for average folks and besides, microcomputers based on the 8088 were cheaper to build. The 6502 and Z80 microprocessors, at the time popular in personal computers, were no match for the higher speed 8088 with its internal 16-bit capability. There seemed to be no contest. The market would be saturated. A Hoover-like promise filled the air that every desktop would one day hold a personal computer.

More importantly, factors including expandability and documented operating systems allowed hundreds of manufacturers to produce computers that were func-

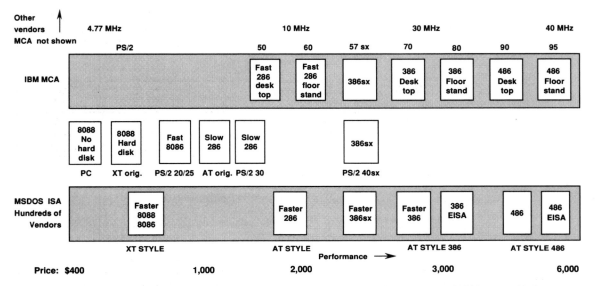

Figure 16. Systems comparison: Here we see the many performance possibilities provided by the different MS-DOS computers and also how much of the total market IBM intends to service. Notice IBM's penetration into both the MCA and ISA markets. Not shown is the smaller number of MS-DOS MCA clones.

tionally identical to IBM models. Collectively MS-DOS computers have become commodity items both in the home and in the office. Later models, based on the Intel 80286, 80386, and 80486, give the MS-DOS computer features that place it in the company of engineering workstations. Also, since Unix runs on Intel-based microcomputers as well as on Motorola-based microprocessors, the dividing lines between home and business computers is blurring to the vanishing point. As mature operating systems, more powerful CPUs, improved graphics displays, and peripherals become available we find microcomputers moving in on the engineering/scientific and higher-level business applications.

MS-DOS computers can be divided into two classes: 1) IBMs, and 2) all other MS-DOS compatibles. Look at the IBM models that initiated the MS-DOS phenomenon. The note in the introduction to this Part highlights the nomenclature used for MS-DOS compatibles presently available. Figure 16 combines IBM's original and PS/2 lines with the wide variety of compatibles in a single performance chart. The chart's purpose is to depict the huge selection offered both from IBM and the hundreds of compatible manufacturers here and abroad. You should note that price ranges and performance comparisons are only guidelines that will not hold for long in a rapidly moving industry.

Original IBM PCs

As mentioned earlier, IBM started the MS-DOS computer craze with the PC line. IBM's ability to mass produce and market the PC, regardless of what was inside, was indeed a masterful business feat. IBM microcomputers can be divided into original units introduced in 1981 and the newer PS/2 product line introduced in 1987.

Because so many of the IBM PC line are still in use, and because they were the fountainhead of the DtC phenomenon, they merit special consideration. DtCs at first were designed for modest use around the home and in elementary business applications.

Model	CPU	Slots	Hard Disk	Floppy Disk Cap.
PC	8088	5	None	160K
XT	8088	8	10 MB	360K
AT	80286	8	20 MB	1.2 MB

Table 2.   Summary of original IBM PCs

Some of the factors that led to their popularity were:

- *Marketing* – They were vigorously marketed by IBM and IBM's backing assured customers of continuing support.

- *Auxiliary chips* – IBM PCs had DMA controllers, used an interrupt controller, and contained a built-in math coprocessor, an 8087. A CPU-integrated coprocessor was not found on other popular DtCs of that period, the Apple II, Radio Shack's TRS-80, and the 8080/Z80-based CP/M systems. Similar chips for the Motorola 68000 were either more expensive because of its full 16-bit data width or were not available at all.

- *Relatively low cost* – Initial PC/XT models based on the Intel 8088 were easy to build, and later models based on newer Intel microprocessors would be upward-object compatible.

- *Simple operating system* – PC-DOS was designed to be simple and adjustable. Although the Intel version 1.0 was a bare minimum operating system, version 2.0 had some of the attributes of larger operating systems such as tree-structured directories and piping, moving data between programs.

- *Video display* – Although early models suffered from poor color graphics performance, they exhibited adequate text performance and video costs were kept down. IBM now produces a range of higher quality and more expensive video display systems.

- *Bus* – A well-documented and easy bus to interface to. It would later become an IBM de facto standard known as the ISA (Industry Standard Architecture) bus.

The attributes above produced a reasonable compromise between performance and cost; ideal conditions to touch off the desktop computer rage. Applications software was easily produced by a mass of companies and individuals who generated it in quantity.

IBM Personal System/2 Workstations

Because other vendors improved considerably on IBM's original computer and in order to stay abreast of new technology, IBM, in 1987, introduced the PS/2 line. Significant features of PS/2s, not found in IBM's original line of PCs, were:

- Support of Intel 80386.
- Reduced integrated circuit count.

- Disk controller, video display, and other I/O functions built into the motherboard.
- 3½" floppy and hard disks.
- Auto resource allocation. Allocation by firmware on each add-on board, which eliminates tedious add-on board switch settings and avoids conflicts with interrupts, DMA, and use of I/O channels.
- Micro Channel Bus. A more advanced bus similar to Apple's NuBus and those found in engineering workstations.
- 200 MB optical disk support on some models.
- Larger in-ROM BIOS (>100K) for improved I/O support.
- Higher performance graphics interfaces and displays. VGA models offer better graphics performance than older CGA and EGA interfaces.
- Wide range of hard disk support from none (Model 20) to 600 MB (Model 80).
- Expandability from two to seven slots.
- Clock speeds from 8 to 40 MHz.

Model	CPU	Bus	Size	Significant Features
25	8086	ISA	Desktop	Low cost for schools, no hard disk
30	8086	ISA	Desktop	Low-cost starter system
30E	80286	ISA	Desktop	80286 with ISA compatibility
40	386SX	ISA	Desktop	ISA compatibility
50	80286	MCA	Desktop	Low-cost office system
50Z	80286	MCA	Desktop	Built-in networking capabilities
57	386SX	MCA	Desktop	SCSI hard disk
60	80286	MCA	Floor model	Better for expansion
70	80386 (80486 plug in)	MCA	Desktop	Excellent price/performance/size tradeoffs
80	80386	MCA	Floor model	Good for expansion
90	80486	MCA	Desktop	XGA display
95	80486	MCA	Floor model	XGA display, network server capability

Table 3. Summary of IBM PS/2s

The summary presented in Table 3 points out the significant differences between PS/2 models. Most importantly, the IBM PS/2 line supports both ISA and MCA buses, and all current Intel microprocessors. Each model number has many different categories supporting different memory expansions, built-in network capability, different CPU speeds, mass storage, floppy disk, and IBM mainframe communications options. Floor standing models have greater expansion capability, offering more slots and disks.

MS-DOS Styles

IBM offers a formidable array of DtCs. However, this is only part of a large whole. There is a thriving MS-DOS world full of compatibles to be seen. Besides IBM, many computer manufacturers have declared support for the MS-DOS DtC. Why do so many manufacturers build MS-DOS computers?

- **Big Blue's marketing power** – The first MS-DOS computers were marketed vigorously by IBM.
- **Hardware documentation** – IBM fully documented its architecture through a complete set of technical reference materials that include complete schematics for the system unit, all interfaces, and IBM-manufactured peripherals.
- **BIOS documentation** – Complete source listings of IBM BIOS ROMs were provided in the technical reference. The excellent documentation of hardware and operating system software made it particularly easy to clone the early IBM PCs.
- **Bus** – Fully documented ISA bus that was not particularly powerful but was easy to interface to hardware and to the software base.
- **Power vs. price** – The first PCs filled the gap between the less powerful 8-bit personal computers and the more powerful workstations of the period. Today's MS-DOS computers represent an excellent power to price ratio.

As a class, MS-DOS compatibles are quite similar to their IBM ancestors. However, they differ in performance. MS-DOS compatibles come in three styles:

- **XT style** – MS-DOS compatible computers similar to the original 8088-based IBM PC and XT, with only basic improvements, particularly in CPU speed.
- **AT style** – MS-DOS compatible computers similar to the original 80286-based IBM AT, with many supporting the 80386 and 80486 microprocessors, and with a host of performance features.
- **MCA style** – The Micro Channel or PS/2-style MS-DOS compatible computers similar to the Micro Channel PS/2 computers.

MS-DOS Computer Architecture

Not only must the MS-DOS compatibles be functionally equivalent to respective IBM DtC product lines, but collectively they must also be compatible with one another.

In any MS-DOS computer, you will find common architectural features. Commonality is what permits these computers to run under the same operating system and therefore to run the same software base. Common attributes will be found in IBM clones, Asian, or performance MS-DOS compatibles. It is the common attributes that characterize MS-DOS computers as a class.

To be compatible with IBM and other MS-DOS computers, a given computer must be functionally equivalent. Functional equivalency means that an applications software base will function the same when running on any computer within the class. From the viewpoint of the software, all the computers are the same.

The following is a list of the basic components of MS-DOS computers that together constitute their characteristic architecture.

- **CPU** – At the heart of every MS-DOS computer will be an Intel 80xxx microprocessor. Other manufacturers are already making these microprocessors.

- **Support chips** – Intel support chips such as the 8255 PIA, 8257 DMA controller, 8253 counter timer, and 8257 interrupt controller will be found in any MS-DOS computer. Lacking these, they will have reverse-engineered VLSI combined equivalents of the chips.

NOTE

In *reverse engineering*, a VLSI device is duplicated not by copying a schematic representation of the internal transistors, but by duplicating the input/output functionality of the device. What is actually inside the duplicate may be quite different, but functionally the device should be identical to the original model.

- *I/O architecture* – The identical mapping of the support chips into the I/O space; or what I/O locations are occupied by the controlling registers of the support chips.

- *Memory architecture* – Similarities in where the various memory structures are situated. MS-DOS computers will have their interrupt vectors at the bottom of real memory, followed successively by their RAM-based operating system, operating programs, video memory, hard and graphics display ROM, EMS switching space, and finally their ROM BIOS at the top of real memory, executable by all 80xxx CPUs.

- *Bus* – The bus (e.g., ISA, Micro Channel, EISA) must have identical pinouts if it is to support the many peripherals that plug into an MS-DOS computer.

- *Interrupt vectors* – Use of the same interrupt structure and corresponding DOS service routines.

- *Mass storage* – Similar or identical floppy disk drive sizes, formats, and controllers. Similar methodology for controlling and organizing hard drives.

- *Graphics display interfaces* – Consistent location of video memory, types of graphics display interfaces (e.g., CGA, EGA, VGA). ROM BIOS graphics display initialization support, equivalent text and APA display modes.

- *Standard interfaces* – Similar serial and parallel printer interface chips, interconnecting cables, I/O channel mapping. RS-232 serial interfaces use the National Semiconductor 8250 or 16450 ACIA (Asynchronous Communications Interface Adapter) chips.

- *BIOS routines* – The same location in memory, RAM, ROM, and similarly connected to the operating system.

The architectural factors listed above do not exist by coincidence. Compatibles must obey many of the architectural rules established in the original IBM PC line.

MS-DOS Compatibles

In addition to classifying MS-DOS compatibles as XT style, AT style, or MCA style, we can also classify them according to time period and manufacturing factors. Although IBM no longer manufactures XT and AT models, you will find them at computer shows and for sale on the open market. Therefore, you should know how to recognize them and understand what you will be getting if you buy one.

IBM Identical

The IBM clones of 1981 to 1985 were for all practical purposes identical to their respective IBM XT and AT PCs with the same specifications listed in Table 2 on page 44. With the early IBM-identical compatibles, the aim was to run IBM operating systems and software written for them right out of the box. Differences were built-in deliberately and solely for the purpose of avoiding copyright and patent violations.

Reverse engineering of support chips also protected against copyright problems. Most of the identical clones were supplied from Asia, particularly Taiwan, and components could be purchased for a fraction of the cost of the corresponding IBM equipment. Identical clones were such close copies of their IBM counterparts that most IBM components were interchangeable in these units. For example, IBM BIOS ROMs and BASIC ROMS would function even in the clone units and vice versa. Patent infringement loomed as an ever-present possibility, but was rarely challenged by IBM.

IBM Improved

There was a period from 1982 to 1987 when compatible computer manufacturers improved the IBM architecture and especially the weak IBM graphics interfaces a bit too much. In order for software to operate on the IBM-improved PCs, graphics routines had to be written specifically for the improved architecture.

> **NOTE**
>
> For a time, the Hercules monochrome graphics interfaces helped bridge the gap between different compatibles because a variety of graphics drivers could be obtained for this interface. As long as software was using the drivers, the software was at least graphics compatible.

Not all of a given program would have to be rewritten, but the software would be sufficiently unique that it would be packaged specifically for a particular product line. For example, Lotus Corporation supplied the 1-2-3 spreadsheet program in a box labeled for the Texas Instruments MS-DOS DtC. This software would not run on an IBM PC or identical clone; neither would the IBM version of 1-2-3 run on the Texas Instruments DtC. Individuals owning the improved compatibles could only hope that a sufficiently large user base would encourage software vendors to write software for their particular compatibles. The notion of installable graphics drivers that could accommodate different system architectures not supported by the operating system was only in its infancy.

> **NOTE**
>
> For speed, the NEC APC incorporated an 8086, rather than the 8088 found in IBM's original PCs. This didn't cause much of a problem. However, the APC also incorporated a graphics display interface based on their 7220 graphics controller chip, rather than IBM's crude CGA and EGA dumb video interfaces. The chip required very special software that wasn't too plentiful. Likewise, the Texas Instruments DtCs incorporated an improved graphics display adapter that was incompatible with IBM's CGA and EGA.

Current MS-DOS compatible purchase decisions will more likely be from one of the following categories.

Asian Compatibles

Hundreds of Asian manufacturers are mass producing MS-DOS compatible computers in every price range. XT and AT compatibles are no longer identical clones; they are improved versions.

- **VLSI random logic replacement** – The auxiliary chips such as interrupt controllers, DMA controllers, CPU, and the random logic that tied these chips together have been replaced by fewer and more reliable VLSI chips.

- **Smaller motherboards** – IBM's original AT motherboard was quite large. You can now purchase similar motherboards one fourth the size.

- **CPU clock speeds** – Most of today's Asian compatibles allow you to run at higher clock speeds. The original XT's 4.77 can run as high as 12 MHz; the AT's 6 MHz goes up to 16 MHz.

- **386/486 compatibles** – During the period that IBM was retooling to begin manufacturing 386-based PCs in their PS/2 Micro Channel product line, MS-DOS compatible vendors began placing 386 and later 486 CPUs in ISA bus boxes. Competition intensified to white heat because IBM was no slouch when it came to VLSI random logic replacement and microminiaturization of components.

- **Wide availability** – Motherboards and various peripheral interfaces and components can be purchased throughout the United States at computer shows and from thousands of local dealers. Chains of stores sell HB DtC hardware and software in supermarket settings. You can either buy the pieces and assemble them yourself or have someone do it for you.

  Asian compatibles are particularly popular in the home and in small business. You can start with a low-cost, cut down unit and build on it, adding a hard drive and a better monitor later. As their performance and reliability improve, you will find increasing numbers of Asian compatibles in the work place.

- **Compatibility** – Because of their relatively tame architecture, Asian computers, as compared to the performance compatibles and even IBM models, exhibit extraordinarily good software compatibility.

Performance Compatibles

Several U.S. and even more Japanese firms produce 80386- and 80486-based compatibles. Differences are mostly in the performance area not involving software compatibility with IBM or Asian models. U.S. and Japanese models are priced competitively with similarly performing IBM PS/2 models but have great difficulty, as does IBM, in challenging the low prices of Asian compatibles. Performance compatibles are found most often in commercial, professional, and engineering applications. Compaq, Zenith, AST, Hewlett Packard, Everex, and ALR are common brand names of performance compatibles.

Generally, you can recognize the performance compatibles by:

- **Higher levels of component integration** – The critical hard disk and graphics display interfaces are often found integrated on the motherboard and closely tied to CPU and memory. 32-bit data paths are commonly used for memory.

- **Higher performance interfaces** – Higher performance interfaces such as ESDI hard disks and intelligent graphics display controllers in display interfaces. High performance and specialized cache memories.

- *Higher cost* – Individual components and supporting hardware, power supplies, and computer cases are not generally replaceable and must be purchased from the original equipment manufacturer (OEM). Thus you'll pay more for replacements and repairs.

- *Less availability of component parts* – It is more difficult to get replacement parts due to less general replacements. You can't buy a heavily discounted Compaq motherboard at a computer show.

Category Blurring

The Asian and performance categories are beginning to blur as Asian manufacturers hop up their 386 and 486 DtC models. This all makes for healthy competition and lower prices across the board.

Most organizations will have some combination of IBM and compatible MS-DOS computers. When a large organization chooses compatibles for purchase, some considerations transcend individual tastes and preferences. Not only do you want to save your staff endless hours of shopping around, you also want consistency. Different models will differ to one degree or another physically or operationally and, of course, price will certainly be a factor. Make sure you review the following to help you narrow the choices.

- *Performance* – Which models provide the necessary performance levels? This is particularly important in network servers, engineering applications, large databases, and DtP applications.

- *Compatibility* – By now, most MS-DOS compatible computer compatibility problems have been solved, however, beware of compatibility problems that are often associated with the higher performance models. Although earlier MS-DOS versions and PC-DOS versions could be used interchangeably, there will be problems with the newer DOS 5.0 and OS/2 that are quite sensitive to the way increased memory is provided in the 80286- and 80386-based systems.

- *Quality* – How reliable is the unit? Ascertain the MTBF (mean time between failures). More expensive units will incorporate more reliable technologies, better motherboard designs, more burn-in testing and reliability. As with other investments, avoid what looks like free lunch.

- *Maintenance* – Consider system unit access for upgrading, particularly of hard disks and floppies. Look at the physical construction of the system box and how it holds the interface boards. Look for availability of contract maintenance and replacement plans. Differences in maintenance requirements, procedures, and spare parts procurement could constitute a logistical nightmare for your maintenance facility.

- *Popularity* – As always, try to choose popular manufacturers.

Volume purchases will reduce cost and help to assure responsive local solutions for knotty problems. Support is essential for the many diversified applications you will install in your DtCs. A popular manufacturer will also guarantee a good spectrum of performance choices under a common support umbrella. While trying to get a foot in the door, the less well known vendors may offer the moon. On the other hand you may be put off by the aloof attitudes of some of the popular vendors.

You will probably fare better if fewer manufacturers are involved in your computer solutions. Institutions will need to balance the specialized and high performance needs that diversified equipment can satisfy against the general needs of the more prevalent organizational operations that fewer models can satisfy. Managers of centralized support facilities will face hard decisions on what makes and models to support. Almost any equipment mix is bound to dismay some staff members; those who have convictions on the most desirable and best systems for their needs will deplore any contrary decision.

AT-Style Computers

AT-style computers are MS-DOS compatibles that implement 80286 and later microprocessors. Most include the ISA bus, and some implement a special 32-bit bus. A given DtC may have a special 32-bit bus or the newer standardized EISA 32-bit implementation. Owing to their longevity, we will concentrate on them for much of the MS-DOS computer discussion.

Table 4 highlights AT-style performance enhancements and their associated compatibility problems.

Feature	Description	Problem
Memory Caches	High speed static memory caches use special controller chips from Intel or from other vendors. Program/data portions used most often are placed here. In some DtC models you can have the BIOS placed in faster shadow RAM for enhanced I/O performance.	Some manufacturer's MS-DOS computer will require system specific MS-DOS versions and BIOS set-up installations of software that manage the hardware. Software compatibility problems will occur with performance software that uses system memory as a cache instead of that on the hard disk interface.
32-bit Memory	Most 80386- and 80486-based models support high performance 32-bit SIMM memory on the motherboard.	Beware of motherboards that use proprietary daughterboards for memory expansion to permit a smaller sized motherboard. Until recently, 32-bit expansion slots used for memory expansion were unique to each manufacturer's 80386-based MS-DOS computer. Most of the better systems implement EISA standard slots for 32-bit expansion, and usually plug all memory into the smaller motherboard. 4 MB SIMM memory modules make this possible.
Special Coprocessors	Sockets are available for more advanced coprocessors such as Weitek.	Remember, your software must support these processors. Even stock coprocessors may be rated at different clock speeds or might have special speed-up hardware. Installation should be performed only by knowledgeable personnel. Some MS-DOS computer users have had to slow down their CPU for it to function with the coprocessor.

Feature	Description	Problem
Mass Storage	Faster, denser, hard drives, improved hard drive interfaces (ESDI, SCSI, and IDE) with cache memory on the interface itself.	There may be incompatibilities between caches and with special diagnostic, formatting, or backup utilities that make intimate use of disk interfaces.
Graphics Display Interfaces	Faster video interfaces with faster RAM and controllers to allow shorter video read and write times.	Different manufacturer's implementations of IBM's CGA, MDA, EGA, and VGA display interfaces may not be compatible at register levels. Software that communicates directly with interface registers may cause problems. Mail order super VGA interfaces come in a variety of increased resolutions. However, they require special drivers and have been known to cause many video problems.
CPU Speed	Faster CPU clock speeds.	Faster CPU cycling can interfere with time sensitive procedures such as disk formatting and some network and communications boards. Also, graphics display and memory add-on boards are sensitive to CPU clock speed and may not function at higher speeds.
Packaging	Sturdier, lighter, smaller; all around better.	Fitting the units with specific ergonomic devices or rack spaces may be difficult. The lunchbox portables often do not physically allow full access to all slots.
Improved Chip Technologies	Surface mount of smaller chips, multiple support chips, DMA controller, interrupt controller, and auxiliary chips on VLSI chips. These chips can reduce the motherboard chip count from >100 to <20, which improves reliability and reduces power consumption.	VLSI equivalents that may not act exactly as original chips. Some require BIOS initialization. Problems may occur in highly specialized software that interacts directly with auxiliary chip functions. Go with the most popular chip sets, such as those from Chips and Technologies.
Operating System	Many vendors of compatible computers provide improved MS-DOS and OS/2 versions.	Differences occur in DOS hidden files and configuration files. Differences in MS-DOS compatible architectures are more sensitive to high MS-DOS versions, beginning with DOS 5.0, and to OS/2. More customizing is required with OS/2.
Improved BIOS Support	Improved BIOS ROMs with better built-in diagnostics and configuration support.	Differences in cache software implementations, EMS drivers, and other BIOS related drivers.

Table 4.   AT-style performance and compatibility

AT-style computers are popular and continue to be so because they are offered by dozens of vendors in a broad range of choices. Performance levels vary from 80286, to 80386, to 80486, all using the popular ISA bus. IBM support of microprocessors on the ISA bus is improving because IBM, who originated the ISA bus, expects a good market for it. There is a compatible to fit almost any budget from reasonably priced clones to quite expensive systems with high performance capabilities.

As you can see, choosing the fastest *and* most compatible AT-style DtC is not a simple matter. Shopping for DtCs should be undertaken with as much care, caution, and consultation as you would exercise when buying any other expensive technical equipment. Go with popular and well-supported systems, which is your best defense against problems such as those recounted above. However, as upgrades occur and new microprocessors are introduced, security and satisfaction may flip to uneasy anxiety. Just when you thought compatibility woes were gone, breakthroughs may thrust more complicated motherboards at you and special peripherals may appear on your wish list. You may pay more, but you will be computing more and troubleshooting less.

AT-Style Upgrades

Among AT-, XT-, and MCA-style computers, the AT style is the most popular and will be used as the model for upgrading; but what is said also applies rather consistently to the other two. IBM provides considerable upgrade documentation and support for MCA-style computers, which, in view of the complications involved in upgrading, convinces many to stick with IBM.

Math Coprocessors

Normally the 8087, 80287, and 80387 coprocessors are used, respectively, with the 8088, 80286, and 80386 microprocessors. The 80486 and later CPUs contain an on-chip math coprocessor, but the SX versions disable it on those 80486 chips that did not pass coprocessor tests. You can buy any number of special coprocessor add-ons that run faster Intel coprocessors on daughter boards, run other makes of improved Intel-type coprocessors that plug into the original coprocessor socket, or use very different coprocessors from yet other manufacturers, Weitek for instance, which may require special sockets. Check your math coprocessor needs carefully and be sure that your DtC has a socket for the one you select and that your software supports it. If software compilers don't support the coprocessor, the coprocessor will not be accessed. Special coprocessors such as Weitek require special compilers.

Special Processors

Your application may require a processor more specialized than the math coprocessor mentioned above. Consider DSP (digital signal processor), FFT (fast Fourier transform) processors, array processors, or even transputers. These processors are sometimes implemented on add-on cards that plug into existing ISA or Micro Channel card slots. For example, Intel's 80860 RISC microprocessors are available on plug-in boards for PS/2s and AT-style computers.

> **NOTE**
> Planning for this type of of upgrade can affect your initial DtC purchase. NeXT and Macintosh DtCs accept DSP coprocessors directly on their motherboards to ensure proximity to the CPUs and software support.

Hard Disks

Most AT-style computer cases have up to six half-height bays for mounting hard drives and/or floppy drives. For disk upgrading you need to be aware of several options:

- *RLL technology* – There are special interfaces with higher density data transfer rates that allow more hard drive storage. RLL interfaces require RLL-certified hard disks for reliability.

- *Data compression boards* – Data compression boards compress data on-the-fly to and from the hard disk, transparently from software. Compression boards may pose a problem when data is lost from the hard disk and must be recovered.

- *Faster hard disk interfaces* – Older technology, the Seagate ST512/406 for instance, has been almost completely replaced by IDE, intelligent ESDI, and SCSI interfaces. Although more expensive, data transfer rates are improved while actually reducing the burden on the DtC's CPU.

- *Built-in disk drive interfaces* – Most performance AT-style personal computers have disk drive interfaces built into the motherboards or closely interfaced to CPU/memory circuitry. Built-in disk drive interfaces are difficult to replace. Hard disks purchased for high performance DtCs are generally more expensive and not easily interchanged.

- *Formatting* – A hard disk should be purchased together with a controller and low-level formatted with its matching interface. A given disk controller can support many different hard disks and a given hard disk can be operated by many different controllers. However, once formatted by a given controller, the hard disk generally cannot be operated by a different controller without reformatting for that controller.

- *Cables* – Most hard disk problems can be traced to bad cables between the hard disk and its interface. Be sure that good, undamaged cables are included in your hard disk purchase.

- *Set-up procedures* – Formatting, partitioning, and setting up of a hard disk is not trivial. The best maneuver is to enlist someone who has done it before, preferably with the same hard disk and interface as the one you purchased. Frequently the hard disk comes with software that will lead you through the entire installation process, so check for this.

Removable Hard Disks and Other Magnetic Media

You can buy 20 MB, 44 MB, and 90 MB Bernoulli removable disk drives that plug into a hard disk slot. Also, tape backup units up to 2.2 gigabytes can fit into a hard disk bay.

Floppy Disks

The hard disk controller in most AT-style computers will support two floppy disks, both 3½" and 5½", and in both high and low densities. You can add a third or even fourth floppy for increased compatibility by using special add-on boards. Newer IDE and SCSI interfaces will support more than two floppy disk drives. Be sure the AT-style computer has sufficient bays for the number of add-on drives you will require.

Graphics Display Interfaces

VGA adapters may be purchased for older XTs and ATs originally outfitted with
low resolution CGA and EGA display adapters. Hundreds of vendors supply such
boards. They come in a wide range of prices and capabilities. The extended VGA
modes also differ widely, and you may not be able to find software drivers.

Memory

Memory upgrades are particularly complicated. Some of the factors to consider are:

- **Extended/expanded** – Which do you need? Which will your CPU support?
- **Memory speed and type** – Are you purchasing chips of appropriate speed for the
  CPU? Are you purchasing the appropriate type (SIMM, SIPP, DIPS)?
- **Motherboard capacity** – How much memory will the motherboard support? The
  more supported it is on the motherboard, the fewer add-on boards will be needed.
  The most effective location for memory is on the motherboard.
- **Memory amount** – How much memory do you really need? Do you need more
  memory for a hard disk software cache or do you in fact need a faster hard drive?

┌─ **EXAMPLE** ──────────────────────────────────┐

Putting an 80386 processor add-on board with 32-bit memory in an 8-bit
XT will accelerate CPU execution quite a bit. You are, however, still
saddled with an 8-bit bus for I/O transfers to and from hard disks and
video interfaces in the rest of the unit. Moreover, the add-on board will
likely be more expensive than simply replacing the entire XT
motherboard with a 386 motherboard. Further, software compatibility
problems may arise from a relatively nonstandard CPU/memory/system
interface, particularly with the newer, more architecturally sensitive operating systems like OS/2.

└──┘

LAN Boards

If you want to network a DtC, you should look into LAN hardware and software.
If family members each want a DtC but you can't afford a large hard drive or another printer, you can buy cut-down systems and interconnect them to share a large
hard disk and printer. Many LAN boards contain boot-up RAM that permits a network DtC to acquire the operating system from the server, precluding the need for
local mass storage. Data can still be saved locally with floppy disk drives on the
remote units. A complete LAN system, such as Artsoft's Lantastic, that includes
software and cables for two DtCs and costs around $300.

CPU upgrades

You can buy an add-on board with a higher power CPU than the one on your
motherboard. An 80386 board with its own 32-bit memory for an old XT will give
it 386-like performance. Also, you can jack up your existing CPU clock frequency

on some AT-style DtCs by simply plugging in a different clock crystal. Upgrades to the 80486 are possible but more complicated because of on-board cache memory requirements. Most CPU upgrades are expensive, and may not be cost effective.

Generally, 32-bit 80386 and 80486 DtCs combine their CPU, memory, hard disk, and sometimes video display interfaces in a closely-tied 32-bit system, impossible to duplicate through after-the-fact CPU upgrades.

Bus Slots

AT-style computers will support older 8-bit XT-style add-on boards, but for increased performance most interfaces, video display, hard disk, and network come in 16-bit versions. Be sure that your AT-style computer has a sufficient mix of 8- and 16-bit slots to handle your needs.

Power Supply

Don't forget that every board you add to a DtC consumes power. Be sure your unit has sufficient power to run whatever it is that you add. Popular power ratings are from 150 watts to 300 watts for a fully loaded DtC. Some power supplies come with dual fans and built-in transient suppressors.

Serial and Parallel Interfaces

Many AT-style computers provide serial and parallel interfaces on the motherboard, but they may be purchased on individual add-on boards included with video display interfaces or on memory add-on boards. Determine how many of each you will need so that you have the proper mix. While there are eight slots in an AT-style computer, they can fill up quickly. When buying add-ons you should know what they include because many of them incorporate multiple functions. Figure 17 shows the most common use of bus slots.

Building Your Own AT-Style Computer

If you are keen on building a DtC, you can do it. Lean back and imagine this: You received a flyer luring you to a computerfest. You decide to go. In an area about the size of a high school gym are hundreds of vendors offering assorted bargains from gadgets and trinkets up to fully loaded 80486 DtCs. The floor is teeming with bargain hunters. Some buyers organize teams equipped with walkie-talkies to pass the news when a hot bargain is spotted. The table below show approximate prices for important DtC components that can be found at a typical computer show.

❬ Computerfest ••• Retail Store ❭	
8088 motherboard	
Stock 4.77 MHz CPU ....$ 20	Switchable 4.77 or 10 MHz ....$ 50
80286 motherboard	
AT clone 60	C and T chips, fits in XT 80
80386 motherboard	
25 MHz 300	33 MHz, built-in static cache 450
80486 motherboard	
25 MHz 800	33 MHz w/added 128K cache 1000

Table 5.   Comparative prices for motherboards

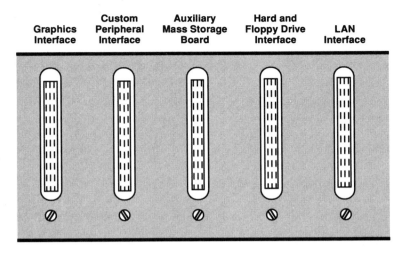

Graphics Interface	Custom Peripheral Interface	Auxiliary Mass Storage Board	Hard and Floppy Drive Interface	LAN Interface

Figure 17. **Typical slot assignments**

⟨ Computerfest ••• Retail Store ⟩		
Hard Disk Drives		
Used 10 MB, no guarantee $ 30	120 MB, guaranteed ....$ 350	
Hard Disk Controller		
8-bit IDE 25	Latest ESDI 16-bit 200	
Floppy Disk Drives		
Straight from Taiwan 55	From U.S. and Japan 100	
Video Interface		
Stock IBM CGA......................20	Good super VGA 150	
Monitor		
Composite green screen.........20	Good multisync analog color 350	
Keyboard		
Off the boat from Taiwan........25	Enhanced high quality 90	
Memory Expansion		
640K for XT............................50	4 MB of SIMM for 386 250	
Math Coprocessor		
8087 for XT............................50	80387 300	
Power Supply		
65 watt 35	250 watt 75	
Case		
Cheap AT box 15	AT-style with 6 drive slots ....100 flashing LEDs and pushbutton switches	

Table 6. **Comparative prices for hard disks and other components**

After you have selected and purchased the necessary parts, install the motherboard in the case with screws. Bend a few metal posts here and there to fit. Maybe you'll need to file the bay where the disk unit mounts. Plug in the boards and you have a do-it-yourself DtC. Be forewarned, however, that assembly can be a harrowing experience because component dimensions vary considerably. A mechanically experienced friend can be of enormous help.

If you know nothing about the insides of a DtC, you might ask the dealer to assemble it for you. You may even get the assembled DtC cheaper than if you bought the parts separately, and get a guarantee to boot. As Table 5 and Table 6 show, you can assemble a low-end MS-DOS computer for as little as $250. Essentially you will have a cut-down XT. For about $1500 you could have a fairly good 80386.

Buy from local dealers even if you pay a little more. If a component has to be exchanged, you won't have to drive many miles or have to rely on the postal service. If components from different dealers are incompatible, each will claim that the others are at fault. If all components come from a single dealer, a more equitable resolution of such a problem is possible.

A large part of this book was drafted on an Asian 386 MS-DOS computer assembled in the manner described above at a cost of about $2000.

AT Style vs. MCA Style

For many, obtaining an MS-DOS compatible reduces to the choice of 1) an AT-style computer assembled from components supplied by a multitude of manufacturers, 2) buying a ready-made performance DtC, or a PS/2 MCA computer from IBM. Not many manufacturers, working on tight budgets, are willing to pay the licensing fees to implement IBM's proprietary Micro Channel. Therefore, there aren't many MCA-style compatibles to consider. Besides, the EISA standard 32-bit bus provides an attractive non-IBM standard for other manufacturers.

AT-Style Advantages

- *ISA compatibility* – Wide availability of expansion products designed for the AT ISA bus. This includes the normal complement of add-on boards as well as special prototyping and experimentation systems.

> **NOTE**
> Global Specialties, a Connecticut firm, sells a board that brings the ISA bus out to a prototyping board for experimentation. Also, many engineering and research organizations have created numerous specialized interfaces to their equipment on ISA boards. The MCA board is smaller and has a denser connector trace spacing than the ISA board, making it more difficult to design outrigger interface boards.

- *Wide selection* – A terrific selection of computers with mind-boggling performance enhancements in a wide price range from hundreds of vendors.

AT-style is suited for:

- *CAD/CAE/CAM applications* – Groups that squeeze every possible drop of performance out of their computers and interface them with a variety of equipments and different computers.

- *Engineering/science* – Primary importance is processing throughput and availability of custom add-on processing and interfacing boards. Most of these individuals are willing to tinker with the technical issues of compatibility and performance enhancement variables found in the AT-style computer.

- **Home use** – Asian compatibles can often be purchased cheaply. Also, interfacing to home and other experimentation with the ISA bus is still practical.

MCA (PS/2) Advantages

- **Easier to support** – Fewer manufacturers make MCA systems, so most purchases are from IBM, which provides reasonably good support.

- **Safety of IBM** – IBM has demonstrated with its RT/6000 that it can compete in the workstation market. Increasingly powerful Micro Channel add-on boards from SCSI hard disk controllers to 3-dimensional graphics interfaces are appearing weekly.

- **IBM mainframe connectivity** – Support for specialized mainframe connectivity features is more likely to come from a combination of proprietary advanced PS/2 ROM BIOS routines and advanced OS/2 versions and interfaces to the Micro Channel bus.

  IBM supports the communications option hardware (including terminal emulator boards and Token Ring network boards) very well. Certain maintenance of these complex boards is essential.

> **NOTE**
>
> The connectivity reasoning given here is mostly hearsay, but such rumors have convinced certain IBM mainframe users to purchase IBM PS/2 equipment. Many individuals have expressed concern about the degree of integration that will come about for IBM's overall computer line.

- **IBM operating system compatibility** – The newer operating system versions are becoming architecturally sensitive, particularly in the way they manage extended memory. An IBM DtC running an IBM operating system is a safe option for those who don't want to bother with different DOS configurations on compatibles, even if performance might suffer.

- **OS/2 support** – Certain support of future functional extensions of OS/2. Although other popular vendors claim they will maintain support of their OS/2 versions, you may be sure that IBM will come through.

- **Micro Channel** – Many argue, all things considered, that the Micro Channel and potential improvements hold the promise of best overall design for MS-DOS computer buses. EISA-based systems must maintain compatibility with the less capable, although currently popular, ISA bus style. Promises of even faster and better Micro Channel buses are continuously in the literature. Also, there is great interest in the 20 Micro Channel audio/visual signals that will become important for future DVI and interactive video applications.

- **MCA board advantages** – MCA boards are smaller and force higher chip densities and lower power, which should ultimately result in higher reliability. This, however, will not transpire without painful and expensive retooling.

Purchasing IBM PS/2

- **IBM connectivity** – Groups that do analyses and conduct management functions in a shared environment between IBM mainframe computers and their desktop units.

• *Administrative applications* – Offices in which performance is not as important as high reliability and accurate maintenance.

Relative Performance Considerations

Many factors need to be considered when you compare the performance of MS-DOS compatibles based on the different Intel microprocessors. Some of these factors will become clear as we look at systems based on the 8088, 80286, 80386, and 80486 microprocessors.

Important general factors that affect performance are:

• Clock speed of the CPU, which is currently 4.77 to 50 MHz.
• Speeds of system RAM and other resources and wait stating.
• Type of hard drive and bus interface used.
• Type of video interface.
• Presence of math coprocessor and its software support.
• Instruction and hard disk cache memory.
• Bus data transfer rates.

If one were to look only at the 8088, 80286, and 80386 microprocessors running at the same clock speed, each performing a simple task, the relative performance would be:

$$8088 = 1.0$$
$$80286 = 4.0 - 5.0$$
$$80386 = 7.0 - 8.0$$
$$80486 = 15.0 - 30.0$$

Feature or Attribute	Microprocessor			
	8088	80286	80386	80486
Clock speeds	As high as 10 MHz	As high as 20 MHz	As high as 40 MHz	As high as 80 MHz
Data bus width	8 bits	16 bits	32 bits	32 bits
Video interfaces	CGA, EGA, VGA, and Super VGA video interfaces are becoming faster; fewer states and quicker screen reads and writes. Extended VGA interfaces incorporating intelligent graphics controllers are becoming popular.			
Memory addressability	1 MB	16 MB	4 GB	
Memory management	Simple 16-bit segmentation scheme	Variable and larger segments	Sophisticated segmentation and paging scheme and virtual 8086 machine capability.	
Math coprocessor values	8087 - 1.0	80287 - 1.8	80387 - 3.0	-

Table 7.   Comparison of microprocessor performance and attributes: Clock speeds and bus widths influence performance. Greater memory addressability and more sophisticated memory management also improve software performance.

> **NOTE**
>
> Depending on the application, the performance of the 80286 and 80386 processors can vary greatly. Performance differences have as much to do with data path width and speed to and from peripherals as instruction execution rates.

As you can see from the above and from Table 7 the biggest jump in processing power is between the 8088 and 80286 systems (other factors not considered).

When all relevant factors are considered, an 80286-based system could be 10 to 15 times more powerful computationally than the stock 8088-based IBM XT, while an 80486-based system could be 30 to 100 times more powerful than the XT. It depends on how you configure the system and what software is running.

The processing speeds of different Intel microprocessors can be measured by IPS, the number of instructions per second that can be processed. Given a problem requiring the use of most machine level instructions, the 4.77 MHz 8088 can execute instructions at about 200 to 300 KIPS (a thousand IPS) while a 33 MHz 80486 can run at 5 to 10 MIPS (a million IPS).

The extent to which special microprocessor features, including memory management, addressability, and coprocessing can use this power depends on how well these features are supported by the operating system and the applications software. For instance, many of the features of the 80386 microprocessor will be unused as long as there is a large 80286 (and 8088) microcomputer user base. Of course, software vendors will always be found who will support a new microprocessor feature.

If you buy an 80486-based system, you could easily be disappointed to find that after spending one or two thousand more than the price of an 80286-based system, the increase in performance less than you expected. This could happen easily if a new 80486 system is not configured properly, or if the appropriate software that can take advantage of this processor is not used. Software products that support special features of the 80386 and 486 microprocessor include DESQview, Windows, FoxBase Pro 386, Borland's Debugger, Mathematica, and IBM's Interleaf Publisher.

A properly configured 80386 or 486 microcomputer is usually software compatible with 80286-based systems and will generally outperform it by at least 3 to 1. Therefore, an 80386-based system is almost always a better buy for those who need the higher performance.

Why Choose an 80386/486-Based Microcomputer?

At present, many DtC users are quite satisfied with 80286 or even 8088 performance levels. Several factors, however, point to an increasing need for the higher performance levels of 80386/486 systems.

- **Memory management** – Newer operating systems – OS/2 and MS-DOS 5.0, and major MS-DOS enhancements such as MS-Windows – will take advantage of the enhanced memory management capability of the 80386 processor. Several stand-alone software products already do. When these memory management capabilities are properly used, performance improves by an order of magnitude. For instance, some database structures can be reorganized by reorganizing memory. The ability of the 80386/486 to reorganize the way it addresses memory translates to an impressive performance enhancement for the special cases and applications that can take advantage of this capability.

Of particular importance is the 80386/486 virtual 8086 capability. Using this capability the Windows and DESQview environments can support multitasking or programs not originally intended to be supported. By virtualizing the entire 8086 environment, including its management of screen memory, MS-DOS graphics programs, not specially written to do so, can even be windowed. Programs written for virtual memory capability will also benefit enormously through the 80386/486 demand paging capability.

- *Addressability* – The 80386/486 can directly address 4 GB of memory. This is 256 times the direct addressability of the 80286 processor. Although few systems support more than 16 MB of memory, some systems will expand to 64 and a few to 128 MB. The problem is finding motherboard and slot space for the memory. As memory densities increase while prices continue to fall, we may expect to find systems with up to 1 GB of main memory at the turn of the century. Future operating systems and applications will undoubtedly gobble up larger addressability. Among such applications are huge databases, AI systems, 3-D graphics, and intensive mathematical systems and simulations.

- *Pure performance* – As more DtC applications software products are being written in higher-level languages and more higher-level application-specific languages evolve for the microcomputer, the increased performance of the 80386/486 will become more important. Many DtC applications programs such as dBASE and Lotus 1-2-3, previously written in assembly language, have been rewritten in the C language for increased functionality and expandability. However, the performance of these products suffers on inadequately powered microcomputers.

  Other products, such as the Excel spreadsheet and WordPerfect word processor, were developed initially in the C language. Higher-level languages, the SQL query language for example, will also require higher performance. Most engineering/scientific, graphics, and large database management applications require the higher levels of functionality provided by fourth and higher generation languages, many with OOP capability. Such higher-level languages demand higher CPU capability, just to plow through the hierarchy.

  Although instruction execution speeds under the current 16-bit MS-DOS and OS/2 support are not much different for the 80286 and 80386, other factors, such as coprocessor support, 32-bit memory, and peripheral interfaces can, nevertheless, improve performance. Soon, the availability of the 150 MIPS 80586 will place even more processing throughput at your disposal. Also, as language compilers support the improved 80386 processor capabilities, DtC applications developed using these compilers will require at least an 80386 processor.

- *Operating systems and networking* – The overhead of improved operating systems, such as OS/2, and networking will require considerable performance from the system microprocessor.

- *80486 upgrade* – It will be relatively easy to upgrade 80386-based systems to 80486 capability because of their inherent similarities. Moreover, the price of a 486 motherboard is not much more than the price of a 386 motherboard with coprocessor.

Several vendors are now packaging moderately-priced microcomputers based on the lower cost 80386SX and 80486SX microprocessor. These systems represent an attractive alternative to the higher cost 80386-based systems and the less expensive and slower 80286-based systems.

Laptop and Notebook Portables

The popular laptop application is use in the field. It is convenient for collecting data, recording meeting minutes, and writing memos. Bring the laptop to the office, plug it into the DtC serial port using communications software to transfer files and programs. Another popular use is presentations and demos at meetings, where a laptop is connected to a viewgraph display peripheral.

Current MS-DOS compatible portables include VGA video displays, up to a 495 MB hard drive, 16 MB of RAM, and 80386 CMOS microprocessors. Battery life is three to five hours between recharges. Units with hard drives run half as long. Most machines can use line current through a converter. Small keyboards may be awkward and expandability, the availability of slots, is limited.

The just introduced flat screen active CRTs, in which each screen dot is an active transistor, can now produce vivid colors comparable to those of a display monitor. Until recently the portable displays were notoriously poor in text and graphics. Now it's a matter of affordability, because a good color display can easily add $2000 to the portable's price tag.

Some notebook MS-DOS computers, using neural network technology, can recognize handwriting on their display screens. These units come with special software for developing interactive applications such as taking orders in restaurants to in-the-field insurance claim adjustments.

The Apple Computer World

The story well-known to all microcomputer enthusiasts is that of Steve Jobs and Steve Wozniak who, working in a garage, designed and built the first Apple computer. Over time, these early Apples evolved into today's popular Macintoshes. What is it about these computers that attracted so much attention and enabled the Apple Corporation to compete in the crowded MS-DOS compatible ring, and lately in the engineering workstation arena?

The history of the Apple computer so far is marked by two eras. The first is the era of the 8-bit Apple II, which continues to be quite popular in some areas. The second era, jolted by rocky upheavals, begins with Apple's initial, relatively unsuccessful attempts to launch the 16- and 32-bit Macintosh line.

Apple's story could be called a saga of feast to famine to feast. The early Apple IIs attained exceptional popularity, but Apple's transition to faster 16- and 32-bit DtCs was marred by several unfortunate failures, notably the Lisa and the Apple III. The Macintosh would support the 68000 microprocessor, but unlike the Lisa, would be an inexpensive (around $2000) appliance-type computer.

But now a third era is dawning for Apple as it couples with IBM in a joint venture. In mid-1991 Apple and IBM announced the formation of a joint software company that would:

- develop an open system software platform.
- design computers based on IBM's RISC chips that are being developed in conjunction with Motorola.
- collaborate on multimedia software.

Whatever comes of this alliance will undoubtedly benefit DtC users, but to what extent its impact will be on the microcomputer industry will not be known for at least two to three years.

The Early Apples

The early Apples were an excellent compromise between the rather drab B/W CP/M and TRS-80 DtCs and the colorful and talkative entertainment computers, the 8-bit Ataris and Commodores of the period. We begin the discussion of the early Apple with its first brush with success, the Apple II.

The Apple II Computer

The Apple appeared around the time of the CP/M computer, the Radio Shack TRS-80, the Commodore, and the Atari. The Apple II, Apple's first popular DtC, was introduced in 1978. It came in several different models, as may be seen in Table 8, and the early ones were quite similar except for memory support, slots, size, and portability.

Model	CPU	Significant Features
Apple I, II+	6502	Six-color graphics, 280 x 192, 7-slot expandability
Apple IIe	6502	Increase in memory support to 128K.
Apple IIc	6502	Smaller size, not expandable, cheaper, built-in 5¼" floppy.
Apple IIc+	6502	Built-in 3½" floppy, internal power supply
Apple II GS	65C816	Enhanced graphics (320 x 200, 256 colors) and sound, plus built-in local talk network capability.
Apple III	6502	Business version of Apple II, not completely compatible. Not popular.
Lisa	68000	Used Xerox graphical user interface, ran integrated software; pricey, poor performance considering the 68000.

Table 8.   Summary of early Apples

The factors that led to the Apple II's popularity in the home and in some businesses were:

- *Heavy marketing* – Apple Computer spared nothing in its advertising campaign, which was aimed especially toward the general consumer and educational markets.

- *Educational usage* – Aggressive marketing included donation of computers to secondary schools, which established a solid Apple II base and favorable bias in school systems nationwide. Success in this environment attracted the attention of a broad audience, including that of software developers, who were quick to spot a burgeoning market and rushed to supply it with easy-to-use software.

Many school systems continue to use the Apple II because of this early exposure. Popularity in this environment is also credited to a rich educational software base that makes good use of Apple II's color capability and even more so to Apple's hospitable and intuitive graphical user interface. Within minutes of first introduction a youngster can produce interesting results on the screen.

- *Microprocessor* – The 8-bit 6502 was a good microprocessor for squeezing a lot out of the early Apple's 64K memory.■ The 6502's 256 zero page registers were put to good use in small Pascal and BASIC implementations. The simplified construction of the registers gave the compilers and interpreters quick access to the 6502.

■ In addition to your program, the 64K contained a 12K BASIC interpreter, 4K of ROM BIOS, 4K of memory mapped I/O, and 16K of screen memory.

- *Expandable system unit* – A well-designed system unit that included keyboard, system motherboard, power supply, and seven well-documented slots for expansion, all packaged in high impact-resistant plastic case.

- *Color capability* – The Apple implemented a 280 by 192 six-color video display. The interface design, although somewhat strange and a bit difficult for software developers to follow, was significantly more straightforward than that found in the entertainment computers, the Atari, Commodore, and Texas Instruments that we talk about later. The other popular CP/M and Radio Shack TRS-80 computers were only black and white.

- *Use by the handicapped* – Due to good expandability and documentation, many Apple IIs benefitted the handicapped and those in special education. Specialized interfaces included speech recognizers and synthesizers for the hearing and speech impaired, keyboard replacement devices for the physically handicapped, text video interfaces for the visually impaired, light pens, wheel chair guidance systems, body switches to control home appliances, to name a few. Many Apple IIs are serving the handicapped today.

Apple II GS

All of the early Apples incorporated an 8-bit data bus, including the Apple GS for peripheral compatibility. The Apple II GS, introduced in 1986, was to provide Apple II users with a more powerful 16-bit DtC that was compatible with the Apple II. The 16-bit 65C816 microprocessor of the GS was object compatible with the 8-bit 6502, yet considerably faster, clocking at 3 MHz compared to the Apple II's 1 MHz. The GS would accept many of the same expansion boards as the Apple II. However, software that used the enhanced graphics and sound capability of the GS would not be backward compatible on the Apple IIs. The Apple II GS did provide users, particularly schools, with highly graphics-oriented educational applications as an affordable alternative to a faster machine with better graphics.

The early Apple IIs did not support hard disks. Other manufacturers supported them with the ProDOS operating system. Most Apple IIs used 5¼" disk drives while the GS and c+ moved up to the higher capacity 3½" drive.

Early Apples could support several MB of memory through a process similar to the one used in MS-DOS computers to support expanded memory. As with MS-DOS computers, special software support was required. When Apple shifted to the 68000 microprocessor for the Macintosh, the software lost popularity.

The Other Apples

A couple of Apples, the Apple III and Lisa, listed in Table 8, never seemed to ripen. The Apple III, introduced in 1980, was a business version of the Apple II. It failed to win public acceptance due largely to its incompatibilities with the Apple II.

In 1983 Apple introduced its first 68000 based DtC, the Lisa, which featured the Xerox GUI interface and ran integrated software. Due to poor software implementation and hardware deficiencies it was not a great performance machine. Besides, it was pricey, around $10,000. Lisa did not succeed.

The Compact Macintosh

■ The Mac is named for the McIntosh apple, grown mostly in Eastern Canada, British Columbia, and New England.

In response to the surging popularity of 16-bit MS-DOS computers brought out by IBM in 1981, Apple three years later, in 1984, introduced its Macintosh.■ Based on the Motorola 68000, it was destined to become a winner. The 68000 is a more powerful microprocessor than the Intel 8088, popular at the time in XT-style MS-DOS computers. As we can see by looking at Figure 10 on page 28, however, the 80286 AT-style computer was also introduced around 1984, and 80286 performance compares well with the 68000. You should be aware by now that lines are being drawn for a great battle between the MS-DOS and Apple computer worlds.

Apple's philosophy at that time was to develop a small, inexpensive, appliance microcomputer based on the powerful 68000 microprocessor. Important features of the Macintosh, according to this philosophy, were:

- Closed architecture without coprocessing in early models.
- Spiffy high-resolution B/W monitors similar in resolution to IBM's EGA.
- Based on 68000 microprocessor.
- Small desktop footprint.
- Graphical user interface oriented and user friendly operating system.■ At the time the GUI was known as a WIMP (Windows, Icon, Menu, Pointing) system.

■ Similar to that found on the Alto in 1973 and Apple's own Lisa, but with better performance.

These characteristics resulted in a body of consistent user friendly software in many applications categories. Apple's operating systems for Macintosh and Macintosh II have typically catered to the user interface and graphics support. The interface and graphics support are no doubt the most important sources of Apple's popularity, which continues to hold steady. Such built-in and consistent support has been lacking on the MS-DOS side until recently.

■ The CPM to MS-DOS transition was between the 8080 and 8088 microprocessors, which were not drastically different.

The early Macintosh computer suffered from a serious lack of software and crippling memory support problems. Software conversion between the Apple II's 6502 and Macintosh 68000 was slow and painful due to the significantly greater capability of the 68000.■

The early compact Macs were built upon the principle of a tightly designed DtC with all required interfaces built into the motherboard. This approach, while limiting expansion, ensured a consistent software base. Software developed for one Macintosh would run on any Macintosh quite simply because all Macintosh implementations were the same. No specialized interfaces or hardware to accommodate. This of course was contrary to the Apple II, which was quite expandable. The size and cost of the Macintosh was reduced by including the monitor and system unit in the same box. As it turned out, since so much was crammed into such a small box, the compact Macintosh was a nightmare to repair. DtC users usually prefer expandability and a choice of peripheral interfaces. Important attributes of the compact Macs are summarized in Table 9.

Model	CPU	Slots	Memory	Feature
Skinny Mac	68000	none	128K	Original Macintosh, 512 x 342 B/W.
Fat Mac	68000	none	512K	Original Macintosh, 512 x 342 B/W.
Plus	68000	none	4 MB	Built-in SCSI interface begins.
SE	68000	one 16-bit	4 MB	Sony sound chips. More combined direct access functions on proprietary chips. Internal supported hard disks start. ADB port with custom VIA (Versatile Interface Adapter chip.
SE/30	68030	one direct	16 MB	Small footprint with 68030.
Classic	68000	none	4 MB	Inexpensive.

Table 9.   Summary of compact Macs

The Mac Classic is an inexpensive return to the early B/W Mac days, but with 4 MB of main memory. Because it uses the 68000, buyers should know that this unit won't support System 7.0 virtual memory.

Let's look at some of the more prominent features of the compact Macs, many of which survive in today's line of Apple computers.

- *Compact size* – Small size is achieved by combining the monitor and its support circuitry in the system unit using highly functional support chips. The monitor support circuitry and power supply circuitry are on the same analog board. Crowded circuitry and the monitor itself being inside the system box made repair or expansion very difficult for non-specialists.

- *Substantial in-ROM support* – Macs have ROMs ranging from 64K to 512K that provide excellent support to the Apple operating system. This relatively large ROM includes the BIOS functions normally found in MS-DOS computer BIOS ROMS, but also contains user interface and graphics support in the form of QuickDraw routines. Built-in graphics support has a profound impact on the nature of applications software available for the Macintosh.

- *Proprietary chips* – The use of chips such as BBU (Bill Bailey Unit) combined floppy, video circuity, and IWM (Integrated Woz Machine) proprietary floppy format is the reason the Macintosh is not widely cloned. The proprietary chips lead to smaller and more efficient motherboards, but more esoteric programming. Most MS-DOS computers implement the industry standard peripheral controller chips or VLSI combinations that are widely available.

- *Apple Desktop Bus connector* – This connector controls multiple daisy chained input peripherals, keyboards, mice, and alternative devices for the handicapped. The Apple Desktop Bus connector is great for interfacing a wide range of input devices. There is no analogous interface for MS-DOS computers.

- *SCSI ports* – Built-in SCSI (Small Computer System Interface) ports for more sophisticated high-speed peripherals. SCSI is becoming an industry standard interface. SCSI support is being built into newer MS-DOS compatibles. However, most users acquire SCSI interfaces by add-on boards, which are not as intimately interfaced to important CPU functions.

- *Serial ports* – Built-in high serial port using Zilog Z8530 SCC, a serial communications controller chip. The SCC is used as a printer/modem port and also for low demand networking of local groups of Macs. MS-DOS computers use the less capable National 8250 SCC chip, which nonetheless is adequate for most RS-232 interface applications.

- *Limited expansion capability* – The SE and SE/30 have a single direct access connector. The direct access bus of the SE/30s brought out important CPU functions – address, data, and control – directly, which is a particularly good interface without an intermediate bus standard in the way. Getting the most out of this type of interface, however, requires considerable developmental skill. MS-DOS computers have an analogous connector in their specialized non-EISA 32-bit connectors.

In general, the Macintosh is a well thought out, highly integrated, and somewhat proprietary DtC in a small package and at low cost. Since the MS-DOS compatible world at the time of the compact Macs was providing users with similar, yet expandable capability and a good microprocessor, the 80286, and a wide choice of peripherals, Apple would have no choice but to open its computer line.

Macintosh II Line

Apple returned with firm determination in 1987 to the business of producing expandable computers in their Macintosh II line. Not only did Mac II have peripheral slots like its ancestor the Apple II, it incorporated the powerful NuBus, jointly developed by Apple and MIT. Implemented with a reliable 96-pin Euro connector, the NuBus has become an industry success story. While MS-DOS compatibles have their EISA and Micro Channel buses, Apples and Mac IIs have the NuBus.

The most important difference between the original compact Mac line and the Mac II line could be called "getting off the appliance kick," summarized below:

- *Monitor separation* – The monitor and monitor circuitry are separated from the system unit. The Mac II has a monitor resting on top of it in the fashion of an MS-DOS computer. Many different graphics interfaces plug into the system unit expansion slots to support many types of monitor interface, and with the same interface flexibilities as the MS-DOS computer.
- *Expandability* – With 3-6 NuBus slots, Apple returned to providing slots for a variety of high-power peripherals, from image processing boards to data acquisition boards.
- *Coprocessor sockets* – Provided standard coprocessor sockets with built-in support of the powerful Motorola math coprocessors, including in-ROM detection and support of the coprocessor.

Model	CPU	Clock MHz	Coproc.	Slots	Memory	Distinctive Features
Original Mac IIs are no longer manufactured.						
Mac II	68020	16	68881	6 NuBus	16 MB	Higher capacity 1.4 MB floppy. Older Macs used 800K SWIM chip, which reads MS-DOS disk format.
Mac IIx	68030	16	68882	6 NuBus	16 MB	68030 support.
Mac IIcx	68030	16	68882	3 NuBus	16 MB	Small footprint.
Modular Macs (the current Mac II line to meet most needs).						
Si	68030	20	none[1]	Direct or NuBus	17 MB	Built-in color interface with sound input and microphone.
Ci	68030	25	68882	3 NuBus	32 MB	Optional cache memory.
F/X	68030	40	68882	6 NuBus, 1 direct[2]	32 MB	Many performance features.
"Low-cost" Color Mac						
LC	68020[3]	16	None	1 Special	10 MB	Apple IIe emulator, built-in color interface, sound input.

Table 10.   **Summary of the Mac II line, past and present**

1. After purchase you can have a NuBus or direct slot added, each with a 68882 coprocessor.
2. The direct slot of the F/X is not compatible with that of the Si or the Se/30.
3. Be careful. System 7.0 virtual memory support requires the 68030 microprocessor. Recall that the special virtual memory capability of the 80386 microprocessor is not found in the earlier 80286 model.

The Modular Macs

The improvements of the modular Mac over its Mac II predecessor is better memory support, sound input capability, and color graphics interfaces built into the motherboard. This is a partial return to the earlier Macintosh philosophy to build as much into the system unit as possible. The built-in display adapters, however, are often criticized as being slow and are often replaced by improved adapters on expansion slots.

The Macintosh F/X

■ An industry buzzword for "special effects."

The Mac F/X■ is a high performance Apple and is intended to compete favorably with the more popular engineering workstations described in the next category. The F/X has highly specialized peripheral controllers including a special DMA SCSI hard disk controller for superior hard disk performance. The F/X uses special 64-bit SIMMS for higher memory performance and has many other performance enhancements not found in the earlier Macs. High-end Macs have performance features that are found only in the very high performance MS-DOS compatibles.

The Mac LC

Some think LC means low cost. The LC is in fact a low-cost color Macintosh with the sound capability of the SI and limited expandability. Also, it can emulate the Apple IIe, which can be very useful because the old Apple II line continues to be quite popular in primary and elementary education. Its limited expandability, only a single special slot that is not compatible with the SE/30's direct slot, should be considered carefully when purchasing this Macintosh.

The Mac Portable

The Macintosh portable uses a 16 MHz low-power 68000 CPU. The Macintosh portable computer includes many of the features of the Macintosh series computers, including the processor direct slot, internal modem, video output port to drive separate monitors, external disk drive port, SCSI port stereo sound port, and ADB bus port as well as RS-232 and RS-422 outputs and Apple Talk capability.

Model Summary

Summarizing the different, popular Apple computers we have:

- **Apple IIs** – First 8-bit color Apples that helped start the DtC revolution through a well thought out, documented, and expandable system.
- **Apple Macintoshes** – 16-bit B/W units are built like appliances, with small footprints and almost everything you need included on the motherboard.
- **Apple Mac IIs** – Larger, more powerful Macintoshes with NuBus expandability more in line with today's MS-DOS computers.
- **Modular Macs** – A good spectrum of Apples, from the relatively self-contained Si to the super powerful, expandable F/X.
- **Mac Classic** – An inexpensive return to the little Macintosh.
- **Mac LC** – Low-cost color with particular good a/v effects.

A solid line of peripherals is also available for the Macintosh line.

> **NOTE**
>
> Solid means well integrated and well matched in performance to the companion system unit. This smaller line of good, though more expensive, peripherals makes it a bit easier to configure Macintosh systems than to configure MS-DOS computers.

You could say that peripherals for the Apple are not as diversified as those for MS-DOS computers, but the ones that are available are generally pretty good.

You can see from the above discussion that the Macintosh line has a selection of CPU, memory support, virtual memory support, and coprocessors very similar to those for MS-DOS computers. What continues to distinguish the Apples from MS-DOS computers is their built-in sound I/O hardware, better built-in graphics display interfaces, built-in ROM graphics, and user interface support.

Apple's Commitments

Apple Computer will continue to build and sell innovative desktop tools for engineering and business. Apple's future plans are to electronically integrate their desktop tools with the products of other major computer manufacturers, including IBM, DEC, and AT&T. Innovations from Apple have included:

- **MacAPPC** – Apple's software implementation of IBM's Logical Unit 6.2 and Physical Unit 2.1 specs.
- **MacWorkStation** – A software platform that allows developers to tie various host computers together with their Macintosh lines for user friendly processing front ends.
- **Macintosh coprocessor platform** – A ready-made add-on board building block card that includes a Motorola 68xxx processor and large amounts of RAM that interface to the NuBus. Vendors can buy this board and add capability for whatever niche they choose.
- **X Windows** – Apple Computer now implements the X Windows windowing standard. This will provide for a more distributed processing capability between workstations.
- **CL/1** – CL/1 is called a connectivity description language. It provides a bidirectional and transparent connection between Macs and potentially all host systems. CL/1 is the PostScript of computer-based communications.

Although there is considerable hype over MS-DOS compatibility modules, boards with Intel microprocessors for the Apple computer are not recommended for running MS-DOS software. The reason for a thumbs down is that these systems were not designed from the ground up to support Intel microprocessors. You would do well to wait patiently for the many new business applications that will be developed to run in the 68xxx environment as Apple continues to popularize these microprocessors.

The joint venture proposed by IBM and Apple Computer to form a software company is expected to have at least two important consequences. One is that the two firms will jointly support a power chip that IBM has under development and the other is that 80xxx and 68xxx software will converge.

Summary of Mac/MS-DOS Comparisons

Performance and architectural similarities can be found between Macintosh and MS-DOS computers in any category you may choose to compare. Both product lines support a wide array of useful software, both are extremely popular, and both are well supported. What then are the major differences between them?

Major Differences

1. **Proprietary design** – Apples have considerable proprietary design features both in in-ROM support and in the chips used in them. This has prevented a compatible market from developing as well as the proliferation of different cost and performance choices. MS-DOS computers are built with standard chip sets, mostly from Intel and Chips and Technology, available to any manufacturer desiring to build an MS-DOS compatible computer. This produces a highly competitive market and a great variety of models and products in the MS-DOS computer world.

2. **Graphics and user interface support** – Apple's operating system provides a good deal of user interface and in-ROM graphics support. Although much of this type of support can be found in MS-DOS computers, it is dispersed in many locations; e.g., in OS/2 Presentation Manager, in Windows, in the MS-DOS operating system enhancer, or in the applications software itself. Support is diluted, because it is coming from so many different directions. Also, due to the higher proliferation of different peripherals, this support is not as well integrated into a single manufacturer's product line.

In the Macintosh line you have in-ROM support of tightly controlled peripheral product lines, many of which are produced by Apple. In comparison, MS-DOS computer peripherals are mostly manufactured by vendors not cognizant of system unit or system software support details. Thus their support is not as well integrated with the respective computer low-level operating system software or computer hardware. This well-integrated software support results in Macintosh applications developers preferring to use built-in support rather than to write their own. This in turn results in a consistent set of compliant software.

Although Apple's look and feel can be obtained on MS-DOS computers by GEM, Windows, and the OS/2 Presentation Manager, the Macintosh look and feel has been bred into its hardware, which has well-integrated graphics interfaces and in-ROM support.

As we try to distinguish between the obvious characteristics of MS-DOS and Apple computers, we find that there isn't much difference. The most significant differences are that MS-DOS computers have a broad manufacturing base while Apple does not; Apple has been dedicated to a graphical user interface from the outset, while MS-DOS has not. Table 11 shows the complexities involved in comparing the two most popular HB computer systems.

FEATURE	MS-DOS	MACINTOSH
Popular operating system	MS-DOS, OS/2 (Windows, Presentation Manager).	Apple DOS 6.0, System 7.0.
Memory	640K limit problem on 8088 units. Virtual support with advanced OS/2 versions and Windows.	Consistent memory support up to 16 MB. Virtual support with System 7.0.
Data formats	None widespread other than ASCII.	ASCII, PostScript, .PIC, and formatted text.
Stock video	16 Color VGA, IBM 8514/A, XGA.	256 and 16.8 million color 640 by 480 display.
Bus	ISA, EISA, Micro Channel.	Direct, NuBus.
Graphics support	Varied; none in MS-DOS, PM in OS/2, Applications provide own support and drivers.	QuickDraw (ROM), and in OS.
Data transfer between programs	Historically, ASCII and lately, cut and paste and DDE with Windows and OS/2 for specific programs.	Cut and paste from the beginning and lately Subscribe and Publish through System 7.0.
Applications software base	Broad and diversified.	Widely varied, however focussed on office applications.
File management support	Varied. Little in MS-DOS, better in OS/2 and Windows, best with utilities.	Good support with Finder.
Compatible market	Hundreds of manufacturers.	None prominent.
Pricing	Wide variance.	Fixed mid to high range.
Networking	Generally provided by add-on boards.	Low-level networking built into most units. High level with add-on boards.
Microprocessor	Intel 80xxx.	Motorola 68xxx.

FEATURE	MS-DOS	MACINTOSH
Unix support	Using AIX.	Using A/UX.
Sound	External, non-standard add-ons.	Audio chips on motherboard supported in-ROM.
User interface	GUIs lately available from different sources: OS/2, MS-DOS, and Windows. Applications software provides its own.	GUI from the beginning and consistent.

Table 11. MS-DOS DtC compared to Macintosh

Viewing the table at a distance, we see more firmness and integrity on the Apple side because there are no possibly quirky compatibles and there is solid in-ROM graphical user interface support. Also important is that Apple doesn't suffer the dual bus standard found with MS-DOS computers. But then, Mac users fight between their NuBus and direct connect slots. Due to a better line of stock video display interfaces, melded effectively with in-ROM graphics support routines, the Macintosh has considerably greater integration in its fully supported graphics options. You can purchase any video display adapter for either machine, including built-in 3-D capability, DVI, and other special video. Special displays will generally require special software support on either platform.

You may admire the Macintosh line because of its pure breeding; indeed,it has few mutations. This is good from a consistency viewpoint, but mutation can produce intriguing variations in species.

As both IBM and Apple undertake to develop general-purpose business, engineering, and home use systems; their software base, operating systems, and architectures appear to converge. And, since software is being developed at significantly higher levels on each of these platforms, we will find increasingly similar software on the two.

Comparable Evolutions

Let's compare two very similar evolutionary paths: that of the 8- to 16-bit Intel-based microcomputers and that of the Apple II to Macintosh line. It was a great leap forward from the 6502-based Apple II to the 68000-based Macintosh computer. This jump can be seen in Figure 10 on page 28. A period of software scarcity ensued because of the radical difference in the microprocessors.

As Intel-based systems jumped from the 8-bit 8080 and Z80 microprocessors to the 16-bit 8088 there was also a period of software scarcity, but not as severe. Software running under CP/M, such as dBASE and WordStar, was converted rather easily to run under MS-DOS on 8088-based PCs. Due to 8088 segmentation, 64K programs were not too difficult to rewrite. Therefore, programs converted from the 8080, limited to 64K, and new programs written for the 8088 under MS-DOS, limited to 64K, came rather quickly. Writing programs larger than 64K meant dealing with 8088 segmentation, which is considerably more difficult, and programs were therefore slow to emerge. Also, the CP/M and early MS-DOS operating systems were philosophically similar operating systems as contrasted with the very different custom operating systems found on both Apple II and Macintosh DtCs, the Macintosh shifting to a GUI-oriented operating system.

Although software conversion to the Macintosh from the Apple II was more difficult than from the Intel 8080 to the 8088, developers of 68000-based software immediately had 16 MB addressability, while in the MS-DOS world, development capabilities passed through three transitions:

1. **64K** – Unsegmented 8088 programming.
2. **640K** – The limit of 8088 addressability using segmentation.
3. **16 MB** – 80286 memory addressability supported differently by OS/2, by individual programs, or by MS-DOS extenders.

These transitions complicated what would have been an orderly software maturation process had Intel simply moved from the 8080 to the 80286. The 64K to 16 MB jump, on the other hand, was a joy to Apple computer software developers.

Computer World Stumbling Blocks

In sum, the Apple and MS-DOS computer worlds have both had difficulties. The MS-DOS world was confronted with the 64K to 640K to 16 MB barriers, while Apple arrived rather late in offering an appropriately usable 68xxx – the Compact Mac.

Now that the MS-DOS and Macintosh worlds are engaged with 32-bit addressability (4 gigabytes) and virtual memory capabilities exceeding trillions of bytes, software and system developers are scrambling to catch up with the increasingly powerful hardware. Apple has its System 7.0 operating system while MS-DOS computers have OS/2 and DOS 5.0 with Windows. How will they pack more memory into their system units and more capability into their applications software? The answers to these questions will become apparent when we look at the changing nature of DtC operating system software and hardware later in this book.

Software transitions among the early 8-bit DtCs were encumbered with applications software that was written predominantly in machine language and was therefore difficult to convert from one microprocessor to another. Today, however, DtC software conversion is a different problem because most of it is written in higher-level languages. Now the problem is fitting applications into the various current high-level environments with Windows and Motif, and in architecturally diverse DtCs. We will touch on these issues later.

DtCs Come of Age

Now, we are happy to report, both the Apple and the MS-DOS computers have become legitimate computer workstations: MS-DOS computers with their 386/486 processors and OS/2 Unix capability; and Apple with its 68030 and 40 processors, System 7.0 software, and A/UX, Apple's Unix. We will now turn to the engineering/production workstation category of DtCs, which, as pointed out earlier, is becoming more difficult to delineate as a clear-cut category.

3.2 Engineering/Production Workstations (EP)

A workstation is a complete computing environment. A complete computing environment is the combination of high-performance hardware, a mature operating system, well-connected applications software, and connectivity with other workstations.

Dominating the scientific/technical field are the powerhouse computer workstations from such manufacturers as DEC, HP, Sun Microsystems, Intergraphics, Silicon Graphics, IBM RT6000, Xerox, and Data General.

The EP DtCs operate the higher-end applications demanding CPU horsepower and connectivity more closely related to mainframes and minicomputers. Yet, EP DtCs are often based on the same CISC microprocessors and coprocessors from Intel and Motorola that are found in the HB and EE categories. You will also find EP DtCs based on the reduced instruction sets (RISC) CPUs when performance in a specific area, say graphics, is crucial.

Sun Microsystems and Mips are the companies leading this technology and they show promise of putting mainframe processing power on desktops by the mid-1990s. The present version of Sun's SPARC (Scalable Processor Architecture) CPU, which evolved from Berkeley's research on RISC technology, has enabled it to become a market leader and DtCs based on it are about 30 times faster than DEC's original VAX or around twice as fast as the fastest MS-DOS 486-based DtC.

Of course, an 80586 chip with 150 MIPS capability will change the microcomputing scene. To add to the confusion we have the possibility of IBM and Apple collaborating on a CPU and an operating system code named Pink. Then there is ACE (Advanced Computing Environment), a sort of United Nations of RISC supporters. The ACE consortium with its growing membership is attempting to focus standards for manufacturing RISC-based computers. Specifications include minimum configurations for memory, storage, audio support, and minimum graphics resolutions of 1024 by 768.

The engineering production DtCs are more serious and centralized computing equipments and they are closely related to, and often difficult to separate from, minicomputers. At least for the present, however, we do not call them minicomputers because many are based on the CISC microprocessors that by definition are what microcomputers are made of. In many cases these computers do not fit on your desktop. Often you will find them resting on the floor next to a desk or near a cluster of desks in a network configuration. Since many of the EP computer vendors provide models that do fit on a desktop we must consider them in our hardware evaluations.

Most EPs operate under the Unix or DEC VMS operating systems through user friendly, windowed work environments such as Motif, Open Look, DECwindows, and Open Desktop.

Engineering and Production Categories

Within the EP category, we can define two types of DtCs: engineering workstations and production computers.

The engineering workstations (EWs) such as Intergraphics, Silicon Graphics, Apollo, and Sun for example are oriented toward the design professions, heavily emphasizing the use of graphics. This is evidenced in their extensive use of math and graphics coprocessors, general dedication of a single unit to a single user and inclusion of computational add-ons that support animated graphics and complex design data input.

The production workstations (PWs) Xerox, DEC, and Data General are oriented toward the larger scientific number crunching, image processing, information processing, and publishing traditionally performed on mainframe and minicomputers. For example, you might find a DEC MicroVax running departmental financial information using a statistical information system like the Statistical Analysis Software from SAS Institute.

Production usage likely when MicroVax is shared as a centralized data server by users with terminals. Also, you might find special page-oriented displays on a Xerox workstation or other general-purpose high-end math coprocessor with slightly less emphasis on special coprocessors. This is not to say that you won't find engineering design applications on DEC workstations, or that you won't do desktop publishing using FrameMaker, for example, on an Apollo engineering workstation.

Engineering/Production Applications Software Base

You will recall the applications areas discussed in hardware/software connection were:

- Writing/Publishing
- Information Management
- Display Graphics
- Engineering/Scientific
- Control/Interface

Although the HB computers do supply applications solutions in each of these categories, the EP computers are better suited for the higher power applications in each area.

In the writing/publishing area we find highly functional technical publishing software such as IBM's Interleaf or FrameMaker from Frame Technology Corporation.

Interleaf is a modular product that builds on a core. The core consists of a text processor, a graphics package, layout tools, composition features, and printer drivers. Tables, equations, advanced graphics packages and other features can be added, building up to a full-featured book publisher. With so much publishing power you will need a workstation to run it. The IBM slightly trimmed version of Interleaf Publisher runs on what we define as an HB computer. But it needs a minimum of 6 MB of RAM, 25 MB of free space on the hard disk, a mouse, a VGA or 8514/A monitor and adapter, and a PostScript printer or typesetter.

■ WYSIWYG or "what you see is what you get" composition systems display documents as graphic images approximating their printed appearance.

FrameMaker is a full-featured WYSIWYG desktop publisher with a complete tool palette for creating figures, geometric primitives, rules, as well as pattern and color fills. ■ The software also manages the task of producing long multichapter documents. This is all integrated into a complete and open publishing software package optimized to take advantage of the distributed computing power of HP Apollo, Sun, DEC, and recently Apple workstations.

In the information management area we find industrial-strength software such as the Informix and Oracle database software. As with the publishing software, the applications are optimized for network operation. Managing large product databases created on the engineering workstations requires heavy duty mass storage and very reliable operation, not yet attained in the HB category.

> **NOTE**
>
> Reliability is not just reliability from a hardware standpoint, but also from an operational standpoint. Software failure occurs often because of mismatched operating system support features, confusion over memory management and network drivers, and other configuration flukes. These problems are mostly due to the immaturity of operating systems and the recent growth pains experienced in the HB class.

The engineering and scientific software category is diversified and complex. Applications such as image processing, data visualization, CAD/CAE, and number crunching generally have similar needs for high-end CPUs, powerful graphics support, and sophistication in math coprocessing and special peripheral areas. Moreover, special products in this category are particularly expensive. You will find more EW applications on HB class computers as the demand for CAD/CAE and image processing grows and HB computers become more reliable and efficient. Many organizations are already running CAD applications on HB computers, using such software as AutoDesk's general-purpose design system AutoCad, and other products for mechanical design, stress analysis, printed circuit board layout, and capture of schematics.

We also see many applications in the control/interface category. In the data acquisition area, acquiring and processing the data in real time is often a requirement, and the higher capacity and faster hard disks and quicker CPUs found in the EPs are necessary to this end. Manufacturing and process control of large plant floors will require the seasoned reliability and performance dominated by the EP category. Reliability in both operating systems and hardware is essential for controlling shop floor robots and other paraphernalia where safety and production economies are paramount. Already, you will find HB computers on shop floors monitoring defects and helping to organize manufacturing processes.

We are beginning to see the HB category handle applications such as those described above, but the hardware and software need to mature a little more before these microcomputers can begin replacing workstations in large numbers.

Engineering Production Workstation Features

Let's look at specific engineering workstations, examine their attributes, and compare them with HB computers. This background will help us see how the two categories are blurring.

Integrated Connectivity

Today's engineering workstations use networking not as an afterthought but as an integral feature of their overall design. Connectivity may be over serial links and terminals hooked to the more powerful workstations thanks to the multiuser, multitasking capability of Unix, or it may be over numbers of workstations in LANS and WANs. Advanced communications support, such as X Windows, and an engineering and network-oriented applications software base provide a strong basis for a well-integrated work environment.

HB DtCs originated in a non-network atmosphere. As network hardware and software diminished in cost, thanks to VLSI-implemented network interfaces and the many network software vendors – 3COM, Banyan, and Novell, to name a few of the more popular ones – pressure increased to network HB DtCs. Networking was accomplished mostly with software and add-on hardware. Neither original operating systems, not MS-DOS or Apple-DOS, provided for network operation, nor for that matter did any of the applications software products written for those operating systems. The industry continues to struggle with network software as newer systems, notably OS/2 and Apple System 7.0, begin to provide network functions for applications developers to use Windows.

Powerful Graphics Capability

Production and particularly engineering workstations usually generate graphics using highly specialized and intelligent graphics interfaces, some of which contain multiple CPUs. Intelligent graphics interfaces relieve the EW's CPU of complex drawing functions that are instead performed by the CPU in the graphics interface.

Historically, HB DtCs use dumb video interfaces that simply map a memory area to the monitor's screen. The DtC's CPU is responsible for drawing images into this memory area. Since current HB DtCs are expandable, a variety of intelligent graphics interfaces has become available in the form of add-on cards. However, their enhanced graphics capabilities are not well supported by the hardware architecture of the DtC's internal logic board, by the operating system, or by the applications software base.

Sophisticated Buses

EPs are generally equipped with sophisticated buses and even multiple buses; for example, separate buses for DMA, CPU data, and video data. Hierarchical bus structures permit multiple CPU boards to share common memory as well as to use their own private memory. Arbitration signals permit multiple processors to access the resources of the same system. The VME bus, for example, found in Sun Microsystem EWs, provides high data transfer rates and flexible data transfer through resource management. Such buses also provide faster integration circuits that buffer and manage the respective signals.

HB DtCs are offering more sophisticated buses – Micro Channel, EISA, NuBus – but these are all single bus systems.

Greater Data Widths

EPs implement full 32- and even 64-bit data paths as well as 32-bit address buses. HB computers will often bus only the first 24 CPU address lines, limiting memory expansion to 16 MB, and will often implement only 8- or 16-bit data channels. Newer HB systems are providing standardized 32-bit data and address capability with EISA, NuBus, and Micro Channel.

High Performance CPUs

EPs implement the more powerful microprocessors and run them faster on their more sophisticated buses. The power and sophistication achieves higher throughput as well as greater integration between the CPU and other important system controllers and processors. EWs are moving from the conventional CISC (complex instruction set CPU) microprocessors to the very fast RISC (reduced instruction set CPU). As more parallel CPU architectures are developed, with multiple CPUs and coprocessors combined on a single chip, we will find them first in EWs. EWs generally start with IPS rates of around 10 MIPS. This is where HB DtCs top out.

■ Many MS-DOS computer software products continue to operate on the 8088 microprocessor.

While HB DtCs implement high-end microprocessors, the current applications software remains compatible with the more conventional CISC microprocessors from Intel and Motorola and maintains backward compatibility to earlier CPUs. As Intel and Motorola microprocessors begin to combine RISC and parallel capability, we will see the DtC applications software base shifting toward the use of that type of CPU architecture.■

EXAMPLE

The Intel 80486 is part RISC and contains an on-board floating point unit (FPU).

Peripheral and System Controllers

High-speed peripheral interfaces (ESDI, SCSI), faster DMA, and cache memory controllers are commonplace on EP workstations. Higher performance peripherals open the way for faster and higher capacity hard disks, increased CPU throughput, and more capable graphics interfaces described earlier.

The newer high-end HB DtCs are beginning to implement more sophisticated system logic boards that integrate system and peripheral controllers, but you will find this only in top-of-the-line models, and even then they are not as well integrated as in the more expensive engineering workstations.

Mature Operating Systems

EPs generally operate under mature operating systems, Unix for example, that provide multitasking, virtual memory support, and other features for using today's enhanced microprocessors. These capabilities allow DtCs to perform important tasks such as printing, networking, applications development, and applications usage concurrently, as well as to operate larger applications software systems.

HB DtCs have historically had well-focused and relatively single-minded operating systems. This is changing in the MS-DOS computer world with Windows and OS/2 with Presentation Manager, and in the Apple world with System 7.0 and the A/UX operating systems.

What Is the Cost?

The attributes mentioned require system integration and professional software development environments. This and the higher cost they entail make it unlikely that they will be found in the home office or basement workshop. EP units are generally priced between $20,000 and $100,000 and software usually starts at $1,000, with typical products costing $5,000 to $10,000.

Merging of Categories

Already we are seeing the HB and EP categories merging as DtC vendors produce higher performance and more cost-effective DtCs, and EP vendors produce low-end workstations. Are the MS-DOS and Apple computers in the HB category complete computing environments? Considering complete product lines, the best answer is – not quite. The following examples show how certain makes of HB DtCs approach workstation capability.

Apple's Engineering/Scientific Applications

Apple's Macintosh II line and particularly its F/X DtC combines open architecture with the NuBus, flexible graphics interface options, higher performance 32-bit Motorola microprocessors, and high speed memory caches. These features, together with the multitasking and virtual memory support of System 7.0, allow the Mac II to compete in the EP category while maintaining compatibility with the very popular Macintosh applications software base. As Apple integrates Unix (A/UX) into its software base, that too will make it more competitive with EPs.

MS-DOS Compatible Workstations

Many vendors, including Sun Microsystems and Intel, are now manufacturing sufficiently powerful 80386- and 80486-based microcomputers that they qualify to be called EPs. Most run well under Unix, although they can also run the current MS-DOS and OS/2 software base. Many of these DtCs maintain ISA compatibility to allow use of ISA add-ons. Intel's computers combine a well-integrated system design using 80486 microprocessors with their own shrink-wrapped Unix. We should expect to see powerful workstations continuing to come from Intel as they manufacture not only their own CPUs, but also their own support chip sets. They also produce a line of non-Unix MS-DOS compatibles and a line of network components.

Since the majority of these Intel CPU based computers implement the ISA bus and can be configured to run MS-DOS, we place these MS-DOS compatibles in the HB category. However, their enhanced performance and Unix capability pushes them toward the EP category.

Low-End Engineering Workstations

Sun Microsystems, a leading manufacturer of EWs, produces low-cost EWs that sell for about $10,000. The high-end F/X by Apple also sells for around $10,000. Both the Apple F/X and low-end Sun models support similar performance features, including SCSI peripheral interfaces, high DMA capability, a sophisticated bus, powerful CPUs, and peripheral controllers. Yet there are differences. Sun implements Ethernet controllers on its logic board, not found on the Apple F/X. The Sun models implement a more sophisticated S bus, which also routes network, SCSI, and other signals not found on Apple's NuBus. More VLSI is found in Sun Microsystem units with higher levels of integration between the CPU and other system functions. Moreover, Sun's graphics interface is more sophisticated than Apple's stock offering.■

IBM's Entry into Engineering Workstations

■ The logic board is in fact the motherboard, the one that accepts most other plug in boards.

IBM is well known as a mainframe and HB DtC manufacturer. Recently, IBM has begun penetrating the engineering workstation market with its R/T (RISC Technology) line of DtCs. IBM's RISC System/6000 is a solid EW entry with a wide range of price/performance models that encompass all of the EW features described above. The 6000 uses an enhanced and upward-compatible Micro Channel bus.

Summary of HB and EP Features

HB DtCs are manufactured for the mass market, so low-cost is the most important objective. These DtCs run the widest variety of software, which is also intended to be low cost, turnkey, and widely available. EPs are manufactured with performance as the primary objective. They are intended for diversified applications in technical engineering and scientific research and in high-end publishing and database management areas. While each category attempts to run software in another, large differences in operating systems, market penetration, and performance make this crossover impractical at present.

EP hardware and software are proprietary, complex, and difficult to develop and support. HB software is often written by independent individuals. While HB software can be, and should be, operated right out of the box, most EP software requires extensive installation and concentrated learning. HB DtCs should be operable by those with little or no experience; EPs require considerable understanding just to turn on and off.

3.3   Entertainment/Education (EE) DtCs

In concise terms, the EE class of computers, Commodore and Atari, combine innovative and usually proprietary hardware to produce a computer particularly good at special audio/visual effects and other specialized applications. EE DtCs are also sometimes referred to as a/v (audio/visual) computers. Due to the hybrid hardware architecture found in these computers they are sometimes unflatteringly called *punk* computers. You know the type: radical clothing, splotches of neon color in the hair, speaking a strange language. But, isn't there room for all? A very different breed of software has evolved for the EE class of computer. Software from high-speed aircraft chase games to serious video studio support, to say nothing of music development and synthesizer systems to stimulate the most sophisticated musician. What is it about the EE class of computers that has made them such a sensational mind-expanding tool?

Today's EE computers produce spectacular and accessible audio/visual effects on a low entry cost computer that is fun to own and a creative experience to run. To answer the question posed above, let's look at major features and comment on the relative merit with HB DtCs.

Novel Performance Architectures

The EE computers have highly specialized architectures with particular focus on graphics such as animation and desktop video.

> **NOTE**
>
> *Desktop video* is a term popularized by evolving applications that combine live video and computer graphics, which are very popular on the Commodore computer because of its built-in and add-on devices that synchronize external video sources with on-board computer graphics.

Many of the performance features found in the high-end HBs and low-end EWs, multiple buses and SCSI interfaces for instance, can be found also in the newer EEs, such as the Commodore 3000. Particularly high performance is obtained by proprietary chips that combine multiple complex functions – DMA, video, hard disk sound – and are therefore difficult to program at low levels. When operating systems and

■ High-level languages can implement audio/visual commands by just pointing to menued commands rather than having to program these features in assembly language.

support software can access these features at higher levels, the burden is less on software developers who must cope with these very complex devices.■

Proprietary chips are the reason we do not find clones of these systems in the open market. Note the similarity with Apple products that also use proprietary devices. Although proprietary to a lesser degree, Apples are still not cloned.

Software

A diverse software base has evolved for the EE DtCs. This software takes advantage of their novel architecture. Many software products are less than $100, yet provide endless hours of enjoyment and learning with fascinating special effects and user interaction with the computer's deepest secrets.

Educational Software

Popularity of DtCs in some school systems is directly related to the availability of low-cost educational software and low-cost entry into desktop computing. Much of the highly visual software, control panels, process control, math and geometry experimentation can be greatly enhanced by the animation capability and sound effects that are well-supported in the EE class.

Most of the educational software is developed for a specific purpose and cannot be modified to meet more general needs. A recent development, however, is aimed at general-purpose software for teachers to use to create custom educational packages that generate images, question-answer-reward modules, and so on.

Voice I/O

Software is appearing for recording, processing, and reproducing an individual's voice. Since most EE computers have built-in audio I/O hardware, software developers have reason to write this type of software. There is a market for it.

Music

Using stereo, complex sound generators, and highly visual software you can dabble at composing and literally write an entire symphony. Later, you can be the conductor as you play back your symphonies. Although the Apple HB computers have built-in music and voice I/O, it is far below the sophistication found in EE computers. Through built-in MIDI (Music Interchange Digital Interface), EE computers are typically hooked up to electronic keyboards, drums, and other musical equipment. Combining good operating system support of MIDI interfaces and complex sound hardware with a great visual display system will allow spectacular musical control systems to be developed on EE computers.

Business Software

Many business software products, including spreadsheets, word processors, desktop publishers, and DBMS programs, have been ported to EE DtCs. In itself this is not a striking development. But when software is modified to take advantage of the EE a/v architectures, lifeless word processors and database managers take on an exciting new life running on an EE computer. Animated graphics fields in your database or music backgrounds and voice prompts in your menu can make an application sparkle.

Support Issues

User group support for EE is not as prevalent as it is for HB computers. There are, however, numerous users groups that have SIGs (special interest groups) that sponsor such activities as music conventions. Magazines and books providing public documentation are also not as prevalent. Some magazines are dedicated to special a/v activities that are popular on the Commodore and Atari DtCs.

Special software configurations, peripheral set-ups, and other operating system adjustments are difficult on the EE computer's special operating system and need greater expertise. This situation should improve as more advanced operating systems acquire features found in the operating systems of other DtC categories. Already, the EE computer operating systems are moving away from their own OS environments toward HB-like environments that have file management, GUIs, and driver installation methodologies.

Although the software described above may be fine for individual applications, it lacks the solid hardware and software support found in the HB category. Therefore, large organizations are reluctant to use what is otherwise excellent computer hardware. Two factors will improve the situation: 1) HB computers will add a/v capabilities, broadening the market for a/v software; and 2), EE computers will evolve to expandable architecture and run on universal operating systems.

Low-Cost Entry

The keyboard and system unit are often combined in an impact-resistant plastic case that is relatively inexpensive ($150 to $500), easy to carry, and occupies little space. If your expansion intentions are conservative, you won't have a problem. However, you should be aware of the following:

- *Power* – Internal power supplies may not be adequate for expansion peripherals. These peripherals usually need their own power supplies, which makes them more expensive.

- *Expansion* – Bus expansion is generally limited to one connector, as in the early compact Macintoshes. An expansion device, such as a hard drive, may have to plug into the side of the unit. Sometimes the expansion edge is continued to another point on the expansion peripheral, which allows yet another peripheral to be plugged in, and so on. This can result in an unwieldy conglomeration of bus-interfaced peripherals. Each peripheral so connected will require its own enclosure and power supply.

In sharp contrast, HB and EP DtCs have system unit boxes with internal bays for a hard disk, tape backup unit, etc., and slots for their respective interfaces.

Expansion problems are somewhat mitigated by SCSI capability, which does not require a system bus interface for each peripheral, but rather allows interfaces to be chained with a relatively simple cable. Each peripheral does not need intimate connection to the DtC's bus, but instead can do with simpler connections to multiple SCSI connectors.■

■ As Apple went from the Compact Mac to the NuBus-equipped Macintosh, we would expect Atari and Commodore to eventually follow suit.

Special User Interface Hardware

A variety of user interfaces including joysticks, light pens, voice I/O, touch screens, and other paraphernalia are often found in the EE category. The software products that use them treat you with surprisingly intuitive friendliness.

Few standards exist for governing the use of special hardware input devices. Standards will develop with the increased use of these devices in the HB class. Already, there are software toolkits for assisting developers in using character recognition screens of notebook computers or built-in ROM support of voice I/O now found in Apple's computer line.

Early Entertainment DtCs

The entertainment category started with the early 8-bit Commodore 64 and Atari 400 computers. Texas Instruments marketed a 16-bit entertainment DtC, the 99/4 based on the TIM 16-bit 9900 microprocessor. The 99/44 won considerable popularity, then waned due to poor documentation of internal capability and TI's redirection of its DtC manufacturing emphasis to MS-DOS compatibles.

Radio Shack produced an EE computer, the Color Computer, based on the very powerful 8-bit Motorola 6809. The Color Computer did not have the graphics and sound power of its Atari and Commodore competitors. It survived because of the 6809, a good BASIC interpreter, relatively good game cartridge support, and Radio Shack marketing. The Color Computer can still be found at Radio Shack stores.

These early entertainment DtCs cost only $100 to $200, providing you didn't use a floppy disk or printer and were content with in-ROM cartridge software primarily devoted to secondary education and games. As we shall see, newer versions of EE computers combine their EE vintage capabilities with support of the HB software base as well as sophistication in desktop video.

Commodore/Atari vs. Early HB Computers

The early Commodore and Atari EE computers were based on the same CPU as the Apple II DtC. Radically different architectures and lack of any operating system that could provide a common basis for compatibility, made software incompatible with any of the 65xx-based machines.

> **NOTE**
>
> The Atari used the MOS technology 6502 as did the Apple II. The Commodore used the 6510 microprocessor, which was object compatible, but added an internal I/O port at the beginning of addressable memory.

While the Apple II computer implemented color graphics and the black and white CP/M computers featured 8-inch disk drives and business software, the early EE architectures featured no-contest graphics and sound capability.

The early Commodore and Atari EEs had potent animation graphics systems and spectacular sound effects provided by custom sound chips. The Commodore's video interface was of the sprite generator type, which could slip relatively simple images around the screen effortlessly and could even detect their collisions. This facility put to shame the performance of dumb interfaces found in the early HB computers.

The Commodore's sound chip could generate 3-tone voices and noise simultaneously in an ADSR envelope (Attack, Decay, Sustain, Release). Contrast that with a single digital bit controlling a speaker in the Apple II.

Early HB computers, the TRS-80, Apple II, CP/M, and early MS-DOS computers, could perform these tricks only with add-on cards. Since these cards were after-the-fact additions, they were not supported by the respective operating systems, languages, or turnkey applications products.

It was primarily the built-in audio/visual features that separated the early Commodore and Atari DtCs from HB DtCs of the period. This distinction continues today, although it is somewhat blurred by add-on graphics boards for both Apple and MS-DOS computers and built-in sound I/O chips in the Apple Macintosh. Even EP workstations are appearing with relatively simple sound chips.

EE Computers Become More Accessible

Referring to Figure 10 on page 28 you will note that around the time the Apple and CP/M machines made the 8- to 16-bit transition, so also did the primary entertainment Atari and Commodore computers. The transition was to the Motorola 68xxx microprocessor line still used in today's EE models.

What really separates the newer 16- and 32-bit EE computers from their 8-bit ancestors, however, is the accessibility of their special a/v effects. Aside from plug-in game cartridges on early EE computers, programmatic access to a/v features was difficult. You were forced to completely understand the underlying nature of the very complex graphics and audio support devices. This understanding could come only from poring over the technical chip specifications. The lack of higher level software support stuck you with having to program the support chip's control registers in Assembly language or BASIC peek and poke statements.■ Some chip functions were supported by BASIC function statements, and these functions were well documented. Programming a/v features was not for the weak of heart or spirit. Today's EE computers have a variety of menu-driven software that free you for creativity. For example:

■ BASIC's peek and poke statements allow you to manipulate memory locations directly, which is how the special effects chip registers appear.

- Play your own custom musical instrument by hand-painting a waveform on your monitor screen with a mouse or light pen.
- Remove scratches in your favorite record album by simply removing the spike on the viewed wave form.
- Merge two CD-ROM program sources, recorded at different times, onto a single recording by aligning their recorded waveforms on screen.
- Create a series of animated computer images for frame-by-frame recording in a video studio. Touch up live video still frames with computer-generated graphics.

All this is accomplished with sophisticated menus, without programming a single line of code.

The newer models, like their predecessors, typically combine system unit and power supply in a rather small system box that is easy to carry around. This keeps the entry cost much lower than that of the newer HB DtCs. When you finish adding floppy and hard drives, interfaces, printers, and monitors, the cost of these systems becomes comparable with moderately-priced HB computers.

EE Computers Compete with EPs

Due to their spectacular graphics architectures, EE computers in some ways can compete on even terms with EP computers. As the EE graphics interface matures with enhanced design graphics capability, image transformations, dense bit planes and lots of colors, higher image resolutions and 3-D capability, the newer EE computers are becoming formidable competitors with low-end workstations. There is no reason why EE computers cannot run the Unix operating system if properly outfitted with lots of memory and a big, fast hard drive.

Newer EE computers, for example the Commodore 3000, combine many features found in advanced HB computers such as SCSI interfaces, high-end Motorola microprocessors, improved internal system interfaces, greater memory expandability and a more sophisticated expansion bus. Commodore's DOS 2.0 implements a fine user interface as well as multitasking.

Low-Cost Entertainment Systems

Going to entertainment extremes are the Nintendo, Nintendo Gameboy, and NEC systems. These little microcomputers incorporate two or three highly specialized VLSI chips that perform all necessary functions: CPU, sound, joystick interface, and sprite graphics. Animation is realistic and you can enjoy superb sound performance and effects. No keyboard, floppy disk, or hard disk is required, which would increase the cost but also allow you to copy game software. Accessories include a joy stick, a light gun, a flexible mat with switches that you can jump on, or an arm band with switches for controlling input.

Inside the game cartridges you will find one or more ROMs that contain game software, while separate ROMs contain graphics sprites and sound effects: bells, gunshots, bongo drums, and animal growls. You can even edit the effects. Sound realism is obtained by recording actual sounds and digitizing them in ROM, which is scanned by the sound hardware to reproduce the original sound. Unnatural sound effects can be developed in various ways as described in Part V.

Entertainment system games are mesmerizing. Ask any child about Nintendo's Super Mario I, II, and III. Once the educational potential of these computers is realized, we can expect to see equally mesmerizing educational game cartridges on sale. Since the game cartridges use the TV set and require no expensive peripherals, complete systems can be purchased for between $100 and $200. Newer systems incorporate CD-ROM for special effects and graphics storage which will allow them to present real video and improved sound effects for spectacular games. Interfaces between these low-cost entertainment computers and the more expensive DtC and other peripherals will provide them with greater flexibility. Imagine developing your own games on a DtC, then downloading them to a game computer for execution.

3.4   Summary of System Comparisons

We have discussed three main DtC categories: the pervasive commodity home/business (HB) computers, the strong and reliable engineering and production (EP) computers, and the a/v special entertainment and education (EE) computers.

The HB DtCs emerged from the microprocessor revolution that began when microcontrollers evolved to 8-bit capability. With slick packaging and maturing operating systems, we find these computers in the home and increasingly in the workplace. The MS-DOS and Apple computers forming this category are so popular we find many households with several networked computers. In the workplace, the HB computer has almost completely replaced pencil and paper; it services a wide array of day-to-day needs from taking notes to keeping spreadsheets of purchase orders.

More heavy-duty engineering/scientific and production applications are being performed on HB computers, although they often chunk larger applications or run the smaller self-contained tasks. HBs are essential for such purposes. Almost anyone can now afford to have one. Not only at work, but also one at home. The benefit of having work capability at home and vice versa is beginning to capture the attention of today's management. More and more of tomorrow's work will be performed on HB computers as wide area network technology improves. Already TV cable systems are being used experimentally to network HB computers.

Table 12 highlights the main points of each system.

Aspect	Applications Category		
	HB	EP	EE
Primary Applications	Personal/Management, Business, Production assistance, Day-to-day activities	Engineering, Scientific, Production	Entertainment, Education, Experiments, Increasing business
Operating Systems	Common, custom	Mature, common	Custom, specialized
Support	Widespread	Vendor specific	Vendor specific
Architecture	Vanilla, common	Performance oriented	Specialized a/v
Environment	Desktop	Desktop/group	Desktop

Table 12. DtC category highlights

EP computers are the industrial strength DtCs that descended directly from mainframes and particularly from the minicomputers of yesterday. Capitalizing on enhanced performance, straight-up operating systems, and improved network technologies, EP computers are found almost exclusively in the workplace. Unlike their mainframe antecedents, however, the EP class of computer runs large applications in a much friendlier environment, in fact, imitating its HB upstart cousin. You could think of the EP DtC as a hybrid: a combination of a friendly HB computer and the relatively intractable mainframe of yesterday. You will be able to find the day-to-day software of HB computers in the EP category as users demand this type of software for their production work.

EE computers bring to desktop computing a fresh and exciting innovation in hardware and software. Although not as popular as HB computers, EE computers lend themselves well to experimentation and to the use of diversified software. The important roles of audio and visual effects are exploited in EE architecture. Unfortunately, maturity and standards are still lacking in the industry for the appropriate use of sound and video. But this will change, and probably soon.

4.0   The Hardware Software Connection

- Matching Areas
- Hardware Performance
- Software Performance
- Hardware Selection

Too often DtC systems hardware components are chosen with insufficient thought about their capability to operate particular software. A basic familiarity with the relationship between software and hardware is necessary to make an intelligent match between the two.

Although the issues and concepts of DtC applications software are many, our focus is on appropriate matches between applications software and DtC hardware. To do this we divide the applications territory into manageable categories, discussing each in terms of its most important characteristics from a hardware standpoint. Also included, for the sake of completeness, are important issues such as data compatibility and major cautions not necessarily related to hardware.

Individual software products number in the thousands, so we have to group them into applications categories.

- Information management
- Writing/publishing
- Display graphics
- Engineering/scientific
- Control/interface

Most of the applications of interest fit in at least one of these categories.

4.1   Matching Areas

Most applications can be relegated to principal areas of impact: program, data, and operation, each having a profound influence on hardware configuration.

- *Program* – Requirements of the program itself: desktop publisher, DBMS program, spreadsheet, CAD package.
- *Data* – The data that the program uses or generates for documents, databases, spreadsheet files, numbers.
- *Operation* – Important factors affecting the operation of the software.

The following tables list the more important configuration factors. The tables, while not exhaustive, are sufficiently complete to give you a feel for the many different considerations you should leaf through mentally when matching your hardware and software needs.

PROGRAM ITEM	FACTOR
Total program size	Mass store
Program memory requirement	OS, memory
Language used (hierarchy)	CPU, mass store, math coprocessor
In-memory size	Memory
Math oriented	Math coprocessor
Graphics oriented	Math coprocessor, graphics coprocessor, CPU, display.
Supplementary utilities (such as dictionaries for word processors)	Mass store, memory, CPU

Table 13.   Program configuration factors

DATA ITEM	FACTOR
Amount of data processed at one time	Memory, mass store, CPU
File or memory oriented data	Memory, mass store
Type (ASCII, binary, custom format)	CPU
Necessary file conversions	CPU/memory
Archiving	Optical disk/tape backup
Combined text and graphics	Printer/CPU
Concurrent usage	Network (control), OS
Entry (imported, hand entered)	GUI, network, display, modem, mouse
Security	Network, OS
How much data on line for reports	Memory, mass store
Type of user	GUIs

Table 14.   Data configuration factors

OPERATIONAL ITEM	FACTOR
Output or reporting capability	Monitor/printer
Multitask with other application	OS, CPU, memory
Use with resident enhancements	Memory, compatibility
Unattended operation	UPS
Output professionalism	Printer/plotter quality
Real time operation	CPU, OS
Signal processing required	Specialized hardware
Location	Vibration, portability, reliability, system unit construction

OPERATIONAL ITEM	FACTOR
Training, maintenance, upgrades	Interfaces to vendors
Special outputs	Plotters, film copy
Required demonstrations	Projection/view graph video
Alternative input	Mouse, voice I/O
Combine output with external video	Video digitizers and cameras
Need for external images	Image digitizers
Math intensive	Math coprocessor

Table 15.   Operational configuration factors

Hardware and Software Performance Levels

If we can think of hardware and software in terms of discrete performance levels (low, medium, and high), we can then begin to match the performance requirements of software with the performance capabilities of the hardware.

Next we shall break down the system hardware and applications software categories into performance levels. Last we present the specific linkage between the two discussing each applications category in terms of significant hardware considerations in the hardware categories.

Hardware Component Performance Levels

For the major hardware categories discussed next, performance levels are divided into low, medium, and high. You are encouraged, at least initially, to fit your own requirements into these levels because they will help you later in the system selection process. Following are the various categories of system components in terms of their performance levels.

CPU

Level	MIPS	Intel	Motorola	RISC
Low	100K	8088	NA	
Medium	1 MB	80286	68000	
High	10 MB+	80386/486	68020,30,40	Sun, SPARC, and Mips CPUs

Table 16.   CPU performance levels: Special-purpose processing devices may be available commercially for your DtC, which can have a profound effect on the CPU requirement.

Before you purchase a DtC, find out if the system can accommodate the following devices:

- **Coprocessors and add-ons** – Math coprocessors and special computational add-ons.

- *Graphics coprocessors* – High end video interfaces.
- *Communications processors* – LAN boards and other communications interfaces; terminal emulator boards, and the like.

MEMORY

Low	–	Applications and data fit in considerably less than 1 MB. In MS-DOS computers only real mode is required.
Medium	–	Applications require up to 4 MB. MS-DOS main programs might fit in real memory. The use of expanded or extended memory is generally required for the data.
High	–	Applications require virtual memory, approaching and sometimes exceeding 16 MB. MS-DOS computers require extenders and 80286 protected mode support or 80386 virtual memory support.

MASS STORAGE

Low	–	10 to 40 MB hard disks with ST506/412 interfaces. No backup capability other than floppies.
Medium	–	40 to 200 MB hard disks with IDE hard drive interfaces. 90 MB supplementary Bernoulli drives and possible tape backup. Low end optical (1 to 2 GB).
High	–	200+ MB hard disk with ESDI/SCSI hard disk interfaces. 1 to 10 GB helical tape backup, optical jukebox (100+ GB) for large datasets. Mainframe mass storage.

DISPLAY

Low	–	Composite monochrome or low resolution color; less than 512 square (IBM's CGA, EGA, MGA, Hercules).
Medium	–	Analog RGB with resolutions of around 512 square and 16 to 64K colors (Apple's 8- and 24-bit color; IBM's VGA and Super VGA).
High	–	Analog RGB with resolutions closer to 1024 square; 64K to 16 million colors, and intelligent graphics interfaces.

PRINTER (OUTPUT)

Low	–	Low-cost nine-wire dot matrix, monochrome ink jet.
Medium	–	Twenty-four wire dot matrix, low-cost laser printer; 6 pen "A" and "D" size plotter; color ink jet.
High	–	High-end laser printer (e.g., HP LaserJet III); 14 pen "D" and larger size plotter.

KEYBOARD

Low	–	Standard Selectric style.
Medium	–	Standard Selectric with additional function keys, separate cursor pad, programmable features such as typematic.
High	–	Multiple keyboards, voice input capability, built-in mouse or position indicators (or position indicated by graphics table).

HARDWARE INTERFACES

Low	–	Serial interfaces for low data rate peripherals <100Kbits/sec such as modems, plotters, older printers. Standard Centronics parallel printer interface.
Medium	–	IEEE 488 or SCSI or high speed serial for faster peripherals such as line printers, higher speed test equipment, some mass storage devices, and specialized peripherals for acquiring data and process control. DMA interfaces.
High	–	ESDI (hard disk), shared memory or high speed DMA for custom peripherals. Customized interfaces for DSP coprocessing devices and custom interfaces to other specialized peripherals.

NETWORKING/COMMUNICATIONS

Low	–	DtC as dumb terminal at low bit rates over phone lines using RS-232 interfaces.
Medium	–	DtC emulating intelligent terminal at higher bit rates. Terminal emulation boards and coaxial connections to mainframe. DtC operating in network or servicing a small network (<10 DtCs).
High	–	DtC as LAN server serving multiple users and serving data and programs to groups. Communications server to mainframe. Host client applications on X Windows.

OPERATING SYSTEM

Low	–	Single task/process (such as MS-DOS).
Medium	–	Single tasking system supplemented with GUIs, shells, extenders, and so on.
High	–	Multitasking such as OS/2 or Unix, multiuser/LAN service, real time operating systems, X Windows operating environment.

Software Performance Levels

As in the case of the major system components, we can look at the major applications categories in terms of their performance levels.

WRITING/PUBLISHING

Low	–	Simple text editors for creating small programs, short memos and drafts, simple lists and charts using block characters.
Medium	–	Word processors for generating styled documents of moderate size (20 to 40 pages).
High	–	Text processors creating large documents with indexes and glossaries. Graphics-based word processors and desktop publishers generating documents and books exceeding 100 pages.

INFORMATION MANAGEMENT

Low	–	Flat file managers, use of spreadsheets for small arithmetic and accounting tasks (purchasing, course grading, lists).
Medium	–	Relational DBMS products for maintaining group level databases. More sophisticated reports sometimes including charts/graphics. Use of high-end spreadsheets for more comprehensive data tracking.

| High | – | Organization-wide databases, catalogs, property lists. Sharing data with mainframes over networks. Sophisticated corporate reports. Large product databases. Reports include highly styled graphics. Reports could be generated on the DtC using data from the mainframe or server in a manner transparent to users. |

DISPLAY GRAPHICS

Low	–	Simple charting and image painting systems for crude viewgraphs, simple line art and box drawings.
Medium	–	Generating charts with spreadsheets. Entry level CAD packages and entry level drawing, presentation, and data charting programs.
High	–	Illustration software for professional publishing, high-end presentation software. Slide show and animated presentations through multimedia, interactive video, and DVI.

ENGINEERING/SCIENTIFIC

| Low | – | Home-grown software written in BASIC or Turbo Pascal for experimentation, playing with data and experimenting with analytical algorithms. |
| Medium | – | Use of spreadsheets for numeric analysis. Low-end CAD packages. Use of DtC for generating proposals and test plans. Low-end graphing, plotting, and analysis programs. |

> **NOTE**
>
> At this point we can look for the classic breakpoint between the HB category and the EW category.

| High | – | Professional CAD/CAE, image processing, AI, analyses with languages such as SAS (Statistical Analysis Software), APL (A Programming Language), and other high-end engineering software programs including Mentor's Analog and Digital Electrical Engineering design and simulation software. |

PROCESS CONTROL

Low	–	Use of DtC for simple experiments, interfacing simple devices, low data rate data acquisition (<1000 samples per second), and particularly, acquisition of low data rate signals that need not be processed in real time as they are acquired.
Medium	–	Use of DtC as integral part of sophisticated systems such as robotics control, interactive video, and small plant process control.
High	–	Use of DtC acquisition for high data rates >1 million samples per second and the need for real time processing of acquired data. Manufacturing control in large plants.

4.2 Matching Application with Hardware

Each applications category has its own particularly important configuration items. Awareness of these critical items will go far to ensure that your purchase at least supports your intended application. Be aware that as you grow with your DtC you will discover new and different applications needs, so a full investigation of what you might want to do with a DtC is important.

Let's look at items by applications category. We can divide the critical configurations into manageable parts. When selecting hardware for a particular application, try to group its needs into meaningful task clusters. The lists presented are not exhaustive, but should give you an idea of the process necessary for matching hardware and software.

Writing/Publishing

The most popular application for microcomputers is assisting individuals in their writing. Products range from simple text editors to full-blown desktop publishing systems with the capability of combined text and graphics images. Outline generators, spelling and grammar checkers, and other enhancements make this applications software both powerful and flexible.

In the writing/publishing applications arena you must be particularly aware of the various software programs that supplement this category:

- *Print controls* – Spoolers, font enhancers, font scaling, and font resolution improvement utilities.

- *Styling and writing aids* – Clip art, dictionaries, thesauruses, outliners, spelling and grammar checkers.

- *Peripheral drivers* – Support for the many printers/scanners, FAX modems, plotters, and more sophisticated publishing equipment such as digital typesetters, photographic image setters, and other composing machines.

Writing/publishing software is often interleaved with database, spreadsheet, and graphics applications, placing a further burden on system hardware. The more recent word processing packages include integrated software functions, enabling you to get more of the job done with a single package.

Further dividing the category, we find distinct software applications:

- *Editors* – Enter and manipulate unformatted ASCII text.

- *Word processors* – Prepare text for printing. Appearance and format oriented. Embedded printer controls, fonts, spacing controls. Good for memos, correspondence, and other short documents.

- *Text/document processors* – Prepare complex documents and books for publication; materials that require tables of contents, indexes, glossaries, and cross references.

- *Desktop publishers* – Appearance and page layout oriented. Combined text and graphics. Low-end DtP systems usually have limited text processing and graphics generating capabilities, and instead have import features for bringing in files from word processors, graphics packages, and spreadsheets or other software that specializes in areas not provided by the desktop publisher. High-end desktop publishers have extensive graphics capabilities built in.

Hardware Factors

APPLICATION	FACTORS
Editors	Display (text) speed.
Word processors	Display speed, printer fonts
Text processors	CPU MIPs, mass storage, memory
Desktop publishers	CPU MIPs, memory, display APA resolution. Interface to high end printers.

Table 17.   Writing/publishing hardware factors

CPU

Low-power CPUs can support text editors quite well, provided that screen scrolling speed is not important. For higher scrolling speeds, necessary for quick browsing of text, higher-level CPU capability and higher data width video interfaces are required. Word processors need at least moderate CPU capability to handle font control and text formatting.

CPUs bog down quickly under the load of full-featured document composition packages. Composition of tables and equations pushes formatting requirements upward. A word or text processor that uses a thesaurus, dictionary, and grammer checking utility will need moderate to high CPU activity. You will find it fretful if you have to spend more than a few minutes to spell check your document when you are facing a deadline. Many text processors can merge graphics and text images, which drives up the CPU requirement considerably. Text processors also need greater CPU capability for processing indexes and tracking in-text cross references. Heavy use of graphics and high levels of font and text control will impose further burdens on the CPU.

Memory

Editors thrive on keeping many active files in memory, which can drive memory requirements up even though most editor programs are quite small. Due to small program size, editors are often operated as adjuncts to other programs, DBMS language compilers and the like. The greatly enhanced functional capability of word processors demands large quantities of memory The sheer size of text processors and their need for large on-line indexing and referencing files makes that demand even stronger. DtP programs have the highest memory requirements because of their size, their interaction with many different data inputs, and the need to keep a large number of fonts on line. DtP programs need considerable overlaying or virtual memory support because of their enormous functionality and size.

Display/Interface

Plain text editors can survive on low capability non-APA displays. However, the number of lines in view can be important when trying to arrange large quantities of draft material. Displays for word processors should be at least 40 lines and preferably a full page, 66 lines. Screen resolution may not be important for text-only input, but higher resolution is easier on the eyes. High resolution becomes a requirement when sophisticated document writing packages are used to create high quality publications. Mid-range displays can manage font control and graphics needs of word processors. But word and text processors with WYSIWYG capabilities require higher resolution and larger displays. Desktop publishers as a rule require the highest resolution displays to get the most out of their extraordinary graphics and text capabilities.

On most DtCs the CPU manages APA display fonts, although some use specialized hardware, graphics controllers, and some even implement display PostScript. Dumb controllers, such as found in the home/business DtC category, will need maximum data width – 16-bit interfaces for AT-style MS-DOS computers – to provide adequate character and graphics update speeds. Monitor resolutions step into the spotlight as word and text processors evolve into DtPs with graphics capabilities. High resolution monochrome monitors with multiple page displays are most appropriate for full-featured desktop publishing. Apple computers are particularly good in this regard.

Interfaces

Text editors generally drive dot matrix printers over the popular, low-cost Centronics parallel interfaces. A word processor's higher-level font capability will perform best with a laser printer, which also operates over the Centronics parallel interface. Some of the higher-end laser printers require more intimate shared memory interfaces to correspond between displayed video and printed output. WYSIWYG capability becomes more important at the DtP level. Some DtPs can interface to more sophisticated Linotronic and Compugraphic typesetters, which will require more expensive interfaces.

PostScript outputs from DtCs can be ported to different typesetters either directly or over a network. This book was drafted on an Asian MS-DOS clone and uploaded to an IBM mainframe with a Compaq. Using a hardwired terminal and the full screen editor on TSO, the copy was coded in IBM's Script General Markup Language. Drafts were printed on a 240 dpi laser printer. As a cost-saving measure, files were often transferred to the Compaq or to a Macintosh IIcx for editing in WordPerfect and then sent back to the mainframe. To prepare reproducible copy the GML-coded files were converted to PostScript, networked to a Macintosh, which transmitted the PostScript files over AppleTalk to a 2400 dpi phototypesetter.

Printer

The outputs from simple text editors are generally rough drafts of documents or program listings and low-cost dot matrix and ink jet printers work fine. If the word processor is used for more professional-looking documents, a more versatile and higher quality printer should be used, such as a 24-pin letter quality dot matrix type or a low-end laser printer. Most DtPs can output high resolution text fonts combined with high resolution graphics. High-end laser printers support PostScript with at least 300 dpi resolution, but 600 dpi is preferred. Your printer should be able to create and scale its own fonts to relieve the DtC's CPU of this process-intensive chore. Software support for printers is becoming more complex as printer requirements become more sophisticated. The selection of fonts and line spacing, and the availability of primitive print commands vary from printer to printer. Make sure that the printer you want is appropriately supported internally by the word processor you plan to use.

Hard Disk

A small hard disk can support a good text editor because small files are easily kept on floppy disks. As the files grow in number and size, storage becomes a problem. When used to prepare large documents and even books, larger hard disks or mainframe connections become important. Thesaurus, dictionary, and fonts need storage space. DtP software needs substantial storage space for fonts and clip art libraries for creating complex publications. Clip art libraries are available on CD-ROM, which makes optical disks important. Printers that can create and scale internal fonts will reduce the mass storage load considerably. Using scalable font technology, a single font will provide all of the sizes required for that typeface, instead of having to individually store many different sizes of the same typeface.

Keyboard

Text editors need a fast keyboard so that text can be entered quickly. A good keyboard feel helps. Word processors can take great advantage of special and function keys, and particularly of programmable keys that can perform repetitive keying sequences. Special keys in the same locations on different keyboards make it easy for data entry personnel to switch workstations without losing productivity. Keyboard layout is important also to destop publishers, but mouse support becomes an even more important requirement for various setups and text movements.

Networks

Some word processing packages can operate effectively on LANs and perform group writing functions. Network functions might include redlining and document summary screens, password protection, and document search and retrieval. Some text processors permit audit trails and revision control and most are available in networked versions.

Data Compatibility

Text editors are generally compatible, since most use ASCII format. Word processors, however, have their own built-in formats and special codes for text formatting. Although many word processors can import and export each other's data formats, there will be a problem when one word processor cannot address another's special capabilities. Transportability of formatted documents between dissimilar packages and between incompatible printers is a frequent problem. Because of the differences in text formats, word and text processing applications cannot be easily shared by different word processors.

DtPs have even more specialized data formats. Desktop publishers require inputs from word processors, graphics illustration packages, and even databases. They have the most complex data compatibility requirements. Those sharing data will want to operate identical software or be prepared to cope with clumsy and involved file conversion problems.

Desktop Publishing

Don't underestimate the difficulty of learning a full-featured desktop publisher and its hardware requirements. Whatever you do in text processing or desktop publishing you must provide intensive support with appropriate resources. You can solve the problem in several ways. You can spend a lot of money enhancing a modest DtC and acquiring an arsenal of programs to satisfy your pre-publication needs. With this approach be prepared to perform like a one-man band. Each program will have idiosyncrasies that you will have to learn. The opposite approach is to select a package that has all, or most of the functions you need built in. In this case too, you can spend a lot of money, both on the full-publishing software package and on the hardware – a high-end workstation – because you will need a robust system. But the payback will be generous because learning one package is easier and running it will be more efficient.

■ Interleaf and FrameMaker are full featured publishers, considerably more sophisticated and expensive than Ventura and PageMaker.

If your principal application is desktop publishing, you will do well to choose products with vintage desktop publishing histories – Interleaf, FrameMaker,■ Ventura, and PageMaker. The same holds for word processors, Wordperfect, Word, and similar historically tested packages. Most DtPs allow sophisticated page layout and control, but this will take a long time to learn and use effectively. Competent use of DtPs require solid training and more than a pinch of artistic talent.

Information Management

Information management involves keeping track of relational and numerical information, retrieving it, and arranging or combining it in appropriate formats. Information management is a necessary component of almost all DtC applications. Scores of information management products are available. Since database management plays such an important role, you should plan for it even if it is not on your initial wish list. Managing databases is a fundamental part of any applications category whether it is the documents produced by a word processor, the images produced by your graphics display software, or the information in an employee data file.

Information Management Software Categories

Further dividing the category, we find the following distinct software applications:

- *Database management* – Categorizing, organizing, tracking and reporting of large information bases. Databases can range from the familiar address book and telephone directory to personnel, and finally to corporate financial information.

- *Product management* – Management of complex product data information. Databases can range from electronic chip libraries to the schematics for building a skyscraper.

- *Office management* – A variety of software for assisting in the office. Applications range from creating and maintaining Rolodexes to the vertical applications of doctors, lawyers, and even green house office management.

- *Project management* – Keeping track of work progress, work flows, critical paths and milestones.

- *Time and work scheduling* – Tracking appointments and scheduling work; managing what you want to do when.

- *Accounting* – Accounting, ledger and financial applications for businesses.

- *PIM (Personal Information Manager)* – Everything from income tax preparation to financial planning and checkbook recordkeeping.

Hardware Factors

APPLICATION	KEY FACTOR
Database management	CPU, networks, memory, mass store, mainframe link
Product data management (documents, CAD parts)	Networks, dissimilar platforms, mass and archival storage
Office management	Software integration
Project management	Program compatibility, flow charts, displays
Time and work scheduling	Ease of use
PIM	Portability, ease of use

Table 18.   Information management hardware factors

CPU

DBMS coprocessing devices are not yet off the laboratory workbench, so CPU requirements for information processing remain directly related to the size and complexity of management programs and particularly, the database files that they manage. File sizes can range from 100K to a gigabyte in size. Most information management applications begin small, but grow quickly. Always overestimate your CPU requirement, starting with a higher-level capability. Some office management and PIM programs operate comfortably with low-end CPUs as long as the files are small and computation is not intensive. For files less than 100K small CPUs will suffice. As you approach 1 MB you'll need medium capability and for larger files you'll need high-end CPUs. Fast hard drives with caches can relieve the CPU to some degree.

Memory

Memory requirements are a critical issue because keeping large amounts of the information in memory quickens the searching, sorting, and indexing functions integral to most information management systems. Because indexes need to be in memory, memory available to the database will be reduced. Nonexecutable memory can often be used to supplement the hard disk when executable memory is not available for manipulating the files. Although most DBMS systems are file oriented, maximum file size is limited by mass storage, not memory. Better efficiency is obtained when as much as possible is brought into memory. Files <100K can be satisfied by low-end memory, those less than 1 MB can operate with medium memory, while those above 1 MB force the high end.

Mass Store

The size required for the hard disk is directly related to the total size of the databases that you want to manipulate. It is a well-known fact that databases grow, and as they grow, hard disk speed quickly becomes a critical factor because at some point the data can no longer fit in memory, and therefore must be shuffled between memory and the hard disk. As files are sorted, indexed, and searched, hard disk activity begins to affect system performance. For handling partitioned or secured databases, it may be necessary to divide the data into reasonably sized chunks. The current 44 and 90 MB Bernoulli cartridges are great for partitioning large datasets. These cartridges should not, however, be used for archival storage because they are unreliable compared to tape back up systems. Management information systems should also be backed up as a safeguard.

Disk caches can improve performance by shuffling back and forth between hard disk and memory. Project management, PIM, and applications using spreadsheet programs are considerably less dependant on the hard disk because they are intended to operate primarily from memory. Also, data files in such applications are usually small.

Display/Interface

Information system applications are often textual, since most of the displayed data is in character form. The display screen will be used for mirroring input data, selecting menued reports, and editing portions of the data. Text-graphics will be used for the graphic interface to create dialog boxes, pull-down and pop-up menus, icons, and so on. Video interface requirements will depend upon how fancy the respective data entry screens are to be: in color, with sliding bars, etc., but should be serviceable by the low- to medium-level video systems. Some information management systems use fairly complex forms ahead of their input data and this can drive up the display requirement. As information management systems become more visual, incorporating images in data fields, that too will drive the need for higher end displays.

Printer

Most information management printouts are text oriented, and some can be supported by dot matrix printers. Many DBMS products. particularly the high-end spreadsheet programs, support more sophisticated report formats with multiple print fonts and APA graphics. Database outputs are often conditioned by DtP products pushing the printer requirement. This trend toward better output quality in information management reports is driving up the printer requirement to high-end lasers and color printers. Printout speed can be crucial when large reports are involved.

Keyboard

Typing skills are important for high volume data entry. Human error during data entry can wreak havoc in information management applications. Therefore, input data verification is mandatory in most database applications. Data generated by other applications packages can sometimes be downloaded and used to satisfy a certain task. Although it's possible to purchase data files or databases that have been created and are maintained by outside vendors, most of the data will be entered through a keyboard.

System Hardware Interfaces

Most of the standard interfaces in this category are satisfactory. Most of the higher-level data connections are handled by network hardware, although there are sometimes special requirements for data entry. Key pads, touch screens, light pens, and LED scanners are often interfaced to data entry software to expedite data entry. Many of these devices can operate over the standard interfaces with appropriate software drivers, but some require custom interfaces.

Networks

Reliable networks are vital to the implementation of information management systems where data must be entered, viewed, and reported at more than one point.

Data Compatibility

Owing to the popularity of information management on DtCs, most products have built-in utilities to convert between the various applications-specific formats; if not, off-the shelf utilities are available for conversion. This is particularly true of relational database management systems that have uncomplicated files, and spreadsheet products. Financial and time project management products may be less compatible with different utilities simply because they are special. It is always a good policy to check whether conversion products can get you between your project manager and your favorite DBMS or spreadsheet program. The larger problem is the conversion between particular implementations.

Application Compatibility

The data stored by an information management system is only a part of the total investment. What may be more difficult to transport is the particular application itself: data entry and verification methodology, user prompting, data sharing mechanisms, output reports, and so on. This database product infrastructure cannot be converted simply from system to system. One of the few standards in this arena is the SQL (Structured Query Language) that does provide a standardized approach to retrieving information from large datasets, yet allows each workstation provide its own user interface.

Database Development

Database development efforts are not trivial. Information management systems are the black hole of software development. Most organizations are beginning to realize that successful operations depend on accurate management of their corporate data and product databases, but turnkey solutions to information management simply do not exist yet. The input, management, and reporting of corporate data involve some of the most intensive software developments, particularly since the data must be shared at so many levels and viewed and reported by so many different individuals. The DtC world is inundated with approaches to information management from the fancy hypercard systems innovated by Apple Computer, to the mainframe DB2 system, to the hundreds of database management products found on business computers: dBASE, DataEase, Paradox, and Object Vision. Data entry personnel and those involved in applications configuration and development are important contributors, and their efforts should not be belittled.

Inappropriate Products

Users often begin DBMS applications with inappropriate software such as spreadsheets and file managers, spending inordinate time trying to restructure the data to fit the product or to develop convoluted techniques for extracting information. Others with very simple, dedicated information tasks use full-power database management packages where spreadsheets, file managers, or even text editors could have done the trick. The most commonly observed problem is not anticipating the need for external configuration at the start of a project. This is particularly true in the DBMS area, since the trade hype focuses on the ease with which inexperienced personnel can operate such a system.

The newer object-oriented information management systems are considerably different from the traditional hierarchical and relational systems of the past. External configuration support entails a wide range of technical competence from software selection and configuration to the details of report writing and printer control. Users are often unaware of the roles that text editors and spreadsheets play in the DBMS process. Text editors and spreadsheets can be used to preassemble data sets in ways that might not be possible once inside the DBMS environment. Sharing data between such software and the DBMS will become an important issue. Using products whose limitations are quickly reached, improper use of mass storage devices, and lack of concern for data entry validation are the major stumbling blocks.

Today's DtC DBMS software allows developers to insert a layer of power and friendliness between the user and the intractable data through powerful software tools. This layer includes filters for separating data of interest, visual organization of data on-screen and in printed outputs, push-button menu selections, windowed graphs of selected data, and an assortment of other customizable features. Current DBM systems are freeing the user from dependence on outside developers, enabling them to customize applications, adding powerful menu-driven configuration processes and treating the added functions and capabilities in an object-oriented fashion.

Display Graphics

What is more fun than drawing pictures with no need for scratch paper, pencils, or erasers? DtC graphics software offer you everything from complex data charts to attention-getting slide shows. Graphics software allows you to generate graphics images on the DtC monitor, on projection monitors, or on hardcopy devices. Graphics images may be plots of scientific or business data, word and picture viewgraphs, flowcharts, free-form drawings, digitized drawings from other sources, and any other text or non-text display. Applications proceed from simple painting packages to business graphics including complex bar and pie charts to the data visualization products. Although there are thousands of DtC graphics products, we break them up into categories for the sake of management.

Representative Graphics Categories

Further dividing the display graphics category, we find the following distinct software applications:

- *Drawing* – Drawing programs allow you to create displays using a set of predefined drawing elements. These elements include:

  - *Clip art* – Object libraries are available for a wide range of picture elements; everything from a space shuttle to a baby's rattle.
  - *Primitive geometric items* – Boxes, circles ellipses, lines, and points.
  - *Text* – Characters in a variety of sizes, typefaces, and special effects such as shading, skewing left or right, rotating, and so on.

  In drawing software the drawings are developed by storing descriptions of individual graphics primitives (lines, boxes, ellipses) in a file. Editing involves selecting, overlaying, modifying, combining, and deleting individual primitives.

- *Paint programs* – A step above the drawing level, painting programs allow you to create graphics images through manipulation at the pixel level. Drawings are developed by coloring individual pixels on the display screen. You can paint broad areas, magnifying portions of the image so that individual pixels (fat bits) can be manipulated with greater certainty. Images might first be scanned in from hard copy or may originate as computer clip art.

- **Presentation** – Presentation software deals primarily with graphics that heavily emphasize textual material. Visuals prepared as 8 by 10 transparencies (viewgraphs) are the meat and potatoes of many meetings. Most commonly these are:

  - Bulleted lists of topics
  - Title slides
  - Organizational charts
  - Schedules
  - System diagrams
  - Bar and pie charts

- **Illustration** – Software to prepare complex illustrations for use by DtP software or other professional applications such as advertising, posters, and the like. Often images can be first captured by video equipment or graphics digitizers. Although illustration software is similar to drawing software, it has much higher functional capability with fonts and it gives precise control over created images.

- **Slide shows and animation software** – Designed for the production of lively and interactive graphics displays consisting of multiple, sequenced graphics images. Slide shows are designed for sequencing relatively different images with sophisticated transitions that result in an animated quality. Required slides are generally imported from scanners. Animation software is designed to generate a more real-life animated sequence, which could even be actual sequences of motion video using special hardware.

- **Flow charts** – Flow charting programs are drawing packages that manipulate flow chart symbols on screen to produce graphic representations of logical steps of processes. If the desired flowcharts are particularly complex, then the more powerful CAD programs might be considered.

- **Data charting** – Data chart programs transform columnar data into presentation graphics, bar graphs, pie charts and line graphs. The graphic facilities of charting programs let you compare multiple columns of data. Generally, data is imported from other software such as numerical analysis, spreadsheets, and database managers.

Hardware Factors

APPLICATION	KEY FACTOR
Drawing	Mouse, mass store (clip art)
Paint	Mouse, display resolution
Presentation	Display type
Illustration	CPU, mass store, display colors/resolution
Slide shows/animation	Special interfaces, CPU
Flow charts	Display resolution

APPLICATION	KEY FACTOR
Data charting	Data compatibility

Table 19. Display hardware graphics factors

CPU

Most graphics display software is written for the HB category of computers. Since the popular video interfaces in this category are dumb, the CPU bears most of the drawing and image manipulation load. Your HB drawing applications will have a direct relationship between display resolutions, total number of pixels, and CPU requirements. On MS-DOS computers this translates to 8088 for CGA interfaces, at least 80286 for EGA and MGA interfaces, and 80386 for VGA interfaces. Above moderate VGA resolutions, even higher power graphics controller interfaces will be needed to handle the higher resolution.

Although drawing and presentation software make good use of clip art, you nevertheless must move those images about your screen, which can drive CPU requirements higher. Illustration programs can perform complex image processing functions on selected portions of an image. These functions can include counting objects and calculating areas, as well as erasing, and contrast and texture variation, which can greatly improve appearance.

Illustration software with its higher levels of functionality and image and font manipulation capability will require high-end CPUs. Data charting packages often present data in 3-D or other modes. A chart of oil production, for example could be done with 3-D images of wells. This type of highly visual capability will oblige you to use higher-end CPUs. Animation software without appropriate multimedia hardware will also require high-end CPUs, while DVI hardware can relieve your CPU's load. Just managing the large data requirements of animated graphics, however, will keep CPU requirements high.

Memory

Most display graphics software packages have moderate requirements since most have no data. CAD drawings are multilevel constructions. On one level you could have information relating to wiring; on another to parts names and vendors. A CAD drawing is usually a complex hierarchy of information, with the drawing itself at the top level. Since most drawing and painting programs are not particularly functional, you can often get by with low to moderate memory requirements. Illustration programs require higher resolution displays, must manage many online fonts, perform complex image functions, and provide high levels of image manipulation. Illustration software may support a large number of fonts that need to be on-line. This forces memory requirements even higher. Many display graphics programs process their images directly in memory, imposing additional burdens on memory. Animation and slide show software require at least moderate memory to buffer the images. Special add-on hardware such as DVI brings its own memory and therefore CPU memory requirements will not be as critical.

Mass Storage

The outputs of display graphics programs may often be stored on floppy disks. Drawing, painting, charting, and presentation programs create moderate sized files, around 100K, and the programs themselves are not too large. Font libraries, clip art libraries, and the higher resolution outputs of most illustration software products will require moderate to high-end hard disk drives.

Animation software using DVI processing capability can compress live video to store up to an hour on a 600 MB optical disk. Shorter segments, up to ten minutes, can be stored on a moderate hard disk. In one instance a record store used its 100 MB hard disk in conjunction with DVI hardware to compress scanned-in record jacket images and audio samples from albums. Illustration programs and development systems for interactive video presentations and associated utilities can each easily occupy 20 MB of a hard disk. And that's not including the data files.

Printers

Display graphics software can make good use of almost any printer. For dot matrix printers, speed and resolution becomes the issue. Although the 24-wire dot matrix printers can supply remarkably highly resolved images, printout speed is very slow. Laser printers can make a great difference here, but color is not yet practical. Ink-jet printers are popular for displaying the moderate resolution output of the display graphics applications. For higher resolution and more accurate output, plotters are often used, although output speeds are quite slow.

Film image recorders are used to capture display graphic output. The image recorders are actually specialized video display devices. Some actually plug right into your video output. Since display graphics applications are often required in color, the big choice will be which color printer to purchase.

Display Interface

Display graphics programs are quite popular in the HB DtC category. Underpowered displays and dumb video interfaces are the rule. This creates a bottleneck in the display area. Although the Apple Macintosh display interfaces have extraordinary color rendering capability as compared to the stock MS-DOS video interfaces, the Mac interfaces are quite slow. Illustration packages can have display requirements rivaling CAD software graphics. The popular MS-DOS interfaces, IBM's VGA, are also slow, considering they display only 16 colors. For an MS-DOS computer be sure to get the widest possible video interface: 16 bits for 80286 and 32 bits for 386/486 systems.

Although increased data width between interface and CPU helps alleviate the display speed problem, the real solution comes with standardization of higher-level graphic display controllers, IBM's XGA for instance. Presentation software products may need special projection and viewgraph displays.

The personal business MS-DOS and Apple DtCs accept add-on graphics interfaces with appropriate power to handle the higher-end graphics requirements of the illustration software products, previously within the scope only of higher-end workstations. In addition to the interfaces, additional software drivers are needed that are not included in the usual complement of operating system software. Installation of these drivers can be complicated and frustrating.

Discontinuity of support software is not as serious a problem in the EP category because most software is designed at the outset to include high performance graphics interfaces. Also, more powerful graphics interfaces are more integrated in the system design and not added as an afterthought.

Keyboard and Mouse Input Devices

Display graphics systems make good use of the mouse; its feel and resolution are important considerations.

System Hardware Interfaces

Display graphics software generally operates on the standard DtC. Some scanners and most plotters operate through the standard serial and parallel interfaces. DVI applications will usually require special add-ons, so your system bus capability and slots become important considerations.

Networks

Moving display graphics images on networks can really eat up network capacity. It may be necessary to cordon off groups using networks for image movements into smaller, isolated groups through intelligent network gateways. The gateways permit high levels of communication between a subnetwork while providing subnetwork communications, to a lesser degree, to the rest of a larger network.

Data Compatibility

There are hundreds of different data formats for graphics images. Multiple standards have evolved in each of the areas mentioned above. There are scads of graphics format conversion utilities, and many graphic products can convert formats internally. To make good use of graphics on DtCs, you could use several drawing graphics products. You could create an image with a paint program for incorporation in a presentation program. If you want to combine product usage, you need to check out data compatibility between the various drawing graphics products. If the graphics products are to be used by desktop publishing software, its compatibility must also be assured.

Engineering Scientific Software

Engineering and scientific (ES) software is a broad category that has been used as long as there have been computers. All major branches of engineering and scientific disciplines have routinely used computers in day-to-day activities for over two decades. Mechanical engineers build cars, ships, and airplanes with their help; civil engineers design and build bridges; and electrical engineers use them for circuit design and analysis. These are only the mainstream examples of ES software. The ES applications described here usually run on the EW class of DtCs. But you will find more of these applications on HB computers as the HB DtC hardware and operating systems mature.

ES software includes all manner of design and analysis programs, the number crunchers, CAD/CAM software, some types of graphics software such as data visualization, and other esoteric forms of software such as those used for medical applications. The need for specialized peripherals and coprocessors complicate matters. Moreover, special products in this category are particularly expensive. Although process control is often included in the ES category, we have created a separate control and interface category because of the unique hardware requirements.

Due to the diversification of software in this category, we show only the more popular categories:

- *CAD (computer-aided design)* – Use of the computer to assist in the design of mechanical, electrical, architectural and other products. The item is drawn on screen with all associated data.

- *CAE (computer-aided engineering)* – Products in the CAE category combine drawing and graphics with powerful engineering simulation and fault analysis. Other capabilities include finite element analysis, testing the strength of complex objects through meshes, electronic circuit simulation, and the design of VLSI chips.

- *Number crunching and analysis* – Not specific to any particular engineering category, these products provide math and plotting support required by most engineering activities. Functions include numeric and symbolic computation, matrix manipulation numerical analysis, curve fitting, nonlinear equation solution, equation editing, and equation plotting.

- *Image processing* – Analysis of images that can range from planet surfaces to medical X-rays.

- *Data visualization* – An emerging software category that helps visualize complex, multidimensional data. Ingenious techniques based on colors, contours, and animations are used to help engineers and scientists visualize the large numerical databases that they gather.

■ This definition of AI is based on that given by Roger Penrose, in *The Emperor's New Mind*.

- *Artificial Intelligence (AI)* – An increasingly important field of science, AI encompasses everything from knowledge bases to pattern recognition using neural network techniques.■ The objective of AI is to imitate human mental activity. AI applications can be found proceeding in five principal directions:

  1. *Robotics* – To solve the practical requirements of industry for mechanical devices to perform complicated tasks with versatility, speed, and reliability that heretofore have demanded human intelligence and dexterity. Also, to perform hazardous tasks safely or to perform tasks under severe conditions.
  2. *Expert systems* – To capture and manage the essential knowledge of an entire profession, such as medical or legal.
  3. *Pattern recognition* – To develop methods similar to those used by the human brain to recognize images, characters, words, and sounds.
  4. *Psychology* – To imitate human behavior for the purpose of learning how the human brain works and how it processes stimuli.
  5. *Philosophy* – To develop insights into the concepts of mind and matter.

- *CASE (computer-aided systems engineering) tools* – CASE technology is the automation of step-by-step methodologies for software and systems development from initial planning to ongoing maintenance. CASE programs are designed to automate the drudgery of managing the development process and free the developer for problem solving. CASE methodologies help to standardize and systematize software development and maintenance by approaching them as an engineering discipline rather than as the whims of individual software developers. CASE tools can be used to develop software in any of the applications categories described in this section.

Hardware Factors

The evolution of EP software is closely related to the development of computer hardware. On the average, computers became 30% faster every year in the 1980s; it is conceivable that speeds could double every year in the 1990s. The major event in CPU improvement is CPU design based on reduced instruction sets (RISC). Sun

Microsystems (SPARC chip), Mips Computer Company (MIPS chip), and IBM are the leading companies in the use of this technology and show promise in putting mainframe processing power on desktops by the mid-1990s.

Other major developments include powerful CPUs with built-in math coprocessors from Intel and Motorola. The present version of Sun's SPARC CPU, which evolved from Berkeley's research on RISC technology, has enabled it to become a market leader and is about 30 times faster that DEC's original VAX, which is around or twice as fast as the fastest MS-DOS 486-based DtC.

Application	Key Factor
CAD	CPU, math, display, plotter mass store
CAE	CPU, math, display
Number crunching and analysis	CPU, math, special math coprocessor
Image processing	CPU, math, mass store
Image processing	CPU, math, mass store
Data visualization (contours)	CPU, math, graphics coprocessor, display, mass store
AI	CPU, math, interfaces
CASE	CPU, networks

Table 20. ES applications hardware factors: Enhanced math capability through math coprocessors or special-purpose computational add-ons.

CPU

CAD, due to intensive graphics, and CAE, due to simulation of complex systems, have extraordinary CPU requirements. Many number crunching systems depend on high-level interpretive languages, such as SAS and APL, and must manipulate large numerical datasets. They too, as a result, are CPU intensive. Such exotic tools as fuzzy logic, used to make robots balance candlesticks, and emulation of neural networks, used to solve recognition problems, require enormous CPU capacity not found in the HB category. EWs often require RISC or application-specific processors, or must be supplemented with special computational add-ons that achieve throughputs rivaling those of supercomputers.

> **NOTE**
>
> Supercomputer add-ons are extraordinarily powerful, incorporating highly parallel array processing or highly specialized processing capability that can equal and exceed that of the more general supercomputers because the add-on is dedicated to a specific computational task.

The fastest CISC CPUs at the highest clock speeds are obligatory for the ES software category. Since high-level languages are used, high-end CPUs are required.

CAD applications and their attendant graphics display needs are more prevalent in the EW category, so the CPU load is not much of a problem. This is because the EW DtCs usually implement higher-end graphics controllers, which relieve the CPU of some of the graphics load. Image processing often involves custom video interface boards, which also assume some of the CPU load, so even moderately-powered CPUs can support image processing. The CPU in this case is relegated to moving the data to and from the image processing hardware.

HB DtCs will often require more than the usual built-in math coprocessors and more specialized computational enhancements such as those described in subsequent parts of this book. Analysis plots will require heavy math due to the large amount of statistical computing, curve fitting, and regression analysis.

Memory

EP applications have high memory requirements. CAD programs start at 20 MB sizes and on-line parts libraries can require a gigabyte of memory. On MS-DOS computers, CAD programs, even those that use extended memory, hog real memory. Many problems are experienced trying to free real memory of TSRs and network drivers using such products as Quarterdeck's QEMM and MS-DOS EMM. QEMM and EMM allow those drivers to operate in upper memory blocks, freeing real memory.

MS-DOS computer users often use spreadsheet and DBMS products to analyze their data, which require considerable expanded memory. Large numerical data bases must be kept in huge memory arrays for processing and intermediate results need to be in memory also. This need to periodically access all portions of a dataset is particularly true of digital signal processing in which a lot of squential data gets shuffled around. Due to this scattered access, the entire data set must be stored in memory.

Mass Store

Ideally, large CAD databases should be manipulated in memory, but because of their large sizes, they must often be shuffled to and from the hard disk; in this case hard disk speed becomes critical. CAD and analysis software may take as many as 40 floppy disks to transport. Individuals attempting CAD applications on MS-DOS computers should begin with fast ESDI drives capable of moving large CAD databases to and from memory. You can wait for one minute on an MS-DOS computer just to load a CAD drawing, often several MB in size, into your extended memory.

Most CAD programs involve complex databases related to their images and have moderate to high memory requirements. Analysis program mass storage requirements are driven primarily by the size of the non-archived data being processed or buffered on the way into your DtC. Of course you can always use magnetic tape, but the data would not be randomly accessible. This can be a problem particularly when processing involves rapid access of data from assorted positions in the data set.

Display Interface

The complex nature of CAD presentations and images being manipulated calls for high end graphics interfaces. Newer analysis software products provide sophisticated 3-D and 4-D output graphics; data visualization is becoming the key issue in the '90s. The requirements on the video interface are extraordinarily high. High resolution and fast response capability is required to perform geometric functions. A great problem arises with high-end graphics requirements of ES software on the typical HB DtC interfaces. The cost of an appropriate interface and monitor can easily exceed the price of the entire DtC system unit.

The high-end graphics processing requirements of image processing, CAD, and data visualization require high levels of integration between graphics display interface, math coprocessors, and CPU. This integration, currently found in the EW category of DtCs, continues to divide the EW and HB DtC categories.

Printer

Dot matrix and low-end laser printers are often used for analysis data printouts. In fact, it is surprising how detailed a CAD-generated electronics schematic can be printed on a 24-wire letter quality dot matrix printer. Most CAD outputs, due to their precision and color requirements, are performed on plotters. Many laser printers support HPGL (Hewlett Packard Graphics Language) and therefore CAD drawings can be plotted on laser printers without additional software driver lashups.

Keyboard

Digitizing tablets are often used for graphics input, and so tablet resolution and response become issues. The keyboard can be supplemented for ordinary command and data input by menued inlays on the graphics tablet.

System Hardware Interfaces

Because of heavy math requirements, specialized computational add-on boards will often be needed to supplement the CPU. Boards include array processors, FFT processors, and DSP digital signal processors. Verify compatibility with other DtC hardware before you commit to these add-ons. Specialized processor add-on hardware promises performance improvements of orders of magnitude, yet must stay compatible with other system hardware. Image processing software will sometimes require specialized interfaces necessary to capture video images.

Networks

Since ES software usually runs large datasets, particularly fast networks – at least greater than 10 MB/sec – are needed to shuffle so much data around. We're not talking about electronic mail, in which 500 byte messages are moved back and forth. CAD files are seldom less than several MB, while electronic parts libraries are seldom less than 1 gigabyte.

Data Compatibility

The complex nature of engineering databases moves data compatibility to the forefront. Each engineering discipline has is own data format needs. The data needs of DtC board connections are quite different from those of bridge structures or finite element meshes. Internal to CAD drawing databases are complex relationships between different drawings as well as between levels within the same drawing. Electronic parts libraries usually contain thousands of names, numbers, and attributes. Product conventions such as PDES (Product Data Exchange Specifications) are slow in coming.

As the design industry awaits standards, a software application known as PDM (Product Data Management) has evolved to help tackle the management of complex product development datasets. Basically, the datasets are encapsulated and managed without internal knowledge of the dataset. Such quantities as release dates, persons responsible, due dates, and authorized sponsors are tracked in what is known as metadatabases. Tracking follows the data from a draft specification to a finished manufactured item. Installed on a network, PDM software can control access to product databases. Control of access is critical, because many individuals will need to access such files for quite different reasons.

OOP technology is being introduced to assist in handling and interrelating the vastly different and complex databases found in the EP category.

Use of HB Computers

Engineers and scientists are beginning to use HB DtCs for analysis tasks. Although CAD and other engineering software can be found for the HB class, the tradeoff will usually be performance for the more utilitarian platform. Stated another way, although CAD applications might be squeezed, the abundance of day to day productivity software makes up for the frustration of operating the engineering software in crowded memory and with ill-equipped operating system support. As HB computers mature and as more HB software is rewritten to operate on the EW computers, HB and EW platforms will become equal.

Control and Interface

DtCs can be used to control other equipment, or to interface between dissimilar equipments. Computer aided manufacturing and experiment control are examples. Traditionally, CAM processes have been driven by custom microcontrollers or minicomputers. However, the DtC is beginning to surround CAM activities. DtCs may be used to preprocess and store CAM data and can serve as controlling computers. DtCs are now common in factories and are used to control scientific processes in laboratories. DtCs are found as embedded controllers or monitors or even interfaces in much larger computing systems.

Control and Interface Categories

We can subdivide the control and interface category this way:

- **Process control** – DtCs are used to control experiments and they play a role in complex manufacturing operations with computer-aided manufacturing.
- **Data acquisition** – Using the DtC to directly interface to and acquire data from other systems.
- **Embedded DtCs** – Using the DtC as a dedicated interface between two other devices, or as a dedicated controller in a larger system.

Hardware Factors

Application	Key Factor
Process control and CAM	Open architecture, reliability, networks
Data acquisition and processing	CPU, DMA/shared memory interfaces
Embedded DtCs	Reliability, shared memory interfaces

Table 21.   **Equipment control and interfacing hardware factors**

An open architecture is particularly important in the control/interface category since the DtC will be used as a platform for a variety of specialized interfaces. Attributes of an open system include:

- Complete documentation of all bus functions permitting hardware designers to develop interfaces.
- Complete documentation of operating system functions available for the support of system resources interrupt levels, DMA channels, memory mapping, and I/O space mapping.
- Provision of parallel bus signal slots for add-on hardware devices.

These attributes are mandatory to allow vendors to develop add-on systems that will cooperate in their use of DtC system resources.

CPU

Most process control systems implement their own specialized coprocessors and interfacing devices, particularly for real time data processing. Therefore the loads that they impose on the DtC CPU can be quite variable. A data acquisition add-on board will usually have its own dedicated microcomputer for data gathering; a DSP board will have its own dedicated high MIPS signal processor chip. Simpler configurations, for instance, an environmental control application may not only be required to gather significant amounts of data but will also have to display flow diagrams, floor plans, and the like.

Memory

CPU memory requirements are often driven by the amount of online data to be processed. For voice recognition systems it is the number of word sets being recognized, for data acquisition systems it is the amount of online data to be analyzed and kept ready. For environmental systems it is the amount of space required to keep a day's data. Although many add-on processing boards control large quantities of their own memory, 1 MB to 4 MB, much of it may have to be shared with the CPU for effective integration.

Mass store

Process control and interface software do not take up much room, but the amount of data collected by a data acquisition application is likely to increase the mass storage requirement. Since many control and interface applications are operated remotely over long periods of time, be sure not to overflow your hard disk. Alternative storage such as Bernoulli cartridge disks or streaming tape systems may be required. Also, for many reasons, you may want to keep important data on hand without having to go to archival storage. For example, an environmental control computer user may want a plot of last month's data quickly without going to archival storage.

Display Interface

Many process control applications will benefit through graphic presentations. Diagrams of processes being controlled, visual alarm panels, oscilloscope representations of signals being acquired or laboratory front panels with graphic knobs sliders and switches controlled by your mouse all require at least a moderate graphics interface.

Printer

The printer will often be used for raw data printouts and for this dot matrix printers suffice. Speed can be important due to the volumes of data output required for quick scanning. If plots of multiple acquired data sets are required, color printers and plotters may be necessary.

Keyboard

The keyboard is often used to control system parameters, so accuracy is particularly important. Keyboard mistakes can have immediate effects that are difficult to correct later on.

System Hardware Interfaces

Process control applications are generally more sensitive to architectural differences – DMA implementations, interrupt levels, I/O map and memory usage, and available slots – and require you to know much more about your system hardware than the previously mentioned software categories.

In the MS-DOS world, the problem is the different ISA and MCA buses. In the Apple world, early Macs were not expandable. The newer Mac IIs, however, have a very expandable NuBus system. Also, since there are few if any third-party Macintoshes, the bus is the same; there are no different versions, and therefore less possibility for compatibility problems. Software is much more abundant for MS-DOS computers – with compilers, software libraries, utilities, and tools – than for most other platforms. Software availability combined with their open architecture is why MS-DOS computers are so popular in engineering and production activities.

Data compatibility

The nature of data in this area extends from customized binary data for machine control and raw input data to highly customized formats found in some environmental control systems. Often ASCII data format is the only possibility for a common format and its use is encouraged. Look for utility software for conversion to the format of the many common data display products: spreadsheets, data charters, and DBMS products. Moving acquired data into these products can greatly enhance analysis capability, particularly when browsing the data for trends.

Software Maturity

Software for control applications is quite diversified and also sometimes poorly written. The unavailability of appropriate languages, subroutine libraries, and little software support of add-on boards is an obstacle. It's easy to buy that data acquisition board, yet getting the associated software to do precisely what you want may be much more difficult. Be sure that technical support of associated software is available and try to find someone who has used the system you are considering.

Be sure too that the support of software provides linkage to other languages, particularly machine language when performance is desired. Many control applications involve highly integrated hardware and software and installation of either can be tedious, even if you can get both hardware and software to work. Board enhancements and bug fixes must be well supported. Good software support of add-on boards should be weighed as heavily as the particular hardware performance claims made by the vendor.

Most vendors supply software with their interface boards. This software is often inadequate for the intended function, or is tied to a specific language library, and must be redeveloped for other languages. Often, special compilers are required to write software that uses the add-on board properly and efficiently. Software customizations occur at the most technical level, often in assembly language, and at the software driver level, and may require extensive programming efforts. The importance of obtaining the right hardware and associated software cannot be overemphasized.

Off-the-Shelf Interfaces

If you wish to design your own interfaces, be aware that your problem may already be solved somewhere in the large variety of off-the-shelf interfaces currently available for DtCs. The lack of centralized technical information on the use of these systems often leads to inappropriate software purchases, or failure to take advantage of the enhanced performance of control systems.

5.0   Data Transfers and Compatibility

■ Removable Media Format
■ Data Format
■ Applications
■ Data Transfers

The end product of DtC activities is usually the processed data. When moving data between applications programs, you need to know something about its internal format as well as the infrastructure of the software to which it is being transferred.

It is important to distinguish between media format, data or file format, and other aspects of data usage in an application. The other aspects are referred to as infrastructure, which may need to be factored in when data is moved between applications programs. From Figure 18 you can see that media format is determined at the disk controller while the data format is established by the application. Applications data is generally moved about the DtC system encapsulated in a specific data or file format. Applications programs convert this data into a presentation format for viewing and printing while the hard disk controller converts it to a media format for storage on a particular medium.

Figure 19 shows that factors beyond data format need to be considered when you move data around. Let's look at media formats, before we investigate some of the issues of data compatibility.

5.1   Removable Media Format

Media format refers to the way data are recorded on a given medium, how magnetic fields are oriented, and how the 1s and 0s appear in recorded form. Some popular hard disk data encoding formats are RLL (run length limited), FM (frequency modulation), and MFM (modified frequency modulation). Media format is generally developed at its controller and is customized for the particular medium being used: hard disk, floppy disk, CD-ROM, or magnetic tape. The applications software should be completely independent of media formats. Media formats are governed by media controllers in conjunction with operating systems.

You need to be concerned about media format when you want to transfer removable media, diskettes, Bernoulli cartridges, and CD ROM disks from computer to computer. We will look more at details of media format, including the non-removable hard disk in a later Part.

The following factors determine the compatibility and usability of data-filled floppy disks, Bernoulli cartridges, or CD-ROMs.

- *Density* – High or low. The number of recorded bits per inch of track length.
- *Tracks* – How many circular tracks of data are there? The popular floppy disks support 40 and 80 tracks.

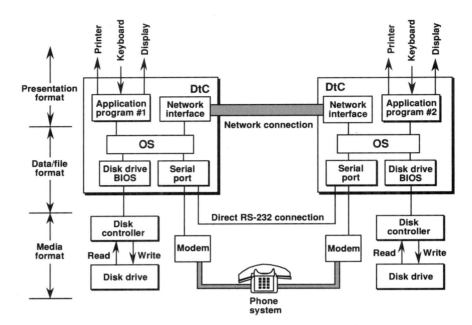

Figure 18. Media, data, and presentation format: From media to presentation, data can take many forms.

- **Size** – The physical size of the diskette 3½", 5¼".
- **OS format** – How the raw recording medium is set up by the operating system before the actual data is written to it. Sectors per track, sector gaps, and sector addressing are established.
- **Hard/soft sectoring** – Sector position is determined by holes in a floppy diskette, while soft sectoring relies on addressing information laid onto the disk tracks.
- **Data encoding** – RLL, FM, and MFM, used for floppy and hard disks.

Removable cartridge formats, Bernoulli for instance, may differ considerably from those described above due to the high data densities and increased need for data redundancy. Most utility software programs such as Norton Utilities and Gibson's SpinWrite will seldom work on this medium. Generally, formatting, erasing, and other utilities are provided by the manufacturer of the medium.

Media Transportability

Different microcomputer systems cannot always read one another's medium, even though physically they look identical in size and mounting. Discord occurs because of differences in interfaces and formatting mechanisms. It is likely that floppy diskettes will soon be compatible across microcomputers. MS-DOS computers, Apple computers, and Sun workstations will read one another's diskettes. Differences in media format that occur across different makes or microcomputer categories can create difficulties or completely prevent the transfer of data between different DtC systems by way of removable floppy disks and tape. Such problems are independent of software programs, and arise from different recording techniques, interfaces, and disk sizes.

Within a given vendor's media, the greater data density disk drives can read the lower data density disks, but not the reverse. For example, on an MS-DOS computer the 1.2 MB 5¼" disk drive will read the 360K floppies, but not the other way around.

Apple Macintosh computers, using appropriate software, will read MS-DOS formatted diskettes. Using appropriate utility software, a Macintosh can create disks in MS-DOS format that can be read by an MS-DOS computer when it is desired to move Macintosh data to an MS-DOS computer. MS-DOS computers cannot read Macintosh native format. This asymmetry in disk format transfer is due to the specialized floppy disk controllers in MS-DOS computers that quite rigorously define the disk format at the controller level. In contrast, Apple computers traditionally use less confining hardware for their disk interfaces and can create almost any disk format.

You can purchase a disk interface for your MS-DOS computer that will enable it to read native Mac-formatted diskettes.

Media Independent Data Transfers

Figure 18 gives a global view of data from disk media to an applications program. Notice that the medium format is beneath the operating system and its communication interface software. In fact the application is completely isolated from the details of media format by the operating system. When a program calls the operating system for data, the operating system drivers talk to the respective media controller, which is ultimately responsible for the particular medium's format. Figure 18 depicts two DtCs that are interconnected by an RS-232 interface directly, by modem, or by a local area network.

Data files can be moved directly between RS-232 ports. Specialized asynchronous communication software products can allow the two DtCs to act as though they were in a LAN. No external hardware other than the existing RS-232 serial interfaces and cabling is required and transmission rates are at the maximum supported by the serial interface hardware if direct connected. For most DtCs this limit is around 100Kbits/sec. Since the RS-232 data ports may be used as seven-bit (128) or eight-bit (256) codes, you must be sure that it is appropriately programmed for seven-bit ASCII or eight-bit binary transmissions.

The communications or networking software essentially redirects data to flow over the communications interfaces rather than to the media controllers. The data that are finally transmitted over the communications interface are media independent. The receiving computer receives the data through a reverse process, without concern for media format. If the data are to be recorded on the other end, then the other computer's operating system, aware of its particular medium, performs the necessary recording.

You can see from Figure 18 that network connections or the serial interface can circumvent media format problems completely because the transfers are at the data byte level. At this level, there is no medium format and therefore no concern about different media on different computers.

Data format is the manner in which a given applications program represents its data, or the manner in which the data is coded into the respective bytes. We will be looking at a number of different data formats: some are designed for no-frills movements of ASCII characters, others, for special formats, can include color, size, font, graphics images, CPU execution codes, and a host of other application-specific information. Formats that are peculiar to a particular vendor's program are program-specific formats, while more general formats that are related to particular application areas, DBMS or graphics, for example, are application specific.

For writing/publishing software, the primary data element is text surrounded by various format codes and included graphics images. For spreadsheets, it's usually numbers surrounded by formulas. For databases, it's information surrounded by relationships, indexes, and report formats. For drawing programs, it's the lines and boxes, or individual pixels that are being represented in the data surrounded by parameters for representations of tables, charts, and graphs. Depending upon the application there will be different types of data representations. Figure 19 shows four popular software categories, the primary data elements, and the program-specific data.

Within the program-specific data you can see the primary data (top of box) as well as the pertinent style and format information (bottom of box) that must be specified to adequately display the data. There are no particular styling and data formatting standards; styling and formatting are different in most vendor's software products even though the products are in the same applications category; e.g., DBMS, word processing, and so on.

Before we treat the subject of data transfers and infrastructure let's look at the most general data format, one that is primarily application independent.

ASCII Codes

ASCII stands for American Standard Code for Information Interchange. Since text and numbers are the universal data quantities transmitted between computers, a general format has been designed to handle these no-frills transmissions. By no frills, we mean just the data, and not how it appears in color, size, font, and so on. You can see the tradeoff immediately. The ability to transfer data vs. the ability to transfer style or other applications-specific information.

ASCII is the most widespread data format. One hundred twenty seven codes are used to represent the alphabet, numbers, punctuation, and some universal printer and modem control characters. Seven binary digits are required to contain these combinations. Hardly a DtC program exists that cannot generate, import, and export ASCII data.

ASCII codes are grouped as follows:

- *00-1F Hex* – Control codes (backspace, line feed, carriage return, escape, form feed, end of file)
- *20 Hex* – Blank (or space)
- *21-2F Hex* – Miscellaneous punctuation
- *30-39 Hex* – Numbers

- **40-5F Hex** – Upper case text characters and miscellaneous symbols/punctuation
- **60-7F Hex** – Lower case text characters and miscellaneous symbols/punctuation
- **80-FF Hex** – Extended ASCII codes (application-specific)

ASCII files are generally referred to as text files and they are ideal for applications in which many users with diverse equipment types must share textual data, electronic mail, for example, where the style or format of the data is not important. The ability to share ASCII is a fundamental requirement of any software package. Sharing of ASCII data can be complicated somewhat by different interpretations of the control codes. For example, some programs use carriage returns and line feeds, hard carriage returns, to terminate lines while others let the software decide line lengths. Although ASCII is an optimum approach to plain text transfers, the mechanism fails miserably when we need to transmit more than textual information: graphics, spreadsheet, number positions, database indexes, and graphics with control information. For complex data transfers we must use applications-specific formats.

Comma Delimited ASCII

Comma delimited ASCII is often used for transmission of record-oriented databases. Comma delimited ASCII works between DBMS systems, or between DBMS and DBMS merge capable word processors. Separation between the different field entries in the data records is signified by commas, or some other agreed-upon character, including blanks. Most database management programs and languages can easily read comma delimited ASCII files.

This is in contrast to fixed length or column formatted fields where spaces are used to keep each field within its own column. Comma delimited files save storage space. Comma delimited and column formatted ASCII may be directly displayed by most operating systems type or list commands without further need of conversion. Column formatted files, however, are easy to manipulate with text editors. Large file sizes of column formatted files, filled with blanks, can be reduced by compression utilities such as ZIP and ARC, that easily squeeze out the blanks for storage and replace them when the files are decompressed. There may be difficulty in sharing comma delimited and comma formatted files with systems, some mainframes for example, that restrict text record lengths to 256 bytes or less.

Extended ASCII

Extended ASCII should be considered a superset of ASCII codes. Through different techniques, we can extend or add to the total number of codes ordinarily representable with seven data bits. The extended codes obtained may be program specific or application specific.

1. *Escape codes* – A larger number of additional codes is obtained by preceding ASCII characters with the code IB hex (ESC). ASCII characters following the ESC code now take on a whole new meaning. The primary uses for these so-called escape codes are:

   - *Printer control* – A relatively standardized set of printer control codes are invoked by the ESC mechanism. For instance ESC E and ESC F turn emphasized and double strike print modes on most dot matrix printers. These special codes can be embedded in the normal text stream to the printer and once encountered will set up special printer operations without affecting processing of normal characters.

- **Full screen display text control** – Escape sequences can be used to control your terminal's text color and cursor position. By transmitting these codes, you can position your remote screen's cursor without extra commands. The codes amount to the normal ASCII characters preceded by the ESC code. Video drivers, designed to recognize these characters, such as MS-DOS's ANSI.SYS, make it easy for software programs to control character color and position through standardized video drivers.

2. **Null codes** – As with the ESC code, the 00 hex (null) code can proceed ASCII characters to yield more codes. Null codes are also somewhat standardized and one popular usage is to represent the special keys on the more sophisticated keyboards. Among such function keys are Alt, Page Up, Page Down, Home, and End.

3. **Add an eighth bit** – By simply adding an eighth bit to the existing seven-bit (pure ASCII) system, one obtains another 128 codes. Actually, this usually takes up no more memory since each ASCII character is stored by the CPU in an eight-bit memory byte; the eighth bit permanently zeroed. The extra codes (80-FF hex) are usually application dependant. For example, MS-DOS computers use upper codes for representing text-graphic characters.

Many programs limit graphics to the use of these special characters for graphics transportability. Although only limited graphics can be obtained, mostly for drawing boxes and lines, any program or video interface that can handle only characters will be able to perform graphics. This is particularly important in MS-DOS applications since MS-DOS provides only text support and doesn't differentiate between the ordinary characters and text-graphic characters. Other programs may draw simple figures with these characters.

Word processors may use the upper characters to define format and style such as boldface type, underlining, text color and other functions. The idea is to use the eighth bit to represent application specific information.

Language compilers might use the extended codes for tokens to represent functions while common text is represented with the usual first 128 ASCII codes. For example the statement

```
PRINT "HELLO"
```

would be represented as 91,48,45,4C,4C,4F where the 91 is the token for print and the remainder is the ASCII code for the word HELLO.

The ASCII format is one of the most general and popular formats. Some of the more application specific formats are actually coded in ASCII.

Application-Specific Formats

Not as universal as pure ASCII, yet more specialized than extended ASCII, these data formats are standardized within a particular applications category to ensure compatibility and data exchange between and among members of similar applications families. This kind of standardization is usually based upon an ASCII representation of a conceptually more complex data type. Let's look at a few examples.

- **DIF** – DIF files are considered a standard for the transmission of row/column oriented data systems. DIF files are particularly specialized at passing spreadsheet data between different spreadsheet programs or between spreadsheet programs and DBMS programs. Printing DIF files as is reveals a sequence of data row-wise, or column-wise with additional positional information to facilitate their recreation at the receiving application.

- *Encapsulated PostScript* – A data format suited for combined text and graphics images. PostScript is the language used for defining and manipulating the images. Encapsulated PostScript is interpreted by a PostScript interpreter usually implemented in your printer. Some video display interfaces can interpret PostScript streams for presentation on your monitor.

When the above datasets are printed with the ordinary display utilities, the coded ASCII characters appear. They will have little meaning unless you understand the underlying mechanism used to transfer the information.

Binary Format

Binary formats are generally program or even hardware specific. Without any further information, a binary format appears as a hopelessly random mix of data codes. Binary format could represent the vectors in a drawing, CPU machine language, a Lotus 1-2-3 data file and even compressed ASCII data.

In binary format, most if not all 256 possibilities in an 8-bit byte (00-FF hex) have meaning and the meanings of the 256 codes will depend upon the specific application. Look at the following examples:

- *Machine language* – The 256 codes translate to opcodes (what the CPU should do) and operands (what it should do it to). Each CPU will have a different machine language. There is no standardization on opcode representations. The operands, however are generally a register number or numerical memory or I/O location. Each 8-bit binary value is normally represented (in printouts and on your video display) by two 4-bit hex data nibbles. For example 10101111 would split to 1010 1111, then to AF hex.

> **NOTE**
>
> Intel hex format is an ASCII representation of binary data, suitable for 7 bit-only data transmissions. Recall that the 128 ASCII codes only required 7 bits for transmission. Two 7-bit ASCII characters are used to represent an 8-bit binary value. To do this, we convert each hex value to an ASCII value. The AF becomes 41,46. The 41 is the ASCII code for "A" and 46 is the ASCII code for "F".

- *Lotus 1-2-3 binary file format* – The spreadsheet program Lotus 1-2-3 uses an internal format where even characters are not represented with conventional ASCII codes, but rather with a complex set of compressed codes. Codes could represent spreadsheet entry position, representation of formulas, printer setups, macros and, of course, the spreadsheet text/number entries themselves. The early version 1.x used the WKS binary format while version 2.x and above used the WK1 format. Although .WKS files can be read by version 2.x, version 1.x won't read WK1 format files. So, just as there is concern that an earlier CPU will not execute the machine language of a later model, there is similar concern with programs that have specific data formats.

- *Compressed data files* – Most compressed data files are in binary format. Files are compressed by noting such things as repeating characters or blanks. Most data compression programs operate between 30-50% compression ratios; the compressed file is up to 1/3 the size of the original. Compressed files are generally not readable by their respective applications programs and must first be decompressed. A popular MS-DOS computer compression format is the ZIP format.

Attempts to view or print binary files without the assistance of the application that generated them will render strange looking character displays. Most text display utilities will render the lower 128 codes as characters, however the upper codes will appear as whatever text-graphics codes the particular display system was intended to use. Thus when a binary file is viewed, a random mix of printable and text-graphics characters appears.

Any ASCII codes embedded in the binary file will show through as characters. There are file viewers that can adapt to the various file formats and present meaningful displays and printouts outside of actually having to operate the application that generated the data. For example, the XTree Gold Professional utility program for MS-DOS computers lets you view dBASE, Lotus, Word Perfect and a variety of other popular application-specific binary files. Within XTree you can see, and within limits interact with the spreadsheet or database, look for particular quantities, and output portions in ASCII.

5.3   Data Transfers

Now that we have peeked at some of the different data formats, let's see what we need to consider when moving data between programs. First, be aware that moving files between applications, although somewhat complicated, is only half of what needs to be done. When moving program-specific data, three things must be considered:

1. The data itself (numbers, characters, images).
2. The style of the data (color, size, font).
3. The infrastructure that defines the personality or usage of the overall application.

The three items are shown in Figure 19. Items 1 and 2 shown at the left are generally collectively contained in what we call the program specific data files that move the data, documents, and images, between different DtC stations. Item 3 is the actual implementation and interaction of the data. Item 3, the high-level infrastructure, may include additional data sets, database indexes, and report formats.

Therefore we have two main considerations when transferring data between applications:

1. **Moving the data** – How to get the data between the applications intact.
2. **Maintaining the infrastructure** – How to preserve the details of the application.

Moving the Data

Each software category (spreadsheets, word processors, database managers, graphics) have particular data representation needs. Within each category there are hundreds of different products accomplishing very much the same thing, yet each program has its unique way of representing its data.

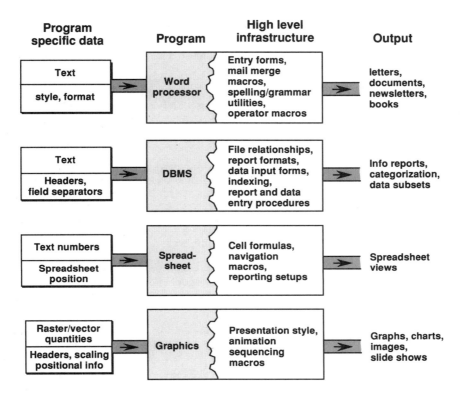

Program specific data	Program	High level infrastructure	Output
Text style, format	Word processor	Entry forms, mail merge macros, spelling/grammar utilities, operator macros	letters, documents, newsletters, books
Text Headers, field separators	DBMS	File relationships, report formats, data input forms, indexing, report and data entry procedures	Info reports, categorization, data subsets
Text numbers Spreadsheet position	Spread- sheet	Cell formulas, navigation macros, reporting setups	Spreadsheet views
Raster/vector quantities Headers, scaling positional info	Graphics	Presentation style, animation sequencing macros	Graphs, charts, images, slide shows

Figure 19. **Program-specific data and application infrastructure:** Formatting is only half the problem; the usage infrastructure must be considered as well.

Program-specific data formats are customized to a specific program's use, and in general cannot be read by other programs in the same applications category except where the program developer has provided internal conversion utilities. Most program-specific formats are in binary or in extended ASCII, with extended codes specific to the particular program.

The major compatibility problem is that each vendor's product uses different codes for the same purpose. One word processor may have codes for functions not even implemented in the other word processor. For example, WordPerfect files cannot be read directly by the Microsoft Word program; the files must be converted to Word format. These conversion (import/export) utilities will hopefully be built into your particular program and will support the popular formats. If they are not, you will have to seek out external conversion utilities that can convert the file to the required format.

The difference in format becomes critical with desktop publishers having so much functional formatting capability. Figure 20 shows how two different word processor programs can make use of the same data file. Notice that it is much easier to use the data file by its parent program than to convert it for use by a program that has different data requirements.

To avoid compatibility and conversion problems, it is always best to use the same vendor's software product on both ends. This is especially important for sharing files with co-workers. When you must deal with different program data formats there are usually two alternatives.

1. ***ASCII conversion*** – For text-based applications (such as word processors, spreadsheets, and DBMS packages). Strip the file to pure ASCII (lower 128 codes). This has the undesirable effect that many of the formatting and special effects (font selection, boldface, underline, spreadsheet formulas, database headers) will be lost and will have to be reconstructed manually within the new program.

2. ***Utility conversion*** – Convert the one program's file format to the other's requirement with a conversion utility. This may have the undesirable effect of incomplete conversion of special codes or characters. Due to the complexity and functional variety of the various DtC applications packages, intelligent file format conversion utilities that can completely transform different formats are far from universal. Therefore, various fix-ups will often be required on the receiving end. To be reasonably safe, use the ASCII conversion.

There are many data format conversion programs on the market. Most are peculiar to a particular applications category. For example, there are conversion utilities that specialize in drawing graphics formats, or DBMS and spreadsheet formats, or word processor formats.

Also be aware that the same applications programs may have specific format problems between different versions of that program. The newer version will generally read the older version's files, but not the reverse. Most programs provide for upgrading file formats to the newer versions, but the reverse may not be true. Thus, even when a group sticks to the same applications package for data file compatibility, problems may still arise when version upgrades occur.

Moving the Infrastructure

When you operate a particular software product and use data, there is much to be considered beyond just the data. The following infrastructure and support logistics are not accounted for in most simple file transfers. Figure 19 shows the file format aspects of moving data as well as infrastructure considerations. Some infrastructure considerations are exclusive to particular applications areas, however the following considerations apply to almost any applications category.

- ***User interface to the data*** – Nature GUI, light bars.
- ***Data input*** – Setups, verification, translations.
- ***Menuing systems*** – Developed for particular user classes.
- ***Peripheral support*** – Drivers, setups.
- ***Reports*** – Output styles and configurations.
- ***User help*** – How user help and menu-driven assistance is implemented.

Programmed configurations – menuing and data entry conventions – tend not to accompany the data, and setting up these configurations are time consuming endeavors.

Since infrastructure is a function of the particular program, it becomes important to choose similar or, better yet, identical products on both ends, as the time involved in setting up a good infrastructure can exceed the actual process of entering the data that is to be viewed, managed, and used by the software.

Considerations within Categories

Let's now look at these principles more closely in a few software applications categories. We will use the very popular word processors for the most in-depth look.

Word Processors

A good word processor may have hundreds of different text-oriented functions and it is unlikely that all functionality will be matched following a data format conversion. The way that columns, page breaks, and line centering is handled, to say nothing of included graphics images and formats, can thwart any sincere format conversion utility.

Figure 20 shows two word processors trying to use the same data file. The data being represented is the word HELLO. Normally these characters are represented by the ASCII codes as shown. Additional codes embedded in the file (the 93H and 94H codes) hold information relating to format; e.g., the characters HELLO will appear in boldface type when printed. Although a simple example, we can see that there are two distinct items carried in the word processor's data file, the text HELLO and the format or style **bold**. In fact, there are dozens of attributes such as type styles and sizes, line quadding and color, that could have been specified.

Different word processors will use entirely different schemes for representing the style of the text being represented. Also, word processor files can have headers describing printer options and other defaults and font descriptions. As shown in the figure, the second word processor uses different codes for the bold facing process (code 88, 89). Therefore you will need to convert between these data formats if you want to transfer the program-specific data files between different word processor programs.

Most word processor packages allow their program-specific formats to be converted to ASCII. What is left following conversion is only the text; all special formatting information must be reinserted.

Users who create their documents originally in ASCII, using text editors, do not have any program-specific format problems. The following scenario exemplifies a common problem these users could confront:

1. User creates ASCII file on text editor and submits to professional for formatting and composition.
2. Using a good word processor or DtP software, the professional changes the ASCII draft into a highly stylized document.
3. The originator needs to make significant textual changed in the document.

Once the document is coded with DtP markup, whether with general markup language tags or with WYSIWYG codes, it is impractical for the originator to use the text editor to make changes in the file. This is because the manuscript is on a text processing computer in coded or formatted form. The computer is not readily accessible to the originator and the formatting would probably be foreign. Conversion of the file back to ASCII would eliminate the format coding. So, instead, the originator must submit changes in written form and forgo personal interaction with the manuscript.

For those who need to create and share documents at all stages of developments the following are the two best options.

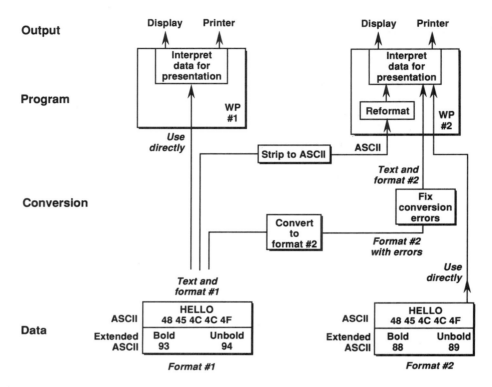

Output

Program

Conversion

Data

Figure 20. **Program-specific data conversion:** Each program should use its own specific data files to avoid tedious file conversions.

1. Originators prepare copy using editors. Copy remains in draft ASCII form until the manuscript is complete. Upon completion and after final approval, the manuscript is processed on a desktop publisher.
2. Everyone assigned to document preparation learns how to operate the word processor, using the same one. Most document composition requirements are made in this step. Should a higher-level of formatting be required, the word processor output can be imported by a desktop publisher for further refinement, which can include all manner of graphics and even equations.

Word processors are being used more and more for various self-contained, automated data entry purposes. To accomplish specific tasks, it is often necessary to program the word processor by means of a macro programming language that can be used to string complicated command sequences together. Programmed macros automate repetitive word and data processing tasks. For example:

- *Mail merge* – Merging word processor files with databases to create form letters.
- *Menu driven forms entry* – Using a functional wordprocessor to enter data into forms.
- *Automate file operations* – Using macros to bring in address headers from an address file, or stock paragraphs and files from other files. All of this can be automated with programmed macros.

The frames around the in-text notes and examples in this book were inserted by macros, as were the bulleted lists and marginal notes.

> **NOTE**
>
> A macro is a time-saving substitution of a complicated sequence of instructions or key presses with a brief command or a single keystroke. Macro in the present context is much more sophisticated. Word processor and spreadsheet macros are more a programming language than simple substitution. Programmed macros are strings of high level commands like search file, load file, and move data, that can be programmatically sequenced as simple statements in programming languages. Commands strung together in this way can invoke other lists of commands, and can do so conditionally. The flexibility of powerful high-level commands is thus combined with the programmability of a programming language.

Spreadsheets

Spreadsheet data transfers include the numbers and text managed by the spreadsheet. Most popular spreadsheet programs have quite reliable import/export utilities built in.

As with word processors, spreadsheet programs have their own built-in macro languages. Automating complicated and often repetitive spreadsheet operations using built-in spreadsheet languages can reduce user apprehension during complicated operations. Some examples of sequences that lend themselves to automation are:

- *Printing* – Printing complicated portions of spreadsheets.
- *Data entry* – Guiding the user to appropriate cells for data entry.
- *Security* – Preventing entry in certain areas, or even restricting the viewing of certain areas.
- *Menuing* – Providing additional menuing (in addition to that already provided by the spreadsheet program) for custom applications.
- *Movements* – Movement to different portions of the spreadsheet.
- *Special functions* – Statistical or other specialized math functions that might not be implemented on the receiving end. For example, some spreadsheet programs support statistical analysis functions.
- *Data extraction* – Extracting data from several worksheets, combining them, and producing a summary sheet that prints itself.

The extent to which spreadsheet users use their spreadsheets directly through their command sets, will limit the problems of applications conversion.

Database Managers

Data transfers usually include the various information files managed by the database software. This may in fact be several related files. As with the other categories, the popular products will have built-in conversion utilities to handle the different data formats; different record headers, data representations, and field separators for example.

DtC DBMS applications are typically highly customized for the particular application and user class and setting up this infrastructure is quite complex.

Database managers use many different file types. Some DBMS managers keep all the files for a particular application in a single file. This includes indexes, data entry forms, report forms, and the actual database files. Others keep these in separate files. Converting between the two extremes can be complicated.

The more important items in a DBMS infrastructure include:

- **Relationships** – The complex relationships that exist between the various database files.
- **Indexes** – DBMS file indexes. Indexes relate between information and location on the hard disk for quicker access.
- **Reports** – The type of reports desired including input screens, and custom output formats that can include images.
- **Data entry, screens, and forms** – How data is entered, verified, and limited.
- **User interface** – How the user is interfaced to the data.

The above are just a few of the things that make a DBMS application unique.

Drawing Graphics

Drawing graphics programs feature different specialties: presentation, painting, and data charting for example. Each program has a unique way of representing graphics images. The diverse nature of graphics formats defies enumeration, so be sure utilities exist to convert to your desired format. The infrastructure of drawing graphics programs is mostly related to how the data is visually presented: type of chart, kind of text for descriptions, orientation, style, superposition of images, and a host of other specifications.

Languages and Source Code

Although you probably do not think of languages as applications, there are nevertheless data format considerations at the source level of the language. In fact, languages are how applications programs were developed in the first place.

Most higher-level languages implement their respect functions with English source function statements that are then compiled into the corresponding CPU's machine language for execution. Source formats within any particular language are executable on different DtCs by respective compilers/interpreters as long as the source code is not machine or platform dependent. Due to the wide range of computer architectures and available compilers, the functions supported by a language compiler, the analog ports, and special graphics commands, may not work on different DtCs.

> **NOTE**
>
> The function of a language compiler is to read source code and convert it to executable machine code; this is not unlike the function of a word processor reading its application-specific file, formatting codes, and rendering readable text on screen or sending it to a printer. In both cases, a software program takes in one form of data and outputs it in another form. In fact, language processor software, editors, compilers, assemblers, linkers, and debuggers treat the language source code as data to create particular applications programs.

As shown in Figure 21, a transportable nucleus is surrounded by subroutine libraries. Although the core is transportable, the libraries are required to support different DtC hardware. Today, each DtC class, whether MS-DOS or Apple, will

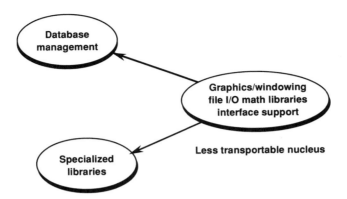

Figure 21. **Traditional medium-level language approach:** Older language compilers surrounded a small transportable core with subroutine libraries for specific DtC architectures and uses.

require special compilers supporting a particular type of DtC hardware and operating system software.

> **NOTE**
>
> Many language compilers/interpreters implement functions that require support from the operating system. For example, Apple's languages take advantage of Apple's ROM-based graphics support routines.

When converting source code to run on different DtC platforms you will need to watch closely for functions that may not be supported on the target system.

Over the next decade languages will evolve to object orientation. The data will become the important factor. The source code will be subservient. What will be needed is a set of class libraries for each machine architecture. The concept is similar to that of a particular operating system providing hardware-specific functions.

The phenomenon of DtC architecture-specific functionality has been historically true of BASIC, which, until the mid '80s was built into ROM on HB computers. The design philosophy of BASIC was to allow users intimate control of the variety of machine interfaces, memory reference, game ports, graphics, serial interfaces, and printer ports on a particular DtC architecture. Figure 22 shows a less transportable core. More architectural functions indigenous to a particular DtC class are supported immediately and directly in the core compiler functions. Highly specialized functions continue to be supported by conventional subroutine libraries.

Other microcomputer languages, Pascal and C, have evolved in this direction. Rather than providing hardware-specific subroutine libraries to account for hardware architecture differences, they are incorporating within the language compiler's core commands necessary to operate machine-specific interfaces. Program efficiency is improved, with no need to call in external routines, and programming is made easier, avoiding the tedium of linking different program portions together. However, transportability of the source code between different categories of microcomputer is reduced. When trying to convert source code on microcomputers, users are well

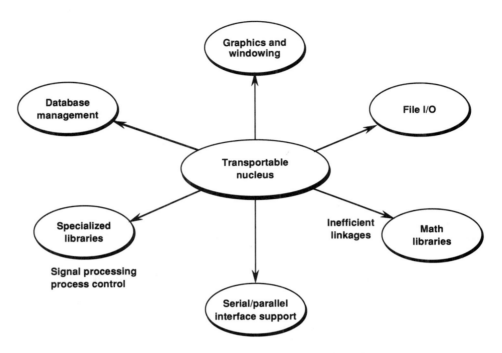

Figure 22. **Contemporary languages on DtCs:** Contemporary language compilers tend to be platform specific, but are benefited by a powerful and easy-to-use core.

advised to consult individuals who are using the particular language on a particular machine to guarantee a better understanding of the compatibility constraints.

Compatibility in today's C language development areas is assured by standardized ANSI (American National Standards Institute) functions. ANSI guarantees portability on a variety of platforms that implement the standard. Subroutine libraries for each platform integrate properly with the core compiler in such areas as parameter passing, variable definitions, and the like.

The extent to which architecturally-specific functions, graphics and specialized I/O functions, are used by a given language, will tie you to a particular DtC system. That is the rub. If you want complete source code transportability, implement only the architecturally tame vanilla core statements like x=20. You will have a program that cannot interact with the outside world, and is therefore of little use.

Within any particular DtC class, MS-DOS, Apple, Mac, or Unix-based engineering workstation, source transportability problems are not too severe because of the similarity of architecture and operating system support of hardware. It's when we cross categories, convert a word processor from an MS-DOS computer to run on a Macintosh, that architectural and operating system differences become critical.

Data Transfers Summary

Many different formats exist simply because of the variety of DtC applications and complex peripheral support requirements. Even within the same software category, there are seldom any data format standards. Whenever possible, you should try to standardize products within each software category if you are going to share data with others. If you must use different software products, and/or different DtC hardware, make popularity the cornerstone of your system. The best data format conversion utilities exist for the most popular software products.

There are several options for program-specific file conversions. One option is to use built-in capability of your software product to import/export data to other applications in the same software category. The advantage is that there is no need to manually convert format or strip to ASCII. The disadvantage is that occasionally formats are not correctly converted. You may opt to strip to ASCII first, then import ASCII into other applications. Most applications can do this, so there is always a way to move at least text and numerical data. Unfortunately, program-specific data formatting is lost and must be recreated on the other end.

Moving data between applications is like moving furniture between houses. Although the moving van trip is important, the real work begins when the van arrives and the furniture must be set up in the new home. Moving data from one application program to another is just the beginning. The infrastructure – the way your application uses, views, menus, and operates – can be very difficult to duplicate in different program and hardware environments.

6.0   Operational Considerations

- DtC Configuration
- Purchase and Set-up
- Troubleshooting
- Maintenance
- Computer Viruses

Many important considerations are often neglected in the process of selecting and operating DtCs. There are common sense procedures for improving your chances of getting what you need and want.

6.1   ABCs of the DtC Configuration Process

When planning a DtC system you should first look to the task that needs to be done. Once you know what the software is to accomplish, you can better select a product able to handle the work in a reasonably friendly fashion and with sufficient power. Of all the features and capabilities that exist in DtC technology you should look first for those that appear on your *must* list. Features you'd like to have should be entered on a *wish* list. Watch for them. If they are valid requirements, they are likely to show up in a future software package.

To select a DtC configuration, while still keeping your wits about you, you should follow these steps:

1. *Identify the needs of your application* – Determine the software category or categories that will accomplish your goals. Many applications categories have significant overlaps.

2. *Review available software that satisfies those needs* – Magazines such as the *Seybold's Outlook on Professional Computing, Database Advisor, Software Digest,* and others mentioned elsewhere in this book provide excellent unbiased software evaluation reports. Trade magazine ads are good awareness tools, but claims should be viewed with caution. Software bulletin boards provide downloading of product demos 24-hours a day.
   Many large organizations maintain a collection of proven software packages that are available for hands-on experimentation. Software vendors will often provide demonstration disks for use on your own DtC system.

3. *Identify the hardware for the candidate software* – If purchasing other makes of compatible or lookalike hardware, consult with individuals who are aware of the various performance and compatibility differences or who are operating the same hardware with the same software. Choose popular and well-supported hardware. What are you using at work? What do your friends use? When problems occur, who do you turn to for help? Where can you have your DtC repaired?

4. *Select a likely configuration, making appropriate trade-offs* – Your selection will have to take into account various organizational policies, departmental recommended software configurations, DtC maintenance constraints, and even legal questions. User groups are usually well versed in this area.

5. *Verify compatibility of components and software* – Watch for compatibility and support of your intended peripherals. Will your software run under the intended operating system? Is it data compatible with other products you are using? If using other manufacturer's lookalike hardware, check with someone else operating the same hardware. Use the most popularly supported peripheral hardware; it's more likely to be supported by hardware drivers.

   Compatibility determination is generally possible only by consulting with individuals running the configuration you have in mind. Be careful not to choose a system based upon a specific compatibility issue within a single applications area; you will probably implement other applications as awareness of other applications areas emerges. Later, applications will likely have different compatibility constraints.

6. *Evaluate hospitality to change, expansion, and reconfiguration* – Reconfiguration can involve inclusion in local area networks, addition of more powerful peripherals that require more sophisticated interfaces, addition of memory, and possible problems of compatibility with future DtC hardware and operating systems. For example, 8088-based systems do not support OS/2.

7. *Make final selection* – You will now be in a position to make an informed decision. The final selection should take into account the potential delay in acquiring DtC equipments. Be aware that DtC hardware needs a variety of software besides the primary applications area. Required software includes the operating system, perhaps a spreadsheet program, editor, computer language, etc.

NOTE

A gulf often separates advertised promise and real-world performance. It pays to be skeptical until claims have been verified in practice. Vendors as a rule provide names of satisfied customers when asked and will arrange on-site demonstrations of their products. Best of all is a demo of *your* work. The vendor's demo is designed by experts and is staged by well-practiced people who know how to impress you. You will make better decisions if you base them on how *your* data is processed.

6.2   System Purchases

When you order your DtC, keep these guidelines in mind:

Remember basic peripherals: Include monitor and interface, memory expansion, printers and interfaces, modems, proper mass storage devices, and floppy disk units.
Anticipate expansion: The system unit box must have enough bus slots to accommodate the number of add-on boards you are sure to need. A prospective buyer should consider future expansion needs when deciding how many bus slots will be sufficient.   Add-on boards include:

• *LAN* – Connection to local area networks.

• *Synchronous Mainframe Links* – Coaxial mainframe connections other than low-level RS-232 connection.

• *Special printer interfaces* – Memory mapped laser printers.

- **High and ultra high resolution video interfaces** – Intelligent, high resolution display interfaces may be required to support CAD/CAE and desktop publishing applications.

- **Special mass storage** – High capacity magnetic removables (Bernoullis, for example), and optical media.

- **Process control and signal processing applications** – These may include voice, signal, video processing, character recognition, and other systems.

Don't forget that you will need sufficient bays for the floppy disk devices, hard disks, and other mass storage devices you choose to add later.

Select software: Include at least the operating system, a good text editor, and perhaps some file organization utilities. Choose your editor or word processor carefully. It will be your most intensively-used software package. You will do everything from creating system files to generating correspondence, memoranda, and reports.

Don't blindly copy someone else's purchase: Talk with individuals who understand the many interactive and overlapping requirements of DtCs. If you are thinking about setting up a system similar to a friend's or colleague's, spend some time using theirs. Find out what they would do differently if they had to buy a system afresh.

Test the hardware: Try out the DtC's monitor and keyboard before you commit to purchase. Bad matches between these peripherals and your working style can make your life miserable and degrade the productivity you should expect from the DtC.

Consider floppy disk compatibility: Order appropriate floppy disk configurations to assure compatibility with other DtCs in your immediate area. Think about whether you will need to move diskettes between home and office systems. You may want to add a different size floppy drive in one or the other system to facilitate transfer.

Include a coprocessor: The system unit usually has a math coprocessor socket. It makes sense to include a coprocessor in the initial purchase. Plugging one in later can sometimes be difficult.

Check the power supply: The power supply that comes with the DtC is adequate for the initial system. But does it have enough pepper to handle expansion items (disk drive, add-on boards, and memory, for example)? Early Macintosh DtCs experienced severe power problems during upgrades, and power supply units often had to be replaced from third-party sources.

Look at the warranties: DtCs usually have one year warranties, while printer warranties are good for only 90 days. Memory interfaces generally carry 2-year warranties.

6.3 Standard Set-Up Procedures

Perform your initial set-up with experienced help. You'll be glad you started off on the right foot.

Cleaning: Work out procedures and make materials available for cleaning disk heads, keyboards, and monitor screens.

Registration forms: Fill out software registration forms to preserve your registration number. This is important to make sure you receive information on updates and to make sure telephone support is available.

Hard drive set-up: Get someone knowledgeable to help you set up your hard drive and learn the basic procedures for setting up such operational parameters as paths, methods for running programs from various subdirectories, etc. Development of these methods is essential for productive use of your system.

File organization: MS-DOS users often supplement rather weak built-in file management capability with a popular file organization tool such as Xtree Gold Professional and Qfiler. See Figure 23. Macintosh users are generally happy with the Mac's built-in point-and-shoot MultiFinder file management capability.

Directory management: Keep your root directory clean. Only a few operating system files are required to reside in your root directory. For MS-DOS users the files would be the COMMAND.COM (command interpreter) file, the AUTOEXEC.BAT file, the CONFIG.SYS file, and two hidden DOS files not ordinarily seen in a directory listing. Keep system files in a subdirectory, DOS files in a DOS subdirectory, batch files in a batch subdirectory, word processor program (and its utilities) in a word processor subdirectory, miscellaneous utility programs in a utility subdirectory, and so on. You'll be glad you did.

Backup: Develop a consistent procedure and schedule for backing up your hard drive. Note that data backup and program backup methods may differ (programs usually can be replaced – data more often cannot). Keep programs and data separated. Use floppies for data backup. Do not rely solely on the hard drive to keep and backup important data.

Floppy disk management: Develop rigorous procedures for floppy disk storage. Organize your program disks by categories.

Program/Data Separation

You should keep programs separate from data. This means keeping your data in a separate subdirectory under the subdirectory of the parent program that generated it. For instance, you might keep your Lotus 1-2-3 .WK1 files in a data subdirectory that branches from your Lotus program directory. If you can, make it a habit to back up your programs and data on floppy diskettes or Bernoulli disks. Also, store your programs and data separately on diskettes and cartridges. Among the reasons why it is important to keep programs separate from data are:

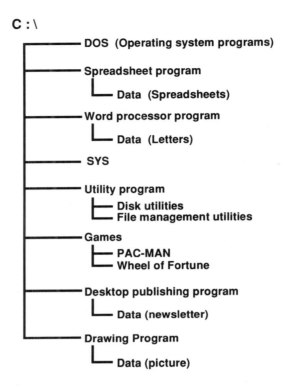

**C : **
- DOS (Operating system programs)
- Spreadsheet program
  - Data (Spreadsheets)
- Word processor program
  - Data (Letters)
- SYS
- Utility program
  - Disk utilities
  - File management utilities
- Games
  - PAC-MAN
  - Wheel of Fortune
- Desktop publishing program
  - Data (newsletter)
- Drawing Program
  - Data (picture)

Figure 23. Tree directory: Typical directory structure showing data stored in appropriate subdirectories for parent programs.

- ***Modularity and organization*** – Program/data segregation assists you in keeping your hard drive better organized, with fewer files in each subdirectory.
- ***Restoring data/programs*** – You will be better able to recreate a damaged hard drive if programs/data are kept separately. Damage from program misuse or insidious attacks by computer viruses will be less likely to affect segregated data. Restoring crashed hard drives will be simpler because program-only hard drive subdirectories are much easier to restore from the original program disks, using normal installation procedures.
- ***Knowing what you have*** – It is easier to inventory your hard drive if programs and data are segregated. Knowing that data and programs are separated is important if hard disk damage occurs. Determination of what was lost is critical to satisfactory recovery.
- ***Backup simplification*** – Data requires more frequent backup than programs do. Keeping your data files separate makes it easier to back them up on a timely schedule.
- ***Software upgrades*** – Program upgrades are more complicated if data files are also located in your program subdirectories.
- ***Program security*** – You will be less likely to accidentally distribute proprietary programs or confidential data if each is on separate disks/subdirectories. Also, accidental erasure of valuable programs/data will be reduced.

Office Environment

■ Concern with the interface between a worker and his working environment is called *ergonomics*.

The industry has given considerable study to providing adequate environmental facilities to DtCs and their users.■ Set up a workstation with attention to the following:

Lighting/glare: Special lighting fixtures are available to reduce room glare and special polarized screen masks may be obtained to reduce reflections from a DtC monitor screen.

Power filters: Power filters can be purchased to reduce the possibility of system failure and data loss due to power line transients.

UPS: An uninterruptible power supply, depicted in Figure 24, can sustain a DtC for up to a half hour in case of power outage. These units are battery-operated power supplies that are charged during normal power availability. Upon power loss, they automatically switch over and apply converted battery power to the DtC.

Workstation support equipment: Investigate ergonomic appliances available through specialty office supply houses. These include desks designed to accommodate DtC terminals, monitors, and keyboards, as well as computer operator chairs. If you spend significant blocks of time staring at a computer screen, whether at home or at the office, don't skimp on your desk and chair. Monitors, chairs, and keyboards set at improper heights put strain on the neck, back, and wrist, causing potentially serious medical problems. Display monitor suspension arms position the screen most conveniently for the user and keep it off the desk and the DtC box. Wrist braces used by many secretaries help to alleviate wrist strain.

6.4   Corporate-Wide Activities

Large organizations usually provide centralized support of user's most common DtC hardware and software needs. When creating such facilities, management must be particularly sensitive to ongoing special needs at group and section levels either because of the type of work being done or because of strict schedules that demand quick turnaround. For routine functions, however, it makes sense to have a central computing facility for maintenance, supply, upgrading, and repair.

DtC Locally Stocked Items

Large organizations stock a variety of DtC related items. Items to consider for local stocking should include:

* *Memory cards* – A variety of expanded and extended memory boards for MS-DOS computers, including various serial, parallel, and real time clock interfaces. Most popular memory chips, SIMMs, and batteries for these boards should also be stocked.
* *Math coprocessor chips* – These are not cheap, so check to see if your software really needs them. Stocking may be a problem because many different coprocessors and clock speeds must be supported.
* *Power cords and power surge protectors* – Power fluctuations and transients can damage valuable components.

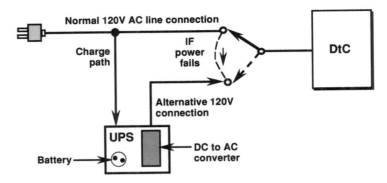

Figure 24. **UPS:** The UPS switches so rapidly upon power failure that equipment does not sense the power loss.

- *Paper* – Computer paper in several sizes including microperf with company logo. Labels and envelopes are also needed. Special smooth-surfaced laser paper is available for preparing reproducible copy. Ordinary paper has surface texture that contributes to fuzzy edges on printed images.
- *LAN boards and transceiver installation kits* – Most corporate DtCs are becoming LANed.
- *Floppy diskettes* – Most of the popular 5¼" and 3½" diskettes in low and high densities should be stocked routinely. For consistency and reliability, select only proven diskette makes. Large organizations should choose vendors based on overall reliability. Cheap floppies will have a profoundly negative impact on an organization's productivity. Also, users will be annoyed with the different packaging of different brands. Differences in labeling and package sizes will require different storage cubes.
- *Removable hard disk cartridges* – 20 MB and 44 MB 5¼" disks and 90 MB Bernoulli cartridges should be available.
- *Digital tape cartridges* – For tape backup systems, carry several popular sizes.
- *Cables* – Parallel and serial interface cables and adapters for most popular DtCs.
- *DtC software* – The most popular software should be stocked locally. Staff members will be relieved of the distraction and time-consuming effort of keeping alert for updates to software and documentation. Your institution should determine what software in the different categories is most widely used.
- *Stockroom software* – A typical assortment of HB software that is carried in quantity by large organizations is given in the following list. Remember that EP software may be managed more efficiently at department level. It is not generally ordered and maintained at enterprise level because of its specialized use and high cost. EE software is not carried at all because of its specialized nature and limited use.

MS-DOS COMPUTERS

OPERATING SYSTEMS

PC-DOS	Current version.
MS-DOS	Current version.
MS-Windows	Current version.

EDITORS

KEDIT	Highly programmable editor.
BRIEF	Programmer's editor.

WRITING/PUBLISHING

DisplayWrite	If widely used in the organization.
Microsoft Word	A Mac-like word processor that runs under Windows.
WordPerfect	Word processor of choice for most MS-DOS users.

INFORMATION MANAGEMENT

DataEase	Easy to develop quick applications.
FoxPro	Specialized applications, popular X-base.
Lotus 1-2-3	Spreadsheet
Microsoft Excel	Spreadsheet for Windows
Paradox	For Windows; powerful and friendly.
SAS	Heavy-duty statistical information management system.

CAD

P-CAD Master Schematic	Master schematics, electronic schematics, and design.
AutoCAD	General-purpose CAD.

DRAWING, GRAPHICS

MS-Power Point for Windows	Great for quick presentations.
Harvard Graphics	Powerful presentation capability.
Lotus FreeLance	Good for drawing and similar in feel to Lotus 1-2-3.
DrawPerfect	Graphics companion to WordPerfect.

UTILITIES

Fastback	Hard disk backup.
Norton Utilities	Hard disk maintenance.
PCTools	General purpose toolkit.
XTree Gold	File management.

COMMUNICATIONS

IBM Personal Communication	3270, 78, 79 emulation program.
PC LAN Program	IBM product.
ProCom	General-purpose for use with modem.

LANGUAGES

MS-Visual BASIC for Windows	Object-oriented BASIC.
MS-Quick BASIC	Popular for small utilities, easy to learn.
Turbo C and Pascal	From Borland; good for a variety of smaller applications.
MS-Assembler	For the adventurous; closely associated with hardware.
MS-Fortran	Scientific programming.
STSC APL	Scientific programming.

APPLE COMPUTERS

WRITING/PUBLISHING

Microsoft Word	Proven Mac word processor.
WordPerfect	For compatibility with MS-DOS version.
MacWrite	Good power and easy to use.

INFORMATION MANAGEMENT

MacProject	Project management.

Microsoft Excel	Spreadsheet.	
DRAWING/GRAPHICS		
MacPaint	Excellent paint software.	
MacDraw	Easy to use drawing software.	
Power Point	Good for presentation graphics.	
UTILITIES		
FastBack	Hard disk backup.	
Pyro	Hard disk backup and repair.	
COMMUNICATIONS		
TCP/Connect	Communications on Ethernet.	

This list demonstrates how pervasive the HB computer has become in the workplace and points out the applications they are put to by the majority of users.

Loaner DtCs

Many organizations provide staff members with loaner DtCs. This policy provides a useful migration path for older DtCs that are ready for retirement. You will notice that older DtCs often undergo a rebirth as many seemingly obsolete machines become vehicles for a variety of auxiliary tasks. For example, an old XT can be pressed into service as a file server in a small local area bulletin board.

Training

Large organizations routinely provide computer training courses for their employees. Short courses are usually given on the more popular software products and DtC operating procedures. Well-planned DtC training programs include application-intensive follow-ups. Also, special away courses are arranged if the office budget allows.

Most organizations maintain a selection of video training products that are designed to walk you through given software packages. Many new or currently popular DtC software products are available for you to try. Hands-on experience is clearly the best way to verify whether a given program or product will satisfy your application needs and personal preferences.

Community colleges that offer courses in personal computing techniques and the use of popular computer software products provide an excellent opportunity for acquiring computer literacy.

Universities are recognizing the need for technical courses in desktop computing. Universities are beginning to offer courses in comparative architecture, interfacing techniques, operating systems, and software applications. Some engineering and computer science curricula require students to own a DtC as a course prerequisite.

Do not overlook the many tutorial videos that are available from software houses and hardware vendors. Videos may even be loaned overnight or over a weekend for viewing at home.

Current Literature

No treatise on DtCs or any other field that literally changes by the hour can remain up to date for long. If DtCs are a part of your workaday world, you should devote some reading time to the current periodicals in the field.

PERIODICALS

- Aldus Magazine
- Byte
- CA Insight
- Communications from the ACM
- Computer Graphics World
- Computer Graphics Today
- ComputerLand Magazine
- Computer Language
- ComputerWorld
- Connect (computer networking)
- The Connection (buyer's guide)
- Data Based Advisor
- Datamation
- DBMS
- Dr. Dobbs Journal
- Electronic Publishing and Printing
- Electronics
- Explain (DB2 users)
- Government Computer News
- IEEE Computer
- IEEE Micro
- Information Center
- Information Week
- InfoWorld
- ITC Desktop
- Language
- Master Pages (Aldus PageMaker tips)
- MacUser
- MacWEEK
- MacWorld
- Microsoft Systems Journal
- PC Computing
- PC Digest
- PC Magazine
- PC Publishing
- PC Tech Journal
- PC Today
- PC Week
- PC World
- Portable Computing
- SAS Communications
- Andrew Seybold's Outlook
- Software Digest
- Software Magazine
- Tekniques (Tektronics tips)
- Thinking Visually (Freelance Plus tips from Lotus)
- Unix World
- WordPerfectionist (WordPerfect Newsletter)

Centralized Maintenance and Configuration Support

A centralized maintenance capability is a must for large organizations. Some of the factors to be considered in setting up such a facility are:

- *Overhead vs. project charges* – Who will pay for the maintenance? Will it be considered general company overhead or will there be a chargeback to individual projects?

- *Limit models* – Try to limit staff to purchasing similar, if not identical, models whenever possible. Slightly different DtC models will frustrate repair and maintenance operations. The problem is acute in the MS-DOS compatible arena due to the thousands of different manufacturers supplying hardware. An institution-wide policy is required to balance individual needs for special units and high performance models with organization-wide needs for standardization.

- *Invest in maintenance* – Don't try to fix everything. Consider contracting for maintenance with repair facilities that promote exchange policies for board-level and peripheral-level repairs. On-site personnel, however, are a must to manage the operation. Functions for a maintenance staff will include equipment burn-ins, establishing maintenance policies, determining acceptable equipments, collecting defective equipment, storing quick replacement components, and other end-user support functions.

- *Department and group maintenance* – Often, due to specialization, individual departments or groups may need to establish their own maintenance capabilities and recruit repair specialists.

- *User sensitivity* – Most DtC users would find it difficult if not traumatic to lose their DtCs. Loaners should be made available in case of breakdown so that ongoing tasks are not interrupted.

6.5   Troubleshooting and Maintenance

If you insist on performing your own maintenance and repair functions, then you should be aware of the following.

Cockpit Problems

The most important thing do when hardware problems are encountered is to remember that most hardware problems turn out to be operator errors or cockpit problems. Therefore, identifying the nature of the problem becomes an important first step. Cockpit problems may be due to:

- *Configuration files* – Improper DOS setup files or improper use of buffers, memory management programs, TSRs, environment parameters, and a host of other power-up parameters will be the first things you want to look at when your system doesn't work right. On MS-DOS computers this would be the `AUTOEXEC.BAT` and `CONFIG.SYS` files in the root directory.
- *Wrong use of default disk drives* – Programs do not know where their data is coming from or going to.
- *Improper software configuration* – Use of improper drivers for the particular peripheral you have. Use of same memory for multiple utilities (disk cache, print spooler).
- *Power out or wrong cables* – No power to peripheral, peripheral plugged into the wrong port, defective data cable, or defective cable connectors at the DtC or peripheral. Inappropriate serial interface speed settings and wrong driver installations exacerbate the problem.
- *Configuration Settings* – Improper add-on board settings can result in subtle problems that may not reveal themselves immediately. Improper memory switch settings, improper parallel and serial interface jumpers, port selections, and bad configuration information in the DtC (board switches set wrong or configuration memory inoperative due to bad batteries) can cause the DtC to become confused about what is connected to it.

System Unit Hardware Problems

Most DtC system unit problems occur in the cable/connector, add-on board, and board to bus connectors. These problems can arise anywhere in the DtC's life cycle, but generally get worse as the DtC ages.

- *Cables* – Cable problems can be caused by shorted pins at the connector, separated pins at the connector, and stretched, broken lines in the cable run. Associated problems can trigger error messages leading you to believe that you have a software problem.
- *Chips* – Heating and cooling of the chips can sometimes unseat them. Often pressing on each socketed chip to make sure it is seated firmly will cure the problem. Every computer maintenance facility should have a RAM tester for DIPs, SIPPs, and SIMMs that also tests for access speed. Marginal RAM access speed will often cause problems. Different manufacturers have different ways of testing and indicating RAM access times.

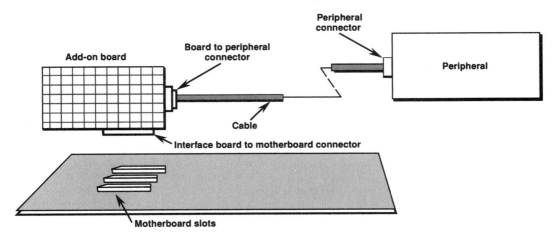

Figure 25. Interface board connectors: Most DtC problems will be traced to poor mating of interface boards and peripheral connectors.

- ***Connectors*** – Bad mating between add-on boards and the motherboard bus slot or between the peripheral cable and the interface board edge connector is common in low-cost DtC equipment. See Figure 25. Careless remating of these connectors can cause serious damage. Some system units have problems when the case is deformed, the weight of a monitor for instance, may cause the internal cards to shift.

  PC (printed circuit) edge connectors are found in MS-DOS and lower-cost computers. PC edge connectors have two opposing rows of spring-loaded contacts that mate to the printed circuit edge on the expansion board. The expansion board signal runs are brought out to flat traces that plug into the connector. This reduces the cost of the expansion boards, but repeated plug-in can wear and even break the traces. Also, loose lateral fit in the board or connector causes adjacent pin shorts and bad connections. To provide more contacts IBM's MCA bus connections are only 0.05 inch apart compared to the 0.1 inch spacing found in the popular ISA connectors. Closer spacing only aggravates the spacing problem that already existed.

  Euro connectors are found in Apple's NuBus, and the more expensive EP class of DtCs. The Euro connector provides connections by rows of deep cylindrical holes mated by an opposing connector with pins on the adapter card. Euro connectors are more expensive, but the design is much more reliable than the PC edge connector. Tolerance problems are minimized and a particularly good connection is made.

When problems occur, note the operating conditions: when, what software, what configuration, and so on. This kind of information will assist maintenance personnel in pinpointing the problem.

Printer Operation and Maintenance

- ***Paper dust*** – Dot matrix printers generate considerable paper dust that should be occasionally cleaned from around the print head.
- ***Manual head movement*** – To avoid stripping gears or breaking rubber belts, print heads should not be moved manually while the printer is turned on.

- *Ribbon jams* – Printer ribbons can jam, stripping printer gears. Ribbons should be replaced when print begins to fade.
- *Head jams* – Print head jams can occur if the print paper is not properly loaded into the printer. Turn off the printer before clearing the problem.
- *Paper advance* – Use printer front panel controls for advancing printer paper. If you need to move the paper manually, turn off the printer power first.
- *Clone printers* – Printer features of the more popular U.S. and Japanese printers are duplicated in less expensive units manufactured in China and Taiwan. Although functionally quite similar, they may require different data cables, interface switch settings, and software drivers.
- *Card stock* – Laser printers should not be fed paper heavier or flimsier than stock within the range recommended by the manufacturer.

Floppy Drive Operation and Maintenance

- *Head alignment* – Disk drives seldom need alignment, however, head cleaning can cure "disk drive not ready" and "data not found" errors.
- *Magnetic fields* – Diskettes are sensitive to magnetic fields that can exist around your monitors, radios, and power cords. They are also sensitive to static.
- *Floppy disk problems* – Diskette problems include bad limit switches in the disk drive unit: write protect, disk lock, zero index, etc. Software products will give different, and sometimes cryptic error messages for these problems.
- *Improper formats* – Improper diskette formatting can cause grief. Different density disks have different formatting requirements, yet the system may allow you to format a disk improperly. High and low density 5¼" diskettes look the same, physically, while the 3½" disks are differentiated by a hole in the diskette jacket.

Video Displays and Display Interfaces

- *Cables* – You may think you have a hardware problem when the problem is actually that the connector on your display monitor is not fully seated. Unplug the connector and plug it in again.
- *Magnetic fields* – Monitors placed close to magnetic fields (or other monitors) will have distorted images. These effects include rippling and color impurities.
- *Shock hazard* – Do not use modified or other non-standard monitors. They may not provide adequate isolation from line voltage, presenting an electrical shock hazard.
- *Improper monitor switch settings* – Multisync monitors often have switches for selecting analog, digital, or even composite inputs. If the switches aren't set correctly you can get a blank or garbled screen. Also, monitors have underscan and overscan switches. If these switches are set improperly, you get a display that looks too big or too small.
- *Improper display interface switch settings* – Video interface switch settings include bus sizing, interrupt usage, default screen modes, monitor type (analog/digital), and other configuration control settings. These must be set according to the type of monitor/system combination you own.
- *Connector mismatches* – Plugging the wrong monitor into your video interface connector can cause damage. Some monitors have the same connectors but require different interfaces. Many interfaces have both analog and digital outputs. Different cables/adapters may be required, depending on the type of monitor.
- *Improper signal usage* – Some monitor cables appear to match an interface but, in fact, do not, so mismatches in signal definitions will cause problems. Many RGB interfaces mix the horizontal and vertical sync on the green signal line. Another

classic problem is running an analog RBG monitor on digital RBG outputs. The pins match fine; the signals are wrong.

- *Display interfaces* – Some common display interface problems include improper memory, which causes speckles and missed characters on the display, improper use of signals by the display to sense the type of interface, and lack of required software drivers and documentation. This is particularly true in the MS-DOS compatible arena where so many manufacturers are building monitors and interfaces.

As always, popularity is important. Purchasing a monitor/interface combination that is popular will ensure that you'll have knowledgeable friends to consult when you have problems. You will be able to borrow cables or swap interfaces to troubleshoot your problem if you know someone who's monitor and interface are the same as yours.

Modems

- *Power connectors* – Power connectors to external modems may be flimsy. They become loose making modem operation intermittent.
- *Null modem* – Flat cables between modem and DtC serial interface may require null modems, depending upon how the serial interface is set up.
- *Switch settings* – Most apparent modem malfunctions are due to inappropriate modem switch, RS-232 interface jumpers, or bad communications software settings.

Serial and Parallel Interfaces

When different serial/parallel printer interface cards are purchased from different manufacturers, or a serial/parallel card is added to the system, it is easy for the DtC to malfunction. DtCs implement the popular serial and parallel interfaces on hard disk interfaces, memory add-ons, and on the motherboard as well as on separate dedicated cards. Each will have its own particular way of specifying I/O address and interrupt usage. You will need to read the documentation carefully when setting up multiple serial/parallel interfaces. It's no wonder that system problems arise because more than one interface has the same I/O address or is trying to use the same interrupt.

Signals on the serial interface connector can be routed to different pin numbers by internal interface jumpers to define terminal or computing equipment types. Misunderstanding of the pinouts causes the equipment to be inoperative, giving the impression that the serial interface is dead. IBM and Macintosh both use different connectors on different computer models, which exacerbates the problem.

Stock IBM serial interfaces implement their serial interface functions by a VLSI ACIA chip manufactured by National Semiconductor. The National chip has been widely reverse-engineered in a variety of styles. In some cases multiple serial and parallel Centronics printer interfaces are implemented on a single chip, increasing reliability and reducing the price of these important interfaces to as low as $10 for an add-on board.

Hard Drives

Hard drives are sensitive to shock. Most of them can be parked safely by utility software that desensitize them to moves. Most newer DtC hard drives automatically park upon power down, but check yours to make sure. Power loss while writing data to your hard disk will usually result in severe data loss.

Many hard drive problems are simply due to bad cables between the hard drive and its interface. When data loss occurs, be aware that any of several available utility programs may breathe life back into an apparently erased hard drive. Often directory/file allocation data is lost, or the ability of the hard drive to boot system software; yet valuable data is still present. Data recovery utility software can resurrect your lost data.

If the data loss is due to a defective hard disk controller, you may need to find another identical controller from the same manufacturer to retrieve your data. Hard disks and their controllers are intimately related.

Keyboards

Keyboards can pick up static, transmit it to your system unit and crash it. This seldom hurts the keyboard, but it may damage your data. Conductive mats on the floor or desktop will eliminate the problem.

Although keyboards are generally quite reliable, the relatively flimsy cable connectors between keyboard and system unit board can cause problems. Often modular phone plugs are used to connect keyboard cables. Be careful not to tug on the cable unless you provide some strain relief. A simple piece of tape under the cable can do wonders to relieve the strain between cable and connector.

Network Interface cards

Network interface cards are complex DtC interfaces, and are therefore likely to exhibit compatibility problems in different DtC models with their different operating systems and support ROMs. Before you invest in these cards, be sure they work in your particular DtC.

A phenomenon called computer viruses is now a matter of concern to DtC users. Your DtC could become infected, so you should be aware of the possibility.

What computer viruses are: Computer viruses are either self-contained, hidden programs or segments added to existing programs. They are designed to be insidious. It is possible to include, in a normally innocent DtC program, code that can damage your data or impair programs residing on your hard drive. The code may be cleverly placed – in a way that is difficult to detect. It can be triggered in several ways: by the passage of time, by particular sequences of key presses, by combinations of system operations, or by a random event. The code could lie dormant for years before becoming virulent. Its most dangerous aspect is its malignancy. It can spread like a cancer.

What computer viruses do: Programs that become infected can, in addition to performing their intended tasks, selectively erase data from the hard drive, crash your system, produce obscene messages, and do other naughty and malicious deeds. Or, they may modify other programs in your system and cause them to misbehave. They can, for example, replicate endlessly and spread throughout your system.

Where viruses come from: Viruses are hatched in the minds of individuals who seem to enjoy wreaking havoc on others. They may be disgruntled employees or devious experimenters. Generally an otherwise perfectly good program is infected with pernicious code and you, innocently, install the deadly program yourself.

How viruses invade your system: The infection can enter your system through a communications network or by a program that you install yourself. Programs in the public domain and even commercial software can contain a virus.

How viruses are detected: Several software products have been advertised that claim to guard against viruses. When a threatening syndrome occurs, the respective DOS function is temporarily halted and a message asks if you really want to do what you are doing. Also, checks can be performed to verify that previously installed programs retain their integrity – that no changes have occurred.

Virus detection mechanisms: Virus detection is difficult and uncertain. Anti-viral mechanisms protect against less devious forms of the infection but are ineffective against virulent forms. Clever programmers may write directly to specific hardware, bypassing the BIOS, and thereby prevent any resident program from discovering the presence of the virus.

How to protect yourself: While there is no effective vaccine to guard against this infection, you can protect your system by following sensible and normal operating procedures. Routinely back up your data and be selective about the programs you admit to your system. Before exposing critical data and programs to them, have public domain programs checked out thoroughly by knowledgeable personnel. If you need to add public domain software to your system, it is a wise practice to obtain copies from individuals who have been using the software and know that it is healthy. Even then you may be devastated by one of the long-term dormant, time-release types of virus. Some of the good practices you should develop not only to protect your programs and data but also to keep them in good order are highlighted earlier.

Extent of the problem: Disturbing accounts have been heard of viral infections attacking wide area LANs. In one instance a virus entered a large computing system, it is thought, by way of a commercial hard drive that contained public domain utilities. In any case, it is wise to be alert to the harm that could ensue from an infected program. Viruses or not, it is always smart to keep programs and data backed up.

A virus called Stoned: The following specific example should convince anyone that a virus can be extremely insidious.

During routine virus checks performed in a company's computing center, the Stoned virus was identified on an IBM XT. Immediately following its discovery, Stoned was cleaned from the XT, but on the same night it reappeared on other XTs in the same company. The virus, it was found, was spread by contaminated floppy disks, not over networks.

The mischief occurs when a system is booted from an infected floppy disk. During the boot process, the system executes code located in the boot sector of the hard disk. If, however, there is a floppy disk in the A drive, the system will load code from the floppy's boot sector. If the floppy disk has the virus on its boot sector, your system becomes infected.

The infection process: Once started, the infection propagates. During the attempted boot, Stoned appends itself to the DOS command processor so that any process initiated by the command processor will install the virus on the respective floppy operated. Given this behavior, Stoned is considered a resident virus. Although cleaning programs will remove it from the partition table, Stoned will remain in memory. Therefore once it is cleaned from the hard disk, be sure to power down the system.

If Stoned is on a floppy and you boot from it, Stoned moves into the hard disk partition table. After you power down, it remains hidden in the system. When you repower the system, Stoned reappends itself to the command processor. Thus, even after a power down, Stoned will continue to reinfect floppy disks because the code will reappear in the partition table.

Damage that can occur: Possible loss of hard disk data. The McAffee documentation indicates that file linkage can be destroyed. The damage you could see would likely be the inability to access the hard disk, or damage similar to that which occurs when you repartition a hard disk and lose all the data. Although there are many data recovery products on the market, it is not known at this time if they would be effective for any damage caused by Stoned. Who boots from floppies? We all do, and most of the time it is accidental. If you leave a floppy in the A: drive and reboot your MS-DOS computer, one of two things happens.

1. *Ordinary disks* – You receive an error message telling you that the system couldn't boot from the disk. Ordinary disks have boot sectors too. If the virus

Stoned is in the boot sector, your system becomes infected during the attempted boot process.

2. **Operating system startup disks** – If Stoned is in the boot sector, the system becomes infected because you will boot Stoned whenever you boot the operating system.

Cleaning Stoned from your system: Many viruses can be removed by commercial software. For example, the McAfee Associates VIRUSCAN contains a program called CLEAN. CLEAN will not only remove the Stoned virus from your partition table, but also hundreds of other viruses that may be lurking on the hard disk. Power down the system immediately after cleaning to remove the resident portion from memory. If you continue to operate without a powerdown, you will continue to infect your floppies. To clean Stoned from your floppies, simply run CLEAN on your floppy. This will remove Stoned and preserve your data. Since the infection is in the boot sector, your data will not be affected. A successful DOS format will also clean the disk, but your data will be removed as well. If you are not sure how to clean the floppy, do not use it, discard it.

- **Protect your floppies** – Write protecting and scanning are the only sure ways to protect floppies.
- **Protect your system** – Routinely, scan your system for viruses. Many systems are configured to automatically run scan programs whenever you power up to ensure a virus test at least each time the system is rebooted.

How the virus spreads: The Stoned virus travels on floppy disks. Any floppy placed into an infected system will have its boot sector written to during any floppy disk operation that would ordinarily light the floppy disk drive LED. Operations include:

- **Executing programs** – Executing any program that reads or writes to the floppy. This includes running virus scan programs. Therefore, operating a scan program on an infected machine will itself infect the floppy disk. Hopefully, that same scan program will identify and clean the virus. Before you clean floppies on a system, make sure that the system itself is clean.

- **Copying** – Copying files to or from the floppy.

- **Directory operations** – Performing an operation such as DIR, MKDIR, RMDIR, and the like.

The Stoned virus does not travel in files or executable programs. Scan routines that look at your programs and data will be ineffective against this virus. The scanning program must look at the hard disk partition table and floppy disk boot sectors to discover the Stoned virus.

7.0   High-Level Considerations

Committing to desktop computing is a serious and expensive proposition for everyone, from large corporations to small companies to individuals. Large organizations are confronted with the need to buy dozens or hundreds or even thousands of units. Moreover, various groupings of desktop computers and workstations will have to be networked. All of this is enormously expensive in terms not only of hardware and software, but also of the manhours involved in planning, budgeting, designing the overall architectures, providing for cabling, and managing hundreds of other associated details. The acquisition problem for individuals is equally ponderous. After house and car, a desktop computer could be the next largest investment to be made.

Whether you are a home enthusiast purchasing a lightly endowed home computer or a manager considering the purchase of thousands of desktop computers for your organization, your choice should be backed by the higher-level perspective contained herein. Through a more intelligent understanding of the many factors affecting the DtC industry, your decision will have a better foundation.

7.1   DtC Limitations

Desktop computer users, despite their dedication and enthusiasm for this approach to productivity, must cope with limitations mostly due to the continuing evolution of the technology. To better use your desktop computer now and in the future, you should better understand its limitations and their underlying reasons. We list them in order of significance.

Mainframe Inertia

Prior to DtCs, computer users were captive to centralized computing environments that did not allow them full control of system resources. This situation, which continued for almost thirty years, led to a collective mainframe orientation that tended to blind users, MIS (Management Information Systems) managers, and software developers to many possibilities. Within the last three years some of these possibilities have begun to be realized, but mature development is still years away. The advent of dedicated desktop workstations with infinite configuration possibilities has opened the door to imaginative applications.

Solution – MIS departments need more familiarity with the rich and interactive development environments that are possible with DtCs.

Immature Operating Systems and Networks

DtC operating systems and networking methodologies are only beginning to become mature. The helter-skelter nature of the software base is mostly due to poor or indifferent support by the operating system.

Solution – Choose applications software that uses most of the of operating system features that have been developed for networks. Software developed for networks has to be robust to avoid network clashes and crashes. Even if you aren't using the networked version of a given manufacturer's software, that software will be more robust.

Isolation of Hardware and Software Developers

Hardware and software developers are still working separately. Chip technology is 10 years ahead of software technology. While this disparity creates enormous opportunities for software developers, the developers tend to take advantage only of selected chip capabilities in solving specific problems.

Solution – Silicon foundries where software is actually implemented in the hardware. Application-specific processors are already emerging. A new age of computer science will encompass both hardware and software principles and their distinctions will vanish.

Limited Integration

Most DtC products are designed as standalones with limited freedom for data interchange. The integrated software packages that attempt to resolve this problem are, in turn, constrained by memory environments. The functions that integrated software supports are less capable than the corresponding functions supported by the standalone packages.

Solution – Choose popular products that support data interchange. The solution to this limitation will ultimately come from improved operating systems supporting data and resource sharing among the applications software base.

Software Obsolescence

Most popular packages evolve stepwise through multiple releases during their useful lifetime. Upgrading is a problem particularly when licenses, floppy disks, manuals, and other paraphernalia must be replaced. Larger organizations find this a particularly vexing problem.

Solution – A good solution is to centralize support of software upgrades for the products most widely used. Choose software products whose data survive product upgrades without major conversions. Later, networked software distribution will help to alleviate the multiple release problem. Continued use of older, proven software products can lead to successful applications. Not everyone needs the latest software version. This entire book was drafted with a 10-year-old editor.

Operating System Immaturity

Current DtC operating systems do not recognize many of the specialized capabilities of modern chip technologies found in today's DtC. This is primarily due to the inability of operating system developers to depend upon the timely and pervasive availability of specific hardware devices. For example, MS-DOS had to be initially developed for the 8088 microprocessor, even though the 80286 and 386 were under development at the time. HB DtCs have typically not provided for multitasking and distributed processing applications.

Solution – Improved OS and OS standards such as OS/2, SAA, X Windows, OSF foundation Unix. Consolidation of hardware standards and performance enhancements to give more DtCs a uniformly higher power capability, necessary to operate the improved operating system and user friendly GUI environments.

Platform Dependence of Software

DtC system architectures vary from the fairly unsophisticated and vanilla MS-DOS computer to the stronger but still relatively tame architecture of the engineering workstations.

The entertainment or audio/visual DtCs such as the Commodore Amiga and Atari computers were designed with highly specialized hardware, making their software bases unique when a/v features are used. This hurt popularity in the business community, mostly because the showtime features were considered unsuitable for business-like computer applications.

Apple Computer followed a broader road. It developed computers that combined sophisticated hardware with a more generalized architecture that could support most major applications categories in business, entertainment, and the engineering and scientific communities. The continuing success of Apple is due to its philosophy of designing system hardware and software as an integrated unit, keeping the user interface at the highest level of importance. MS-DOS computer manufacturers and software developers have finally recognized the value of this approach, as attested to by the effort now brought to bear on Windows.

Improved operating system and development language technology will narrow the compatibility gap between software operating on different platforms. The best software products already operate across different platforms: Apple, MS-DOS computers, Unix boxes. Client/server architecture will also help alleviate the problem of platform diversification affecting software compatibility. The approach of providing a happy medium between highly specialized hardware and software compatibility among different system units with operating system support will strongly unify the software base.

Factors and Recommendations

The following cautions and recommendations are considered to be important. Disregarding them may lead to costly mistakes. These precautions have been developed over many years of direct participation in the evolution and revolution of DtCs since their inception in the '70s. The only difference between today's problems and those of yesterday is that of scale. If only one warning applies to your situation, this book will have served its purpose.

Product Popularity

Buy a product according to its user base, paying attention to those that are popular. By far the most important consideration is company-wide and industry-wide support when you have problems.

With software, try to stick with the popular vendors and resist the temptation for flashy new products. Newer products with a small user base are buggy and help resources will be scarce. These products may never mature; they are often pulled from the market before follow-on versions are released and they never become useful.

For hardware stick with popular workstation products. These include IBM, Apple, Sun, HP Apollo, and Silicon Graphics workstations. When purchasing compatibles, be aware of the various compatibility issues and purchase accordingly. Don't purchase only for speed. Think also of compatibility.

Let hardware and software compatibility be the major driving forces, for in the long run compatibility will win out over speed as the more important advantage.

Operating Systems

The most frustrating software bottleneck, the 640K limitation on today's MS-DOS DtC software base is gradually abating as newer operating systems finally support the advanced features of 80386 and above microprocessors. MS-DOS users should plan for an improved software base and cope, without going overboard, with transitional software in the interim.

Software Development

DtC computers lend themselves to development of applications that are useful only to the originator. This is due to the straightforward accessibility of many DtC software packages. Often times, the originator or a user of the result tries to peddle the application as something suitable for production use by multiple users.

Applications development and use should be viewed the same for the DtC and the mainframe in this respect. Development projects must be well defined and appropriate documentation prepared as the development proceeds. Individual software development projects will spread through an organization, and if not controlled will ultimately wreak havoc due to lack of planning and attendant data cross usage problems. Remember that the software will need to be tested through as many possible user activities as possible. The scenario you leave out will be the one that fails you when you least expect it. Careful planning at the outset will help software projects to be better organized and to be more fruitful in the long run.

Networking

Networking DtCs is not a panacea. The advantages to networking are numerous, but they do not appear immediately when you hook DtCs in a network. Trained technical personnel are necessary for administering DtC network hardware, software, and particularly the specialized configurations required in today's networks.

Today's DtC networks are rudimentary information distribution mechanisms. Tomorrow's networks will implement much more sophisticated hardware protocols and will allow high levels of interactivity between workstations. Developing, configuring, and administering software for these environments will demand competent technical and managerial personnel.

Acceptance

Many jobs functionally warrant automation, for which effective DtC solutions already exist. But administrative roadblocks often arise that prevent implementation of these solutions. Examples include requirements for specialized equipment for classified data processing, the ban on bringing laptop DtCs into many facilities such as military installations, and the general suspicion with which ADP procurements are viewed. Don't expect the existence of DtC solutions for a processing problem to guarantee acceptance of that solution.

Organizational Cooperation

Creative interdepartmental assessments and technical information dissemination mechanisms – users groups, technical newsletters, and the like – can minimize redundant activities in large organizations. The establishment of a centralized support facility can at least focus these efforts without duplication. Particularly important is the centralization of maintenance, software licensing, and major component acquisition.

Support Requirements

Almost invariably management underestimates the installation, development, and administration of software, hardware, networks, stockrooms, training, and other related support functions related to DtCs. These needs will continue to press because almost everyone in the organization will eventually need a DtC as a basic tool for carrying out work assignments.

Appropriate Power Ranges

In every software and hardware category there are a range of products that accomplish the limited basic tasks such as simple text editing, as ell as more involved tasks such as desktop publishing. For maximum efficiency, it is important to match the product to the actual complexity of the task.

Compatibility

Avoid using different applications software products within the same software category to process the same set of data. DtC software products are not sufficiently compatible to allow rapid data transfer or effective conversions. This is especially true for large applications. Software products that perform highly specialized functions such as graphics and special peripheral I/O generally do this without the help of the operating system. These products are likely to be less compatible among different hardware platforms. In the software world, and particularly the MS-DOS computer compatible world, lookalike products are generally cheaper, and improve on the original in some way. Subtle compatibility problems may arise that outweigh the benefits of having bought the lookalike product.

The lookalikes are usually compatible with a single version of a major product so that as newer versions of the original are offered, the lookalike product may become out of date. Due to subtle differences, lookalike products are difficult to maintain; they may go obsolete, and they may introduce subtle operating differences in systems that incorporate them. This is not to say you shouldn't buy compatible products. You should, however, limit your purchase to the fewest number of the most popular models once particular performance needs have been established.

For example: One organization limited its purchases of MS-DOS compatible computers to a couple of high performance brands to alleviate maintenance problems. Another organization chose a particular database manager product for most of its information management to alleviate data and applications conversions among many products.

7.2   *Future Trends*

Some of the more important trends noted in the industry are presented for your inspection. Placing time frames on trends is risky business, but the types of changes described are inevitable. The considerations expressed previously will be greatly moderated by these future events. We present trends categorically. The limitations identified above will be gradually resolved as the various technologies mature. These predictions are based upon an assessment of emerging technologies as viewed at the time this book was written.

Hardware

As always, hardware technology will precede required software.

Memory

Memory densities are increasing while cost per bit decreases.

■ Products currently identified as productivity software will become built-in features of the traditional major packages.

- *1 year* – Expanded memory boards and related special-purpose software for MS-DOS computers will be phased out as the newer operating systems support the larger conventional addressable memory of the 80286 and 80386 microprocessors. ■
- *5 years* – Memory densities will increase to 64 Mbit separate components. The average workstation will contain 64 MB of memory. The cost of 64 MB memory will be comparable to 4 Mbits today.
- *10 years* – Intelligent memory devices that are now being developed will be readily available. These devices will have their own built-in computational capability, and when linked in large numbers will provide distributed processing networks.

CPU

- *This year* – The Intel 80486 and Motorola 68040 microprocessors are becoming the standard CPU for most small computer workstations. More advanced CPUs are being readied for market by Intel and Motorola.
- *1 year* – The Intel 80586 will become popular in DtC workstations.
- *5 years* – Advances in CPU processing power will be combined with special-purpose coprocessors (graphics, databases, array processors) and peripherals resulting in DtCs with computational capability that will rival and exceed that of our current mainframes.
- *5 years* – CPUs will be developed that will reach one billion instructions per second. Already 100+ MIPS RISC CPUs are available.
- *20 years* – It will be no longer possible to distinguish between CPU and special processing devices as independent entities. Intel's 80786, scheduled for the turn of the century, is rumored to contain DVI capability.

Mass Storage

Optical disk technologies have become competitive with the proven magnetic technologies. Optical technology has given rise to increasing competition with magnetic technologies, forcing prices down and densities up. Home users can purchase 100 MB hard drives for around $300. Not uncommon are 200-500 MB magnetic hard drives on DtCs.

- **1 year** – WORM (write once read many) optical technologies will be properly supported by commercial applications software to provide DtC-based electronic file cabinets and software libraries.
- **5 years** – Read/write optical technologies will become practical. This will provide mainframe storage capacity on DtCs, causing less dependency on central mass storage facilities.
- **10 years** – Optical technologies with no moving parts. Holographic techniques for mass data storage; storage volumes becoming virtually unlimited.
- **20 years** – Neural networks. Electronic devices at molecular level or even lower, at the electron level. Real computer brains, perhaps even with conciousness.

Printers

Laser printers are becoming mandatory peripherals for many new DtC applications software products including desktop publishers and CAD software.

- **5 years** – Most DtC users will have dedicated laser printers.
- **5 years** – Color laser printers will be popularly available, revolutionizing the way publications and artwork are generated.
- **10 years** – Decreasing need for printouts, as all work can be stored and viewed at everyone's workstation and transmitted over wide area networks to remote workstations.

Video Displays

- **Now** – Oversized displays for CAD and desktop publishing.
- **5 years** – Better than TV quality graphics with lifelike animation.
- **10 years** – Wrap-around displays capable of displaying all of your current work activities. These will include touch panels.
- **20 years** – Direct visual input to the human brain, especially applicable to the visually impaired.

Special Peripherals

- **5 years** – Handwriting optical character readers.
- **10 years** – Voice typewriter. Voice coprocessors capable of full contextual speech recognition and synthesis of realistic voice at low bit rates.

System Architectures

DtC system architectures continue to mimic their mainframe predecessors for a time. As developers and users become more sophisticated, however, the nature of these architectures will adapt to meet the special needs of dedicated workstations.

- **5 years** – More effective use of coprocessors through higher speed bus architectures. Offloading from CPU special functions such as database management, voice recognition, graphics, and communications as standards emerge in these areas. Improved bus standards, Futurebus, will help move different system architectures and peripherals together.

- **10 years** – Practical parallel processing architectures, such as matrix connected microprocessors, will require innovation in the area of software tools and compilers. It is fine to have powerful hardware, but it must be readily accessible to and usable by the average user.

- **10+ years** – Personal silicon foundries. The DtC provides an excellent environment for special-purpose devices. Special functions placed on silicon deriving basic power and software nurturing from the host DtC can reach performance levels exceeding the most powerful general-purpose super computer. What is still missing is the ability to develop these special-purpose devices quickly and interface them consistently with DtC buses. There is considerable work going on in this area, and silicon compiling is becoming available to some individuals. Already you can imagine a DtC interfaced with an inexpensive chip foundry. After entering appropriate functional descriptions, a device is created. This device is then plugged into a standard DtC interface that has appropriate DMA, interrupt, and other bus features.

- **10+ years** – Optical computing will become a reality. Already optical computers are being prototyped. VLSI devices, similar in size to today's silicon chips, will instead fabricate light-transmitting materials in chip form. Photon transmission, rather than electron, will be used for signal transmission. Current chip fabrication technologies can and will be adapted to the manufacture of optical chips. Another powerful fabrication technology allows placing microminiature mechanical devices in harmony with digital devices on silicon. Some day (under the control of a DtC, of course), these miniature devices may free our bodies of diseases, improve our vision, and enhance our thinking.

- **20+ years** – All software functions will be performed in hardware. At this point software will finally have closed the gap with hardware. The business of writing software to fit general-purpose hardware will continue to diminish; the current trend for workstations to be a distributed processing system made up of intelligent components and peripherals will culminate in systems that have no visible distinction between hardware and software. For instance, a workstation might perform tasks such as database management, 3-D graphics presentation and manipulation, and text processing all of which would be represented by adaptive hardware devices that are intelligent enough to form a social organization necessary to solve given problems. Humans will be able to interact with workstations in the same manner as they interact with other humans. To reach this level, hardware and software cannot be developed by independent groups.

Networking

Networks will incorporate greater numbers of computers and encompass larger geographic areas. Facilities will use DtC networks to perform those multi-user data sharing tasks that were previously in the domain of mainframes and minicomputers. To attain the data rates necessary for true distributed processing (100 Mbits/sec), most local area networks will need optical fiber connections. Networking will be accomplished by riding piggyback on other information services including telephone systems, cable TV, and satellite dishes. Network services are already being expanded to include merging of voice and video with the traditional computer data.

- **Now** – Use of home computer for shopping, entertainment, banking, remote home control, and child day care.
- **5 years** – Access to more sophisticated information services and sources incorporating graphics; more user friendly; incorporate live video.
- **5 years** – Significant work at home over networks.
- **5 years** – Software trial, purchase, and update over networks.
- **5 years** – Multi-media data processing and display over networks.
- **5 years** – New network standards such as FDDI (Fiber-optic Distributed Data Interface) will routinely support >100 Mbit/second data rates and protocols necessary for distributed processing. Users at any workstation will be able to manipulate

and view programs operating at other workstations. Optical network interfaces for all DtCs.

- **5 years** – Significant improvement in data compression techniques will permit practical transmission of data and images over telephone lines. Compression factors of up to 10,000 to 1 are said to be possible through fractal encoding and decoding schemes. You may be able to download your favorite video over a phone line.

> **NOTE**
>
> Complex image data sets are created in practical applications of chaos and fractal geometry with simple recursive generators. The implication in data compression is that a complex image or data set can be divided into much smaller sets that can later be regenerated through recursive iterations. Encoding and decoding algorithms are particularly complex, and therefore require extraordinary computing power. Already, competition for data bandwidth makes these techniques worth pursuing.

- **10-20 years** – Today's simple networking will evolve into true distributed processing in which the participating workstations will begin to resemble a social enterprise.

Software

Text Processing

- **Now** – Most popular text-oriented word processors will include graphics merge capability. More user friendly desktop publishing software are becoming available for MS-DOS compatibles.
- **5 years** – Manipulative systems that let the user interact with keyboard, voice I/O or touch panel video displays to create and manipulate integrated text and graphics. All text and graphics development capabilities will be integrated unlike today's systems where crude methodologies exist for importing the various components necessary to create complex documents. The impact of this on the average user will be intuitive systems for pointing, placing, and manipulating text and graphic images. Also, low-cost peripherals will enable users to digitize their own photographs into these documents easily. Handwriting OCR will be incorporated into the text processing environment.

Information Processing

- **Now** – A databases may be shared by several DtC users with a dedicated data server, which stores and manipulates data in the database. Other DtC workstations can query this database (and tools exist to customize this process to individual user needs – menus, screens, etc.). Once subsets of the served database are received, other tools (Lotus 1-2-3, X-base) can process the data further.
- **5 years** – Support will exist for a networked database that is not data server dependant, rather the database resides throughout the network with different pieces on different DtCs. A query results in automatic acquisition of those portions of the data from whatever sources are required to satisfy the query.
- **5 years** – User friendly fully integrated approaches to information processing that incorporate spreadsheets, word processors, database managers and graphics programs in highly integrated and friendly environments.

- **5 years** – Graphical information systems (such as HyperCard) will become more practical, especially when combined with multi-media, including video disks and CD ROMs.
- **10 years** – Networks will enable multiple users in workgroups to simultaneously interact with the same databases, documents, and images. Imagine working on a memo or database query with your partner across town; his image in the upper left hand corner of your DtC screen, the two of you creating and modifying a document interactively.

CAD/CAE and Graphics Software

- **5 years** – Better graphics performance will permit manipulative systems for more creative construction of complex figures including 3-D capabilities and animation simulations, similar to that found only on larger computers at this time. Today's systems are still cumbersome and difficult to use. Virtual reality will find many practical applications on the DtC.
- **10 years** – Graphics simulations of complex physical systems at your workstation. You may be viewing what's running on other systems, but this will be transparent.

AI Software

- **5 years** – Expert system shells that can capture integrated verbal and graphical representations. For example, a system that can be taught by a human expert to identify the integrity of a mechanical component from strain patterns. Systems such as this one are currently experimental, and operate only on larger computers; DtC software will make AI more tractable for manipulation.
- **5 years** – Flexible educational software will allow a teacher to dynamically configure a system to meet a student's immediate needs.
- **10 years** – Voice, visual, and acoustic pattern recognition, which will allow the computer to be used as a platform for serious robotics development.
- **20 years** – DtCs will recognize their operators visually.

Applications Development

- **10 years** – Applications generators will allow development of significant information management systems by non-programming users.
- **20 years** – Applications will be built into the hardware. At most, configuring these applications will be required.

Workstation Software

- **5 years** – Universally similar software. HB and EP software will look so alike that if you covered the system unit, you would not be able to tell which system is running the software. Top of the line HB and EP DtCs will have similar over-all hardware potential and will run under operating systems that support multitasking and distributed processing.

Through new VLSI chip sets introduced by Texas Instruments, interfacing to Apple's NuBus and the MS-DOS bus will be simplified. Systems combining both Apple and IBM buses have already been produced. The recent IBM and Apple collaborative agreement should be beneficial to DtC users.

As operating systems, software, and networks continue to become similar for the different workstation platforms, it will become important that the different platforms have similar computational power. More specifically, when you prepare to buy a platform, a Sun, Apollo, Apple, or an MS-DOS computer, consider hardware performance factors such as CPU strength and graphics capability. Be sure that equivalent software products will run on these different workstations at comparable performance levels.

Operating Systems

- **1 year** – Full user interface, windowing, and graphics support provided by most operating systems.
- **5 years** – Support of multiple concurrent applications with good memory management and performance across the board using high-end CISC and RISC CPUs.
- **5-10 years** – Support for distributed processing over networks built into operating systems.
- **5-10 years** – Standardization in microcomputer operating systems (OS/2, Unix).
- **10-20 years** – Full network integration support, a network that is as easy to use as a single workstation.
- **20+ years** – The operating system will no longer be a distinguishable software entity.

PART

II

Part II. Hardware Fundamentals

Given the complexity and rapid evolution of the desktop computer it is easy to understand why so many users are so bewildered. Successful desktop computing applications are erected on the pillars of performance, compatibility, reliability, and supportability. In this construct, system hardware, operating system, and applications software are intimately related components, each contributing to the final product, whatever it may be. With a dollop of the right kind of insight, you will find technical issues easier to understand and hardware/software selection decisions easier to reach. To control the destiny of your particular application, you need to know the ropes.

Like Detroit automobiles, today's desktop computers are mass-produced on factory assembly lines. Buying a car or a DtC is a serious investment. In both cases it is important to know enough so that when you look under the hood you know what you are seeing. The microcomputer consists of components that are designed to function together to achieve a predetermined end. The principal components are the CPU, memory, and input/output (I/O) interfaces. There is also a variety of auxiliary devices and a communications bus. All of these components need to be placed in perspective so that you are able to understand DtCs and use them to your advantage.

A searching look inside a microcomputer is required to learn more about the strengths and weaknesses of its essential components. Figure 26 displays the key components found inside the system unit box. The CPU is the main controller. The math coprocessor and the DMA controller, used for block memory transfers, are interconnected. An interrupt controller, which manages outside events, can be used to interrupt CPU processing. A counter timer develops necessary system timing and interrupt signals. Hooked up to the bus are the memory and the standard serial and parallel I/O interfaces. Keyboard, video, and mass storage interfaces are not shown. They are described together with peripherals elsewhere in this book.

Let's look at the basic microcomputer components, see how they work, and learn why they are connected the way they are. Specifically, we will examine:

- *Microprocessors (CPUs)* – Literally the workhorses of the microcomputer world, how they exercise overall system control.
- *Support chips* – The major VLSI chips found in the system unit to complement the CPU.
- *Addressing* – How devices are called to establish communications.
- *Memory* – Physical types, expansion, and its management.
- *Buses* – How they carry signal and data traffic throughout the system.
- *Interfaces* – The different types and how they connect your peripherals to vital internal system resources.

- *Interrupts* – Their importance and use in DtCs.

Discussions and recommendations in other portions of the book assume that you have read Part II, or that you are sufficiently versed in the basics to skip it.

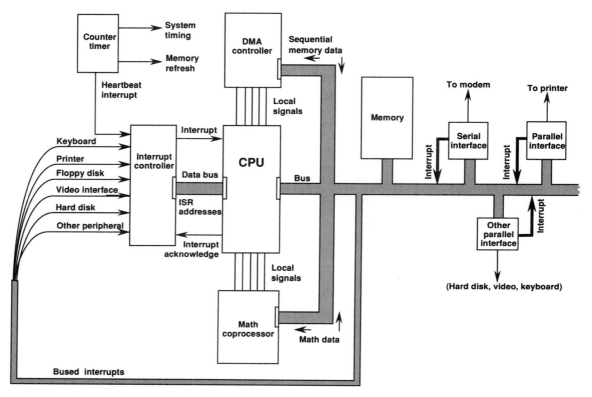

Figure 26.   Internal system components: Although the CPU is only a small part of a DtC, it is the single most important component.

1.0   Microprocessors

As a technological breakthrough, the microprocessor rivals the creation of the wheel, the concoction of gunpowder, the discovery of electricity, and the invention of the transistor. Since its arrival on the scene, it has had a profound effect on our lives. Practically everything that is automated incorporates one or more of them. Indeed, the microprocessor is the main component of the desktop computer. Now this little wonder is not only automating our lives, it is expanding our minds. We should look closer at these tiny giants and marvel at how far they have come in their brief 20 years of evolution.

The market is flooded with many types of microprocessor. To simplify matters, this discussion focuses on the two most popular vendors, Motorola and Intel, concentrating specifically on 16- and 32-bit CPUs. We saw in Figure 26 that the CPU is the focal point of the DtC system. A closer look at the CPU in Figure 27 reveals the particular significance of the CPU: device addressing and communication. Memory, data, and devices are selected by the CPU's address lines. Once selected, data flows over the data lines. The more address lines, the more devices that can be selected. The more data lines, the more parallel data can flow.

Although microprocessors use many other signals and system-specific control functions, their performance ultimately hinges on addressability and data width. Therefore, our CPU discussions focus primarily on those two parameters.

1.1   Microprocessors of the '70s

Early 4-Bit Microprocessors

The first microprocessors were designed to replace complex logic in machine controllers, elevators, traffic lights, and the like. The idea was to program the complex logical operations of these devices so that you could change operational characteristics without having to replace banks of relays.

The first of these microprocessors was the Intel 4004. The 4004 had a 4-bit data width and addressed 64K of memory with its 16 address lines. It contained no operating system as such, but a program in ROM carried out a narrow range of specific tasks. Upon closer examination it was seen that these microprocessors exhibited capabilities similar to those of general-purpose CPUs: they had instruction sets and program execution, and soon their purpose was reconsidered in terms of conventional data processing. Data processing became more feasible with 8-bit character-oriented microprocessors and a general-purpose operating system that could load and store programs and data.

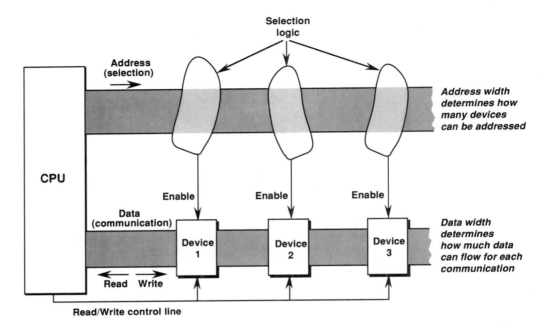

Figure 27. Addressing and data communications: The CPU is the grand master of the DtC. Its capability defines the system's overall performance.

> **NOTE**
> When a microprocessor is referred to as a 4-, 8-, 16-, or 32-bit CPU, the bit reference is to *data width*.

Later 8-Bit Microprocessors

The first 8-bit microprocessors promoted microcomputers from simple process controllers to data processors. Although limited, these microprocessors began the tradition of personal computing. The following microprocessors all addressed 64K of memory with 16 address lines.

- *6502 MOS technology* – The 6502 was found in the early Apple II and a similar CPU was used in the early Commodore computers. The 6502 treated a 256-byte memory area as if it were an arrangement of CPU registers. The 256 bytes weren't exactly register-level instructions, but they were faster than regular memory instructions because they had special one-byte addresses. This treatment, combined with its improved memory addressing modes (over the 8080 and 6800), is why the first generation Apple II and Commodore computers performed as well as they did, despite their limited memory resources.

- *8008* – First Intel 8-bit microprocessor. Used in process control.

- *8080* – Similar to the 8008, popular in first-generation business microcomputers under the CP/M operating system.

- **Z80** – Produced by Zilog Company. Enhanced 8080, more instructions, upward object-compatible. ■ The Z80's popularity was enhanced by Radio Shack incorporating it in their heavily marketed TRS-80 personal computer. Although Radio Shack's operating system (TRS-DOS) was specially developed for the TRS-80, hundreds of vendors, including Radio Shack, embraced the CP/M operating system upgraded to run on the Z80, which further popularized it.

- **6800 Motorola** – The 6800 was mostly used for low-level process control. No standard operating system was developed for the 6800, nor did any computer manufacturer promote it in the marketplace.

- **6809 Motorola** – Enhanced 6800, but not upward object-compatible with the 6800. The 6809 is the most powerful 8-bit microprocessor. Found on dedicated interfaces, controllers, and embedded systems. Radio Shack opted for the 6809 in its low-cost color computer. A Unix-like operating system, OS/9, was developed later for this little 8-bit wonder.

In order to perform data processing, systems based on these microprocessors all functioned under rudimentary operating systems. These operating systems ran different programs in RAM to achieve a computing capability greater than that of their 4-bit ROM-based predecessors.

The original 16-bit processors from the two major microprocessor chip vendors, Motorola and Intel, discussed next, *were not* upward object-compatible with their 8-bit predecessors.

1.2   Intel 80xxx Microprocessors

The first Intel 16-bit processor, the 8088, was clearly inferior to Motorola's first 16-bit entry, the 68000. Due to IBM's support in 1981, however, the 8088 quickly became popular, primarily in lower-end computing applications. More advanced models, 8086, 80186, 80286, 80386, 80486, and 80586 compare favorably with the Motorola 68xxx series.

8088

The 8088 addresses 1 MB of memory with 20 address lines, and has 16-bit data paths internally, but brings out only eight data lines. Therefore 16-bit data quantities must be funneled through an 8-bit path. Excessive degradation is avoided through instruction queuing. No memory management capability exists other than a primitive 64K segmenting system through a few segment registers. Instruction execution speed at 5 MHz clock rate is approximately 300 K/sec.

The original IBM PC and XT, no longer marketed by IBM, were based on the 8088 microprocessor. Using a simple memory management scheme called *segmentation*, illustrated in Figure 28, a programmer could place 64K program and data areas anywhere in the 8088's 1 MB address range.

XT-style motherboards featuring the 8088 microprocessor cost about $50, not much more than a pocket calculator. Of course, a bare bones XT requires a case, a power supply, a floppy disk drive, and a monitor. But you can have all of that for about $300, the price of a VCR. As we shall see, however, the 8088 microprocessor

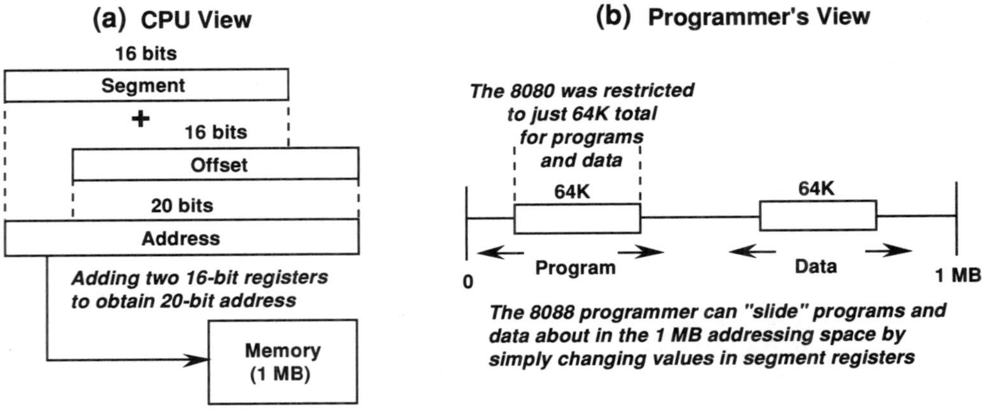

Figure 28. Segmentation in the Intel 8088: The 20-bit address is developed by adding a 16-bit segment to a 16-bit offset, which results in a 20-bit address. By simply readjusting the segment registers, the entire 64K program and data areas can be slid anywhere in the 1 MB addressable memory. The offset is developed through the ordinary effective address operands as in the 8088's predecessor, the 8080. In fact, 8088 assembly language looks like that of the 8080, since instruction addresses continue to be only 16-bits wide. The difference lies in the segment registers, which extend the 16-bit offsets throughout the 1 MB addressable memory. By ignoring the segment registers, programming the 8088 is quite similar to programming the 8080, which helps with the conversion of software between the 8080 and 8088 microprocessors.

is primitive by today's standards, so you will probably want to invest in something more sophisticated.

8086

The 8086 is identical to the 8088 except that all 16 data bits are brought out. This improves performance by around 80% at similar clock speeds. The IBM PS/2 Model 30 is based on this microprocessor.

80186

Similar to the 8086, except that much of the surrounding hardware necessary to develop a microcomputer based on this chip is contained within the chip itself. The 80186 microprocessor became popular for single-board microcomputer and dedicated processing functions such as LAN boards and graphics controllers.

80286

Still a 16-bit microprocessor, but a significant departure from the 8086/186: including 24 address lines for 16 MB of direct memory addressability; more sophisticated instructions; and relatively sophisticated memory management capability. IBM's extinct AT, Personal System/2 Models 50 and 60, and a variety of other vendor's AT-style desktop computers use this microprocessor. The 80286 is the first Intel microprocessor to support multitasking from within using memory protection mechanisms, context switching, and other hardware and software devices specifically intended to support multiple processes running on a single CPU. Also, virtual memory support is possible through internal 32-bit virtual memory addressing. The 80286's improved segmentation is shown in Figure 29. Although lesser

Intel microprocessors can simulate this environment in software, getting a DtC to multitask is an oppressive burden if the right hardware isn't in place.

While the 80386/486 CPUs far surpass the capability of the 80286 processor, the 80286 is quite a step above the 8088. Due to the increasing popularity of 80386/486-based DtCs, 286 motherboards are very inexpensive.

The segmentation capability of the 80286 is more flexible than the 8088. Segments can be sized and segment registers are implemented through pointers to memory. Pointers allow for a greater number of more flexible segment registers, which is essential for managing multiple programs operating concurrently in memory.

The 8088 develops a 20-bit address by simply adding a CPU segment register with a 16-bit program counter value, which serves as the offset. The 80286 develops its 24-bit address through a more sophisticated procedure, summarized in Figure 29. While the offset is still a 16-bit quantity, the segment portion of the address resides in an 8-byte segment descriptor table that is also in CPU memory. The table not only contains the segment value, which is then added to the offset to obtain the physical 24-bit address, but it also contains additional bits that determine access, read/write privilege levels, and other pieces of information needed to implement virtual memory.

While a virtual address can be specified as an internal CPU register value, a *physical address* must ultimately be created. The physical address, through physical address lines, literally triggers the physical memory to execute the program. The final output from the adder in Figure 29 is manifested on 24 physical address wires. Addresses that appear in the segment descriptor table can be virtual; that is, they do not necessarily result in physical address line values pointing to data that is in fact in executable memory. Many virtual addresses will point to code that is not in physical memory. When the CPU attempts to execute such code that is not in memory, an exception interrupt is issued. Before continuing with the instruction stream, the interrupt triggers a sequence of events that brings these non-physical virtual program portions stored on the hard disk into physical memory, where they can execute.

> ### EXAMPLE
> By analogy, think of a bank's cash on hand as physical memory, and the bank's total cash worth, which is mostly out on loans, as the virtual program portions stored on disk. If someone wants to draw out money that is not covered by cash, the bank will have to go out and get the cash from other sources, just as the CPU must access the disk to execute program portions not located in executable memory. While the banking system depends on a small percentage of cash on hand, a virtual memory system depends on executable memory that is considerably smaller than virtual memory.

80386

The 80386 is significantly more powerful that the 80286. It has a full 32-bit data path, and 32-bit direct addressability plus additional 14-bit virtual addressing capability. Improvements over the 80286 include:

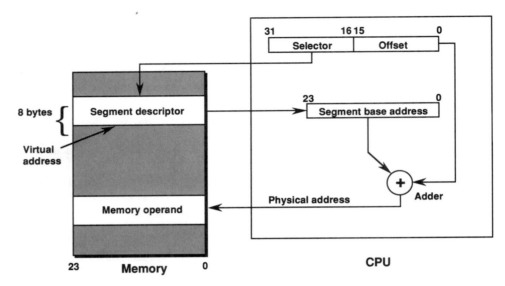

Figure 29.   Improved segmentation in the 80286

- Page-mapped virtual memory for mainframe-like memory management. Although not absolutely essential for implementing multitasking and virtual memory, paging allows considerably more flexibility in manipulating memory than the segmentation scheme provided in the 80286 microprocessor. Paging splits memory into fine 4K pages, which can then be jockeyed about the memory map with ease and precision. Paging is implemented beneath and is compatible with a segmentation scheme similar to that for the 80286. See Figure 30. The ability to disable paging allows applications that run on the 80286 to run on the 80386.

- Improved text management facilities (text-oriented instructions).

- Huge direct addressability (4 gigabyte).

- I/O protection bit maps for protection of I/O devices.

- Internal hardware breakpoint exception capability for debugging. Interrupts internal to the 80386 occur when additional registers are set and used to compare address and data conditions on the fly. When the conditions are met, the interrupt occurs, and debugging routines can be executed. Thus, break points can be built in without modifying the existing code and programs being debugged can operate in real time.

- More sophisticated instruction set.

- VM (virtual machine) mode. The VM mode allows the 80386 to behave as though it consisted of multiple 8086s, each capable of operating independently to the point of running different operating systems. The Windows environment takes advantage of this 80386 capability to run multiple concurrent MS-DOS applications programs.

- Instruction queuing. An improved 15 instruction pre-fetch register allows instructions that are likely to be executed to be pre-loaded during other bus operations. Queuing is also found in earlier 16-bit Intel microprocessors, although it is not nearly as efficient.

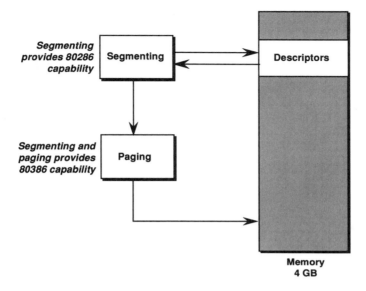

Figure 30.   Paging in the 80386:   The 80386 adds paging capability, further enhancing its ability to manage memory.

80386SX

This is a special version of the 80386 microprocessor that brings out only 24 address lines and 16 data lines (like the 80286). Using this chip, vendors are able to manufacture low-cost 80386-like systems or upgrade 80286-based systems to 80386-like capability.

DtCs based on the 80386 are now quite popular because of increasing applications software and operating system support of its unique memory management capabilities, and because of its greater speed as compared to the 80286. A variety of low-power 80386 and 80386SX CPUs are available for laptop DtCs. Newer versions can actually stop execution (analogous to a car idling) during power down modes, using practically no power. Also, recent price drops and other vendor's reverse-engineered 80386 equivalents have greatly reduced the cost of an 80386-based DtC.

80486

The 80486 is similar to the 80386 with the following exceptions:

- A math coprocessor is built into the CPU chip and is no longer a separate chip as with earlier 80xxxs.
- Due to the combined CISC/RISC design, throughput is twice that of the 80386 at the same clock speed.
- 8K instruction and 8K data caches are built into the CPU.

The built-in coprocessor of the 80486 adds considerable cost to the CPU. However, you do get a significant improvement in speed and performance. The real jump in CPU capability from the 80286 to 80386/80486 is in the memory management area. Efficient memory management is needed to support the really powerful capabilities of Windows and the OS/2 operating system. The significant fact is that the 80286 is being left behind because it is slower and cannot manage memory as well as the 80386/486. All major vendors of compatibles, including IBM itself, support the 80486 CPU in their DtC models.

Now here come the critical decision points. A coprocessor for an 80386 will cost from $200 to $800. If you decide to add a coprocessor, you have many options; with the 80486 you already have one built-in. If you want your 80386 to also have speed, you face an additional investment of five hundred to two thousand dollars to reach the performance level of an 80486. At the very least, if you buy an 80386, check to see if a 486 upgrade is possible.

EXAMPLE

IBM's Power Platform is a 486 board that upgrades their PS/2 Model 70 DtC to the level of an 80486 CPU.

All of the capabilities of the 80386 and 486 microprocessors will probably not be fully harnessed by the majority of the software base for several years.

Cut-down versions of the 80486 CPU (the 486SX) disable defective math coprocessors enabling the chip to sell for much less than the full 486 version. As with the 386SX chip, the modified 486 chip versions give users increased purchasing flexibility. The DtC buyer can have the speed of the 486 CPU without buying a coprocessor. And like the 386, 486-based DtCs provide a plug-in coprocessor socket. It is interesting that we already have DtC applications software that will run *only* on the 80386 or 486.

1.3   Intel CPUs of the '90s

80586

The 80586 will permit 80xxx system capability and also provide high-end RISC capability exceeding 150 MIPS performance. Features will include:

- **More transistors** – Three million transistors. The 80486 topped out at around one million.
- **Scalar architecture** – A highly parallel architecture that performs a lot of work with only a few instructions per clock cycle.
- **RISC instructions** – The 80586 will implement Intel's RISC instruction set.
- **CISC compatibility** – Included logic permits the execution of the large 80xxx software base.
- **150+ MIPS** – As the 80586 can execute multiple instructions per clock cycle, a 50 MHz clock can produce these high MIPS.

Other processors capable of one or less instructions per clock must push clock speeds to exhorbitant levels to attain high MIPS. Higher clock speeds are more difficult to implement throughout a system and cause more radio frequency interference. One way of getting around high-speed clock problems is to make the CPU do more per clock cycle, as is the case with the 80586. Another way is to let the CPU run faster internally, yet operate the vital bus interface signals at lower frequencies. For example, newer 486 chips can run at 66 MHz internally. However, external bus signals continue to operate at 33 MHz. Using such a chip, you could breathe new life into a 486 DtC while maintaining 33 MHz compatibility with the rest of the system hardware.

Year	Chip	Data Width	Ad-dress Width	Addressability		IPS	Clock (typi-cal)	Motorola equiv.	Significant dif-ferences from predecessor
				Di-rect	Vir-tual				
Low power, 8086 class:									
1982	8088	8/16	20	1 MB	N/A	300K	5 MHz	none	Simple segmen-tation.
1982	8086	16	20	1 MB	N/A	600K	10 MHz	none	Full 16-bit data output.
1982	80186	16	20	1 MB	N/A	600K	10 MHz	none	Single chip 8086 computer.
Medium power, 80286 class:									
1985	80286	16	24	16 MB	1 GB	1.5 M	12 MHz	68000	Multitasking sup-port in in-structions and hardware. Im-proved segmen-tation.
High power, 80386 class:									
1987	80386	32	32	4 GB	64 TB	5 M	25 MHz	68030	Demand paging added to seg-mentation. Vir-tual 8086 capability.
1990	80486	32	32	4 GB	64 TB	15 M	40 MHz	68040	Built-in cache and math coprocessor.
Super Power, 80586-plus class:									
1992	80586	32/64				150 M	100 MHz	68050	RISC perform-ance.
2000	80786	256	64			2 G	250 MHz		DVI capability.

Table 22.   Intel CPU power levels.: The microprocessors are divided into three classes, based on addressability and data width. A fourth emerging super class is also indicated; information, however, is scarce.

Legend: 1: G = gigabyte = one billion bytes = 500 thousand pages of 80x24 text.

2: T = terabyte = one trillion bytes = 500 million pages of 80x24 text.

3: Features of 80586 and 80786 are based on speculation and rumor. Power will have to be defined after they arrive and are put to use.

80786

Purely speculative at this point and discussed at a recent Intel seminar was the x86 megaprocessor. Some have dubbed this chip the 80786, and these are the tentative specifications:

- **100 million transistors** – Using a 0.1 micron technology. Currently, solid state devices occupying a one micron (one millionth of an inch on a side) space are considered high tech.
- **DVI capability** – Real time video and 3-D graphics capability will be implemented on chip.
- **Performance enhancement** – Using a 2 MB internal cache memory, and operating at 250 MHz, this chip will deliver 2 G instructions per second.
- **Math capability** – Two floating point vector processors running at one thousand Mflops (million floating point operations per second).
- **Parallel processing** – Four parallel 64-bit CPUs operating at 750 MIPS each.
- **256-bit external data width** – This should answer most who question if future systems will go beyond 32-bit data widths.

All of the above are to be implemented on a one inch square die, the size of the active silicon.

1.4 Motorola 68xxx Series Microprocessors

Unlike the Intel 80xxx microprocessor line, which began with the relatively weak 8088 microprocessor, the Motorola 68xxx line has always been a solid performer, and it has been adopted for engineering workstations from the beginning of the 16-bit revolution. With the appearance of the 80286 Intel processor, the disparity between these two lines has all but disappeared as Unix begins to penetrate the MS-DOS-compatible world.

The Motorola's 68xxx 16- and 32-bit microprocessors are upward object-compatible. However, they are not upward object-compatible with their 8-bit predecessors, the 6800 and 6809. The 68000 microprocessor has 32-bit internal data paths, addresses 16 MB of memory, and is a much more capable microprocessor than Intel's first 16-bit entry, the 8088. The 68000 quickly found its way into relatively expensive engineering workstations that run CAD/CAE and other engineering/scientific applications under the Unix operating system.

Apple Computer was one of the first companies to design a low-cost DtC, the Macintosh, based on the 68000. Apple's Mac II and later series used later model 68020, 30, and 40 microprocessors. The 68020 and 68030 microprocessors are higher performance versions, include full 32-bit data and address widths, and have many other sophisticated features. The 68030 has built-in memory management that compares favorably with that of the 80386. The newer 68040 also compares favorably with Intel's 80486. As with Intel, more advanced chips are in the making.

The Macintosh and Macintosh II lines adopted the 68xxx series of Motorola chips while their predecessor, the Apple II computer, relied on the 6502 processor. Consequently, Macs are unable to run software that was written for the Apple II. Significant differences between the 6502 and 68000 microprocessors and the Apple II and Macintosh operating systems led to a temporary shortage of software. Now, however, software is abundant for Macintosh systems. In contrast, the change from the 8080 to the 8088 Intel microprocessor was not as painful, since the differences in the microprocessors and operating systems (CP/M to MS-DOS) were not as significant.

1.5   Why Did IBM Choose the 8088?

IBM chose the Intel 8088 in 1981 to begin its PC line even though higher performance 16-bit Motorola microprocessors were available and already popular at that time. The reasons for going with the 8088 were clearly pragmatic and were probably driven by the following factors:

- *Inexpensive design* – The ability to design less-expensive DtCs around the 8088 due to its 8-bit data bus and the popularity of 8-bit interface chips.

- *8080/Z80 software base* – At the time there was a large body of 64K 8080- and Z80-based applications running on the Radio Shack TRS-80 and CP/M microcomputers. Converting these programs to 8088 object code was made easier because the 8088 64K relative segments and translation utilities were available from Intel, manufacturer of both the 8080 and 8088 microprocessors.

- *Ownership ties* – IBM would acquire an interest in the Intel Corporation.

- *Object compatibility* – The entire line of PCs was based on the 8088 and 8086 microprocessors; planned 80xxx microprocessors would be upward object-compatible, each running on its predecessor's machine language, and would encompass a wide range of computer applications.

- *Operating system availability* – Availability of the 8088 microprocessor stimulated the concurrent development of three operating systems: CP/M, UCSD Pascal, and QD-DOS.

  - *CP/M* – The 8080 CP/M 80 was easily rewritten by Digital Research Corporation for the 8088, becoming CP/M 86.

  - *UCSD Pascal* – An operating system known as UCSD (University of California, San Diego) Pascal appeared rather quickly for the IBM PC. The experimental Pascal-based system included an assembler and a P-code compiler. The compiler brought the Pascal code down to an intermediate language (P-code) that could be generated also from other languages, Fortran and BASIC. P-code instructions executed on a hypothetical, optimized computer known as a stack machine. The stack machine code was converted to 8088 code on the fly, using a small interpreter. Thus, converting UCSD Pascal to run on 8088 systems involved, at most, the rewriting of a relatively small interpreter.

  - *QD-DOS* – An operating system developed by Seattle Computer Corporation in a brief two-month period and called *Quick 'n' Dirty* DOS. It was shelved until Microsoft purchased it and tweaked it into MS-DOS. The full story is told elsewhere in this book.

Although the 8088 was not as powerful as its contemporary 68000 microprocessor, compared to its 8-bit predecessors it did have some good features. It had exclusive math coprocessor instructions, on board multiply/divide, internal error exception handling, and higher clock speeds.

It must have been IBM's intention to build a personal computer a cut above those already popular 8-bit DtCs (such as Apple II, Radio Shack TRS-80, and the 8-bit Commodores and Ataris), and yet not as powerful or expensive as the developing engineering workstations based on the more powerful Motorola 68000. Although many did not think much of IBM's initial PC offerings, the PC did have many features not found on most of the earlier 8-bit DtCs – features of the more expensive 68xxx-based workstations of that period:

- Bus slots suitable for expansion.
- Math coprocessor.
- DMA controller for faster data movement than was possible by the CPU alone.
- Interrupt controller rather than the usual one or two interrupts to allow better usage of peripherals.
- Open architecture with bus, system design, BIOS ROM, and completely documented operating system, which made it easy to build add-on hardware (and software).

In 1981 no one but IBM could put these engineering workstation features into a low-cost personal computer. IBM's marketing strategy coupled with the accessibility to the internal workings of IBM's product line ensured a phenomenal software base and spawned the clone generation – resulting in the MS-DOS computer revolution witnessed today.

IBM's Intel philosophy appears to be working well. MS-DOS and DtC applications software development have been relatively stable since 1981. But this stability may change with the recent cooperative agreement reached by IBM and Apple to develop open platform products.

1.6   RISCs

RISCs (reduced instruction set CPUs) are CPUs with instruction sets that are smaller and more efficient than those of conventional CISC (complex instruction set CPU) processors. Popular chip vendors, like Intel and Motorola, are producing RISCs with instruction execution rates of 25 to 70 MIPS.■

■ Current Intel and Motorola 80486 and 68040 CPUs execute at the rate of 5 to 15 MIPS.

The problem with CISC CPUs is that the majority of time is spent executing a small group of general-purpose instructions. The RISC CPU uses the chip real estate, which is normally used to implement infrequent instructions, to make a smaller set of frequently used instructions execute quicker. This gain in speed will offset the additional time required to emulate the infrequent instructions.

In order to realize maximum benefits from RISC CPUs, we need particularly sophisticated compilers. The traditional CISC compilers take great advantage of the rich machine language functionality of CISC processors to obtain functionality at the high language level. RISC compilers, however, have very limited CPU instruction sets to work with. For example, a CISC compiler would implement arrays and array indexing in high-level language by taking advantage of the CISC CPU's flexible addressing modes and register capability. Flexible high level branching such as CASE and DO WHILE statements are created from the flexible CISC jump and call machine language commands. RISC processors have only primitive branching, testing, and register movement machine instructions, but they compensate with exceptionally fast processing of these weaker instructions. RISC processors can be of particular advantage if care is taken to write appropriate compilers or dedicated machine language programs that can squeeze functionality from rapid but banal machine instructions.

Given the general-purpose nature of DtC software, it will take time to depreciate the enormous investment in Intel 80xxx and Motorola 68xxx microprocessors. RISC CPUs are implemented in smart peripherals such as laser printers, OCR (optical character recognition) systems, and specialized engineering workstations, where dedicated and efficient execution is mandatory. Intel's 80486 CPU is part RISC and part CISC.

Both Intel and Motorola, as well as other vendors, are manufacturing high-powered RISC microprocessors. For example, Intel's 80860 RISC processor includes three parallel math coprocessors and 3-D graphics capability, all built into the same chip. By placing more functions on the same chip, interprocess communication speed improves because there are no DtC board electronics in the way. IBM Wizard add-on boards operate 80860 RISC processors to supplement IBM PS/2 computer's CPU capability. The Wizard board is an excellent example of synergism between CISC and RISC processing in the same DtC. The PS/2 line 80xxx CISC processors execute the ordinary home and business software while appropriately written engineering and graphics applications can use the Wizard board.

1.7 ASICs

Another breed of processor chip, known as ASIC (application specific integrated circuit), is making its debut in the peripherals marketplace. Here, the notions of general-purpose CPU architecture and instruction sets are abandoned; the ASIC is designed with a specific application in mind. Each may vary considerably from one application to another.

Although most general-purpose compilers and software development tools cannot be used on such processors, custom software and firmware for the intended task operate with great efficiency.

> **EXAMPLE**
>
> The newer HP LaserJet printers use an ASIC processor. Both the architecture and instruction set are specialized for character and graphics printing, achieving special effects that greatly enhance the final product. By modulating the sizes of its dots, the LaserJet III rivals the print quality of a 600-dpi printer. The ability to print dots of different sizes is especially advantageous in producing smooth curves.

1.8 Microprocessor Wrap-up

Numerous evaluations have been made of the higher-end Intel and Motorola microprocessors. The consensus opinion is that the advanced models of both are so sophisticated that comparisons are difficult, given the types of applications currently found on microcomputers. Each chip set is more than adequate for most DtC applications. Both Intel and Motorola CISC CPUs have significantly improved memory management compared to earlier models.

The telling difference that occasionally emerges from these evaluations is that higher-end Intel chips lean toward memory management and multiprocessing similar to that found on mainframe computers, while the higher-end Motorola CPUs are oriented toward high-performance dedicated workstation applications. Both chips support a variety of sophisticated coprocessing devices.

Every year or so we are dazzled by the appearance of yet another microprocessor, more sophisticated and captivating than any before it. First came the 8-bit micros that opened the gates of computing to everyman. Next came the 16-bit Intel and Motorola microprocessors that addressed more memory and ran faster. Then came the 32-bit models with exceptional ability to manage memory, which brought mainframe-like capabilities – virtual memory and multitasking – to the desktop. The next round of new microprocessors will include built-in image and video processing, parallel processing, application-specific processing, high throughput, and we can only imagine what else. The cycles seem to have five-year periods. Currently, we are in the multitasking/virtual memory period.

2.0 Special Function Chips

- Cache Controllers
- Graphics Coprocessors
- Interrupt Controllers
- Counter Timers
- DMA Controllers
- Math Coprocessors
- ACIA Chips

The special function chips breath life into your DtC; each assisting in its own particular specialty just like tireless workers in a finely tuned production line.

Inside every DtC is a set of powerful VLSI devices that define its hardware personality. The circuitry and logic embedded in special function chips can easily be an order of magnitude greater than that contained in the CPU. A better understanding of these chips can help you capitalize on your system's performance as well as add more applications to your repertoire.

Many hardware factors besides CPU type and speed come into play when you buy and use a DtC. A host of special function chips supplement the CPU, glue your system interfaces together, and perform auxiliary tasks for effective system operation. Some of these chips are initialized automatically when you power up, so they require little or no attention; others may involve configurations that affect system performance. Let's look at the chips found in most DtCs.

2.1 Cache Controllers

Cache controllers are complex pieces of VLSI logic. The purpose of the cache controller is to keep in its local memory data and instructions that are most used by the CPU. Caches work because of a phenomenon known as the locality of execution principle. The principle states that in a Von Neuman architecture the CPU tends to access the same memory locations over and over again.■ Others have noted the same phenomenon. The Bradford distribution that comes from information science is virtually identical to the 80/20 rule, which states that in a large collection of useful things, as in a stock room or library, 20 percent of the items will be asked for 80 percent of the time. Similar ratios hold for many other phenomena in human activity.

■ A Von Neuman computer executes its instructions sequentially.

A cache controller uses extremely fast static RAM as its area for instruction and data storage (see Figure 43 on page 231). This local cache is around 1/20th the size of the executable memory ordinarily implemented in slower dynamic RAM. When the CPU gets data from memory, the cache controller checks to see if the information is already in the static cache. This check is performed using very fast comparative circuitry that looks at current and previous CPU addresses. If data is in cache memory, the cache memory system can deliver it to the CPU with no delay. This situation is called a cache hit. If, however, the required data is not in the cache, the CPU will require an access to slower memory. This situation is called a cache miss.

Data retrieved during a cache miss is also written into the cache's faster memory. If the CPU again requires this data, the locality principle ensures that there will be no delay. In order to write new data into the cache, other data must be flushed. How well the controller manages the process of writing and flushing, preserving the most accessed instructions and data, determines just how much it can improve system performance.

In many situations the CPU will execute tight loops, repeatedly fetching and executing the same few instructions. Also, the CPU is likely to use many of the same memory locations such as counters and pointers, repeatedly. The cache controllers attempt to store these often-accessed memory objects in fast RAM for immediate reuse.

Cache Size

In an MS-DOS computer, a cache of 640K real memory would be ideal. For MS-DOS software, most programs and data accessed would in fact be in the cache, leaving no need for a cache controller at all. Rather, all commonly used directly accessible memory would be fast static memory. This would be exceedingly expensive since static RAM is about ten times more costly than dynamic RAM. Although there is widely varying opinion about how much cache is required, most agree that the curve is not linear. The greatest speed improvement occurs with the initial addition of cache, e.g., 32K in an MS-DOS computer. Improvements do occur beyond that, but they are not as significant. While you might see a 15% speed improvement with a 32K cache, you might see only 20% with a 64K cache. The improvement will depend largely on the type of software executing and how the locality of execution principle holds for the particular application.

Cache Performance Expectations

Cache controllers can sometimes become confused, rendering them ineffective. The following are a few situations that might impede the cache controller's ability to manage its memory.

- *Multitasking software* – Many different and unrelated programs are being executed concurrently.

- *Peripherals that update memory* – Through direct memory access, peripherals can affect memory in ways not connected with what the CPU might be doing. A process known as *snooping* can be used by the cache controller to determine if this is going on.

- *Sequential search software* – You might be operating software (such as DBMS or spreadsheets) that sequentially search large amounts of memory, which confuses the cache controller designed for the locality of access principle mentioned earlier. Sequential searches over large memory areas flush useful data from cache memory.

Since these and other complications can occur, it is easy to mispredict how much a system will benefit from a cache controller. Different methodologies can be used to manage the flow of data between controller, system memory, and CPU. There are also different types of cache controllers, and their performance and cost vary considerably.

Cache improvements are so enmeshed in complexity you can abandon any hope of calculating empirically, or of using intuition to predict how well a particular cache controller system combination will improve system performance. Instead, try the software you plan to run on a specific DtC system with a specific cache implementation and compare this with other implementations both with and without cache. Then determine under what specific configuration and data sets the application operates the fastest.

2.2 Graphics Coprocessors

Intelligent display interfaces ease the CPU's burden in generating and manipulating complex graphics images, which can include text functions. Before confronting graphics coprocessor chips, look first at the two main types of DtC graphics display interfaces: *dumb* and *intelligent*. Figure 31 shows how both dumb and intelligent display interfaces appear from a system point of view. The dumb display interface simply scans a memory area while the intelligent interface can do this scanning as well as develop and manipulate graphics images without the concentrated effort of the CPU. Intelligent video interfaces are often implemented by specially designed high speed microcontrollers and other logic, using scores of special function chips. More recently, the graphics coprocessor (one or two VLSI chips) can perform most of the desired graphics functionality in a modern intelligent graphics display interface.

Dumb Interfaces

Most home and business (HB) DtCs implement dumb video interfaces. Since dumb interfaces scan a memory area whose contents are manipulated by the CPU, it is a relatively low-cost and somewhat standardized software interface for text and graphics display needs. The dumb interface, however, places the entire burden of generating and manipulating text and graphics on the CPU. As intelligent interfaces, driven by graphics coprocessor chips, become supported by more DtC applications, more sophisticated CAD, graphics, and desktop publishing applications will become prevalent on DtCs.

Intelligent Interfaces

Intelligent display interfaces perform graphics functions internally with little or no help from the CPU. These functions are being combined onto fewer and fewer VLSI devices, known as graphics coprocessors, thereby becoming less expensive and more reliable. Intelligent display interface graphics coprocessor chips typically perform these functions:

- *Multiple-bit planing* – More than one image can be stored and manipulated logically. Images can be slid in front of or behind other images, lines of parts of images can be hidden by overlaying, and surfaces can be altered in size, shape, and texture.
- *2-D and 3-D image manipulation* – Rotating, scaling, and performing other complex transformations on images.
- *Image enhancement* – Contouring, contrasting, and other processes can be performed on the stored image.
- *Text manipulation* – Some chips even handle text of multiple fonts, sizes, colors, and rotations.

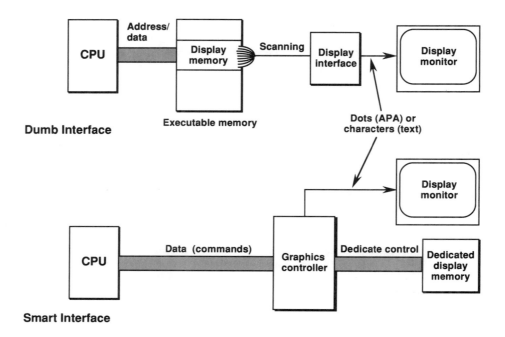

Figure 31. Dumb vs. intelligent display interfaces: The dumb interface makes the CPU do imagery, while the intelligent interface, usually implemented by a graphics coprocessor chip, assumes more of the graphics responsibility itself.

- **Windowing** – Ability to manipulate large screen areas quickly to give objects motion effects.

Of course, a dumb video interface can implement the above functions, but doing so places the entire burden of rotating, windowing, and text generating on the CPU, and these functions become impossibly slow. This fact is painfully obvious to those running CAD software on HB DtCs that incorporate dumb video interfaces.

Often, intelligent display interfaces use multiple VLSI chips, which might be implanted on large circuit boards, with each chip performing a particular function: creating graphics, color tinting, scanning, synchronizing display. In the more expensive EP DtCs, more chip real estate might be found in the intelligent display interface hardware than on the CPU board itself. This is one of the factors that has kept EP computer prices high.

Intel, Texas Instruments, National Semiconductor, and other chip manufacturers have developed powerful graphics coprocessors like the Intel 82786 and TMS 34010 on single chips, or on a few associated chips. These chips have been popular for years in the more expensive EP DtCs; only now are they finding their way into HB DtCs.

Software Support

HB DtCs cannot support good graphics because they do not popularly implement intelligent display interfaces. Developing good software that can take advantage of such an interface is extremely difficult. Why develop such software on DtCs that do not commonly support high-end graphics or whose users do not need high-end graphics? As more powerful graphics functions are consolidated on single chips, high-end graphics functionality will appear on lower-cost HB DtCs, and will also bring the price of engineering workstations down. Also, DtP applications are forcing the high-end graphics performance issue on otherwise graphics-immune users. An example is IBM's XGA smart graphics video interface found on its Model 90 and 95 DtC, which represents an MS-DOS computer climbing up to the EP class of DtCs.

For some time, the EP DtC class has implemented graphics using intelligent display interface hardware to increase graphics performance for the more sophisticated CAD and graphics applications. Due to the diversification of such devices, operating system support is lacking and each device must be supported by specific software drivers. Boards with intelligent display interfaces have been available for several years for the MS-DOS or Macintosh computer, but they are not supported by the low-end software base.

Higher-performance DtC graphics applications involving millions of pixels per second are beyond the capability of any DtC's CPU alone. Higher-performance graphics applications on the HB DtCs will depend on appropriate use of intelligent display interfaces. Moreover, DtCs incorporating intelligent display interfaces implemented by Intel, TI, or some other standardized graphics coprocessor chip set, will be more amenable to a more standardized software base. It is surprising how well the APA Macintosh DtCs make use of their 68xxx CPUs despite popular use of dumb video interfaces.

2.3   Interrupt Controllers

The early XT-class MS-DOS computers had interrupt capabilities exceeding those of the lower-priced Apple, Radio Shack TRS-80, and CP/M DtCs in the early '80s. Newer HB computers use more and higher performance interrupt controllers. For DtCs that use a variety of peripherals, good interrupt performance is essential to allow interleaved processing of multiple independent tasks. As DtCs are integrated into real time process control and data acquisition applications, interrupt handling becomes more important.

Why Interrupt Controllers Are Necessary

Most microprocessors have connections for two hardware interrupts. One of these interrupts, usually called INT, can be enabled or disabled under software control; the other, usually called NMI (non-maskable interrupt), cannot be disabled. The NMI is usually reserved for peripherals to report serious conditions to the CPU, such as memory errors or other faults, to which the CPU responds by shutting itself down. The INT is used to support peripherals when they desire quick action by the CPU. Although there is usually only one INT connection to the microprocessor, there are methodologies by which a single INT can be expanded into multiple interrupts. Figure 32 and the following describe how peripherals can share a single INT line.

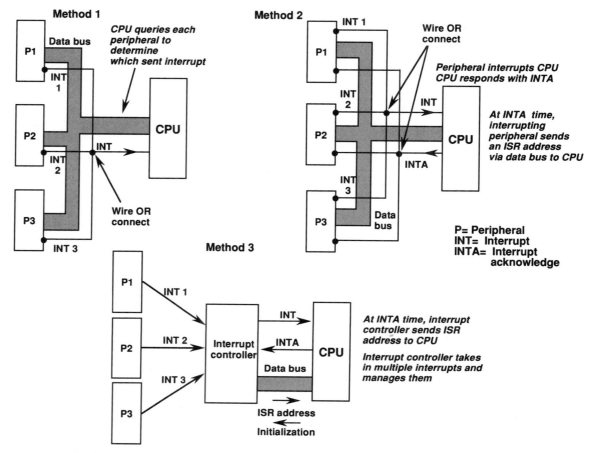

Figure 32. Interrupt methodologies: Method 1 forces the CPU to query each peripheral to find out which one sent the interrupt. The querying is accomplished over the data bus by I/O mapped status registers in each peripheral. In method 2, the peripheral actually sends the interrupt service routine address over the data bus at INTA time (the time when the CPU acknowledges the interrupt and expects such an address). In method 3, the interrupt controller manages all of the interrupts and takes care of sending interrupt addresses, relieving the CPU and peripherals of the responsibility.

■ A wire *OR* connects several output signals to a common input. All wires actually touch, but each output device has special circuitry that prevents cpntention.

1. **Method 1** – Each peripheral connects to the same CPU INT line through a wire OR connection. ■ When a particular peripheral activates the INT line the CPU must first query each peripheral, through I/O registers contained in the peripheral, to determine which one requires service. Once this is ascertained, the appropriate interrupt service routine executes. This method requires no special hardware, but does take longer because the CPU must query each peripheral.

2. **Method 2** – Peripherals supply their own interrupt routine address. As before, all peripherals share the same INT line. In addition, each peripheral has the ability to place an interrupt service routine address on the data bus during interrupt acknowledge time. Following an interrupt, a bused line INTA (interrupt acknowledge)

is issued by the CPU. The peripheral that issued the interrupt will use this signal to place a unique address on the data bus that the CPU will read at INTA time to formulate the address of the interrupt service routine. That routine will then be executed. The problem with this method is that few peripherals have the capability of supplying interrupt addresses in the manner stated. A dot matrix printer, for example, cannot supply its own interrupt address.

3. **Method 3** – An interrupt controller is placed between the peripherals and the single INT line of the CPU. Figure 32 shows the interrupt controller between the CPU and peripherals. The controller provides individual interrupt lines that are bused giving each peripheral its own interrupt line.

The controller issues interrupt service routine addresses during INTA time, freeing peripherals from this function. Each peripheral simply connects to its own unique interrupt line on the controller. The controller issues the interrupt to the CPU and appropriate interrupt address at INTA time depending upon which controller lines are activated. Figure 26 on page 162 shows the interrupt controller, including interrupt signal busing from a system perspective.

Interrupt Controller Functions

It makes sense to centralize the significant interrupt functions into a single chip interrupt controller rather than to have each peripheral perform these functions. Most interrupt controllers can provide the following capabilities:

- **Programming ISR addresses** – The address that will be issued by the controller upon each interrupt is programmable.

- **Masking** – The controller can be programmed to ignore any of its incoming interrupts. For example, you may allow the keyboard interrupt, while disallowing interrupts from the RS-232 serial interface.

- **Setting priorities** – The controller can be programmed to place different priorities on incoming interrupt lines. For example, the controller can assign a higher priority to an interrupt driven by the hard disk than to an interrupt driven by the printer. While the printer service routine executes, the controller will react to a hard disk interrupt, sending the CPU off to service the hard disk. During execution of the hard disk routine, the printer interrupt will be paused until the hard disk interrupt finishes.

The end user does not typically perform the above functions: they are part of the initialization process that occurs when the DtC powers up. BIOS routines oversee the appropriate interrupt controller configuration set up. There are occasions, however, when specialized or aberrant programs might change the configuration. This can cause particularly strange DtC behavior, sometimes requiring repowering to restore the original configuration.

Interrupt controllers can be cascaded to allow even more interrupts. For example, XT-style MS-DOS computers implement a single 8-interrupt controller, while AT-style computers implement two 8-interrupt controllers. With more interrupts to use, there is less of a chance that you will run out of available interrupts. This is one of the many reasons prospective DtC buyers move toward higher-level and more expensive models.

2.4   Counter Timers

Most DtCs implement a VLSI chip that can create general-purpose timing signals. Counter timers are programmable event generators. Whenever a repeating signal or time delay is required, the counter timer can perform this function and free the DtC's CPU to do more important things. Following are examples:

- **Repeating signals** – The counter timer can be programmed to generate repeating signals. For example, the heartbeat interrupt described later is usually triggered by repeating signals from a counter timer. Some system's dynamic memory refreshing is accomplished by repeating signals from a counter timer. Counter timers also generate signals for time keeping and audio prompting signals.

- **Programmed time delays** – Rather than writing software that has your DtC twiddling its thumbs for a time delay, you can use your counter timer. The counter timer can be programmed to count down an internal clock, after which it creates an interrupt. The CPU need only tell the counter timer to start. When the counter timer finishes the countdown, it interrupts the CPU. During the countdown process, the CPU is free to perform other tasks. Some higher-level languages have timer, delay, and sound commands that interact directly with the counter timer, ridding you of the drudgery of having to understand how it works.

Most counter timers have several individual, programmable counters that appear as 16-bit registers to the programmer. Initializing the counter timer consists of programming the registers with numbers constituting the required delays, pulse frequencies, and timing values.

2.5   DMA Controllers

MS-DOS computers were the first personal computers to implement not only interrupt controllers, but also this very important device. The DMA controller moves data between contiguous memory locations and I/O devices, or from one block of contiguous CPU addressable memory to another. The DMA controller is an expert in sequential data transfers to and from contiguous memory locations. It was designed for that purpose. Therefore, the DMA controller provides transfers to and from mass storage devices faster than the general-purpose CPU can. The data to be transferred must be in consecutive memory locations. And if it is, the DMA controller will transfer it very quickly. If the data to be moved is not contiguous in memory, the CPU will have to make the transfer, using CPU port I/O.

Using the DMA controller properly and having a bus structure that supports higher transfer rates will improve system performance significantly. As with the interrupt controller, cascading DMA controllers will provide more channels of DMA. Moving data rapidly about the DtC and its peripherals is essential for real time data acquisition and processing, especially with DBMS packages, which call upon the hard disk to move large amounts of data to and from memory. Provided that these transfers are of consecutive bytes, the DMA controller can transfer them much more efficiently.

The more sophisticated bus structures and other architectural advances found in today's DtCs are beginning to provide a suitable platform for supporting the high data rates possible with DMA controllers. This will give these DtCs the performance required for the more advanced scientific and engineering applications found on the EP DtC class.

Multiple Channels

DMA controllers can provide high-speed transfers for multiple channels. Each channel can support its own transfer and these transfers can occur concurrently. For example, the hard disk moves a block of data into memory, video memory moves a block of information into its memory from system memory, and a program moves a block of data from one part of memory to another. All of this can be happening while the CPU continues to execute its code. Handshaking signals between the CPU and DMA controller orchestrate this movement with the help of the DMA controller expertly interleaving multiple transfer activities. How efficient the DMA controller is with these multiple activities is a sign of its quality. If you were to time how long it took to perform a particular software task with or without a DMA activity going on at the same time, the difference in time would seldom exceed one percent.

What Is a DMA Channel?

Each DMA channel has an individual capability to move data. Behind each channel is a register set that can generate consecutive addresses. These addresses replace addresses that the CPU would ordinarily create.

Each DMA channel has two bus lines dedicated to it. As Figure 33 shows, one line, DRQ, is for the DMA transfer request and the other line, DMA acknowledge, DACK, is for the DMA controller to acknowledge the request and begin the transfer. Since each channel of DMA will use two bus lines, the more DMA channels required, the more bus lines required.

Prior to usage, each DMA channel is initialized for the starting address and the number of bytes to be transferred. If the peripheral wants a transfer from channel 1, it sends a signal on the bused DRQ1 line. Following this, the DMA controller checks with the CPU, and if the CPU is not using the bus, the DMA controller takes over. The DMA controller then activates the DACK1 line, the acknowledge for channel 1, and places the data to be moved on the data bus and the first address on the address bus. The peripheral uses the DACK1 line to gate the data. The cycle repeats for the next consecutive address and so on until the entire transfer has been completed.

As shown in Figure 33, peripherals that incorporate DMA do not use the address bus to select them for connection to the data bus. Instead, DMA peripherals use the DMA request and acknowledge signals for selection and control. The request signal asks for a transfer to take place. The acknowledge signal gates the data that the DMA controller placed on the data bus into or out of the peripheral. The data comes from or goes to consecutive locations in a block of memory somewhere in the DtC, a byte at a time.

┌── **NOTE** ──┐

Read and *write* DMA transfers can be made. The read transfer sends data to the peripheral from consecutive memory locations while the write transfer sends data to consecutive memory locations from the peripherals. Reading or writing is from the memory's standpoint and the distinction is accomplished by the system's read/write control lines. In

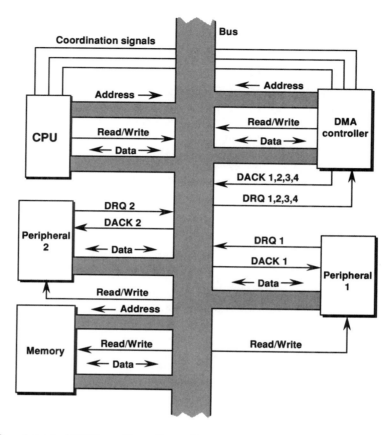

Figure 33. A typical DMA configuration: For sequential data transfers the DMA controller takes control of the bus and moves data between memory and peripherals.

addition to commandeering the system's address and data lines, the DMA controller also commandeers the read and write control lines.

The above DMA data transfer scenario might sound a bit confusing. DMA is nothing more than a communications methodology between peripherals requiring data and a device (the DMA controller) that can supply the data faster than the CPU to contiguous memory locations. A DMA controller has the following character-istics:

- *Burst rate* – How fast can it transfer data in burst mode? A DMA controller can be programmed to not demand a DRQ request for each byte transferred but rather to move data quickly following the first DRQ request.

- *Memory to memory transfer* – Can the controller move data between two ad-dressable memory blocks? Some MS-DOS computers, notably the XT style, cannot perform this essential function.

- *Data width* – What is the DMA controller's data width? XT-style MS-DOS comput-ers have 8-bit capability, while the AT-style computers have 16-bit capability.

- **Number of channels** – How many channels of DMA does the DtC support? XT-style computers support four channels with one while AT-style computers support eight channels through two DMA controllers.

- **Addressability** – How many bytes can be transferred sequentially? Many MS-DOS computers, notably 8088- and 80286-based DtCs, cannot transfer more than 64K at a time.

- **Handshaking** – What kind of signals from the controller are bused? Can it notify the bus when it is done; can it control interrupts?

- **Scattering/gathering** – Some DMA controllers can actually spray data into and out of memory in a more sophisticated manner than a sequential transfer. But, it will never be as flexible as the DtC CPU.

2.6   Math Coprocessors

The decade of the 1980s has seen a thousandfold increase in the numerical processing capability of DtCs. Through appropriate use of math-coprocessor hardware, a relatively inexpensive HB DtC can have math performance to rival a minicomputer.

The CPU of a DtC is a general-purpose processing device that excels in the overall management of system resources, program execution, and data management; it is not specialized for math. It will never perform math as successfully as a device designed specifically for math functions.

Most CPUs can add, subtract, multiply, and divide. Due to the CPU's internal ALU bit-width limitations, usually 32 bits, only limited precision can be obtained. Greater precision can be achieved through repetitive algorithms that manipulate more bits a few at a time.

Floating point math can allow very large numbers using a limited number of bits. In floating point math, a few exponent bits represent a power of ten while more mantissa bits represent the actual number by which the exponent multiplies. The mantissa bits carry the precision while the exponent bits carry the size, thus attaining a balanced compromise between size and precision.

Whether high precision or large numbers are the focus, the associated binary operations necessary when the data width is limited are cumbersome and time-consuming. Worse, to do exponential and trigonometric transcendental functions, the already overworked CPU must perform hundreds of add, subtract, multiply, and divide operations just for a single function calculation.

For example, a power series function for *sin(x)* is:

$$\sin(x) = \frac{1}{X^3} - \frac{1}{X^5} + \frac{1}{X^7}$$

and on to an infinite number of terms. To obtain accuracy and precision, a large number of terms must be included. Notice how each term requires an increasing number of multiplications ($X^7 = X * X * X * X * X * X * X$).

Math coprocessors supplement the CPU by taking over math functions. Most math coprocessors operate in conjunction with the CPU. Cooperation is attained through control signals between it and the CPU. See Figure 26. In some systems, the 80xxx coprocessors for example, the math coprocessor's instructions are intermixed with the CPU's ordinary instructions. The coprocessor recognizes these instructions and takes over for the CPU, not only performing the associated math much faster, but also letting the CPU continue to perform its own functions in parallel. If a math coprocessor is not installed in the DtC, other means, such as extra CPU software must be provided to do math.

Today's math coprocessors perform the common add, subtract, multiply, and divide functions much quicker than the CPU, but this is only the beginning. In addition they perform transcendental functions, hyperbolic functions, logical functions, max and min functions, modulus, and many other popular general-purpose math functions. Moreover, they do this at high precision *and* in one fell swoop.

Most software can recognize whether or not you have a math coprocessor installed and provide the appropriate code for either possibility. Numerical performance of DtCs has improved by a factor of several thousand over the last decade. The table below compares the 8-bit Z80, popularized in the Radio Shack TRS-80, with the latest Intel CPUs and coprocessors.

Numerical Performance Comparisons

Z80 8-bit CPU/no coprocessor	2K Whetstone
8088 CPU/8087 coprocessor	20K
80286 CPU/80287 coprocessor	200K
80386 CPU/80387 coprocessor	2M
80386 CPU/83D87 coprocessor	3M
80386 CPU/Weitek 3167 coprocessor	5M
80486 CPU/Weitek 4167 coprocessor	15M
80860 CPU/has coprocessor	20M Whetstone

■ *Whetstone* is a standard performance benchmark for mathematical floating point operations, expressed as whetstones per second.

For purposes of comparison, the 10-20M Whetstone figures are comparable in performance to a DEC VAX 9000 series minicomputer costing hundreds of thousands of dollars.■

Acquiring a Math Coprocessor

Since a coprocessor sells for several hundred dollars, you need to choose it carefully. Determining whether or not you need a math coprocessor is relatively simple: Is your application math oriented, does it support a math coprocessor, and does it operate sufficiently faster to justify the cost of the coprocessor? While an 8087 math coprocessor might cost you only $50, it can improve an 8088-based XT's math performance considerably for those applications that know how to use it. For higher-end coprocessors, you can easily spend from $200–$2000 depending on the vendor, type, speed, and system integration.

Be aware that some applications may require specialized math capability beyond that of your math coprocessor. Many different types of specialized computational add-ons can be found, some of which are described later.

Math coprocessors usually plug into available sockets in the DtC. The math coprocessor may not be the remedy you thought if other factors are not considered when putting a total system together. The coprocessor may be able to perform math quickly, but the arguments and answers must still be moved to and from the coprocessor by the CPU. Therefore, your math coprocessor can benefit from many of the traditional system performance enhancements. These include cache memory, interleaved memory, bus performance, DMA capability, fast interrupt response and other features that speed up a CPU's ability to move data quickly. All can supplement the math coprocessor's quick math capability.

Different Types of Coprocessors

For this discussion we look at the popular Intel coprocessors found in MS-DOS computers.

Stock coprocessors: Those manufactured by Intel for supplementing their own line of microprocessors. For the 8088 microprocessor there is the 8087 coprocessor; the 80287 and 80387 coprocessors are for 80286 and 80386 microprocessors respectively. Intel's 80486 microprocessor has an 80387-compatible coprocessor built into the CPU. The Intel 80860 RISC CPU also has a built-in coprocessor. Neither the 80860 nor its internal coprocessor are compatible with their previous Intel counterparts.

The stock coprocessor will serve you well if:

- Spreadsheets are getting large and recalculation time is becoming a problem.
- You are experimenting with fractals, which require highly repetitive calculations.
- You operate the conventional software base that supports the standard Intel coprocessors.

Improved stock coprocessors: Manufactured by other vendors, these coprocessors are object-compatible; they execute the same instructions identically with the Intel coprocessor, but are faster and/or achieve higher precision. The CYRIX FasMath 83D87 is such a coprocessor. Its 90-bit precision exceeds that of the Intel 80387's 80 bits and it is said to be two to three times faster. Of course, you will have to pay more for the performance, and there is always the risk of incompatibility with future software written for the Intel coprocessor even though the current software base may be well tested for compatibility.

If you are a serious math user, and you are willing to spend more money, an improved coprocessor is for you. You will still have compatibility with the conventional software base.

Special coprocessors: Vendors produce coprocessors with better capabilities in certain areas (such as vector math). For example, the Weitek 3167/4167 coprocessors are not compatible with the Intel 80387 but outperform it in many math functions. The Weitek is a memory-mapped device, supporting a 64K array space in the DtC system's memory map. From a hardware point of view, because the Weitek sockets are supersets of the 80387 socket, the same socket can accommodate either chip. The chips are not software compatible; each chip requires its own software support. Some DtCs have sockets for both Intel and Weitek processors and can operate both concurrently.

If you require the specialized capabilities of this processor, you should purchase the specialized software and compilers that take advantage of its capabilities.

Precision vs. Speed

The Intel coprocessors have at least 80 bits of internal precision, and can perform high precision calculations much more quickly than the CPU. This can result in a speed-up of orders of magnitude compared to the CPU's capability. Many applications do not require such high precision; graphics or FFT (fast Fourier transforms). Many coprocessors, Weitek for example, support 64 bits of precision and have modes for 32 bits. This speeds them up considerably, and makes them more appropriate for applications where speed, not precision, is essential.

So, how much faster will your software run? Just because a coprocessor could perform a *sin(x)* function a thousand times faster than the CPU doesn't mean that CAD software is going to run a thousand times faster. In addition to the CPU performing non-math functions during a CAD session, even math-specific functions need considerable overhead. For example, the CPU must assemble arguments that exceed the system data width a piece at a time for transmission to the coprocessor. An 80-bit argument will require three 32-bit words on an 80386 DtC and six 16-bit words on an 80286 DtC. The answer must also be handled piecemeal.

Piecemeal transfers as well as other problems will affect the math processing speed. You may notice when recalculating a large spreadsheet or performing a large matrix inversion with MathCad software that response is significantly below the actual difference in a function compute time. Count on the coprocessor to improve a DtC's math performance by a factor of from 3 to 10. A ratio of 10 to 1 is equivalent to the difference between an hour of computing time and only six minutes.

Software Compatibility

The Intel coprocessors are object-compatible as we go up the line just as their respective CPUs are object-compatible. Improved coprocessors have demonstrated high levels of software compatibility with slight differences in such things as round-off error where they tend to be better than their Intel counterparts. Deliberately different coprocessors (such as the Weitek) are not software compatible and require their own specific compilers and applications. This is worthwhile, however, when you consider their enhanced performance in math areas, particularly in vector processing.

2.7   RS-232 Serial Interface Chips

The RS-232 serial interface, described later in the interfaces section, is often implemented on a single VLSI chip. The early terminology for such single chip serial interfaces was UART (universal asynchronous receiver transmitter), while today's devices are called ACIAs (asynchronous communication interface adapter). The latter are more sophisticated and include additional enhancements such as interrupt control, and programmable bit rate generators not found on the earlier UARTs.

■ BIOS is the basic I/O system software. It is often referred to as the kernel.

ACIA chips are quite reliable and relatively simple to program. They have programmable bit rates, programmable interrupts, and a variety of other special functions that can communicate with a modem. Basic support for these chips will be found in BIOS since these chips are usually an integral part of the DtC system.■ MS-DOS computers, for example, incorporate the very popular National Semiconductor 8250 and 16450 ACIA chips. Often due to performance or more sophisticated needs, the serial interface may need to be supported by a different more sophisticated chip. In these cases, special drivers will be required and compatibility problems are likely to occur since most software must communicate with the serial interface and this communication is often specific to the National Semiconductor chips.

The ACIA chip is isolated from serial interface connectors by receiver and driver chips. These driver chips are what usually become damaged by electrical storms or other static discharges. Those who like to fix their own systems should purchase serial interfaces where these chips are socketed so that they can be replaced. Don't be too concerned if your serial interface is on a plug-in board; these boards may cost only $20. But if the serial interface is an integral part of the DtC motherboard, the driver chips cannot be easily replaced. Fixing a bad driver in that case could mean replacing the entire motherboard.

2.8   Chip Consolidation

Chip manufacturers now produce on a single VLSI die most of the logic circuitry, often called random logic glue, necessary to combine the various major chips found separately in today's DtCs. The manner in which this is done can affect compatibility. Now such previously separate functions as the RS-232 interface, Centronics parallel interface, interrupt controller, DMA controller, cache controller, and address decoding are colocated on single VLSI chips.

Integration results in a smaller motherboard and higher reliability. Today's DtC motherboards are scarcely larger than the page you are reading and fit into a compact profile cases that take up only a small portion of your desktop. Miniaturization can be credited to consolidation of random logic functions onto single VLSI chips. The trend of functional consolidation will continue until all of a DtC's functionality is on a single chip. Already, the CPU, math coprocessor, and graphics coprocessor are consolidated on the 80860 CPU.

Occasionally, compatibility differences can occur when the relatively standardized VLSI chips such as DMA controllers and interrupt controllers are combined into single chips, particularly in the area of chip initialization. Hopefully, each DtC system's BIOS will account for the differences and software will use BIOS functions to initialize these chips. If software talks directly to these devices rather than using the BIOS for isolation, then software could be rendered system specific. A host of insidious problems show up when reverse-engineered consolidated chips are slightly different from their original counterparts. As always, be sure that the intended software operates correctly on the intended DtC model.

Chip consolidation is a particular problem in the MS-DOS computer category due to the large number of producers, each manufacturing their own particular motherboards. There are currently thousands of U.S., Japanese, and Asian producers of MS-DOS computers, each company with its own mix of chip consolidations. Several vendors, OPTI for example, or Chips and Technologies, produce relatively standardized consolidated chip sets.

3.0 CPU Addressing and Device Selection

The most fundamental concept at work in your microcomputer is how communication between the CPU and the rest of the system is orchestrated. If all components match each other well, you will realize the best performance your DtC can offer. If an underpowered or mismatched component should happen to be in the way, a chokepoint is created in the system and performance will suffer.

Everything that we hook up to a microcomputer – whether it be memory, hard disk interfaces, printers, or mice – needs to be able to communicate with the CPU. In order for the CPU to contact its empire of slave devices, the CPU must know where to reach each device. A scheme known as addressing provides location information. Just as every home and office has a unique postal address, every microcomputer device must have a unique address. This address, or binary identifier, is used by the CPU, by way of the bus, to call up and connect to each device whenever communication is needed.

In the paragraphs that follow, the intent is to provide a strong technical understanding of the concept of addressing and device selection. Such an understanding is fundamental to much of what follows in this chapter. Particularly this is:

- *How the CPU selects memory and devices* – The CPU selects memory cells as well as peripheral devices using its addressing capability. Later, when we discuss interfacing, we will need a clear understanding of device selection with the CPU.

- *The importance of the CPU's addressing capability* – The CPU is the overall system manager, so most system performance capabilities hinge on the CPU's capability of getting at or addressing the many devices in the DtC.

- *Directly vs. indirectly addressable memory* – We need a firm technical foundation to be able to understand the difference between directly addressable (primary) and indirectly addressable (secondary) memory. Understanding at this level will help you to appreciate the complex tradeoffs of using both memory types.

3.1 Binary Signals

What address lines actually carry are binary signals that can either be in a "1" state or a "0" state.

The decimal value of a binary number is obtained by multiplying the weights of each bit by the bit coefficient and adding the results. The weight of each binary place is 2 raised to the power of the bit position's number. You can see that the bits further to the left carry more weight, which is why they are called *most significant*. The bits to the right carry less weight, and are thus called *least significant*. Let's look at the binary number 10011 and see what makes it equal to 19 decimal:

Binary Numbers

1	0	0	1	1	Binary Number
4	3	2	1	0	Bit Position
2^4	2^3	2^2	2^1	2^0	Bit Weight
16	8	4	2	1	Decimal/Bit value
1(16)	+0(8)	+0(4)	+1(2)	+ 1(1)	Add weights
16	**+0**	**+0**	**+2**	**+1**	**= 19 Decimal Equivalent**

If we look at the highest number representable with 5 binary places, we would have the binary number 11111 or

16	+8	+4	+2	+1 = 31

Counting 00000 as a number, we therefore have 32 possible binary numbers (or states) that can be represented by a 5 place binary number (or $2^n = 2^5 = 32$).

Next we need to know that the address lines in a digital computer can carry two different signals: a 0 and a 1. The 0 is usually represented by a voltage between 0 and 0.8 volts and the 1 is represented by a voltage between 2.5 and 5 volts. Selection devices, such as the NAND gates depicted in Figure 34 use these signals as their inputs. We now have one of the keys to understanding addressability and device selection. We know how many different quantities (or addresses) can be represented or selected by *n* address lines. That quantity is 2^n.

> **NOTE**
>
> The actual number of possible addresses is obtained by counting the number of address lines and raising two to the power of that number. In a two state system, 2^n values can be specified using *n* wires. Thus, the 8088 with 20 address lines directly addresses 2^{20} or 1 MB of memory.

Before going on to device selection, let's conclude with a look at decimal and hex (hexadecimal) numbers. The table in the margin shows the relationship between decimal, binary, and hexadecimal numbers.◼

Hex	Binary	Decimal
0	0000	0
1	0001	1
2	0010	2
3	0011	3
4	0100	4
5	0101	5
6	0110	6
7	0111	7
8	1000	8
9	1001	9
A	1010	10
B	1011	11
C	1100	12
D	1101	13
E	1110	14
F	1111	15

Decimal Numbers

In the decimal system, numbers behave like this:

4	5	2	0	6	Digit Number
4	3	2	1	0	Digit Position
10^4	10^3	10^2	10^1	10^0	Digit Weight
10000	1000	100	10	1	Decimal Value
4(10000)	5(1000)	2(100)	0(10)	6(1)	Add Weights
40000	**+5000**	**+200**	**+0**	**+6**	**= 45,206**

We use the same process for a binary and a decimal number. The difference is that the weights of each coefficient are obtained by raising 10 to the power of the digit number position.

Hex Numbers

The hexadecimal number system is based on 16, represented by digits 0 through 9 and characters A through F. Each hex character has a four-place binary counterpart. In the hex system, hex 0 is equivalent to binary 0000 or decimal 0, hex 2 is equivalent to binary 0010 or decimal 2, and hex F is equivalent to binary 1111 or decimal 15. For example, the expression 1011 stands for

```
(1 x 8) + (0 x 4) + (1 x 2) + (1 x 1) =
8 + 0 + 2 + 1 = 11 = B HEX.
```

The hexadecimal system raises 16 to the power of the digit place. The hex number 9EAB would be:

(9)	(E)	(A)	(B)
$9(16^3)$	$+14(16^2)$	$10(16^1)$	$11(16^0)$
9(4096)	+14(256)	+10(16)	+11(1)
?	?	?	?	*Use your calculator*

We have seen what constitutes a binary number, and we can now imagine binary signals appearing on CPU address lines. Binary signals are used on the address lines for the sole purpose of selection. The selection process is for two main purposes: fetching instructions and moving data.

NOTE

Other bus masters can control address lines. The DMA controller is one possible bus master. Some DtCs provide additional bus signals that can allow a number of different bus masters to have control of the bus according to an arbitration scheme.

What Is Selection?

Here's how selection works. Every device that needs to communicate with the CPU comes with a logic circuit that is connected to the address bus. In each case, the logic is designed to respond only to a specific address. When a given device recognizes its address, the device connects to the data bus to communicate and perform its function. Depending on the state of additional control lines (read/write), communication proceeds either to the device from the CPU (write), or from the device to the CPU (read). Figure 27 on page 164 shows several devices connected in that manner. Since there is only one data bus between the devices and the CPU, only one device at a time can be selected or on line.

A Detailed Selection Example

As mentioned previously, the CPU selects devices using its address lines. Figure 34 displays a detailed example of the process of device selection using a simple three-address system.

Address Lines			State
A_2	A_1	A_0	
0	0	0	0
0	0	1	1
0	1	0	2
0	1	1	3
1	0	0	4
1	0	1	5
1	1	0	6
1	1	1	7
0	0	0	8

This lowly three-address system can only contain 8 devices. Since $n = 3$, the address lines can have as many as 2^3 or 8 different logic states. The 8 different states are shown in the margin.■

Figure 34 shows the 8 possible devices that are to be selectable by the CPU; each connected to selection logic that can decode (or detect) a unique address. Note that when a device gets selected, it can then communicate with the data bus.

The Decoding Process

To understand the decoding process, we need to know how the selection logic, the NAND gates shown in Figure 34, perform the job.

Notice the CS on each device has a bar over it. The bar designates an active low condition. The active low condition means that when the connected wire, normally in a logic 1 state, goes to the low logic state, the device will be selected. Now let's see what it takes for any given CS input to change from a 1 to a 0.

The NAND gate

To know what makes the CS input go to a 0, we need to understand how the NAND gate works. The NAND gate is really an AND gate with an inverter. The inverter is shown as a bubble at the tip of the NAND gate. The reader may be more familiar with the AND function, which yields a 1 when all of its inputs are 1.

The NAND gate will yield the necessary logic 0 output only when all of its inputs are logic 1. Not just one or two, but all of the inputs. Note that the inputs to the NAND gate are connected either directly or by inverters to the address bus.

Recall that when the inputs to a device's NAND gate are all 1, will the device get selected. Next, look at the device at address 2 (binary 010). This NAND gate

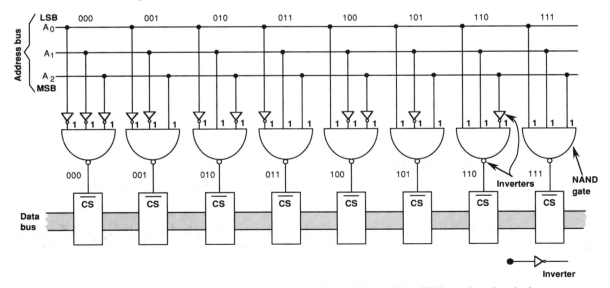

Figure 34. Selecting devices through address decoding: The CPU reaches its devices through a process known as address decoding. An address is sent, it is recognized by the device selection logic, and the selected device communicates.

has inverters appropriately placed on address lines A0 and A2 so that when the requisite 010 appears on the address bus, the two 0s are converted to 1s. The A1 line is already a 1 and is connected directly to its NAND gate input. We now have a system of logic that will recognize a 2 on the address bus. The 2 will cause the inputs of the NAND gate connected to the device at "2" to all become 1s; the NAND gate output will go to 0, and the device at "2" will get selected. What places the 010 on the address bus? The CPU or DMA controller, of course.

The Tristate Condition

What does it really mean to select a device? When we say a device is selected, it is meant that it is actually connected to the data bus. Therefore, there must be a method that would electrically allow a given device to connect to the data bus when selected. This method is known as tristate logic. Only one device at a time can connect. To connect two devices would be like asking several people the same question and trying to hear everyone's answer at once.

Bistate logic can produce 1s or 0s for communications states. Tristate logic has a third state as well. In this third state, the logic is actually electrically disconnected and unable to transmit either a 1 or a 0. It behaves as though it were detached from the bus, thereby allowing another device elsewhere in the system to be connected, not tristated, to the bus. In fact, only one device at a time is ever connected; all others are tristated. As the CPU executes instructions, the tristate on/off process occurs millions of times per second as memory is executed and data is sent throughout the system.

The CPU can write to several devices simultaneously without bus contention problems. The tristate concept really applies to CPU read operations. When reading, it cannot tolerate more than one device at a time trying to communicate.

Address Decoding Saves Wires

The process by which the NAND gates detect one of eight possible devices according to only three wires is known as address decoding. With only a three-line system, you might have a problem appreciating the utility of address decoding. But, imagine if you had 16 million different devices to select, as would be the case in an 80286-based microcomputer. Were it not for the fact that 16 million different unique addresses could be encoded on 16 address wires, to be decoded at each device location, the 16 MB system would require 16 million wires; each to select one device or memory cell.

Pursuing the principle of decoding further and looking at a more realistic 16 MB memory system, see Figure 35.

3.2   Effective Addresses and Addressing Modes

Now that we've seen how the CPU address lines select devices, we need to know why and how the CPU develops these addresses. The address lines and selection process described previously are used for two main purposes: fetching instructions and moving data.

Fetching Instructions

Sequential address are used for executing programs. Programs consist of memory bytes or words that must be accessed and read into the CPU sequentially. Normally, the CPU sequences its address lines as instructions are fetched from memory, one after the other. The instructions usually come in two parts; an operation code, and an operand. The op code tells the CPU what kind of operation to perform, and the operand tells it what number to use. In many cases, the operand specifies an address to which the CPU is directed to send or receive data. Thus, we arrive at the next important use of addressing; moving data.

Moving Data

Program instructions usually call for the CPU to fetch data from the outside world (read), or to send something to the outside world (write). The address of the device to which the CPU is to communicate is usually contained in a previously fetched program instruction, and now the CPU is responding to the instruction. The address can also be derived. Such an address that targets data is known as an *effective address*.

Effective Addresses

A CPU's capability of developing effective addresses, called its addressing mode capability, is a critically important CPU performance attribute. After all, this is the CPU's only means for directing where it receives and sends data.

The effective address can be considered the target of a CPU action. It is the address where important data is sent or received. This address could signify a memory location or a device. Sometimes, the effective address is located in the actual instruction stream and is called an immediate address. For more flexibility, the effective address might be calculated by the CPU based on the contents of other addresses.

For example, effective addresses can be created by adding the contents of different memory locations (basing), or by getting the address from memory locations pointed to by other memory locations (indirection), or by creating the addresses based on the contents of memory locations a number of locations away from a given memory location (indexing), or even by a combination of indexed and indirect. The different modes of creating effective addresses are known as the CPU's addressing modes. The more flexible it is at creating effective addresses, the better the CPU.

3.3   Addressing Summary

A methodology has been described that allows your CPU to communicate with a number of devices through a process known as addressing. The CPU reaches its memory and peripherals by specifying on its address bus an encoded address that all devices watch for. When a given device address comes up, a selection process begins and the device is able to communicate over the data bus. In this way an orderly flow of information from a myriad of different devices can proceed in the computer. The addressing capability of the CPU is an important attribute for describing it.

4.0 Memory

Appropriate memory usage and management by applications software and the operating system is essential to successfully implement the DtC. Proper configuration of memory – having the right kind in the right amount in the right place – will turn a computing bane into a computing boon.

Unfortunately, one can't run down to the neighborhood computer store, buy a pound or two of memory, and happily ever after run applications. Memory configuring requires understanding of hardware and software capabilities and limitations. You will need to recognize the different kinds of memory chips and their speeds. Also, you will need to look at memory from the application and operating system points of view. Finally, you will need to consider the many ways to support and enhance memory. Discussions include:

- *Physical memory* – Looking at memory at the chip level.
- *Primary and secondary memory* – The competing uses of primary executable memory and types of non-executable secondary memory.
- *CPU memory support* – Different CPU's capabilities of addressing and supporting memory as well as constraints imposed by the operating system.
- *MS-DOS memory* – The different forms of MS-DOS computer memory, expanded and extended.
- *Memory enhancement* – How to enhance the existing memory support provided by the operating system.

As a rule: the faster the memory, the higher the price. There is more to memory, however, than cost and speed. We will first look at the chips and types of memory found in a system unit and on peripheral interfaces. Next, we will discuss memory concepts. Finally, we offer various methodologies for maximizing use of executable memory in today's DtCs, focusing on MS-DOS compatibles where memory problems are the most critical.

4.1 Physical Memory

Although the subject of memory can be treated at many different levels, its physical form – the chips that you plug into the motherboard – are of two primary types: RAM and ROM.

RAM (Read/Write Memory)

RAM is where your programs and data are executed. Contrary to the opinion of many computer users, the term *RAM* does not stand for random access memory, and if it does, it ought not to. The expansion is misleading; both RAM and ROM are random access, also called directly addressable, memory. RAM and ROM got caught up in the industry's penchant for acronyms and ROM has the misfortune of appearing not to be randomly accessible even though it actually is. The real difference between RAM and ROM is that RAM can be written to while ROM is read-only. RAM can be changed by simply writing over its previous contents. Current DtCs require anywhere from 256K to 64 MB of RAM. RAM memory comes in two major types: *dynamic* and *static*. The dynamic is the common memory where programs and data reside, while the faster static memory is for special-purpose functions such as execution and disk caches, and fast video memory.

Dynamic RAM

When you load programs, create datasets, and multitask programs, you are doing this in dynamic RAM (DRAM) memory. When you upgrade your DtC from 1 MB to 4 MB to 16 MB and higher, you are adding DRAM memory. Most DtC memory is dynamic. Dynamic RAM (DRAM) provides high-density, low-cost, and low power-consuming RAM. This is not without penalty. Dynamic RAM can be thought of as a capacitor, which slowly discharges and periodically needs a refreshing charge. Dynamic memory is refreshed by reading it periodically. This refresh activity is done transparently by hardware in the DtC and is usually of no concern to you or your applications software. In most DtCs, the refreshing function never consumes more than 1% of a CPU's processing. In some rare cases, applications programs interfere with the refresh process and cause a system to crash.■ Another penalty of dynamic RAM is its slower access time compared to static RAM.

■ For example, memory to memory transfers using the DMA controller on an XT-style computer will interfere with the refreshing process also supported by the DMA controller.

> **NOTE**
>
> *Random access time* is the time it takes for data to become valid once addressed in memory. Typical access times for DtC DRAM memories are from 70 nsec in 33 MHz 486-based DtCs to the slower 300 nsec DRAM used in the older 5 MHz 8088-based PCs. Static memories can have access times below 10 nsec, while ROM access time is between 200 and 500 nsec. Although the memory speed is most related to CPU clock speed (the faster the CPU, the quicker must be the access time), there are other factors that might need to be considered. These factors include memory location, vendor type, and whether or not the DtC implements wait states.

DRAM has been quadrupling in density approximately once every two years. Currently, 1-4 Mbit DRAMs are popular and 16-64 Mbit DRAMs are being developed. Most DtC RAM memory comes on small circuit boards with a byte (8 bits plus 1 parity bit) of DRAM on each board. These boards, known as SIMMs (single inline memory module), plug into connector strips on most DtC motherboards and this is typically how you add memory. There are two different kinds of SIMM: one type with a PC board edge, and the other type, called a SIP, with protruding pins. The SIP is the more reliable of the two, but it is more difficult to plug in. Not long ago, DtC memory was added by plugging memory boards into the standard bus connectors or special daughter boards on custom connectors.■

■ Certain types of memory (expanded) are still added in this fashion.

Divorcing memory expansion from the bus connectors allows a more intimate interface between memory and CPU. Some DtCs access DRAM memory on alternate clock cycles, or alternate DRAM banks through a process called *interleaving*, to improve memory access speed. Add-on memory expansion cards seldom allow this type of access. Usually, you need a certain minimum amount of memory in order to have two main banks to alternate. The minimum amount may be 1 MB, 4 MB, or 8 MB.

Since SIMMs ordinarily plug into a DtC's motherboard, an important shopping point becomes the amount of this memory the motherboard will hold. On 32-bit systems, you need to add memory in 32-bit wide chunks to get the necessary 32-bit wide memory. RAM comes in 4-byte wide increments. For example:

1 MB = four 256K by 9-bit modules
4 MB = four 1 MB by 9-bit modules
8 MB = two groups of four 1 MB by 9-bit modules

Most motherboards will permit at least 16 MB to be plugged in, although some others will have you plug 8 MB into the motherboard and the other 8 MB into a 32-bit bus connector board. This board-connected memory will cost more due to the additional plug-in board. If you plan to go to 16 MB or beyond, choose a motherboard that will let you go that far with motherboard plug-in SIMMs.

At midyear 1991, IBM and Siemens AG, a major German electronics firm, announced a joint venture to manufacture some of the world's most advance computer chips, among which is a 16 MB DRAM. This additional competition should have a positive effect on Intel, Motorola, and other chip manufacturers.

The cost of DRAM is now around $50-$70 per megabyte, with its per-byte cost continuing to drop while its density (bits per chip) continues to increase. It is, therefore, truly one of today's better bargains.

Static RAM

Static RAM is super fast read/write memory with much quicker access times than DRAM memory. Static RAM is available with access times as low as 10 nsec. Its quick access time allows static RAM to operate at much higher clock frequencies than DRAM. Faster sequencing provides commensurately faster program and data execution in static memory. Static RAM acts like a latch – it does not discharge its contents – and therefore does not require refreshing. It uses more power, costs more, has quicker access times, and is found in DtCs in which performance is an important consideration. As we shall discuss later, many DtCs permit use of this very fast static RAM for performance-improving hardware disk and execution caches.

Due to different types, speeds, applications, and complications, as well as the need to plan for the future, DRAM and static RAM should be added only with the advice of competent professionals.

> **EXAMPLE**
>
> If you are planning to upgrade a 25 MHz 80386 DtC to a 33 MHz model, you should buy a 70 rather than an 80 nsec DRAM chip. If you continue using the 80 nsec chip, you may need to operate that DtC using wait states to slow it.

ROM (Read Only Memory)

ROM is where the vital system-support software is located, regardless of the type of operating system or application software you are running. You can think of ROM as having intrinsic design characteristics. Every time you power up your system, those ROM characteristics will come into play.

ROM contains routines that initialize the motherboard's auxiliary chips, test the memory, and support the more common serial and parallel interfaces. This hardware will always be a part of the DtC, so it makes sense to place its support in firmware. ■

■ Firmware is a term used for software that is hard-wired or permanently burned into ROM. Firmware is hard software.

NOTE

The EP DtC class and most minicomputers incorporate ROM in order to bootstrap the larger I/O support system – the kernel – to RAM from the hard disk. Most HB DtCs incorporate a large portion of their I/O system BIOS in ROM. Apple, Commodore, and Atari EE computers consider graphics and user interface support as fundamental as I/O support and place it also in ROM.

BIOS routines used most often, such as hard disk and video display interface support, are copied into a DRAM called shadow RAM. Access times for DRAM are shorter than for ROM, so performance of the hard disk and video support routines will improve.

Figure 44 shows a separation between motherboard components and the slots that the peripherals plug into. Many peripheral interface boards contain their own ROMs for support of their built-in functions. Video interface, hard disk interface, or that special voice recognition board will likely have its own dedicated ROM for initialization and support. When operating such add-ons, you will have to be concerned that memory space occupied by its ROMs do not conflict with one another or conflict with your system BIOS ROM or DRAM.

EPROM (Electrically Programmable Read Only Memory)

Whereas ROMs must be programmed at the factory, a special type of ROM known as EPROM can be erased and reprogrammed by you. Such ROMS come in 16, 32, 64, 128, 256 and 512K byte sizes. With a hardware add-on board available at most computer dealers for less than $100, you can program your own EPROMS, electrically, using included software. Additional sockets allow such conveniences as copying other EPROMs or ROMs. To erase the EPROM, you need to expose it to ultraviolet light. UV erasers cost about $50. Most EPROMS are pin for pin compatible with the ROM chips that they can replace. For those who don't like the way their ROMS behave, new BIOS ROMS can be programmed in EPROM. Programming a ROM is at best difficult and copyright infringement is a possibility. Many DtC ROM BIOS and peripheral BIOS ROMs are already of the EPROM type to allow easier upgrading.

EAROM (Electrically Alterable Read Only Memory)

Another form of ROM known as EAROM adds to EPROM the capability of electrical erasure. Special hardware is not required to operate EAROM chips and they are often used as nonvolatile RAM memory in notebook computers. Writing to EAROM takes milliseconds, but reading is fast. EAROM is best used for storage of important utilities or small datasets.

Memory Failures and Testing

Although today's memory technology has come a long way, you may still experience memory problems. The following are some of the many factors that need to be considered when evaluating memory reliability and performance.

- *Different vendors* – Different vendor's RAM chips are not the same. Reliability varies, so buy RAM from manufacturers with proven chip technology track records, or from manufacturers your friends have used with satisfactory results in similar environments. Popular names, such as Texas Instruments, Motorola, and the Japanese NEC (Nippon Electric Corporation) DRAM have reputations for reliability. RAMs of less well-known manufacturers may be less expensive, but may not be as well tested.

- *Wrong access time* – Fast CPU clocks need equally fast RAM access times. Selective wait stating can be used to slow the CPU down for slower memory areas, but this defeats the purpose of having a fast CPU.

> **NOTE**
>
> Wait states can be selectively inserted for particular (slow) memory areas or peripheral interfaces. This slows the CPU only when a particular memory or interface is accessed. Otherwise the CPU runs at full speed.

- *Conflicts* – Peripheral memory is often inadvertantly mapped to the same addresses as system DRAM or other interface memory. The resulting conflicts can cause the DtC to appear as though it had a bad memory, when in fact two areas of memory are fighting over bus control.

- *Memory testing* – The only sure way to test memory is to operate memory similar to the way your programs do. Most memory testing programs simply write to, then read memory locations. Code execution causes a different type of memory flexing. Therefore, many memory test programs do not flush out the problems that will occur when you run programs.

- *Interface board memory conflicts* – Interface boards will often require static or fast DRAM memory to accomplish their buffering and execution. Often this memory is shared because it is also addressed and accessed by the DtC's CPU. This memory is also subject to the CPU's memory access speed, and inadequate access times can cause problems. For example, the video interface may have worked on the 12 MHz 80286-based DtC, but it may not work on your new 33 MHz 80486-based DtC even though it plugs into the bus just fine. Problems such as flickering, and missed pixels on the video display can be due to slow memory on the display interface. System crashes can result from improperly-configured interface board ROM memory.

4.2 Primary vs. Secondary Memory

You can conceptualize memory as something that resides in a hardware component or as an operating system resource. Both views will be useful later when we begin to examine memory management methodologies. When trying to understand how a DtC uses memory, it is best to think of memory as existing in two forms. These forms and their specific functions are:

- **_Primary, directly accessible, memory_** – Primary memory is memory that is directly addressable and therefore directly accessible to the CPU. Given that it is directly addressable, it is executable. Executable memory is the CPU's work area, where programs are executed and the data processing takes place. Each cell of executable memory can be selected individually by the CPU. When the computer is turned off, all data and programs existing in this space are lost.

- **_Secondary, indirectly addressable, memory_** – Secondary memory is not directly addressable or accessible to your CPU. Portions of it at a time might be, but by and large, secondary memory is not immediately available for program and data execution. Secondary memory can also be called indirectly addressable or indirectly accessible memory. Secondary memory is used as storage space for programs and data files. Since all information in executable memory vanishes when power is shut off, computer users need a holding area for applications they wish to save; this is why we have hard disks. Secondary memory is used to supplement executable memory in a variety of other ways also, as will later be seen. Expanded memory and software caches can be considered secondary memory, but they lose their data when powered down.

Primary Memory

To be executed or processed by the CPU, programs must exist in memory that is connected directly to the CPU's address lines. Each memory cell or device must be able to respond to a unique and possibly random address from the CPU. This is because software programs never provide predictable sequential access to memory and data. The intimate selectability of devices through the CPU addressing system is known as _direct addressing_. Think of directly addressable memory as being in the execution spotlight of the CPU.

This is not the case with programs and data sequentially stored on a hard disk or in other memory areas not directly connected to the CPU. These must first be moved into directly addressable memory to be executed.

Primary memory is connected to the CPU's address lines such that each byte is _immediately_ accessible to the CPU. The number of devices or words of memory that can be connected in this fashion is limited to 2^n, where n is the number of address lines implemented by the CPU. Thus 2^n becomes an important limit to how much memory a given system can have at any given moment to support program execution. The 80286 with 24 address lines directly addresses 2^{24} or 16 MB of memory, and the 80386 with 32 address lines can directly address 2^{32} or 4 gigabytes of memory. The extent of addressibility has little meaning, however, unless the operating system knows how to use it.

A Primary Memory Example

Figure 35 depicts executable memory in an 80286 system. Imagine that there are sixteen 1-MB RAM chips, each one connected to its own decoder. The MSBs (most significant bits) 23 through A20 select the particular RAM chip, while the LSBs (least significant bits) select a particular byte within the RAM chip. When the MSBs become equal to an E (hex) or binary _1110_, the E decoder's output will be a _0_, which selects its particular RAM chip. We have a total of 24 address lines, which are able to select 2^{24} or 16 M different items. With four address lines for chip selection, we can select 16 different chips. With 20 address lines going into each chip, there can be 2^{20} or 1 MB in each chip. Thus we have the 16 MB of memory, distributed among 16 different RAM chips.

Notice how the MSBs A20-A23 of the address bus select the particular memory chip out of 16 other possible 1-MB devices that could be selected with those four lines. The LSBs A0-A19 of the address bus select one of a possible 2^{20} devices (memory bytes) through internal selection logic within the memory chip itself. Any of the 1 million bytes within any of the 16 chips is directly accessible by the CPU. As the CPU gathers instructions and data, it uses its memory read and write control lines in conjunction with its address bus.

> **NOTE**
>
> Later, there is a discussion of I/O control lines that give access to another realm known as the I/O space.

When a particular chip gets selected, its internal circuitry leaves the tristate condition and the chip can communicate with the bus. See Figure 35. The selected chip looks at the lower 20 address lines to get one particular byte out of a possible 1 MB.

MSBs are used to select devices at a higher level (more bytes per device) while the LSBs are used to get at byte locations within the devices. In this example, the additional four address lines (A20-A23) are involved in the process of directly addressing the 16 MB or memory. It is these additional four lines on an 80286 CPU that allow it to access 16 MB of memory directly.

Primary Memory Competing Uses

Many software enhancements and utilities come into memory from the disk when needed, act on existing files, and then depart without conflict. Then, there are software functions that need to occupy memory at the same time. It is this necessity that causes us so much grief. The many competing uses for primary memory are:

- *Applications software packages* – The work space required for the executing program (spreadsheet, database, word processor). Under MS-DOS, program size is usually limited to 640K; however, larger programs can be accommodated using overlays or extended memory.

- *Data* – The size of active memory areas dedicated to data. For word processors, this is the text being manipulated; for database management systems, the files being sorted, queried, entered; for spreadsheet programs, the in-memory spreadsheet; for graphics programs, the image being manipulated; for engineering software, the current analysis data. Many DtC programs must be file oriented due to the lack of primary memory.■

■ Provisions for larger-than-memory data files are accommodated by working on these data-sets piecemeal from large disk files.

- *Resident enhancement software* – Software used to provide capabilities not originally provided by the applications programs and not found in the operating system. Many enhancement programs are kept resident in memory to act quickly, and as such, take up vital memory space. These include notepads, calculators, schedulers, and a variety of other useful functions.

- *Peripheral aids* – Print caches, font utilities, keyboard enhancers, and a host of programs that improve or enhance a peripheral's performance.

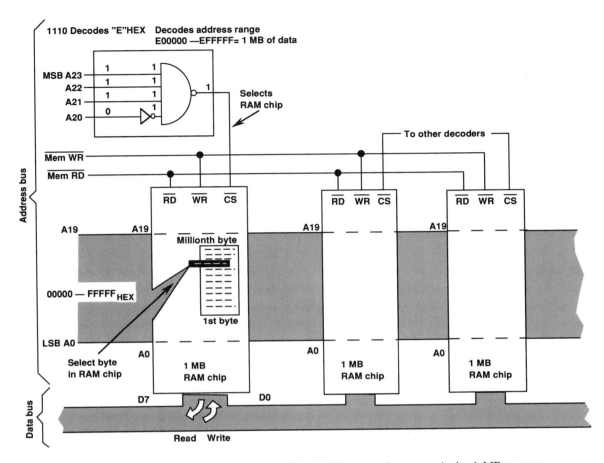

Figure 35. An actual memory system: The NAND gate selects a particular 1 MB memory chip out of a possible 16. Once selected, a particular byte within the chip is selected by the lower 20 address lines and shuffled to the data bus for communication with the CPU.

- *Data aids* – Programs that check, smooth, convert, or otherwise manipulate data. Many programs require their own built-in grammar aids and spelling checkers to check input data instantaneously. Although much of these programs can be off line on the hard disk, parts of these programs need to be in executable memory along with the primary application.

- *Operating system aids* – Software that provides support for program execution modes not found in the operating system. These include multitasking add-ons such as DESQview, and software disk caches.

- *Operating system* – The operating system itself takes up a portion of executable memory. On MS-DOS computers this is about 100K, while for Unix it is no less than 1 MB.

- **Add-in products** – Products that provide additional capability to software. For example, some programs have add-in word processors and report generator aids. These take up executable memory.

- **Auxiliary RAM** – The not-so-obvious use of RAM for keyboard buffers, video memory areas, macro buffers, the microprocessor's stack, interrupt vectors, and other operating system functions.

- **LAN drivers and buffer areas** – LAN drivers extend existing I/O drivers to act over a network. To speed data transfers, memory buffers may be required.

The need for primary memory space increases when each of the above needs to be executable at any time. Although proper support by the operating system and applications programs at the outset will help mediate the contention for space, your DtC will always have a crying need for primary memory. Later, we shall see that through virtual memory, programs larger than primary memory can actually be allowed to execute with portions being stored in secondary memory. Usually the secondary memory will be a hard disk.

Secondary Memory

Indirectly addressable, or what we shall call secondary memory, is memory that is not directly accessible to the CPU. Unlike executable primary memory, there is a middleman between the CPU and secondary memory, never allowing the memory to be immediately available. Secondary memory space is located behind an interface, as if on the other side of a door that the CPU cannot go through. In order for programs and data in secondary memory to be executed by the CPU, they must first be brought through the interface into the CPU's directly addressable memory space.

> **NOTE**
>
> It is possible that the peripheral interface has an internal memory that is commonly addressed by both the CPU and its controller. This is called *shared memory*. Shared memory is an effective way to couple data between two CPUs, each with its own local address and data bus. With shared memory, the doorway is bigger so that access is faster to memory locations and data retrieval.
>
> Shared memory, however, must be on the respective peripheral's interface board in order to be connected to the CPUs of both the DtC and the interface. On-motherboard memory cannot be shared with a peripheral.

Secondary memory is necessary because not all of your many programs and data can fit in the execution spotlight at all times. Due to operating system constraints, CPU addressing limitations, as well as financial considerations, a DtC user rarely has all the primary memory needed. Secondary memory provides a place for programs and data to stay to be called up when needed; by analogy, not unlike actors in a play waiting in the wings for their cue to step onstage.

The advantage of secondary memory is that its size is not limited by the number of address lines on the CPU. The disadvantage is that detachment from those same lines prevents the CPU from controlling the secondary memory directly. Without direct addressing, secondary memory is denied the CPU's internal hardware mech-

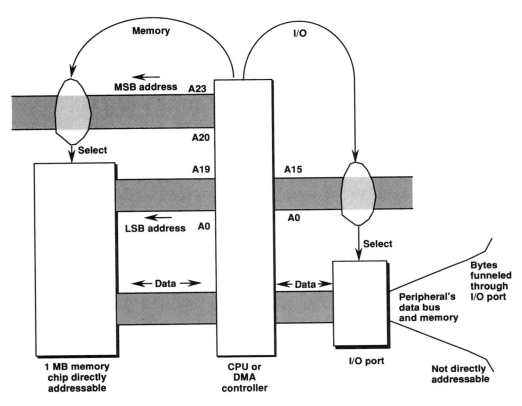

Figure 36. Primary and secondary memory: While executable memory is easy to reach by the CPU, secondary memory may have to pass through a narrow I/O doorway.

anisms for managing memory such as paging and segmentation, and it is denied the richness of CPU memory instructions.

An 8088 CPU can only directly address 1 MB of memory, but its hard drive could be many times that size. The same 8088 CPU could access 32 MB of expanded memory (another form of secondary memory). An intelligent graphics controller connected to the same CPU could access 4 MB of its own memory. Having indirect memory is like having a tin of caviar without a can opener. There's wonderful stuff inside, but how do you get at it?

Secondary memory is usually hidden from your CPU's addressability by some form of a controlled interface. Although the interface controller may perceive the secondary memory as directly addressable, the DtC's CPU may not. Data must be shuffled into the CPU's addressable memory through an interface. Given this fact, the size and speed of the interface doorway becomes critical. For example, as depicted in Figure 36, the doorway between executable and secondary memory could be as narrow as a single data word. This type of interface is known as port I/O.

Figure 36 is a combined look at primary and secondary memory. The 80286-based system is implementing primary memory and a single I/O port. In the memory map, there is a 1 MB memory chip. The 1 MB memory chip is similar to that shown in Figure 35. Notice how the secondary memory is not directly accessible or executable by the CPU; it is hiding behind an I/O port. The CPU must pull bytes from secondary memory through the narrow I/O port in a manner determined by whatever interface lies behind the port, and not in a manner controllable by the CPU's address lines. Actually, a portion of CPU memory can be shared by both CPU and peripheral. As we shall see later, shared memory is an optimal scheme, but one that is difficult to implement.

Two types of secondary memory are:

- **Hard disk** – The sequential bytes of data stored on a hard disk can be considered secondary memory. Programs and data stored on the hard disk are hidden from the direct addressability of the CPU behind the hard disk interface. The disk interface can shuffle data between its own cache memory and the CPU's memory using DMA transfers, or there could even be a shared memory between the CPU and the disk interface.

- **Bank-switched memory** – Bank-switched memory can be considered secondary memory since most of it is not directly accessible by your CPU. Only a part at a time can be switched into the CPU's addressing capability. The switching can instantaneously place hundreds of thousands of bytes at a time into the CPU execution spotlight. This is in contrast with the slower data transfer rates possible from the hard disk. Data stored on it must be whisked off serially before finally being transferred into CPU memory.

In many microcomputers, you will find other remote memory areas segregated from the CPU. Although the CPU will need some form of access to the memory, the respective controller will have the most direct control. For example:

- **Hardware disk cache memory** – The memory buffers on the hard disk interface are not directly accessible to the CPU, and therefore could be considered secondary memory. This cache memory is, however, directly accessible by the hard disk controller. Direct accessability results in optimal performance between controller, cache memory, and the hard disk, necessary for getting data in and out of the rapidly spinning disk platter. Once it is off the platter, however, a less direct interface can get the data over to the CPU. Later, we will have more to say about hard disk caches.

- **Intelligent display interface video memory** – Memory controlled by an intelligent graphics interface is usually not directly addressable by the CPU. It is directly accessible by the intelligent graphics interface, which needs that control for construction of graphics entities in this memory. In Part V, we will see how intelligent display interfaces manage their memory.

Bank-Switched Memory

Bank switching has been used since the early Apple II and CP/M microcomputers, providing a means to supplement those system's meager 64K memory resources. A board containing 3 MB of memory plugged into a 1970s Apple II. Because MS-DOS expanded memory is a form of bank-switched memory, let's look closely at this kind of secondary memory.

With bank switching, a near limitless amount of memory is tucked away in a memory reservoir. When needed, this memory can be almost instantaneously elec-

■ The software switch is simply a register in the I/O space; from the CPU's viewpoint it is an external device. The switch permits different memory banks, one at a time, to be connected to the CPU.

tronically switched by a software switch into the CPU's available addressing space. ■ In an MS-DOS computer, this memory is known as expanded memory.

Data can be moved more quickly by bank switching than by the mechanical hard disk and its primarily sequential interface. Bank switching instantly places an entire block of memory into an area of primary memory.

With bank-switched memory, the CPU is allowed to directly address banks of memory, any one of which can be as large as the addressing limit of the CPU. The CPU can access more memory than its number of address lines would indicate. The problem is that only one bank at a time can be directly accessed. You still cannot execute a program larger than the addressing limit of the CPU because problems would occur whenever a program spanned more than one memory bank.

While you cannot execute programs or process data in the banks not connected, you can *store* programs and data there. By rapidly switching the banks into and out of CPU addressability, each program can be made to execute for a while, then stem out of the way while the next program is switched in and so on. Specifically, bank-switched memory can:

- act like a very fast hard disk (software disk enhancers to be described later).
- store many smaller-than-executable memory programs to be brought into executable memory one at a time for a bit of execution, and thus multitask. The DESQview MS-DOS enhancer accomplishes this trick.
- allow your main program to have more than the CPU's addressable memory limit of data stored out in bank-switched memory. Using special software drivers, this data can be used.

EXAMPLE

A similar situation exists in a television set. A hundred or so television stations are available on a TV's antenna. The stations are out there somewhere, but you can select only one at a time to view. Likewise, through bank switching, a CPU can select which bank of memory will be connected to its address lines. See Figure 37.

The problem with bank-switched memory is that it is an afterthought. If you really need to support more directly accessible memory, you need to build more addressability into the CPU initially.

In fact, if you need that much memory, wouldn't it be more effective to simply use a CPU with more address lines in the first place? These lines would be internal to that CPU and mechanisms, registers, or instructions designed into the CPU could affect them, exerting more intimate control by paging and segmentation. But then, just purchasing a CPU with more address lines will not solve the problem if the operating system or programs don't know how to use them.

Continuing the television analogy, getting that better CPU would correspond to purchasing a state-of-the-art television that allows you to view more than one channel (bank) at a time on the same viewing screen. If you were in the business of monitoring the networks, you would want to see all of the stations at once. Likewise, if a CPU had to manage more than one program in memory at the same time, it would need to have more control. Rather than switching banks of memory, why not just put all the programs into one directly executable memory area? As

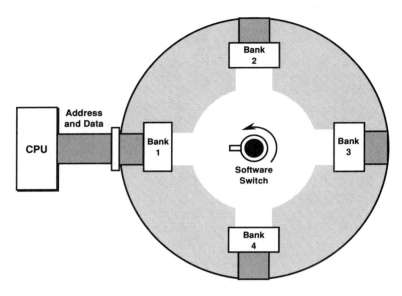

Figure 37. Bank switching: With bank switching, an entire memory block can be placed into the CPU's direct accessibility immediately.

we shall see, Windows extends the capabilities of MS-DOS to do just that in primary memory called *extended memory*.

> **NOTE**
>
> Shuffling programs in and out of the hard disk is much more frustrating to a CPU than working with directly accessible memory or even switching memory banks. However, it is more justifiable to use the hard drive as a reservoir since this form of memory is much cheaper per MB and can be added to almost any DtC in almost any quantity. A 100 MB hard drive costs around $500 while 100 MB of DRAM memory costs around $5000. 500-1000 MB hard disks are popular on today's DtCs. Imagine the cost of putting 1 gigabyte of any type DRAM memory into a DtC.

Of course, it may not be feasible to get a better CPU, or the CPU you need can't be used by the operating software, or may not even exist. So instead, you add bank-switched memory for its speed. It is not the most efficient solution, but it will provide the needed memory.

It is important to understand the concept of bank-switched memory because a special form of it, expanded memory, is the popular secondary memory used in MS-DOS computers. As we shall see later, expanded memory is switched into the first 1 MB of memory, addressable by all 80xxx CPUs.

Summary of Executable vs. Secondary Memory

Secondary memory is the basis for such contrivances as expanded memory, RAMdisks, and other hardware/software devices, each of which supplement executable memory and enhance a system's performance. The manner in which the operating system and applications software shuffles programs from the wings to center stage will determine overall throughput. Secondary memory is of great concern to us since it is used to supplement the finite directly addressable memory in its grand act of executing programs. For example, virtual memory discussed in the next Part is actually a highly articulated use of the hard disk's storage capability.

And thus we have the tradeoff between executable and secondary memory. Executable memory is immediately available to the CPU; but it forgets, and requires special attention by the operating system in order to execute programs efficiently. Secondary memory, more distant from the CPU, but usually more abundant and easier to support by the operating system, is always ready and willing to supplement executable memory.

4.3   CPU Executable Memory Support

Today's popular microprocessors differ in their capability of supporting executable memory. The descriptions offered below are independent of any operating system or applications software base that could short-change the capability.

INTEL	Direct	Virtual	MOTOROLA	Direct	Virtual
8088	1 MB	None			
80286	16 MB	1 GB	68000	16 MB	None
80386/486	4 GB	64 TB	68020/30/40	4 GB	64 TB

Table 23.   Directly addressable and virtual memory: Comparison of Intel and Motorola microprocessors.

Motorola 68xxx Microprocessors

As shown in Table 23, 68xxx-based applications have always enjoyed a directly addressable memory of at least 16 MB. With the introduction of the 68000, this support was captured in the engineering workstations of the period. Lower-cost DtCs, based on the 68000, including early and recent Macintosh offerings as well as Commodore and Atari models, are not able to support the full 16 MB. The problem was not the CPU's fault, but rather that you could not install it into the system box because of:

- *Lack of physical space* – To keep the cost of these so-called commodity computers low, the vendors put only about one megabyte of memory on the motherboard, with little or no expansion infrastructure such as slots and power supply. The rationale is that the lower cost of fewer slots is an acceptable tradeoff in view of the applications this type of computer supports.

- *Lack of bused address lines* – The number of bused address lines to connect to the memory is limited. Even today's DtCs seldom bus more than 24 of the CPU's direct address lines, thereby capping memory expansion at 16 MB, regardless of CPU capability.

Intel 80xxx microprocessors

For Intel-based DtCs – we shall restrict our attention to MS-DOS computers – the problem is much more serious. In the table above you will see that the first microprocessor in the compatible series can support no more than a 1 MB directly addressable memory space.

The following is a comparison of the increasingly powerful memory support modes of the Intel 80xxx microprocessors:

- **8088/8086** – The 8088 addresses 1 MB of memory, which is called real memory. The MS-DOS industry speaks of a 640K limitation due to the upper portion, which we later describe as UMB memory, being used for video display, ROM BIOS, and other dedicated functions.

- **80286** – This processor can operate like the 8088 in what is called real mode. The 80286 also operates in protected mode. In protected mode its additional four address lines and sophisticated internal memory management capability begin to provide the type of support today's larger programs and multitasking operating systems require. In protected mode the 80286 accesses an additional 15 MB of memory known as extended memory. Through an improved memory segmentation scheme it can slide memory around more flexibly than the 8088 CPU can. This improved memory management capability makes the 80286 processor better at multitasking and virtual memory usage.

- **80386/486** – These are premier memory managers that can address 4 gigabytes of memory directly with their 32 address lines and manage 64 terabytes of virtual memory. Also, the 80386 can look like multiple 8086 CPUs in *virtual 8086* mode. In this mode, each emulated 8086 has its own dedicated 640K memory area taken from extended and virtual memories. Through additional paging capability the 80386 can slice and dice memory into chunks as small as 4K. This managment capability is being tapped by individual applications programs, the OS/2 and Unix operating systems, and MS-DOS enhancements such as Windows and Quarterdeck's DESQview.

Real-Mode Memory

Real memory is the first MB of memory, which is directly addressable by all 8088, 80286, and 80386/486 microprocessors. Real mode is an 80286 CPU capability that, when enabled, makes the 80286 chip look like an 8086, addressing only the first megabyte of memory, and following 8088 segment addressing rules.

Intel CPUs and all MS-DOS computers must have real-mode memory to survive, since it is their common execution area. Figure 38 shows the commonality of real memory. Common addressability stems from the fact that all 80xxx CPUs can implement the same form of addressability on their first 20 address lines. Notice that successive CPUs in the Intel series have increasing addressability: the 8088/86 – 20 address lines; the 80286 – 24 address lines; and the 80386/486 – 32 address lines.

The first 16-bit Intel microprocessor, the 8088, was a weakling compared to its Motorola contemporary, the 68000. The 8088 implemented only 20 address lines and therefore could address only real memory. Since MS-DOS was developed originally to support the 8088 processor, programs that rely exclusively on MS-DOS memory management can execute only in the first 0-1 MB memory region. New MS-DOS versions, Windows, and OS/2, allow program execution in extended memory, supported by the 80286 and later CPUs. However, the type and level of support varies considerably.

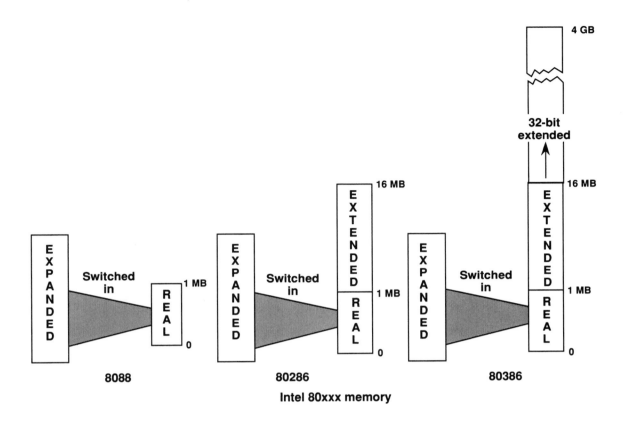

Figure 38. Extended and expanded memory: All 80xxx microprocessors can use expanded memory because it is switched from within real memory that is common to them all.

Even if your DtC has an 80386, which is capable of supporting 4 gigabytes of executable memory, under MS-DOS you might still have to squeeze most of your programs into the first 1 MB of memory.

■ OS/2 and MS-DOS use real memory differently.

Figure 39 shows the manifold uses of real memory in an MS-DOS computer and the demands placed upon it.■ You can see that real memory is split into two main constituents: DOS memory and upper memory.

DOS Memory: DOS memory is the memory from 0 to 640K. This memory is crammed with important functions. Most important, it is where the operating system and applications programs execute. Since it is the first and best supported memory for executing programs and data, vendors fight for possession of it so that they can stuff their programs into it. In DOS memory programs are guaranteed to execute regardless of MS-DOS computer configuration. From the bottom up, DOS memory contains:

- *Interrupt vectors* – First, we find the 256 four-byte interrupt vectors that point to the important MS-DOS software routines.

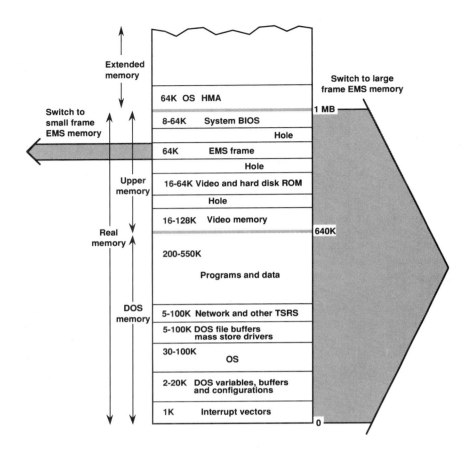

Figure 39. Real memory usage: Real memory, within every MS-DOS computer, must perform many functions. After all system demands have been satisfied, your programs have at most only half of the 1 MB left for themselves.

- *DOS variables* – Next comes an area used by DOS for its variables, buffers for the keyboard, a couple of text fonts, and configuration information storage.
- *DOS* – This area stores the resident portion of the operating system.
- *Device drivers* – In this area go the device drivers used to support the add-on mass storage devices and memory buffers for the hard disk.
- *TSRs* – Next you will load various utilitarian TSRs (terminate and stay resident) routines that provide added operating system functionality. Particularly, the network drivers will go here.
- *Programs and data* – Next, and of principal interest to you, come programs and data. There may not be much room for your programs given all of the items mentioned above.

Upper Memory (Upper Memory Block – UMB): Upper memory is the 384K of real memory above DOS memory, between 640K and the 1 MB ceiling. The UMB is frequently reserved for important ROM routines and video memory. Referring to Figure 39, let's look at the UMB in more detail:

- *Video memory* – This is memory that is mapped to the video screen by the video interface hardware, or the source of the monitor's characters and graphics. IBM has reserved a 128K area in the UMB for its video interface memory. Although VGA and super VGA interfaces can support up to several MB of memory, these larger memories are usually bank switched from within the 128K portion. Some intelligent graphics controllers actually use a portion of the 128K as a window into their individually controlled memories.
- *Video and hard disk BIOS* – Above video memory you will find the hard disk BIOS routines when on the hard disk controller. Also in this area are video interface initialization and switching routines.
- *EMS frame* – Next, you should find the EMS frame. This 64K portion of memory is where expanded memory, discussed later, is switched.
- *Holes* – In the UMB are blocks of memory that are not used by anything, and are therefore empty. As we shall see later, these blocks can be filled with RAM to execute TSRs and network drivers. UMB holes can be from a few bytes to 130K or so of contiguous memory.

The 64K of extended memory just above real memory, known as high memory, is often used by software such as Windows, DESQview, and MS-DOS 5.0 to execute part of their program kernels through special drivers to avoid using scarce DOS memory for this function. To use extended memory, you will have to run an 80286 or later CPU in protected mode.

Real Mode vs. Protected Mode

The 8088 supports only 1 MB of direct addressability, and does this with limited segmentation. Intel microprocessors beyond the 8088 can operate in two modes:

1. *Real mode* – In which they behave like an 8088 microprocessor.
2. *Protected mode* – Which supports extended memory.

■ A similar situation occurred when the 8080 was upgraded to the 8088 microprocessor. Programmers had to deal with segmentation for the first time.

In real mode, the 80286 microprocessor can be forced into an 8088-like mode where its four additional address lines and enhanced segmentation behind those address lines are effectively disabled. In this mode, 8088 programs can be executed on the 80286 CPU without modification.■ Likewise, the 80386/486 CPUs can act like 80286 CPUs in real mode by defeating their paging capability. Although this allows 8088/8086 programs to execute on the better CPUs, they are restricted to the 0-1 MB real-mode memory region. Real-mode operation permits the large real-mode software base to operate on all of the 80xxx microprocessors, albeit not very effectively. The capability for real mode operation exists to maintain upward object-compatibility. Even if you have the latest 80486 CPU, you may still need to operate software intended for the 8088.

Protected-mode operation uses the more sophisticated segmentation capability of the 80286 microprocessor and allows its 24 address lines to access the full 16 MB (2^{24} bytes) of memory. This memory is called *extended memory*. The 80386 microprocessor can operate in this protected mode by circumventing its paging and its additional eight address lines. To operate in protected mode, real-mode software products must be rewritten.

Soon, protected mode will be exhausted as we seek the masterful memory management capabilities of the 80386. Already, OS/2 version 2.0 takes advantage of the full 32-bit addressability of the 80386 microprocessor. How this will affect the protected mode software base is yet to be determined. The 80386 memory above 16 MB is called *32-bit extended memory*.

Looking at Figure 38, notice the different amounts of primary memory supported by the different 80xxx CPUs. Real, extended, and 32-bit extended are all executable primary memory. However, the only primary memory fully supported by MS-DOS, and therefore supported by the entire MS-DOS software base, is real-mode memory. Current versions of OS/2 support only extended memory. View supported executable memory as a precious resource whether it be the real-mode memory supported by MS-DOS, the extended memory supported by MS-Windows and early OS/2 versions, or the 32-bit extended memory supported by OS/2 Version 2.0.

Operating system supported executable memory is a precious resource because it can be used cooperatively by the applications software base. Just because a CPU can support and manage memory does not mean that programs will be able to take advantage of the capability. If programs individually, through makeshift fixups such as DOS extenders or their own custom memory management routines, use available memory resources, you will be sure to encounter complicated problems and a lack of software cooperation. Also, note in Figure 38 that a form of memory known as expanded memory, bank switched into real memory, is available to all 80xxx CPUs.

Breaking the 640K Barrier

It is clear that a great deal is going on within the real memory region, and that is where the infamous 640K limit resides. As if that weren't bad enough, the increased addressability of 80286 and 80386 microprocessors is left unreachable and unused by a large portion of the software base. A significant portion of real memory is unavailable even for program execution.

Looking at Figure 39 and reviewing the usage of real memory, you can see that 384K of the available 1 MB real-mode memory is used for the system's BIOS ROM, video memory, and other dedicated purposes. Therefore, programs written to operate under the MS-DOS umbrella are restricted to a total program plus data space of 640K. Worse, the MS-DOS operating system will occupy another 100K or so. Now you're down to 540K and you haven't installed network drivers yet.

You are not as constrained as a fish trapped under ice is, and software developers may override this limit in several different ways:

1. **Enhance the existing MS-DOS operating system** – Enhance MS-DOS to support greater than 1 MB of memory and write applications programs to take advantage of this. MS-DOS 4.0 provides drivers allowing programs that know how to use these drivers to access 32 MB of expanded memory primarily for their data areas. This expanded memory support works for all 80xxx microprocessors. MS-DOS 5.0 will allow you to load several programs in extended memory and execute these programs one at a time in carousel fashion. Microsoft Windows takes MS-DOS to new heights in its ability to support the 80286/386/486 in protected mode and it even supports 80386/486 virtual 8086 mode.

2. **Get a new operating system** – Create a new operating system from the ground up intended to support extended memory and the enhanced memory management capabilities of 80286 and above CPUs. Eliminate the 8088 microprocessor completely. The eventual performance improvements and reduction of confusing fixes that use real mode memory are worth the phase out. OS/2, Unix, and Windows NT running on MS-DOS compatibles are examples of this.

3. **Develop new software** – Create applications programs that individually know how to support extended memory and use MS-DOS mainly to be loaded. This requires quite a technical investment, and software developers are reluctant to devote time to such an endeavor, particularly in light of newer operating systems such as OS/2 that provide centralized methods for using memory consistently available to all programs. Besides, for proper use of extended memory, programs will need to cooperate and be written according to specifications that meet the operating system's support capability. ■ If not, they will monopolize memory and resist being able to operate with other programs that do know how to share memory.

■ VCPI (virtual control program interface) and XMS (extended memory specification) are such specifications.

Some of the fixes described above (MS-DOS 5.0 carousel mode or Windows 80386 virtual processor mode) can operate existing MS-DOS software unchanged. In order to really take advantage of the capability of Windows or OS/2, software must be redesigned for a new operating system.

4.4   MS-DOS Computer Memory

The two primary RAM resources for MS-DOS computers are extended and expanded memory. To correctly view these two types of memory, you need to realize that extended memory is an increase of executable memory, while expanded memory simply relies on bank switching to fool the CPU into accessing more memory.

- **Extended memory** – Extended memory is additional, directly addressable memory. Since the 80286 CPU has 4 more address lines than the 8088, the 80286 can directly address 16 MB of memory. See Figure 35 on page 205 You could say that extended memory is proper because it connects to the CPU in a way that permits the CPU complete and direct access to all of it. However, since an 8088-based system can't have it, expanded memory has become quite popular.

- **Expanded memory** – Expanded memory cannot be directly addressed in its entirety. Expanded memory is actually a form of bank-switched memory, switched into the lower 1 MB of memory accessible to all 80xxx CPUs. Expanded memory only connects, is switched, to the lower 20 address lines of the 80xxx CPUs. At most, only 1 MB at a time of it can be directly addressed by the respective CPU. This may seem a large disadvantage, and it is. The benefit is that all 80xxx CPUs have the lower 20 address lines and can all implement expanded memory.

Extended Memory

Extended memory is directly addressable, executable memory beyond one megabyte in 80286 and above systems. In order to access extended memory, 80286 and above microprocessors have to be placed in protected mode, so that they can use the improved segmentation needed to activate the microprocessors' additional address lines.

Extended memory is directly addressable, in its entirety, by the CPU. All of the memory management capability of the CPU can be directly exercised on extended memory. It is all executable and through proper operating system support can execute large programs and data sets, often in their entirety, without shuffling to the hard disk or other secondary memory.

Applications for Extended Memory

Applications for extended memory fall into several categories.

- **Proper protected-mode operation** – Use this memory for proper program execution. This will rule out the 8088 microprocessor, but the improvements in performance and diminishing alternatives complications (expanded memory usage) will be worth it.

- **Programs larger than 640K** – Executables can now be greater than 640K. Also, multiple 640K programs will be much easier to execute by multitasking, and even by virtual memory. Programs may support this mode individually through extenders under MS-DOS, or may be rewritten to allow Windows, OS/2, and even Unix to manage the memory for better cooperation.

- **Programs with large data areas** – Put them into executable memory in the first place. Many programs use extended memory for sorting and other CPU-intensive functions. As described above, programs will do this individually under MS-DOS, or cooperatively under OS/2.

- **Software disk enhancers** – Even if you cannot execute your programs in extended memory, you can always use it to emulate a fast hard disk.

The proper use of extended memory is becoming a reality through newer operating systems such as OS/2, Unix on a DtC, or through operating MS-DOS with the Microsoft Windows.

Operating Expanded Applications Using Extended Memory

Even though you have an 80386 or above DtC, you may want to run the many programs that support expanded memory due to its popularity. Through software emulation, extended memory can be made to act precisely like expanded memory on 80386 and above systems. This is done with additional software drivers that emulate expanded memory with extended memory and 80386/486's memory management capability. Applications that use EMS drivers can use the same drivers, operated identically, even though you have extended memory on your system. There is, however, a speed penalty in the emulation that you won't have if you use extended memory in the first place.

How to Add Extended Memory

- **8088/86** – Don't even try. The 8088 does not directly address more than 1 MB of memory. Remember that it has only 20 address lines.

- **80286** – Most 80286-based systems, due primarily to age, have you add extended memory on boards plugged into bus slots. Newer 80286 systems permit you to add this memory directly to the motherboard.

- **80386/486** – Most 80386/486 systems allow you to add 1-32 MB of extended memory by plugging SIMMs right into the motherboard. On the motherboard, the full 32-bit data transfer mode of the 80386 is incorporated. Therefore, if you are using 1 MB SIMMs, you need to add memory in 4 MB increments. To have only 1 MB of 32-bit memory, you would need to use 256K parts. Some 80386/486 systems have a special 32-bit connector for plugging in extended memory in addition to the memory on the motherboard. Also, the EISA connectors, described later, provide for 32-bit memory addition. For the best possible interfacing fit to the CPU it is best to plug memory into the motherboard.

Expanded Memory

The 640K problem discussed previously can be lessened for all MS-DOS users by expanded memory. The switching method discussed earlier has a history dating back to the early 8-bit microprocessors that needed to expand their meager 64K of directly addressable memory.

Expanded memory has two advantages over extended memory:

- *It works with 8088-based systems* – Expanded memory can be added to all 80xxx-based microcomputers, including the 8088. See Figure 38.
- *There is no bused address line limitation* – Expanded memory can be added as long as at least 20 address lines are bused in the system.

Expanded memory is really just an elegant form of bank switching. Expanded memory is switched into a directly addressable area in the first 1 MB space and thus can be operated by all Intel 80xxx microprocessors. The LIM 4.0 Specification spells out the process for software developers.

> **NOTE**
>
> **LIM 4.0 EMS Specification**
>
> The LIM (Lotus, Intel, Microsoft) EMS (expanded memory specification) 4.0 describes how to create EMS software drivers for expanded memory boards. The drivers isolate the applications programmers who want to use expanded memory from the specific hardware details of implementation. Developers simply use a standard set of functions that allow them to allocate this memory almost as if it were a hard disk. See Figure 40.
>
> Developers are able to create programs that can access up to 32 MB of memory, 64K at a time, despite the 8088/8086 microprocessor limitation of only 1 MB of direct addressability. The software operates identically on all 80xxx microprocessors without modification. This is executable all at the same time, but it must be brought into the 640K executable area through a switching area before it can be executed. MS-DOS 4.0 provides EMS support internally, but for previous versions you will need to install EMS drivers in the CONFIG.SYS file.

Two Types of Expanded Memory

Two types of EMS memory, small frame and large frame, differ in how EMS memory is switched into your executable memory. As shown in Figure 39, the small frame bank bank-switch doorway occupies 64K in the upper memory block between video memory and the BIOS ROM (usually from E0000 hex to EFFFF hex). The large frame bank-switch doorway can be anywhere in real memory.

The EMS reservoir can contain up to 32 MB of memory that can be used as secondary memory to store your programs and data, much like a hard disk. The difference, is the speed at which this program and data material can be moved into the execution memory spotlight.

The EMS reservoir is divided into 16K pages. Transfers between the reservoir and the doorway take place instantaneously by an electronic switch controlled by registers in the I/O space. The switch appears to the CPU as a group of accessible I/O registers that define the pages that will be switched into the switching window. Instructions are sent to the registers by the CPU and this tells the electronic switch

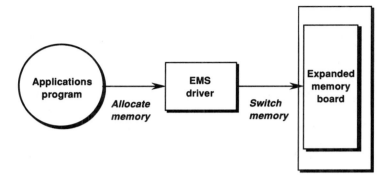

Figure 40. EMS drivers

which of the EMS pages it should place into the executable switching area. With the above background, let's compare small and large frame EMS memory.

Small Frame

In small frame expanded memory, a 64K switching window is located in the UMB (see Figure 39 on page 214). This 64K doorway is known as the EMS frame buffer. On 8088 and 80286 systems, the frame buffer must be located on an external EMS memory board, and there can be no other system memory in the frame buffer's location.

Once switched into the switching window, a program slice or data chunk can be executed in the window if it is less than 64K in size. Larger than 64K MS-DOS programs that might be stored in the expanded memory reservoir will need to be executed in DOS memory in the 0-640K region of real memory. The larger-than-64K programs can be brought into the 640K execution spotlight, 64K at a time through the switching window. Although the switching process is practically instantaneous, the 64K program chunks must be moved from the switching area to DOS memory by slower CPU-controlled block memory transfers, or in some systems, DMA transfers.

For reasons outlined above, small frame expanded memory is outdated by its 64K limitation. It simply isn't efficient for multitasking large programs. The time taken to shuffle programs larger than 64K between EMS and DOS memory is prohibitively long. Figure 41 depicts small frame expanded memory as being used mostly for program data areas.

Large Frame EMS

As shown in Figure 39 on page 214, large frame EMS can implement its switching window anywhere in real memory. Thus entire MS-DOS programs can be quickly switched into and out of the real memory executable memory space. This is much better than small frame switching, particularly if you wish to execute several programs concurrently. This is how Quarterdeck's DESQview MS-DOS multitasking enhancement program works as it brings each program into the execution spotlight for a bit of execution and then goes to the next.

Large frame switching is accomplished in two ways depending on the CPU type.

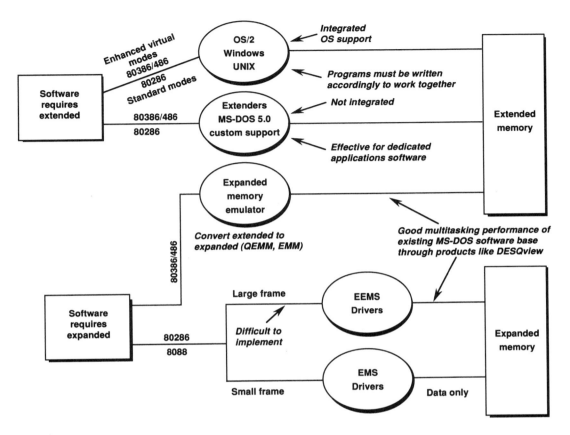

Figure 41. MS-DOS computer memory usage: The upper part of the figure shows the most desirable and integrated solutions, while the lower part shows the less integrated yet necessary solutions to overcome everyone's need for memory.

- *8088 and 80286 MS-DOS computers* – As indicated previously, the EMS switching window cannot be occupied by any other system memory. Also, the window must be located on the EMS board due to its intimate relationship (proximity to the electronic switch) that controls the EMS memory reservoir. If the switch window is going to be extended into DOS memory, DOS motherboard memory in the switch window must be disabled.

  The disabled motherboard memory will be wasted. This is not a problem since memory is cheap. What will be a problem is if you cannot disable the required motherboard DOS memory due to a lack of motherboard memory configurability. Given that you can disable the requisite memory, you will be in for a complex setup as mechanical switches on the motherboard will require special settings. Also, there are a load of switches on the EMS board that must be set to determine the window position. Complicating this setup is the fact that many EMS boards also provide extended memory capability and there are switches that determine how much and where the extended memory is shared.

- *Large Frame with 80386/486 MS-DOS Computers* – The memory management capability of the 80386/486 CPUs uses extended memory as if it were expanded memory. Instead of expanded memory on a board somewhere being switched through the frame buffer, the extended memory is remapped internally by the CPU. The remapping can be to anywhere in real memory, and therefore large frame EMS memory can be accomplished. You won't have to disable motherboard memory, set switches, purchase an additional (and expensive) EMS memory board, set switches on that board, and then pray that everything works. Instead, you simply install a software driver (QEMM from Quarterdeck Software, for example), and perform all of the specific installations without ever opening the hood of your DtC. The enhanced capability opens many options and many possible setups, some of which may be complicated; but at least the setups are all in software.

Not only can the 80386 use extended memory as expanded memory, remapping it into the frame buffer; but as we shall see later, the holes in the UMB can be filled with extended memory giving the crammed TSRs and network drivers a place to execute. You may have the advantage of OS/2 support of extended memory and the current support of expanded memory boards with the same extended memory.

> **NOTE**
>
> Consider the irony, how complicated things have become. Extended memory should have been used in the first place for large programs, being made to appear as the less CPU-intimate expanded memory. Now programs and operating systems that cannot get off the expanded memory habit can still have expanded memory by using extended memory.

Figure 41 shows how the applications program that wants expanded memory uses extended memory by conventional expanded memory drivers in conjunction with an expanded memory emulator driver. Software such as DESQview's QEMM, MS-DOS 5.0's EMM, and Windows take advantage of the 80386/486 memory management capability to make extended memory act like expanded memory. The figure also shows the more straightforward approach: using protected mode extended memory as is in the first place.

Figure 41 shows an 80386 processor with an applications base working together under a well-chosen operating system as the best memory solution. Various coping mechanisms are suggested in the lower part of the figure. One method uses extended memory through various fixes such as DOS extenders and improved MS-DOS versions such as 5.0. The bottom part of the figure shows the expanded memory that all processors can use and the variety of applicable usage methodologies. Notice that the *data only* solution, bottom right, uses small frame memory. All solutions above the small frame EMS can support large programs and multitasking. However, the best solution is the most integrated one, using an operating system that supports an 80386/486 CPU.

Applications for Expanded Memory

Recall that the main justification for expanded memory is the fact that it can be implemented on the 8088 microprocessor. On 80286 and above microprocessors with proper operating system support, extended memory can be used to accomplish the expanded applications described below.

- **Software disk enhancers** – Expanded memory works fine for implementing these functions since random access to the entire memory area is not required when RAM memory is emulating a hard disk.

- *Print spoolers* – Temporary storage for data to be printed. Use of a fast hard disk could work as well.

- *Program data areas* – Data-intensive programs, each smaller than 640K, can make good use of expanded memory for their large spreadsheets, databases, and documents. Rather than shuffling between hard disk and executable memory, the shuffling takes place between expanded memory and executable memory. The respective programs must be written specifically to use expanded memory through EMS drivers. Programs such as dBASE, WordPerfect, and Lotus 1-2-3 can use expanded memory.

- *Multitasking* – Multiple MS-DOS programs, each less than 640K, can execute concurrently using expanded memory without modifications to these programs. For example, the DESQview MS-DOS enhancement alternately brings these programs into the executable 640K area and allows them to execute in round-robin fashion. Users of programs such as Lotus, dBASE, and WordPerfect can run *all* of these programs concurrently. This works much better with large frame expanded memory due to the extraordinary amount of program shuffling that would be required through a 64K switching window.

- *Program swapping* – Program swapping may be more sensible than running several programs concurrently. Often, you don't really want multiple programs to execute concurrently, but rather have them all remain ready in memory. This allows you to operate several programs at different times without having to continually load and unload them, which often involves tedious setups. They are simply left in memory and you switch between them at will by simple key presses. MS-DOS 5.0 and standard 286-mode Windows provide this capability using extended memory. Applications programs are swapped between main memory and expanded memory. This can be faster than swapping them between executable memory and the hard disk.

Problems with Expanded Memory Method

The popularity of EMS memory is fading as the 8088 is phased out and extended memory is welcomed by the industry. OS/2, Windows, and MS-DOS 5.0 support extended memory and developers are embracing this support.

Technically, expanded memory is not a sound way to increase a system's memory because it depends on mechanisms outside the internal memory management capability of the microprocessor. It is an ad-hoc solution, and limited in comparison to extended memory.

So here is the rub. Although extended memory is better from a pure design point of view, expanded memory has become quite popular because of:

1. *Tool-up time* – It is easier to write programs that use EMS drivers to individually rather than cooperatively execute under newer protected-mode environments such as OS/2. Many MS-DOS applications programs use expanded memory for their larger than executable memory data areas, which is relatively simple. This has permitted them to get on the air faster and it requires less tool-up time than do applications using OS/2 support of extended memory.

2. *8088-based computers* – Many 8088-based computers still in service cannot use extended memory.

3. *MS-DOS enhancements* – Many MS-DOS enhancements, such as DESQview, allow unmodified programs to multitask using expanded memory. Many users ac-

cept this alternative as they await applications to be rewritten under OS/2 or Windows.

Adding Expanded Memory to a System

■ Some expanded memory boards have the ability to be configured as extended memory or backfill conventional memory.

- *8088 and 80286 systems* – You must purchase expansion memory boards that plug into the system's bus. Boards come in 8- and 16-bit data widths for these different systems. ■
- *80386/486 systems* – Extended memory can be made to emulate expanded memory through the use of software drivers. You may also add regulation expanded memory boards to an 80386 if you really want to.

MS-DOS Memory Confusion Summary

The limited support of extended memory by applications programs due to the lack of this support in MS-DOS has led to a plethora of add-on expanded memory software options and hardware add-on boards. Since all 80xxx microprocessors may implement expanded memory, the approach has become quite popular. Many users opt for extended memory, supported by an increasing number of stand-alone programs and other programs under Windows and OS/2, expecting that this support will drive the marketplace. Others want expanded memory to be supported now. 80386 users boast that extended memory can also act as expanded memory.

MS-DOS 5.0 will support extended memory, but only in a carousel fashion. You can load multiple programs in extended memory and execute any of them one at a time, as if they were records in a jukebox. Windows and OS/2 provide adequate support of extended memory to those programs written to use it.

Table 22 on page 171 shows that an abrupt separation occurs between medium and high power microprocessors as their direct memory addressability makes a spectacular leap from 16 MB to 4 gigabytes.

■ It is one thing to say an operating system will support 4 gigabyte memory and yet another to plug 4 gigabytes of memory into a system. At today's memory costs (about $60 per MB) 4 gigabytes would cost $240,000, to say nothing of how you would actually plug it in.

When we move to the Motorola 68020 and above and the Intel 80386 and above, 16 MB of directly executable memory expands to 4 gigabytes of directly executable memory (32 address lines).■ As programs continue to demand more and more memory we should all plan for the next plateau. We've already seen how troublesome the difference between the 8088 and 80286 memory support capability is. We should brace ourselves for what will happen when we finally consume the 16 MB directly accessible memory of the 68000 and 80286 processors.

In the near future, you will need to consider greater than 16 MB support capability since many of today's systems provide for as much as 64 MB of motherboard memory. It is likely that future DtC applications will use increased executable memory resources as well as depend more on virtual memory techniques. Virtual memory, a grandiose scheme of managing primary and secondary memory, will be discussed in detail in a later part. Memory will continue to go down in cost, more address lines will be bused, and a system's conventional memory requirements will continue to double every year or so. Hard disks are becoming faster, larger, and cheaper. Their mix will depend a lot on the relative cost between hard disk and random access memory. In either case, you will need to start thinking about it.

4.5   *Memory Enhancements*

A variety of techniques are available to enhance the performance of your existing software base. We separate them into two categories:

- *Software disk enhancers* – Tricks for using available executable memory with additional software to assist performance. These make up for operating system or software shortcomings in using memory.

- *Hardware caches* – Hardware caches use special high-speed memory to provide improvements that are completely automatic. You need not install any special software or drivers, nor be concerned about an operating system's weaknesses; the caches do their job.

Software Disk Enhancers

Although you ordinarily think of the hard disk as a place for long-term storage of programs and data, it is also used as a short-term storage for the purpose of dynamically shuffling programs and data between executable memory and this long-term storage. Shorter term secondary storage is needed to hold programs. Executable memory isn't large enough to hold *all* of the programs that we may want to execute in a given time period, so we kick them into and out of executable memory from the hard disk as needed. If executable memory were large enough, we could simply load all of the programs into it and quickly run them one at a time, or even concurrently, as required.

Moreover, executable memory is seldom large enough to hold the complete data set that a given applications program may want to manipulate, whether it be a database to sort, a document to rearrange, or a graphics image to fix. Instead, the program usually works on the data a chunk at a time from the hard disk. Working with large datasets can be excruciatingly painful; you may need to sort a 10 MB file and yet be able to hold only 300K of it in memory at any given time. If executable memory were large enough, the program would simply place the entire data set into executable memory and with the magnificent memory management capability of a late model CPU promptly operate on the entire data set all at once. This would be the fastest and most efficient method, for the CPU with its paging, segmentation, and other capabilities is the master shuffler.

As it turns out, there may be DRAM memory not executable but nevertheless available to help with the above shuffling process. This DRAM memory may be laying around, unused for two reasons:

1. Extended memory cannot be used as executable memory because you are, sadly, running the 80286/386 or 486 in real mode. You are using only the 0-1 MB real mode memory for compatibility across the entire 80xxx line, which must include the 8088 microprocessor.

2. You have added expanded memory to an 80xxx microcomputer to run software that popularly uses expanded memory for multitasking or large data areas, and you're not using it all for that software.

Why not use this memory, since it can't be executed, to act like a fast hard disk? This is precisely what software disk enhancers do.

Software disk enhancers are replacements to hard disk drivers that enable an amount of DRAM memory to act as though it were a fast mass storage device. The idea is to speed up the operating system's ability to get programs into memory, or the process of an applications program getting large files into memory, or the overlaying process. Figure 42 depicts this process. Notice how the operating system's or applications program's calls for hard disk access are redirected to come from unused DRAM memory instead of from the hard disk. This process is transparent to the software.■

You may wonder how the files and data get into the DRAM memory in the first place. There are two different types of software disk enhancers and the difference is related to how that happens:

■ Software programs are not modified. Instead, the external hard disk driver software is modified when you install the disk enhancer driver. The driver takes care of the details of redirecting the program's disk requests to instead be satisfied from the memory.

1. *RAMdisk* – For the RAMdisk, you must copy these files from hard disk to the RAMdisk. Operationally, the RAMdisk is considered as another disk drive. In fact, software simply perceives the RAMdisk as the next highest drive letter in the disk drive chain. For example, if you had an a: and b: floppy, and a c: hard disk, the RAMdisk would become the d: drive.

The advantage of a RAMdisk is that you may need another logical disk drive for intermediate operations or to help organize utilities storage, or to provide a temporary place for disk copying procedures. You could place in it editors, resident utilities, and other programs that always need to be brought in and out of executable memory rapidly.

The disadvantage is that since the RAMdisk acts just like a hard drive, you could forget that the RAMdisk is actually RAM memory that will vanish, destroying your data when you turn the system off or lose power.

2. *Software disk cache* – A software disk cache is a DRAM memory area automatically used to store programs and data *most often used*. Here a modified disk driver takes care of the details of placing into the RAM area programs, data, and files based on how often they are requested. Those required the most will more likely be found in memory. Although you are not responsible for managing the process of getting data into the cache, you will need to tell the driver how big to make the cache. The cache size needs to equal the total size of programs and data that you execute most frequently. The cache can be as large as your available extended or expanded memory.

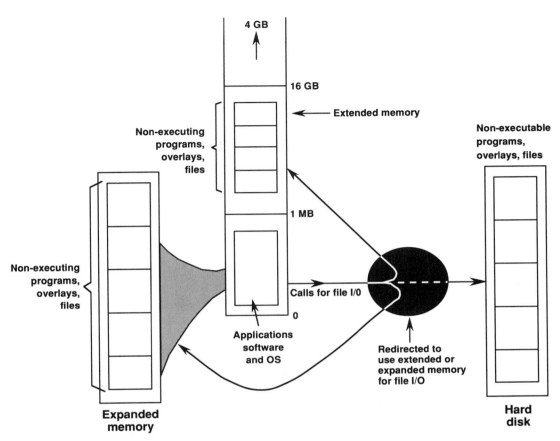

Figure 42. **Software disk enhancers:** Software disk enhancers can appear to your software as a fast hard disk, but actually they are unused DRAM memory areas.

With write-through capability, data written to the software cache is also written to the hard disk. Thus you will not lose valuable data in a power outage. You do not need to copy anything anywhere, the software takes care of it based on usage. Both RAMdisks and software caches reduce wear and tear on the hard disk and provide silent file access.

> **NOTE**
>
> Software disk enhancements are not always faster than the hard drives they supplement. Some hard drives use direct memory access, a vary fast data transfer methodology, and quick seek times that can exceed the CPU's capability for moving data between memory. Also, redirected software drivers may not be efficient. Remember, software disk caches must replace software requests for the hard disk transparently. There-fore, the random access nature of the RAM in a software disk cache cannot be fully realized.

Not Really Virtual Memory

You could say that software disk caches are a greatly simplified form of virtual memory whereby you can manipulate data whose total combined size exceeds executable memory. The software cache process, however does not take advantage of CPU capabilities in memory management, nor does it provide the mechanism by which single or multiple programs can each be larger than executable memory. With the following examples, we look at what can be done with software disk enhancers.

1. *RAMdisk application* – You need to sort a 2 MB file greater than executable memory. You copy the file to be sorted from the hard disk to the RAMdisk and tell dBASE that the file is on the d: drive (the RAMdisk). dBASE sorts the file, and you notice that the hard disk is silent during the process. Following the sort, you copy the sorted file back to the hard disk where it is safe. Actually, dBASE shuffled the file between the RAMdisk and executable memory and when it was finished, it placed the file, as it became sorted, back onto the RAMdisk.

2. *Software cache application* – You need to sort the same 2 MB file. You tell dBASE to begin the sort (the file is on the hard disk). The sort begins, and as portions of the file to be sorted are brought into executable memory, they are also brought into the cache. As these portions are repeatedly required, they are brought from cache to executable memory, and you notice hard disk activity decreasing. As the file becomes sorted, it is written back to the hard disk as well as to the cache. You get the file sorted faster, without needing to copy it to RAMdisk first, and back to the hard disk, as in the previous example.

3. **Running more than one program** – You load into memory your favorite word processor, WordPerfect, which takes a few seconds. Then, you need to execute a dBASE program. You leave WordPerfect and load dBASE, which takes a few more seconds. While using dBASE you note that the dBASE overlay files are executing without much hard disk access and seem to be getting into executable memory faster. Having finished with dBASE, you need to execute WordPerfect once more. Now, you notice it only takes one second to load. Faster response occurs because the dBASE overlays and the WordPerfect program, after the initial load, were shuffled between cache and executable memory instead of between hard disk and executable memory.

Software Disk Enhancement Problem

Software disk enhancers are really a temporary fix to the much larger problem of MS-DOS's inability to support the larger memory models implemented by the more advanced 80xxx microprocessors. The more executable memory that a system supports, the more you will require, and the larger your programs will require. When programs exceed 16 MB, the virtual capability of the 80286 will be required. When programs exceed 4 gigabytes, or when you just can't have enough memory on your 80386-based system, virtual memory or the above caching techniques will continue to be required.

What should have happened in the above example with WordPerfect and dBASE is that an 80286 and above CPU loaded both WordPerfect and dBASE into executable extended memory, allowing both programs to exist simultaneously. You should have been able to toggle between them instantaneously, and even execute them concurrently. The dBASE file should have been loaded in its entirety into extended memory and sorted right in place. It would have taken much less time than shuffling between extended memory and the smaller real memory where only 100K or 200K a time could be sorted.

Improved operating systems would let us perform these activities quite differently. For example, on an 80286 or above microprocessor under OS/2, both WordPerfect and dBASE could be loaded into extended memory, could execute concurrently, and could even share the same video screen. If we had an 80386/80486 microprocessor running under Windows, using the 80386 virtual processor mode, each program could have its own virtual 8086 microprocessor implemented using extended memory. If limited to an 8088 microprocessor, we could run under the DESQview enhancement where both programs would execute concurrently, alternately being switched into executable memory from expanded memory.

Hardware Disk and Execution Caches

While software disk caches help you cope with not having enough executable memory, or the operating system's inability to support what you do have, hardware caches improve a system's performance regardless of executable memory concerns. Hardware caches, as the name suggests, operate below and independent of software. Since they are separate from software, they do not require special software drivers to fool programs, nor do they need any operating system support other than the initialization of cache controllers. Two types of these are:

1. *Hardware disk cache* – Some hard disk controllers use a high speed cache memory buffer right on the hard disk interface. This memory is local to, controlled by, and highly integrated with the hard disk controller CPU. Close integration with the hard disk controller provides hard disk performance improvements beyond that possible with the previously described software disk caches. This memory is expensive and not commonly directly accessible by the DtC's CPU. Like the software cache, it is used to store often-used hard disk data.■

■ Sometimes part of the disk cache memory is shared and directly accessible by the DtC's CPU. DMA transfers between a shared memory interface and main memory allows extraordinarily high data transfer rates between the hard disk interface and executable memory.

■ You may recall that the 80486 microprocessor has 16K of cache built right into the chip.

2. *Hardware CPU instruction execution cache* – The hardware CPU instruction execution cache will make all of your programs run faster. Unlike the hardware disk cache, the CPU instruction cache is executable. Rather than improving hard disk performance, the hardware CPU instruction cache improves CPU performance. Do not add the CPU cache if the problem is a slow hard disk. The instruction cache improves the performance of software already loaded into executable memory. It operates by a special controller chip installed between the CPU and executable memory. The controller manages the cache to keep code most often executed by the CPU in the CPU instruction cache. This memory is very fast and expensive static RAM.■

> **NOTE**
>
> The *locality of execution* principle states that most software programs execute in localized areas, or tightly coupled program loops, in memory. If these smaller program loops could be stored in very fast memory, performance would improve. On an MS-DOS computer restricted to 640K of executable memory, the largest practical cache size would be 640K, and real-mode DRAM memory could simply be replaced with faster static memory. But that would be expensive. With only 32K of cache memory and a good controller you can obtain an 85% hit rate, i.e., 85% of the time, a needed instruction will be found in the cache.

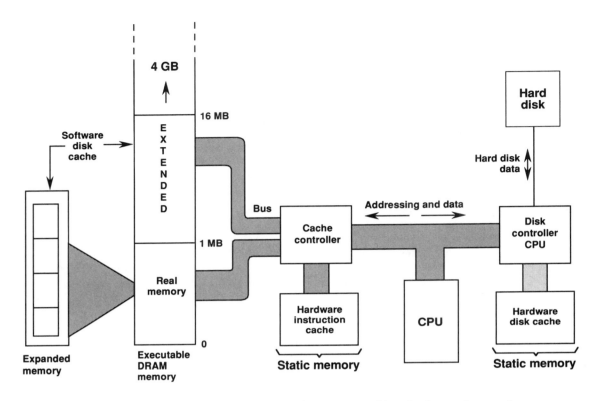

Figure 43. Hardware caches: Performance improvement without having to change software.

Experimentation shows that this hit rate translates to software executing form 15-25% faster than without the cache.

A controller between the CPU and DRAM memory manages the process of keeping the most-used instructions in the cache memory. This is accomplished entirely by the controller and is *not* the responsibility of the operating system or software. Regardless of problems with inadequate operating system support of executable memory, a hardware cache will almost always improve system performance. Ask yourself: How much is the improvement? How much does it cost? and Do I really need it?◼ The performance improvement you will get by implementing the CPU instruction execution cache will depend a lot on the particular type of software you are operating. Your software may be slow because of inadequate graphics display interfaces or slow hard disks. Or, your software program's operation syndrome (discussed earlier) may not take advantage of the cache controller's capability.

◼ You could get the same improvement by purchasing a 33 MHz without a hardware cache rather than a 25 MHz CPU with a cache. The 33 MHz CPU, however, will require a faster memory throughout the DRAM memory system.

Because a hardware cache and controller both need high speed static memory, adding a hardware cache can easily increase the cost of a DtC system by 10%.

Hardware vs. Software Caches

Figure 43 shows the relationship between hardware caches and other memory used for software caches. Access to the hardware instruction cache is controlled by the cache controller; it is not the responsibility of the CPU. Therefore, the operating system and applications software need not even know it exists. The hardware disk cache is taken care of by the disk controller CPU and again, applications software does not worry about it. In contrast, the software caches described earlier required user-installed drivers.

4.6 Memory Summary

The issues of memory support are complex, and intimately tied to both the applications program's and the operating system's ability to support it. In MS-DOS computers, the issues can get quite sticky due to the 8088's poor memory support and inconsistent support of the better CPU's memory management capability. Because software and operating system geared up to that processor, later processor's support has become quite complicated. Even today, much of the MS-DOS computer software base continues to suffer because it executes mostly in the first 0-16 MB of memory. There are many temporary solutions to the problem while the 8088 microprocessor is phased out and the MS-DOS operating system its enhancements and replacements begin to more adequately support memory.

5.0 Buses

- Signals
- Structures

The bus, like your arteries and veins, carry the very life's blood of a DtC to the peripheral interfaces. A well designed and documented bus is essential for the synergistic combination of a DtC and its many complex peripherals.

As you can see in Figure 26 on page 162 and in Figure 44, a variety of signals are generated within a system motherboard. Although most of them come from the CPU, other signals – power, arbitration, and timing – are generated by other components. A methodology is required to make these important signals available in a consistent manner by establishing pathways to devices outside the design of the motherboard. These pathways between the internal components are known as the bus.

The bus is a set of conductors that interconnects the components of a microcomputer and carries all communications signals throughout the system unit, much like the human nervous system carries electrical impulses from the brain to various parts of the body. The bus could be considered a modular separation of essential computer CPU and memory functions from add-on devices that vary from application to application. A good bus system is what makes the DtC the synergistic combination of computer and peripherals that it is. Systems that do not adequately provide this service, that have poor bus documentation, lack of sufficient signals on connectors, or not enough bus connectors, will suffer with poor expandability.

As we shall see, the CPU is one of the many possible managers of the bus. Direct memory access (DMA), graphics, and other coprocessors may also exercise control over the bus.■

◼ If you need to move a lot of contiguous data from one memory block to another, the operating system may call upon a DMA controller, a device specialized in such data transfers, rather than the general-purpose CPU.

5.1 Bus Signals

The lines and groups of lines that make up the bus carry different types of signals. Most of the bus lines of the system are buffered, that is, they are strengthened by digital amplifiers so that they can connect to and drive a variety of devices requiring reliable digital inputs. At the highest level, buses can be divided into three functional groups: address, data, and control buses.

Address lines

Address lines direct addressing signals from the CPU or other system controller to the devices that are connected to the common communication data bus. Devices can be memory cells, peripherals, or anything else that needs to be connected and controlled. Multiple address lines can be used to select multiple devices. The more address lines, the more devices can be selected, and thus the more capability and

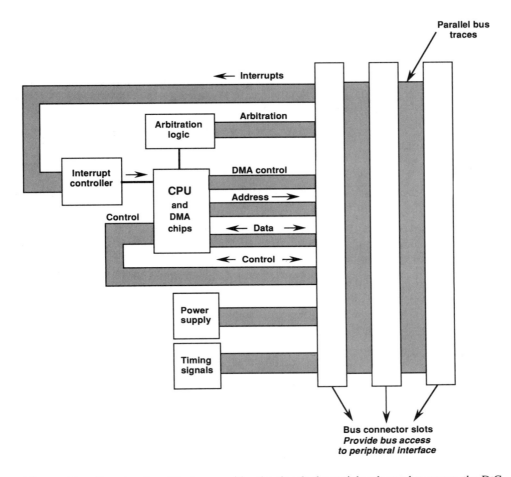

Figure 44. **Bus signals:** The bus provides the signals the peripherals need to access the DtC.

versatility is available to the system. Since each address line can have either of two states at any time (a one or a zero), the number of possible addresses on n lines is 2^n. Recall the earlier discussion in addressing.

Data lines

Data lines are pathways for communicating to and from devices and the CPU once the devices have been selected by the address bus. Data width is a fundamental measurement of processing capability. As a rule, the larger it is, the more in-parallel processing capability there is.

Data width is what we refer to when we define a microprocessor as an 8-, 16-, or 32-bit system. When describing data width in terms of a complete system, however, we must consider the following:

- **CPU registers** – Most importantly, the internal size of the respective microprocessor's registers, and therefore the quantity of data handled in parallel by most operations related to the microprocessor.

- **Data lines** – The number of data lines brought out of the microprocessor and accessible by other devices. For example, the 8088 microprocessor has internal 16-bit register width but brings out only 8 data lines. This reduces its processing throughput by forcing it to deal with quantities two serial bytes at a time.

- **Bused data lines** – The number of data lines bused throughout the system. Peripherals can take advantage of only the width of data brought out to the bus to which they are connected. An 8088 microcomputer will bus the eight data lines from the CPU following buffering and amplification.

- **Coprocessor data width** – Many coprocessors have large internal data widths. For example, the 8087 coprocessor has 80-bit register data widths.

Since a system's data width is a composite of many individual quantities, *width* can be a confusing and subjective term. Figure 45 shows an 8088, 16-bit microprocessor connected to an 80-bit coprocessor by an 8-bit bus. Although arguments will be passed eight bits or less at a time, math processing will take place more rapidly by this configuration than if the processing were done internally by a 16-bit microprocessor without a math coprocessor. The arguments are slowed on the 8-bit bus, but the 80-bit path internal to the coprocessor makes up for the difference, and then some.

Intel's Memory, I/O Signals

In a microcomputer, the two major areas to communicate with are memory, where programs and data reside, and I/O, where everything else resides. Memory and I/O signals allow the CPU to indicate whether a memory or I/O device is being accessed. I/O devices are registers that lie between the CPU and the peripherals on the peripheral interfaces. By communicating with these registers you can print characters, position the hard disk on a particular sector, set up the video interface's display characteristics, or send characters to a modem through the serial interface. Within these interfaces are registers that are similar in function to memory locations.

> **NOTE**
>
> Registers, like memory, can be written to and read from. Instead of storing programs and data, however, registers are used to send commands, receive status conditions from peripherals, or act as go-betweens for the communication of data to and from peripherals.

Motorola and other microprocessors implement their I/O devices in their memory map. In the memory map the CPU can operate devices with the same deftness it uses to operate memory. Intel, however, has an I/O map distinct from the memory map. Since the same address bus is used to access both types of devices, separate control lines are used to establish two different sets of device locations – those in the memory space and those in the I/O space.

In order to differentiate between memory and I/O communications, the CPU implements two different types of instructions: memory and I/O. If the programmer wants to address a memory device, a memory instruction is used; if an I/O device is desired, an I/O instruction is used.

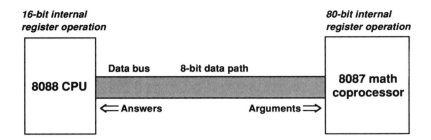

By analogy, imagine two people (devices) both living on Main street, but each in a different city, one in Chicago (memory) and one in Cleveland (I/O). Thus, the system designer designates in which space (city) a given device will be by letting the appropriate control line (along with the correct "street" address) select the device. Figure 46 shows separate and memory mapped I/O.

From a hardware viewpoint the separation manifests itself as two additional control lines on the bus. From a software viewpoint the separation manifests as additional I/O instructions.

Advocates of memory mapped I/O argue that in any microprocessor (Intel or other), the largest number and greatest variety of instructions are memory oriented. Thus, I/O devices that can be located only in the memory map can be controlled more flexibly. They also argue that the number of possible I/O devices is that of direct memory addressability excluding what is used for programs and data. The separate I/O camp concedes that the separate I/O spaces are considerably smaller than the memory map of the same CPU.

Advocates of Intel's separate I/O space argue that the Intel I/O instructions are customized for doing the sort of things that I/O devices do, such as character processing and string processing. Also, they argue that in Intel systems all I/O devices can be placed in their own identifiable map and instructions that reference them are easy to identify by their unique mnemonics.

Unless you are programming at lower levels, both applications software and the operating system will protect you from the details just recounted. However, when you need to program a system's devices, troubleshoot interface malfunctions, or interface to a new device, understanding this separation becomes paramount.

Read/Write

Read/write signals control the direction in which data is moving on the data bus. The read signal instructs a device to send data to the CPU to be read by the CPU. The write signal instructs the device to receive data from the data bus, written to by the CPU.

DMA Signals

The DMA, using its sequential memory data transfer capabilities, generates request and acknowledge signals that control data transfers. The DMA controller takes control of the address, data, and read/write control lines from the CPU. The DMA

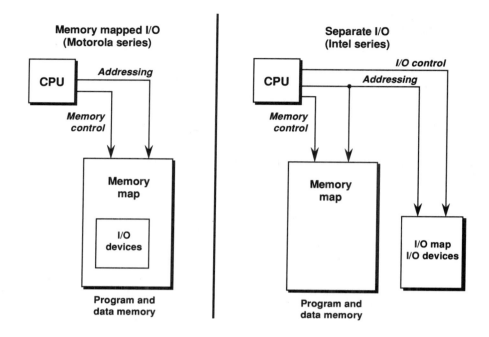

Figure 46. **Separate and memory mapped I/O:** Intel CPUs separate memory and I/O by using separate control lines for for memory and I/O, each activated by a different type of instructions.

controller requires peripherals to request data transfers and it acknowledges them with a signal that tells the peripheral the data is ready. Multi-channel controllers implement several request and acknowledge signals. This is discussed in greater detail elsewhere in this Part.

Interrupts

Peripherals and internal system components cause the CPU to execute interrupt service routines (ISR) when respective interrupt lines are activated. Each interrupt wire points the CPU to an ISR corresponding to the required function, such as reading the hard disk or sending another character to the printer. Important peripherals can thus attract immediate attention. When an interrupt occurs, the CPU marks its place and drops whatever it is doing in order to service the interrupt. After servicing, the CPU resumes its previous operation. The more interrupt lines implemented and bused, the better the system. Usually, as shown in Figure 26 on page 162, an interrupt controller is inserted between the bused interrupt lines and the CPU. Interrupt controller chips manage interrupts and queue them in priority order for overall system control. Interrupts can be masked by hardware or software controls.

Wait States

Different devices operate at different speeds. Peripherals that operate slower than the CPU need to issue wait instructions to the CPU. The CPU idles while the peripheral device prepares data. When the device catches up, the CPU proceeds. The need for wait states depends on how fast the CPU moves from instruction to instruction and how fast the peripherals respond. Video interface memory may be a bit sluggish and slows the CPU, while the hard disk interface buffer memory is just fine and requires no wait states.

Bus Control and Arbitration

Bus control and arbitration signals permit multiple processors, including digital signal processors, graphics, network controllers, DMA controllers, and multiple CPUs, to share system resources over the bus. Bus signals separate the sophisticated Micro Channel, NuBus, and EISA buses from the rudimentary ISA bus found in AT-style computers. Older DtCs gave the CPU control over everything in the system, limiting most data transfer to the ability of the CPU and, at most, a DMA controller to move bytes. The newer buses allow any bus master to move data around in the system by an arbitration scheme that uses a central arbitration point (CAP).

Power

Power signals are usually bused. Five volts, at the highest current rating, power the microcomputer's logic and memory. Floppy and hard disk motors are powered by 12V and the RS-232 signal transceivers use plus and minus 12V. The power lines can be bused throughout the system as are other signals. Power lines tend to be heavier than signal lines because they carry more current. Often, when plug-in boards or peripherals such as hard disk motors require lots of power, the power is supplied by individual cables rather than by the bus. Power loss due to breaks in the bus can cause some plug-in boards to lose power while others remain alive. Problems of this nature can be quite difficult to troubleshoot.

5.2 Bus Structures

Open and Closed Bus Architectures

An open architecture is one that is sufficiently well-documented that manufacturers can readily design, build, and market special and general-purpose add-on cards. A closed architecture is one in which there is no parallel bus, or if one exists, it is not sufficiently documented for outside vendors to manufacture interfacing equipment. The early IBM and MS-DOS compatible PCs and Apple IIs implemented a relatively simple, but well-documented open bus that led to thousands of add-on boards. These early boards had limited interactivity with host functions, particularly in the area of memory and processor sharing. But their simplicity paved the way for the design of low-cost computers and peripherals, thereby contributing to the emergence of the DtC as a commodity.

MS-DOS Compatible Buses

The major bus types for MS-DOS compatible computers are the ISA (industry standard architecture), the EISA (extended ISA), which is a 32-bit extension to the ISA bus and the totally different MCA bus (Micro Channel architecture).

The ISA Bus

The ISA bus is no doubt the most popular bus in the computer industry in terms of the number of computer units sold that incorporate it.

You will find the ISA bus in most MS-DOS compatible home computers. Its origins trace back to the introduction of the PC/XT line of IBM computers. The ISA bus is low cost, relatively unsophisticated, and lacking the bus control and arbitration capability of the EISA and MCA buses.

Due to the addressability and bused data width difference between the 8088 and 80286 microprocessors, two different buses were created for IBM's original XT- and AT-based DtCs. For the 8088-based XT, a 62-pin connector was used to carry the bus signals to interface boards. The 62-pin connector brought out the 8088's 20 address lines, 8 data lines, 4 DMA channels, 6 interrupts, other signals, and power.

For IBM's 80286-based AT, the same 62-pin connector was extended to provide for an upward-compatible superset with the additional 4 address lines, 8 data lines for the 80286 microprocessor, as well as additional interrupt and DMA signals, provided on a separate connector. Boards originally purchased for the 8-bit 8088 XT-style computers could also be plugged into IBM's AT computer.

■ AT style is a class of MS-DOS compatible computers that incorporate the ISA bus architecture and implement 80286, 386, and 486 microprocessors.

Although IBM XT and AT computers are no longer manufactured, the ISA bus standard lives on in many AT-style MS-DOS compatible computers from scores of Asian and U.S. manufacturers.■

The EISA Bus

A standard 32-bit superset of 8- and 16-bit buses was long in coming because IBM discontinued use of the ISA bus in the AT and has only recently reinstituted it in the newer 80386SX models. Thankfully, dozens of other manufacturers have put 80386 and 80486 microprocessors in boxes that include the 8- and 16-bit ISA connectors. It was therefore inevitable that a standard would evolve for a 32-bit connector that is an upward-compatible superset of the ISA 8- and 16-bit connectors. This standard is the EISA bus. Note in Figure 47 how the EISA bus simply adds a special upward-compatible connector for the additional 16 address and data lines of the 80386/486 CPUs and other signals.

Prior to EISA, many AT-style compatibles implemented their own 32-bit connectors, so there were many different types. The connector was usually used to add additional memory to these early AT-style compatibles. A 32-bit memory interface is an important performance requirement and the high density SIMM chip motherboard add-ons were not yet a reality. These compatibles are still available, but each may require its own particular type of 32-bit memory expansion board.

Since the EISA connector is an upward-compatible superset of the 16-bit ISA connector, you can continue to resurrect ancient 8-bit add-on boards as well as newer 16-bit add-ons. This upward compatibility has caused the ISA/EISA bus to flourish in a world of continuously improving AT-style computers. Figure 47 shows how more data and address lines are added as we move from the 8- to the 16- to the 32-bit EISA connectors.

Although the EISA connector shown appears to be longer than the 16-bit AT connector, it is actually the same length. The third block in the EISA connector is

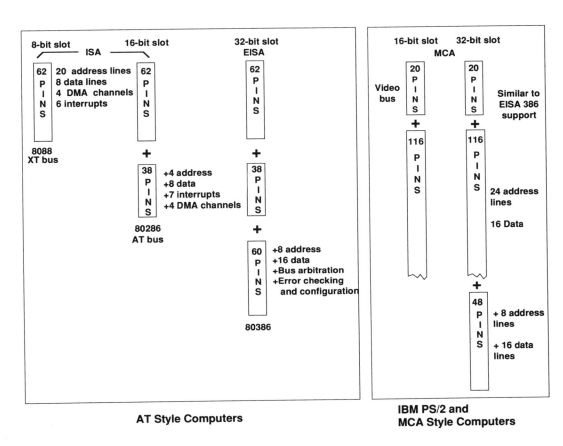

Figure 47. **ISA/EISA vs. MCA buses:** Notice that the ISA/EISA bus standard is completely different than the MCA bus standard.

implemented as the second (higher) row of the DtC edge pins on a taller connector accessible only to EISA boards. Regular AT boards simply plug the EISA connector's lower row of contacts near the motherboard as on the regular AT connector. For example, XT-style 8-bit boards plug into AT-style 16-bit connectors. Both AT-style 16-bit boards and 32-bit EISA boards will plug into the EISA connector.

How does the 80286 or 80386 microprocessor know what type of board is plugged into the bus? A common bus signal informs the CPU on a board-by-board basis what type of data transfer is required for that particular board. Using this control signal, the CPU appropriately sends 1, 2, or 4 bytes at a time down the 8-, 16-, or 32-bit bus. Thus, you can have a mix of 8-, 16-, or 32-bit data width boards on an EISA-bused DtC. This is quite a feat indeed.

Only the more expensive and higher performance 80386/486-based AT-style computers incorporate the EISA standard bus connector. This is because only particular high-speed peripherals, graphics interfaces, and network controllers require the full 32-bit connection to the bus, and these peripherals are not likely to be found in or on a home computer.

EISA-bused DtCs incorporate a mix of 8- and 16-bit ISA connectors as well as a few EISA connectors, and you can plug older 8-bit and 16-bit boards into the EISA connector. If you do this, however, be aware of two things:

1. You won't be taking advantage of 32-bit data width.

2. Other features of the EISA bus, such as self configuration, error checking, and bus arbitration, won't be accessible.

It might make more sense to leave those 8- and 16-bit boards in an older DtC and recycle them to another member of your organization or household. Naturally, we all want a 32-bit connection to memory, which is the most frequently accessed device by the CPU, but this is usually accomplished by a motherboard connection. The motherboard provides a more intimate link to the CPU than is possible with the bus connector. Special non-bus sockets on the motherboard permit plugging in SIMMs for this CPU connection.

Many AT-style compatibles incorporate their own specialized 32-bit bus connectors, sometimes used for memory expansion, although most do also provide for SIMMs.

The MCA Bus

The MCA, IBM's proprietary 32-bit bus, was created for its new PS/2 line of personal computers. The MCA bus is perhaps IBM's best technological achievement in the past five years. It represents a four-year effort involving thousands of designers and engineers. The MCA bus was originally designed to ameliorate three common problems: the personal computer bus was susceptible to radio frequency noise, it was unable to share resources among multiple processors, and it was unable to share interrupts.

Most importantly, the MCA bus is a complete rework of the ISA bus and is incompatible with it. As shown in Figure 47, ISA/EISA add-on boards will *not* plug into the MCA bus, and MCA add-on boards will *not* plug into the ISA/EISA bus. IBM felt that it was worth abandoning compatibility for a complete and improved bus. Some of the MCA bus's main features, most of which are also incorporated in the EISA bus, are:

- Improved memory and I/O transfer cycles in 8-, 16-, and 32-bit modes.
- Distributed grounding patterns to reduce radio-frequency emissions and stabilize logic levels. This will become more important as microprocessor clock speeds exceed 25 MHz.
- Automatic peripheral configuration; no more switch settings.
- Shared interrupts between cards.
- Bus arbitration mechanism. Up to 15 processors can share the bus using a fairness algorithm.
- Optimized signal placement at the connector, which simplifies interfacing with VLSI devices.
- Direct support of audio signals on the bus. These signals can be used by modems, voice chips, and sound chips.
- Support of video signals on the bus. This provides more flexibility for graphics add-on boards and video usage (interactive video).
- Extendability, because many signals on the 132-pin bus are not used.

- Support of multiple processors on the bus.
- 0.05" pin spacing (vs. 0.1" spacing of the older bus) allows for more signals on a smaller add-on board. The smaller tolerances may be a problem for amateurs who fabricate their own add-on boards.

EISA vs. MCA

■ Some vendors offer boards with an ISA/EISA connector on one side and an MCA connector on the other allowing the board to be plugged into either an AT-style or MCA DtC.

Both EISA and MCA buses provide distinct advantages over the older ISA bus system. ■ There is, however, a continuing debate between MCA and EISA. IBM has used aggressive marketing strategies for the PS/2 line incorporating the MCA bus. The main advantages are that MCA has been in existence longer than EISA and more MCA add-on boards are available than EISA boards. The new MCA design is a plus; not only does it improve upon an older bus, it is not subject to the older one's weaknesses.

In support of the EISA bus, compatibility with the very popular world of the AT-style computers is a major selling point. There are, by far, more manufacturers of AT-style computers, particularly when we consider the Asian clone market. Since the MCA bus is a proprietary IBM bus, a licensing fee must be paid to IBM before the bus can be incorporated into a DtC. Many DtC vendors operate at such a low margin that they cannot afford to pay the fee.

Apple's NuBus

Found in the Macintosh II line, the NuBus is thought by many to be equal in sophistication to IBM's Micro Channel. If you are serious about high-power add-ons for the Macintosh, you had better make sure that it has NuBus capability. Some of the lower-cost Macs do not implement the NuBus.

Futurebus+

The Futurebus+ standard is currently being formulated by the IEEE Microprocessor Standards Committee for the next generation of multi-microprocessor, parallel architecture DtC systems. Futurebus+ is planned to be architecturally independent, fault tolerant, scalable, and autoconfigurable.

5.3   Bus Summary

The buses just described all provide for a more sophisticated DtC. The increased sophistication can be summarized as follows:

- ***Multiprocessing*** – Multiple processors can share system resources through bus arbitration schemes.
- ***Auto-configuration*** – Provide add-on board auto-configuration and usage of vital system resources (interrupts, DMA).
- ***Higher speed*** – Dramatically increased bus data transfer rates. Higher speed allows data to move faster between the CPU and others and between peripherals.

Although it is more complicated to interface to the newer buses than to the previous generation of DtC buses such as the ISA, chip vendors including Western Digital, Intel, and Chips and Technologies provide VLSI chips that simplify interfacing.

Boards for systems implementing EISA and MCA are difficult to design and tool. Disappearing are the days when the hobbyist could design interfaces in the basement workshop and play with them on a DtC. Since the EISA allows experimentation, many hardware-oriented university computer courses continue to use EISA AT-style computers.

Before the EISA, MCA, and NuBus, there was a line of sophisticated standard buses such as Motorola's VME bus, Intel's Multibus, and others, which long ago implemented the advanced features now attributed to EISA, MCA, and NuBus. What is important, however, is that the earlier buses were not found in home and office computers. They were found in expensive minicomputers and engineering workstations. The improved buses of today's DtCs when coupled with other important advances such as high resolution video displays, fast hard disks, improved CPUs, and multitasking operating systems are all part of a continuing equalization process. This process is blurring the distinctions between DtCs and crumbling the dividing wall between DtCs and what has been traditionally defined as workstations.

The MCA, EISA, NuBus, and VME are evolving bus standards. As processing demands continue, upward-compatible improvements in these buses will inevitably occur. The degree of compatibility between different versions will always be a vital issue. Moreover, an important factor for the future of buses will be their ability to support higher clock speeds of the newer CISC, RISC, and ASIC processors and to allow these processors to share a DtC's resources. Already Intel is manufacturing CPUs that can operate at clock speeds well above 50 MHz, exceeding the capability of today's ISA bus. As CPU clock speeds increase and add-on boards become more sophisticated the older bus standards will fade away, and the need to provide upward-compatible solutions will be replaced by a newer set of bus standards. Apple's NuBus and IBM's MCA bus represent this trend.

Although the newer buses boast such high-level capabilities as multiprocessing and light-speed bus transfers, the huge commercial software base hardly uses such capabilities. While there are many special-purpose applications of multiprocessing, for example, networking and heavy-duty math processing, it will be years before the commercial software market catches up to the capabilities many DtC buses now provide. The appearance of video, audio, and resource sharing signals on DtC buses will herald a new breed of applications software. You will see software that connects with a TV or VCR camera and software that communicates with new hardware incorporating application-specific processors dedicated to database management, text manipulation, data acquisition, and a host of other functions.

6.0   Interfaces

An interface is the divider between independent systems across which they communicate or act upon one another. It is a sort of "talk across," a gossip fence that neighbors lean on when they exchange important information on important events. While an interface separates devices it also joins them for a given purpose. There are several kinds of interface. Hardware interfaces are wires and plugs that interconnect devices; software interfaces are languages, codes, and messages; user interfaces are display screens, keyboards, mice, and other input devices. Almost anything that allows one component of a system to talk to another component can be called an interface.

A DtC system has a CPU, memory, and other components. Peripherals are also likely to have these components. In order to speak to one another there must be an interface, a portal between the DtC and its peripherals. DtC interfaces have varying degrees of intimacy, performance, bus signal access, speed, and protection. As always, there will be a coin-flip: some will favor performance, others standardization.

You can think of an interface as an interpreter that converts the internal signals and data of a device into a neutral form for communication. The neutral data can then be passed to a receiving device where it can be reconstituted for use by that device.

> **NOTE**
>
> An analogous situation has already been discussed. A complex internal data format was converted to a neutral ASCII format for transmission to another program. Within the ASCII format there was no program-specific information. On the receiving end the ASCII data had to be reconstituted. Just as a neutral file format is an intermediary between two software programs, so is an interface an intermediary between two different hardware systems that need to transfer data. Neutral ASCII data format entails a loss of program-specific data and the interface loses hardware-specific knowledge or connection intimacy between the two interfaced systems.

Interfaces are found between a DtC's internal components as well as between these components and the outside world, or the DtC's peripheral interfaces. Peripherals are the focus of the following discussion as we look at various ways that DtCs communicate with them. The connection between internal DtC signals and the interface occurs most often at the DtC's bus. The term *bus interface* is used to characterize this type of interconnection. The interface will generally be contained in an add-on board that plugs into the DtC bus. Most often there is an electrical connection between the DtC bus and the interface and another between the interface and the peripheral.

The primary purpose of a bus interface is to accept data from the DtC's bus and make it available to a peripheral and also to provide data to the DtC bus from a peripheral at a given time. Peripheral interfaces conduct standard signals between the peripherals of the DtC and other equipment, just as household electrical systems carry a standard voltage.

If you were to inspect a DtC system's signals and buses, you would confront a flurry of seemingly random activity. Millions of addresses per second and millions of available data bytes wander around the data bus. The activity, however, is far from random. The various interfaces talk to the CPU, or to one another at a rapid pace; each device reacting only to its own calling address. Figure 48 depicts a DtC and peripheral communicating through their respective interfaces, each controlling the transmissions using *handshaking* signals.

Each system's address and data bus do not connect to one another, but rather communicate through the respective bus interfaces. In addition to the data that flows between these systems, the handshaking signals permit data flow control so that data is sent no faster than the receiving computer can process it. Signals such as strobes, request/acknowledge, busy, and interrupts will be used as these handshaking signals. Depending upon the type of interface between the two systems (DtC and peripheral) the DtC CPU may either need to be directly involved with the transfers, as with the CPU port I/O, or not too concerned at all, as with the DMA and shared memory.

6.1   Fundamental Interface Types

Interfacing spans different levels of sophistication; it can comprise elaborate schemes for multiple peripherals to share system resources as well as simple schemes for the CPU to communicate with its peripherals. The main interface types include CPU port I/O, DMA, and shared memory as shown in Figure 49. The CPU port I/O makes for flexible but slow communications; DMA yields faster transfer

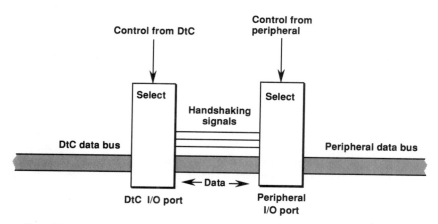

Figure 48.   The general interface: Interfaces allow communication between dissimilar systems, each system having some responsibility for controlling the flow of data.

without flexibility; while shared memory provides the most intimate interface, but is more difficult to implement. Let's look at each in detail.

CPU Port I/O

This is the simplest level to implement. The CPU is used to directly write to or read from the peripheral. The interface of the peripheral is set up as a single directly accessible device, a port. The port appears to the CPU as a single addressable register.

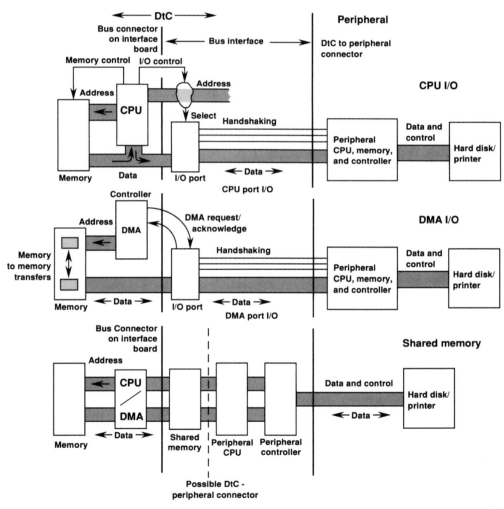

Figure 49. Three fundamental interface types: Port I/O places the data transfer responsibility on the CPU, while with DMA transfers, the DMA controller takes over. With shared memory, data exists in both systems simultaneously.

The interface connects to the address bus and watches for a particular address from the CPU. When this address occurs, the device connects to the bus for data communications. Recall the earlier discussion on device selection. The DtC CPU acts as the go-between, reading data from the peripheral through the port and writing it to memory or reading data from memory and writing it to the peripheral through the port. In the following example, the CPU port I/O is implemented by both the DtC and peripheral, a printer for instance.

EXAMPLE

CPU PORT I/O

Figure 50 shows the DtC and printer communicating data through parallel CPU port I/O interfaces implementing strobe and busy status signals.

We join the action as the printer prints its last character and the printer status goes from *busy* to *not busy*. The *not busy* event triggers an interrupt in the DtC CPU, disengaging it from its current task to execute the following code:

```
OUT 300, 65
```

Upon code execution, the CPU places the binary equivalent of *300* on its address bus. At the same time the CPU places a *65*, the ASCII code of the character (the letter A) to be printed, on its data bus. The address *300* actuates the interface and causes it to capture the *65* that has been placed on the data bus. The interface transfers the *65* from the D (data bus) side to the Q (peripheral) side of the interface latch. On the Q side, the character *65* is trapped, waiting for the printer to read it. Following the capture, the DtC CPU returns to what it had been doing prior to the interrupt.

No other device in the DtC reacts to the *300* address since other DtC devices each have their own address. As a result of the CPU write action, the DtC interface generates the strobe signal. The strobe signal becomes an interrupt to the printer CPU.

On sensing strobe interrupt, the printer CPU stops whatever it is doing to execute the code:

```
CHARACTER = INP(500)
```

This code causes the printer CPU to place a *500*, its interface location, on its address bus. The printers interface reacts by passing through to the printer data bus the *65* that is latched in the DtC interface and connected to the printer interface by cabling. At this instant, the printer CPU

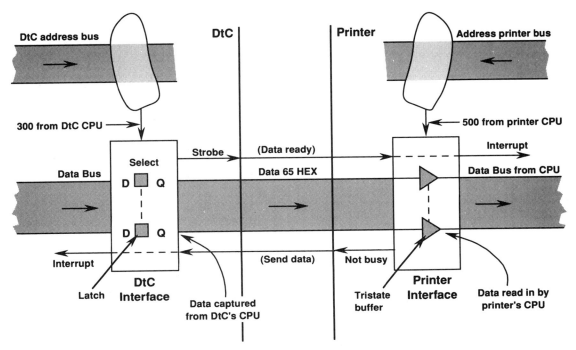

Figure 50. **CPU port I/O example:** Using CPU port I/O, the CPU must be the data mover.

captures the *65* and sends it through another interface, not shown, to the printer head.

Thus the DtC interface captured the character from its bus and made it available to the printer CPU by the printer interface. Through the interfaces, two completely different microcomputers communicated. And all of this occurred in microseconds.

Use of Interrupts

The DtC does not check for a busy printer, nor does the printer check for a received character. The *event* of the printer not being busy triggers the DtC CPU to transmit the next character and the *event* of receiving a character triggers an interrupt to the printer CPU to print that character. There is no waiting. While the printer is busy, the DtC can be off doing something else, and while the printer is waiting for another character, it can be forming the previous character. Proper use of interrupts on both sides is the key to immediate processing.

The example above, a basic and easy to implement interface, shows how different computer systems communicate through interfaces, and should help to solidify the notion of direct and indirect addressability.

Referring to the discussion on direct and indirect addressability, notice that memory resources in the printer are *not* directly addressable by the DtC CPU and conversely, memory in the DtC is not directly addressable by the printer CPU. Most interfaces, including the one in our example, appear as a single register capable of passing one data word at a time, occupying a single I/O address. This type of interface is known as PIO (port I/O) interfaces. 8- 16-, or 32-bit transfers can occur in parallel, depending on the respective system's data widths. 80386-based systems, for example, often have 32-bit interfaces to their faster peripherals: hard disks, graphics interfaces, and memory. Although data throughput can be increased by the wider 32-bit data transfers, data must pass through both the respective CPU and a portal that is quite narrow when you consider that each communicating system might have megabytes of its own internal directly addressable memory. Thus, the interface can be a bottleneck in the process of information transfer between DtCs and peripherals, or even between coupled DtCs through long haul or local area networks. Direct memory access and shared memory interfaces, which are described next, can help alleviate the CPU-driven port I/O bottleneck.

DMA

Direct memory access is an efficient way to move data between two devices. Through direct memory access the DtC can get data from a peripheral into and out of its memory quickly and without a CPU as an intermediary. The DMA controller shares the bus with the CPU and masterminds successive read/write transfers between the peripheral and DtC memory. The transfers are at a much higher rate than would be possible using the CPU as an intermediary, as is the case with CPU port I/O. The DMA controller can transfer data between the peripheral interface and DtC system memory while the DtC CPU is otherwise occupied. In most cases both the CPU and the DMA controller can be using the same bus concurrently with only a minor CPU slowdown.

The DMA acts in two primary ways:

1. **DMA port I/O** – The DMA controller moves data to and from a single word register port from and to DtC directly addressable memory. The DMA controller doesn't care when or how the data arrives at the register; it simply places the incoming words into sequential DtC memory locations. This type of transfer is called a *write transfer*. In the other case, the DMA controller can send bytes from sequential memory locations in the DtC to a single word register. This type of transfer is called a *read transfer*.

> **NOTE**
>
> A *write transfer* refers to bytes received through the port and written to the DtC memory by the DMA controller. A *read transfer* refers to the bytes picked up by the DMA controller reading the DtC memory for sending to the DMA port.

DMA port I/O is similar to CPU port I/O. The outside data passes into and out of DtC memory by way of a single, word-wide register. The difference with DMA port I/O is the speed at which the data can flow. DMA port I/O transfers are much faster than those made by the CPU because the DMA controller specializes in sequential transfers; that is, the bytes transferred must be to and from contiguous memory locations. Request and acknowledge signals between the peripheral and the DMA controller are the handshaking signals that control the flow. DMA request and acknowledge signals act like the busy and strobe lines described in the previous example of CPU port I/O. Figure 49 does not show how the peripheral is moving data on its side. It could be using its own CPU port I/O, DMA port I/O, or a variety of other methods for gathering up and distributing data on its end of the communication. In any case, both interfaces will synchronize their activities with handshaking lines so that the data receiver can keep up with the data transmitter.

2. **Block transfers** – The DMA controller not only controls the passage of data between DtC memory and port registers, but it can also perform memory-to-memory transfers within the memory of a given DtC. Figure 49 depicts block memory transfers occurring between different parts of DtC memory. The transfer can take place only if both memory blocks are directly addressable. The DMA controller can quickly move data between different memory areas. The ability to do this has great merit, because situations involving sorting, graphics constructions, interface buffering, and moving data from EMS switching frames to executable memory can benefit greatly from quick block memory transfers.

If the peripheral and DtC share memory, the shared memory will be addressable by the DtC DMA controller. Then, DMA memory to memory transfers can move data between the shared memory and directly addressable memory elsewhere in the DtC.

Since the typical DMA controller has four sets of addressing registers, also known as channels, it can move data between four different memory areas and four respective port registers, each connected to a different peripheral concurrently. Or it could perform block transfers between two pairs of memory blocks concurrently. And it can do this while the CPU is executing instructions.

As long as the transfers are from contiguous memory locations, the DMA controller can transfer more efficiently than the CPU can. Programs and data are often stored in contiguous memory. Graphics images are often stored in blocks of contiguous memory locations, requiring block transfers between the display interface memory, a form of shared memory, and the memory blocks in the DtC.

Although direct memory access is faster than the CPU interface, DMA transfers lack flexibility. You may need to perform a translation on the data while you move it from one place to another; maybe scale it, bias it, change its color, shape, or density. Or you may need to transfer data that is sprinkled about in memory and not in contiguous locations. The DMA controller specializes in fast, contiguous memory data transfers; it is not capable of data processing. For data processing, the CPU of the DtC or the CPU on the interface board must get into the act.

Shared Memory

Peripherals will often need to directly address a block of memory in the DtC, or the DtC may need to address a block of memory in the peripheral. Shared memory is an effective way to couple data between two CPUs, each with its own local address and data buses. With shared memory, the interface doorway is much bigger than the CPU port I/O and DMA port I/O interface types. In fact, with shared memory, the interface portal becomes equally addressable by both systems and data isn't really transferred at all between the two. It exists in, and is shared by, both systems at the same time.

Since shared memory usually needs to be controlled by the CPUs of both the DtC and the peripheral, the physical location of the shared memory on bus interfaces will be on the interface board. This way the memory can be controlled by DtC address and data lines, carried on the bus, and by the peripheral controller, located on the board. The shared memory cannot be the DtC system memory since that cannot be controlled by the peripheral's address and data lines. When using shared memory interfaces, DtC system memory must not occupy the addressing range of the shared memory on the interface or bus conflicts will occur.

Shared memory could be memory that is commonly addressed by both the CPU of the DtC and the controller of the secondary device, the hard disk. The EMS frame buffer is a shared memory between the EMS board and DtC on-board memory. Shared memory will often be found in video interfaces and other peripherals.

Many signal processing boards share memory with the DtC. Signal processing software can be stored on the DtC hard disk and loaded directly onto the signal processing board as if it were any other DtC memory area. You might, for example, develop some signal processing routines using a cross compiler operating on the DtC. As the compilation process completes, the signal processing program is placed into DtC memory. The signal processor CPU can immediately run this code because it directly addresses the same memory. There is no data transfer, as such. Both the DtC CPU and signal processor CPU can operate in the same memory, with the DtC creating the program and the signal processor executing the program.

Also, data might be stored in the common memory, as when a voice recognition and synthesis add-on board stores voice data in shared memory. The CPU of the DtC can manage word-recognition sets, display screens, possibly a floor plan in a voice-controlled home control system, distribute voice recognition algorithms, and compress voice files to the shared memory. The voice synthesis and recognition board CPU will execute the algorithms to do what it does best, recognize, synthesize, and compress voice data. Here, we have an effective share between the higher-level processing capability of the DtC and the lower-level processing capability of an add-on board.

By now you might think that shared memory is a panacea. This would be true were it not for the fact that shared memory interfaces are difficult to implement. The reason is that both the peripheral and the DtC addressing and data communicating capabilities must be merged on the same interface board. This merge can be accomplished if the interface and interface CPU are located inside the DtC. But how can memory be shared between a laser printer located some distance away? It can be done if we run the address and data buses of the laser printer CPU back to the DtC. Figure 49 on page 245 shows a possible DtC-to-peripheral connector where the peripheral CPU is not on the bus interface, but rather is contained in the peripheral. Notice how the intimate addressing signals must pass between DtC and peripheral over the interface cable. When the peripheral CPU and controller are on the interface board, data and control pass to the hard disk or printer from the DtC-to-peripheral connector.

Using DMA block transfers or CPU port I/O, programs and data located elsewhere in DtC memory can be transferred rapidly to and from the common memory area.

Figure 49 depicts the three fundamental types of interface: CPU I/O, DMA port, and shared memory found on desktop computers. See how the CPU I/O uses the CPU as an intermediary in data movement, which allows additional processing to take place. The DMA controller speeds consecutive memory data through the interface but can't process the data. In the shared memory interface, there is no transfer of data taking place. Data simply exists in directly addressable form in both systems. In all cases, what is important is how data gets from the executable memory of the DtC to the executable memory of the peripheral interface.

Type	Speed	Processing	Interface Sophistication
PIO	Slow	Whatever a CPU can do	Low
DMA	Fast	Contiguous transfers only	Medium
Shared Memory	Instantaneous	Whatever both CPUs can do	High

Table 24.   The nature of three types of interface: From the table, the compromise should be clear between speed and complexity of the interface as well as between speed and processing capability.

6.2   *Popular Interfaces*

Popular peripheral interfaces are:

Parallel printer interface: Most dot matrix printers plug into the parallel interface found on most DtCs with only minor cable differences. The interface provides for high speed parallel data transfer between the DtC and printer. The *Centronics* parallel interface is considered a standard type and is typically implemented as a CPU port I/O interface.

RS-232 serial interface: Used for the low-speed modem, mice, and plotters. Most of these lower-speed peripherals plug into the serial RS-232 interfaces found on most DtCs. Null modems may be required to account for proper operation. The RS-232 serial interface is also a CPU port I/O type interface.

Keyboard interface: Keyboard interfaces are similar to the RS-232 serial interface. Inside the keyboard, a microprocessor converts the key presses from row/column array connections in serial codes that are converted back into parallel data bytes in the keyboard interface for access by the CPU. The keyboard interface is usually implemented as a CPU port I/O interface.

Hard disk interface: The hard disk and hard disk interface usually come in matched pairs for a specific DtC. Hard disk interfaces sometimes share some memory with the DtC. Since the shared memory is directly addressable by the DtC, shared memory data can be shuffled between shared memory and the rest of its executable memory by CPU action or if transfers of consecutive memory locations are allowed, by DMA memory-to-memory action. Look at Figure 49 on page 245 and imagine that the interface CPU is the hard disk controller. Notice the shared memory that is directly addressable by the DtC CPU or its DMA controller.

Other hard disk controllers will ship data bytes quickly through a parallel port on the hard disk. The DtC will implement DMA port I/O to scoop up the rapidly arriving bytes of data, placing the data in contiguous DtC memory locations. Look again at the figure and this time imagine that the register on the DtC side is receiving bytes rapidly from the hard disk interface. On the hard disk interface side, DMA port I/O might occur between its unshared memory and its parallel port. The hard disk interface could be using *any* means of assembling bytes in rapid order. The DMA controller will pick up the bytes as they arrive and place them in DtC contiguous executable memory locations. The CPU then executes the data in its own time.

The ESDI, enhanced system device interface, is a popular high-performance hard disk interface. The general-purpose SCSI, small computer systems interface, is used also as a hard disk interface.

Graphics monitor interface: The graphics interface connects the graphics monitor to the DtC. One of the more sophisticated interfaces, it must manage a large memory area in which images are stored. The memory, or part of it, is often shared with DtC memory and methods described for the hard disk interface will be implemented to move between this memory and other memory in the DtC. The less sophisticated dumb video interfaces scan this memory out to the display leaving the DtC CPU in charge of getting images into it. The intelligent graphics interfaces draw and manipulate the memory images directly, saving the more general-purpose CPU from this chore.

While all DtCs require a graphics display monitor, there are many different types. The older monitors are driven by low-resolution single wire composite video signals while the newer monitors require separate analog red, green, and blue signals as well as digital synchronization signals. Moreover, different display resolutions require different horizontal and vertical synchronizing signals. Early IBM monitors, the CGA, MDA, and EGA required digital color signals, complicating any quest for standardization. Fortunately, today's multisync graphics monitors can adapt to many of these differences and we can use the same monitor on different DtCs. Connector pinouts – red, green, blue color signals, horizontal and vertical sync – are becoming standardized with only a few different connectors and adapters. We will say more about graphics interfaces in a later Part.

Interface Standardization vs. Performance

All of the interfaces mentioned above connect to a DtC internal bus. While the buses are completely different in different classes of DtCs, the interfaces bring signals to the outside world according to certain conventions. For the serial interface, the convention is known as RS-232. For parallel printer interfaces, the convention is known as the Centronics standard. Because of their high level of standardization and popularity, the RS-232 and Centronics parallel printer interfaces will be discussed later in detail.

Several different types of cables may be used to connect a monitor to a system unit and different signals may pass over them; however, the cables and signals are standardized. Single wire composite video is a standardized video signal that is connected with a standard RG-59 75-ohm or RG-58 50-ohm coaxial cable while many analog RGB monitors use a standardized 9- or 15-pin cable to carry the RGB and sync signals.

The hard disk interface may connect to the hard disk with one of several types of cable, as discussed later. The popular SCSI, ESDI, ST-512/406, and IDE con-

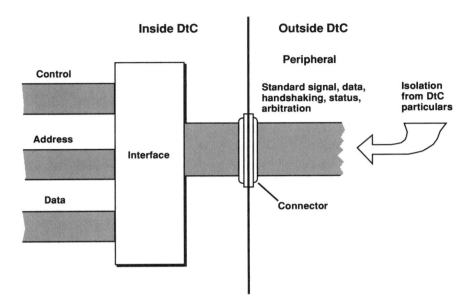

Figure 51. Standardization with interfaces: An interface relieves the peripheral from details within a given DtC system. Standardized peripherals are less intimately interfaced.

trollers implement different cables between the hard disk interface and the drive itself.

The bus interface serves as a shield between the peripheral and the DtC internal bus. In Figure 51, looking into the serial interface connector, you see the same RS-232 type signals, speeds, and voltages regardless of what computer is behind the interface connector. You can plug the modem that implements these signals into almost any DtC. The shielding effect, however, is not without penalty. By isolating the peripheral from the more intimate internal DtC signals, you keep it from effective coupling with the internal components of the DtC and other peripheral interfaces.

While a modem and dot matrix printer will plug into most standard RS-232 and Centronics parallel printer interfaces, the hard disk and video display will probably not be so compliant. The graphics interface to monitor, or the hard disk interface to hard disk data connections are more intimate connections than the serial interface to modem connection. Intimate connection is essential for the high data rates that must occur between the DtC CPU and the video interface memory. The more specialized the peripheral, the less common, or neutral, the interface, and the more difficult is the interchange between different DtC interfaces.

Specialized Peripherals and DtC Standardization

Highly specialized peripherals: character and voice recognizers, data acquisition systems, and signal processors, for example, require a highly specialized interface such as shared memory, or require a more direct contact with the DtC's specific capabilities – memory, CPU, DMA, interrupts – than can be provided by the more common interfaces. The special peripheral and interface board come as a matched pair designed for one another and a particular DtC bus. If you are going to make use of this type of peripheral, you need to be more concerned about consistency in the choice of DtC platforms than if you use peripherals not matched to particular DtCs. The RS-232 serial, the Centronics parallel printer, and now the SCSI interface are well standardized and are included with most DtC purchases. Often these interfaces are built right into the DtC motherboard, which saves vital bus connectors for the more specialized peripheral interfaces. Due to their popularity, these interfaces are usually supported by the operating system, applications, and programming languages. Software products that use these interfaces through BIOS drivers that support them are assured the highest degree of compatibility among different microcomputer systems.

Since the RS-232 and Centronics parallel interface are general purpose, they do not offer the most efficient use of a given microcomputer architecture (DMA, interrupts, memory resources, or direct communication with other peripheral interfaces), nor do they allow particularly high speed transfer of data. It is this compromise – lack of intimacy for general-purpose operation – that characterizes the standard interfaces.

Other, more specialized interfaces are becoming popular and therefore standardized. Examples are the SCSI, a high speed, intelligent interface used mostly for hard disks and networks; the MIDI (musical interchange digital interface); and the IEEE 488 test instrument interface. Also, there are interfaces that can bridge between the DtC bus and the bus of other more specialized microcomputer systems such as the STD (standard) bus used by many process control systems. As microcomputer manufacturers provide sophisticated functionality in their microcomputer hardware, specialized, standard interfaces will bridge the gap between efficiency and generality. Standard interfaces to DVI, voice synthesis and recognition, and other special hardware will occur as these functions become more popular.

Serial and Parallel Interfaces

The important distinction between serial and parallel interfaces is the manner in which data words are transmitted. The parallel interface moves multiple bits at a time between the DtC and peripheral, while the serial interface uses a single data channel. After data is captured from the bus, the bits move in single file along one channel (serial), or the bits move several abreast along that many channels (parallel).

The Centronics parallel printer interface, for example, captures 8-bit bytes (representing characters) and sends them en masse to the printer. The printer then reads these signals a full byte at a time. When 16- or 32-bit words are transmitted in parallel between the DtC and the peripheral, the speed of the interface is even higher.

For modem use, the serial RS-232 interface converts parallel bytes into a serial bit stream to be sent to the modem and ultimately over the phone lines. Two single data paths are used: one for transmitting and one for receiving. Since the phone system works this way for voice transmissions, there is no need for eight phone lines to transmit computer data.

Add-on Interface Boards vs. Built-in Interfaces

Peripheral interfaces are most often located on boards that plug into the DtC bus connectors. Bus interface boards contain the circuitry necessary to select, buffer, and protect the peripheral and connect it to DtC-bused signals on demand. When correctly interfaced, the peripheral can talk to the CPU, memory, or any other device connected to the bus.

The most common interfaces, the serial RS-232, the parallel printer and keyboard interfaces and sometimes graphics and hard disk interfaces, are an integral part of the DtC motherboard. On-motherboard location frees the valuable bus connectors to hook up to the less common peripheral interfaces. Some DtCs (Macintosh, Atari, Amiga) provide practically all of the popular interfaces on the motherboard and provide only one or two bus connectors. This reduces the cost and size of the units, but can restrict their flexibility in interfacing to a wide range of peripherals.

Built-in interfaces may be difficult or impossible to change. For example, say you don't like your built-in display interface; it doesn't have enough resolution or colors. You buy a bus-connected display interface and plug it into your system's bus. Hopefully you will be able to disable the interface on the motherboard so that the two interfaces do not conflict with each other's use of memory, interrupts, DMA, or I/O registers. If you need to add a different serial, parallel, graphics, or hard disk interface by using a bus-interfaced add-on board, you must be able to resolve conflicts that might occur with those interfaces found on the motherboard.

On the advantage side, building in the interfaces can reduce the cost and size of the DtC system. With built-in interfaces you require fewer bus connectors. Also, the interfaces may connect to signals not bused and provide a more intimate and integrated interface than bus interfaces provide. This is particularly true of hard disk, graphics, and memory interfaces, which are being built into the system motherboard to share use of the DtC system resources.

6.3   Important Bus Interface Signals

The bus signals listed earlier may take on a clearer meaning when described from the point of view of the peripheral bus interfaces.

- **Address** – Address lines are used to separate and select the myriad of devices that may be interfaced to the DtC. This includes the internal memory as well as the I/O registers in the peripheral interfaces.

- **Data** – Once selected, the data bus will be used to transfer the information. Intel 80xxx systems will transfer 8-, 16-, or 32-bits of data per transfer depending upon whether an 8088/86, 80286, or 80386/486 commands the transfer. Using additional bused signals the CPU and peripheral will agree on the appropriate transfer data width.

- **Interrupts** – The peripheral may want the kind of instant CPU service that is available only through interrupts. Rather than having the CPU poll, the peripheral can tug on an interrupt line, which immediately yanks the CPU away from what it was doing to service the peripheral.■ To do this, however, the peripheral needs access to a bused interrupt line. These lines are shown in Figure 26 on page 162. The previous interface example illustrated the use of interrupts by a peripheral on both ends of a communication.

■ The CPU determines that a peripheral needs service by polling, that is, by repeatedly reading the peripheral for service requests using CPU port I/O.

- **DMA control** – Signals that invoke and acknowledge DMA chip control of data transfers. These transfers are much quicker than CPU transfers, but there will be tradeoffs.

- **Bus arbitration** – When multiple peripherals must concurrently share system resources, a method of arbitration permits this to occur in an orderly fashion. To accomplish the necessary handshaking between devices and the system, bus arbitration signals are used.

6.4   Potential Interface Conflicts

Conflicts can occur when multiple boards try to control the same bus signals. These contentions or "bus wars" can bring a system to a standstill and can even damage interface boards. Worse, these conflicts are often initially diagnosed as software problems. The user makes elaborate changes in software configurations, but the problems persist. Finally, in desperation, the frustrated user pops the hood of the DtC, looks at the interface board technical manuals, and discovers improper board hardware settings. Reconfiguring the interface boards through switches and jumpers forces the boards to cooperate in resource use, and all becomes well.

The NuBus, Micro Channel, and EISA bus interface boards can be configured to use the appropriate bus signals cooperatively by software initialization. These initializations are serialized in firmware on each interface board, relieving users from the tedious and frustrating chore of board setups.

Buses that do not implement autoconfiguration, the MS-DOS ISA, for example, continue to experience signal contention problems such as:

- **Interrupts** – More than one peripheral vying for the same interrupt line can cause trouble. Peripherals can sometimes use the same bused interrupt line if there is a method for sharing. If each interface is able to tristate its interrupt connection to the bus under software control, multiple boards can share a single bused interrupt as long as only one board at a time is enabled.

- **DMA** – As with interrupts, contention for the same DMA control signals can be problematic. Multiple boards must not be connected to the same DMA control signals unless they can be electrically connected only one at a time under software control.

- **Controller I/O registers** – Controller I/O registers serve two purposes. One is to communicate such information as mode, type of transfer, and rate of transfer. The other is to provide the portal through which the data actually passes. If more than one controller is mapped into the same I/O locations, the controllers try to connect to the same data bus, and bus contention occurs with possible damage to the interface. When the CPU tries to read the multiple devices all chattering at once at a single I/O address, the CPU sees gibberish.

- **Memory** – Peripheral controllers may contain ROM memory that the CPU uses for initialization and control routines. Also, the interface may contain dual-ported memory for easy access by the DtC and the peripheral CPU. As with I/O channel addresses, this interface memory must not belong to the same addresses as memory on the other interface boards or on the system memory. Extended and expanded memory drivers use memory in complicated ways, making it difficult to track down memory conflict problems.

Multiprocessing

This is the most sophisticated type of interface technology. In multiprocessing, one or more processing agents or peripheral interfaces can control DtC resources by sharing the system bus. This requires higher levels of software and bus capability than are currently found in the lower-cost DtCs. In fact, it is the multiprocessing capability more than any other capability – graphics, mass storage, CPU speed, or memory addressability – that separates HB computers from EP computers. More advanced buses such as Motorola's VME bus, and the HB computer buses such as Micro Channel, EISA, and NuBus can support multiprocessing. Having the right bus, however, is only the starting point. The interfaces, operating system, and applications software must also be multiprocessing-aware.

6.5 Standardized Interfaces

The previous discussion should convince you that outside devices can be connected to DtCs in many ways. If general-purpose peripherals are to connect to different DtCs, provisions and compromises will have to be made, or what are known as generic interfaces will have to be used. By limiting bus access, generic interfaces can account for differences between different DtCs. The disadvantage, however, is poor access to internal system resources.

RS-232 Serial Interface

The early dit-dah-dit Morse code telegraph keys and later, teletypewriters, used a communications technology quite similar to today's RS-232 serial interface. Communications were serial, using a single data channel over a long copper wire between transmitting stations. For telegraphy, the same wire was used for both sending and receiving. After all, you wouldn't be sending on your key while you were listening. The old ASR 33 teletypewriter was a popular way of sending messages back and forth. Later, when computers came on the scene, simple ASR 33 serial interfaces between computers and these teletypewriters allowed hard copy printouts of programs and data entered in those computers. In those days, bit rates of 75 or 110 bits per second were considered high speed telecommunications.

Since computers still need to communicate with single-channel phone systems using modems, the need for the RS-232 serial interface persists, though at substantially higher rates. Also, a single channel, your phone connection, is used. Figure 52 shows a bird's eye view of the RS-232 serial interface with a connection to a peripheral.

The two principal means shown in Figure 53 to implement the RS-232 interface are 1) connecting the RS-232 interfaces of two equipments with a hard wire or 2) connecting them by modem. The modem converts the digital RS-232 signals to signals appropriate for a phone system. As we shall see, when direct connecting between RS-232 equipments, a null modem, an interconnection box, is often required to adjust the wires between the two directly-connected equipments.

Figure 54 shows a typical serial interface implemented with a VLSI asynchronous communication interface adapter (ACIA). Addressed data registers inside the ACIA can be read or written to by the CPU. The ASCII code of the character to be transmitted is written to the data out register, which converts it into a serial bit stream that includes the character as well as synchronizing bits and a parity bit. Conversely, incoming serial data is reassembled into a parallel byte that can be read by the CPU from the read register. Most ACIA chips can implement and control interrupts.

As shown in Figure 54, the RS-232 interface includes logic level converters. A DtC's internal logic levels are typically 0V for a logic 0 and 5V for a logic 1, whereas RS-232 signals are +3V to +12V for a logic 0 and -3V to -12V for a logic 1. The larger differences in logic levels permit easier discrimination of logic levels and therefore more reliable operation over longer cable lengths. Serial interface interconnecting cables can be longer than the parallel printer interface cables.

The important characteristics of the RS-232 serial interface are:

- *General-purpose communications methodology* – The RS-232 serial interface provides the lowest common communications denominator between computers and between computers and peripherals.

- *Asynchronous interface* – No separate channel is needed to synchronize transmitting and receiving systems. Synchronism is on a character-by-character basis with each character carrying extra synchronizing bits called *start* and *stop* bits. Precise timing between transmitter and receiver is not required. In fact, the transmitting and receiving interface clocks can be off by as much as three percent and the interface will still function. The extra synchronizing bit takes up the slack.

- *Error detection and correction* – The only error handling provided at the hardware level is single bit parity error, which will identify only the fact that a single error, actually an odd number of errors, has occurred in a single character. It is up to the communications software to recover from the error. Higher levels of software pro-

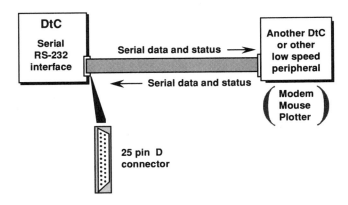

Figure 52. **RS-232 interface overview:** The RS-232 serial interface is used for bidirectional, low-cost communications between equipments.

tocol can be used to check blocks of data and retransmit if there is an error. Two popular software protocols are Xmodem and Kermit. The method is reliable, and is used to transmit large files where errors cannot be tolerated.

- *Long haul communications* – Use the serial interface and modem to move data between distant computers over phone lines and between dissimilar equipments that don't need intimate control or high speed communications.

- *Remote computer control* – By RS-232 interfaced terminals where high levels of interaction with the remote software are not required. Many multitasking operating systems support multiple users over RS-232 interfaces running at 9600 bits/sec.

- *Low data rates* – Due to the nature of communicating channels such as serial interfaces, phone systems, modems, and low-quality transmission lines, these communications have low data rate requirements between 300-200 Kbits/second.

- *Low cost* – Low-cost hook ups, low-cost cabling and connectors, and availability of appropriate interfaces, including modem, on many personal computers.

- *Single chip implementation* – Except for final signal conditioning, the typical RS-232 serial interface is implemented with a single VLSI chip, a UART or an

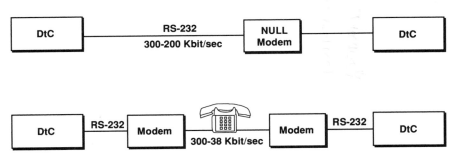

Figure 53. **Modem and direct RS-232 connection:** The direct RS-232 connection permits higher data transfers but can not transmit around the world. A modem is needed for that.

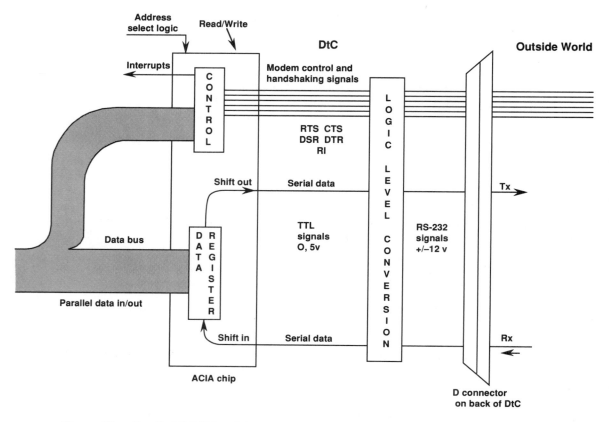

Figure 54. Detailed RS-232 serial interface: The RS-232 interface is usually implemented by an ACIA chip, which is a glorified serial to parallel to serial converter.

ACIA. The ACIA chips are more sophisticated than the UARTs, combining a UART with additional interrupt handling, bit clocks, status bits, and other nice features.

- *Availability* – Most DtCs have built-in serial interfaces. The interfaces are often combined with the parallel printer interface, real time clocks, and even expansion memory on some DtCs. Today, you can purchase an add-on board for an MS-DOS computer with two RS-232 serial and two parallel printer interfaces for less than $20. Serial and parallel printer interfaces are included also in IDE disk controllers.

- *Applications* – The serial interface is for slow peripherals. These include impact printers, plotters, mice, and long haul modems. Transmission speeds of up to 9600 bits/second prevail, although in special cases, up to 200 Kbits/second is possible. The serial interface converts parallel internal bus data transmissions to single or duplex channel operations suitable for single channel commercial phone systems, using a modem.

- *Data rates* – Data rates range from 75 bits per second to over 200 Kbits per second.

• *Simple cables* – For direct connections between equipments, as few as three wires can do the job for two-way communications. Also, cable lengths can be 50 feet long, and sometimes up to 1000 feet, depending on transmission bit rate, without special interfaces.

Table 25 displays popular RS-232 bit rates and applications. Figure 53 compares direct connection and modem transmission speeds.

BIT RATE	APPLICATION
75-110	Older TTY equipments
300	Yesterday's (1970s) modems. Phonetic speech synthesizers can operate at this rate.
1200	Yesterday's (1980s) modems; very reliable phone communication.
2400	Today's low-cost modems (around $100). Many DtCs have 2400 bps modems built in.
9600[1]	Today's more expensive modems; special features and higher cost. The typical throughput rate for direct connected applications. Fax modems.
100K-200K	High end of serial RS-232 communications. Direct connection only; low-cost serial RS-232 networks.
50K to 1.54 M[2]	Leased digital phone lines. Low-cost serial directly connected networks.

Table 25. RS-232 bit rates: Note[1] The 38 Kbit/second rate shown in Figure 53 is an effective transfer rate, which includes data compression performed by the modem. Note[2] The high end, 1.54 M, will require special non-RS-232 communications interfaces.

Supported Peripherals

Peripherals that are commonly supported by the RS-232 serial interface:

• *Printers* – The older low-speed daisy wheel printers and teletypewriters are still supported by the RS-232 serial interface. Most of these have been replaced by the faster dot matrix printers requiring the Centronics parallel printer interface and laser printers requiring the Centronics or more specialized parallel interfaces.

• *Plotters* – Plotters typically implement an internal high-level plotting language. They accomplish a lot of work per command, and the work takes time. For example, you can command a plotter to draw circles, large letters, or lines, and it will take care of the dreary details of plotting these items. Sending these high-level commands, for example HPGL Hewlett Packard graphics language, to an HP compatible plotter over the relatively slow RS-232 serial interface may be quite acceptable. The serial interface is not the bottleneck. The bottleneck will be the speed at which the plotter plots. A simple serial interface print spool program could make the whole operation transparent to the requesting application, with the plotter backlog accomplished in the background using interrupts.■

■ A print spooler is a software device that routes data to be printed to a memory or hard disk area ahead of the slower printer. This allows the slow printing process and other software to operate concurrently.

- *Modems* – It makes sense to use the serial interface here since only a single channel is available on the phone line and the data rates of 300 to 9600 Kbits per second do not demand a faster interface.

- *Mice* – Since a mouse is used primarily as a pointing device, position updates of 100 per second are often adequate. A serial interface operating at 9600 bits/second can easily provide this data rate. A high resolution mouse or digitizing tablet, which provides more accurate positioning and screen drawing capability, might require a custom parallel interface.

- *Character recognizers* – Some of the lower-cost, limited-font, stand-alone character recognizers can use the RS-232 interfaces, since the recognized character data is sent to the DtC in ASCII format. More often, however, the character recognition function is more closely integrated with a DtC (shared memory for downloading recognition parameters, and algorithms) and the interface is implemented as an add-on board, which then connects to the scanner pad or table hardware.

- *Scanners/digitizers* – Occasionally, low-cost image scanners will use RS-232 serial interfaces to transport digitized images to a DtC. This is in an effort to keep the total scanner cost down. It is more likely that a specialized parallel interface will be used due to the density of APA scanned image data sets.

RS-232 Signals and Pinouts

Figure 52 displays a typical hookup between two RS-232 interfaced equipments.

Table 26 lists the more common RS-232 signals and respective pin numbers you would see on the popular 25-pin D connector used in most computers. The MS-DOS computers are popularizing a 9-pin connector, also shown in Table 26.

Abbr.	Pin No. on 25-Pin Connector	Pin No. on 9-Pin Connector	Signal Description
Outbound Signals			
TX (M)	Pin 2	Pin 3	Transmit Data. Data goes out on this line.
RTS	Pin 4	Pin 7	Request to send. Requests data from opposing computer/peripheral.
DTR (M)	Pin 20	Pin 4	Data terminal ready. Higher level data request.
Inbound Signals			
RX (M)	Pin 3	Pin 2	Receive Data. Data comes in on this line.
CTS	Pin 5	Pin 8	Clear to send. Indicates permission to send data.
DSR (M)	Pin 6	Pin 6	Data set ready. Higher level permission to send data.

Abbr.	Pin No. on 25-Pin Connector	Pin No. on 9-Pin Connector	Signal Description
RI (M)	Pin 22	Pin 9	Ring Indicator. Detection of the phone ring signal by the modem.
RL (M)	Pin 8	Pin 13	Received line signal. Indicates a dial tone has been received by the modem.
Ground	Pin 7	Pin 5	Common ground.

Table 26.   RS-232 serial interface signal nomenclature: Note[1] Signals designated with an M are implemented through the modem and are not typically used in direct connect applications. Note[2] The pinouts refer to the configuration data terminal equipment.

There are separate wires RX and TX for receiving and transmitting signals at the digital RS-232 level. The modem, however, converts these incoming and outgoing digital signals to two or more different analog frequencies for transmission on analog phone lines. Thus, we can have duplex communications on a single phone circuit.

In performing its functions, the modem provides even higher isolation of system details. Remember that the RS-232 serial interface isolated you from DtC bus details. Likewise, the modem isolates you from RS-232 level signal details. Once you get the modem working, and once your partner in Germany gets his modem working, plugging each into a modular phone jack is rarely traumatic. This must be so, or worldwide modem communications would not exist.

Problems with the RS-232C Standard

The RS-232-C standard defines the signal names and voltages, line lengths, and connection methods for the RS-232 serial interface. Table 26 lists the most often used RS-232 signals. However, knowing signal names and characteristics is not enough to keep you out of trouble when using the RS-232 interface. RS-232 interfaced equipments seldom work the first time they are hooked up. You could, for example, experience equipment designation confusion. Figure 52 and Table 26 show that unlike the Centronics parallel printer interface, the connections between two RS-232 serially interfaced equipments are symmetrical. The RS-232 interface supports identical two-way communications, and the convention that is popularly applied looks like this:

An equipment can be considered either a data terminal or computing equipment, depending on which convention is used. The convention determines the pinouts at the RS-232 interface. For historical reasons, the DtC is often considered a data terminal. Likewise, most peripherals are considered data terminal eqipment. For example, the two equipments in Figure 55, a DtC and a plotter, are viewed as data terminals. Each RS-232 interface has identical pinouts. In order for communications to take place between DtC and plotter, signal reversals must occur. This is where the null modem comes into play. The null modem reverses the appropriate signals so that proper signal directions TRANSMIT on the DtC, go to RECEIVE on the plotter, and so on.

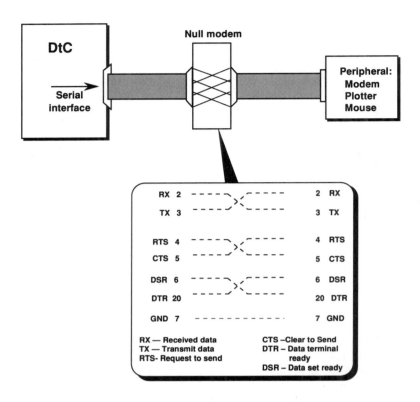

Figure 55. Null modem: The null modem is simply a box that makes it easy to reroute RS-232 signals between equipments.

In fact, the null modem can reroute RS-232 signals between two equipments. Often, handshaking lines (CTS, RTS, DTR, DSR) are not implemented within the interfaces and have to be faked, connected to fixed signals, in order for respective interfaces to function.

Another way to fix the problem of same equipment designations is to redesignate the DtC as computing equipment such that pin 3 on its RS-232 interface comes out as the TX, transmit line. This rewiring can be accomplished with switches inside the DtC on the serial interface.

Other sources of confusion include:

- **Handshake implementation** – Proper implementation of the handshake lines that control data flow between equipments.

- **Transmission parameters** – Getting transmitting bit rates, parity, and framing parameters correct on both ends of the communication.

- **Connectors** – Most vendors use the 25-pin D connectors, but many computer and peripheral manufacturers take liberties with connector type and pin assignments. Vendors will use other connectors or different pinouts. For example, AT-style and MCA-style MS-DOS computers use the 9-pin D connector shown in Table 26 on page 262. The Apple Macintosh uses a European 8-pin DIN connector.

Before you plug the new peripheral into the RS-232 serial interface and find that it doesn't work, check the cable and connectors to be sure that you are using the proper software drivers. Also be sure that the transmission parameters are correct. The lack of rigorous standards and the potential for errors makes RS-232 serial communications a troublesome area for nonexperts.

Part of the appeal of local area networks is the more controlled environment of intra-computer hookups, which often require only a single conductor (and shield) coaxial cable between networked DtCs. This alleviates the hassles discussed above, but new complexities arise since so many computers can be hooked up in so many more flexible ways. The cost is administrative software complexity that, as we shall see, can make the problems indicated above appear insignificant.

Sharing RS-232 Interfaces and Peripherals

■ *Supported* means that operating system commands are provided for setting up and using these interfaces.

Most MS-DOS computers incorporate two (and a few incorporate four) interfaces, while OS/2 and Unix machines can support an unlimited number.■ So many DtC peripherals use the RS-232 serial interface that there is often no alternative but to share the interfaces that you do have. One of two methods shown in Figure 56 may be used to provide for peripheral sharing.

Method 1 - Software configuration: This method is appropriate when the number of peripherals does not exceed the number of available interfaces. Connect peripherals to each available RS-232 interface (COM ports) and set up each application to communicate with its own COM port (COM1: or COM2:) through internal menu selection and configuration.

The advantage of this method is that applications programs will automatically access their desired COM ports, and therefore, their desired peripherals without manual operator switching operations. Further, there is less cabling, fewer connectors, and no switches required.

Method 2 - Sharing a single COM port by switching: This method is required when you have more peripherals than available COM ports. Simply connect the switch to one serial port and peripherals requiring the serial interface to the switch output connectors. Manually select which peripheral you desire to be connected. The switch shown in Figure 56 switches all 25 lines of the cables between the DtC and the connected peripherals. A two-peripheral RS-232 serial D connector switch costs around $15.

The advantage of method 2 is that applications will not need to be individually configured. Just set up all programs to use the COM1 port and switch to the appropriate peripheral when required. Also, you can support any number of peripherals on the same port with an appropriately large switch.

Even though you may have sufficient COM ports to connect each peripheral to its own port, you may still want to switch a single port. This will avoid having to configure applications differently according to which peripheral they will use. It might be just as easy to throw a manual switch.

Another need for switching arises when one peripheral must service several different DtCs. For this purpose, the manual switch may be used in reverse as Figure 57 shows.

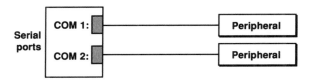

Method #1
Connect each peripheral directly to communication port

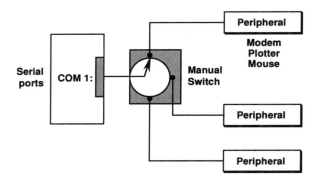

Method #2
Share a single communication port by switching

Figure 56. **Switching multiple peripherals:** A serial interface is not required for each serial peripheral.

More sophisticated electronic switches, actually a custom microcontroller, can automatically switch the peripheral to whatever DtC is sending to it. Moreover, these electronic switches can react to special commands from individual DtCs for setting up buffers in the switch and other useful features. These switches are considerably more expensive than manual switches. They are useful when all you need is a reliable way for several DtCs to share an expensive laser printer and you don't need the ultimate flexibility provided by a more expensive LAN configuration for printer sharing. Remember the electronic switch; it will do a good deal but will fall short of separating the printouts at the common printer.

Parallel Printer Interface

The Centronics is a popular parallel printer interface. Most parallel printer interfaces identify their data according to a standard arrangement indicated in Table 27, known as the Centronics standard from the early popularity of Centronics printers.

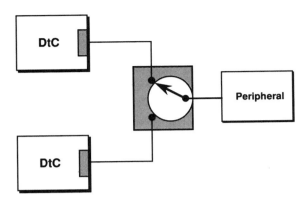

Figure 57. Using the peripheral switch in reverse: Many DtCs may need to be connected to a common peripheral.

Signals from DtC to Printer		
Data	Pins 2-9	Eight parallel data lines.
STB	Pin 1	A strobe that tells the printer when data is valid.
INIT	Pin 16	An initialization signal that resets the printer.
Auto Feed	Pin 14	Controls how printer reacts to carriage returns and line feeds.
Signals from Printer to DtC		
Busy	Pin 11	Printer cannot accept more characters; it is busy.
Ack	Pin 10	Acknowledgement that printer has received a character.
PE	Pin 12	Printer is on line and ready.
Err	Pin 15	Printer is out of paper or has a malfunction.

Table 27. Signals usually found on a 25-pin Centronics D connector

The parallel printer interface is typically used for dot matrix and laser printers. It is considerably faster and less difficult to hook up and use than is the RS-232 serial interface. This interface hooks up printers near a computer and is not intended to be as multi-purpose as the RS-232 interface. The greater speed comes about because a byte (character) at a time is transferred in parallel across the interface, best for local peripheral operations. The slower RS-232 serial interface has only one data channel and longer distance intended operation. The parallel interface will support cable lengths up to 50 feet without special buffering circuitry. Figure 58 is a bird's eye view of a parallel printer interface connected to a printer.

Figure 59 displays a typical parallel printer interface in detail. The data lines send characters to the printer and the status lines report back its condition. The data channel occupies one CPU port I/O register while the status lines occupy another. The data and status registers are shown as individual data registers. To send char-

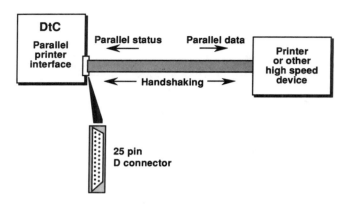

Figure 58. **Parallel printer interface overview:** The Centronics interface is a popular low-cost printer interface.

acters to the printer, the DtC CPU must write to the character data register. To read printer status, such as `out of paper` or `printer ready`, the CPU reads the status data register. In Figure 50 on page 247, the data register is the one located at address 300. The status register is not shown. Not only are there parallel data paths out of the interface (character data lines), but there are also parallel data paths into the interface (5 status lines). This makes it possible to use most parallel printer interfaces for a more general two-way communications interface, as is the case with low-cost LAN hardware. All you will need is a special cable and a fifty dollar software program.

There are many different types of parallel interfaces. Their main feature is that they connect multiple data bits to the bus in parallel. This is in contrast to the serial interface, which converts the DtC parallel data into serial data for transmission. A typical parallel printer interface and its more common interface signals are shown in Figure 59.

Note that the Centronics parallel printer interface is a special case of a parallel interface. Parallel interfaces can be wider than one byte and can support DMA. Following are several important characteristics of the Centronics parallel printer interface.

- *Parallel interface* – Bytes (characters) are transmitted 8 bits at a time to the printer. Several bits of printer status is also received in parallel from the printer.

- *Low cost* – Like the serial interface, the Centronics parallel printer interface is usually implemented with a VLSI chip, known as a parallel interface adapter.

- *No internal data clocking* – Unlike the RS-232 interface, which requires matching speeds, parity, and framing on both ends of the communication, the Centronics interface requires just a strobe to the printer, telling it that data is ready, and an acknowledge from the printer, telling the DtC to send the next character. For the handshaking signals, see Table 27 and Figure 59.

- *No DMA or shared memory* – DMA and shared memory (possible attributes of the general parallel interface) are not implemented on the Centronics parallel printer

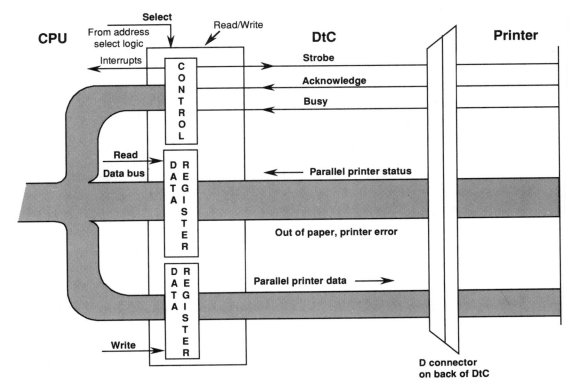

Figure 59. Detailed parallel printer interface

interface. Interrupts, however, can be implemented by the interface as shown in Figure 50 on page 247.

Supported Peripherals

Peripherals commonly supported by the Centronics parallel printer interfaces are:

- **Printers** – Although the serial interface has historically supported the older daisy wheel and Selectric printers, today's DtC printers perform APA graphics and therefore require much higher data rates than are possible over RS-232 serial interfaces. Most APA printers can use the Centronics parallel interface. Some laser printers can require more specialized interfaces, those which can map printer and system memory together for WYSIWYG operational capability that is highly integrated with video interface memory. Although PostScript is a high-level language for doing APA graphics and text, many commands are nevertheless required to print complex text and graphics images. The Centronics parallel interface is typically the minimum requirement for laser printers that implement PostScript.

- **Low-cost LANs** – Its bidirectional capability allows the Centronics parallel printer interface to be used as a relatively high-speed interface for a low-cost local area network connecting two computers. Figure 59 shows parallel and bidirectional character data and status information between an interface and a printer. If the printer were replaced with another DtC with its printer interface appropriately connected to what were printer lines, we would have a decent parallel data communication path between the two computers.

> **NOTE**
>
> The status lines of one interface would have to be connected to the data lines of the other and vice versa.

- *Voice output* – Some vendors' voice digitizing hardware plug right into the Centronics parallel printer interface. In a little box that hangs off the parallel interface, an A/D converter converts digitized speech into an analog sound signal that is fed to a speaker. Ordinary printer signals pass through a connector on the other side. This type of interface is not expensive and it can give a DtC human-sounding speech, providing you have the memory to store it. Through a companion recording device, you can even record your own voice.

Centronics Printer Interface Signals and Pinouts

Figure 58 displays a typical hookup between a DtC and a Centronics-compatible printer. Table 27 describes signals that are usually found on a 25-pin D connector of a Centronics printer interface.

The signals include character data to the printer, handshaking lines to control data flow, and status lines that report the printer's condition. You may wonder how DtCs implementing the same 25-pin D connector for both RS-232 and parallel printer interfaces help you to differentiate the connectors. It goes like this: The differentiation depends on the different sex of the connectors. The serial interface output connector is usually male, and the cable connector is female. The parallel printer interface output connector is female, and the cable connector male. Also, it is impossible to plug a serial cable into a Centronics-style printer because the printer input connector is flat-edge, which is a different type.

Problems with the Centronics Standard

The Centronics parallel printer interface has been standardized by a specification that calls out the connector type, signal lines, eight parallel data lines from computer to printer, parallel status lines from printer to computer, handshaking, and other auxiliary lines. The major problem with this interface, and similar to problems associated with the RS-232 serial interface, is the difference in printer status, interface configuration switches, and certain handshaking signals (ACK, BUSY) whose polarities and usage have not been completely standardized. To avoid such problems, printer purchases should always include a cable for the DtC and a guarantee from the vendor of trouble-free operation of a specific printer with a specific DtC.

Sharing Centronics Parallel Ports

The considerations for sharing the Centronics parallel interface are similar to those described for the serial interface.

Serial and Centronics Parallel Interface Summary

Table 28 compares the features of the serial RS-232 and Centronics parallel interfaces.

Feature	RS-232 Serial	Centronics parallel printer
Speed	300-200 Kbits/sec	Up to 1 MB/second.
Distance	50 feet direct connect; around the world by modem	Up to 15 feet. Greater distances possible with special adapters.
Channels	One out, one in	One byte out, 5 bits in.
Usage	Modems, mice, plotters	High speed printers.
OS Support	Yes	Yes

Table 28.   RS-232 and Centronics parallel printer interface characteristics

Since both the RS-232 and Centronics parallel printer interfaces are supported by the operating system, the following benefits are realized:

- *Configuration* – Configuration of interfaces, bit rates, and parity by commands built into the operating system.

- *Redirection* – Applications that use the operating system support of these interfaces can easily be redirected. For example, a program expecting input from the keyboard could instead get redirected input from the serial interface. This is what makes remote control software for DtCs possible. Software printing to the Centronics parallel printer port could just as well print to a DOS file.

- *Network sharing* – Peripherals using the RS-232 and Centronics parallel printer interface can easily be shared over a network. These interfaces are supported by the operating system, and therefore can be redirected to operate over a network.

Appropriate Peripheral Sharing

The need to interconnect more DtCs and peripherals and to perform these connections with greater user transparency makes LANs the most practical method for peripheral sharing. The above material has been presented to make you aware that low-cost set ups exist for connecting relatively small numbers of DtCs and peripherals together by standard interfaces and simple switches. Thus, you have an administrative swap between the inexpensive and simple switches and higher cost and greater software complexity of local area networks.

IEEE 488 Interfaces

The IEEE (Institute for Electrical and Electronic Engineers) 488 interface is more versatile than the parallel printer interface. The IEEE 488 interface main attributes include:

- *Multiple peripheral support* – Several peripherals can be chained to a single IEEE 488 interface. These peripherals can communicate with the DtC by handshaking, addressing, and arbitration signal lines implemented by the interface.

- *Test equipment interface* – The interface and its supporting commands are primarily designed for data communications between test equipment.

- *Full bidirectional* – Supports 8-bit data transmissions in both directions (read and write).

The IEEE interface is also known as the GPIB (General Purpose Interface Bus).

Operating the IEEE 488 Interface

Operating the IEEE 488 interface involves more expertise than conventional, single peripheral, parallel interfaces. There is a command structure associated with this interface and a language that must be learned. Most HP computers and test equipments implement this language in their built-in BASIC languages, and you will find an inherent integration between the various equipments that use the IEEE 488 interface.

IEEE 488 interfaces are also available for many DtCs as plug-in boards, although they are not well supported in software. To use them, you need to install cryptic drivers and hope that communication between the DtC and the test equipment is successful.

Data Compatibility with the IEEE 488

Most test equipments are microcomputers in their own right, and some even have floppy disks. Disk media formats between these test equipments and DtC floppy disks are sometimes incompatible. File transfers between test equipment and the DtC often require direct connections of the IEEE 488 interfaces on the test equipment and the DtC. The data being transmitted could be in binary format, and receiving software on the DtC must be able to handle this format. Problems occur when sequential file software on the receiving DtC that is expecting ASCII data reacts strangely to the binary data. This can include such effects as false EOF (end of file), which can abruptly terminate the transmission mid-stream and cause other frustrating behavior.

SCSI

An SCSI (small computer system interface) is an intelligent general-purpose interface that can handle many details of data transfer not possible with other interfaces. The SCSI (pronounced "scuzzy") interface is an attempt to offer the best of two worlds: a standardized interface and good access to internal DtC system capability. This combined capability is primarily what is making SCSI such a popular and widespread interface for the demanding needs of today's DtC peripheral. The details include DMA transfers, complex memory transfers, and complex strings of interconnected peripherals. SCSIs are microcomputers in their own right; they support multitasking and asynchronous as well as synchronous data transmission, and they offer a wide range of performance alternatives. Their popularity is growing apace with the increasing variety and complexity of peripherals and as the need increases to relieve the demands on the CPU. The SCSI is becoming popular in the support of local area networks with the help of a newcomer called a *nodem*, discussed elsewhere.

The SCSI is providing standardization for hooking up higher-speed peripherals. DtCs are implementing this and other intelligent interfaces to permit easier interchange of mass storage and other high-speed peripherals between DtCs that incorporate the SCSI. Later, when we discuss hard disks, we will take a closer look at the SCSI in the context of other hard disk interfaces.

MIDI

The MIDI is a special but standard serial interface for controlling computerized musical instruments. MIDI is a specification for how the various parameters (tone, pitch, velocity, blend, status) will be transmitted between computer-controlled instruments. With a data rate of 32 KHz, what is transmitted is not the music content, but rather the control of synthesizing devices on the instrument that generate the musical waveforms. MIDI interfaces are available for most desktop computers.

6.6 *Interface Summary*

There are two main classes of interfaces: the customized device-specific interfaces for higher- speed sophisticated peripherals and the lower speed but very popular standard interfaces.

The difference between using standard and custom interfaces is that custom interfaces provide intimate access to more system functions but are more complex and difficult to manage. Since highly-specialized peripherals are matched to their custom interfaces, they will only plug into a specific DtC class. For example, the scanner/fax modem combination board for an MS-DOS computer will *not* plug into an Apple Macintosh computer.

Standard interfaces allow less intimate contact between peripheral and DtC system resources, and can be operated on almost any microcomputer. The standard interfaces usually come with the DtC. Irritating differences, however, can frustrate users of these interfaces.

7.0   Interrupt Processing

We think of computers as obedient servants to the programs that we write. The CPU slaves from coded instruction to coded instruction accomplishing our specific tasks. There are times, however, when its attention needs to be focused on other, perhaps more immediate tasks. There is a need to break the CPU's work cycle, tap it on the shoulder, to do tasks outside its ordinary realm.

The key to successful CPU functionality is interrupt processing. These tasks may be servicing important peripherals that cannot wait, performing tasks not originally planned, or just getting away from a specific application to do work more appropriately done external to that application. For these reasons we need the interrupt. Interrupts play an essential role in desktop computing because they:

- allow programs to be interrupted asynchronously, that is, at any time, by external events.
- offer an escape route that developers can use to add to programs extra features that were not originally planned.
- provide a means by which multiple concurrent programs can execute.
- provide a shorthand notation for calling executable code without knowing the location or even the content at development time.

7.1   What Is an Interrupt?

An interrupt may be thought of as a disturbance in the ordinary flow of program execution, a temporary diversion for the CPU. First, we will look at the call instruction, cousin to the interrupt.

Program Branching and the Call Instruction

Any computer program is simply a flow of mostly sequential instructions in memory. Each instruction tells the CPU what to do next. If all instructions were sequential, there would be no need to choose one option over another, depending on conditions. Since choices almost invariably exist, we have the notion of *branching*. By branching from one path to another, a different set of code can be executed. Many branches are conditional, or they can be made to depend on conditions that can be tested. A particular type of branch instruction known as the *call* allows a branch to be taken so that the CPU remembers where in memory it was executing when the call instruction was sent (see Figure 60).■

■ Actually, the return address is placed in an area of memory managed by the CPU and known as the *stack*.

The call instruction has only to specify the location in memory of the code to be executed. At the end of the called code must be a return instruction. When the

CPU executes the return, it finds and gets from the stack the storage location in memory of the code that was being executed at the time of the call instruction. The CPU continues execution at that point. As with any branch instruction, the call can be conditional. This is a flexible way to modularize program functions by using multiple subroutines, each accomplishing specific functions. A spreadsheet program or a word processor could contain hundreds if not thousands of such subroutines.

7.2 Interrupts

Software Interrupt

You could think of a software interrupt as a shorthand call instruction. The address of the subroutine, known as an interrupt service routine (ISR), is not in the software interrupt instruction, but is in a memory area, known as an interrupt vector table, that is located outside the execution area of an applications program and is managed by the CPU.

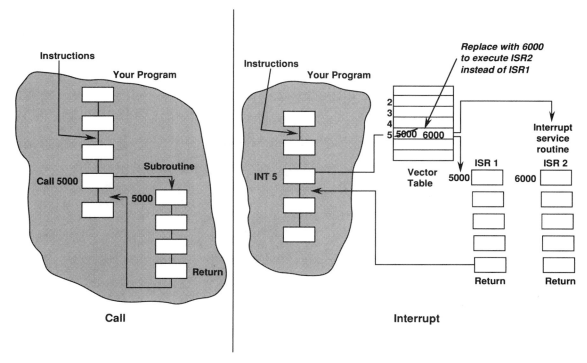

Figure 60. The call vs. the software interrupt: The call specifies the location where CPU execution should be diverted, while the software interrupt uses an indirect address through an address table.

Because this address is external to a program, it can be managed without knowing anything about that program. For example, the table address can be changed,
calling a different, perhaps improved routine. No change in the applications program
is required to pull this off. Or, perhaps, additional code needs to be added to the
existing interrupt service routine. Just add the code and move the return to the end
of the code. Although we might not know where the interrupt instruction is in
memory, we do know where the table is.

The software interrupt is explicit in the sense that it is a program instruction. This
is in contrast to the hardware interrupt, which is invoked by a wire to the CPU. The
software interrupt is synchronous because it calls for an activity at a particular time,
related to the application in which it is located. To sew such an instruction into an
application's code requires an intimate knowledge of the application.

As we shall see, the software interrupt is a convenient way for software to call
upon the operating system for services that might change. Rather than changing the
code in each application that might request a particular service, the memory pointer
(interrupt vector) to the routine is changed instead to point to the changed service.
This way we can make adjustments to the service routines without affecting the
software base. Figure 61 shows such an adjustment.

Hardware Interrupt

Unlike the software interrupt, the hardware interrupt is activated by a wire connected to the CPU. There is no need to place explicit code in the program to get the
CPU to go off and do something else. Invoking this interrupt is akin to clapping
your hands to get attention. The hardware interrupt is an asynchronous process –
there is no advance notice to an executing applications program when the hardware
interrupt will occur. The usefulness of the hardware interrupt is that we needn't
know anything about the applications program running when the interrupt occurs.
The CPU will remember what code it was executing and following the interrupt the
CPU will continue processing as if nothing had happened.

The ISR executed as a result of a hardware interrupt can be specified through
an interrupt vector table as described above. The address can also be specified by
the peripheral requesting CPU service, or by the interrupt controller.

In summary, there are three ways to divert the CPU:

1. *Call instruction* – Directs CPU execution to an area of memory that is specified
in the instruction.

2. *Software interrupt instruction* – Directs execution to an area indirectly specified
somewhere else in memory.

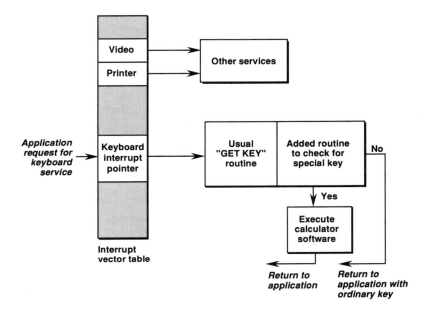

Figure 61.   Adding capability using interrupts: Capability of a software program may be enhanced using predictable interrupts.

3. *Hardware interrupt* – Not an instruction at all; the hardware interrupt signals the CPU to divert its execution over wires connected to the CPU or an interrupt controller. The address of the executing code is usually supplied by the interrupt controller or a peripheral.

Figure 60 shows the fundamental difference between the call instruction and the software interrupt. The hardware interrupt is independent of any specific application code (see Figure 62), whereas the software interrupt must be explicitly called for by the interrupt instruction that must be sewn into the program.

Responding to Asynchronous Events

Many peripherals require service at times not known by the programs you are executing. The hardware interrupt precludes the need for software having to poll the hardware. Otherwise they would waste time continuously reading the registers of the peripheral to determine whether or not the peripheral needed service. Precisely when the peripheral needs service, the peripheral interrupts the CPU and receives service immediately.

┌─ *EXAMPLE* ───┐

Fire Alarm You need to monitor your house for fire. You want to use a DtC for this purpose and you also want to do your usual word processing. You don't care that your word processor is temporarily suspended while the fire is being extinguished.

No Interrupt For programs that do not use a known interrupt, you will need to modify each of the programs you operate (no easy trick) to additionally perform the fire alarm check.

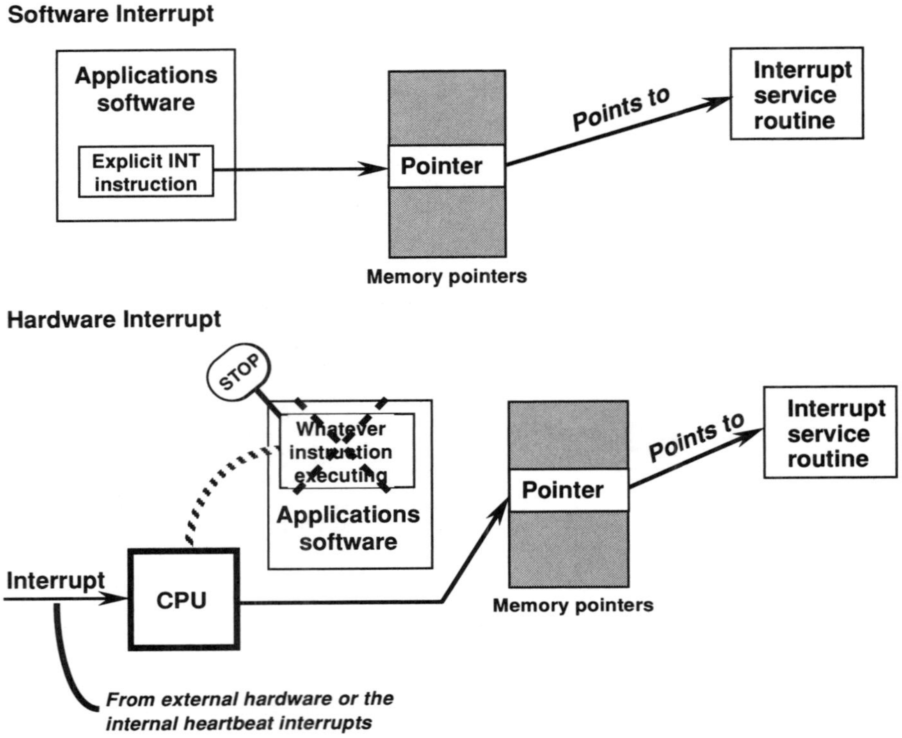

Figure 62.   Software and hardware interrupts: Sofware interrupts are designed to call for planned activities in an executing program and are therefore accomplished by instructions explicitly located in the program. Hardware interrupts, usually for events extraneous to the currently executing program, are implemented by hard wires connected to the CPU, and can force the CPU to an interrupt service routine independent of the executing program.

With Software Interrupts You can hope that each applications program that you operate makes use of a particular interrupt often enough to permit its respective service routine to test the fire alarm. Most MS-DOS programs check their keyboard buffers repeatedly using a keyboard interrupt. Becuse the keyboard interrupt is reached by an interrupt vector table entry, you will be able to find the keyboard service routine easily. Knowing where the routine is, you can add the code that tests for the fire alarm there, and all progrms that use the keyboard will test for the fire alarm.

With Hardware Interrupts Hook up the fire alarm to a bused hardware interrupt line and install a fire alarm service routine pointed to by the respective interrupt pointer. When an alarm occurs, the CPU is interrupted and the ISR executes immediately. No need to test for the alarm with software. There is no need to perform any modifications to applications programs or hope that all applications you run perform periodic software interrupts. Even if a bused interrupt line is not available you can still use hardware interrupts. This is because most systems implement an internal, non-bused, periodic interrupt known as the *heartbeat interrupt*, discussed later.

TSR Programs

TSR programs are after-the-fact enhancements to an application or operating system. Perhaps you need a calculator to pop up on screen and you want it to happen from within your favorite word processor.

Since most applications programs either check the keyboard frequently, using a software interrupt, or immediately react to a hardware interrupt from the keyboard, you have a way of taking control during the resulting keyboard processing to allow the calculator software to be executed.

Using an interrupt is like catching a fish as it jumps out of the water. You don't know where the application is executing; under the surface you don't know where the fish is. But once the fish is in the air – as long as the program uses the keyboard interrupt – you can find the keyboard service routine (catch the fish) and modify this routine to check for a special key that, when pressed, will cause the calculator software to present a calculator. While the calculator software is executing, your previous application is not. Later we shall see how to use interrupts to do more than one thing concurrently.

> **NOTE**
>
> The TSR discussion demonstrates a single tasking operating system mentality. A good multitasking operating system would load the calculator as a separate task and execute concurrently in its own screen window.

Figure 61 displays how, using the interrupt, you might add this additional calculator function to an existing application (spreadsheet, word processor) not knowing anything about that application.

Concurrent Processing

If we extend the notion of interrupts, we can perform more than one task at a time, concurrently or alternating. Before, we had to do one thing or another separately, and never at the same time.

Imagine that you need an extra, background job to be performed while you are running an important foreground program. The background job might be a print spooler that empties a memory area to the printer, or it could be a software clock ticking hours and minutes while you type on a word processor. Or it might be sending a file, a few bytes at a time, to a distant mainframe. Whatever the task, it can be accomplished by periodically interrupting the CPU during the execution of the foreground task. During each interrupt, the CPU goes off and works a bit on the background task, and then returns to the foreground.

What we need is a way to periodically generate a hardware interrupt to the CPU that can divide its attention between or among tasks. Such an interrupt is the *heartbeat interrupt.*

The Heartbeat Interrupt

The heartbeat interrupt is a periodic hardware interrupt that comes from within the system unit of the DtC. Referring to Figure 26 on page 162, note how the heartbeat interrupt signal comes from an internal counter timer, rather than from an external source over the bus. Now we have what we need: a continuously recurring interrupt independent of the bus and peripherals. The interrupt can be used to control the CPU, diverting it to other tasks. The diversion is transparent to the executing software, the same as with the bused hardware interrupt.

The utility of the heartbeat interrupt is that it can be used to permit, even guarantee, departure from an existing program to perform other concurrent tasks, or after-the-fact software functions. The only other escape route would be periodic software interrupts from these applications programs that cannot be guaranteed on an external bused interrupt, which might not be available. Remember the fish out of water?

A Heartbeat Interrupt Example

Look at the bottom of Figure 62 and the incoming CPU interrupt as a heartbeat interrupt. The routine shown in the figure will be executed according to the rate at which the heartbeat hardware interrupt is generated.

Return now to the fire alarm. As discussed earlier, the proper way to implement the alarm is to have the fire tester issue a bused hardware interrupt when a fire is detected. If there is no bused interrupt, use the heartbeat interrupt. The heartbeat interrupt will still get the CPU's attention periodically to break off its current task to test the fire detector by way of a port register. To see this more clearly, look at Figure 61 and think of the vector table pointer shown there as a pointer to the fire alarm test. Think of the incoming request as being generated by the heartbeat interrupt. Think of the test routine as the fire test routine.

If there is a fire, the test is *yes*, and we execute the `call the fire department` routine that trips the alarm for firefighters to respond. If there is no fire, we resume the interrupted applications program. How often the interrupt occurs is determined by how often the counter-timer chip generates a pulse that triggers the heartbeat interrupt. The frequency of the counter-timer pulse is programmable, so you can preset the repetition rate. For a file alarm, once per minute may be acceptable.

Notice the important difference between the heartbeat interrupt method and the direct bused interrupt method. With the heartbeat interrupt the fire alarm must be tested periodically, while with the bused interrupt the CPU is roused immediately when a fire occurs. There is no need for testing. The testing overhead on the CPU probably won't be more than about 1%, so this method isn't bad, and it works without a bused interrupt. Notice also, as with any hardware interrupt there is a guarantee of leaving the executing code either to test for the alarm, in the heartbeat method, or to immediately execute the alarm routine, in the bused interrupt.

Other Heartbeat Applications

The routine executed by the heartbeat interrupt could be a clock routine used by the operating system to keep track of time, or even a scheduler program that could permit many different programs to execute concurrently. Of course, programs could, if it were planned, call for external service periodically just for the purpose of concurrent operation. Later, we will discuss a variety of methods for corralling software to perform a variety of functions not originally planned for.

The interrupt provides a vital form of communication to the CPU from the external events and equipments permitting the CPU to rapidly change its course to perform multiple and often unconnected operations. One measure of CPU capability is how quickly it can go from one task to another. This capability is known as context switching. Software interrupts permit software developers the convenience of simple references to software routines and flexibility in software installation. Hardware interrupts permit the CPU to quickly respond to asynchronous and unexpected events.

PART

III

Part III. Operating Systems

The operating system is the controller of the DtC and its resources. It must be an able manager of DtC hardware as well as a friendly go-between for applications programs. Today's operating systems are being improved in many ways. Improvements result in a friendlier but changing software nature. To understand the many applications software tradeoffs and limitations you need to understand the operating system's evolving role, and how you can assist that evolution toward a higher plane.

In the simplest instance, a computer does not need an operating system. Today's toys and games have chips that drive hardware directly. In a desktop computer, however, we need an operating system to supervise the complex activity that goes on inside. When you boot a DtC, the operating system gets ready to execute commands, to supervise the flow of program tasks and data during processing, and to make sure the programs obey the traffic laws and don't collide and hurt one another.

The operating system manages individual jobs for the user, loading programs and files as needed and putting them away. As task manager in a multitasking environment, the operating system makes sure that programs execute according to schedule, allocating resources as they become available to on-going tasks that need them. As data manager, the operating system keeps meticulous track of where data is stored so that programs can access and share data from known locations and formats. Finally, as communications manager, it outputs information to a screen or routes it to a printer, and in a networked environment it makes sure that the correct information is transmitted to and received by the appropriate users.

The more functions supported by the operating system, the fewer will have to be supplied by the individual applications packages. If the operating system doesn't provide peripheral I/O support, memory management, data sharing, or graphical user interfaces, each individual software program will need to supply the support. It is likely that each will provide that support differently. As a consequence, software cost is increased, software becomes less integrated, the software developer has a tougher job, and both time and memory are lost to the user when such support functions must be loaded together with the software every time a program is operated.

Several types of operating system can be distinguished in terms of major DtC applications categories: HB (home and business), EP (engineering and production), and EE (entertainment and education). Several facets of DtC operating systems deserve exploration, namely:

- Purpose
- System support capability
- History and evolution
- Enhancement
- Comparison

Software of immediate interest is of two types: one is system software and the other applications software. The latter, applications software, is found in a wide variety of forms and performs a wide variety of functions for satisfying the particular needs of the users. There are, however, common needs that all applications share. How well an operating system meets the common needs determines the success of the applications software base.

1.0   Operating System Overview

An operating system runs the computer, telling it how to receive input; display and print output; find, store, and keep track of information; and handle communications. Because of its central role in computers, it has attracted a great deal of developer attention and effort to make it faster, more capable, and easier to master. In the light of rapidly developing computer technology, profound improvements are being achieved not only with operating systems, but with the applications software that depends on the operating system and its adjuncts.

The operating system provides the functions needed to manage computer resources as well as communication between applications programs. Although each applications software package *could* perform this resource management task for itself, and in fact some do, this does not make sense from a modular design standpoint. What *does* make sense is to let the applications software package perform functions that produce the work you need, such as word processing and database management, and let the operating system tend to the resource management details of the particular microcomputer being used.

We could think of an application, then, as running *under* the operating system; that is, using operating system functions rather than its own to communicate with other applications and to access specific microcomputer hardware resources. Software packages that use operating system functions extensively will get along better with each other. Unencumbered by architectural specifics, they can be transported more easily between different computers. Conversely, applications packages that try to encompass many system level details are hard to manage. Moreover, the division of labor allows developers to concentrate on achieving higher levels of functionality necessary to do a particular job without being mired in system specifications.

1.1   Early Operating Systems

In the beginning, thirty years or so ago, there were no microcomputer operating systems as we now know them. Programmers wrote their own input/output routines. In most cases the programmer was responsible for every task performed by the computer without the benefit of an operating system that could perform many common tasks during program execution.

The first microprocessor of interest, a 4-bit chip, ran dedicated hardware in simple process control environments; hence its operating system was not an operating system at all, but rather a dedicated program running in a ROM environment.

Software compatibility between various systems was not important because each process control computer performed only its own dedicated task.

The transition from 4- to 8-bit microprocessors resulted in microcomputer systems that could process data in relatively simple ways; but as these systems developed and proliferated, the need emerged for operating systems that could supervise higher-level software.

The Intel Corporation's 8080 microprocessor was the first 8-bit microprocessor to run under a standard operating system. The operating system, called CP/M (Control Program/Microcomputer), was the first microcomputer operating system to use consistent techniques for isolating applications software from hardware architectural details. Isolation of software from hardware means independence of one from the other.

NOTE

Standardization of an operating system is where the fundamental tradeoff between compatibility and performance originates. There were hundreds of 8080/Z80 microcomputer manufacturers; each with its own architecture – location of of I/O devices, uses of memory, and a host of other system-specific features. Software vendors wanted their software to operate on all 8080/Z80 microcomputers, and the CP/M operating system could provide the operating environment to accomodate them.

Since CP/M was written entirely in machine language, it was not portable between different CPUs. Since most systems were based on the same 8080/Z80 CPU, portability was not an issue. The problem was running the same software on different microcomputer systems based on the same 8080/Z80 CPU.

Standardization means that all hardware-specific support functions peculiar to a particular microcomputer were sequestered in a small well-defined portion of the total operating system, the BIOS. When the operating system needed to be rewritten for different architecture, only the BIOS needed to be modified. The remaining operating system functions, dealing primarily with file management and program loading, would use the BIOS. See Figure 63.

By confining the hardware support functions to the BIOS, the CP/M applications software base could be easily transported between the hundreds of different 8080/Z80-based microcomputers. The portability held if the programs limited their I/O to only functions supported by the BIOS. The BIOS I/O support was primarily simple text functions. The consequence of transportability was that the limited I/O programs did not allow for spectacular software.

■ Text based means that OS functions were available for displaying and printing text, with no built-in functions for graphics.

The infant CP/M operating system was text-based and addressed only the hardware resource category.■ CP/M provided a simple load and go mechanism to load and execute programs one at a time. The operating system kept track of available executable memory, and if the file was small enough to fit, it was loaded and immediately executed. A simple file management system maintained program and data files within the capacity of the disks. Only the 8080/Z80 CPUs, with 64K memory and no memory management, and the 8088 CPU, with its limited segmentation, were supported by CP/M. The rules for how applications software could use CP/M to control the hardware were well defined and did not vary from one microcomputer implementation to another.

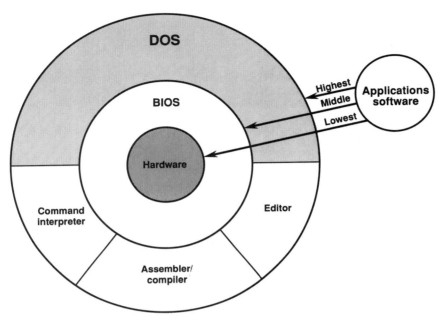

Figure 63. Shielding software from hardware: The operating system (shown in the outer ring) and applications programs are isolated from the fundamental system hardware by the BIOS. Although the figure exemplifies MS-DOS, other operating systems are similar.

MS-DOS, which drew from CP/M, is one of today's most popular DtC operating systems. Yet it still provides only text and primitive hardware support. Operating systems such as Unix, OS/2, Windows, and Apple's DOS provide improved support in many resource categories beyond MS-DOS's text and hardware limits. Recent operating system developments include the support of graphics, data, memory, and CPU resources. These topics will be our focus in the following sections. Particularly, we will look at the many enhancements for and alternatives to MS-DOS, the operating system that has become a household item. But first, let's look at some definitions, other important operating systems, and a few basic concepts.

1.2 Resource Categories

In order to compare operating systems, we must first define the major categories of resources that an operating system should be able to manage for your applications software base. Later, we will look at the popular operating systems in terms of these categories.

- *Hardware* – From the highest perspective, hardware can be separated into two major blocks.

  1. *The system unit* – Containing the CPU, memory, buses, standard interfaces, and support chips.
  2. *Peripheral interfaces* – Interfaces to a vast array of peripherals.

- **Memory** – The resource that programs need in order to execute. The hard disk, cache memory, virtual memory, expanded memory, and protected memory are forms the OS needs to understand and support if it is to deal successfully with applications.

- **CPU** – To be an effective commander, the CPU must be able to manage itself. It must be able to apportion its capabilities among many different software tasks for increased functionality.

- **Data** – The reason for computing is to arrange, rearrange, or refine data. Individual programs need strong OS support to manipulate, move, and process data files. Not only must data be shared between applications on the same computer, but also between multiple different computers in networks. The sharing of data over networks is the essence of the enterprise computing model.

- **Graphics and user interface** – The support of graphics and the user interface by the operating system is the key to interactive, interesting, and useful applications. Graphics and the user interface are tightly coupled because graphics play a vital role in establishing a good user interface. The days of text-only operating systems are ending. The great advantage of a graphical user interface is that it provides quickly recognizable and easily learnable cues to available options. Users can begin doing productive work within minutes of first exposure to a good GUI. Once a well-rounded graphics capability is supported universally by operating systems, we will have reached a new height of friendly, visual computing.

1.3 Operating System Support Components

A computer operating system should provide support in many different areas: file manager, shell, system component and peripheral I/O support, memory management, graphical user interface, means for integrating programs, and certain auxiliary tools. We shall look at each in turn.

File Manager

The file manager (FM) is the most important component of the operating system; it takes care of all programs and data. A file manager is a large set of routines for accessing and manipulating data files. The files could be located on a remote network disk, or could be I/O devices acting like files. The file manager supports file naming, directories and subdirectories, copying, device I/O, and routing.

Some operating systems have you enter FM commands from a non-informative prompt, while others guide you with visually appealing prompting screens. Although MS-DOS provides relatively good file management capability, the user interface to such management has historically been poor. Newer versions and a number of enhancements make file management a more pleasing visual encounter, improving greatly on the rudimentary prompting capability of the operating system.

On the Macintosh, the file manager is known as the *MultiFinder*. The Mac has provided fine ROM-based user interface and graphics support from the beginning; its file management consists of simply pointing to a folder icon to open a file.

File management is Unix's strongest suit. In fact, under Unix, a powerful FM treats programs, data, and peripherals as similar entities or files, thereby providing a strong communications link between programs, the hard disk, and other devices such as printers and video disks.

The BIOS (Basic Input/Output System) Kernel

The kernel of an operating system separates the operating system and applications software from DtC fundamental hardware. Minicomputers and EP class DtCs implement their I/O system support in a RAM-based kernel, bootstrapped from a mass storage device. When the HB class DtCs began as diskless microcomputers, their operating systems were a combination of a ROM BASIC and a ROM BIOS. Since there was no disk, the I/O support had to be in ROM.

The BIOS is a set of individual machine language routines, usuaaly found in ROM on the microcomputer motherboard, that interact with microcomputer hardware and peripheral interfaces at the lowest level. By using these routines, applications programs and higher level operating system components such as the file manager do not need to know the nitty gritty DtC hardware details.

The term *basic input/output system* originated with the CP/M operating system where only the essential I/O capability of a microcomputer was supported. The term carried over to the MS-DOS computers in which BIOS ROMs even today provide only modest additional capability relegated to custom chip initialization and performance enhancement hardware control. *BIOS* is a misnomer when applied to the Unix and other large OS kernels, which provide considerably more I/O functionality, or when applied to the higher-level graphics support found in the Macintosh and Commodore Amiga. *BIOS* is used here because it is well known in the industry and by the general public.

BIOS functions support:

- *System initialization* – Functions include initial programming of special function chips, installation of pointers to system interrupt software, tests of the motherboard including memory, and determination of on-board interfaces and their integrity. Also, you will find basic time keeping routines for updating system clocks and providing other timing signals in the DtC.

- *Basic mass storage support* – The BIOS will usually provide elemental support of included floppy disks and mass storage devices. On some DtCs, floppy disk and hard drive interfaces are not a part of the basic motherboard. BIOS support of these hard disk interfaces (or other auxiliary devices such as Bernoulli boxes and optical drives) may be found in ROMs on each interface board.

- *Standard interface support* – Since most DtCs include the standard serial and parallel printer interfaces, there are general-purpose BIOS routines that support these interfaces. MS-DOS BIOS support in this area is minimal and only text based. If a program is going to need more sophisticated support for laser printers, for example, it will need to supply its own routines in drivers.

- *Video interface support* – In MS-DOS computers, text support for the early video interfaces (found on all systems) is in motherboard BIOS ROM, while BIOS for the more sophisticated video boards (EGA, VGA, and above) is in display interface board ROM. The BIOS support includes initialization of different display modes and primitive text support. Apple's BIOS support of display interfaces is considerably more flexible and includes extensive APA (All Points Addressable) support of graphics, fonts, and user interface functions. The Apple Macintosh BIOS also supports its versatile and sophisticated interfaces (SCSI, Apple Desktop Bus, AppleTalk). The interfaces as well as APA fonts are supported in ROM. In the Unix operating system, graphics support is provided by C routines either custom developed or supplied by the integrating environment. MS-DOS computer graphics support is now being provided by Windows and OS/2.

Several manufacturers produce BIOS ROMs for MS-DOS computers. Part of your MS-DOS purchase decision might be the support found in BIOS ROM. Therefore, it pays to determine which manufacturer's ROM is best for the purpose you have in mind. Popular BIOS manufacturers are Pheonix, AMI, and Award. Capabilities you may want to consider include:

- *Separate I/O speeds* – Separate programming of I/O channel clock speeds and access times. Another means for matching slower peripherals to the system unit.

- *CPU speeds and wait states* – Several CPU speed options may be provided to allow more flexible speed configuration. Sometimes you will want to let up on the CPU throttle or insert wait states to match the CPU to slow memory, peripherals, or software.

- *Shadow RAM* – This is a technique for downloading ROM software into RAM for quicker execution. Shadow RAM works particularly well in replacing video drivers.

- *Instruction cache options* – The ability to select different hardware cache configurations and caching approaches. Cache controllers are sophisticated and often configurable.

- *Chip set initializations* – Many vendors incorporate large scale VLSI chips that amalgorize auxiliary chip functions. Through BIOS support, the different chip sets found on different MS-DOS computers can be initialized and accommodated. The chip sets accommodate a variety of system performance adjustments including memory speed, timing, I/O channel speeds and mapping shadow RAM. Chips and Technology and Opti are two such vendors.

- *BIOS adjustments* – They are usually found at two levels: a rough mode for the novice, and a fine tune mode for the expert. There is wide variation in the amount and type of support in different manufacturer's BIOS ROMs. Of course, the amount of support will also depend on the sophistication and adjustability of the motherboard design. Adjustments are saved in a special CMOS RAM chip that is maintained by a battery back up.

The Unix kernel is modified for use on MS-DOS computers to take advantage of the ROM BIOS, which makes Xenix, IBM's AIX, and other DtC-based Unix kernels somewhat similar to the MS-DOS computer BIOS.

Device Drivers

■ C is a favorite language for such intensive purposes as program routines because of its code efficiency (small size) and speed on microcomputers.

Device drivers are program routines, usually written in machine code or in the C programming language, that control the operation of peripheral devices such as printers, mice, and display screens.■

Device drivers are similar to BIOS routines, except that their purpose is to match particular applications with peripherals not found in the common microcomputer system unit. Some drivers, particularly those required by the DtC itself, come with the operating system. Drivers make it possible for an operating system to work with different peripherals and configurations. But with the enormous selection of peripherals on the market, it is impossible to include every driver every user may need. Device drivers are often included with a given applications program to be installed in a way that is appropriate to the specific microcomputer and peripheral configuration.

Device drivers usually load into RAM to increase flexibility for matching so many programs with so many peripherals. Each driver, of course, is unique to a given device. A printer driver, for example, contains the instructions necessary to change type fonts, advance paper through the printer, insert indentions and line spaces, and eject the page when it is full.

Most MS-DOS applications programs find the BIOS support provided for standard serial and printer interfaces too limited. The use of custom printer interfaces and the need for text and graphics printer control intimately tied to each application makes it necessary to have specific printer drivers for each applications program. Likewise, the lack of MS-DOS graphics support severely limits the use of text-only routines found among MS-DOS computer BIOS routines. Therefore, each application program comes with its own unique set of graphics drivers, one for each of several graphics interfaces. You install necessary drivers on your system for the microcomputer and peripheral configuration. Graphics and user interface support found in Windows and OS/2 are relieving developers of the tedious chore of providing their own graphics support or of using uncommon graphics subroutine libraries. Instead, common support by the operating system will guarantee a more consistent use of graphics and cooperation (windowing, data sharing).

The Apple Macintosh provides considerable graphics, user interface, and peripheral support, albeit for a small number of peripherals, in its ROM BIOS. The result of this extensive ROM support is a consistent user's perception of the ways of working with the Macintosh applications software base.

Shells

A shell is an intermediary between a user and an operating system. Typically, a shell is an add-on program that provides a menu-style or graphical icon interface that makes it easier to enter commands. A shell provides friendly access to the operating system's file manager by translating ordinary language commands into codes that the operating system can understand and respond to. The shell asks for input, interprets commands, and relays your intentions to the operating system.

The Default Shell

The default shell is what the operating system uses when it powers up. When you enter commands at operating system prompts, the program that is listening is the default shell. Once you execute a given program, your session can be driven completely by that program, which pushes the shell aside. Seldom, however, will you execute an isolated program. As your computational skill increases, you will find yourself executing an assortment of programs, sometimes concurrently.

In the Unix operating system the default shell is highly programmable, while in MS-DOS computers the shell is a rather weak command processor. The ability to replace or modify the default shell with enhanced versions can customize the most important software interface – the one between you and the programs that you run. The default shell can be autopiloted by batch files in MS-DOS computers and shell scripts in the Unix operating system. The MS-DOS batching capability is limited compared to the highly programmable Unix shell scripts. This allows for preprogrammed and complex command scenarios to be automated. Script files can be stored on hard disk where they will be easily accessible to simplify or replace keyboard input.

The Shell Game

The typical DtC user has limited control over the look and feel of a shell. In order to customize, you must be able to replace the operating system default shell. MS-DOS users have a choice of commercial shells from simple file management helpers like XTree and QFiler to more sophisticated enhancements like DESQview and Windows. Such shells are more than just a fancy interface to the operating system. They include supplements to the operating system that allow it to support multitasking, share data between programs, and display the outputs of multiple programs on the same screen (windowing).

The graphical orientation of the Macintosh shell, The Desktop, is inviting, although not very customizable. Surrendering your power to program the user interface was the implicit bargain made when choosing the Macintosh. And remember that while you are not in control of the particular look and feel, that look and feel *is* a popular one. Moreover, a simple operating system does not have to be programmable to be comfortably useful. Besides, you can always run Apple's Unix on your Macintosh.

If you do need a highly customized shell, and you like to program, the Unix shell capability may be right for you. With Unix you can program your own custom shell or use a ready-made GUI shell.

Memory Management

In the best of all possible computing worlds, we would have an unlimited amount of directly addressable memory. Abundant directly addressable memory would:

- allow programs of unlimited size to run continuously.
- allow files of unlimited size to be worked on directly.
- allow multiple programs to run concurrently.

In this computing scenario, secondary memory would be needed only for long-term storage. The problem is that we don't live in the best of all possible computing worlds. Directly accessible memory is not able to accomplish all that is needed because operating systems provide varying support of a given CPU's memory management capability and executable memory is more expensive than secondary memory. To offset these limitations, enterprising DtC users have devised a variety of schemes for getting the most out of the limited executable memory.

Simple Memory Management

The easy way to handle programs is to run programs whose total size does not exceed executable memory and to run only one program at a time. Each program to be executed is loaded into memory as it is required, erasing the previous program. When the previous program is needed again, it is brought back into memory, erasing the current program. And so on. Historically, this is how MS-DOS and other single-tasking operating systems work. Because of this lack of memory management maturity and flexibility we find ourselves having to cram most of the executables into small memory areas.

Sophisticated DtC users can't be satisfied with this one-at-a-time method. Their ultimate goal is to run multiple concurrent programs, each potentially larger than executable memory, using as much directly accessible memory as possible and treating the mass storage as a virtual memory resource. Appropriate operating system functions would manage the programs and split up memory to minimize the amount of transfer between the hard disk and executable memory.

Some operating systems can provide just enough capability to load and run programs one at a time; other operating systems can provide full virtual memory capability. While most of us have experienced the load and go capabilities of CP/M, MS-DOS, and other HB computer operating systems, we should look at the ultimate memory management capability found in the Unix or VMS and lately in the OS/2 and Apple System 7.0 operating systems.

MS-DOS and Apple computers have both experienced problems with memory usage. Until recently, neither manufacturer's operating system has supported virtual memory or multitasking other than through crude enhancements. Help is on the way, however, in the form of Microsoft's Windows NT (New Technology) and a 32-bit version of OS/2 for MS-DOS computers and Apple's System 7.0, which will support virtual memory and 4 gigabyte addressable memory. We all look forward to this, but until then we need to know where we have come from and how we are handling memory matters now.

Virtual Memory

Virtual memory may be one of the most misunderstood capabilities of an operating system. Therefore, we shall discuss virtual memory from a few different viewpoints: its history, its technical features, how the DtC industry is grappling with trying to implement it, and particularly, why it is so essential.

Virtual memory is an elegant scheme to manage the expensive executable and less expensive secondary memory for optimum use. With virtual memory you can execute one or more programs larger than executable memory by using low-cost secondary memory as though it were able to execute programs. We've all used hard disks for long-term storage of programs and data; thinking of the hard disk as an executable resource, however, is quite a bit more than that.

As we know, programs can only be executed in directly addressable (executable) memory. The operating system is responsible for bringing the programs from secondary storage out to directly addressable memory, where they can be executed. An MS-DOS computer user may not think about what goes on when the Lotus 1-2-3 program is loaded from the hard disk and is executed. The fact that the size of this program (or its overlays) cannot be larger than executable memory, however, is a problem that frustrates software developers and users and has many complicated solutions. The most efficient of these solutions is virtual memory.

> **NOTE**
> Recall that executable memory is directly addressable memory. The amount depends on how many address lines are brought out by the CPU and to what extent the addressability is supported by the operating system.

In the pre-DtC days, computers were huge expensive machines, taking up entire rooms and costing hundreds of thousands of dollars. Obviously, it was impractical for each worker to have his own mammoth computer. The single computing resource power was shared using multiple display terminals each connected to the mainframe through low-speed serial communication ports. Each user wanted the computer to himself, and wanted a lot of executable memory. Executable memory was costly, however, so there was never enough to go around.

Another problem was that individual users did not want to concern themselves with the limits of executable memory. They wanted to develop and use programs that could be arbitrarily large and therefore bigger than the executable memory on that distant computer. After all, they didn't buy the computer, so why should they have to worry about such details?

An operating system was needed that could solve these problems by managing the limited executable memory resources at a high level. It would be able to:

1. Allow more than one program at a time to execute in memory (multitask).
2. Allow each user an apparently infinite executable memory resource (multiuse).

To successfully accomplish the above, the computer would need to have colossal executable memory resources, or at least, it would have to be able to simulate such a resource. This simulation is virtual memory.

Virtual memory is like a store system. In order to be sold (executed), goods (programs) must be on the store shelves (executable memory). The display shelves don't have room to display every item in stock. The warehouse (secondary memory) holds the long term storage items and excess inventory until they are needed for display (execution). It is good practice to keep the best sellers (portions of programs that execute the most) on the shelf. With this warehouse system, the total inventory of any given product line can be larger than shelf space; similarly, programs that are larger than executable memory can be stored in secondary memory. Multiple programs can execute concurrently in memory just as multiple product brands can be displayed side by side on the shelf.

The virtual memory system divides its executable memory into finely resolved pages, that is, equal chunks of memory. This organizes executable areas according to their specific requirements, and minimizes costly transfers. Without paging, virtual memory is still possible, it just isn't as efficiently organized.

Virtual memory lets you run a program that requires more memory than is installed on your system. You can have several programs running simultaneously, even when there isn't enough memory for all of them to be resident simultaneously. Also, it makes it simple to run programs that have greater-than-executable memory requirements. A given software task's memory space is divided into pages. Some of these pages are resident in physical memory while the rest are stored on hard disk. When a task requires a page that is not currently in memory, a page-fault exception interrupt occurs, and the operating system suspends execution of the task while it loads in the page, swapping out other pages if necessary, and lets the task continue execution.

A CPU can advertise more memory, by internal register bookkeeping, than it actually addresses. When a program portion is requested that is not in memory, an exception interrupt occurs, and the item is brought in from secondary memory.

> **NOTE**
>
> Recall the discussion of bank switching where programs larger than addressable memory could not be executed due to the lack of internal CPU mechanisms.

As more and more users attempt to share the executable resource, the shuffling becomes more costly, until finally each user experiences long response delays. Fortunately, this problem goes away when each user has an individual computer, or does it?

The first microcomputer operating systems supported a relatively low-power, but nevertheless individual, computing resource. Most of us were happy to run the early text-based word processors, spreadsheets, and database managers on the early microcomputers, later dubbed PCs. Simple single-tasking operating systems such as CP/M and MS-DOS were just the ticket. These early operating systems evolved with an emphasis on running one simple program at a time. Since PCs were inexpensive enough for everyone to own one, there was only one user per microcomputer. There was no need for virtual memory.

And besides, although virtual memory gives a computer magnificent capability for managing executable memory, it is not trivial to implement, nor is it absolutely necessary for accomplishing multitasking. As long as each program is limited in size to executable memory, and it is swapped in its entirety with other programs, we can enjoy multitasking using simple operating system enhancements.

As microprocessors became more powerful, Unix and its engineering and scientific software base was installed on 68000-based engineering workstations of the late '70s and '80s. Through Unix, the microcomputer can be given virtual memory capability. Lower-cost DtCs based on the 8- bit microprocessors, and the 16-bit Intel 8088 were not sufficiently powerful to run Unix, nor did they need to.

DtC user needs have lately become more sophisticated. DtC users do need a multitasking, virtual memory operating system. The following are some examples:

- **Networks** – The need to run programs distributed in a network requires multitasking.
- **Windowing** – The need for multiple programs to cooperate and communicate in a single, friendly environment requires multitasking.
- **Program size** – With programs operating in higher-level languages and environments, memory consumption has risen dramatically.
- **Graphics** – Increasing usage of graphics and their manipulation have driven program memory sizes.

Looking at virtual memory in terms of the CPU resources required to properly support it should help us in understanding why it is long in coming on the less sophisticated microcomputers and operating systems.

Virtual memory is not so much a form of memory as a methodology by which programs can think that they have more than the directly executable limit (2^n, where n is the number of CPU address lines). What happens is that the code is shuffled in and out of directly executable memory from secondary memory, usually on hard disk, as required by the operating system. Thus, programs can be written that are larger than memory and the operating system will take care of such details as getting code into memory as it is required for execution. Figure 64 shows several larger-than-memory programs being executed.

The process of initiating virtual memory is by no means just a flip of the switch endeavor; it requires three important technical investments:

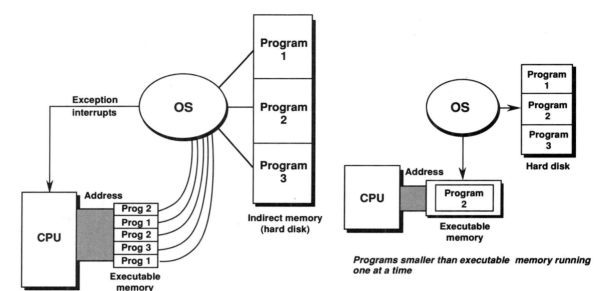

Exception interrupts

OS

Program 1

Program 2

Program 3

Indirect memory (hard disk)

Address

CPU

Prog 2
Prog 1
Prog 2
Prog 3
Prog 1

Executable memory

Programs larger than executable memory running concurrently

OS

Program 1

Program 2

Program 3

Hard disk

Address

CPU

Program 2

Executable memory

Programs smaller than executable memory running one at a time

Figure 64. OS with and without virtual memory capability: The figure shows virtual memory wherein one can run multiple programs, any one of which may be larger than executable memory. At right is the MS-DOS limitation, without enhancement, running only smaller than executable size programs.

- Considerable CPU hardware resources
- Sophisticated software development techniques
- Sophisticated operating system

Virtual memory has been standard fare on the traditional mainframe, the more powerful minicomputers, and the engineering and production workstations under Unix and other operating systems. In the realm of microcomputing, however, virtual memory remains a tantalus, a locked box without a key. For a CPU to perform multitasking with virtual memory, the CPU must have and the operating system must support:

- *Additional addressing registers* – Registers inside the microprocessor can specify virtual addresses larger than can be represented on the microprocessor's physical address lines. Thus, programs larger than 2^n can be managed by the CPU.

- *Paging capability* – The CPU can split executable memory into a series of small (512 to 4K) pages and for the sake of efficiency, the operating system can allow different pages to belong to different programs. By appropriately splitting up addressable memory into segments and pages, which requires particular microprocessor hardware, the operating system can manage many programs, each competing for memory resources.

- *Exception interrupts* – The operating system must allow incomplete programs to exist and execute in memory. The CPU will generate internal interrupts when incomplete programs reach a point where code does not exist in executable memory. The operating system can then bring code, transparent to the program, into memory from the hard disk when the program requires it. Exception interrupts are created from within the CPU, unlike interrupts that are prompted by external events. The interrupts must occur from within to allow the operating system to bring missing code in to executable memory without upsetting the currently executing program.

■ Virtual compilers allow you to develop code that is limited in size by the CPU's virtual memory capability and not by its physical address lines. An 80286 processor can run 1 gigabyte programs even though it only directly addresses 16 MB, or an 80386 could run programs that were 64 terabytes even though it addresses only 4 gigabytes.

You can well imagine that virtual memory requires an entirely different approach to the development of software than simple load/execute/unload software. In order to take advantage of the features just described, programs need to be developed using special tools. Virtual memory compilers can create code that can be managed in a virtual memory environment.■ Extenders can be woven into program code that can better manipulate the internal CPU capabilities, irrespective of the operating system.

So, what can we do? You should now realize that you cannot simply take a bunch of individual programs, such as the currently popular MS-DOS computer software base, throw them into a new operating system, such as OS/2 or Unix, and expect them to share virtual memory resources. Nevertheless, it is surprising to what lengths the MS-DOS computer industry has gone, short of creating a complete virtual memory system, to better use the memory of the MS-DOS software base. Later, we will look at more complete renovation of MS-DOS software to take advantage of MS-Windows and the OS/2 operating system.

Overlaying

Overlaying is a popular technique used by programs that need to be larger than executable memory, but without the higher technical investment of virtual memory. Using overlaying, a single program that would otherwise be larger than executable memory is split up into a main executable and overlays, each of which is smaller than executable memory. The main executable always resides in memory.

┌─ **EXAMPLE** ───┐
The dBASE database programming language interpreter is composed
of a main executable (dBASE.EXE) and several overlays (.ovl) files.
These were created with a C compiler, which provided the overlaying
capability. The overlay manager is contained in the dBASE.EXE executable.
└──┘

The overlaying process is controlled by compiling and linking the program with an overlay manager. The linker builds the overlay structure. Most medium-level language (C, Fortran, Pascal, BASIC) compilers provide overlaying capability when you develop code. Basically, you split up the program into a main program executable and one or more overlays, each less than total executable memory. As the main executable requires the overlays, the overlay manager software brings the necessary overlays into and out of memory. This is similar to calling subroutines, except that the subroutines need not be in executable memory.

Like virtual memory, overlaying is a method of sharing executable memory and hard disk resources. The difference is that the capability is provided by the developmental language rather than by the operating system. Figure 65 displays the overlay manager fielding the executable's requests for overlays. Overlaying is not as efficient as virtual memory because the overlays are often large and are not related to hardware in the CPU as are the pages of virtual memory. Only the main executable is recognized by the operating system.

Each language compiler will require different overlay strategies and implementation details, none of which are cooperative in any sense. Were the operating system, instead, responsible for managing memory resources and if each respective application called upon it for resources when required, we would have a more cooperative environment. This cooperation is one of the many improvements to the MS-DOS operating system made by Windows or the MS-DOS replacement, OS/2. The primary difference between overlays and memory supported by the operating system is the cooperative effect of multiple concurrent programs sharing the limited executable memory resource, all relying on a central figure, the operating system, to take care of the details of shuffling executable code into and out of indirectly accessible memory.

High-Level Peripheral Support

The more we can depend on the operating system to support peripherals, (particularly video display and printer output), the lighter will be the burden on the software. Of course, the operating system will never be able to support each and every peripheral device's idiosyncrasies. But it should, at least, support the higher levels of activity most programs require that are independent of the particular hardware, including:

- *Graphics* – Graphics functions such as rotations and transformations. By selecting a standard graphics language like PHIGS (Programmer Hierarchical Interactive Graphics System) as part of the operating system, graphics can be supported. At a high level, the operating system can perform these operations, and the specific commands necessary for a given device can be generated through lower-level drivers. Why should each program have to perform the same high-level operations independently?

- *PostScript* – Manipulation and formatting in PostScript is also machine independent at higher levels.

- *Drivers* – The operating system should manage peripheral drivers so that each application is not obliged to bring its own set of drivers. The multiplicity of drivers should be administered by the operating system, with each program having access to them. Of course, this level of cooperation between software vendors will be hard to realize. Also, efficiency between an application and its driver often forces individual developers to use their own custom drivers. OS/2, for example, provides its own facilities for managing printer drivers.

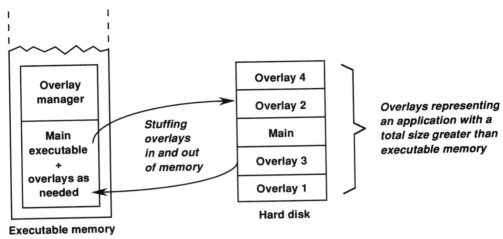

Figure 65. Overlays: An overlay manager can manage the process of bringing overlays to memory from secondary storage. Although the total overlay size can exceed executable memory size, no single overlay can.

Auxiliary Tools and Support Features

Most operating systems include the following tools necessary to make adjustments and perform rudimentary troubleshooting.

Text Editors

Preparation of textual material with computer assistance has several levels of sophistication. At the most elementary level the text editor is used to create batch and configuration files for the operating system. At a higher level an editor is required to build text files, correct errors, and to move, insert, copy, or otherwise alter written matter.

Among many important editorial functions are these:

- Duplicate one or more lines
- Delete characters/lines/blocks/files
- Find characters or character strings
- Insert characters or extended text
- Merge files
- Move text from place to place
- Make single or global replacements
- Page up and down in a file
- Set tabs
- Undo

At higher levels are word processors, document writing programs, and desktop publishers. These packages offer, in addition to editorial functions, orthographic and rhetorical aids (e.g., spelling checkers and thesauruses), graphics, and page layout features. Unix provides a built-in desktop publishing capability.

Most operating systems include an editor for the purpose of setting up batch processing and configuration files. Such editors usually have minimal capabilities, handy only for the simplest input and editing tasks. Most users, therefore, choose other, more powerful editors, purchased separately.

Assemblers/Compilers

Rudimentary assemblers and debuggers (programs that let you look at and manipulate machine-specific code) are included in most operating systems. But, as with the editor, you will probably choose to buy more worthy assemblers separately. The Unix operating system, itself written mostly in C, provides C compiling capability and a substantial set of program development utilities.

Graphical User Interfaces

At its unfriendliest, a shell's user interface presents a single character prompt that reveals little. At its friendliest, the shell allows you to point a mouse and select icons, pull down menus, move light bars, point to functions to be performed by the file manager, and execute programs. This type of picture-oriented shell is also known as a graphical user interface (GUI).

A GUI provides even the most naive user simple and obvious access to computer files, programs, and functions, and ready means for doing productive work. It allows attention to be focused on the task rather than on the method to be used. Perhaps the most important benefit of a GUI is often overlooked – it puts fun into mundane tasks for both the old hand and the novice.

A graphical user interface is an environment developed for a user to operate a microcomputer with minimal anxiety and frustration. A GUI provides easy access to programs, data, and information stored in various files; to manipulate them productively; and to put them safely away when done. Everyone knows what a GUI is – can recognize it instantly – but few comprehend it in entirety. The visual parts often distract attention from other, equally important functions that make up a GUI. GUIs have these major attributes in common:

1. Graphic orientation with icons and other visual elements
2. Direct visual/manual manipulation of on-screen elements
3. Object/action sequence of task execution
4. Bit-mapped displays that show output in WYSIWYG form
5. Consistency across applications and platforms

Most of these attributes relate to the GUI facet that is exposed visually to the user. Among the not so apparent characteristics are important management functions. To one degree or another, a respectable GUI provides file management, print management, and program management. Item 5 in the list above is perhaps the most important factor to novice users. Once you learn to manipulate and use one application, you are well on your way to using others because all of them will have the same look and feel.

The visual parts of a GUI are designed to simulate a desktop, a worktable in miniature with recognizable graphics representations of objects called *icons* laid out in an orderly array for easy selection. The simulation is often called a *desktop metaphor*, conveying the notion that the display screen resembles a desktop or is analogous to it.

The Macintosh, for example, simulates an office on the computer screen with pictures of manila folders to represent data files and a trash basket for files and scraps to be deleted. The Macintosh trash basket exhibits bulging sides whenever it is holding discarded material.

An icon can represent an application, directory, file, or other object.■ A list of selectable functions that are available is called a *menu*. A menu that drops down from a menu bar when a function is selected is called a *drop-down* or *pull-down* menu. One that appears when an item from a list is selected is called a *pop-up* menu. Pop-ups and pull-downs display secondary lists of options.

A window is an area on a screen used to display icons, menus, or to run an application. A window consists of a title bar that displays the name of the window, a menu bar that lists several options, and scroll bars that allow you to move matter up, down, left, and right inside the window. Most windows have buttons in one or more corners for resizing the window, moving it from place to place on the screen, and for closing it when done.

A good GUI is intuitive; that is, once initiated, a user does not have to refer to documentation to continue. Everything a user needs: files, paths, options, and functions are displayed on screen, so very little guesswork is involved. While it is easy to get started, a GUI is not completely free of mysteries. A newcomer will need some introductory prepping. The GUI documentation should be studied and some tutoring by an old hand will save a great deal of time.

If starting with Windows, a novice is well advised to become familiar with the built-in help feature. While a lot of navigation through menus is accomplished with a mouse, many functions involve keyboard keys. Windows Help explains the use of special keys.

Originally, microcomputer operating systems (MS-DOS, CP/M, Unix) were merely text-based program starter environments. You simply typed the name of a program, and it ran. The need for better user interface between the operating system and its control of software brought on an explosion of graphical user interfaces.

> **NOTE**
>
> Although many different operating system enhancements are lumped into what many call the GUI, the reader is cautioned that most operating systems provide many functions besides the GUI. For example, the Unix multitasking and data sharing functions existed long before it ever had a GUI. OS/2's data sharing capabilities are implemented outside its GUI (the Presentation Manager).

The idea of a graphical user interface glimmered first in the mid-1970s at PARC, the Palo Alto Research Center of the Xerox Corporation. It was the most dramatic feature of the Xerox Star workstation. The Star had advanced and innovative features, but it was expensive. Although marketed intensively, it never became a commercial success. The Apple Lisa, offered for sale in 1983, was not widely accepted by the buying public, even though it had a well-developed and eye-catching GUI. A year later Apple introduced the Macintosh. It was smaller and cheaper than the Lisa, and much more successful. The friendly graphical user interface deserves much of the credit for the widespread popularity of the Macintosh.

The proven marketability of the Macintosh GUI did not escape the notice of others. Microsoft began work on its Windows product in 1983, hard on the heels of Lisa and in anticipation of the Macintosh. The Windows development effort took

■ Software products such as MS Windows Express can be used to develop custom icons.

much longer than expected, the better part of two and a half years. The first version of Windows appeared on computer store shelves in November 1985, fully a year and a half after the promised delivery date. The following year release 1.03 became available.◼

◼ Interim releases included a European version and another in which several bugs had been fixed.

Most importantly it offered support for additional printing devices, including PostScript laser printers. On 2 April 1987, the day IBM announced PS/2, Microsoft introduced Windows 1.04, which supported the PS/2 VGA and the IBM mouse.

At this point IBM and Microsoft began joint development of OS/2 and Presentation Manager. The highlights of that undertaking may be found later. Windows and Presentation Manager are basically the same. Windows, for whatever differences there are, is generalized while Presentation Manager is intended for IBM-intensive installations.

MS-DOS computer users (without such graphics and user interface support) are sometimes pleasantly surprised to learn that a consistency is at work within a series of integrated software (such as the GeoWorks Ensemble desktop aid). Suddenly a warmth begins to pervade the application, because in moving from one function/operation/product to another, the territory remains consistently familiar to the user and thereby friendly.

Integrating Environments

There is much more to a good operating system than just pushing buttons to start a program. An important capability of an operating system is its ability to help programs work together. If programs are written to use the additional capability afforded by the operating system, they contribute to a well-integrated and friendly software base. Of course, this places a burden on developers, who must take more into consideration than when developing independent programs. A programmer must, for example, adjust program interfaces to fit into windows and give the program two-way message ability. Running individually, programs call upon the operating system for services, but seldom listen for anything. Now, programs must react to messages from the operating system telling them when they can execute, where they can display graphics, and when and where they should send data. The functions described below help programs operate seamlessly. Rather than one program coming in, running, and going out followed by another program coming in, running, and going out, we have:

- **Clipboards** – Software devices that allow programs to exchange data intuitively.
- **Data sharing** – Methods for programs to automatically share data. An operating system should provide for data sharing as an intention, not as an afterthought.
- **Windowing functions** – More than one program can display output on the screen. Output can even be displayed on different computers on a network in the X Windows environment.
- **General graphics support** – Not only to support the graphical interface to the operating system, but also to provide programs with the graphics functions that they need.

◼ The programs run alternately, but the time slicing occurs so rapidly it appears that the programs are running simultaneously.

- **Multitasking support** – Means by which more than one program can run at any given time.◼

Many competing integrating environments are available for the leading DtC platforms and operating systems. Although most of these environments differ in appearance and function, they benefit the user who wishes a specific look and feel. Moreover, as software products are developed that can operate in more than one environment, what becomes important is the data that they generate rather than the interface presented. In some cases, products will need to be developed differently for each environment. The overwhelming requirement, however, will be sharing data between the products over networks.

Arguments arise for and against having integration support within the operating system, instead of each application coming up with its own. Integrated environment supporters claim that it is easier to develop applications with good user interfaces and graphics capability when the support for this is provided by the operating system. Programs will have consistent user interfaces, may be able to share data, and even share windows on the same screen. According to this scenario, the dawn of a new day of obedient software is at hand.

Opponents contend that more efficiency can be obtained if groups of programs provide their own integration. Development may be more difficult, but efficiency is served when application-specific interfaces are in place.

Three types of integrating environments predominate: one is based on kernels, the second is network dependent, and the third is embedded in software packages. A sampling of the kernel and network types can be presented this way:

Kernel-Based Integrating Environments

Kernel-based systems are intimately linked to hardware and operating systems, which limits their portability. The following integrating environments are kernel-based:

Name	Source/Platform
DeskMate	Tandy Radio Shack
The Desktop	Apple Macintosh
DESQview	Quarterdeck
GEM/3 Desktop	Digital Research, Inc.
Intuition	Amiga
New Wave	Hewlett-Packard
Presentation Manager	IBM OS/2
Sun View	Sun Microsystems
Toolkit	Apple Macintosh
Windows	Microsoft

Microsoft Windows: Windows is a Macintosh-like graphical environment intended to enhance the existing MS-DOS operating system. MS-DOS programs need to be rewritten to be windowed in the environment. However, existing programs can take advantage of other features such as multitasking. Windows, the current best seller among MS-DOS enhancements, is truly a remarkable breakthrough for the MS-DOS community. Perhaps the most welcome of its many new features is its advanced memory management capabilities. Windows is about as close as Microsoft could get to the Apple GUI without duplicating its power and friendliness exactly.

Regardless of the widespread infatuation with it, Windows is not appropriate for all MS-DOS users. It should surprise no one that to some, the MS-DOS prompt, once they know how to navigate in that operating system, is a highly efficient user interface. Moreover, not all MS-DOS programs work in Windows and Windows has an appetite for memory. These drawbacks may be enough to make Windows a hindrance rather than a help in many practical situations. Windows' friendliness may in fact get in the way of productivity. On the other hand, in a not too different situation, Windows may be an indispensable productivity booster to an application.

MS-Windows is not just a windowing product. It is also a Program Manager, with a program execution shell that displays icons representing programs and applications. The Program Manager panel contains icons for the Windows File Manager, a Control Panel, Print Manager, a Clipboard, an MS-DOS prompt (for MS-DOS users who simply cannot let go), and a Windows Setup.

The File Manager displays a directory tree of all your files. Each directory is represented by a file folder, and folders containing more than one file or subdirectory are marked with a tiny plus sign – a nice touch. The Control Panel gives you access to screen colors, so you can change the decor of your display, even to small details such as different colors for active and inactive title bars and the color of text characters in the active window. You can even wallpaper the background with several attractive patterns.

Point to Fonts and click to see the half dozen typefaces that come with the Windows package. Other icons in the Control Panel allow you to check your ports, printer, 386 enhancements, and keyboard. You can select icons that let you alter mouse speed. You can also modify the keyboard layout, switch measurements from the English system to metric, and alter the formats of dates, time, currency, and decimal numbers.

The Program Manager Accessories panel gives access to a blank file for creating a document, to Paintbrush for sketching graphics, as well as to a notepad, cardfile, calendar, calculator, and clock. A Terminal icon allows you to set up a telephone dialing function, to program function keys, to perform text transfers and to carry on communications activities.

Each Windows panel has a Help option that gives information on the feature being used and provides how-to instructions. A click on Help on the Clipboard window displays a pop-up menu. Selecting Procedures and one of the topics in that panel displays instructions on how to cut and paste within documents, between documents, and between applications. Also contained within Windows is a complete set of graphics support routines similar to the OS/2 Presentation Manager.

Ease of use extends from start to finish. The Setup program analyzes the configuration of the DtC and chooses one of three operating modes that is best for your computer. The modes are *real*, *standard*, and *enhanced 386*.

- **Real mode** – Called WIN/R, this is the 8086/8088 mode. It runs applications inside the 640K of real memory. While you can mouse around with multiple DOS and Windows programs, real memory is too confining to be practical.

- **Standard mode** – Called WIN/S, this is the 286 mode. It multitasks *only* applications that have been written for Windows 3.0. All of the memory in the system, including the 16 MB of extended memory, is available for programs and data. MS-DOS applications can run in carousel fashion only.

- **386 enhanced mode** – Called WIN/3, this mode runs on 386 DtCs and needs at least 2 MB of memory for good performance. Multitasking includes both Windows and DOS applications. All of the RAM in the system is available for data and programs, and disk space is used as virtual RAM if needed. Virtual 8086 machines can be set up in memory so that many unmodified MS-DOS applications run as if each had its own 600K environment.

The setup program automatically creates folders for programs on the hard disk. When Windows 3.0 is installed, it automatically creates folders for your programs. A double click on the folder and on an icon starts the program.

OS/2 Presentation Manager: This is very similar to Windows. A sophisticated set of user and graphics support software libraries. MS-DOS programs must be rewritten to use Presentation Manager. Microsoft is writing a Windows version that will run on OS/2 instead of Presentation Manager.

DESQview: DESQview, from Quarterdeck Systems, is an attractive compromise between switching over to another operating system or purchasing integrated software in order to achieve integration. DESQview is the best environment for those who would rather fight than switch, and continue operating their favorite MS-DOS programs with the comfortable level of integration provided by DESQview.

Hewlett-Packard NewWave: NewWave is a file manager and scheduler that is based on Windows 2.0 and runs on MS-DOS computers. As an object manager it merges data from different applications at predetermined times and produces compound documents. Built-in hot links update data in related documents whenever data in one of the source files is updated. Automatic procedures called *agents* trigger programs at preselected times to gather data from diverse sources and generate reports.

GEM/3 Desktop: Graphics Environment Manager is from Digital Research. A GEM-like system was developed also for MS-DOS computers that operated a series of friendly software products. The Ventura Desktop Publisher can run under GEM. GEM also runs on Atari DtCs.

Commodore Amiga Intuition: This flexible windowing environment is for Commodore computers. It uses exceptionally good ROM-based graphics support found in the Commodore.

Macintosh Desktop: A friendly, mouse-driven environment for managing programs and data files. Apple has implemented this friendly environment from the beginning on the Macintosh line. Desktop takes advantage of the extensive ROM-based interface support found in the Mac.

Network-Based Integrating Environments

Network-based systems are not only portable, but can run on one platform and display results on one of a different architecture. The most serious drawback of network-based integrating environments is that they must move large quantities of data constantly across the network just to keep displays fresh and responsive. The following implement network-based integrating environments:

Name	Source/Platform
Motif	Open Systems Foundation (OSF)
NeXTStep	NeXT
Open Look	Sun Microsystems
Open View	Sun Microsystems
Open Windows	Sun Microsystems
X Windows	MIT

Two of the major players in this environment are Open Look and OSF/Motif.

DECwindows Desktop Environment: Digital Equipment Corporation's view of enterprise-wide computing is based on the desktop environment concept, which conforms to a wide range of networking, graphics, operating system interface, user interface, and document exchange standards. DEC is following the OSF/Motif GUI model. Two of the important aspects of this environment are integration of heterogeneous equipment (MS-DOS and VAX workstations) and distribution of applications to remote locations in a network. Macintosh is supported also.

Components of the Desktop include an X Windows system, an X User Interface, CDA Services, Desktop Accessories, Utilities, and an MS-DOS extension.

- *Session manager* – Supports the look and feel of the user session (keyboard definition, screen color, etc.)
- *Window manager* – Controls look and feel of the windows as you use them (style, title bar contents).
- *Terminal emulator* – Lets the window emulate a variety of DEC terminals (VT100, VT220, etc.).
- *Desktop applications and utilities* – Set of utilities that come with the windows environment (clock, calculator, calendar, etc.).

OSF/Motif: Motif is Open Software Foundation's version of the X Windows development toolkit. It has the look and feel of a system proposed by HP and Microsoft. It emulates the look and feel of IBM/Microsoft's Presentation Manager. It's a direct competitor of Open Look.

It's also a graphical user interface specification, great for writing Windows applications that will run on different platforms over networks such as PC, VAX, HP/Apple, etc.

Open Look (XView and AT&T Open Look): Open Look is a graphical user interface specification originally introduced by Sun Microsystems and backed by AT&T. The goal is to define a graphical user interface standard for Unix workstations. The two current major implementations are Sun's XView and AT&T's Open Look. It is a direct competitor of OSF/Motif.

Embedded Integrating Environments

You can purchase software that within its ambit integrates several software functions. Since the functions are written and coordinated by the same software developer, seamless operation between several software functions can be achieved.

Integrated software packages such as GeoWorks Ensemble and FrameWork provide internal windowing support and do not need assistance from the operating system. The type of windowing can be customized for the software functions being implemented. The level of windowing integration possible in such products can be greater than any achieved through external windowing environments. This is because external environments must provide for general software needs, while integrated packages can concentrate on display functions specialized to only those few software functions that they feature.

Enable: An integration of word processing, database management, spreadsheet, graphics, and communications capabilities. Enable provides reasonably good and well-integrated support across many significant software functions. It is easy to use.

FrameWork: An Ashton-Tate product, FrameWork is similar in function to Enable. Both FrameWork and Enable implement their own internal languages for increased customization.

Symphony: Lotus Development Corporation's integrated spreadsheet, database, graphics, and word processor. Its emphasis is on the spreadsheet, with a sophisticated capability of placing forms ahead of spreadsheets to simplify data entry and searching.

GeoWorks Ensemble: Primarily a collection of personal information management tools: address and telephone book, spreadsheet, word processor, scheduler, and a collection of games. Ensemble is an excellent example of how friendly an embedded integrating environment can be.

Borland's SideKick: This product includes a notepad, calculator, scheduler, phone book, and file manager. It also supports a laser printer for spectacular outputs. And, SideKick operates underneath your usual programs as a TSR program.

> **NOTE**
> Embedded integrating environments are also found in PageMaker, Excel, Micrografx Designer, Ventura Publisher, Interleaf, and others, and are inextricably tied to their packages.

Different Modes

Many argue that combining so many important software functions in one software package must lead to inadequate functionality in some areas. Some are willing to pay a power penalty for good integration. Others operate individual software programs such as word processors, spreadsheets, and database managers without integration. Yet others are operating individual programs that attain their integration through a centralized support.

Some software developers are beginning to understand that while many users need an important software function at a high level, they also need a sprinkling of other capabilities at a lower level. This way the software function of interest is done well, but other capabilities are included just in case they are needed. For example, WordPerfect is for word processing, but it also has some graphics and desktop publishing capabilities. Excel is a spreadsheet program, but it has good presentation graphics features. If you don't like the graphics capabilities of Excel or WordPerfect you can always operate other programs that specialize in presentation graphics. Don't be surprised when you find some spreadsheet capability in a presentation graphics program. The ideal situation would be for the operating system to provide the integration and the applications developer to provide the functionality.

2.0   Operating Systems Categories

- Home and Business
- Education
- Entertainment
- Engineering and Production

The different feel and applications areas of the different DtC categories is not due only to their difference in architecture. Just as important is the nature of their operating systems.

2.1   Home and Business

The HB operating system is not very programmable – a feature we shall see is of paramount importance in the EP category. Instead, the intent is simply to run a variety of software. Users of these operating systems want to plug in software as they would an audio cassette, select what they want and play it; making use of preprogrammed software and using the computer as a labor saver. Much of the preprogrammed software has programmability built in through application-specific languages. The operating system stays as is. It does *not* get programmed.

MS-DOS – Precursors and Successors

CP/M was first written in 8080 assembly language. It was the first operating system to provide centralized hardware support for software applications and won such widespread favor that computers using the operating system became known as CP/M computers. PC-DOS followed CP/M and originally was quite similar to it. PC-DOS was also written in 8088 assembly language. The IBM PC-DOS and its MS-DOS version will both run on the 80286 (acting like an 8088 chip in real mode) and on the 80386/486 (emulating the 80286 in real mode). Operating at 8088 levels precludes use of the advanced 80xxx microprocessor capabilities.

Although MS-DOS computers, originally clones of the IBM PC line, are built by many different manufacturers, they are practically identical from the viewpoint of software. Indeed, the ability to run the MS-DOS software base requires that MS-DOS computers be similar. Because MS-DOS is specific to the 8088 microprocessor, it does not support important enhancements found in the 80286 and later Intel microprocessors. MS-DOS lacks support of most of the resource categories mentioned in the beginning of this Part. Later we will focus on MS-DOS weaknesses and look at solutions.

The open architecture of MS-DOS computers and their consequent popularity, has made the possible combinations of peripheral equipment practically endless. It has been difficult to provide support for peripherals within the MS-DOS operating system. Instead, peripheral support is provided by drivers that are unique to each application. Other DtC operating systems (Atari, Amiga, Macintosh) are not required to support such a diversity of peripherals, and therefore much of their peripheral support can be found in ROM.

MS-DOS computers are a commodity item. Hundreds of manufacturers in several countries are producing MS-DOS computers that are compatible. Differences among MS-DOS computers (and their IBM counterparts) are largely in the realm of performance. As a result of massive proliferation, MS-DOS computers are readily available, at relatively low cost, with a seemingly infinite choice of peripheral enhancements. In Asia alone there are more than a thousand manufacturers of MS-DOS computer components.

The MS-DOS software base is abundant and diverse, and difficult to manage. Software installations can be complex due to the diversification and the user is burdened with the details of matching various combinations of system unit and peripheral. Hundreds of software products are available in every software category, so there is bound to be something suitable for almost any need. From a managerial standpoint, however, there is little consistency in the multitude of software approaches and solutions.

It is this diversity – this multiheaded dragon – that plagues those who would build an operating system to manage every possible peripheral, user interface, and software type.

What we must remember is that it will be difficult to have it both ways, that is,

1. to run anything we want in any way we want with any peripheral we want, *and*
2. to dump most software support functions onto the operating system.

Providing more functional support (by OS/2 and MS-DOS/Windows) will help to tame the diverse MS-DOS applications software base. Some will be pleased; others irritated. We will probably always have both forms of operating systems – the patchworked MS-DOS and the strict OS/2.

Combined Text and Graphical Interfaces

MS-DOS computers have endured a long history of non-APA or text-only software and corresponding video display hardware. The early video interfaces were mostly text oriented with only limited graphics capability. The text-only support restricted display screens to 80 by 25 characters. As a consequence, each MS-DOS applications program had to provide its own user interface and graphics capability, which has led to a proliferation of disparate and often user unfriendly programs. Of course, this has also led to the tremendous variety of applications available for MS-DOS computers.

Since graphics has become so important to software applications, the need for each application to have its own graphics support has frustrated the growth of the applications software base. APA support is provided in Windows and in OS/2.

MS-DOS with Microsoft Windows

Microsoft Windows is a considerable adjunct to MS-DOS. It adds several important features:

- Support of extended memory
- Multitasking
- A graphical user interface
- Data sharing (clipboard)
- Windowing

MS-Windows was designed for those who want an improved MS-DOS, without sacrificing their existing MS-DOS software base.

OS/2 with Presentation Manager

Frustrated with keeping MS-DOS going, IBM and Microsoft developed the OS/2 operating system. In many respects, OS/2 is revolutionary, having capabilities that compete favorably with the powerful Unix operating system. The ties with MS-DOS were severed inasmuch as OS/2 requires the 80286 protected mode to operate. Although previous 8088-based software can run under OS/2 (in the MS-DOS box), OS/2 will not operate on an 8088 microcomputer.

Apple's Operating System and Graphical Interface

Apple Computer has long recognized the importance of supporting the user interface and graphics from within an operating system. Apple's OS has historically provided support for:

- **Data sharing** – Moving data between programs using the Clipboard. MS-DOS computers usually share data by files.
- **Presentation/GUI** – User friendly selection of programs and data with icons and menus.
- **Windowing** – The sharing of the video screen by different programs.

Apple's APA Graphics Support

User interface and graphics support is so fundamental in Apple's operating system that it is found in firmware (ROM). From the beginning, Apple decided to support the more difficult APA video interfaces and printers. Vendors tend to take advantage of this APA support to ease their respective development burdens in the graphics and presentations areas. Since this support is within Apple's operating system, programs that use it will behave consistently.

There is no particular reason why MS-DOS programs cannot be written to resemble Macintosh programs, and some in fact do. It simply takes more effort at the applications-development level. The developmental burden will ease with the built-in support found in Windows and OS/2, however, the support cannot be as intrinsic as it is in the ROM-based systems of the Apple Macintosh.

Apple's Peripheral Support

Apple's in-ROM support extends well into its peripheral line, due to a more limited assortment of powerful peripherals. Although several vendors produce Apple peripherals, Apple's own peripherals are good, albeit expensive. This limited peripheral base is well supported by the operating system. The tradeoff with Apple software is: less diversity in supported peripherals vs. better built-in support for those peripherals that are supported.

2.2 Education and Entertainment Computers

The immense diversity of EE computers presents a unique problem for developers and vendors of operating systems and software.

The two main EE computer vendors are Commodore, with the Amiga, and Atari. The Atari and Commodore DtCs are significantly different from microcomputers described as HB and EP. Although EEs are based on the 68xxx microprocessors, they differ from each other in all other respects. The architectures of these computers evolved in a competitive environment where focus was driven by meeting users special needs.

Examples of these needs include:

- **High resolution graphics** – Oriented toward animation effects.
- **Special user interface** – Specialized user interfaces supporting their unique applications base. Trackballs, gamepads, and other nifty input devices.
- **Speech synthesis** – Built-in hardware for synthesizing phonetic or digitized speech.
- **Music chips** – Chips specialized in generating complex waveforms. Some of these can synthesize most musical instruments and include multiple channels and stereo effects.
- **Specialized buses** – DMA for speech processing, different memory buses for multitasking.■

■ We do not include Apple Macintosh in this category even though their models do support sound chips. Compared to the Atari and Amiga DtCs architectures, however, the Macintosh is tame.

Most of the above functions are supported in ROM with BIOS routines that are customized to the particular DtC. Moreover, the Atari's hardware and ROM support is completely different from that of the Amiga, and for that matter different from Apple's Macintosh. Programs written to take advantage of these special features either directly or through the ROM BIOS will not be compatible with other highly specialized EE DtCs. Their specialization makes it unlikely that a general-purpose operating system such as Unix will be operated by most EE computer owners to afford compatibility. It is difficult or impossible to write applications that will run on more than one of these significantly different systems while trying to use the special features of each.■

■ Although Unix is available in this class, it will be difficult for text-based software under Unix to take advantage of special features described.

Special Effects Programming

Software development requires a different programming talent in the world of audio/visual effects. Programmers need to interact with complex devices and be knowledgeable about how to manage the audio/visual effects supported on these computers.

Integrating sound and animation has been the hallmark of Atari and Commodore DtCs from the beginning.

A/V Capability for MS-DOS Computers

a/v hardware is becoming available for MS-DOS computers. Intel's DVI (Digital Video Interactive) system is a set of boards added to an MS-DOS computer that combines live motion video and audio with software applications.

The MS-DOS add-on hardware is not as hospitable as EE a/v hardware because the a/v capability wasn't built into the computer or the operating system from the start. Since this hardware is added after the fact, it is not as well integrated with the rest of the DtC hardware, nor its operating system.

■ Apple's latest Macintosh computers are providing reasonable levels of integrated audio/visual hardware.

Although there have been improvements in MS-DOS computers, with the MCA bus a/v signals, the support of Intel DVI, and increased interest in a/v applications, it will still be a while before the levels of integration on Atari and Commodore computers become possible on the more popular HB computers.■

Summarizing the Audio/Visual Approach

Software running under the EE DtC architectures and operating systems will take advantage of special features, and will achieve higher performance than software that runs under the more controlled architectures of the HB and EW categories.

Unfortunately, no standards exist for the significantly different EE computers. Each has its own custom array of hardware, software, peripherals, repair methodologies, and, sometimes, local area network hardware. Software using special features is not transportable between these computers. If one of these computers becomes popular (like MS-DOS computers or the Apple Macintosh line), the lack of compatibility between different vendor's models would become academic. Software that must transport to other computers will have to be written to be insensitive to different architectures. In this form, the applications will lack the spectacular performance for which they are known.

EE computers are rarely imitated. To prevent imitation, EE computer vendors usually hold back system information that is necessary for cloning and further ensure hands-off by vigilant control over patents, copyrights, and proprietary BIOS ROMs. The more common peripherals (printers, video, mass storage) are provided by the original vendor. These peripherals are more expensive than generic brands because of limited production. Often, a better match between peripheral and computer offsets the additional cost. Since there is more freedom to customize architecture, the EE computers are supported by a more customized operating system with more intensive built-in peripheral support.

In the constrained peripheral environment discussed above, software developers can concentrate more on their applications and less on supporting a multitude of system unit and peripheral combinations. Instead, a single, high-performance system with better integrated peripherals and interfaces runs the software base. Better matches between applications software and peripherals are the rule. Within a given manufacturer's line, software is less abundant, but is often more consistent and efficient than HB computer software. Such specialized software includes:

- *Music systems* – Music development systems using MIDI interfaces and electronic keyboards, as well as built-in sound generators.
- *Desktop video* – Combining live video from video disks and cameras and using this with computer graphics for spectacular graphics shows, training software, and other applications requiring live video usage.

The EE computer provides a spectacular computing environment. Highly integrated audio/visual effects are second nature to these computers. Running the more bland software base of the HB computer, often available for the EE, is self-defeating. An EE purchase should, rather, be motivated by the EE-oriented software base for which these computers were designed.

2.3   Engineering and Production

Engineering and production workstations are required for high-order tasks including CAD, CAE, artificial intelligence, desktop publishing, and management of large databases. Such DtCs combine well-integrated system architectures with powerful

CPUs and good networking capability. What they need is a mature and powerful operating system.

Although many operating systems are associated with the higher-level DtCs found in the scientific technical areas, let's focus on the most popular operating system found in this category, Unix.

3.0 Focus on Unix

Unix is traditionally at home on the more powerful microcomputers and workstations, on minicomputers, and even on mainframes and supercomputers. With the arrival of microprocessor chips with adequate power and cross-platform communication, Unix is becoming a force in the DtC environment.

Unix was born in a Bell Laboratories research group in the late '60s. Ken Thompson and Dennis Richie performed most of the groundbreaking in a project known as MULTICS (Multiplexed Information and Computing Environment), a visionary computer environment for the time. Jokingly, it was also called Many Unnecessarily Large Tables in Core Simultaneously. Unix began as a curiosity, but soon spread throughout AT&T and to the university environment, particularly Berkeley in California. The karma, if you will, of Unix irresistibly attracted student experimentation and enhancement.

Unix was originally developed for the larger minicomputers and, in particular, the DEC line. Unix is now becoming popular on microcomputers as microprocessors come up to sufficient power levels to operate it. The following chronology summarizes its history.

- *1960* – First appearance
- *1970* – Popular on DEC computers
- *1980s* – Popularity develops on engineering workstations (Sun, Apollo)
- *Late '80s* – Versions of Unix appear on popular business computers (MS-DOS and Macintosh)

Unix is found on such original engineering workstation vendors as Apollo and Sun, NCR, AT&T, Prime, and more recently on MS-DOS computers using Microsoft's and SCO's (Santa Cruz Operation) Xenix and IBM's AIX. More specialized graphics workstations operating under Unix are the Graphics Workstations of Silicon Graphics and Pixar.

3.1 *Early Unix*

The first Unix versions came with complete source code, written in the C programming language, and documentation. The early versions were small and most of the algorithms were relatively simple. Unix manuals were readable and only a few pages long. The energetic user could confidently modify and tinker with Unix, something a sensible individual would not dare to undertake with other operating systems.

Historically, Unix applications have been text-based, with minimal graphics support. Newer "binary" Unix versions running on the more popular engineering workstations (Sun, HP-Apollo), support operating environments that include graphics and windowing (X Windows, Open Look).

The transition of Unix from text only to text and graphics is analogous to MS-DOS, a text-based operating system, becoming graphical. MS-DOS, however, lacks most of the more important functional characteristics that separate MS-DOS and Unix. Unix was implemented on 68xxx-based microcomputers before the 80xxx microcomputers. This was because the initial Motorola microprocessors were much more powerful than the initial Intel entries. Beginning with the Intel 80286, and now 80386/486 microprocessors, Unix can run on MS-DOS computers.

3.2   Inside Unix

Written originally in assembly language, Unix was subsequently rewritten and enhanced in the C programming language. Thus Unix is free of dependency on any given CPU.

The benefit from high-level language implementation is threefold:

◼ MS-DOS and APPLE-DOS are written mostly in assembly (machine) language and are therefore locked to their microprocessors

1. **Operating system transportability** – Unix is more easily ported to different microcomputers. Even those with different microprocessors.◼ Because Unix (with the exception of a small machine language portion) is written in C, it can be re-written to accommodate other microprocessors with considerably less difficulty than the operating systems written in a given microprocessor's machine language. Due to its portability, Unix is often the only practical choice when creating operating systems for new or specialized microcomputer systems. Unix is open and well documented, so it can run new computer engines ranging from microcomputers to supercomputers using parallel and distributed processors to toaster ovens. To the extent that there are so many different microprocessors (CISC, RISC, ASIC, even Parallel Multiprocessors), this is an important characteristic.

2. **Better functionality** – As compared to operating systems developed in assembly language. Programming the operating system in a higher language generally results in higher functionality because the developer is free of microprocessor-specific details.

3. **Better applications transportability** – Most Unix applications are also developed in C. The applications software base is developed over a uniform set of libraries, some of which are also used by the operating system. This results in a solid integration of software function with operating system function. Quite simply, C-based software can easily use OS resources. More importantly, the applications software base transports well between considerably different Unix platforms.

Unix-based applications program transportability applies particularly to text-based applications. As with the MS-DOS operating system, there is a continuing need for graphics standards.

The Unix Kernel

In Unix and other operating systems, the term kernel is used to describe the hardware-dependant part of the operating system. The basic functions of the Unix kernel and the HB DtC's BIOS are the same. Both separate the operating system and programs from specifics of a DtC's fundamental hardware. Figure 63 on page

287shows the MS-DOS operating system in relation to the BIOS. A similar diagram for Unix would have the kernel where the BIOS would be shown with another ring around it. This new ring would contain the Unix shell and a set of built-in Unix functions discussed later. The outer layer would contain the compiler, applications programs, and the user's programs. The middle two rings compose what is thought of as the Unix operating system. The Unix kernel for all its similarities to the BIOS encompasses many tasks which MS-DOS leaves to add-on environments. For example, Unix provides such features as scheduling for devices, inter-process communication, and virtual memory management between processes. The Unix kernel started out rather small at around 10K; and was intended to be simple. It has, however, become large, seldom less than 100K, and convoluted. Adding new features or modifying old ones is a challenge. Granted, many of these features are necessary for the Unix multitasking environment and were not necessary for the MS-DOS single user environments. Many add-on environments for MS-DOS are incorporating these features.

The Mach kernel, essentially a revamped Unix kernel, was written by a group of researchers at Carnegie-Mellon University to streamline the convoluted Unix kernel so that it would perform its fundamental tasks well. Other, more complex functions are handled by code that resides outside the kernel. You could call the Mach kernel an object-oriented kernel since it is based around a set of abstract objects that describe executing programs. The objects are tasks, threads, ports, and messages, which can all communicate. The Mach kernel itself is not inherently Unix compatible, however, you can build a compatible Unix system around it. This was done for the NeXT computer. The Unix-compliant Mach operating system, with its friendly GUI, is used on the NeXT computer.

Unix Versions

Unix comes in many different versions (28 according to one count), which often confounds software developers who want to run their programs across the Unix board. Among these only a half-dozen or so receive substantial broad-based support. These versions include:

- AT&T's System V
- Microsoft's and SCO's (Santa Cruz Operation) XENIX for MS-DOS computers
- Berkeley's Unix
- IBM's AIX
- Hewlett Packard's HP-UX
- DEC's Ultrix
- Apple's AUX (Unix with an Apple in its mouth)

Pressure is being applied for the industry to agree to and standardize a single Unix version. A unified Unix coupled with a standard GUI will win widespread acceptance as an extremely powerful operating system. Among more than a dozen recognizable Unix systems, two major Unix standards are currently in direct competition.

- **Open Software Foundation** – The Foundation, out of Cambridge Massachusetts, with key members from DEC, Hewlett Packard, and IBM. The GUI is Motif. This Unix version uses the Mach kernel from Carnegie-Mellon University.

- **Unix International** – This standard emanates from Parsippany, New Jersey with AT&T Sun and Intel as supporting members. This Unix is based on the AT&T System V Release 4.0; X Windows is the GUI.

Unix Hardware Requirements

Unix needs to be operated on a workstation, that is, a multitasking computer with at least 4 MB of RAM, a pointing device, disk storage of at least 100 MB, and at least a 3 MIPS CPU.

Now you can see why Unix was not supportable on the popular home and business DtCs of the pre-1990 era. Today's 80386/486 DtCs, and Apple's Macintosh HB computers do, however, meet the Unix requirements.

Learning Unix on MS-DOS Computers

Through Minix, developed by Andrew Tanenbaum at Vrije Universitaet in Amsterdam, modest MS-DOS computers can experiment with Unix. The version has no AT&T source code, so it is free from licensing restrictions. Minix is a great way to get familiar with Unix. An $80.00 version can run from floppies on MS-DOS DtCs.

3.3   Unix Features

Several important and well-conceived features of the Unix operating system have earned it sweeping popularity in the scientific and engineering areas. If these capabilities are packaged attractively for the less computer-oriented individual, Unix may be accepted into the business world and flourish on home and business microcomputers.

1. **Unification of file, device, and interprocess I/O** – Unix makes heavy use of such process communication software constructs as pipes and filters. Using these software devices, one program's output can easily be another's input. Devices appear as files, which means that they can be manipulated as if they were files.

   Individual Unix programs can be simple; they can hook up to one another easily and combine to perform considerably intense functions. Under Unix, you can save and write data to a disk or tape and the individual driver will take care of the work. The Unix function WRITE () works the same way in every case.

   > **EXAMPLE**
   >
   > Under Unix, a spelling checker could be a conglomeration of simple software functions, well connected by a complex set of pipes. A flexible combination of well-connected software functions may be provided to the user by a set of Unix shell scripts. Under MS-DOS, you simply purchase a complete and independent spelling check program (such as *Webster's Dictionary*).

   The advantage of Unix applications development is that a custom spelling environment can be created under Unix with good communication with other programs. Of course this will take a developmental skill acquired by few common folk. In contrast, MS-DOS applications such as Lotus 1-2-3, dBASE, and WordPerfect are complete and powerful entities, but they do not communicate well among themselves, and they accomplish specialized functions.

   As MS-DOS applications are developed under Windows or OS/2, they too will communicate better. Macintosh applications developed under its operating system

The Macintosh uses PostScript and PIC file formats, which communicate well. Under 7.0, the publish and subscribe functions will assist data communications.

LS is the Unix version of the MS-DOS DIR (Directory) command.

Shell, in this context, is a language.

7.0 will communicate well, however, there is still the problem of being stuck with individual pre-set applications packages. ■

2. **Multiple asynchronous processes** – Unix supports multiple users – usually by terminals – each appearing to have complete computer resources and, through multitasking, each user can operate multiple, interconnected tasks. A single microcomputer can support multiple terminals much like the mainframe computer does. The terminals are typically low cost and character oriented.

3. **Unix supports multitasking** – Under Unix each user can operate multiple, concurrent software processes. A simple `LS` (List) command creates a process. ■

4. **Default shell replacement** – The default shell used to start and control programs can easily be replaced or customized under Unix.

EXAMPLE

When launching a Unix command the & before the command tells Unix that it does not have to wait to finish the current command before beginning the next. Thus you can launch multiple concurrent processes by simply typing commands, one after another.

Using a shell script you can create your own shell. ■ You can stylize the Unix interface completely on a per-user basis and autopilot an assortment of complex interconnected Unix processes. The result can be a set of highly specialized functions.

• **MS-DOS and Unix shells compared** – Unix shell scripts are similar to the common programming languages with such constructs as do loop clauses and variables. In MS-DOS computers, batch files are used to autopilot its command processor.

Although you can auto-pilot your MS-DOS operating system's command processor through these *bat* files, you have only rudimentary control and parameter passing capability compared to Unix shell scripts. You can, however, replace MS-DOS batching capability with enhanced batch processors (such as found in the Norton Utilities). Moreover, the default shell can be replaced with others (such as XTree, QFiler, or even the GUI of MS-Windows.

Both operating systems, Unix and MS-DOS through enhancements, provide a lot of shell customization capability. The major difference is that with Unix, a competent user can customize and closely associate the shell with the operating system, while in MS-DOS, the shell is used right out of the box.

• **Popular text-based Unix shells** – The Bourne shell by Steven Bourne of Bell labs is one of the simpler Unix shells while the Korn shell by David Korn of Bell Labs is the more popular.

5. **Hierarchical file system** – Unix supports a hierarchical file system of considerable flexibility. File hierarchies can be complex and structure hierarchy is implied in the file name through a series of extensions. Although the MS-DOS operating system provides hierarchical directories patterned after Unix, they are not as flexible, nor as amenable to file manipulation between them.

6. **Building block/software tools approach** – Unix is a programmer's environment. Rather than being monolithic, in the manner of MS-DOS and Apple-DOS, Unix combines a number of small utilities that can be joined as needs demand. Most agree that Unix is written by programmers for programmers. To appropriately use

Unix Features   319

Unix, you must be familiar with system calls, libraries, languages and tools, and the manual. Many ad hoc utilities can be combined quickly to build and integrate software subsystems. The MAKE command provides built-in S/W configuration management, for example.

Through a consistent set of commands and software libraries, Unix takes a building block approach to software development. The output of one program may easily be the input of another. Unix lends itself to tinkering. New tools and applications are easy to write once you get the hang of using the tools. Even with new languages, such as the object oriented C++ or Modulo 3. The source code and documentation is there to study, and there are plenty of university courses. The emphasis is on lots of software tools to build anything instead of trying to find the right thing already made. As with MS-DOS, there are vast amounts of public domain enhancements and tools for the Unix operating system.

Unix is *not* geared towards helping you get work done. Unix *is* oriented toward helping you understand the system so that your solution fits into a Unix-style solution. This leads to a considerably different type of solution from one you might find on other systems; it is customized toward very specific solutions.

7. *Dominant file type is text* – As such, these files are easily modified with editors over relatively unsophisticated terminals. Once you know how to use an editor, you can edit and control everything. Of course, this popularity of text-based applications must be taken in the light of popular graphics applications. Under Unix, as with other operating systems there are evolving graphics standards. Of course, once the standards are established, they will apply across the largest cross section of computers known.

8. *Communications protocols* – Unix supports from the simple two point asynchronous communications we all exercise when we use our modems to dial up other computers to the sophisticated high-speed Ethernet networking. Unix was developed to connect a variety of computers together, whether across a building, or country to country on packet-switched networks.

9. *Scientific computation* – Unix was created for scientific computation and data processing for technical development at Bell Labs. Computer science education could include many different courses from "Introduction to Programming" to "Compiler Design" under Unix using 30-40 lessons and sample programs.

10. *Transportability* – Software developed under Unix and ANSI standards stands a good chance of running on a diversity of computers. The diversified operating systems of computers such as Atari and Commodore do not boast such common transportability of software between very different computers.

Unix Beyond Text-Only Applications

As is the case of MS-DOS, Unix has historically been a text-oriented operating system and has enjoyed great software portability.

Inasmuch as the bulk of Unix applications software is text oriented, non-text applications are not a serious problem. Lately, a new breed of engineering applications software is appearing that makes heavy use of graphics. This graphics software merits the same concern for graphics and user interface support in Unix workstations as it has in MS-DOS and Apple computers. And, as with the MS-DOS and Macintosh computers and EE workstations, there are different kinds of program integrating environments for Unix. Two major standards have emerged in the Unix world:

1. Open Software Foundation's Motif

2. Unix International's Open Look

Indeed, when these environments are coupled with the aforementioned Unix functionality, rather spectacular applications possibilities arise.

For example: view a radar image of a countryside right on your workstation and assemble a complex set of signal processing functions by simply looking at a set of icons on the same screen. These icons represent the various complex math processing functions. Use a mouse to connect the various processes and direct data flow into and out of the various processes. In another window view a graphical representation of the image after appropriate filtering and color rendering performed by a more powerful workstation elsewhere.

Unix Networking Capability

Thanks to Unix's ability to treat files, processes, and hardware similarly, networks are a natural environment for it. X Windows, developed at MIT, provides Unix systems with a distributed processing capability not equalled by most HB computer operating systems.

> **NOTE**
>
> X Windows was developed jointly by DEC and MIT at Project Athena. X is based on the W window system written at Stanford. For example: a program on one Unix box can call code on another Unix machine to execute a subroutine call, using the X-11 network protocol. The ability for code on one machine to call code on another computer is one basis for distributed processing.

Unix Tools/Functions:

A few of the popular Unix tools/functions are summarized to show what the Unix environment is like. Unix is definitely a programmers operating system.

- *yacc (yet another compiler)* – A compiler used to build language compilers.
- *lex (lexical analyzer)* – Scanner or tokenizer. Reads input stream breaking it into tokens. Lex recognizes patterns and grammars powerful enough to define almost all programming languages. Lex, however, is not powerful enough to describe languages such as English.
- *lint* – Checks programs prior to compiling for syntax, bad use of variables, etc.
- *termcap (terminal capabilities)* – A library that supports terminal-independent character graphics.
- *curses* – High-level interface to termcap. Curses is a management library that can print formatted strings with rudimentary windowing capability. Curses is limited to character graphics.
- *cc* – C compiler issued with Unix.
- *make* – Creates an executable file from a set of source files by managing the compilation process. Provides basic S/W configuration management.
- *ed* – The basic Unix line editor.
- *vi* – A popular Unix full-screen editor. Available on all Unix systems.
- *emacs* – More general-purpose third party editor. Can display multiple windows. Available as a public domain S/W package that can be obtained without cost.
- *INIT* – First process created at startup. Creates all other necessary processes as well as login for each terminal. INIT is the parent to all Unix processes.
- *CRON* – General-purpose background task scheduler. For example, you can ask CRON to run a program every hour.

- *Troff* – Built-in desktop publishing capability.
- *Graphics* – Unix has rudimentary built-in plotting capability.
- *Built-in utilities* – Built-in spell checking, references, and dictionary.

Popular Unix Commercial Software

Although Unix's strongest suit is it ability to run highly customized software for specific purposes, a variety of commercial software is available. Packages include:

- *CAD/CAM* – A large variety of CAD/CAM packages handling every engineering discipline.
- *DtP* – FrameMaker and the Interleaf technical publishing software.
- *DBMS* – The 4GL Informix and Oracle Database Manager.
- *Graphics*– Popular software includes AT&T's Precision Visuals, and Data Business Vision.
- *DWB (Documenter's Workbench)* – From AT&T, includes graphics (graphs) pic (pictures) and other programs that allow you to set up graphics in troff easily.
- *VLSI design software* – A variety of VLSI design and implementation software.
- *Image processing* – Such image processing software as Precision Visuals, visuals and template graphics software.
- *Symbolic math* – The Macsyma system.
- *Spreadsheets* – 20/20 Access technology and many programs in the public domain software area.

Unix applications are being written in C++, an object-oriented programming language. With the Unix toolchest, you can browse your favorite network and have desired programs delivered overnight by network.

Unix on HB Computers

With more capable MS-DOS computers (80386 and 80486 processors), Apple computers (68040 CPUs), and better hard disks, Unix is now popularly operated on HB computers. MS-DOS Unix systems include the SCO (Santa Cruz Operation) part of Microsoft's Xenix and DEC's Ultrix, Venix sold by VentureCom, and PC/IX written by Interactive Systems Corporation and sold by IBM are some Unix versions available for an MS-DOS computer. Intel has a shrink-wrapped Unix for its MS-DOS computers. Of course, you can also stick with MS-DOS and add software that gives some functions of Unix such as development tools, writer's-programmer's workbench, etc. For as low as $2000, you can purchase an MS-DOS computer sufficiently powerful to operate Unix. Eight years ago this hardware would have cost $25,000.

Most non-MS-DOS Unix computers even have plug-in 80xxx boards that enable MS-DOS applications with ordinary Unix functionality. And do not forget Apple's A/UX.

Real Time Unix

Real time operating systems are the mainstays of dedicated, embedded computers performing intensive, high-speed functions. Since the Unix software base is primarily technical, the need to combine real time processing with the commercial Unix software base is obvious.

Unix is not a real time operating system; however, a version from Concurrent Computer Corps – Real Time Unix – is available. Currently, OSI/POSIX is working on a real time Unix interface that will be a standard on all POSIX compatible

Unixes. To combine a real time capability with Unix yields the promise of real time processing with access to an enormous Unix software base.

Operating Unix, however, is not always practical on the typical embedded real time computer that you might find in a flight controller because of the typical lack of memory and shortage of hard disk resources in such devices.

Solutions to the problem are:

1. Use real time operating systems designed for embedded computers such as Intel's iRMX or Ready System's VRTX, thereby gaining functions tailored for efficient real time processing. Of course, you sacrifice the Unix software base.

2. Place Unix and a real time operating system on different computers and processors connected by hardware – networks, special interfaces – and software links. This approach is expensive because you need two separate computers.

3. A newer solution allows Unix and a real time operating system to operate concurrently with Intel 80386's multiprocessing capabilities. This is done with a common memory area for communications between the real time processing and conventional Unix-based processing.

Real time operating systems are event driven and make considerable use of interrupt processing. The entire operating system is designed around the need for quick response to multiple asynchronous events. This is not the typical operating scenario for the common DtC, which is why we do not find real time operating systems on DtCs. There is, however, a need to combine real time operating system capability with systems such as MS-DOS and Unix. Such combinations can make the enormous applications software base running under these operating systems available for real time applications.

3.4 Unix in Summary

Unix has historically been an operating system for programmers. Unix's tremendous I/O support, multitasking capability and substantial hierarchical file management capability coupled with an array of tools for putting together complex applications in the form of building blocks has popularized it in the engineering, scientific, and academic arena, the playground of problem solvers.

Recent changes to Unix include improved integrating environments, GUIs, and commercial pre-programmed software packages similar to those found on MS-DOS and Apple computers, but much more powerful. The portability of Unix to any computing environment (including MS-DOS) and an increasing number of popular commercial software products promotes Unix to a contender for everyone's desktop. The many versions of Unix are coalescing toward two major standards, the Open Software Foundation and Unix International. Should these two standards merge, the last critical barrier in current Unix applications compatibility will break down.

There are drawbacks to using Unix in business DtCs. The sheer complexity and need for hard disk and RAM resources are effective deterrents. As DtCs increase in power, this becomes less of a problem. The networking power and flexibility of Unix has developers rushing to cover its complexity and broaden its appeal, embracing the standards of new visual user interfaces for the more casual home and business computer user.

Unix provides a rich set of utilities for getting applications running quickly. There's an underlying serve-yourself philosophy. You build the application with with robust tools; you get great flexibility, but you need programming skills. Unix remains a complex system to administer: adding new users, configuring networks, and so on. Then again, the IBM and Microsoft answer to Unix, OS/2, is not trivial either. Unix offers a huge number of obscure options for every command, which gives it a power that can overwhelm beginning user. The popularity and portability of the C programming language continues to keep interest in Unix high.

4.0 Focus on MS-DOS

Three factors assured the acceptance of MS-DOS by a broad population of microcomputer users: it had a low price tag, it was backed by IBM, and it had a familiar feel, reminiscent of CP/M. Both CP/M and MS-DOS divide the microcomputer system unit into three parts: a BIOS, a disk operating system, and a command interpreter. MS-DOS is an inherently simple operating system that has attracted enormous popularity. In recent years it has built a huge installed user base. Because of the size of the potential MS-DOS market, numerous applications software packages have been written for it, as well as many innovative enhancements to the system itself.

The current ferment over operating systems is rooted in the origin and development of MS-DOS. To appreciate what is happening now, we should look at:

- ***MS-DOS history*** – where MS-DOS came from.
- ***MS-DOS development*** – sequential versions.
- ***MS-DOS internals*** – a view from inside the system and how it supports the diverse clans of MS-DOS computers.
- ***MS-DOS enhancements*** – software attempts to correct inherent MS-DOS weaknesses; creative strategies to surmount shortcomings include DESQview, MS-Windows, and a Swiss army knife assortment of add-on utilities. Some of these inventions turned out to be extremely important and far-reaching.

NOTE

WAS IST DOS?

DOS simply means *Disk Operating System*. Through preponderance of usage, many people assume DOS stands for Microsoft's MS-DOS or IBM's PC-DOS. But before PC-DOS there was Apple DOS, the operating system used in Apple II. Its later DOS was called ProDOS. The Tandy Radio Shack TRS-80 Model III called its disk operating system TRS-DOS.

Other computers have DOSes too. Amiga, for example, runs AmigaDOS. Ataris come close with TOS for their operating system. In general, however, a reference to a "DOS machine" usually means an IBM Personal Computer or compatible clone. In those early days, the DOS (refer back to Figure 63 on page 287) was the majority of the operating system. Although it provided basic support for getting programs in and out and managing files, it fell short of today's operating systems, which provide much, much more. Therefore, it was fair to call those early systems by a different name – DOS.

- *OS/2* – a completely rewritten MS-DOS, contrasted with MS-DOS.
- *OS/2 PM vs. Windows* – a choice between enhancing MS-DOS with Windows or replacing it with OS/2 and Presentation Manager.

4.1   Early MS-DOS

MS-DOS was created in 1981 to support the new Intel 16-bit microcomputer system. The previous 8-bit Intel 8080 microprocessor had been supported by the CP/M-80 operating system.   Since the 8088 was not object compatible with the older 8080 microprocessor, a new operating system had to be constructed. MS-DOS is considered to have an open architecture because it is well documented, straightforward, relatively simple, and well structured. Individuals who need to modify it find it compliant. A version of MS-DOS (PC-DOS) was also written that provided exclusive support for IBM-manufactured 8088-based microcomputers.

MS-DOS – An Era of Errors

When IBM first announced the PC in 1981 three different operating systems were available (not including Unix, of course): the CP/M-86, the 16-bit version of the popular 8-bit system; the P-System, a Pascal-based system; and a new product called *PC-DOS* by Microsoft, Inc. At first, CP/M-86 appeared to dominate, having already received wide acceptance and having a huge installed base in the 8-bit world. It was certainly the system of choice among the more experienced PC developers. The first applications to hit the market for the IBM PC were little more than OS ports from CP/M-80 (the 8-bit version).

CP/M-86 would probably have grown in popularity and acceptance and might have become the most supported of the operating systems for the 8088/8086 class of computers – except for one major factor. The CP/M-86 and the P-System each cost $300.00, while IBM offered PC-DOS for a mere $40.00. What tipped the scale in PC-DOS's favor, of course, was not only the price, but also Big Blue's name behind the product. All three packages provided approximately the same functional capabilities. Part of the difference in cost was due to the development tools built into CP/M-86 and the P-System, which were optional extras for PC-DOS; e.g., assemblers and compilers. PC-DOS was co-marketed by Microsoft as *MS-DOS* to operate on the MS-DOS compatibles. This is the name used in the following discussion.

The reason the huge user base accepted MS-DOS and an important factor in understanding the evolution of both software and hardware advancement (or lack of advancement) during the past eight years rests in the source and history of the package.

The story begins in 1980, with the Seattle Computer Corporation, a hardware-oriented company that developed one of the first 8086-based CPU boards for the then widely supported S-100 bus. This bus was driven mainly by the CP/M 8-bit disk operating system. At that time there was no 16-bit OS available, since CP/M-86 had not been released as scheduled by Digital Research Corporation.

Seattle Computer, faced with the dilemma of not being able to sell its CPU, mounted an effort to write a disk operating system for the 8086-based family. This package, known within the company as *QD-DOS* (Quick and Dirty Disk Operating System), was nearing completion after approximately two months of programming, when CP/M-86 was released. Favoring the much wider popularity and support of

CP/M, the Seattle firm shelved QD-DOS, considering it a lost cause. About six months later, to its surprise, Microsoft offered to buy the defunct package for a project undertaken with an unnamed partner. Seattle Computer gladly obliged, selling the system for a reported $100,000. It was soon announced by Microsoft as MS-DOS Version 1.0, in much the same form it had been as QD-DOS. It was apparent to most experienced PC users that it was a thinly disguised copy of the 8-bit CP/M with a few minor internal system differences.

Seattle Computer, basically a hardware company, did not want to market operating system software outside of bundling it for the purpose of selling its CPU board. At the same time the company was tasked with delivering a product significantly different from the vastly popular CP/M in order to avoid legal difficulties with Digital Research, which was at that time a powerful corporation. QD-DOS was written specifically for and tailored to the Seattle S-100 CPU board. For whatever reasons, the Seattle developers of QD-DOS chose to ignore Intel's warnings about certain "reserved" memory locations within the 8086 memory map and used these locations for software I/O interrupt vectors. Use of these vectors would later haunt Microsoft and IBM because it rendered MS-DOS incompatible with later additions to the 8086 family of processors that would allow memory expansions beyond one MB.

It is now well known that MS-DOS took the PC industry by storm, burying the long-time favorite CP/M and building an installed software base never before equalled by any class of computer. Unfortunately, this vast treasury of software was written for an operating system that allowed little room for growth and improvement. Both IBM and Microsoft found themselves locked tightly to the huge base of "IBM compatible" software and were swept before the tide with little control over the direction of hardware or operating system evolution except for minor enhancements here and there. For the most part, the currently popular MS-DOS Version 3.3 is architecturally the same as it was seven years ago when it was known as QD-DOS. The newer versions 4.x and 5.x begin to remove this stigma with their improved user interfaces. Version 6.0, as we shall see later, will be quite different.

Capabilities such as multitasking and extended memory support have been well within the scope of DtC hardware for some time, but have not been implemented because there was no way to maintain software compatibility under MS-DOS. It became obvious around 1985 that a totally new operating system would be necessary in order to keep pace with equipment advancements. Microsoft and IBM decided that software compatibility, though a highly desired feature, would not be the main driving design criterion for the new system.

Having enjoyed, or suffered, many names through its development cycle, including ADOS, MS-DOS Version 4, and MS-DOS Version 5, the completely rewritten OS/2 is now marketed by both Microsoft and IBM. While OS/2 allows DOS programs to run in a compatibility window, that is as far as the similarity goes. It is a completely new package with capabilities not likely to become outdated for several years. The most important factor is that for the first time in a long time the operating system will be back in control instead of the applications software. It remains to be seen what impact this will have on performance and overall effectiveness. However, the positive aspect of the change is a well-written standard interface between user, software, and hardware, flexible enough to withstand a generation or two of computer evolutions. But the fight is on as MS-DOS 6.0 and Windows NT step into the ring.

MS-DOS Versions

The table shows the versions of MS-DOS and PC-DOS.

Ver-sion	Date	Description
1.1	1982	Double-sided floppy disk support, bug fixes.
2.0	1983	Hard disk and tree structured directory support.
2.1	1983	PC-DOS only for PC Jr.
3.0	1984	1.2 MB disk drive support.
3.1	1984	Microsoft network support.
3.2	1985	PC, XT, AT advanced media support (3½" disks).
3.3	1987/88	Multiple 32 MB hard disk support, improved commands.
OS/2	1988/91	80286 and later MS-DOS computers. Significant improvements and size in all definable areas.
4.x	1988	Provides user interface improvements, LIM 4.0 support, and support of hard drives larger than 32 MB.
5.x	1991	Extended memory support (carousel fashion); improved utilities similar to those found in add-on products such as QFiler and XTree. Improved user interface.
6.x	1992	Will run by Windows NT kernel. When combined with Windows 4.0, will become a significant operating system.

Table 29. MS-DOS/PC-DOS versions:
Note 1. PC-DOS versions supported exact clones of PC, XT, and AT.
Note 2. MS-DOS versions supported MS-DOS compatibles.

MS-DOS Components

MS-DOS contains the same elements as other microcomputer operating systems. These include:

- **BIOS** – MS-DOS computers provide support to the system unit components and the usual built-in peripheral interfaces with a ROM BIOS. Support includes keyboard, serial and printer interfaces, video (text), floppy disk, and hard disk interfaces and auxiliary system board chips. BIOS ROMS sizes are 8K (XT style), 20K (AT style), and 100K (MCA style). The larger BIOS of the MCA style is sometimes called the ABIOS (Advanced BIOS); the larger size being necessary for improved graphics, communications, and networking support not found in the BIOS of the earlier IBM models. The Windows NT BIOS (kernel) is 128K.

- **Drivers** – The more specific routines that can be easily installed, changed, and enhanced. Included are RAM-based routines for alternative or enhanced application-specific I/O routines. For example, the WordPerfect word processor comes with over 200 printer drivers that match WordPerfect to a specific printer. WordPerfect drivers replace the more general BIOS printer routine for a better match.

- **DOS (Disk Operating System)** – Most machine-independent DOS functions occur within a specific interrupt known as DOS interrupt 21. The DOS could be called MS-DOS' File Manager.

- **Command processor** – The command processor interprets DOS commands. It is an executable file called COMMAND.COM. Each new version of MS-DOS requires an appropriately updated version of COMMAND.COM. Many operator problems occur when MS-DOS upgrades occur without upgrading this important file. COMMAND.COM is MS-DOS's default shell.

- **Editor** – The editor is called EDLIN.COM. This editor should be used only for crude text editing functions, and if no other editors (e. g., Qedit, Kedit) are available. Fortunately, EDLIN has been replaced in MS-DOS 5.x with a greatly improved full screen editor.

- **Assembler/compiler** – The only built-in capability is found in DEBUG.COM, which includes a rudimentary assembler, disassembler, and machine language debug capability. Most users developing assembly language on MS-DOS DtCs use Microsoft or Borland separate assembler and debugging tools.

4.2   Inside MS-DOS

MS-DOS accommodates differences in MS-DOS computer system units through its BIOS. The safest place for system software support is in the ROM BIOS, because it is an integral part of the system unit and because different MS-DOS computer vendors handle things differently.

System functions such as keyboard support, support of built-in parallel and serial interfaces, auxiliary system board chip programming, and initialization are among the important tasks performed by the BIOS. Applications programs use the BIOS according to a set of firmly established rules, ensuring their operation on different MS-DOS computers. Knowing the rules allows us to enhance MS-DOS through explicit pathways.

Functions will be compatible on different MS-DOS computers as long as the program has:

1. Defined location of BIOS routine pointers.
2. Correspondence between BIOS routine and BIOS pointer.
3. Defined methodology for passing arguments (data).

Location of BIOS Routine Pointers

The Intel 80xxx microprocessor line implements a 256 software interrupt structure. Pointers to interrupt service routines are kept in what is called an interrupt vector table in the first 1K (1024 decimal) memory locations as shown in Figure 66. Each pointer is a four-byte quantity.

> ┌─── **NOTE** ───┐
> The four-byte quantity consists of two 16-bit words, a segment and an offset, that are picked up by the microprocessor upon interrupt. The microprocessor adds the segment (shifted 4 bits left) to the offset, forming a 20-bit quantity that is used as the address. When interrupt

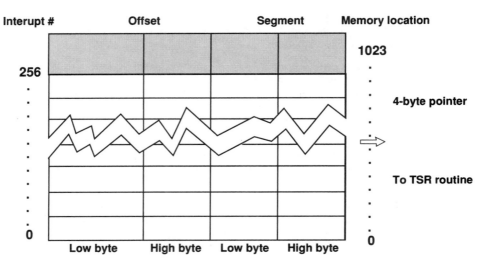

Figure 66. MS-DOS interrupt vector table: The interrupt vector is a waystation, a place to interact with system ISR capabilities and to know where the various system support ISRs are.

xx is executed, the service routine or driver pointed to by table entry xx is executed.

Manufacturers of different 80xxx-based MS-DOS computers cannot choose the location of this table in memory; it is an integral part of 80xxx microprocessor design. The first requirement then, consistent location of the driver table in system memory, is a given in MS-DOS computers. The vector table is a waystation that always contains pointers to the system board I/O routines in any MS-DOS system.

BIOS Routine and Pointer Correspondence

Anyone designing MS-DOS systems must abide by the standards for which vector points to which routine. BIOS conventions are published by Microsoft and it is in the best interest of MS-DOS system designers to arrange their BIOS routine software accordingly. See Figure 67. BIOS systems that do not conform will not run the large body of MS-DOS applications software.

Table 30 shows some of the more popular BIOS routines and their corresponding interrupt vector numbers.

VECTOR # (HEX)	PURPOSE
5	Print screen operation
10	Video text display operations
13	Disk I/O
14	Communications (serial) functions
16	Keyboard functions
17	Printer I/O
1A	Time of day and date functions

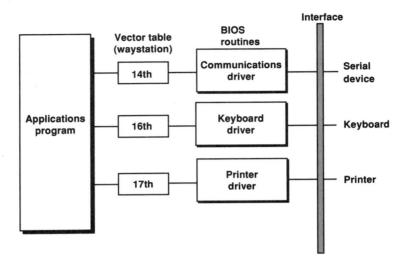

Figure 67. **MS-DOS pointer-driver correspondence:** In any MS-DOS computer you will find pointers at the same vector table locations pointing to generic drivers for the same peripheral types.

VECTOR # (HEX)	PURPOSE
21	Higher-level DOS (file manager) functions

Table 30. Selected BIOS functions

Figure 67 shows the methodology of assigning particular vectors or pointers to particular BIOS routines. The applications programmer desiring to perform I/O to a particular device invokes the appropriate driver by its corresponding interrupt number.

Methodology for Passing Arguments

According to this published convention, characters to be printed, viewed, sent to floppy, etc. are passed in defined microprocessor registers. The convention allows an operating system or a software developer to communicate with a particular device without knowing anything specific about it.

The methods discussed here provide a flexible environment for changing the basic system interfaces. When different or enhanced support is required, a new routine can easily be installed without worrying where the old routine is located. Simply install the new device driver with a few keystrokes.

The Rules and Redirection

The following examples demonstrate how the rules are applied to perform redirection. Redirection reroutes a program, causing it to behave in a way different from the one for which it was written. The usual operating system BIOS functions can be modified or enhanced for different purposes. To use redirection, however, we must depend on the fact that programs use the fundamental BIOS routines and abide by its rules. Here are some examples:

- **Keyboard** – Most MS-DOS TSR programs require that MS-DOS applications use the published keyboard BIOS routines. As programs call for keyboard services, they can be extended with additional capabilities. Utility programs such as SideKick are called in this manner.

- **Printer** – Most MS-DOS versions support a BIOS text dump routine through software interrupt 5 that dumps the text displayed on screen to the printer. The routine is typically ROM based. The program GRAPHICS.COM, supplied on an MS-DOS disk, can be used to supplement the ROM BIOS text dump routine. When you install GRAPHICS.COM, depicted in Figure 68, the existing ROM routine is replaced by one that is in RAM. Now a dot matrix printer can print graphics images as well as text that appear on the monitor screen. Type GRAPHICS at the MS-DOS prompt to replace the interrupt 5 vector and install the RAM-resident GRAPHICS.COM.■

- **Network routines** – To extend the capability of a printer, serial interface, and even mass storage devices used throughout a network. Usage of BIOS routines by software is redirected to act over the network rather than just within the DtC.

- **Video text routines** – The DESQview program depends on the way MS-DOS programs use the text BIOS routines supplied by the OS to window their text output. Many programs can display outputs in Windows, sharing the display screen.

> ■ Ordinarily, you execute an MS-DOS program when you type its name at the DOS prompt. The GRAPHIC.COM program, however, is a TSR program which, instead of executing, modifies the interrupt 5 vector and places itself into memory, awaiting interrupt 5.

Later, we will see that playing by the rules does not guarantee success, because certain programs may ignore the rules for the sake of efficiency.

4.3   The MS-DOS File Manager and DOS Drivers

Regardless of the specific type of MS-DOS computer, you have a variety of common file management capabilities. These include:

- Copying files between mass storage devices or other peripherals.
- Showing file content of mass storage devices.
- Storing and retrieving data on mass storage devices and peripherals.
- Naming and renaming files.
- Managing hierarchical file structures.
- Text-only support of serial and parallel printer interfaces and video display.

With the OS supporting these functions, programs are further distanced from a need to know about the hardware of a particular MS-DOS computer. The part of MS-DOS responsible for these functions is conveniently called the File Manager (FM). This part of MS-DOS, also known as *The DOS*, is its major component.

DOS Interrupt 21

> ■ File manager functions are *not* hardware specific. The FM uses the separate BIOS routines that isolate it from specific hardware functions.

In MS-DOS, most file manager functions are implemented within the granddaddy of MS-DOS interrupts – 21 hex. See Figure 69.

Functions implemented by interrupt 21 are also known as DOS-level functions. DOS-level functions make heavy use of many of the individual BIOS routines discussed previously.■ The difference, however, is that at the DOS level it is a well organized and collective, rather than individual, usage of BIOS routines. This collective, higher-level aspect is depicted in Figure 63 on page 287.

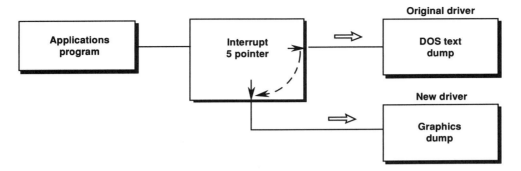

Figure 68. **Replacing a BIOS routine:** Installing a new driver includes loading the driver into memory and changing the interrupt vector table address to point to the new driver.

DOS-level functions such as DIR or COPY formats make use of lower-level system-specific BIOS routines to accomplish the higher-level functions of file management. Since the parallel printer port, serial interface, and video screen are places, besides the hard disk, to send files, primitive support for these devices are provided at the DOS level.

Using functions within the DOS interrupt 21, applications developers and the MS-DOS operating system have complete control of required disk and file management capabilities, without worrying about the particular differences that exist between floppy drives, hard drives, network drives, and optical drives.

Since DOS 21 functions, in turn, use BIOS functions, the DOS functions are truly isolated from system hardware peculiarities. Thus, the MS-DOS FM or DOS, which is the most important and complicated part of MS-DOS, can be moved from one MS-DOS computer to another without much rewriting. It is the BIOS routines that will more likely make up for the differences found in different MS-DOS computers.

By organizing the common file management functions under an easily configurable umbrella, the MS-DOS operating system allows the common FM and peripheral support to act over the RS-232 serial communications port, high-speed network, or alternative mass storage devices such as removable cartridge drives or optical disk drives. Common OS supported interfaces can be enhanced, extended, or otherwise improved.

DOS Level Driver Installation

DOS-level drivers are routines that can extend DOS functions. Since all MS-DOS computers require the general-purpose DOS functions, the ability to manipulate and adjust the DOS drivers is paramount.

To add a DOS driver to an MS-DOS computer, place the name of the driver in the root directory CONFIG.SYS file. The CONFIG.SYS file is used during boot-up to configure the devices supported under the file manager, and this determines the type and capability of an MS-DOS computer's file I/O. The form of this entry is:

```
DEVICE=NEWDEVICE.SYS
```

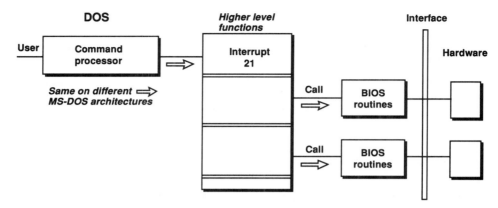

Figure 69. DOS interrupt 21 (hex): Interrupt 21 provides most of the MS-DOS file management functions.

The driver itself NEWDEVICE.SYS is a program that must be made available to MS-DOS by copying it to the hard drive in an appropriate subdirectory. This method of driver replacement is more advanced, yet easier for the end-user than BIOS-level enhancements, such as GRAPHICS.COM.

The table below shows what the CONFIG.SYS file would look like after adding new DOS devices to the configuration. NANCY.SYS is an improved text-only video driver that writes characters faster to the screen than the MS-DOS supplied ANSI.SYS. RCD.SYS is the name of the driver software associated with the Bernoulli disk drive, while SMARTDRV.SYS sets up a disk cache and INET.SYS gives access to a hard disk on the network server. These SYS files are supplied by the interface vendors (Bernoulli disks, network boards) and must be copied to the hard drive. The first two entries, buffers and files, have to do with DOS file management behavior and are typical entries in most CONFIG.SYS files.

```
Buffers = 30   ..................... Sets up a DOS supported software disk cache
Files = 20   ................................... Sets up DOS management of open files
Break = ON   ................... Allows programs to use the DOS break function
Lastdrive = m:   ............................. Set up so last drive in list becomes m:
DEVICE = NANCY.SYS   ........................ Faster text driver than ANSI.SYS
DEVICE = RCD.SYS   .................. Bernoulli removable cartridge (drive e:)
DEVICE = SMARTDRV.SYS 2048   .......................... Set up a disk cache
DEVICE = inet.sys   ............................................. Network Drive (drive m:)
```

Now, in addition to internal c: and d: hard disks, there can be an e: drive, which is a removable cartridge disk drive; a software disk cache (SMARTDRV); and an m: drive, which is on the network server. All of the file management capabilities of the operating system have now been extended to include additional drives, one of which is not even in your office.■

■ Built-in hard drives are usually already configured since they are supported by special ROM BIOS routines.

When you type dir m: at the DOS prompt, you get the directory of the m: drive on the network server. The m: drive could be in another building, or even in another country. For a better directory, use Windows or a file management utility such as XTree Gold Professional. They can act over the network and display a visual directory of the m: network drive.

Application-Specific Drivers

The FM functions are managed by the MS-DOS operating system for the most common peripherals. As long as the peripherals can be connected to the Centronics parallel printer and RS-232 serial interfaces and can use the relatively primitive DOS support, applications can run the peripherals directly or even over a network.

But how do programs account for the differences that will exist when you hook up a graphics display? or a feature-packed printer? or a speech recognizer? These will need application-specific drivers.

Under CP/M and in the early transition to MS-DOS, software was considerably better behaved. It was text-only and used low-speed interfaces, and so the operating system was expected to supply all of an applications program's needs. Indeed this *was* the case when you ran simple language compilers, dBASE, and WordStar programs that had no great aspirations for complex peripherals or graphics. And, they used the standard generic interfaces.

Today, however, this is seldom the case, as more software products become performance and graphics oriented. The demise of text-only software products was inevitable, and it is the new capabilities that compromise the original intent of MS-DOS: to support basic software on a few different MS-DOS computers with the text-only graphics interfaces and character-oriented dot matrix printers.

The drivers supplied by each applications software program run the different peripherals (printers, monitors, and special-purpose devices) needed in the given application. Since each applications program has particular needs for peripheral devices, each requires a unique set of software drivers that communicate directly with the peripherals and interfaces. BIOS routines and DOS functions are not used because they are general purpose and therefore not capable of high-speed or otherwise specialized operations. Moreover, there are no existing BIOS or DOS functions for communicating with the special hardware, interface, or peripheral.

Talking directly to the hardware provides speed and efficiency without the overhead of calling upon general BIOS routines that are not familiar with application needs. Thus, we have application-specific drivers commanding hardware directly. Most DtC software products come with their own set of drivers on separate disks, and you must carry out an installation procedure in which you define your particular system and peripheral configuration.

4.4   Demanding Software

Well-behaved software is text-only, using standard interfaces supported by DOS and BIOS routines. The other type is performance software with graphics, windowing, and high-performance communications that need more than MS-DOS can support. The programs that require such support must provide their own, non-cooperatively. Today's software imposes demands on MS-DOS that the system cannot meet.These demands include

- *Graphics interface support* – Graphics support of standard IBM graphics interfaces (CGA, EGA, MDA, MCGA, VGA, XGA).

- *Graphics and text support* – Graphics *and* text support for hundreds of other vendor's enhanced video interfaces (SVGA, TARGA). These include support of high-resolution graphics, 24-bit color, and built-in graphics coprocessors.

- *Popular peripherals* – Plotters, mice, fax modems, and speech synthesis and re-cognition.

- *Graphics* – Graphics are not supported by current MS-DOS versions except for simple pixel set and reset functions. Today's software demands include higher-level graphics function support for 3-D, animation, rotation, translation, polygon manipulation, and combined WYSIWYG and APA text and graphics.

- *Windowing* – Flexible placement of text and graphics in multiple portions of the screen, each independent of the other.

- *Direct access to serial and parallel interfaces* – For high transmission rates, or other specialized interface control problems.

- *Specialized peripheral interfaces* – Support of special peripheral interfaces such as A/D converters and data acquisition scanners not supported by the BIOS.

- *Laser printers* – Custom interfaces mapping screen memories into printer memo-ries, or use of existing parallel and serial interfaces at speeds higher than DOS functions can support.

Transportability vs. Efficiency

The need for application-specific drivers poses the classic "no way out" dilemma. DtC users want transportable programs that can take advantage of different computer architectures.

The tradeoff is between software being independent of specific architecture and the ability for the software to efficiently support specific features and peripherals. MS-DOS represents a compromise in allowing a certain amount of architectural independence while maintaining reasonable support of peripheral diversification. In order to attain this balance, MS-DOS computer internal architectures are not as diverse as computers in the EE category. All MS-DOS computer internal architecture must be supported by a common operating system available to a large software base. The word *vanilla* is often used to describe the architecture of MS-DOS computers.

To find a way out of this dilemma, applications programs will need to call upon the hardware directly through self-contained application-specific I/O drivers, abandoning the general-purpose DOS and BIOS routines.

In the foreseeable future, however, we will have to settle for a compromise between the operating system being able to support the specific needs of the entire applications software base and the operating system (MS-DOS) handling almost nothing application specific, where the programs have to take care of everything.

The need for application-specific drivers can be lessened through one of the following:

1. *Use of integrated or series software* – Purchasing software where more than one function (spreadsheet, graphics) is integrated into a single package, or supported similarly over several individual packages by the same vendor. That vendor will provide drivers for the whole system of programs that can work with many periph-erals. Then driver installation can cover more than one application.

2. ***Improve operating system support*** – Run software in an operating system environment that centrally provides better peripheral support. Windows provides high-level graphics support for MS-DOS software that is made to use it. For I/O devices, a standard bus interface structure may help the operating system support multiple devices. Such higher-level support is found in the OS/2 Presentation Manager and in Windows.

Levels of Isolation

We can define three levels of isolation that the MS-DOS operating system provides to software, shown in Figure 63 on page 287.

Highest level: Programs using the DOS functions are the most transportable. They can operate on any MS-DOS computer and can operate over networks. There is virtually no need for developers to have hardware-specific information to use these functions.

Medium level: Use BIOS functions directly. By using the BIOS functions outside of the file manager, programs may be a bit more efficient, but will not be redirectable over a network, or to alternative devices.

Lowest level: No general operating system support, which is also known as writing directly to hardware. This is potentially the most efficient, but the least transportable. Programs seldom write directly to the system hardware because it would render the software peculiar to a given MS-DOS computer system unit. Rather than do this, applications programs come with their own application-specific drivers. It is the drivers that write to the hardware.

Even within applications programs, there is a methodology for isolating higher-level functions from the specifics of the hardware. As newer peripherals become available, additional drivers are supplied by each vendor.

The isolation levels in Figure 63 could, with only minor modifications, apply to any operating system. For Unix, the BIOS would become a more powerful kernel, and a more powerful set of operating system functions would surround that kernel, including a user-defined set of functions.

MS-DOS Shortcomings

MS-DOS supports the wide variety of system unit and peripheral combinations through its BIOS, DOS functions, and application-specific drivers. The following summarizes MS-DOS major shortcomings.

- ***Lack of higher-level graphics and user interface support*** – No OS supported graphics or user interface routines. Each program must supply its own. Since application-specific drivers are outside the realm of the usual MS-DOS support mechanisms, they are generally not controllable, or extendable beyond the particular application.

- ***Lack of collective peripheral support*** – Wouldn't it be nice if all peripheral drivers could be managed by the operating system? Once the drivers were centralized in the operating system, every program could use them. Disk drives and video interfaces would be supported through more generalized bus interfaces (SCSI, for example) and this would allow the operating system to work with more devices. Improvements to operating systems are already beginning to support peripheral requirements at higher levels through high-level graphics primitives and text and graphics languages, such as PostScript. Also, driver support is being provided by the operating system rather than by individual programs through OS/2.

- *Lack of common data support* – Programs cannot share data internally through common memory buffers. Instead, programs must share data by the cumbersome method of saving and loading to disk files. On disk, this data is intractable. As we shall see, yesterday's individual-function software products are integrating data sharing functions internally. Also, integrated products are attacking this problem on an individual basis. Techniques that differ between different integrated products force users and organizations into vast retraining schemes.

- *Lack of windowing support* – Programs cannot share video resources. Although there are integrated programs that combine several software functions that window internally, this support is not provided by the operating system. The windowing cooperation is restricted to those integrated software products that perform windowing, and the nature of the windowing varies from product to product.

- *Lack of memory support* – Poor support of available memory. The lack of protected mode memory support by the operating system forces many MS-DOS applications to survive in the contemptibly small 640K memory area. Although some individual programs take on protected mode and virtual memory support themselves (Paradox VROOM technology, DataEase support of extended memory), these programs tend not to cooperate in their use of this memory. When these programs are operated in MS-DOS enhancement environments such as DESQview or Windows, unpredictable behavior results.

- *Lack of program control support* – No support of multitasking. The lack of MS-DOS OS virtual memory support and other Intel microprocessor features, prohibit MS-DOS programs from running concurrently. Techniques are available for running simple background functions, but they are not full-power multitasking applications.

Later, we shall see what an MS-DOS computer user can do about the problems just recounted.

4.5 MS-DOS Computer Architecture Variations

The MS-DOS operating system is unique insofar as it is designed to operate on virtually thousands of computers, each slightly different from the other. Because of this, MS-DOS can never get too intimate with specific hardware details. The BIOS steps in for system unit functions, and software drivers handle specific peripherals.

Software that is designed to run unmodified on the multitude of MS-DOS computers have the following general characteristics:

Standard video interface usage: Most applications software will support the MDA/CGA, EGA, and VGA interfaces according to how IBM implements these interfaces. This support will include the more powerful IBM's 8514/A and the XGA video interfaces as they become affordable and popular. MS-DOS computers that use these interfaces claim compatibility at two levels:

1. *BIOS compatibility* – Software using BIOS functions to initialize video interfaces and display characters will be compatible and will work in character-based windowed environments.

2. *Register compatibility* – Software bypasses the BIOS and speaks directly to the interface. This will render the software specific to a particular video interface.

Most MS-DOS video interfaces require initialization, which is performed by the BIOS or by software supplied with the interface. Initializations or mode changes are performed by applications software using BIOS functions, which assures compatibility. If an applications program performs its own video interface initialization, it must talk directly to the video interface registers; it will then only operate on MS-DOS computers that are register compatible.

Standard I/O: Compatibility is assured when I/O occurs through standard serial and parallel interfaces, since it assumed that IBM-compatible interfaces such as the 8250 ACIA for the serial interface and a compatible Centronics Parallel interface is incorporated.

Auxiliary chip initialization: The BIOS initializes the chip at power-up to preclude system-specific software.

Historically, MS-DOS computers varied considerably because vendors went to great lengths to improve on the initial shortcomings of the early IBM PCs. Notable examples are the Hewlett-Packard (HP-150) with its touch screen display, and the early TI Professional that incorporated a video interface with more colors and resolution than IBM's CGA. The Tandy 200 was based on the 80186 microprocessor, while the NEC APC incorporated a graphics coprocessor that was not compatible with stock IBM video interfaces. The Columbia Data Products PC incorporated serial interfaces that did not use the National 8250 ACIA chip. The DEC Rainbow had dual microprocessors (a Z80 for running CP/M and an 8088 for MS-DOS) and variable speed drives requiring specially formatted diskettes.

In those days, IBM had the MS-DOS computer market share and vendors wrote their software first to operate on IBM PCs. Software written for these computers had to be specific to them since BIOS support of additional features was either not available or difficult to provide. Generally speaking, software written for IBM PCs could not be operated on these machines and vice versa. Vendors write software for the largest user base, which limited availability on different models. Different versions of the popular software products (for example, 1-2-3, WordPerfect, and dBASE) were required for each of the different vendor's MS-DOS computers.

4.6   Current MS-DOS

The situation has changed considerably now that the IBM PC no longer monopolizes the MS-DOS computer market. MS-DOS computer producers go to great lengths to manufacture functionally-equivalent hardware, particularly for AT-style units. Since many IBM PCs have a Micro Channel bus, an IBM-specific mouse, and use a considerable amount of proprietary BIOS software, users sometimes find that their software operates with better compatibility on the non-IBM MS-DOS computers. Differences that do exist between MS-DOS compatibles are well supported in the BIOS as well as in the OS versions. MS-DOS computers fall into three categories:

1. Original IBM PCs, ATs, and the high-performance PS/2s.
2. High-performance DtCs from such vendors as Compaq and Everex.
3. Low-cost, generic medium performance MS-DOS computers from Asia.

Original IBM PCs, ATs, and PS/2s should operate IBM software with few problems. IBM software, however, is only a small portion of the total MS-DOS computer software base. Proprietary Micro Channel bus features, the larger proprietary bus, or the custom, built-in mouse may cause compatibility problems in the higher-performance PS/2 line. Although the problems are rare, they are usually difficult to solve.

High-performance DtCs exhibit a higher level of compatibility problem simply beacuse their users are more sophisticated and tend to operate a more complex array of software. Also, they operate in more complex modes, using more TSR programs, operating DOS extenders, running as network servers in networks, or operating multitasking software.

EXAMPLE

A file transfer program causes a system crash every other time it is used, but only when the file size exceeds approximately 1 MB. The problem occurs only when operating with the Quarterdeck QEMM memory manager, and only on a Compaq.

A high-end CAD software package cannot access the b: drive floppy disk from within, however DOS access works fine. The problem turned out to be an incorrect ROM BIOS version on the Compaq DtC.

What is common about both of these problems is that they occur on high-performance DtCs and are not likely to be seen by the typical home user.

Since the low-cost, generic MS-DOS computers are only recently becoming peformance oriented, their system board designs still have less sophistication in caching systems and CPU to coprocessor coupling, and less sophisticated hard disk and memory interfaces. The standard line of well-tested software is operated on these PCs, making users less likely to encounter compatibility problems in the first place.

MS-DOS vs. PC-DOS

Most of us prefer to use the operating system supplied by the computer manufacturer: PC-DOS for IBM equipment, and the more generic MS-DOS for the thousands of MS-DOS computers now on the market. Identical MS-DOS and PC-DOS revisions numbers are equivalent. PC-DOS and IBM PCs will operate under MS-DOS. Be aware, however, that because PC-DOS is an IBM-supported product and MS-DOS is a Microsoft-supported product, differences do exist between the same revisions of PC-DOS and MS-DOS. These can include:

- *Memory management sensitivity* – DOS 5.x will be sensitive to the differences in the way MS-DOS compatibles and IBM PCs support the extended addressability of 80286 and above CPUs. You'll probably want to use PC DOS for the IBM PCs and MS-DOS for the MS-DOS compatibles. A high-performance compatible such as a Compaq may need a customized version of MS-DOS.

- *Supplemental software difference* – Utility software provided with MS-DOS including cache drivers, expanded memory support, mouse support, low-level disk format utilities, system set up (drive types, clock, I/O channel speeds, wait stating) may be system specific. Problems have been noted with programs operating differently under the various extended memory management software available for MS-DOS computers.

- *Syntax* – Minor command syntax differences between PC-DOS and MS-DOS versions and between generic versions of MS-DOS frustrate users who use both systems.

- *BASIC interpreter* – Included with PC-DOS is a BASIC interpreter that is designed to work with and enhance IBM's ROM-based BASIC. The MS-DOS BASIC interpreter (formerly called GW – George Washington BASIC) is completely disk based, executing entirely in RAM. If you run the PC-DOS BASIC on an MS-DOS compatible without the ROM BASIC, the system crashes. Another problem is that IBM and GW BASIC interpreters are not completely compatible version for version. Users of program shells and communications programs written in interpretive GW BASIC will likely experience minor compatibility problems. Since many BASIC applications are now being developed in Microsoft QuikBASIC (designed to operate on all MS-DOS computers), this compatibility problem is not so serious. MS-DOS 5.x now includes QuikBASIC, which has replaced the BASIC interpreter.

MS-DOS 4.x

MS-DOS 4.x is similar to MS-DOS 3.3 with the following enhancements:

- *Graphics-based DOS shell* – The shell can display directory structure as a graphical tree and can menu program selection. This new DOS feature has been available previously through such utilities as XTree and QFiler. These enhancements should ease the transition to OS/2.
- *Large disk support* – Support for large-capacity hard disks (1024 MB partitions as compared to the previous 32 MB of DOS 3.3.)
- *Expanded memory support* – Support of the LIM EMS specification 4.x.
- *More DOS functions* – Thirty new and enhanced DOS functions.

> **NOTE**
>
> Some think MS-DOS 4.x was a bomb. Many thankfully skipped it to go directly to MS-DOS 5.x. It was worth the wait.

MS-DOS 5.x

This new DOS can offer some of the functionality of OS/2 without its complexity and size. MS-DOS 5.x confirms Microsoft's ongoing commitment to support MS-DOS. MS-DOS will continue to be popular as IBM's OS/2 develops. Many users will want to run their old software under version 5.x as vendors regroup and prepare software for OS/2.

MS-DOS 5.x is similar to 4.x with the following enhancements:

- *Improved graphics-based DOS shell* – Many additional utilities including file compression, copying, and display have been added.
- *Extended memory support* – Multiple DOS programs can be executed out of extended memory in carousel fashion. This is adequate for users who need to switch between programs, but who do not necessarily need to operate them concurrently.
- *Text editor* – The almost universally disparaged EDLIN has been replaced with a real text editor. Also replaced is the BASIC interpreter. Taking its place is the excellent QuikBASIC interpreter that features full-screen editing and structural programming capability.
- *Navigation aids* – A new DIR command can be used to search across multiple directories for files and arrange the results by name, date, time, or size. A program called DOSKEY saves commands entered for later retrieval.

- **Command stack retrieval** – A program called DOSKEY stacks keyboard-entered commands for recall and reuse. It also saves macros consisting of frequently used strings of commands. This is an improvement over the previous function key 3 retrieval of DOS commands.
- **Undo features** – Two new, built-in features are *undelete* and *unformat*. The first restores files that have been accidentally deleted and the second unformats disks that have been inadvertently formatted. Formerly, these features had to be provided by third-party software, such as Norton Utilities.
- **Help** – Finally, well-designed online help is available for all DOS commands. While the syntax remains as spooky as ever, you no longer need to refer to a manual for explanations.

MS-DOS 5.x is intended for 286- and 386-based MS-DOS DtCs with at least 1 MB of RAM. Although MS-DOS 5.x does not break the galling 640K barrier, it does assuage the nuisance by relieving some operating system demands on conventional low memory. Among the most welcome improvements are the built-ins that eliminate the need for add-on software.

MS-DOS 5.x can load into the high memory area, which MS-DOS programs do not normally use. About 45K of usable real memory are released in this manner. The freed memory space may be used by memory resident programs. On 386 machines with at least 1 MB of RAM, MS-DOS 5.x will even load device drivers into the upper memory area using the extended memory manager (EMM), leaving still more DOS memory free. Prior to MS-DOS version 5.x, users had to use other vendor's extended memory managers such as Quarterdeck QEMM or Qualitas 386Max.

Anyone running Windows exclusively may not see much difference between MS-DOS 4.x and MS-DOS 5.x. But for users who run a mix of Windows and MS-DOS applications, the availability of extra memory will be instantly and dramatically apparent, especially if they have been crowding the limit of DOS memory. Memory availability with MS-DOS 4.x and 5.x are compared below. Typical approximate values are:

	DOS 4.x	DOS 5.x
Real Mode	490K	566K
Standard Mode	503K	579K
386 Enhanced Mode	550K	617K
Outside Windows	560K	626K

These figures do not account for any TSRs or drivers that may be loaded on a particular DtC. On 386 and 486 machines with MS-DOS 5.x, TSRs and drivers may be loaded into upper memory blocks, so even more RAM may be freed.

Some attention has been paid to ease of use. A graphics based shell has been added to help manipulate and execute programs. Task switching, while not true multitasking, is a welcome convenience. Several programs may be loaded at once and worked alternately, switching from one to another with simple keystrokes.

MS-DOS 5.x does not do away with all third party help. Qualitas, for example, offers 386Max and BlueMax, memory maximizers for MS-DOS 5.x as well as for MS-DOS 3.0 and up. The BlueMax software optimizes memory and manages to recover additional high memory during program loading. TSR instancing lets you run multiple Windows sessions without conflict. BlueMax runs on 386 and 486 MS-DOS compatibles or PS/2s with 256K of extended memory.

DOS power users who are used to DESQview, OmniView, Software Carousel and other task switching software packages may not be impressed by MS-DOS 5.x's task switching capability. But others will find task switching built into the DOS environment a welcome convenience, something they will soon find they cannot do without.

Announced as this book went to press, DOS 6.x will be coupled with the Windows NT kernel to become a significant operating system.

4.7 MS-DOS in Summary

MS-DOS is primarily an end-user operating system that is portable only between Intel-based microcomputers.

> **NOTE**
>
> *End-user software* is intended for a specific purpose and is not changeable, configurable, or easy to integrate with other software. Just take it out of the box and run it. If you like the software, everything is fine, but you will not be able to customize your own software in this environment.

MS-DOS was not designed initially to be expanded to the levels that it has reached. Current attempts to add capabilities similar to those found in the more sophisticated operating systems such as Unix are only marginally successful. MS-DOS was designed to run software programs one-at-a-time out-of-the box, and as such relies mostly on the user interface, graphics, and data conversion support delivered by programs operated under it. MS-DOS was never designed for high levels of customization or to allow software developers great flexibility.

MS-DOS was originally intended to support the 8088 microprocessor, and newer microcomputers suffer under MS-DOS. A variety of supplemental software makes the problems with MS-DOS bearable. Through constant version improvements and, as we shall see, through software products like DESQview, Windows, and other memory support utilities, users can be productive under the MS-DOS operating system.

The issues involved in MS-DOS compatibility are particularly complex due to the proliferation of these computers. The problems are seldom related to actual hardware differences, but rather to the large number of different users, configurations, and set-up software that can easily confuse even the most knowledgeable systems specialist. The determination of what software will run on which MS-DOS machine cannot be made by reading software ads or from hearsay. Individuals running given packages on identical systems with the same peripheral configuration as yours are the best assurance that the packages will run on your configuration. Today, most compatibility problems on the lower-performance hardware and the very popular end-user spreadsheet and word processor software have been ironed out. Particularly complex problems, however, exist in the higher-performance networked software, CAD/CAE, and the engineering and scientific classes. Many problems continue without solutions even as improved software versions are produced. Since MS-DOS software is typically singularly designed, problems of cooperation between multiple software and data compatibility continue.

If your main interest is operating the many popular turnkey MS-DOS programs individually, each intended for its own specific task and with little capability for integration with other software, then MS-DOS is an appropriate operating system. If issues of data compatibility, windowing, multitasking, and a consistent user interface across software categories is important to you, then MS-DOS will likely disappoint you until it is completely redesigned. Currently the best attempt at improving MS-DOS is MS-Windows, and the best complete redesign is OS/2. As we shall see, these solutions are not without their own problems. Due to the vast popularity of MS-DOS computers and their considerable hardware performance improvements we can be assured that a popular, well-designed operating system will soon emerge.

Looking ahead, however, MS/DOS with Windows, the completely new OS/2, and several Unix variants are becoming popular operating systems for those who strive to reach for the best. The recent agreement reached by IBM and Apple Computer may lead to an entirely new and different operating system.

5.0   MS-DOS Enhancements

- Memory Support
- Multitasking Features
- Windowing
- File Management
- Data Sharing
- Graphics and GUI

Many MS-DOS users will go to great lengths to improve their operating systems. Here we present the often confusing but powerful array of fix-ups to the Microsoft disk operating system.

Several improvements to the MS-DOS operating system deserve careful examination. The improvements range from simple utilities that perform functions not provided by MS-DOS to its complete replacement, OS/2. Although there are hundreds of comparison categories, we focus on the support categories described earlier:

- *Memory* – From real-mode only to full-bore paged virtual memory support.
- *Multitasking* – From one-at-a-time programs to multitasking several programs; each program capable of multiple software tasks.
- *Windowing* – From one program at a time to using the display for multiple graphics windows.
- *File management* – From the dot prompt of MS-DOS to high-performance file systems and graphical directories.
- *User interface and graphics* – From the dot prompt of MS-DOS to built-in support for graphics and user interface.
- *Data exchange* – From ASCII file sharing to highly-integrated data exchanges between multitasking applications.
- *Other features* – Other important characteristics such as improved driver support and call interfaces.

Enhancement of support in the areas recounted above can occur in different ways for the MS-DOS computer user. The simplest involves enhancement of existing MS-DOS software; the next, more sophisticated, relies on MS-DOS but requires rewriting the software in order to take advantage of MS-DOS enhancements; and finally, the option of giving up MS-DOS in favor of OS/2.

Coping methods abound and thousands of software products are available that repair or enhance the capabilities of the very popular MS-DOS operating system. To keep the discussion in bounds, we confine it to the most common methodologies; ones that fall into these two categories:

1. *MS-DOS regular* – The enhancements are tailored to the existing MS-DOS operating system and allow existing MS-DOS programs improved functionality and better cooperation, but do not force the existing software base to be rewritten. The old crate is kept together with baling wire and duct tape.

2. *MS-DOS enhanced* – The enhancements to MS-DOS beyond MS-DOS regular that allow higher levels of cooperation. However, existing MS-DOS programs must be significantly rewritten to use the enhancements. In order to have seamless operation of multiple software functions, they will either have to be integrated initially

or operated in an environment that contributes toward integration. You'll need to purchase new software, but you'll still use a lot of the previously written MS-DOS software.

You may give up on MS-DOS and opt to invest in a completely new operating system, OS/2 for example. In doing so, you will discover functionality previously unknown with MS-DOS. You will learn new and complex computer science concepts and begin to appreciate what an operating system can do. You will need to acquire more expensive software, but the payback will be that the software will work efficiently and productively for you. In this vein, let's briefly consider DESQview, Windows, and OS/2 in the regular and enhanced MS-DOS environments:

DESQview (MS-DOS regular): A product developed by Quarterdeck software in the mid '80s that greatly enhances the operation of existing MS-DOS software. DESQview provides windowing support of character-based software, allows MS-DOS programs to multitask, and even provides data sharing capabilities beyond file sharing. Almost miraculously, all of this is accomplished without requiring any rewrites of the MS-DOS software. This means that you can run your existing MS-DOS software, unmodified, and enjoy high levels of integration. This is quite a feat. However, the increased cooperation is nowhere near that which can be provided when an operating system and its software are written for integration from the start. For those interested in continuing to run the existing MS-DOS software base with added functionality, DESQview would be a popular choice.

MS-Windows (MS-DOS enhanced): A dramatic improvement to MS-DOS is Microsoft Windows. Being an addition to MS-DOS, MS-Windows is at this point considered an enhancement. It provides such important features as APA windowing, more sophisticated memory support, and built-in graphics and user interface support that were non-existent in MS-DOS. However, to take best advantage of Windows enhancements, the software must be rewritten. Windows and OS/2 place great responsibility on the software developer. Even so, Windows provides many useful features to enhance operation of the existing MS-DOS software base.

OS/2 (MS-DOS enhanced): A complete replacement of MS-DOS. Although existing MS-DOS programs can run under OS/2 in real mode, the primary intent is to provide the levels of sophistication that the Unix operating system has. OS/2 is truly a software developer's operating system. As with Windows, programs must be written exclusively for OS/2 to be able to take advantage of it. OS/2 is so much more sophisticated than MS-DOS that the casual MS-DOS end-user will likely never understand most of the technical differences.

Developers, on the other hand, will require extensive retraining in developmental concepts not too different from those used by Unix and even Macintosh developers. Developers will have to use more sophisticated software principles than previously required under the single-tasking simple MS-DOS. Unique to OS/2 are its dramatically different, yet important ties to the MS-DOS software base. This relationship should provide a reasonable tradeoff between providing the end-user with run-out-of-the-box software and providing developers with a powerful high-end means for developing custom applications software that are becoming increasingly important in the DtC user community.

Memory support enhancements are fundamental to program execution and are likely to affect all MS-DOS users.

The MS-DOS operating system was originally designed to operate programs and data in the first 640K of the 1 MB of memory addressable by the 8088/8086 microprocessor. A variety of enhancements and methodologies are available to assist in better using 80286/386 CPU memory capabilities as well asin helping the 8088 along.

Extended Memory Managers

You can buy software products designed to make more efficient use of available memory. Although it is easy to use extended and expanded memory as disk caches, more sophisticated methods permit software to execute and use memory more straightforwardly, through direct access or by special management of available resources.

■ MS-DOS 5.x has a similar capability in its EMM memory manager.

MS-DOS software products such as Quarterdeck QEMM and Qualitas 386Max install like any installable device driver and provide a number of useful functions. ■ The more significant include:

Upper Memory Use

The memory between the 640K limit and 1 MB is generally referred to as *upper memory*. Since this memory is real, software designed for real mode operation can be operated in upper memory. Unfortunately, available memory slots in this region are not contiguous – the holes are small and scattered – and seldom is a hole greater than 128K. Figure 70 that shows the high memory holes being filled from extended memory using the QEMM memory manager. ■ Notice also, that extended memory used for this purpose is not available for other uses.

■ As discussed in the last Part, it is possible to emulate expanded memory with extended memory.

To operate an MS-DOS program in the high memory region, the program must be able to fit into one of the holes. Using the specialized memory management capability of the 80386/486, not possible with lesser processors, extended memory can be shuffled into the high memory holes that might exist in the 640K to 1 MB memory region. Although the high memory region supports ROM BIOS, video interface memory, and other board-supplied BIOS routines such as hard disk and video interface BIOS, there is usually 50-100K of usable space remaining.

> **NOTE**
>
> 8088- and 80286-based microcomputers can also support program execution in high memory, however, the memory must be physically installed in the holes and cannot be emulated with extended memory.

Although only small MS-DOS programs can execute in the upper memory block, there can still be a benefit. Many MS-DOS software programs such as TSRs and network drivers that would otherwise crowd the 640K memory area may be well within the size of holes in the upper memory block. Freeing up more of the 640K

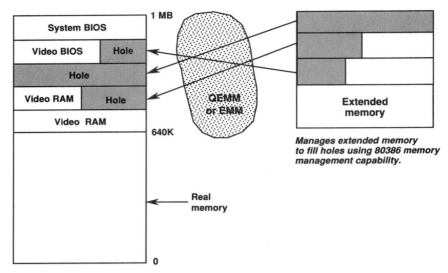

Figure 70.   Upper memory holes: There are unused areas in real memory that can be used for small programs.

region means that you can run larger MS-DOS programs without interference from drivers.

Memory Testing and Reporting

Software such as Quarterdeck Manifest can provide conveniently displayed tables of information concerning the amounts and use of software by extended and expanded memory. Included in the tables are usage of the BIOS, the number of times written to and read from, and other kinds of information. This information becomes particularly useful when troubleshooting memory usage and management problems.

> ┌─ **NOTE** ─────────────────────────────
> Extended memory managers can apportion extended memory as purely extended, as emulated expanded, or as a combination of both.

High Memory

High memory is the first 64K block of extended memory at the boundary between real and extended memory, discussed in the last Part. This memory area is used by products such as DESQview, Windows, and MS-DOS 5.x to execute a portion of the operating system, thereby freeing more of real memory.

Shadow RAM

Shadow RAM is a process for replacing the slower ROM BIOS memories with fast extended memory. The ROMs are copied into extended memory, and disconnected, and extended memory is mapped into the regions previously occupied by the ROMs. Critical BIOS routines can execute much faster in RAM than in ROM. Shadowing will usually result in considerable I/O speed improvements for those programs that use the ROM functions. The most dramatic effect is seen on programs using the character-based video BIOS routines. Quicker screen scrolling is most apparent.

Of course, to realize the speed improvements, programs have to have been using BIOS routines in the first place. As discussed earlier, these routines are often bypassed, which makes shadow RAM ineffective. Both shadow RAM and the above high memory usage subtract from the available extended memory pool size, however the amount (usually around 256K) is negligible in MS-DOS computers typically implementing 4 MB and above of extended memory.

DOS Extenders

Extenders are software products that MS-DOS programs can use to access extended memory, while still allowing programs to execute under current versions of MS-DOS. Extenders are considered MS-DOS enhanced because the MS-DOS program must be written to include the use of an extender. The rewrite is not extensive, but it is necessary. You cannot use memory extenders with non-extended MS-DOS programs.

Extenders are software products that enable the use of 80286 and above CPUs in protected mode and extended memory by MS-DOS programs written to use the extender. Most extenders use the XMS (Extended Memory Specification) to guarantee software compatibility with other products and environments supporting XMS. The extender software is welded into the respective application by the software developer during the compilation process. You simply purchase the end-use software already set up. For instance, the DataEase and PCAD MS-DOS software products both use DOS extenders. Programs can use extended memory even though the MS-DOS operating system does not support it. Although you launch your program from MS-DOS, soon the extender takes control and provides the functionality for protected mode operation. Upon leaving the program, protected mode is turned off and you are returned to real mode.

EMS Drivers

EMS drivers permit the use of expanded memory for data manipulations for those programs that know how to use the EMS drivers. DESQview, described next, takes the EMS driver notion one step further by allowing multitasking in EMS memory. Recall that expanded memory can be emulated with extended memory on 80386 DtCs.

Memory Management with DESQview

The DESQview software product from Quarterdeck enhances the use of expanded memory of the existing MS-DOS software base by allowing programs to multitask. Although the programs don't actually execute *in* expanded memory, they are shuffled between it and real memory where they do execute.

- *8088 systems* – DESQview supports expanded memory on 8088 microcomputers. Using this memory, you can multitask your existing MS-DOS applications.
- *80286 systems* – Similar to the above, but faster.
- *80386/486 systems* – Similar to the above, but extended memory is used to emulate the expanded memory needed for multitasking. A large frame switching window can be used that results in considerable efficiency when swapping large programs in and out of real memory.

Since all software actually executes in real memory, you can multitask your existing MS-DOS software base and this can be done on all 80xxx CPUs.

Memory Management with Windows

In addition to supporting the functions described above, Windows does considerably more in the memory management area. The enhancements are found in three primary Windows modes, real mode for support of 8088 CPUs, standard mode for support of 80286 CPUs, and enhanced memory management mode for support of 80386/486 CPUs.

- *Real mode* – Programs execute in real memory, but expanded memory support is provided for those programs that use it.

■ Programs written for Windows are called Windows programs and those written for OS/2 are called OS/2 programs.

- *Standard mode* – Extended memory is available for multitasking MS-Windows programs. ■ Non-windows MS-DOS programs can be executed in real memory, where they freeze MS-Windows programs and take over the entire video screen. MS-DOS programs requiring expanded memory will need expanded memory boards. Expanded/extended emulation is not possible with 80286 microprocessors.

- *Enhanced memory management mode* – Windows really shines in this mode without streaking.

In addition to the functions mentioned above, the enhanced mode supports the following:

- *Virtual 8086 mode* – Ordinary MS-DOS applications can multitask on separate virtual 8086 CPUs using the virtual 8086 mode of the 80386. This is in addition to the multitasking MS-Windows applications. Moreover, MS-DOS programs can share screen windows with Windows APA programs.

- *Virtual memory support* – A primitive form of virtual memory – a swap file – is maintained on hard disk when the active program size exceeds usable memory. The swapping action is not fine grained and can be likened to a print spooler. The swapping area can be several times the size of the total extended memory. Also, the virtual memory is available to any MS-DOS program. An MS-DOS program requiring 16 MB of expanded memory could have this amount even though an 80386-based computer only implemented 4 MB of extended memory.

- *Screen virtualization* – The video memory itself can be virtualizied, so that even original MS-DOS graphics programs can be windowed. The DESQview program also provides this capability on 80386-based DtCs. Now, you should begin to feel that perhaps anything less than an 80386 CPU is not worth buying.

Compatibility problems arise with the use of enhanced memory software. Some MS-DOS computer vendors provide their own memory management programs (for example, Compaq CEM), while generic versions exist (Quarterdeck QEMM) with greater overall flexibility. Some MS-DOS programs provide their own extended memory support and this can conflict with the support provided by DESQview or Windows. Some programs use extended memory through non-standard mechanisms. VCPI (Virtual Control Program Interface) and the Extended Memory Specification (XMS) define how to use extended memory appropriately to avoid conflicts. Programs using extenders may not function in the Windows enhanced memory mode if they are not designed correctly. Extended memory support provided by Windows can be in conflict with other memory managers that you may have installed.

When operating high-performance software, you must understand a variety of configurations. Many MS-DOS enhancement systems provide for special allocation of extended and expanded memory, and these configurations are necessary for proper software operation. When you encounter memory management conflict problems, you should be aware of the following:

- **Conflict potential** – Certain situations can result in memory usage and management conflicts. Just because a particular program itself knows how to use extended memory doesn't mean that it will cooperate with the external memory management schemes provided by an enhanced operating system.

- **Driver awareness** – You need to understand how the various drivers (network, video, memory management) interact. Do they need to be installed in any particular order? Will they work together? Which MS-DOS computer are you using? Do you know anyone else who has been successful with a similar configuration? Are you prepared to call the software vendor with the specifics of your problem? Can you afford to wait for the next driver or support software revision that may solve the problem? Never think that reporting the problem is not useful. There are so many combinations of software, drivers, system units, peripherals, that your problem could very well be unique.

- **Real memory problems** – Do not forget that no matter how loaded a system is with extended and expanded memory, no matter how much extended memory you have, you can still easily run out of real memory. Although you may think you are using extended memory, much of the software can execute only in the 640K region, and you may simply be filling it up. We are in a period of transition as more programs are able to use advanced CPU memory management and better operating systems evolve. When in doubt about memory size, various utility programs can give detailed reports on software's memory usage.

Memory Support Summary

Although there are many different ways to support the various 80xxx memory modes with existing MS-DOS software, their number and mutual incompatibilities confuse the issues. The most sophisticated memory support strategy is provided by OS/2 in its 2.x Version, which provides top of the line paged virtual memory for a new software base plus a virtual 8086 mode to allow multitasking of your existing MS-DOS software base. Staunch MS-DOS users, however, will continue to find a safe haven for their existing software bases in the DESQview and Windows enhancements. Windows NT and MS-DOS 6.0 promise top of the line memory support also.

5.2 Multitasking Features

The original intent of the MS-DOS operating system was to run only one program at a time. With powerful hardware and more sophisticated applications, users now need to operate software concurrently. To meet this challenge, different techniques and software have evolved to make multitasking possible.

Although the value of multitasking is dubious on XT-style DtCs because the 8088 lacks performance and memory management capability, the carousel function using expanded memory has considerable merit and is quite popular. The door to multitasking begins to open with the 80286 and later CPUs, and it is here that the more sophisticated multitasking operating systems such as OS/2, Unix, and enhancements to MS-DOS such as DESQview and Windows can begin to provide the necessary performance and memory management support.

We now look at several different methodologies, ranging from simple multitasking to complex multithreaded multitasking of OS/2.

Terminate and Stay Resident Functions (TSRs)

TSRs are a popular nuisance for many MS-DOS users. A constant dread is the imminance of a memory collapse that follows inordinate use of a TSR. You can use a TSR to increase the functionality of a given software program. In this case another software program lurks behind the scenes, ready to leap into action when you hit a special key. When the TSR function executes, your foreground program freezes, then restarts when the TSR function is complete. Although concurrent processing does not occur, it appears that two software processes have occurred where originally there was one. This is the most trivial case of multitasking.

Another method uses the heartbeat interrupt to periodically exit the foreground program to perform a background task. Here, you can execute a TSR periodically, according to the repetition rate of the heartbeat interrupt. The function being performed by the interrupt appears to be executing at the same time as the foreground software function. In this simple case of multitasking, the foreground task could be a word processor or spreadsheet, and the background task could be the TSR or interrupt service routine that gets executed as a result of the periodic interrupt. The routine may be a software clock, a test of a temperature sensor, printing a buffer of characters, or executing other functions concurrently with your main programs.

Simulated Multitasking with Carousel Software

Many MS-DOS enhancement programs permit you to load more than one program at a time. You can switch between software programs like clicking a slide projector. Only one program runs at a time, the others can remain in memory, ready to jump in when called.

Although this is not multitasking, there is nevertheless an advantage. Programs need not be loaded and unloaded each time they are required. You can leave a spreadsheet in the middle of a complex set up and run a word processor. When done with it, you can leave and return to the spreadsheet, which has been preserved in the state it was when you left it. All this is accomplished with simple key presses. For example, an `ALT 2` might turn on your word processor, `ALT 3` your spreadsheet, and `ALT 5` your modem communication software. This context-switching capability is powerful and is supported by a number of MS-DOS add-on products. Also, MS-DOS 5.x has this capability built in. Depending upon the software and the CPU, expanded or extended memory may be used.

Multitasking with DESQview

■ MS-DOS programs do not yield control unless interrupted or exited. A program gives up control when you enter `quit` or hit an escape key, which also terminates the program. The heartbeat interrupt keeps the existing configuration and state.

DESQview takes advantage of the heartbeat interrupt and allows several MS-DOS programs to concurrently execute through a mechanism known as preemptive multitasking.■

Ordinarily, MS-DOS permits only one program to execute at a time. When an MS-DOS program is executing, it takes control of the CPU and the only way to exit that program is through an interrupt. When DESQview is loaded, it becomes the foreground program and it takes control of the CPU. You then tell DESQview which programs you wish to multitask and DESQview loads programs alternately, allowing each to execute for a number of timer tick interrupts. Because of the interrupts,

DESQview is guaranteed to get its control back from each executing program that it releases.

DESQview brings each program into real memory from expanded memory and allows that program to execute for so many interrupt ticks. This is called time slicing, or *preemptive* multitasking. Then the next program is brought in, and so on in round robin fashion, each program consecutively executing. You can execute a large number of MS-DOS programs in this fashion as long as you have expanded memory. Of course, the efficiency of each is compromised since each has to share the CPU. Moreover, there is a considerable overhead that DESQview incurs in scheduling the process. Although more than one concurrently executing programs can display its text output, only one at a time can be in the foreground, controlled by mouse or keyboard.

You can customize each program through a variety of set up parameters that include program size, use of video memory, and multitasking parameters. Also, with DESQview, you can execute programs in carousel fashion, bringing one to the foreground and freezing the others in memory.

DESQview uses memory as follows:

- *8088* – Programs are swapped into real memory from expanded memory for execution using time slicing. This process is inefficient, so a small frame EMS switching window will be needed.
- *80286* – Similar to the 8088 but faster.
- *80386* – EMS memory is emulated with extended memory and a large frame switching window is possible, allowing considerable efficiency when multitasking.

Since DESQview uses preemptive multitasking, you can multitask your existing MS-DOS software base. Through its Windowing capability, concurrently executing programs can also display their outputs on different parts of the video screen.

In preemptive multitasking, the multitasking program does what the name suggests, it abruptly cuts in and takes control of each executing program in turn. The operating system scheduler software gives each program several clock ticks to execute. In *cooperative multitasking*, executing programs drive their own execution process by requesting chunks of CPU time. Most programs can be made to multitask using the preemptive methodology, without recourse to explicit internal coding. This is how MS-DOS enhancers such as DESQview need to operate the existing software base. Cooperative or non-preemptive multitasking requires programs that ask for CPU resources and that are event driven, which means they have to be written that way in the first place. Windows uses cooperative while OS/2 uses preemptive multitasking.

With cooperative multitasking, programs can have direct control of CPU execution time, obtaining it when it is really needed; less when other programs might benefit more. However, since programs can control the multitasking process, they can accidentally take over completely, thereby monopolizing or even locking the CPU. Also, programs must be written to multitask from the start.

On the pro-preemptive side, since the operating system is in control of execution sharing, the sharing can be globally controlled, able to consider programs, preferences, and the needs of peripherals. However, efficiency is lost when programs are switched in mid-function. Since each program is generally in control of the switching process, the CPU state must be saved. Context switching can be costly in execution time spent on saving and restoring CPU states, rather than performing the needed software function. Better CPUs (80386/486) are considerably more efficient at context switching because they implement specific context-switching instructions.

> **EXAMPLE**
>
> Multitasking might benefit the typical MS-DOS user who needs to combine two otherwise uncooperative programs. Perhaps you need to transfer a large file over a low bit-rate RS-232 interface to a distant bulletin board. Ordinarily you would have to wait 15 minutes while a communications program performs the transfer, which ties up your DtC. Rather than wait for OS/2, you buy DESQview. DESQview lets you edit the next file while the previous file is being transferred. The editor and communications programs execute concurrently under the DESQview environment.

Multitasking with Windows

Unlike DESQview, Windows supports cooperative multitasking. Each program asks for processing time from the operating system and the CPU is parceled out. Since programs are written initially for multitasking, there is no need for preemptive multitasking.

In real (8088) mode, Windows supports cooperative multitasking for Windows programs, but total size of multitasking programs cannot exceed 640K. Multitasking programs can use expanded memory for their data areas. Also, MS-DOS programs can execute in real memory. When MS-DOS programs are executing, they take complete control of the screen and real memory.

In standard 80286 mode, programs written for Windows can multitask cooperatively and each may exceed 640K, going up to the 16 MB extended memory limit. MS-DOS programs will take control and must execute in real memory.

Enhanced mode (80386/486) is where Windows shines and competes with OS/2's multitasking capability. With the virtual 8086 microprocessors that come with the 80386 CPU, multiple DOS applications can use preemptive multitasking to run, each on its own virtual 8086 CPU. At the same time, Windows programs can cooperatively multitask in standard mode.

Multitasking Summary

MS-DOS users have two alternatives for multitasking: DESQview, which is intended to multitask existing MS-DOS programs, and Windows with its increased multitasking capability for both Windows and MS-DOS programs. OS/2, the ultimate in multitasking, provides internal support, using threads, for programs that multitask. You could think of multitasking in terms of solution levels: low — DESQview, medium — current Windows, and high — OS/2.

> **NOTE**
>
> ### Threads and Multitasking
> Through a process known as threading, applications programs can spawn processes that execute concurrently. A program can use threads to multitask its own internal functions. This kind of multitasking is at a finer level than multitasking different programs. Through threads, a

program can take better advantage of the CPU, allowing it to chip away at multiple, overlapping, and time consuming processes as you sit thinking about the next step.

Example

Call up a particular program. A menu is displayed. As you query and receive basic help on a particular item on the menu, the remainder of the program is loaded into memory. While one spreadsheet is recalculating, you make new entries in another, while yet another spreadsheet is printing. All of these activities take place automatically as you select them, however, you do not control the sequence or priorities. This is established by the operating system, the availability of I/O, and other factors.

Users familiar with both Windows 3.0 and DESQview multitasking of MS-DOS programs often swear by the latter, faulting Windows for being too slow at multitasking.

5.3   Windowing

The ability of MS-DOS operating system environments to support windowing is complicated by the fact that both character- and graphics-oriented video display systems and software have changed over the years. Although MS-DOS was not intended to window applications, there are several ways that windowing can be accomplished under MS-DOS.

A window in the world of DtCs is a rectangular area on a display screen in which you can run an application, track its status, and see the results. Two or more windows displayed checkerboard style are said to be *tiled*. MS-Windows 2.0 used this mode to display its windows. Windows may also overlap, shingle-style, which is known as *cascading*. Windows can be resized and repositioned on the screen for convenience. A window overlaid by others may be moved to the top of the cascade whenever work is to be done in that window.

Windowing is the capability of microcomputer software to apportion parts of a single video display to two or more applications without conflict. The wide appeal of windowing is that once you learn how to run one window program, you are well on your way to knowing how to run all of them.

Windowing with DESQview

Since MS-DOS is a text-oriented operating system, most MS-DOS software from the standpoint of the operating system is character based. Text-oriented software products that perform their text functions by OS supported BIOS functions can be rechanneled into user selectable windows by enhanced video drivers provided by the DESQview system.

In Figure 71, the programs using the BIOS text support are rechanneled to the more sophisticated DESQview text support routines. DESQview's scheduler knows which program is executing (sending characters), and a memory buffer is used to further manage the excess characters coming from the programs to be windowed. Ordinarily, the programs would have used the BIOS support to fill the video screen, while ignoring other programs. Now, through easy to use DESQview functions, you can decide not only where a program will be able to show its characters, but also

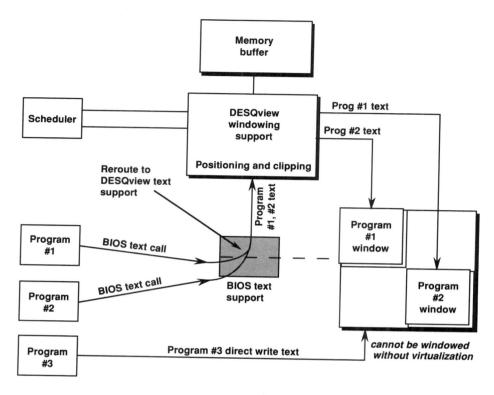

Figure 71. **Character-based windowing:** Programs using OS-supported text functions can be windowed – even on an 8088 CPU.

what portion of the program's full screen will be presented in its DESQview window. The programs are required to use the BIOS, and therefore their calls for support can be rechanneled. Program #3 cannot be rechanneled, since it writes directly to screen memory. DESQview can still run this program, but the program will commandeer the video screen.

Since most MS-DOS applications use the BIOS support for character processing, character transmissions can be trapped and redirected to multiple screen areas.

> **EXAMPLE**
>
> **AN ANALOGY**
> Imagine a theater with reserved seating. When ticket holders arrive at the theater, they are shown to their seats by ushers, who make sure they reach their seats regardless of the order in which they arrive. If intruders without tickets try to grab seats, conflicts occur that must be resolved before the show can begin.

In the DESQview environment on 8088 and 80286 DtCs, graphics (APA) programs cannot be windowed because MS-DOS does not provide a central graphics support facility that can be rechanneled. Instead, the individual software products must supply their own graphics drivers. For hundreds of different vendors to agree on a common approach to graphics is a hopeless expectation. Each program does graphics differently, so there is no practical way to rechannel graphics into windows.

On an 80386/486 DtC, DESQview can even window an MS-DOS graphics program. It does this by a technique called video memory screen virtualization, similar to the one used by Windows.

Windowing with Macintosh

In the Macintosh world windowing is old hat. There has never been a text mode, and graphics support is centrally located in ROM. Perhaps the strongest appeal of a Macintosh is that it is a complete system. All of its parts are designed from the start to fit together. Apple has the longest experience with windowing technology, and continues to lead in the GUI race with its new System 7.0.

Windowing with Windows

The outstanding features of Windows 3.0 are windowing with icons, multitasking, and breaking the 640K program ceiling.

With internal support of graphics and windowing functions, Windows provides power, in all modes, for allowing programs to share the display screen. Programs that run under Windows fall into two main categories:

1. *Windows programs* – Programs written to the Windows graphics specifications can share your video screen the most intimately, and this can be done with 80286 and above CPUs. Since Windows programs are cooperating in their common use of graphics support routines, they can easily share screen windows. For example, as you change window size, the contents of your screen window will shrink in proportion so that an entire page rather than a blocked portion continues to be displayed.

2. *MS-DOS original graphics programs* – For MS-DOS graphics programs not written for Windows, windowing is still possible, providing you are operating in the 80386 enhanced mode. Windows and DESQview can virtualize the display screen's video memory using the 80386's virtual memory capability.
   This is what happens: Each program that is operating behaves as though it has its own video memory because each program runs on a virtual 8086. Although the real-mode programs seem to write to the video interface real-mode memory, they are in fact writing to separate virtualized memory areas in extended memory. Thus, there is no conflict. Additional software manages the different virtual screen areas into windows and, finally, does write portions of each program's virtualized video memory into the real video memory. Windows even detects screen mode changes. You could be operating one program in a text mode, the other in a graphics mode, and still window the two. Windows converts the text outputs to APA data streams to make them analogous to APA graphics outputs.

The following was demonstrated on an Asian 386 MS-DOS compatible operating Windows 3.0 in enhanced mode:

- dBASE was listing a text file in a small window. dBASE uses the standard BIOS text routines.
- IBM's Personal Editor was displaying a file in another window in CGA mode. PE does not use the standard BIOS video display routines.
- Mandel, a public domain Mandelbrot program, was creating a colorful Mandelbrot set in EGA mode in another window.

- Microsoft's BASIC interpreter was displaying text in screen mode 0, a CGA text mode. Text characters are written directly to memory using BASIC poke commands.
- Microsoft's BASIC interpreter was displaying a graphics image in screen 2, a CGA APA graphics mode. BASIC poke commands are used here also.

Those who think they understand MS-DOS computer hardware, video display modes, and the MS-DOS operating system might say this is not possible, yet it was done. Windows recognized the different screen modes because they were set up by standard BIOS routines that Windows can intercept. Each program was writing to different virtualized memory areas. Finally, Windows was smart enough to arrange the outputs of the different program into a single memory area, the video display memory in real memory, so that all programs were windowed. Those who say Windows' only utility is operating Windows programs should take a closer look at its capabilities.

Moreover, each windowed area was not a shrunken image, but rather a blocked portion of each program's screen output. In order for each window to display the full program's output, shrinking proportionately in size, the programs themselves will have to cooperate, or be written especially for Windows.

Cooperation is required for more intimate windowing, graphics control, and data sharing. Figure 73 shows the advantages of software cooperating through centralized OS support functions. Still, it is surprising how much windows can do with ordinary unmodified MS-DOS programs.

Windowing with OS/2 Presentation Manager

Through its Presentation Manager (PM), OS/2 provides windowing capabilities to OS/2 programs similar to the way Windows provides these capabilities to DOS programs. Character-based MS-DOS programs can even window with OS/2 APA applications. OS/2 does not cater to original MS-DOS graphics programs as Windows does. OS/2 APA programs must be written according to PM specifications in order to be windowed.

While PM has the look and feel of MS-Windows, it is fundamentally different. Windows runs on top of DOS, whereas PM is integrated into OS/2. In addition to windowing, MS-Windows must compensate DOS for some of its weaknesses and limitations. PM does not share this problem; PM is not constrained by OS/2.

> **NOTE**
>
> "Running on top of" means that Windows is loaded by MS-DOS and uses MS-DOS file management functions and its BIOS. Windows NT, however, will be supported by its own considerably rewritten kernel. Indeed, MS-DOS will run on top of the Windows NT kernel.

Each PM program runs in its own window, which can be enlarged to fill the entire screen or shrunk to the size of an icon. A Presentation Manager window is quite similar to a Windows window. It has the familiar title bar across the top with menu selections directly below. As with MS-Windows, options may be selected either by mouse or by keyboard keys. Selection of an option produces a drop-down menu with more options. Dialog boxes appear for some options. The user can fill in text fields and punch buttons to specify commands.

Windowing with X Windows

X Windows is a protocol for passing messages to and from a program that is executing on a system and a display. Its purpose is to let workstations display output in multiple windows from more than one network server. X Windows use of client and server are the reverse of the practice in LAN networks. In LAN usage, a server is a network component that provides services to a requesting workstation. In X Windows the server is the software on the workstation that manages the display produced by the application. The client in X Windows is the application that tells the server what to put in the window and how to manipulate it. In short, the client produces the show and the server stages it.

The technology is widely used. More and more open systems features are being offered. Visionware Ltd. of Cambridge, England is marketing XVision 4.0 that turns a PC into an X Windows server running MIT's X11.4 protocols. With a Windows 3.0 interface, a user can run both Unix and DOS applications, and can cut and paste between them. Windows that have been overlaid can be stored and quickly restored. X Windows will be discussed further in the next Part.

5.4   File Management

Closely associated with windowing are graphics and user interface functions. Simple fixes to MS-DOS improve the user interface. Windows and OS/2 provide similar capabilities in this area.

File Manager Support Software for MS-DOS

File managers such as the XTree Gold Professional and QFiler utilities are included here since they improve your interface with the MS-DOS operating system. Although they are low in the spectrum of graphics and user interface enhancements, they nevertheless provide a friendly environment to operate MS-DOS programs and view disk directories.

XTree Gold Professional adds more than a hundred separate file display features. Capabilities include pruning and grafting subdirectories, displaying custom file formats, dual directory displays, a flexible editor, program execution menus, mass copy, delete, and move capability. In short, the XTree program gives the user complete and friendly access to the MS-DOS file management system. Although MS-DOS 5.x has pretty good visual displays, it doesn't hold a candle to XTree. Indeed, there are many users that prefer XTree capabilities to those found in Windows.

In fact, any of the MS-DOS enhancements are likely to be bettered by other vendors, who have a vested interest in a single improvement area. Quarterdeck QEMM will likely be better at memory management than MS-DOS EMM, the public domain program PCED is more flexible than the built in DOSKEY capability of MS-DOS, and the list goes on. You may face a tradeoff between integrating all capability within a single operating system, or seeking enhancements that individually are more powerful than what is found in the operating system.

File Management with Windows and OS/2

Windows and OS/2 significantly improve the interface between user and operating system and the manner in which this is done, from a user's perspective, is quite similar. Both involve a graphical user interface with icons, buttons, and other devices that provide an intuitive way to load, execute, and manipulate programs and data.

The File Manager in Windows 3.0 replaces the old and cumbersome MS-DOS Executive.

File Management with X Windows

X Windows provides a FileView that allows the user to manipulate, edit, delete, and execute files. You can add filters to display only certain files. The FileView automatically determines the type of operation to perform on a file. The user can execute a program simply by clicking on its name with the mouse.

The graphical user interface has icons, buttons, and other devices for easy loading and executing of programs and data.

5.5   Data Sharing

Data sharing occurs when different workstations use the same data for different pupuses. Data sharing through MS-DOS is limited to the MS-DOS capability of file management. As long as you can get data into file, you can share it with other programs. Important aspects are the ways in which MS-DOS can be fooled into higher levels of data sharing and sophisticated approaches to data that have become possible with MS-DOS Windows and the new OS/2.

File Sharing

MS-DOS provides the simplest way to share data, which is to move disk files about. Program one generates a file in a format that program two can understand and saves it to a disk file. Program one is exited and program two, the one that requires the data, is executed. Providing program two can import and convert the particular format (most can at least import ASCII) your problem is solved. This process is tedious at best because you have to exit and reload programs repeatedly, losing precious program setups (files loaded, printers selected) and awkwardly bouncing between the two programs.

Sharing Character Data in Video Memory

■ MS-DOS video interfaces scan a specific and known portion of CPU memory. In doing so, the video interface maps this area to the display screen. Every character presented on the display monitor comes from a known location in memory.

Data can be shared because all character-based MS-DOS programs place characters to be displayed into a known memory area.■

Whether software writes directly to this memory, or uses BIOS functions, a TSR program (like SideKick) can be popped up and used to scoop up characters from any portion of this memory. These characters can be made into a disk file, or temporarily stored in a memory buffer. Some TSR screen capture utilities allow you to set a keyboard key combination that can later invoke this data when you want to move it to another application. The data transmission occurs by the keyboard interrupt. The receiving application does not need to be modified to receive this data and is fooled into thinking that the data was entered by the keyboard.

For example: You are operating program one and see a column of numbers that you would like to move into another program. While in this program, using a unique key combination, you invoke a TSR utility that prompts you to mark off an area on your screen. Then you are asked to select a key combination to invoke the characters so indicated. You say ALT 5. When running program two, you hit the key ALT 5 and as if by magic, the characters previously trapped are fed into program two through keyboard drivers as if they came from the keyboard.

Another method simply takes the trapped characters and allows you to save them as an ASCII disk file. When operating program two, you rely on its ability to read in an ASCII disk file.

Successful operation of the above schemes depends on the fact the software operating is text oriented. This is because the area of memory captured contains ASCII character codes, and your keyboard drivers expect ASCII characters, not APA dots entered through your keyboard. If programs display text using APA graphics modes, all bets are off and the above methods cannot be used.

The methods are cumbersome, and only treat the transfer of ASCII data between applications. Since many of us operate graphics programs and APA desktop publishers, it is hard to become excited over text-only methods.

On Macintosh and Windows programs, all software is APA, and a clipboard is used to hold data. The data can be text or graphics, and as long as both programs implement the clipboard function, that's all there is to it.

Video Memory Data Sharing

Being able to display text in known memory areas can lead to interesting applications. Some programming languages support TSR environments that can look at on-screen text, independent of how it got there, and perform actions depending on what is seen.■

■ The languages are often called mouse languages because they provide existing mouse drivers with this increased functionality.

EXAMPLE

Your software presents cryptic prompts at various points, expecting you to choose one of many equally cryptic responses. Your TSR program could recognize the prompt and present a menu of plain English responses that you could point to with your mouse. Click on one of them, the mouse menu disappears, and the correct syntactical response, created for you by the TSR, will be fed to the originally requesting program by the keyboard driver. It would happen as if you had typed it, only a lot faster and more reliably. What would have been a complicated scenario becomes much easier.

Thus, mouse- and menu-driven functions that were not originally planned for can still be provided. Of course, it would be better to plan menu-driven environments from the start to be correctly integrated to the rest of the application.

TSR environments for automating software can be of use to the handicapped who want to operate existing software bases but are unable to keyboard or see the screen clearly.

Problems with Video Memory Data Sharing

Video memory data sharing only works with ASCII text. Graphics are not supported. Only data that is written to video memory – displayed on the monitor – can be moved. The TSR transfer utilities are not aware of internal data and processing. Data must enter the receiving application as though it were typed through the keyboard, which can lead to complications when you want flexibility of data position.

Data Transfer with DESQview

DESQview also permits data transfers between programs not originally designed for it. DESQview has built-in capabilities, such as those just described, for capturing and moving character data from video memory.

DESQview supports concurrent execution and display to video memory. Both transmitting and receiving programs are displayed on the same video screen, which simplifies the process of marking and moving text from one program to another.

Invoke DESQview by a key press, mark out the text from the area of the screen that program one is displaying. Engage program two and use its cursor to point to where you want the data to go. Then you hit a DESQview key, and the previously marked off data pours into program two by its keyboard driver. Again, the receiving program must be fooled into thinking that the data is coming from the keyboard.

Data Transfer with X Windows

X Windows also has built-in capabilities to move data between applications. Using the mouse you can cut data from one window and paste it into another. This is a powerful feature that allows the user to move data easily between applications even if they are running on different DtCs in a network.

Integrated Software Solution

Data manipulation problems can be alleviated with integrated software. Integrated software packages plan for data sharing internally, so that internal formats, sharing of areas, and display methods can be well coordinated between the different software functions. The functions are written at the same time, by the same developers.

To graph a portion of a spreadsheet in Lotus 1-2-3, simply pull down a window over the numbers, hit a button, and there is the graph. Internally, Lotus 1-2-3 took care of the details of data movement, formatting, and finally, graphing, all at the press of a button. Seamless data transfer methods are possible because they are being used for a limited number of applications. The highest levels of integration are possible. However, you are forced to use the particular software functions that are included in the package.

Moving Data with Windows and OS/2

In Microsoft Windows and OS/2, the approach is taken that if you really want flexible data movement between your software, that software will have to be written in the first place to do so. Let's look at two popular methods of data transfer to appreciate why existing MS-DOS character-based software could not support these methods.

Clipboards

The clipboard is a software mechanism for exchanging data in certain formats between programs that implement the clipboard function. Text or graphics may be *clipped* or *cut* from one file, stored temporarily on a clipboard, and then retrieved and literally *pasted* into another file. Cutting and pasting can be performed also within the same file, which is nothing more than moving something from one place in a file to another. It is also possible to copy something and insert it elsewhere. In this case the material remains in its original location and only the copy or duplicate is moved.

First, programs implementing the clipboard must operate in text and graphics APA modes, as they always have on the Macintosh. Second, programs are written specifically to implement the clipboard. Through the clipboard – a common place in system memory – text and graphics to be moved can be wrapped in a box and the box moved to an on-screen clipboard icon. In the receiving program these data do not arrive through a keyboard driver as with DESQview data transfer, but are acquired by the receiving program as though they had been originated there. Therefore, the data will be appropriately integrated into the existing data of that program. For example, if an image is moved into a document, text presently in that position will flow around the imported image.

The benefit of data transfer is that both text and graphics can be moved between applications. The process is intuitive and well integrated. Unfortunately, supported clipboard data formats, how the programs represent the text and graphics internally, are limited. You can't move images or text fonts between any two programs, unless the particular format is supported.

Dynamic Data Exchange (DDE)

With DDE, processed data, and not data images or text, is moved between applications. To describe it as movement is incorrect. The connection is more accurately a linkage, or hookup between programs.

EXAMPLE

Let's say you are running Windows. In one screen window you have created an Excel pie chart from a few columns of spreadsheet data. In another window you are operating Microsoft Word, where you have placed (through appropriate apparatus) a copy of the pie chart. Now you go back to the spreadsheet, and change a few numbers in one of the columns. The Excel pie chart immediately changes. The pie chart image in your Word document changes also. The change occurred because both programs were designed to exchange data dynamically.

Deep in the code of both programs are the calling and receiving mechanisms that make this possible. Long before the program ever hit the street, these capabilities were expressly built in. The development of these capabilities certainly added complexity to both packages, but the payoff is increased flexibility and better integration.

Looking at Figure 72, notice that with DDE, programs dynamically share the data that is used to create the image. Thus, as the spreadsheet data is changed, both the spreadsheet pie chart and the document spreadsheet change. This is because both programs are multitasking and both programs are continuously looking at the shared data through their respective links. With the clipboard, a more traditional data transfer is taking place. Program one gets the data and places it in the clipboard's memory, and program two gets the data from the clipboard.

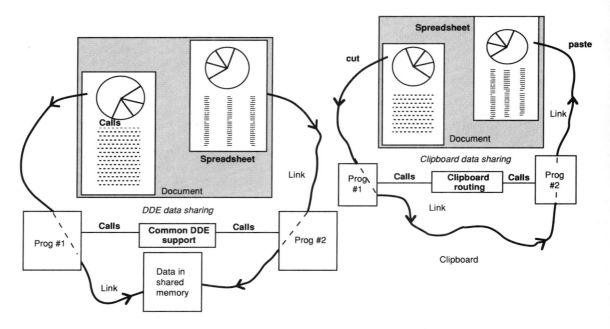

Figure 72. DDE vs. clipboard data sharing: With the clipboard, you deliberately perform a cut and paste operation. With DDE, data is dynamically exchanged between programs.

Although the figure shows both DDE programs displaying on a single DtC video screen, they could just as well be on different screens in a local area network.

- **DDE in OS/2** – OS/2's Presentation Manager provides data movement functions similar to those possessed by Windows. OS/2's enhanced sophistication in multi-tasking and I/O control makes the control of data between applications more complex. Such software constructs as semaphores and queues will accommodate higher level data control and developers will commensurately require higher levels of training to implement data exchanges under more complicated conditions.

- **DDE on the Macintosh** – The Macintosh has had its clipboard from the beginning. DDE-like data transfers are called *publishing* and *subscribing* in the Mac's System 7.0 operating system.

5.6 Graphics and GUI Support

MS-DOS needs a great deal of assistance for graphics. Its handling of graphics is currently limited to BIOS functions that assist in setting or resetting individual pixels. It provides no support of special text fonts, or more complicated graphics primitives, or user interface constructions (menus, buttons, dialogue boxes).

Each program must supply its own graphics and user interface. Each program supplies a set of drivers that help to isolate the program from the hardware details of the interface. Then it is up to the application to use the drivers to develop the various images and dialogue boxes that are found in most graphics-oriented applications.

This leads to a diverse and difficult to manage set of software as compared to that found under Windows, in Presentation Manager of OS/2, or on the Macintosh, which provides this support in the operating system.

Figure 73 shows two applications that take advantage of the functionality built into the operating system, while two others use their own capabilities independently. There are in fact two levels of functionality.

The higher level includes functions for creating graphics, for windowing, and for sending data to defined screen areas, to draw circles and to manage printing fonts. These functions are implemented at a sufficiently high level that specific hardware information such as printer or monitor type is not necessary.

On the lower level, drivers must talk to the hardware, the printers and video display interfaces, for initialization and for the details necessary to implement the drawing and printing functions. Since all cooperative programs use the same high-level functions, they can be coupled to the hardware through a single set of hardware drivers with each driver connected to a particular peripheral. Each non-cooperative program requires its own set of drivers.

The interface between high- and low-level driver functions is clearly specified, so developers will develop consistent code permitting the hardware drivers to convert the higher-level software functions to the final commands that control the particular hardware peripheral.

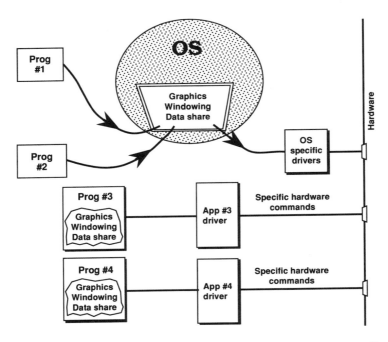

Figure 73. Independent vs. cooperative software: Software that uses centralized OS support can cooperate.

Meta Drivers – Graphics Support

An alternative between software cooperating in the Windows or OS/2 environments and each developer writing graphics routines, is the meta drivers. A large TSR driver is installed (by you) that provides the graphics and user interfaces required by programs. Since the driver is external to the application, it may be modified, new features added, and bugs fixed without modifying the programs that use it. Meta drivers are not general purpose and are not developed by the OS vendor, but rather by a few language vendors. For example, meta drivers exist for certain C and Pascal compilers that developers may use to support their end-user products. As a user, you simply load the TSR prior to loading the application. Meta drivers work only with a limited number of compilers, and are not universally used by software developers.

Windows and OS/2 – Graphics Support within the OS

Graphics support is provided within the operating system. The support is for those universal graphics functions not specific to any particular video interface.

Both Windows and OS/2 provide a large assortment of built in functions for performing graphics on MS-DOS computers. Using call interface functions, developers can implement graphics and user interfaces that call upon the OS for functions, instead of providing their own custom graphics libraries or routines. This results in a level of integration between software products far beyond what could be accomplished through separate developmental efforts.

6.0 Focus on OS/2

Whereas MS-DOS more or less came together, OS/2 was designed from the ground up to take advantage of specific microprocessors and to include features known to be needed in practice. In a real sense, OS/2 has strengths similar to those of Unix. Showing concern for MS-DOS users, OS/2 designers offered an easy upgrade path. Many familiar MS-DOS commands and functions have been kept, and a dual boot mode has been provided to allow MS-DOS users to continue running MS-DOS programs while they gradually migrate their tasks to OS/2.

Anyone who has observed the microcomputer scene for a time will acknowledge the passing parade of hardware and software, in which the new, the bigger, and the better continually replace the old, the not as big, and the not so good. This holds also for operating systems. CP/M, in its prime, literally buried other operating systems with its popularity. Along came MS-DOS, which rather handily "did in" CP/M. One of the principal reasons that MS-DOS so completely overwhelmed CP/M had nothing to do with the technical quality or capability of one system over the other. An important upgrade of CP/M was simply late in coming, whereas MS-DOS, despite its flaws and shortcomings, was ready to market. Not to be overlooked, of course, was IBM's backing and a substantial price difference: $40.00 for MS-DOS as compared to $300.00 for CP/M.

The time will surely come for MS-DOS to fade away. OS/2 or some other operating system will supersede it. Industry observers have conjured different scenarios as to what might happen. The market will shift and realign itself; no doubt about that. But what the share may be for OS/2, Macintosh, Unix, or other contenders remains pure speculation. The falling per megabyte cost of memory will play a leading role in how the next act plays out. It has been announced that Microsoft will subsume MS-DOS into Windows to produce a 32-bit hybrid operating system called Windows NT. The robustness of the competition is certain to win converts from the inherently weak MS-DOS kernel regardless of how well it is bolstered by Windows and other supporting adjuncts.

The great difference between MS-DOS and OS/2 rests heavily on how they came into being, on the levels of chip technology then and now, and on the profound changes that have occurred in user environments. MS-DOS was invented in a partial vacuum with respect to both user experience and DtC technology. There was no microcomputer user population to speak of, and therefore only guesses as to what users' needs might be. Some opinions expressed at that time were quite off target. When the original MS-DOS was being released, Bill Gates, of Microsoft, is reported to have said: "640K ought to be enough for anyone."■

■ The significance of 640K is that 64K was the largest memory requirement at that time, and ten times that amount was thought to be more than sufficient for foreseeable needs.

The scurry to introduce a disk operating system into PCs was IBM's doing. Disk operating systems were already quite common in minicomputers. The key factor that convinced IBM to move into the microcomputer market was the news that Apple's revenues would soon exceed those of IBM's chief mainframe rival, Amdahl. While growth of the microcomputer market was forecast, the phenomenal explosion that did occur was quite unexpected.

The microcomputer world was never to be the same again. Desktop computer usage has spread through every cranny of both business and private activities. User's needs became clearly definable. The design assumptions made for OS/2 were therefore well founded.

- **Graphics** – Where bare text and numbers were once sufficient, graphics had become indespensable.
- **Networking** – Microcomputer to host communications had branched to other microcomputers and even to other hosts.
- **GUI** – The user population included all manner of computer literacy, ignorance, and sophistication, so a hospitable graphical user interface had become supremely important.
- **Multitasking** – Multitasking was recognized as a useful mode of operation. Multiple OS/2 programs can execute using extended memory while an MS-DOS program executes in real memory. Program isolation ensures that if one program crashes, others will continue to run.
- **Memory** – The need for large memory addressing could no longer be neglected. The 80286 provides 16 MB while the 80386 yields a whopping 4 gigabytes. The MS-DOS 640K is truly miniscule in comparison.

The new processors and their descendants open enormous opportunities for enhancing desktop computing in virtually every way. The 80286 and 80386 microprocessors for which OS/2 was designed, in addition to significant new memory management functions, provide for multitasking, program isolation, virtual memory, interprocess communication, networking, and file sharing. Most exciting for system developers are opportunities for multiuser and multimedia applications.

6.1   OS/2 – Beginnings

On 2 April 1987, IBM announced Personal System 2, which superseded the old PC line. The significance of that event was not so much the new line as the new operating system and bus architecture. The operating system was OS/2, a joint development by IBM and Microsoft, made possible by the arrival of the Intel 80286 and 80386 microprocessors. Neither IBM nor Microsoft made any secret of it. OS/2 was the operating system of the future and was intended to replace MS-DOS and PC-DOS. While some interested parties hailed the new operating system as a breakthrough to new and higher levels of desktop computing, others greeted the announcement with skepticism and apprehension. What was to happen to the huge MS-DOS user population and the wealth of versatile and economical MS-DOS software?

Ensuing events, while not contradicting the declaration that OS/2 was in and MS-DOS was out, indefinitely postponed the replacement. Five years later MS-DOS is still alive and well, and OS/2 is still struggling for a secure foothold. The phenomenal success of Microsoft Windows imbued MS-DOS with extraordinary vigor and extended its life beyond anyone's expectation. That success also served to distract significant attention and effort from OS/2, thereby slowing its development.

NOTE

Who Was First?

OS/2 was not the first to:
- **Work around the 640K barrier:** Some applications can switch memory according to the LIM EMS (Lotus/Intel/Microsoft expanded memory specification) and use 32 MB of memory tucked into a hole in the 640K memory map.
- **MS-DOS multitask:** Quarterdeck DESQview and Microsoft Windows can run on MS-DOS and multitask some MS-DOS applications.
- **Switch the 80286 between real and protected modes:** Several MS-DOS extenders are available that switch the 80286 to protected mode so that 16 MB of extended memory can be used.

The concept of OS/2 traces back to the beginning of the multitasking version of MS-DOS, early in 1983. It was called Version 3.0. When the single-tasking MS-DOS update was ready to ship, it acquired the Version 3.0 tag, and the multitasking version, still in the works, became 4.0. But then a special version of MS-DOS was completed. This too was a multitasking system, but only in real mode, which limited system memory to 640K. Customers for this version, which became MS-DOS 4.0, were equipment manufacturers who used it for special purposes.

NOTE

Microsoft DOS 5.x includes a windows-like environment. It features menu options with which users can load up to 14 MS-DOS applications and toggle from one to another. MS-DOS 5.x runs in real mode, so only one application can be executing at one time, similar to what Software Carousel does.

As a consequence, the full-feature multitasking version became known as 5.x (or ADOS, short for Advanced DOS) and alternatively as 286DOS. It was this version of DOS that IBM and Microsoft agreed to develop together. An ideal partnership – wouldn't you say? What could be more fitting than a prestigious hardware manufacturer teaming up with an established software house? The agreement provides for joint ownership, so that each company has full rights to market the product. At this point it became known as CP/DOS, which was changed finally to OS/2.

A serious and potentially unnerving conclusion one could leap to on hearing the OS/2 announcement is: King DOS is dead! Long live King OS! This presumes, of course, that OS and DOS are contenders, only one of which can survive. On reflection, however, other conclusions may be reached. One is that Microsoft and IBM are advancing a more hospitable operating system that would complement PC-DOS rather than destroy it. It must be stressed, however, that enthusiastic spokespersons for OS/2, representing both IBM and Microsoft, initially proclaimed that OS/2 was a replacement for DOS.

What made the announcement even more profound was that it came on the heels of IBM's launching of, perhaps, its most daring and ambitious master plan for future computing – the System Application Architecture. The SAA concept rests on four principles: 1) common user access, 2) common programming interface, 3) common communications support, and 4) common applications. Who could quarrel with such noble vision? Moreover, Microsoft and IBM were committed to it, and some felt the concept could hardly rest in stronger hands.

In view of the accelerating drift from centralized computing to distributed processing and more recently to cooperative processing, which irrevocably moved desktop computing to center stage in the business world, SAA made a great deal of sense. Information systems managers greeted the idea warmly. They saw SAA as a forerunner of a global system that would be coherent and hospitable across many dimensions. With passing time, however, the progress toward realization of SAA goals has been disappointingly slow. Some observers are losing heart. Some even predict that instead of MS-DOS, OS/2 might fail and die.

Headlined repeatedly in computing trade journals and weeklies was concern for OS/2's well-being, based largely on the perception that the phenomenal success of Windows was prompting Microsoft to rethink its marketing strategy. Users, software developers, commentators, and others debated publicly and took sides for or against this or that aspect of OS/2. Opinion fed by speculation resolved into a widely held belief that Microsoft was abandoning its commitments to OS/2 in order to cash in on Windows.

In an effort to set the record straight, IBM with Microsoft's concurrence issued a news release on 17 September 1990 in White Plains, New York, which reads in part:

> "Today's announcement clarifies the roles of both companies [IBM and Microsoft] toward providing a range of operating platforms to meet the varied requirements of desktop customers," said James A. Cannavino, IBM Vice President and General Manager, Personal Systems. "By focusing IBM's development efforts in this manner, we are better able to achieve this goal."
>
> "In order to improve the efficiency of development efforts, IBM will have the primary role for developing 16-bit and 32-bit OS/2, with Microsoft making development contributions. Microsoft continues to develop Windows and will be the primary developer for DOS. Both companies intend to contribute to the development of a 32-bit version of OS/2 that is portable to other computer instruction sets, such as RISC (Reduced Instruction Set Computing). Microsoft will have the primary role of developing this portable version, with IBM making development contributions. All of these products will be cross-licensed by both companies."
>
> "IBM also reaffirmed its intention to reduce the entry requirements for OS/2 to 2 MB, to converge LAN Manager and LAN Server and to make the functions of OS/2 EE and LAN server available to all IBM and OEM OS/2 users. In addition, IBM will begin delivering limited shipments of a 32-bit version of OS/2 to selected accounts in 1990, and the product will be generally available in 1991."

The news release continues with the reiteration that DOS remains a significant platform for entry level systems; Windows serves as a graphical solution for DOS users; and OS/2 is an advanced function operating system with full multitasking in a graphical environment that is ideal for mission critical, line-of-business applications that rely on servers.

Microsoft's Chairman and CEO Bill Gates issued a statement of affirmation, which reads in part:

"We are excited about IBM's announcement today reaffirming our relationship and outlining the expansion of our cross-license agreement for present and future versions of DOS, Windows and OS/2."

"Together, IBM and Microsoft will provide a family of PC operating systems that is compatible and scalable from entry level PCs to high-end, advanced PC platforms. . ."

The pronouncements of renewed commitment to OS/2 by both IBM and Microsoft failed to quell the rumors and speculation. In fact, the *Wall Street Journal* flatly reported on 28 January 1991 that *"Microsoft . . . is dropping OS/2, a software program that four years ago it declared would replace DOS as the system that controls the basic operations of the personal computer."*

An excited call to Microsoft in Redmond, Washington, brought the response that the *Wall Street Journal* was grossly mistaken and that Microsoft was *not* withdrawing support from OS/2. Nevertheless, the OS/2 story continued to experience strange twists and was far from over. Almost every computer weekly of that period carried one or more "gloom and doom" stories on OS/2.

Meanwhile OS/2, while struggling, is surviving, gradually acquired more applications software and attracted more customers. A Forrester Research, Inc., forecast in late 1990 indicated that OS/2 would pass DOS in sales in the U.S. by 1993, although both DOS and Windows sales would remain strong.

Despite the assurances by IBM and Microsoft that all is well in their relationship, there is unquestionably a business and marketing realignment on both sides. Microsoft is looking forward to an advanced 32-bit operating system in a networked environment. In line with this effort it is courting Digital Equipment Corporation and Compaq as partners. IBM, on the other hand, seems to be interested in attracting software developers to stand in for Microsoft. Apple Computer seems willing to fill the void.

OS/2 Family Tree

The term *family* is appropriately descriptive of OS/2 and the PS/2 line of IBM computers because they represent the second generation of microcomputers, the first being the DOS-based PCs.

OS/2 comes in three versions, with two basic editions of Version 1. The two editions are called Standard and Extended. Microsoft licenses OS/2 Standard Edition to manufacturers, providing them with OEM binary adaptation kits that they use to customize OS/2 for their hardware designs. The Extended Edition is licensed by IBM. It has unique components that have been developed by IBM outside the IBM/Microsoft Joint Development Agreement.

Extended Edition features include database support for SQL (Structured Query Language) and DB2 (Data Base 2). Connectivity features include network support for IBM mainframes and minicomputers. Extended Edition is thus aimed at intensively IBM-oriented environments. OS/2 and Presentation Manager, its graphical user interface, both conform to the IBM Systems Applications Architecture (SAA), IBM's concept of every worker and workstation linked directly to every other worker and workstation in an organization regardless of hardware mix.

OS/2 Release 1 Standard Edition SE

Standard Edition 1.0, the first release of OS/2, is the operating system kernel. It displays a simple menu and a Program Selector, and it responds to function keys. As the kernel, it supports essential system functions such as file I/O, memory management, multitasking, interprocess communication, character video output, and both keyboard and mouse input. A cache is included for AT-compatibles and several hard disk partition schemes are supported, as are third party graphics and communications drivers.

- *8088* – OS/2 will not operate on 8088-based (XT-style) MS-DOS computers.

- *80286/80386* – Full protected mode support using 16 MB extended memory. A single MS-DOS program can execute in a limited amount (around 500K) of real memory, while software written for OS/2 Version 1.x can multitask in extended memory. Paged virtual memory up to 1 gigabyte is supported to supplement executable memory; the most active pages being stored in RAM. A 16:16 segmentation scheme severely limits individual program's execution flexibility compared to the full 32-bit capability of Version 2.x.

Version 1.1 replaces the Program Selector with Presentation Manager, a graphical user interface that resembles Windows 2.0. PM conforms to the common user access principle of IBM's SAA. PM is an important feature of OS/2, and the success of the operating system depends a great deal on how users respond to its windowing capabilities. Multilayered windows are essential for multitasking.

In addition to shared memory, system semaphores, and threads, Version 1.1 has Unix-style pipes, a PM clipboard, and a Dynamic Data Exchange (DDE) feature. Pipes are important communications paths over LANs, but they are used also between programs running on the same machine. The clipboard is used to cut matter from one program and paste it into another. The DDE allows programs to request data from other programs and receive responses transparently.

A full-screen editor is provided that is superior to EDLIN, and can be used to create and edit ASCII format files as well as system files and programs. An excellent HELP system is included along with a tutorial.

One drawback of SE Version 1.2 is that it is memory hungry. It requires 12 MB of disk space if all features are installed. However, it is capable of preemptive multitasking, has a new Desktop Manager, and an improved File Manager.

The Desktop Manager replaces the earlier Task Manager and Start Programs windows. Programs are listed in groups in the Desktop Manager window. The groups can be opened on startup or opened by the user. Programs can be moved from one group to another simply by pointing, dragging, and clicking with a mouse.

An interesting and useful feature is an online reference system that answers questions about commands, formats, and parameters. The meanings of error messages and possible corrective responses are displayed on the screen. IBM's Structured Query Language is supported, giving the system a relational database capability.

A new SAA Dialog Manager that conforms to the Common User Access principles of SAA is incorporated as a productivity tool for user-developed applications. Also incorporated are several printer drivers.

SE Version 1.3 is a further improvement over 1.1 and 1.2. It is both smaller and faster. It can run two OS/2 and one MS-DOS application simultaneously on a 2 MB machine. But while a minimum of 2 MB of memory is required, 4 MB are recommended. EE 1.3, meanwhile, needs at least 3 MB.

For the price, there is power to be had. Up to 27 hard drives may be linked. New features include a built-in Adobe Type Manager and enhanced drivers for the Hewlett-Packard LaserJet, Epson, PostScript, and IBM LaserPrinter printers. A new LAN server is provided for Windows 3.0 clients.

By incorporating SAA features and Common User Access, EE Version 1.3 ensures a company-wide interface and platform for shared DtC/mainframe applications. Running multiple MS-DOS applications concurrently will become feasible on the 32-bit OS/2 Version 2.0, if and when it is released.

OS/2 Release 1 Extended Edition (EE)

EE Version 1 contains SE features plus components added by IBM, including a Communications Manager and Database Manager in Version 1.0. Version 1.1 includes several enhancements, as does 1.2. The latter, in particular, has improved database management features and LAN enhancements. LAN support for Remote Data Services, a new SNA gateway, asynchronous protocols, and Ethernet support have been added. While IBM is reluctant to support Windows, it has included client support for Windows 3.0 in IBM's LAN Server in OS/2 Version 1.3. Support has been added also for Cobol/2, Pascal/2, and Fortran/2, as well as interfaces for a Query Manager and business graphics.

The procedures language REXX, which is included in the Standard Edition, appears also in the Extended Edition, as does Easel, a full-featured PM application. Easel is a high-level language that is used to develop PM applications without requiring the developer to know the details of PM primitives and device-level code.

- 8088 – Not supported.
- 80286 – Not supported.
- 80386 – A 32-bit addressing mode of the 80386 is supported.

A virtual 8086 mode similar to that found in Windows enhanced memory mode can support multiple MS-DOS programs, each having a complete 600K 8086 virtual CPU. Since each MS-DOS program is completely encapsulated, having its own 8086, an errant program cannot hurt the rest of the system, even when its 8086 virtual CPU is terminated.

Both versions support any given program executing threads. Software processes can spawn children; and those children can spawn grandchildren and so on. Therefore a complex executing hierarchy can be produced by a single OS/2 program.

Rather than the 16:16 arrangement – 16 bits of segment and 16 bits of offset – to attain a physical 32-bit address, OS/2 uses what is called a flat addressing mode. Offsets are now 32 bits wide and occupy a full 32-bit address range. This permits compilers and applications programs to directly support 1 gigabyte program sizes and eliminates the complex process of programmers having to use segmentation. Internally, OS/2 manages the large programs by paged virtual memory. This is the ultimate form of virtual memory.

Version 1.3 of the Extended Edition has a new LAN server option; implements corporate-wide systems application architecture with its Common User Interface;

runs on more, different microcomputers than version 1.2; includes enhanced driver support for Hewlett-Packard LaserJet, Epson, PostScript, and IBM LaserPrinter; has built-in Adobe Type Manager with scalable PostScript fonts, and has a significantly improved Memory Manager.

OS/2 Version 2 Highlights

IBM has assumed the principal responsibility for the 32-bit OS/2 Version 2.0. This version is highly modular, with such functions as file management, graphical user interface, and network connections snapping into place as needed. A binary compatibility layer allows Windows applications to run as is under OS/2. The system is portable, with multithreading and multitasking features contained in the kernel. Developers writing software for the workstation market, SAS Institute, Inc., for example, say they prefer writing for OS/2 Version 2.0 and its flat memory model. As we shall see, this is probably a wise position to take under existing circumstances.

An IBM spokesman is quoted as introducing OS/2 Version 2.0 as "a better Windows than Windows, a better DOS than DOS, and a better OS/2 than OS/2." At an unveiling early in 1991, OS/2 running on an Intel 80386-based machine with 2 MB of memory ran an OS/2 and a DOS application simultaneously. On a 386-based PS/2 Model 70 with 6 MB of memory it executed Windows applications faster than the same machine booted with a native version of Windows 3.0.

OS/2 Version 3 Highlights

Version 3.0 of OS/2 is a full 32-bit operating system intended for 80386, 80386sx, and 80486 microprocessors. Microsoft is concentrating on this version, having relinquished its interest in OS/2 Version 2.0 entirely to IBM. Native support is included for both Windows and Presentation Manager. Testers have been quite pleased that OS/2 and MS-DOS applications run easily side-by-side. Windows-compatible applications also run successfully.

Microsoft has concentrated effort to make OS/2 3.0 portable across different CPUs and platforms; e.g., Intel's 80860 RISC CPU, IBM's RS-6000 RISC-based DtC, and Sun's RISC-based SPARC DtC. Several successful tests have been run on different processors. Microsoft appears to be aiming also at a 32-bit Windows package based on a kernel referred to as *New Technology*, or NT, with multitasking and multithreading capabilities.

While shortening its overall committment to OS/2, Microsoft continues to invest selectively in the operating system. It is concentrating effort in LAN Manager and SQL Server, both of which depend on OS/2. Microsoft Word for OS/2 is also on its way.

DOS Compatibility Mode

The DOS compatibility mode rightly belongs to the beginnings of the OS/2 story. It is a thoughtful convenience provided by IBM and Microsoft for DOS users. While it offers no advantage for running DOS programs, it provides a transition for DOS users who are moving on to OS/2. Only external programs run under both DOS and OS/2 in the dual mode. Except for these, DOS programs will not run in OS/2 mode and OS/2 programs will not run in DOS mode.

OS/2 has two command processors: one for itself, the OS/2 mode, and one for DOS, the real mode. At one end, then, OS/2 interfaces with DOS; at the other, following IBM's commitment to upward compatibility through SAA, OS/2 paves the compatibility road from DOS to workstations to minicomputers and even to mainframes. A well-behaved SAA program should be able to run on all platforms – a worthy goal for any operating system.

The DOS mode in OS/2 is essentially a DOS 3.3 emulator, so most programs that run on 3.3 will run in DOS compatibility mode. DOS programs that cannot handle interruptions during execution will *not* run without some reprogramming. Compatible DOS programs run because OS/2 can switch the 80286 microprocesor to 8086 real mode that DOS uses. OS/2, meanwhile, does not have the familiar DOS memory limitation of 640K. Instead, it can use up to 16 MB, and if more is needed, the Memory Manager can swap inactive segments to disk. Data too can be stored temporarily in cache.

When an OS/2 system is booted, DOS-mode memory is reserved and the DOS command processor is loaded. DOS mode starts when a DOS command is issued. A DOS program runs only when it is in the foreground. When a switch is made to OS/2 mode, the DOS session is suspended. In Version 2.0, however, there is a multiple virtual DOS mode in which DOS and OS/2 can run concurrently, with up to 16 DOS sessions.

The DOS mode allows those familiar with DOS to continue with it, initiating work or migrating work to OS/2 at leisure and only if OS/2 has appropriate software, capacity, and features for the task and can handle the work better.

6.2   OS/2 Components

The principal components of OS/2 are:

- The Kernel
- Memory Manager
- File Manager
- Database Manager
- Communications Manager
- Presentation Manager

Such a list of components infers a modular construction to the system, and that inference is correct.

Memory Manager

OS/2 can have up to 16 MB of physical memory and up to 1 gigabyte of virtual memory. The layout of the OS/2 memory map is shown in Figure 74. Memory is controlled by two tables: the local descriptor table (LDT) that holds descriptions of the memory space of the current task and the global descriptor table (GDT) that holds descriptions of memory space for all tasks in the system. These two tables are used to allocate memory, to implement memory protection, and to sense whether a task is inside or outside the memory space.

Under OS/2 a program must request memory allocation in advance. Each memory request made by a program must reference a segment selector, which in turn references the GDT or the LDT. In order for OS/2 or a program to reference a memory location, that location must be present as a description in one of the memory tables.

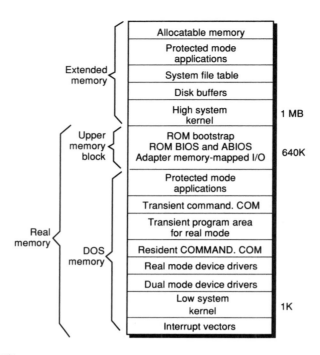

Figure 74. OS/2 memory map: Notice the difference from the memory maps presented for MS-DOS. There is increased use of real memory by the OS and applications programs using real and protected memory.

Memory segments may be fixed, as for the kernel, data, and interrupt time code for device drivers; discardable, which means that a segment does not have to be backed up if swapped out; or marked for loading on demand. Segment swapping can be disabled or determined by *least recently used* or *least frequently used* algorithms. OS/2 will compress scattered space into contiguous free space, if necessary.

OS/2 provides memory management automatically and transparently, allowing for a wide diversity of system calls by applications. Services are available for allocating and freeing segments, including those over 64K, subdividing segments into blocks, sharing segments among processes, and creating segments to be written and executed.

Protection mechanisms are included that isolate tasks from each other in separate address spaces, and within tasks strict rules are enforced between code and data segments at different privilege levels.

File Manager

The File Manager, a Presentation Manager application, allows users to copy and move files. Using a mouse, a click on a file and then on a target directory moves the file. The process is similar to that on a Macintosh.

Files and subdirectories can be organized and sorted in various ways. Data files and executable programs can be associated so that loading one will automatically load the other.

The OS/2 File Manager is compatible with DOS. Hard disks and floppies formatted on one can be read by the other. There is no longer a 32 MB partition limit; under OS/2 partitions can hold multiple files up to 314 MB.

Database Manager

The Database Manager (DBM) can import spreadsheet data and information from many other sources, process them, and display them in many different forms. As it stands, the Database Manager may be useful to DB2 developers, who can write their applications on a PC and upload the results to an IBM mainframe. But when a network server environment is established, the Database Manager becomes truly important.

Access to databases is controlled by a database administrator by means of the User Profile Management System that defines each user's access rights and privileges. Authorization and privilege for reading, writing, and altering database data is recorded in a catalog and maintained by the Database Manager, which checks all transactions by user's ID against the authorization catalog.

A Query Manager has been added. It is a tool that provides quick-and-easy access to the powerful OS/2 user functions that are in keeping with SAA.

Communication and Networking

According to IBM's SAA concept, every user should be connected to every other user in a system. This is another way of saying that every user in an organization should have access to all information and resources needed to do the job. By the same token, the results of that job must be deposited in the system for use by others. In these terms, networking becomes a crucial component.

In a large organization today, one almost inevitably finds a mix of platforms and operating systems, which turns networking into a complex problem. But, as demonstrated by ARPANET, dissimilar computers with different operating systems can be interconnected and can communicate. IBM is relying more and more on Novell's NetWare for its PC networking system.

- *Communications and connectivity* – Some enterprises mandate the system that is to be used corporation-wide, although most enterprises allow local units to select and acquire their own computing equipment. In both cases communications and connectivity issues are critical for multiple workstations to share data and talk to each other and a mainframe. In a heterogeneous workplace, the communications problem can become complicated because of the mix of equipment that must interface when carrying out corporate-wide tasks.

  In one interconnectivity solution, the Macintosh Classic computer equipped with Apple SuperDrive reads and writes to and from PC-DOS, OS/2, and ProDOS files.

- *Sharing resources* – The benefit of resource sharing is moving the drive toward good networking. A feature that is especially appealing to users is the possibility of regaining some mainframe convenience. A program can be installed on the network and downloaded as needed to a workstation. The system administrator then has the responsibility for maintenance and installing upgrades as they become available.

- *Networking* – As murky as the PM/Windows enigma is the one surrounding OS/2's LAN Manager. The outcome rests squarely on IBM's degree of commitment. It appears that some LAN Manager functions are slated to move to OS/2, some to Windows, and some to DOS, resulting in a distributed model. Meanwhile IBM opened the Systems Network Architecture door to non-IBM LANS and computers. IBM's Advanced Peer-to-Peer Network scheme for OS/2 allows direct communication among all members of a network and any device on the network to be configured as a node. Novell and Apple both announced that they would support IBM's APPN, thus allowing Mac and other users access to SNA resources and to routing and directory services. On the other hand, developers will be able to write SNA applications with Mac interfaces and integrate AppleTalk into SNA networks.

Presentation Manager (PM)

Presentation Manager is OS/2's graphical user interface. It features windowing, pull-down and pop-up menus, and scroll bars and works best with a mouse but can be fully controlled from the keyboard. The four direction keys and the enter key on the keyboard may be used in lieu of a mouse.

Presentation Manager has an Application Program Interface. The PM API is big and takes time to learn. It has approximately 500 function calls; about half go to the Graphics Programming Interface and half go to the windowing and user interface component. There is a friendly fall-back position: a programmer can accept default action without knowing all of the API calls. How well the applications are written will determine how Presentation Manager will appear and appeal to users. Applications can be written in COBOL and Smalltalk as well as in C and Assembler.

PM works a lot like Windows 2.0, but where Windows runs on top of MS-DOS, PM is integrated into the OS/2 system. Each running program in a PM session occupies its own window, and each window can be positioned individually and zoomed up and down in size. A window typically has a title bar across the top and below it a menu bar from which options may be selected either by mouse or keyboard keys. The options bring down other menus, some of which invoke dialog boxes with fill-ins and buttons that represent program commands.

6.3   Software Development

One of the most strident complaints against OS/2 by industry critics is that it has no applications software. This is far from true. Up to a thousand OS/2 software programs are already on the market and over 2300 companies have enrolled in the IBM Developer Assistance Program. As OS/2 develops through its succeeding versions, it becomes richer in SAA content.

The Programmer's Toolkit being offered by IBM and the OS/2 PM Toolkit from Microsoft are helping applications developers write programs that conform to SAA, thereby ensuring vertical compatibility across many levels of computing hardware. IBM has an active, ongoing program for providing programming tools and information to encourage OS/2 software development. IBM is working also with firms that want to market other tools and languages for more advanced applications development.

Only a sampling of software is presented here in various applications areas simply to show that software is becoming available across the board. Any list of products made one day invariably becomes obsolete the next. While a few may fall by the wayside, many more will be added.

- *Business-ware* – Stone and Webster Engineering of Boston has come out with Production Scheduling Advisor, a production scheduling and inventory management system for Presentation Manager. The package combines graphics, a spreadsheet, an expert system, and linear programming. Project WorkBench Advisor is another product with an OS/2 version.

Lotus' Notes, a workgroup information management product, supports OS/2 1.2 Extended Edition.

- **CAD** – AutoCAD, a computer-aided design package, offers a separate OS/2 version. Among related packages is Micrografx Designer for OS/2, which also runs under Presentation Manager.

- **CASE tools** – Computer-aided software engineering (CASE) technology is being encouraged by IBM for application to OS/2 software. Whereas most CASE activity has focused on the mini-to-mainframe area, more and more attention lately has shifted toward microcomputers. OS/2 is an attractive target because of its systems perspectives.

    CASE:W, from CaseWorks of Atlanta, prototypes and generates intermediate APP files that are transportable to OS/2 with CASE:PM.

- **Communications** – Novell's NetWare Requester runs on OS/2, beginning with Version 1.2. Corporate Microsystems provides MLINK Runtime and MLINK Developer for asynchronous communications, crosslinking between DOS, Unix, Xenix, OS/2, and Mac platforms.

    AppleTalk protocols are by design independent of workstations and operating systems, so MS-DOS, OS/2, and Macintosh DtCs can talk to each other. IBM's System Network Architecture integrates DtC and mainframe networks. Apple is participating in IBM's Advanced Program-to-Program Communications, including LU 6.2 and PU 2.1 protocols, that allow DtCs to conduct task-to-task communications with other processors.

- **Databases** – Paradox for OS/2 from Borland has good database query tools and can retrieve data from an SQL source. It can also generate forms, graphics, tables, and reports. Among others is R:BASE for OS/2, a programmable relational database management system, and SideKick from Borland International, which is a PM product. Q&A, from Symantec, creates databases for mailings, invoicing, customer tracking, inventory, and expense reports. Microrim, Oracle, dBASE, and Quattro are other examples.

- **Desktop publishing** – Ventura Publisher Gold Series, from Xerox, comes in an OS/2 version as does Aldus PageMaker. PageMaker 3.0 for OS/2 was first shipped in late summer of 1989. Using preemptive multitasking, PageMaker responds smoothly to the user while performing background activities. When loading text and graphics, the user does not have to wait until loading completes, as must be done in the Windows version. The user can start working on a file as soon as a page becomes available.

- **Spreadsheets** – Microsoft has itself made a significant upgrade of its Excel spreadsheet with a version for OS/2. Lotus 1-2-3/G is following suit. Wingz, a spreadsheet, database, and graphics package offers a Presentation Manager version. A nice feature that is appearing in spreadsheets is the ability to group them into sets, such that data changes on one are reflected in all members of the set.

- **Graphics** – Freelance Graphics now comes with an OS/2 graphical user interface and full charting and presentation capabilities, clip art, drawing tools, and a text editor with a spelling checker. Harvard Graphics supports OS/2 and Presentation Manager.

- **Word processors** – WordPerfect began marketing an interim version of its word processor for OS/2 almost two years ago. WordPerfect 5.0 for OS/2 looks and feels very much like the MS-DOS version. It supports over 400 printers. It uses threads to prepare documents for printing in the background. An interesting difference between the MS-DOS and OS/2 versions is that the hyphenation module is built in to the OS/2 version, whereas it is a separate add-on in the MS-DOS version.

  The general markup language TextWrite is available on both the Standard and Extended Editions of OS/2. Other examples are MultiMate, DisplayWrite, and Wordstar.

  Sage Software recently announced a mouse-controlled, programmable Sage Professional Editor that runs under MS-DOS, OS/2, and in dual mode; all versions are packaged in one box.

New software packages for OS/2 are appearing regularly so that it's only a matter of time before users will be able to find and run almost any application they wish on an OS/2 computer.

6.4 OS/2 in Summary

While the debate over OS/2 vs. DOS is far from settled, several issues have become clear. OS/2 and MS-DOS are not mortal foes, only one of which can survive. Despite dire predictions to the contrary, each has a secure place in the microcomputing world. DOS with Windows or Windows with DOS can enjoy an indefinite life expectancy in the realms of small standalone DtC applications. DOS users in such environments may never need to change. OS/2 occupies a comfortable and natural position in enterprise computing environments: in organizations that have large scale tasks and who must build their own business-critical applications. Preemptive multitasking, large memory space, comprehensive interprocess communications, and excellent security are a few of the ideal qualifications that information systems managers require for systems in which quantities of information and data are moved back and forth repeatedly over networks.

OS/2 and DOS (or whatever DOS evolves into) will coexist virtually everywhere. Individuals running independent tasks will use DOS with Windows, while those running large scale interdependent organizational tasks will use OS/2. Few companies today, if any, are totally committed to a single brand of micocomputer. Walk across any company floor or through any corporate hall and you are likely to see IBMs and compatibles, Macintoshes, Sun and Apollo workstations, and more. With the advent of open systems, individual users may freely choose any DtC they wish without excluding themselves from their microcomputing community. This also means that DOS, OS/2, Unix, and Apple System 7 may converse freely whenever they need to talk to one another.

> **NOTE**
>
> People who are running applications successfully on DOS with Windows and have no need for specific OS/2, Unix, or Macintosh features can stay with DOS without penalty.

The reality of MS-DOS limitations cannot be ignored. With per-bit memory costs declining and ever more powerful microprocessors becoming available, MS-DOS will need to completely grow up or it will eventually go the way of black and white film and television receivers. They're around, but not nearly as universal as they once were.

Many organizations are currently evaluating their systems and options, wondering whether to hold their MS-DOS cards or bet on OS/2. There seems to be a general feeling held by some systems managers that OS/2 is yet unproved and lacks applications software. So an early committment to OS/2 is risky.

User Factors

Since OS/2 is intended to be the upgrade path for DOS users, we can speculate a bit about what DOS users might do. For the sake of discussion, the DOS user population can be divided into three camps. One we can call the corporate group, another the intermediate group, and the third made up of independents.

Many standalone DtC users are inextricably committed to DOS, as they should be. They largely work alone; they do not need to be interconnected to other DtCs. Such users have tailored their computers to fit the applications they are running and little more is required. They are comfortable with DOS and the enhancements and extensions that it offers. As long as the DOS installed user base remains anywhere near its present size, it will attract software developers who will offer upgrades of existing software and endeavor to create new applications. Whatever this software might be, and there will continue to be a lot of it, it will run on DOS machines and millions of DOS users will be happy. Since they will have no incentive to switch to OS/2, they will remain bound to DOS. This group probably includes the majority of private DOS computer users.

Some characteristics of those who will stay with MS-DOS:

- Those who enjoy reveling in lots of different software.
- Users who do not run large applications and run only one application at a time. Among these are individuals who run successful applications, relying on the maturity and stability of MS-DOS and available software. With a familiar system that performs as expected, why change?
- Those who are largely or completely independent of other users and do not need network communications.
- Those who may be interested in OS/2 but who do not have hardware that will support it and can't afford to upgrade. OS/2 needs at least an 80286 microprocessor, and an 80386 is highly recommended.
- DtC users who have OS/2-compatible hardware but do not yet see appropriate software on the OS/2 market. These users will switch only when particularly attractive software appears that requires OS/2 capabilities.

The intermediate group is populated by DOS-based users who have industrial strength applications to run. This group may elect to suffer temporarily, to continue with DOS, using products like DESQview and QEMM if need be to give them power and flexibility, for example, for CAD/CAM applications. They will, however, watch developments on the OS/2 front. Just as soon as the right mix of products becomes available, they will seriously consider switching to OS/2. The intermediate group is particularly interested in the newer Windows NT system.

Among the corporate group are those running large programs or who have special needs that do not run smoothly in DOS. Members of this group will seriously consider changing. The choice need not be OS/2; it could be Unix or AIX or Windows NT. Remember that the latter systems have X Windows. OS/2 will be a good choice for custom applications in which mainframe processing has to be moved to DtCs and through networks.

Still other computer users may opt for OS/2 because of corporate decisions or because OS/2 either provides particular features now, or is expected to in the near future. Among these are forward-looking planners who see SAA carrying their applications comfortably to the turn of the century.

Some characteristics of the group that will switch to OS/2:

- **High rollers** – People unconstrained or not disuaded by affordability concerns. OS/2 needs a respectable amount of memory and hard drive capacity to start, whereas DOS can get by, at least initially, with much less, even with Windows.
- **Multitaskers** – Anyone running applications that require frequent switching between two or more programs or who need to move quantities of data and send it to high-resolution output devices.
- **Platform crossers** – Those whose work takes them from one platform to another or involves different computing levels, e.g., from DtCs to workstations to minicomputers to mainframes and back, if and when OS/2 runs on these and other computers.
- **Networkers** – Users interconnected with departmental databases and corporate management information systems who need frequent or continuous communication with other desktop computers and workstations and who need ready access to mainframe databases.

The reality of modern business computing is that multiple diverse platforms will be required, each type optimized for specialized task areas. The toughest job that managers face is finding ways for the diversified components to coexist and function productively in complex interrelated systems.

Evolutionary Trends

OS/2, its predecessor, or its descendant may win out as the IBM standard operating system through the turn of the century. The need for such a system is strong and IBM's commitment to it is great. The future of OS/2 appears assured. The vast army of DOS users, on the other hand, will ensure the longevity of DOS. A probable breakdown of the OS/2 and DOS market could very well be this:

- **Market share** – In terms of units sold, the largest share of the DOS/Windows market will be at mid-level to low- and entry-level desktop computing, in the price range of two to five thousand dollars.
- **Windowing availability** – Windows-like applications will be virtually universal on DtCs at all levels, including workstations. MS-Windows will prevail at the lower end.
- **OS/2 uses** – OS/2 will prevail at the workstation level, microcomputers ranging from about 8 to 12 thousand dollars. In effect, OS/2 belongs to the high end of desktop computing largely because of its SAA features.
- **OS/2 needs** – OS/2 supplemented with a robust Presentation Manager will be the operating system of choice for organizations with hybrid needs; e.g., entities that have heavy duty business needs *and* industrial strength technical applications *and* connectivity requirements.
- **OS/2 attraction** – Conversion to OS/2 will increase when software availability for OS/2 reaches some critical mass, and memory cost drops to some affordability level.

The evolution of the OS/2 operating system is prodded by and is in step with the DtC evolution in the workplace. In large organizations there is a local aspect to that evolution and a distributed one. Locally there is a stong need to customize DtC hardware and software to suit particular tasks or functions. While customization favors productivity and innovation, it inevitably results in a mix of DtC configurations and produces a wonderous menagerie of equipment.

Having opened the door to efficiency and productivity, it must not be closed on the other half of the problem. At least some local organizational units must mesh with larger organizational concerns. There must be a linkage to corporate intelligence so that necessary information can be shared in a timely manner. So while it is nice to have custom tools to do specific tasks locally, organizationally the array of tools may look hodge-podge. This is the problem addressed by the open systems concept in general and specifically by IBM's System Application Architecture, which seeks to make cross-platform connectivity universal. Different computers with different operating systems working together and allowing users to run programs locally or remotely, watching the results on their own screens is the ultimate goal.

New technology will undoubtedly lead also to multimedia systems that merge sight and sound and touch in synergistic ways we can only imagine. Whether such advances become predominantly local, predominantly distributed, or equally both is a soon-to-be answered question. Already CD-ROM applications are appearing that are destined to play important roles in future DtC scenarios. Supplemented by local and remote networked resources, DtCs are becoming indispensable personalized information centers. However the details eventually play out, desktop computing is undergoing a growth spurt and is evolving into a higher technological form.

7.0   Focus on Apple

- System 7 Features
- Memory
- File Management
- Desktop Features
- Resource Sharing
- Networking
- Multitasking

Advanced DOS and Windows users, especially those with high-end applications, will need to pay greater attention to events transpiring in the Apple Macintosh world. No longer can that microcomputing camp be ignored by Apple outsiders. Strong indications have appeared that Apple is shifting more of its efforts to software and systems development, away from hardware. As a consequence, Apple and Microsoft are suddenly formidable head-to-head competitors. By the same token, Apple and IBM now have synergistic interests, and they are beginning to talk about them.

Apple operating systems are based on Motorola 68xxx microprocessors. System 7 is based on the Motorola 68030 chip. Microcomputer users owe a great debt to Xerox and Apple for the graphical user interface, to Xerox for the concept and to Apple for making it available on a commercial scale. As good as the Apple Macintosh GUI was when it was first introduced in 1984, it became even better when System 7 hit the market in May of 1991. System 7 deserves a look.

7.1   Apple System 7 Features

Memory

Macs equipped with 32-bit ROMs can support up to 128 MB of RAM and virtual memory. The Macintosh IIfx, IIci, and IIsi can address as much as 4 gigabytes of RAM or can use virtual memory if actual memory is not available. Older Macs are limited to 8 MB. The MultiFinder and disk cache are not options; they come with the system. If you did not use MultiFinder with your System 6, you will probably need more memory when you upgrade to System 7.

Cache Memory

The amount of disk cache and virtual memory are selectable on the control panel. Minimum cache is 16K and default is 128K; it cannot be turned off.

Virtual Memory

To use virtual memory you need a 68030 microprocessor or a 68020 microprocessor with a Page Memory Unit. The amount of RAM selected should be less than total system RAM. To use virtual memory, you have to set up a partition on the hard disk, the size of which must be equal to system RAM plus the virtual memory selected.

Since the use of disk space as RAM is not as fast as physical RAM, it is probably a good idea to deactivate virtual memory unless you need it. System 7 supports

32-bit addressing on Mac IIci, IIsi, and IIfx, so users can have up to 128 MB of physical RAM to run applications.

Memory Allocation

An About This Macintosh option selectable from the Apple menu displays a graphic representation of your memory allocations.

File Management

MultiFinder and Outline

MultiFinder searches for files throughout the system and Outline displays files and folders in a hierarchical arrangement. The Find command searches for files not only by name but also by size, type, label, or by date of creation or modification.

The display of items in the Finder is governed by the View control panel. Icons can be arranged in rows or in stairstep fashion. View can also arrange listings in predetermined hierarchical order.

Make Alias Feature

A potentially very useful feature in System 7 allows you to assign a nickname, or alias, to a file and thereby make that file available to workstations on a network. For example, a hard disk on a network can be given an alias, identified by an appropriate icon, and the alias can then be used to access the original hard drive from any workstation on the network.

> **NOTE**
>
> The term *aliasing* used in System 7 literature to mean nicknaming of files should not be confused with the use of the same term to refer to the jaggedness of sloping lines on display terminals.

Balloon Help and Help Menu

One of the more imaginative features of System 7 is its context-sensitive Balloon Help. Point to any item on the screen and a cartoon balloon appears with a brief description of the item. Moreover, the content of the balloon changes when conditions change.

In addition to the balloons there is a pull-down help menu that Apple newcomers will find particularly useful. Help is available within System 7 applications without having to leave them.

Type Management and Desktop Publishing Features

System 7 eliminates the jaggedness of on-screen characters. Apple's TrueType scalable type technology comes with the operating system. TrueType is Apple's font rendering software. In addition, PostScript, bit-mapped fonts, and Adobe Type Manager are supported, and you can mix fonts in the same document.

Many System 7 features are particularly suited to desktop publishing. Among them are a word processor for generating and editing text, a drawing program for making sketches, a paint program, a process for retouching scanned photographic images, and a page layout program that puts the different text and graphics objects together.

Using the desktop publishing features, including AppleEvents and Publish and Subscribe, described later, one can produce various kinds of compound documents. Complex documents and large ones are best handled with high-end Macintoshes. Users of low-end Macintoshes will suffer noticeable sluggishness.

Desktop Accessories

Desktop accessories of System 7 include a notepad, scrapbook, calculator, and alarm clock.

7.2   Inside Apple System 7

According to John Scully, CEO of Apple Computer Inc., System 7 is the most tested product ever introduced by Apple. Care has been taken to integrate all of its parts neatly into the whole. It is not at all the mixed bag, referring to DOS and Windows, no doubt, that exists in other environments.

Proud as Apple can be of the polish it has put on the Macintosh and System 7, historically the company's view has been restricted to desktops; it has lacked a solid mainframe connection. With the emergence of enterprise computing, in which custom productivity applications are handled by DtCs while corporate data are still processed by mainframes, Apple needs to shuck its proprietary hoopskirts if it hopes to break into the mainstream of the industry.

Apple is doing just that. With System 7, Apple is becoming a worthy contender in the client/server marketplace. It has begun to license some of its advanced technology to developers and is actively exploring partnership possibilities in certain market areas.

File, Data, and Resource Sharing

The System 7 Sharing Setup panel of displays options for file sharing and option linking. Simply selecting and clicking on the AppleShare icon on the Chooser display and logging on connects the Mac to System 7 Interapplication Communications. With several Macs interconnected, dynamic links are created for passing data between them.

Publish and Subscribe

Publish and Subscribe works only for applications that have been written for it. Custom graphics with the latest data can be imported and merged into reports because files linked in applications that include the Publish and Subscribe feature are updated automatically.

Changes to an original document are automatically inserted in all linked documents. Publish and Subscribe also extends data sharing across networks. When you publish a document or part of one, the system creates an Edition file.

As an example, suppose you select data from a spreadsheet and create an Edition file. This file is automatically updated whenever the original file is updated. The Edition file may then be imported, or "subscribed to," by a spreadsheet on another Mac. Whenever the original data is updated, the corresponding data in the second spreadsheet will also be updated, automatically. Updating, moreover, may be turned off and on.

AppleEvents Resource Sharing

AppleEvents is an application communication protocol that provides applications with the capability of sharing resources and processing, back and forth. Data from a database can be sent to a spreadsheet for processing and have the results returned to the database.

Networking and Communications

Networking

Macs on an AppleTalk network can use FileShare to share files and folders. Macs with system 6 and DtCs with AppleTalk adapter boards can also use the FileShare facility. AppleShare and a dedicated server are not needed. All networking features are included in System 7 for AppleTalk, EtherTalk, and TokenTalk if you have Ethernet or token ring cards installed.

Communication

System 7 comes with a Data Access Language that paves the way for further data exchange when the Mac is connected to an IBM or VAX host system.

Multitasking

Dynamic Data Exchange

Publish and Subscribe extends data sharing across networks. When you publish a document or part of one, the system creates an Edition file. The Subscribe command is used to seek out and retrieve the Edition file. Whenever the original document is updated and saved, the linked Edition file is updated as well.

TeachText Text Reader

System 7 has a feature called TeachText, a text reader that lets you create and read text files. It can read color PICT files as well.

AppleEvents

AppleEvent applications can request services and products from other applications. For example, a text processing application could send data to another application and recieve graphics in return.

8.0   Choosing an Operating System

Bigger, more powerful, and more sophisticated is not always better; in fact, quite the opposite. In practice, few programs or systems are used near capacity. In most instances, a select number of functions or features, say twenty out of a hundred, are used almost always; the rest hardly ever, if ever. So it is with operating systems. Features you will never use do nothing but occupy space in your computer. The ideal operating system, then, is one that is strong in features you will use and spartan in all others.

8.1   Selection Factors

MS-DOS Considerations

Many users will be content with the not too well integrated but very rich MS-DOS software base. This software runs fairly well on 8088- and 80286-based DtCs, although 8088-based units are practically out of production and 80286 sales are declining. If you are doing what many MS-DOS computer users do – text editing, word processing, home finances, small spreadsheets, language experimentation, small utilities development, medium-size databases, games, and medium-level graphics applications, you will remain content with the current MS-DOS operating systems and its newer version 5.x.

Microsoft's announced intent to blend MS-DOS and Windows into the homogenous mid-range package, Windows NT, has been viewed by some observers as opportunism; a reneging on a solemn promise. The result of Microsoft's new position with regard to OS/2, they argue, in effect shoves OS/2 toward the high end of the microcomputer market, into corporate environments. IBM does not seem to mind this assessment, perhaps because that is where OS/2 naturally belongs. Besides, IBM itself has a hefty investment and interest in DOS.

DOS under these circumstances is becoming something quite different from what it used to be. Much of DOS's invigoration is due to memory expansion and extension and, of course, to a graphical user interface. From now on when we speak of DOS, a GUI is implied, whether it is the more expensive Microsoft Windows or a less pricey GeoWorks Ensemble. For an interesting revelation, compare Quarterdeck DESQview or Sun NeWS GUI.

Windows for DOS gives DOS users something akin to the graphical user interface long enjoyed by Mac users. With over two million Windows units sold in just a few months, and still going strong, Microsoft is firmly committed to DOS/Windows, which should bring joy and comfort to the huge DOS user population.

But we should not become so enamored of Windows that we accept it as a magic Midas touch, turning everything into pure gold. DOS and Windows both have a few uglies. First, DOS is a text-oriented system that has inherent problems handling graphics. It needs massive memory enhancement to compete in this arena. Second, adding networking software under DOS significantly reduces the memory available to DOS applications. Third, one could easily suppose that all DOS programs run in Windows. Not so. In fact, neither Windows nor OS/2 are yet supplied with sufficiently varied software to be smug toward one another. Lots of Novell network software runs under OS/2 and not under Windows.

> **NOTE**
>
> Cogent Data Technology has Open Windows, drivers for Novell NetWare, TCP/IP, and LAN Manager that run on an MS-Windows workstation. Using a 386 memory manager such as QEMM, all the modules may be placed in high memory. A user can open a window for each server and seamlessly move data between windows and their respective servers. This is another example of how fickle the microcomputer scene can be: a statement that is true one moment turns false the next.

The same holds for Lotus Notes, a lot of Reflection and Turbo software, and Software Publishing InfoAlliance, a program that integrates data from many sources for OS/2 network users, and literally dozens of other software products.

Microsoft's strength with DOS comes from the stack of diversified software that has accumulated for it over the years. Most of this software survives not only because it serves its purpose well, but also because it has been steadily improved. Admitting this, one cannot deny that the stack is grievously topheavy. Like a pyramid standing on its point, it is unbalanced and all the more precarious because the supporting apex is an inherently weak operating system.

DOS with Windows is a star performer in many respects, but often in a kludgy way because it is in fact a quilt of many patches. Before you can start doing serious work on an MS-DOS computer, almost invariably you find you need more memory. For more memory add an expansion board, to use an 80386 or 80486 chip add an accelerator board, to speed-up processing add a coprocessor, and so on and on. You wind up with a strange one-of-a-kind construction that may just barely hold together.

Years ago there was a popular cartoonist, Rube Goldberg, who was fond of and famous for inventing incredibly outlandish and complicated machines that would perform the simplest of tasks in an absurdly convoluted manner. MS-DOS is reminiscent of such a machine in a perverse sort of way; it is a basically very simple operating system, that through countless enhancements and extensions and other encrustations, has become an enormously complicated system that goes to great lengths to perform rather straightforward tasks.

If the structure is so shaky, what props it up?

- *Availability* – The proliferation of DOS computers available at prices ranging from absurdly cheap Asian models to fairly substantial but still reasonably priced full-feature performance models.

- **Upgradability** – The proliferation of add-ons and add-ins, also at reasonable prices, that put muscle into a PC-DOS computer for almost any application one can think of.
- **Software availability** – The proliferation of software at affordable prices and much more that is actually free.
- **Multitasking** – Low-level multitasking now available with MS-DOS and Windows. Looking ahead, MS-DOS 5.x includes a file manager.
- **More memory** – MS-DOS memory extension to 16 MB, made possible by second and subsequent generations of Intel microprocessors: 80286, 80386, and later. However, shortage of memory will still be an issue for graphics processing and networking.

> **NOTE**
>
> Most DOS extenders are produced by three companies: Eclipse Computer Solutions, Inc., Phar Lap Software, Inc., and Rational Systems. Since DOS programs have to be relinked or rewritten to take advantage of DOS extenders, the products are geared toward software developers rather than directly to DtC users. Lotus and DataEase both use the Rational DOS/16 MB extender, which is transparent to users. Digital Equipment Corporation uses an extender in server software to transform a DOS microcomputer into an X Window terminal. DESQview and all modes of MS-Windows run under the Phar Lap 286/DOS extender. Memory managers are useful as well. Quarterdeck QEMM memory manager releases working space in the first megabyte of DOS memory and fits buffers, network drivers, disk cache, TSRs, and other utilities into areas above the 640K barrier.

- **GUI** – Supporting it most of all is the Windows integrating environment with a graphical user interface that is good enough to challenge the former market favorite, the Macintosh Desktop.

So the answer is: No, MS-DOS is not dead. Far from it! Sales projections by Dataquest, Inc., indicate that MS-DOS will have a three-to-one edge over OS/2 going into 1992, with Mac and Unix workstation installations trailing, in that order. Worldwide projections indicate that DOS sales will begin falling off in 1993, while OS/2 sales will begin to climb rapidly. Unix at the same time will experience a steady but moderate growth. A recent DataQuest forecast sees OS/2 sales increasing annually by 20% and equalling DOS sales by 1994. The big break in favor of OS/2 will occur when the per-bit cost of a 4 MB RAM chip falls to that of a 1 MB chip today. We can only speculate on the effects of Windows NT on the MS-DOS world.

MS-DOS occupies a strong position in the microcomputing world in standalone applications, and this strength will undoubtedly persist indefinitely. Microsoft's own sales projections indicate they will market 18 million copies of DOS in 1991, which will swell the world-wide DOS installed base to almost 80 million. If there is no need for large and complex applications and no problem develops, DtC users will have no reason to change. Many interesting and useful things are possible with DOS with a relatively low investment. The initiation into DOS is cheaper than it is into either OS/2 or Unix. For many first-timers, DOS could well be the *only* entry into the desktop computing world.

Later, when needs grow (as they surely will) and if money becomes available, almost any enhancement can be found at an affordable price to make the system bigger, faster, or more productive. Here a bare-bones MS-DOS user has a decided advantage. Enhancement possibilities for a shoestring DOS DtC are enormous. A DOS user can pick and choose to fit his wallet in all manner of software products and hardware enhancements. A huge stock of DOS software can be acquired literally for nothing. To make sure this situation continues, Microsoft will refrain from doing anything that will hurt DOS's compatibility with thousands of programs.

But there is a limit to upward tailoring. While it is possible to increase DOS's power with add-ons, add-ins, extensions, and expansions, eventually the system begins bogging down. For intensive users, DOS will have to juggle resources to such an extent it will become sluggish. Also, some avenues are simply not open for DOS to grow into. The money spent on enhancing an initially bare bones system can mount to a sizeable sum, leading one to rethink the strategy of starting small.

IBM is definitely committed to Presentation Manager and its support of SAA. Many developers have thrown their support to SAA and are working on PM applications. Windows, you must know, does not support SAA.

OS/2 Considerations

When you think about it, OS/2 with Presentation Manager and DOS with Windows are not true head-to-head competitors. In fact, OS/2 is more similar to operating systems written for minicomputers and mainframes than it is to any written for desktop computers. Both Microsoft and IBM appear to agree that OS/2 is an upscale operating system, more comfortably viewed in the company of high-end microcomputers, workstations, and the like. At the same time MS-DOS is being clearly categorized as the entry level operating system. However, the fact that OS/2 is initially more expensive than DOS with Windows may not be so one-sided in the long run when you figure the cost of the memory and hardware that must be added to an MS-DOS computer to muscle it up to workhorse level.

In reality, then, OS/2 is not an immediate replacement for MS-DOS, but rather a step up to a higher bit-width model. To make the transition easier, many DOS command names and functions have been retained in OS/2. The change from one regime to the other was not to be precipitous, and in fact considerable care was taken to make the transition to the higher level of microcomputing a relatively painless one. From the IBM side, DOS was not being abandoned, but rather bridged to OS/2 for anyone wishing to cross over. Inclusion of the DOS compatibility mode supports this conclusion.

OS/2's chief differences from DOS are in the way OS/2 manages its sphere of work: files, tasks, memory, and multitasking. Also, OS/2 differs in features such as its Communication Manager and the Windows-like Presentation Manager. The principal advantages of OS/2 over DOS are:

- Larger memory and improved memory management; programs run faster.
- Disk caching; large programs can run more efficiently.
- Mixing of graphics and text.
- High-resolution windowing with color, multiple fonts in different sizes and styles.
- Bigger spreadsheets, longer documents, larger databases.
- True multitasking. OS/2 can run a dozen programs at once, plus a DOS program.

Unix Considerations

Unix could develop into an upscale option for DOS users, inasmuch as Unix versions are appearing for such products as Word, WordPerfect, Lotus 1-2-3, Foxbase,

Norton Utilities, Multimate, Multiplan, dBASE IV, and DataEase, among others. Moreover, a Unix workstation can have a DOS mode just like OS/2. Soft PC, for example, emulates the DOS environment on almost any non-Intel workstation, giving it DOS compatibility.

Microsoft, SCO (Santa Cruz Operations), and Hewlett-Packard are working on a Unix version of Presentation Manager, including its full Application Program Interface.

Unix and its IBM counterpart AIX represent an operating system that fits into the workstation area, the territory that spans the gap between minicomputers and microcomputers. This is the territory of advanced applications that call for integrated database, communications, and graphics subsystems, as well as high-end applications development – for CAD, CAM, and such.

Since IBM already has AIX, why a high-end OS/2?

- *User oriented* – OS/2 is user oriented, whereas AIX is oriented more toward technical applications. AIX is scalable to workstations, to minicomputers, and to the largest mainframe, but so is OS/2.

- *User friendly* – OS/2 is feasible for less sophisticated users; AIX requires a higher degree of computer expertise.

- *Networking versatility* – OS/2 fits in with simple LAN networking as well as to SNA networking more easily than AIX, although IBM hopes to integrate AIX with OS/2 networking strategies.

- *Database compatible* – IBM database software plus many third party database systems fit the OS/2 approach more neatly.

- *SAA compatible* – OS/2 ensures compatibility in the SAA environment.

An interesting problem arises in the software market. With almost universal portability becoming a reality – from DOS to OS/2 to Unix to Apple – software houses are suddenly faced with unexpected competition. Packages designed specifically for one platform are now threatened by packages from other platforms because of portability. As an example, Ventura Publisher for the Mac is marketing in direct competition with PageMaker and QuarkXPress, desktop publishers that are well entrenched in the Mac world. The Mac edition of Ventura will be able to import files from DOS GEM, Windows, and OS/2 editions of Ventura.

Software upgrading is becoming a matter of survival. A new grab-bag of features will have to be added just to stay even. Also, something may have to be done to make the product even more attractive. Competition could become more fierce than it is today and some software packages will surely fall in combat.

Macintosh Considerations

The phenomenal success of Microsoft Windows got Apple's undivided attention. Its strongest suit, the super-friendly GUI, was being seriously challenged. Apple has always been a sort of loner; aloof from the rest of the microcomputing world. Moreover the hardware, until lately, was quite pricey. Lower prices and the release of System 7 helped to stave off judgement day, but not for long. Apple is now actively seeking alliances wherever mutual benefit may appear. Even IBM is included as a possible business partner.

Apple Computer Inc., according to its president, Michael Spindler, is transforming itself from predominantly a hardware vendor into an operating system company that also happens to sell hardware. The new posture forms the rationale for Apple and IBM to consider cooperative technological and business ventures. Some valuable goods can be laid on the bargaining table:

IBM's Trade Ware	Apple's Trade Ware
Network protocols	AppleTalk
RISC chip	Publish and Subscribe
Hi-tech chips	Pink OOP system
OS/2 components	Two-dimensional modeling
Mainframe experience	

The Macintosh operating system has been modified to run on other than Motorola 68xxx chips. Also, data exchanges and communications across platforms, Apples included, are rapidly becoming commonplace. Developments along these lines make information systems managers less cautious about investing in Apple equipment for tasks that Macintosh may be especially suited to do.

Macintosh System 7 and a profound change in Apple Computer's attitude promise to swing a broader user base in Apple's favor. In the 1980s Apple was a proprietary company with essentially a single product. With solid technology that was appealing to a substantial market, Apple was able to maintain a strong position in the microcomputing market. A proprietary stance is no longer tenable. In the 1990s Apple will not be able to isolate itself from the mainstream of the industry.

The Macintosh Nutek chip set is a newcomer, similar to the set of chips developed to allow MS-DOS computer vendors to easily build compatible MS-DOS computers. Such chip sets have been long in coming due to Apple's proprietary ROM BIOS versions and its tenacity in suing anyone attempting to clone a Macintosh. Because of the increased demand for Apple computers and the competitive marketplace, there seems ample room for a Mac clone to appear.

Moreover, the possibility exists for the Macintosh operating system to run on Intel DtCs. Apple is exploring the feasibility of licensing the Macintosh operating system to run on Intel systems.

8.2   Choosing Parts and Pieces

The CPU

OS/2

OS/2 1.x requires at least an 80286 while 2.x requires the 80386/486 processors. Windows enhanced memory mode requires the 80386/486 CPUs. For appropriate memory support as well as the increased performance requirements, you will be better off with 80386 CPUs.

MS-DOS

Unlike MS-DOS and MS-Windows, with OS/2 there may be increased sensitivity to differing MS-DOS computer architectures due to OS/2's decreased reliance on BIOS I/O functionality. It will probably not be as easy to operate generic OS/2 versions on a wide class of MS-DOS computers (IBM; Japanese, American, and Asian compatibles) as it was to operate the MS-DOS and PC-DOS operating systems. Before you purchase your MS-DOS compatible, be sure that there is a version of OS/2 that will support it.

Memory

Both OS/2 and Windows require larger amounts of extended memory. Although both can support expanded memory, you should outfit your new MS-DOS computer with at least 4 MB of memory. Also, check if your system unit can be expanded to the full 16 MB of extended memory. 80386-based units can emulate expanded memory with extended memory.

Mass Storage

Existing 10-40 MB hard drives on older DtCs will need to be upgraded to 80 MB and more. Also, faster hard disks will be required for virtual memory support and increased use of the hard disk for file swapping. The following will drive the size and speed of these upgrades:

- *OS size* – OS/2 can require from 3-7 MB of hard disk space.
- *Virtual memory support* – How much of the hard disk will support virtual memory?
- *Multitasking* – How many programs and how large will they be in total? How much expanded/extended memory is required for data areas and how does the hard disk supplement this memory?
- *Database applications* – Increasing numbers of DBMS applications supporting larger databases will become popular. Client/server applications will also drive hard disk sizes.
- *Network and communications servers* – Storing network-wide data requires considerable hard disk space.
- *Graphics/CAD* – Increased hard disk space for image and drawing storage.

Bus

The two operating systems perform well on both ISA and MCA buses. Both buses are quite popular and are undergoing enhancements that are transparent at the OS level.

8.3 Operating System Comparisons

If you had difficulty sorting out the methodologies, complexities, and problems discussed above, you are not alone. The confusion is symptomatic of the bottom-up approach of repairing MS-DOS. It seems like a strong system, but it lacks a good foundation and infrastructure.

OS/2 and Windows Sophistication

Many MS-DOS users are locked into their respective operating systems and environments. However, it's always interesting to speculate on what a switch could be like. The MS-DOS DtC user has many choices: stay with MS-DOS; upgrade to MS-Windows; purchase OS/2; or even convert to Unix.

Software Development

Most of the enhancements ascribed to the Windows and OS/2 operating systems have required that existing software be rewritten. Rewriting software involves a very different approach to software development. The traditional set of MS-DOS software is one way, it asked the operating system to perform functions for it, but it never performed any at the operating system's request. The software would issue countless interrupts, each calling upon the operating system to do something, but it never asked for permission, or if any other process would be affected.

Under Windows and OS/2, software development methodology must become two way or *event driven*. The developer must create software that can operate as a result of many external events that occur. Programs need permission from the OS to perform tasks, and must keep the operating system apprised of their activities. Considerations for event-driven software include:

- *Mouse inputs* – Which program has control of the mouse and which is looking at what is coming in?
- *Screen size* – How much room has been given for the program to display its output? This is necessary to appropriately create and size graphics and text.
- *Compute time* – Multitasking necessitates coordination between multiple programs to properly divide the time. How much CPU time is required? What priority is needed for internal I/O tasks?
- *I/O* – How to synchronize multiple program requirements for singular system resources, resource allocation, and priority. Use of sophisticated chains of I/O; how to ask for I/O, distinguishing virtual I/O from real I/O.
- *Fonts* – Which fonts are being used, and where are they stored?

The greater software responsibility and the different development philosophy make applications for MS-Windows and OS/2 much more time consuming to develop. It is no wonder that OS/2 and Windows programs are long in coming. As the MS-DOS developer community becomes accustomed to the new techniques and concepts for cooperative and well-designed software, more software products will become available. The public domain, currently devoid of such software, will experience a surge in offerings as hobbyists and developers alike try their hand at Windows and OS/2 software.

MS-DOS to MS-Windows to OS/2

As we move from the existing MS-DOS software to rewritten MS-DOS software, the complexity of software development increases. The benefit to the user is increased throughput, software integration, and hopefully, productivity. Although OS/2 provides a variety of tools to automate user functions for end-user applications, OS/2 is still more of a developmental operating system, very similar to Unix, and therefore more difficult to install and operate. It is definitely not yet for the casual user.■

■ A "lite" OS/2, version 1.3, may make the transition easier.

General Features

Table 31 below shows the primary differences between MS-DOS alone, MS-DOS with DESQview and MS-Windows enhancements, and finally OS/2.

FEATURE	MS-DOS	DESQview
CPU/memory	Real, carousel extended	Expanded/extended
Multitasking	TSRs, preemptive	Any MS-DOS, preemptive

FEATURE	MS-DOS	DESQview
Graphics support	None	None
Data share	Files	Video share

FEATURE	WINDOWS	OS/2
CPU memory	Protected mode, VM=8086 mode (3.0), 32-bit flat (4.0)	Page mode, VM-8086 (2.0), 32-bit flat (2.0)
Multitask	MS-Windows cooperative, MS-DOS preemptive	OS/2 preemptive, MS-DOS preemptive threads
Graphics	APA + vector	APA + vector
Data share	DDE	DDE

Table 31.   Major operating system features

Both MS-Windows and OS/2 provide significant enhancements to the MS-DOS operating system. As Windows and OS/2 evolve, one can presume that the similar capabilities will finally merge into one comprehensive operating system.

Multitasking Support

Both OS/2 and Windows have the ability to allocate processor time between many different tasks. Currently, OS/2 has more powerful built-in features to coordinate software multitasking with I/O activities common to all tasks. With OS/2 applications, programmers will have a reliable, standard mechanism to implement. Current MS-DOS users kludge this feature with second-party multitasking software, using DESQview, for instance. Lacking standards, however, these systems are sometimes unreliable and a usage methodology does not exist.

Call Interface

Both OS/2 and Windows provide a higher-level programming interface: the call interface. With OS/2, applications obtain operating system services by calling procedures and passing arguments to a stack. This technique is used by most high-level languages and will provide better portability as well as flexibility when obtaining operating system services. The interrupt mechanism used by MS-DOS often necessitated assembly language programming and constrained argument passing to a limited number of processor registers.

Extended I/O Support

An extensive set of console device interfaces for the video, keyboard, and mouse are available. These functions can be easily extended and enhanced, making it easier to give software more centralized I/O capability and flexibility. Support of I/O must be an integral part of the operating system. Since multiple programs can perform I/O using the same devices, a more sophisticated I/O strategy is needed. While current MS-Windows provides more device drivers, OS/2 provides a more solid infrastructure for implementing I/O.

DLLs (Dynamic Link Libraries)

Both Windows and OS/2 support dynamic linking, which allows executable memory to call software libraries (also known as run time libraries) that were not previously linked to the executable.

> **NOTE**
>
> ### LIBRARIES AND LINKING
> Libraries are modules of software code for accomplishing specific functions. Software is developed using general-purpose languages that attain specificity by linking to additional programs. When the higher-level language is compiled and converted to assembly language, the linking process connects the library functions that must be in memory as machine language references. Machine language from the general software functions and from library functions must agree on memory locations.

Instead, the linkage is set up when the calling program invokes the subroutine, with no need to recompile. This allows subroutines to be packaged, maintained, and distributed independently of their calling programs. Specific advantages are:

- *Packaging* – Subroutine functions can be packaged independently of their calling executable, thus reducing executable sizes.

- *Multiple usage* – More than one program can share a dynalink file. The common software functions of printer and I/O support, and graphics and text support routines can be provided by dynalink files. This will cause a more consistent software base. Not only can programs use dynalink files, but the operating system itself can use this methodology.

- *Upgrade control* – Upgrades to the dynalink files can be accomplished without changes to the main executable. Improvements to dynalink files can impact across multiple software programs.

Since the dynalink file must be linked at execution time, it may slow down the execution speed of programs that use the files. There will be a need, then, for faster CPUs.

Interprocess Communications

Interprocess communication is supported through a variety of sophisticated techniques. These include the use of pipes, queues, files, semaphores, shared memory, and standard naming conventions. The task of managing resources shared between programs will be eased by a consistent methodology for programs to share data. Under MS-DOS, this process is ad hoc with enhancement TSR programs moving data between applications, rather than programs sharing data in the first place.

The OS/2 Extended Edition contains built-in functions for supporting communications between workstations and mainframe computers. Connectivity will allow DtC programs more direct and flexible access to data stored on other workstations or mainframes. The newer client/server network architectures are a step in this direction.

User Interface Support

A variety of methods are available for creating friendly interfaces to your software. They include application windowing, user dialogues, selection buttons, control panels, DOS command entry lines, icons, buttons, window layout, and clipboards. Also a friendly shell provides for starting, switching, and otherwise controlling programs. Previous applications written under MS-DOS had to implement these functions their own way. Now that these functions are included in the operating system, applications programmers can more easily concentrate on improving software friendliness.

Graphics Support

Graphics support in the operating system are callable routines that applications programs can use. Although individual I/O drivers will be required to communicate with specific hardware, OS graphics support will take care of most software's hardware-independent graphics needs. The independent functions are implemented by dynalink libraries that can be improved easily.

Graphics primitives are lines, polylines, boxes, arcs, pies, fillets, splines, dithered fills, areas, palates, and image captures. More sophisticated capabilities include color, backgrounds, device-independent colors, and mixing transformations, rotations, scaling, translating, and clipping. Enhanced text support includes multiple fonts, character widths, halftones, and PostScript. MS-DOS software could accomplish all of this, but each program had to provide the functions through custom programming or the use of non-standard language libraries from a variety of vendors. Now that this level of graphics sophistication is supported by the operating system, applications developers include higher functional levels with less programming. This will lead to a more consistently sophisticated graphics software base. Although earlier versions of OS/2 implementing GDI graphics have more sophisticated functionality than Windows GPI graphics, later versions, OS/2.0 and Windows 4.0, will be quite similar in power.

CPU Support

The more advanced CPU modes are being supported by both Windows and OS/2. This includes support of 32 bit-flat models, extended memory, virtual memory, and the use of separate virtual 8086 processes.

Windows and OS/2 Effect on Applications Software

Eventually, more users will benefit from Windows and OS/2 because applications can perform data sharing, multitasking, graphics, and virtual memory in a less ad hoc environment than was possible with MS-DOS alone or the myriad of add-on software kludges that attempted these functions non-cooperatively.

Newer versions of Windows and OS/2 will change the type of software operating on microcomputers. The software will be more structurally reliable and consistent. Fortunately, both Windows and OS/2 provide back doors where the rebel MS-DOS software with all of its peculiarities and richness can still operate. The new software will probably appear in three stages:

1. **MS-DOS software** – Existing MS-DOS applications ported to the OS/2 and Windows environments running in virtual 8086 environments.

2. **Poor Windows and OS/2 software** – Poorly written software with more concern for speed and memory than for the appropriateuse of enhanced functional support

■ Many OS/2 and Windows users complain of sluggish response when multitasking a few programs, even on the latest 486 DtCs.

provided by Windows and OS/2. Developing software under the new environments will require considerable retraining and a change of philosophy. ■

3. *Good Windows and OS/2 software* – As developers and users learn how to use the newer operating systems, software will improve. More capable CPUs (486, 586, and higher) will make the burden of additional OS overhead less noticeable.

It will take several years for the maturation process to complete. Improved CPU capabilities will match developer's improved developmental capabilities. However, 5 or 10 years in the DtC business could see radical changes in parallel processing and AI techniques that will again revolutionize the way we develop and use DtC software. In the meantime, many users will be satisfied with the existing base of MS-DOS applications.

All applications areas will eventually benefit from the improved operating systems. Those applications most profoundly affected will be:

* *CAD and DtP* – These applications require extensive graphics and enhanced memory support.
* *IBM mainframe software* – A variety of graphics, statistical (SAS), and other mainframe applications can be shared on DtCs with OS/2 connectivity options.
* *Database* – Built-in DBMS support – OS/2 DB2, SQL client/server, and LAN manager – provide the higher levels of support necessary to share databases over networks.

MS-DOS and Windows or OS/2?

Windows 3.0 has been released at a time when it whets the appetite of MS-DOS users who crave a friendly environment and the accoutrements of cooperative software. It satisfies some of their most pressing needs. But under the polished surface is still the relatively weak MS-DOS operating system. Then comes Windows NT. Many think OS/2 is "better" because it has been redesigned from the top down for multitasking, it has a multithread architecture, a 32-bit programming model, high-performance file system, and a rich graphics programming interface with powerful developmental tools. Yet when one looks to the future, one sees planned Windows improvements that, at least on the surface, appear to make it comparable to OS/2.

Lists of applications are written for Windows and more lists for OS/2. Many of your favorite software products appear on both lists. Early versions of Windows are considerably less expensive than those of OS/2, and this is also true of the software products developed for them. Eventually, developers and users will have little tolerance for two major operating system environments that are similar and yet different at the same time. The wary MS-DOS user might well be advised to purchase a DtC that appropriately supports either environment (80386 CPU, 4 MB memory, good performance), but continue to use the existing MS-DOS software base. Be sure to do the following when you upgrade:

* *Software* – Purchase popular software that will be upgraded in step with future operating systems.
* *Hardware* – Purchase hardware capable of supporting the enhanced operational modes the OS will support. If possible, obtain compatibility guarantees.
* *Networks* – Investigate thoroughly the modes of network operation and check on compatibility with other networked operating systems, such as Unix or VMS.

Some will choose Windows because of the lower initial cost and because more MS-DOS programs have converted to the Windows environment. Some will choose OS/2 because of its advertised connectivity with IBM mainframe software, networks, and distributed applications. Some will just stay with current MS-DOS versions and wait for the industry to shake out.

Windows 3.0 client workstations communicating with servers running OS/2 should become quite popular. Power users who demand better foundations for graphical desktops will find the move from Windows 3.0 to OS/2 a smooth one.

In many cases MS-DOS by itself has minimal operating system functionality. Its file system, many agree, needs a thorough overhaul. Fortunately, new MD-DOS versions have solved hard disk size limitations and are addressing poor memory and file management support. But while you can raise the functionality of MS-DOS to increasingly higher levels, the highest reachable level will not be as high as with the completely rewritten OS/2.

Windows NT

The announced Windows NT (New Technology) has most MS-DOS users quite excited. The Windows NT kernel is based on the Unix Mach kernel. The NT kernel is essentially a redesigned OS/2 kernel and is around 128K in size. The NT kernel will support Windows version 4.0, MS-DOS 6.0, the OS/2 shell, or an application-specific user's GUI. Microsoft is developing what may provide the best of all worlds, a Mach-like kernel and compatibility with most operating environments.

Windows is growing up to be more than an MS-DOS enhancement, it is becoming a major operating system. MS-DOS 6.0, which will ship with Windows NT, will run with the help of the Windows NT kernel rather than Windows running by MS-DOS file management functions and its BIOS. In fact, even OS/2 and other systems will run on top of Windows NT, which is quite a role reversal. Currently Windows is tied to the MS-DOS file manager structure. Windows NT will use the same high-performance file format as found in OS/2. NT will be POSIX, ACE, and C2 security compliant – a definite advantage in most user communities.

OS/2 or Unix?

This is a tough call. Both operating systems are sophisticated. Although Unix has a longer history, OS/2 is more oriented toward the business applications found on DtCs. OS/2 permits the existing MS-DOS software base to coexist with higher-level software developed under OS/2. OS/2 can be an end user's as well as a developer's operating system. Software can be developed under the same operating system as it operates on. This is not the case with MS-DOS software developed in mainframe and Unix environments.

For the present, it seems assured that those who use Unix will stay with Unix and those beginning with MS-DOS will stay with it, upgrading to Windows or OS/2. Both Unix and OS/2 operating systems will invade the other's software applications camps, and in five or ten years, may coalesce. As the particular hardware platform becomes less important, so also will the particular operating system. Competition and users needs will drive all operating systems and hardware platforms to support all software.

Apple Macintosh?

The Apple Macintosh user has a choice between Apple System 7 and AUX operating systems. System 7 provides functions similar to those provided by OS/2, with 32-bit virtual memory, application data sharing, and an improved Finder (Apple's program starting and use shell). The AUX (Unix) operating system combines the advantages of Unix with Apple's widely acclaimed look and feel.

Comparative Costs

It will cost more to operate Windows and OS/2 applications.

- *Hardware* – Users will want larger and faster hard disks, increased memory requirements, faster and later model CPUs, better graphics interfaces, and more expensive printers with PostScript support.
- *Retraining* – Users will have to be retrained and there will be a loss of productivity they acclimate to the new operating systems. The upgrade to both Windows and OS/2 will become more difficult as the amount of control the user has over applications increases.
- *Network support* – Systems running OS/2 and Windows will be more likely to be in LAN configurations requiring additional LAN hardware and software.

Of course, all of the devices described above depend on applications developers using the techniques in a consistent manner. Also, a single environment must emerge, or if multiple environments continue, they must be compatible.

PART
IV

Part IV. Networking the DtC

In the early years of the personal computer, users celebrated their independence from the mainframe and revelled in their individual computing havens. Today, the real productivity enhancement is the combination of distinct computing capability and connectivity through local area networks.

What can be more interactive than a desktop computer, with its responsive software and synergistic peripherals? A system of interconnected DtCs that can share resources with user transparency is a good answer. Two or more interconnected computers that can communicate and interact form a configuration known as a network. A local area network is one restricted to a small area, serving a given constituency, and may include workstations, file servers, and print servers, as well as gateways and bridges to other networks.

The immediate and primary focus is on local area networks, the single most important productivity enhancement besides the DtC itself. Other communications methods such as mainframe to terminal and wide area networks will also be discussed. In particular:

Networking orientation: looks at how local area networks evolved from the earlier star connected mainframes and terminals and how PCs played an early role in mainframe communications. A look at a typical office LAN with some important user considerations follows.

Network configurations: will give you a better understanding of the dimensionality of local area networks as we investigate different topologies, LAN interconnections, and server types. You will see that LANs are not intractable sets of connected computers, but infinitely configurable systems of computing elements with adjustable connectivity and power.

Distributed processing on networks: shows the particulars of how the DtCs are connected and what they can do when connected. A network of DtCs can produce applications different from and more flexible than those possible on individual workstations.

X Windows: discusses a standardized and powerful methodology for operating applications across a network of DtCs. Although many think of networks as file and data conduits, a local area network can be much more than that.

Network software and hardware: examines specific hardware and software and how these two interrelate. Although hardware is important for connectivity, it is the software that characterizes a LAN and gives it power greater than the sum of its individual DtC nodes. In this section, we also look at network administration, consider security requirements, and examine evolving network standards.

Networking Orientation

The personal nature of DtCs – the capacity of a machine to conform to your way of doing things – is what makes DtCs so popular. Harnessing these marvels to problem solving in the business environment calls for well-configured networks so that data and information can move quickly, smoothly, and reliably between workstations.

What office workers find so attractive about the DtC environment is that they can select from a variety of machines and operating systems and that they have the flexibility to run the particular applications software they prefer. When office information processing evolved from a central terminal-to-mainframe system to the current environment of many independent microcomputers, it left some data processing requirements inadequately supported. The attractions of variety and choice that make the DtC so appealing are the very things that frustrate communication in the office when DtCs need to exchange information or share printers.

◨ This is sometimes humorously called Nike Net – running disks around in tennis shoes.

Moving information between machines may consist of simply copying a file from one machine onto a diskette and physically transporting it to another machine.◨ This approach won't work, however, when media formats are incompatible or when the volume of information being transferred is too large. A manual diskette transfer system becomes completely ineffective when multiple users want to share information simultaneously.

Riding in like the cavalry to save the day, the networking process provides sophisticated intercomputer information transfer and peripheral sharing. Approaches to networking microcomputers range from trivial to elegant, and represent a revolution in office automation – the advent of the long-awaited distributed processing environment.

The driving force behind microcomputer networks is not so much the availability of new communications technologies as it is the availability of standardized personal computers. The needs of the office-computer user are defining what services microcomputer networking technology must provide.

Local Area Networks for DtCs

The DtC LAN environment provides the most comprehensive set of services currently available to the DtC user. Ideally, the DtC LAN should provide the best qualities of both the standalone microcomputer and the traditional terminal-to-mainframe environment. Indeed, DtC LAN technology is evolving rapidly, with a number of useful services currently available and others on the horizon.

Computer networks are broadly classified into two types: LANs and WANs. WANs, wide area networks, also called long-haul networks, connect computers across long distances.

> **NOTE**
>
> The prototype WAN, ARPANET, was an experiment sponsored by the Defense Advanced Research Projects Agency, in cooperation with a number of research institutions and defense contractors. DARPA's network research was initiated in 1969 and was ultimately so successful that it has evolved into two separate packet-switched networks: Defense Data Network (DDN), an operational military network; and the Internet, an experimental but widely used research network. Other large WANs include TYMNET and Sprint Telenet.

LANs interconnect computers and other information processing devices in a local geographic area – an office, a building, a campus, or a military base. The devices and wiring system that comprise a LAN are usually owned and administered by a single organization, whereas WANs are often owned jointly. Data transmission speeds on LANs are typically much faster than WAN transmission rates. LANs have the following special characteristics:

- *Connections* – A LAN often connects similar computing equipment that run under the same operating system or a network operating system (NOS). More general-purpose LANs such as Ethernet can be used to interconnect a greater variety of computers. General Ethernet LANs can be interconnected to more specific networks such as AppleTalk, with a network bridge. See the example in Figure 75.

- *Cables* – The design of most LANs requires that LAN-connected devices share a common transmission cable.

- *Transparent program and data transfer* – LANs allow file storage and retrieval from any mass store device anywhere in the LAN. This is usually accomplished by redirector software on each LAN DtC. The redirection software takes requests for files that would ordinarily have to be processed by mass store drives on a local DtC and reroutes the requests through the network to mass store units on other DtCs. Transparent file transfer is the cornerstone of the DtC LAN advantage.

- *Transparent peripheral sharing* – Printers, modems, and plotters can be shared transparently as though they were connected to your own DtC.

- *DtC bus-specific interfaces* – Since LAN boards plug into the DtC bus, different boards are required for different bus architectures (AT/ISA, Micro Channel, EISA, NuBus and so on). Specialized processors located on the LAN boards offload from the DtC CPU the details of data trafficking on the network. Some are firmware programmable; others are completely customized VLSI.

- *Simple interconnect* – Connecting LANed DtCs from a hardware standpoint involves installing network boards, running cable (everything from twisted pair to optical fiber) between workstation units, and providing repeaters for longer distance hookups.

As we shall see, the differences between WANs and LANs are significant from both a design and administration perspective.

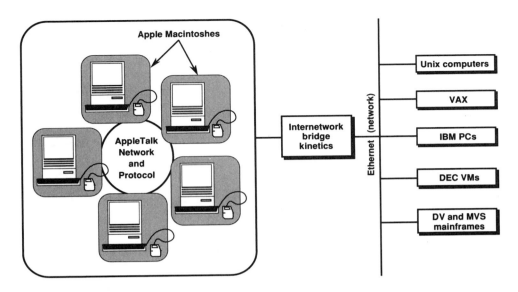

Figure 75. AppleTalk/Ethernet LAN

The Evolution of LANs

The first important LANs were terminals connected to mainframes and minis. Before LAN technology, most terminals were connected to computers using the serial RS-232 standard in combination with asynchronous transmission technology. An individual RS-232 cable for each terminal was connected to the central computer. The large quantity of cabling required made the RS-232 approach both awkward and expensive.

The Development of Ethernet

In the late 1970s, Xerox, Intel, and DEC teamed to develop a method for sharing the bandwidth of a coaxial cable among multiple machines. The resulting system, called Ethernet, used baseband signalling on a thick cable. Multiple transmissions were obtained by the CSMA/CD (carrier sense multiple access/collision detect) media access control system. Special transceivers were required to connect devices into the Ethernet cable. Early terminal-to-computer Ethernet systems used RS-232 cabling between terminals and a nearby Ethernet interface device called a terminal server or terminal controller. The interface device containing the transceiver was then connected into the Ethernet backbone cable. The cable was in turn connected to other interface devices at various locations and ultimately into one or more computer systems. By 1983, these systems were widely used to save terminal wiring costs and to permit a single terminal to access multiple computers.

The DtC as a Dumb Terminal

At about the same time, DtC resident asynchronous terminal emulation programs permitted DtCs to access central computers by mimicking the asynchronous terminals that the computers expected to talk to.

Through modems connected to the RS-232 serial interfaces and communications programs, the DtC can act as a dumb terminal. DtC users can:

- access bulletin board systems for public domain software and commercial information sources like the CompuServe and the Sears/IBM Prodigy Network.
- upload and download small files from other computers.
- emulate a terminal to a wide variety of computers.

A DtC user can contact someone anywhere in the world with a modem and the commercial phone system. Modem communication can be done on a standalone computer; it's inexpensive and it does not require any administration. It is, however, too slow to move large quantities of information, it doesn't facilitate true networking of devices among many users, and it has poor file sharing capability.

Modem transmissions often use a store and forward methodology in which a second computer serves as a temporary storage facility. Since binary and extended ASCII files are equipment and application specific and are therefore usually not subject to local rules, they cannot be typed or executed for verification on the store and forward host. When errors occur in the files, respective applications crash or yield cryptic error messages. Transmitting such files with the higher level protocol such as Zmodem or Kermit ensures integrity. Users needing to transmit large files between identical DtCs commonly try other methods; trading floppy disks or Bernoulli cartridges for absolute integrity.

In the applications recounted, DtC processing power was largely underused because terminal emulation mode required that actual processing be performed exclusively in the central computer. Consequently, DtC users were forced to fit into the mold of the traditional timesharing system and were subject to the same system resource restrictions as any other terminal user. Nevertheless, asynchronous communication for DtCs is a useful technology where inexpensive and general-purpose communication is needed.

Intelligent Terminals

Addressing the limitations of asynchronous technology, IBM and other computer manufacturers developed intelligent terminals using synchronous interfaces. Unlike the asynchronous RS-232 interface, synchronous interfaces transmit at data rates in the Mbit/sec range over a coaxial cable. The higher-level synchronous protocol permits:

- improved error detection and correction.
- support for full screen input data editing at the terminal with minimal interaction with the mainframe.
- increased data transfer rates.
- offload of communications management from the mainframe to the communications controller.

Synchronous communications require that both sending and receiving devices are synchronized before transmission of data is started. Data is usually sent in blocks or packets unlike the character-by-character data transmission style of the RS-232 interface. Table 32 on page 457 describes a synchronous link level just above the physical layer. The links HDLC, SDLC, and BISYNC are synchronous. Synchronous implementations have reliable data transfer, flow control, and error detection and retransmission. Since synchronous communication systems have more sophisticated protocols and error-checking mechanisms, the preprocessing hardware detects and corrects data errors, seldom bothering the user unless the equipment fails. Sophisticated hardware doesn't exist on asynchronous networks, so software executing in the DtC CPU must check the errors.

While IBM is the leader in this technology, other manufacturers provide similar systems. However, since many synchronous technologies use proprietary communications methods, terminal support tends to be confined to a single manufacturer's environment.

IBM's synchronous controllers require coaxial cable connections or synchronous modems, which presents a hardware interface different from the one RS-232 asynchronous devices provide.

The Intelligent DtC Terminal

In addition to emulating a dumb terminal, the DtC can provide an excellent platform for emulating intelligent terminals. The intelligent terminal's synchronous protocol requires considerably more CPU resources than the typical DtC can supply. Specialized boards such as IRMA and Forte, costing $500 to $1000, interface between the DtC and the mainframe synchronous controller. More complicated than RS-232 interfaces, the intelligent terminal emulation boards contain:

- *Special processors* – Special processors that are located on the terminal emulator boards offload the details of protocol and terminal emulation from the DtC CPU. Some of these boards are programmable while others use customized VLSI.
- *Synchronous interface* – Special hardware provides the interface to a coaxial cable or synchronous modem for remote connection across telephone lines.

Intelligent terminal emulator boards must be selected carefully to secure the required level of intelligent terminal emulation. Many companies other than IBM manufacture these boards with particular feature improvements. Compatibility problems can occur between different manufacturer's boards. Also, differences between a DtC's keyboard and monitor resolution and those of the terminal being emulated can create problems.

Combined Intelligent Terminal Emulation and LAN Capabilities

Using the emulation board to configure a DtC as a synchronous terminal gives you intelligent terminal emulation as well as standalone computing capability. However, before you rush out and purchase a terminal emulator board, be aware that LAN technology can provide intelligent terminal emulation as well as a means to communicate with other DtCs.

As Figure 76 shows, a LAN can supply intelligent terminal emulation in two ways:

1. An IBM mainframe computer is also connected to a DtC token ring LAN. All DtCs can then communicate with the mainframe.

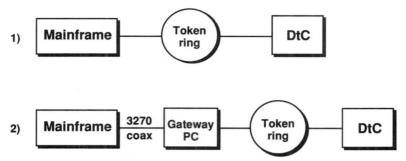

Figure 76. Gaining access to the mainframe by a LAN

2. One DtC in the LAN operates as a gateway connecting to the IBM mainframe by a 3270 coaxial cable or synchronous modem. All DtCs on the token ring LAN connected to this DtC can now communicate with the mainframe.

NOTE

Most DtC LAN environments also support IBM's 327x intelligent terminal emulation across Ethernet or ARCNet topologies connected to an SNA gateway.

Enter the LAN

Despite the limits of asynchronous and synchronous terminal emulation, DtC users had one important advantage over terminal users. They could run many applications on their own machines without interacting with the central computer. As programs such as Lotus 1-2-3, WordPerfect, dBASE, and Turbo Pascal became available, users began to see that many of their needed applications programs, and certainly the least intimidating, were available on their desks. A revolution had begun, and a new class of user was developing. With control of a dedicated computer and a set of application tools as good as the ones available on the mainframe, the user was looking for a way to build simple DtC networks that would share data and programs among like-minded office workers.

The obvious way to meet the needs of the new user class was to create a DtC LAN. It would have to be low-cost, MS-DOS compatible, and easy to install, since many developing networks would be rogues, initially unsupported by data processing departments. Early DtC LAN products included Sytek PC Network, developed for IBM, 3Com Etherlink boards and 3+ Network Operating System, and Novell SNet. IBM PC Network used an unusual analog baseband CSMA/CD system. 3Com stuck with the Ethernet approach and Novell initially tried a proprietary star topology with a 68000-based device as the switch and file server.

All of these early products used the PC/XT or compatible clone as the workstation of choice. The IBM PC's open architecture played a key role in allowing other manufacturers access to the hardware specifications required to design PC bus-compatible network interface cards. The hardware interface and underlying transmission methodology proved to be the easier part of the task. As we shall see, the pioneering work of these early DtC LAN architects is far from complete.

A Sample DtC LAN System

The typical DtC LAN found in an office environment interconnects from 5 to 50 microcomputers. These computers are often similar, belonging to one general class such as MS-DOS compatibles. One or more centralized data storage devices known as file servers might be connected. Additional devices that could be shared by LAN users include laser printers and modems. As shown in Figure 77 LAN-connected communication servers provide DtC users with access to minicomputers, mainframes, or wide area networks.

What the LAN User Sees

When you implement a DtC LAN an obvious question to ask is how the user interface will change as DtCs connect into the network. The answer is that the user interface may change substantially or it may not change at all.

The LAN designer must have a clear idea of what services the LAN will provide as well as of the level of sophistication of the user community. A realistic division of sophistication splits users into two groups: novice users and power users. Novice users tend to have minimal computer understanding, running only one or two applications programs. Most important, novice users are unfamiliar with the DtC operating system. Power users are familiar with the operating system, understand something of the internal functions of software and hardware, and are capable of tailoring their own system interface as required.

The differing needs of these two groups may prompt the LAN designer to create two different LAN user interfaces. For the novice user, the interface should appear as similar as possible to the existing interface. Ideally, the novice user would be unaware that the microcomputer has been connected to a LAN. Applications programs would execute as before, file and drive names would remain the same, and printers and other peripherals would be accessed as they had been when the DtC was a standalone workstation. A menu interface would present the LAN services for the novice to choose. Finally, no new actions would be required to connect the DtC into the LAN, aside from security procedures such as password entry. Novices need to know no more about the internal functions of the LAN than they need to know about the internal functions of their own DtCs.

Power users, on the other hand, can appreciate the additional services and flexibility the LAN provides. They should have the option of customizing their own LAN interfaces. Power users may prefer the command line interface to a menu interface because they can have greater flexibility of interaction during the LAN login process. Under no circumstances, however, should the LAN design permit any reasonable action by either class of user to adversely affect LAN operations.

In the large-LAN environment, the power user should be viewed as an important resource for the LAN designer and administrator. The power user can function both as a valuable information source for identifying LAN requirements and as an informal secondary trainer of novice users.

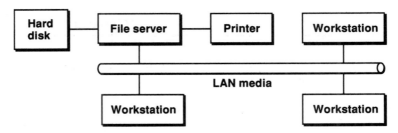

Figure 77.   A sample LAN

What a LAN Can and Cannot Do

In order to decide if a LAN is a needed addition to your computing environment, you should know what you can reasonably expect from DtC LAN technology. The most important reasons to implement a DtC LAN in the office are to:

1. Enable users to easily exchange and share DtC-oriented data and programs.
2. Allow DtC users efficient access to external systems such as minicomputers, mainframes and other networks.
3. Facilitate economical and dependable backup of important data.
4. Create an environment to support distributed applications such as multiuser databases, accounting systems, and increasingly, electronic mail.

LANs certainly have features that enhance the DtC environment. LANs will reduce applications software costs and administrative effort, reduce cost per megabyte for hard disk space, increase hard disk reliability, and centralize administration. Access to data can be strictly enforced, permitting different classes of user to have different privileges: some with read only, others with read and write. Sharing yields a saving on per user costs for running peripherals such as laser printers and plotters, which is a significant expense in some environments.

The features described above may not justify the cost of a DtC LAN, especially since there can be challenges involved. Some problems simply are not solved by LANs:

- *LAN for security* – A LAN creates more security problems than it eliminates.
- *LAN for universal information exchange* – Using a LAN so that any two computers can communicate won't work if file formats are incompatible.
- *LAN to simplify DtC administration* – Networks add a level of complication in software and file access administration.
- *LAN to replace a large computer database* – A LAN file server may not have the speed or capacity to adequately handle very large databases.

Network Configurations

Transmission systems have significant impact upon LAN performance. The theory of LAN data transmission must therefore be understood by those involved in LAN design and procurement. Another consideration is the difference in cost of the various wiring schemes.

A LAN topology is a geometric configuration of LAN media. Different types of electronic signal are used as well as various methods of queuing multiple users who are attempting to access the same network. These and related issues are considered next.

Network Geometries

In the DtC LAN world, the common topologies are bus, ring, star, and distributed star.

The Bus

Figure 78 illustrates the simplest topology, the bus. A bus-based LAN uses a single cable that must be installed to pass nearby each device in the network. Short drop cables connect each individual DtC to the central bus cable. A device called a *transceiver* (transmitter/receiver) controls the microcomputer's interaction with the bus.

The Ring

The ring topology requires the installation of wiring concentrators called *multiple access units* (MAUs) at intervals around the network. Each MAU serves as an access point for 8 or more DtCs, which are connected to the MAU using twisted pair drop cables. See Figure 79.

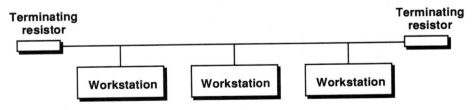

Figure 78. Bus topology

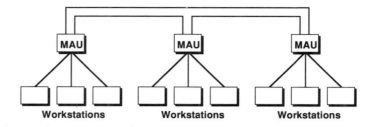

Figure 79. Ring topology

The LAN signals are regenerated in the DtC token interface boards or external repeaters. The ring gets its name from the backbone wiring that interconnects the MAUs, forming a ring, so that each LAN message will eventually return to the MAU and the DtC from which it was originally transmitted. The backbone media may be fiber optic cable or twisted pair. A high speed ring-based technology is becoming available that is similar to IBM's token ring. Fiber optic distributed data interface uses dual redundant rings, and provides transmission rates of 100 Mbps.

The Star

At one time the star was a common DtC LAN topology, but its popularity has waned. The star is unique in that it requires a highly intelligent centralized switching device to route information between star-connected DtCs. Each DtC must use an individual cable to connect it to the central switch. See Figure 80. Such a system works well where there are a limited number of LAN devices being served, but can be expensive to wire and administer when the number of devices grows beyond ten or twenty.

Star LANs provide an attractive topology in an environment where one cabling system is required to support both data and telephone signals. Such systems use a telephone-oriented private branch exchange (PBX) to perform the central switching. The data transfer rates in PBX-based systems are frequently 64 Kbits/sec, slower than rates provided by other LAN topologies. The star topology is insensitive to single point failure.

The Distributed Star

The distributed star extends the limitations of the star topology using multiple interconnected central devices to create a topology that functions as a network of stars. See Figure 81. The intelligence of each central hub is closer to the repeater

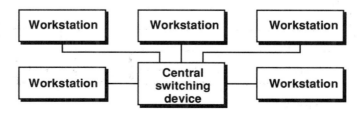

Figure 80. Star topology

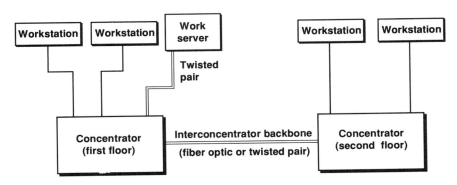

Figure 81. Distributed star topology

function of the ring's MAU than to the switching capability of the star's central switch.

One distributed star technology transmits Ethernet packets over unshielded twisted pair. The cabling scheme, 10BASET, has been adopted as a new subset of the IEEE 802.3 standard.

Baseband, Broadband, and BPS

Any of the media previously described, except fiber optic cable, can carry a data signal by baseband or by broadband. Each media type has a theoretical maximum bandwidth, which is the largest amount of information that can be carried per unit time. Bandwidth is expressed in the number of bits that can be conveyed per second (bps). This can lead to occasional confusion because many data transfer rates within computers, especially disk transfer rates, are expressed in *bytes per second* (Bps). Bytes per second is a useful indicator of data transfer rates since bytes per second translates roughly to characters per second (cps).

Given the limitations of maximum bandwidth, data can be transferred across the media either as a single signal, transmitted as rapidly as the media's bandwidth allows, or as several signals, simultaneously transmitted with each using a portion of the bandwidth known as a band or data channel. The single signal method is known as baseband signaling, and the multiple signal method is known as broadband signaling.

Baseband signaling uses a digital signal similar to the one used internally by a microcomputer. Broadband signaling requires an analog technique, frequency division modulation (FM), which is used in conjunction with frequency division multiplexing, similar to the way cable TV channels share the cable. Since broadband has to convert from the computer's digital signal to analog and back, the technology is more expensive than baseband. As a result, most DtC LAN systems use baseband signaling.

Why use broadband at all? Broadband has two special characteristics. First, its aggregate bandwidth is greater than most existing baseband systems, making it attractive if many high speed data channels must be carried on a single cable. Secondly, because broadband systems use cable TV technology, they can carry closed circuit TV and voice channels along with data traffic. These two capabilities make broadband the ideal choice for large institutions installing one plant or campus-wide cable to carry data, voice, and TV signals. Such systems are frequently called backbones, and can be used to interconnect individual baseband LANs through special baseband to broadband converters called RF modems.

Media Access Control

Media access control (MAC) is the method by which a computer or other LAN-connected device transmits and receives data on the LAN. MAC is the set of rules that define how a station must talk and listen on a medium that is normally shared by many devices. Because most DtC LAN systems are baseband systems, there is a limit of one signal or message on the wire at any given time. This limitation makes it essential that individual devices follow rules governing how and when a device can talk on the LAN. A collision between two devices talking simultaneously will garble LAN messages, which in turn will cause the two devices to retransmit the messages.

Two fundamentally different MAC systems exist in the DtC LAN environment: *carrier sense multiple access/collision detect* and *token passing*. Carrier sense multiple access/collision detect (CSMA/CD) is a MAC system that functions in a manner analogous to a group of people having an informal conversation. Any device wishing to transmit a message simply listens to the LAN and waits for a break in message traffic. When a break occurs, the station begins transmitting its message, while simultaneously monitoring the LAN – this is the CSMA part. If there is no conflict, the transmitting station will hear its own message being transmitted. If a different signal is detected, a collision has occurred between the transmitting station and one or more other stations that are also transmitting – this is the CD part. When the collision is detected, the transmitting station ceases transmission, waits a brief random time interval, listens for a space on the LAN, and attempts to retransmit. The process repeats until the message is successfully transmitted or until the transmitting station gives up.

Token passing controls media access through a more deterministic approach. A short message called a *token* is passed from device to device. The order by which a station receives the token is based either upon the station's physical location on the LAN or upon a unique station address, depending on the specific system in use. All LANs use a station addressing scheme to identify the source and destination of a message. Only the current holder of the token message is permitted to transmit data on the LAN. After a fixed period, the token holder must cease transmission and pass the token to the next station.

CSMA/CD and token passing LANs have decidedly different characteristics, which may become important in certain environments. CSMA/CD systems are simple and inexpensive to implement on the DtC resident network interface boards that support them. In addition, CSMA/CD systems are available from many vendors and adhere to international standards. CSMA/CD has the notable disadvantage of non-deterministic behavior. When the LAN is heavily loaded with traffic, it reaches a point where it stops transmitting data. That point is difficult for LAN designers to predict because it depends upon how much data is being transmitted across the LAN. Degradation can occur in a CSMA/CD system with as few as 50 stations connected. Applications that demand a real time network response, such as process control on a factory assembly line, tend not to use CSMA/CD systems.

The degradation characteristics of token passing LANs are more linear: the LAN slows down gradually and predictably as its traffic load increases. Most token passing schemes allow for station priorities, permitting critical devices to transmit at the expense of non-critical devices whenever the LAN becomes heavily loaded. The tradeoff is that token passing hardware requires more intelligence and therefore is more expensive. Further, token passing systems are currently available from only a few vendors. Additional requirements, such as mainframe computer interface support, may cause one MAC method to be preferred over another.

LAN Architectures

DtC LAN architecture encompasses more than the underlying hardware platform. In fact, the media, signaling system, and media access control methodology together play only a minor role in determining DtC LAN capabilities and performance. The personality of a LAN is determined largely by how its workstations share resources.

Having created the first generation of DtC LAN products, a growing group of vendors set about to develop a more comprehensive DtC LAN architecture. The vendors quickly divided into two camps – the proponents of a peer-to-peer approach, and those who champion a server-oriented LAN.

In the peer-to-peer LAN, one DtC uses files or peripherals physically installed or connected to another DtC. The server-oriented LAN uses one or more centralized devices or *file servers*. File servers provide shared file space, printer access and print queue management, user validation, and LAN administration capabilities. While the file server may appear to replace the minicomputer in the traditional terminal-to-mini environment, there is one critical difference. The file server manages access to shared file space, but applications programs are transferred from the file server across the LAN and are executed in the user's DtC.

Thus, in both the peer-to-peer and server-oriented DtC LAN, a degree of distributed processing exists that is unprecedented in previous information processing system architectures. The merits of each approach deserve more detailed discussion.

Server-Oriented LANs

Server is a fairly recent computer networking term derived from queuing theory. The term indicates that some service is available from the network to a group of clients. A server can be a computer, if the computer is dedicated to providing a single service, or a server can be an application that provides a service and resides in a computer along with unrelated applications. A client may be either a human user or some other entity, perhaps an applications program, that requires the service provided by the server. In the DtC LAN environment, client programs are workstation resident, while server programs reside in the server computer, as shown in Figure 82.

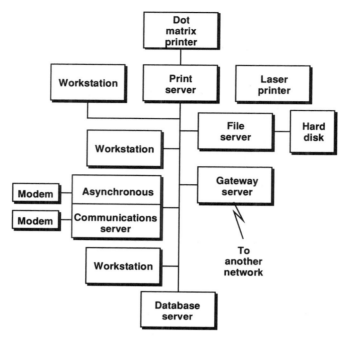

Figure 82. **Server-oriented LAN:** In the server-oriented LAN, file access, and printer control is centralized.

The File Server

The most common server function is file service. The DtC LAN file server provides functions similar to those provided by the file management elements of a minicomputer operating system. The functions normally include identification and validation of a login and password, file access control at the read and write levels, administration, accounting, and security.

File server hardware varies widely. The most popular is an 80386/486- or 68030/40-based microcomputer. A substantial LAN file server requires a moderately powerful microprocessor, but more important, the file server must be able to move large quantities of data rapidly to and from the disk. To satisfy this requirement, file servers often have at least 16-bit data buses, special disk coprocessor boards, and quick access, large capacity disk drives. The speed, capacity, and reliability of file server disk drives merit special consideration because of the number of users depending on them in a server-based DtC LAN.

Recently, a new class of file server has emerged, designed for use on large LANs. These are super servers designed to run high-end network operating systems supporting more than 100 workstations, often providing enough memory to run shared applications in conjunction with the network operating system. They frequently augment conventional DtC technology with parallel processing, proprietary buses, and coprocessors. Super servers may supply fault-tolerant features normally found in mainframe computers. Prices for a fully-equipped super server range from $10,000 to $30,000.

The Print Server

Along with file sharing, most DtC LANs facilitate printer sharing. The print server capability in a server-oriented DtC LAN may be provided as a secondary service by the file server device, or may be available on one or more print server devices. The central function of the print server is to mediate printer access by LAN users.

Access to printers is usually controlled by a print queue, which is an ordered list of documents waiting to be printed. Simple print servers maintain a single queue for each network printer, while sophisticated print servers maintain several prioritized queues per printer. Users having access to higher priority queues can have their documents printed ahead of less privileged users. The print queue administrator interface permits a queue to be stopped, restarted, and reordered by designated personnel.

Print servers that are simply software components on file server devices can be implemented on less powerful types of microcomputers such as an IBM XT. The only special requirement of a print server device is that it must contain enough disk space to queue the print files and enough parallel and serial ports to accommodate the printers that it manages.

Most shared network printers cannot be connected directly to LANs, but must be connected indirectly through a print server device. This presents a problem when a printer needs to be placed at some remote location along the LAN. Several solutions to this problem are discussed later.

Other Types of Servers

As the distributed architecture of the DtC LAN matures, new types of servers are emerging.

Communications servers provide LAN-connected DtCs access to computers or other networks external to the LAN. Communications servers are generally dedicated devices. One variety is the asynchronous communications server (ACS). An ACS resembles a DtC and contains from two to sixteen modems. A LAN server controls access to this pool of modems and allows authorized modem users to use one as if it were connected directly to the workstation. In turn, the ACS modems provide access to any external asynchronous system, including bulletin boards, remote LANs and WANs, and mini or mainframe computers with asynchronous ports.

Another type of communications server acts as a gateway between the DtC LAN and a dissimilar computer or network. Gateway servers are available for connecting DtC LANs to IBM SNA- and 3270-oriented systems, DECnet, TCP/IP, and X.25 networks. Methods for using gateway servers to interconnect DtC LANs with other types of computers and networks will be dealt with later.

A class of server that is being watched with keen interest by the DtC LAN community, is the *database server*. A database server is a LAN-connected distributed processing device that handles database management by first interacting with a client component in the workstation, in order to formulate database transactions. The transactions are then applied to a shared database under the management of the database server software. The database may physically reside on the database server, or on a separate file server. The database server has the potential for improving DtC LAN databases in several significant ways. First, the limited portion of the database processing currently performed within the file server could be removed to another, more specialized device. Secondly, the problem of database integrity could be managed more efficiently by a device that has been optimized for a particular database system and query language.

Peer-to-Peer LANs

In contrast to the server-oriented DtC LAN, the peer-to-peer LAN, shown in Figure 83, is a fully democratic system, without centralized control or file management. It uses a less formal architecture with minimum central administration required. Shared file space can be drawn from individual users workstations or from a central server. Shared printers are usually connected to a user's DtC, though some peer-to-peer systems support dedicated print servers.

File sharing in this environment requires interaction by two network users. First, the user who is making the file available must enter a command to offer the directory for network access. This command will specify access conditions, e.g., write-to access or read-only access, for files used by others. Subsequently, a user on a different DtC wishing to access that file would enter a complementary command, stating the location of the file, the file name, and perhaps a password. To avoid having to enter the commands each time access to the shared file is required, the commands can be executed automatically with a command file.■

■ The procedures are simpler in the AppleTalk/AppleShare environment.

The simplicity and limitations of the peer-to-peer approach may be viewed as an asset or as a liability in comparison with a server-oriented LAN. The selection of one architecture over the other depends largely upon administrative requirements. The networking of a small work group of five to ten users can be accomplished with a peer-to-peer system. The assumption is that the users know each other, can be trusted not to violate each other's private files, and are competent enough to avoid practices that could impair the network. Once the network is up and running, the task of administering this loosely coupled network can be divided among the users.

When a larger number of DtCs require interconnection, when security or data integrity become important and a greater variety of LAN services are planned, or when central administration is to be imposed, a server-oriented LAN is usually needed. The server-oriented architecture has the following advantages over the peer-to-peer system:

- The server is dedicated to file and print services. Other workstations in the LAN are not burdened with file and print service.
- Server-oriented file access control capabilities are more sophisticated, allowing the network administrator to assign a range of access privileges within a given database to different users.
- Important files can be physically protected by locking the file server.
- Users are not dependent upon others for access to appropriate files.
- The LAN will be managed by a central authority, facilitating organized addition and deletion of users, system accounting procedures, disk space allocation, shared disk backup, and print queue management.

Peer-to-peer LANs are more successful in small informal environments, while server-oriented LANs are more appropriate for large numbers of users, or where the LAN is an integral part of an organization's information management system.

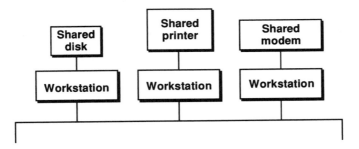

Figure 83.   Peer-to-peer LAN: The peer-to-peer LAN distributes file and print services throughout the LAN.

Low-Cost LANs Using Standard Interfaces

RS-232 serial and parallel printer interfaces can be used for low-cost sharing of a few DtCs over short distances. Using serial interfaces, flat cables, and an inexpensive software package ($150), you can outfit DtCs to share files, disks, and other peripherals by chaining them together through their serial interfaces. RS-232 LAN software is not intended to replace the full capability of a true DtC LAN, but rather to provide a low-cost alternative for linking two or three DtCs that need to share information at low speed. You can connect a laptop to an office DtC after a business trip to download information, or to your personal DtC at home. Only the server DtC would need a hard drive. Asynchronous LANs may be particularly suited for connecting a portable DtC to an office DtC when you need to move files between respective hard drives. Bit rates around 100 Kbits/second are possible with these systems. The Brooklyn Bridge is an example of a serial LAN software package.

Low-cost systems suffer from several shortcomings:

- *Media access control* – Low-cost systems have poor mechanisms, if any, for operating multiple units in parallel. They also have poor or no file management methodology.

- *Reliability* – There is little or no error checking capability in the interface hardware, therefore the capability must be relegated to software, seriously affecting transmission rates.

- *Speed* – Speed is usually limited to less than 200 Kbits/second. Although low speed may be tolerated in simple two computer master/slave configurations, it will not be acceptable for larger numbers of more interactive DtCs.

DtC LANs are now being viewed as one component in a larger internetwork environment. DtC LAN services such as E-Mail, file transfers, and distributed databases are driving the requirement for internetwork connections. Interconnection of computer networks is never a simple proposition, and it becomes particularly complicated when the networks in question use differing protocol standards.

Bridges

Two or more similar LANs can often be interconnected with a MAC (media access) layer bridge, so named because it bridges two LANs that have a common MAC layer protocol, for example, IEEE 802.3. This relatively simple and inexpensive microcomputer-based device is configured as a station on both LANs being bridged, as shown in Figure 84.

When the bridge is initialized, its internal software begins to monitor the traffic on both LANs, noting the source station addresses contained within the packet headers. The bridge constructs a model of the network based on this information, which it stores internally in tables. With location information on active stations, the bridge can make decisions as to whether the destination of a given packet is local or remote. Packets that contain local destination addresses are not forwarded by the bridge. Packets that contain addresses that are foreign to the bridge are, by default, passed to the other LAN. This prevents locally bound packets from being needlessly transmitted to the other LAN. The level of traffic on both networks is reduced, while still permitting inter-LAN communication as required. Today's bridges are essentially plug and play devices, but the auto-learning mode can be overridden by manually configuring the bridge to filter out the packets coming from or going to specific stations.

A variation of this approach, called remote bridging, may be used to interconnect two remotely located LANs. This configuration requires a bridge to be connected to each LAN and a communication link between the bridges. In addition to filtering and forwarding, the exterior sides of both bridges contain communication hardware

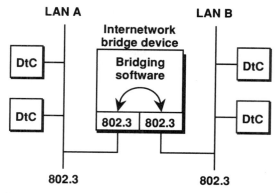

Figure 84. **Bridge between similar networks**

for transmission across wide area links such as dedicated 56 Kbps or T1 telephone lines. When forwarding a packet from one LAN to the other, the bridge will encapsulate the LAN packet in an appropriate long-haul protocol such as HDLC or X.25 in order to ensure reliable transmission over long distance media. Upon receipt, the remote bridge strips off the long-haul control information and transmits the original packet across its own LAN to the receiving station.

Routers

Routers perform a function similar to that of bridges, but by a different means. A router contains an internal map of the internet, which is obtained manually or automatically from an external source. When a packet is received by a router, the layer-two MAC header is discarded, and the layer-three network/internet header is inspected for destination network and station. If the destination network is directly connected to the router, the router constructs a new MAC-layer header containing the station number as the destination address, and forwards the packet through the appropriate port to the station.

If the destination network is not directly connected to the router, the router uses its internal routing table to determine the address of another router – on one of its directly connected networks – that can provide a path to the ultimate destination. The router then constructs a new MAC-layer header, using the address of the next router as the destination station address, and forwards the packet. If no path exists, the packet is discarded.

Inasmuch as routers can understand and construct a variety of layer-two headers, a router can be used to connect networks that use different MAC-layer header formats. A single router could route between an Ethernet 802.3, token ring 802.5, and an X.25 wide area network. The requirement for a common protocol between the various networks is pushed up one level, to layer three, and is different from the bridge, which connects networks with a common MAC layer protocol. The Ethernet, token ring, and bridge. The Ethernet, token ring, and X.2 networks would have to support a common internet protocol such as IP. A new type of router, called a multiprotocol router, can differentiate between several internet protocols, e.g., IP, IPX, and AppleTalk, and route all of them correctly.

Gateways

Gateways are used to interconnect two very dissimilar networks. Gateways are used where the two environments have neither layer-two nor layer-three protocols in common, when neither a bridge nor a router will solve the problem. Gateway systems are designed for interconnecting two specific environments, and internally they contain two complete protocol stacks. A packet arriving from one network is passed up through the incoming protocol stack, dissected, converted to the outgoing protocol format, and then passed down through the outbound stack.

Common implementations include PC LAN to SNA, PC LAN to DECNet, and PC LAN to TCP/IP gateways. High cost, low throughput due to protocol conversion overhead, and inflexibility make gateways the interconnection method of last resort.

Summary of Interconnection Methods

Clearly, both bridges and routers are viable methods. Bridges are less expensive, are faster, and require little expertise to configure and manage. Since bridges don't

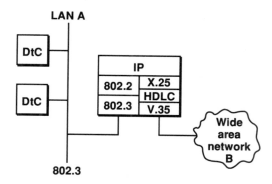

Figure 85. **Routing between dissimilar networks**

use layer-three header information and don't otherwise modify the packet, a mixture of internet protocols may be bridged transparently.

Routers, on the other hand, have the flexibility to support a variety of MAC layer protocols, and can be used to interconnect a larger number of networks. See Figure 85. A bridge may be characterized as a load management device; a router is a more comprehensive network management tool. In particular, security policy and network performance problems can be managed more effectively with a router, given the available expertise. Many large internet environments use bridges to manage loads within departments, with one or more routers interconnecting the departments.

A new device is available that combines the capabilities of the bridge and the router. A *brouter* applies routing functions to incoming packets that contain routable layer-three header information. For non-routable packets, the brouter functions as a MAC-layer bridge. Using bridges, routers, and gateways, DtC LAN designers can connect various types of new or existing networks, with alternatives often possible. Consider the problem of a DtC LAN that uses a proprietary LAN protocol, say Novell's IPX, for file and printer sharing, but which must also provide TCP/IP services so that DtC users can login to a LAN-connected Unix host. One approach would be to install an IPX to TCP/IP gateway on the LAN. DtC users would speak IPX to the gateway, which would convert the IPX packets into IP packets and forward them to the Unix machine. An alternative would be to convert each DtC into a TCP/IP host by installing software on the workstation to provide both IPX and TCP/IP services. In that case, the DtC would speak IPX to the Novell file servers and IP to the Unix host.

The implementer of a DtC LAN that will ultimately be connected to larger computers and networks should consider carefully the impact of SNA, the ISO standards, and TCP/IP when planning the network. The interconnection advantages gained by implementing a TCP/IP- or SNA-oriented DtC LAN must be weighed against the simplicity of installing an autonomous LAN with vendor-specific protocols. That is why it is essential to establish, early in the definition of DtC LAN requirements, whether or not there is a need for interconnecting to standards-oriented computers and networks. If the need exists, that requirement will have a substantial impact upon vendor and product selection.

Distributed Processing on Networks

Executing remotely stored programs and data locally or viewing and controlling remote applications as though they were on your own DtC are some of the exciting benefits that distributed processing technology now offers to LAN users.

The theory behind distributed processing is that multiple computers can be loosely coupled into a functioning data processing system that will work better than the traditional centralized timesharing system. Distributed processing can:

- reduce communications costs, since only centralized data needs to move over expensive long-distance phone lines.
- reduce the bottleneck of a large number of users vying for the central computer processor resources.
- increase system robustness because the loss of one processor would not bring the entire system to a halt.
- reduce dependence on any single vendor, since a mixture of systems can communicate using a standardized communications methodology such as X or SQL.

Whether many individuals access a single mainframe computer over dumb terminals or many DtC users use intelligent resources over a network, distributed processing is *the* way to share computing resources.

Distributed processing can occur at many levels and involve many different hardware and software devices. However it is accomplished, programs and data are shared over a system of computing devices. Computing systems can range from those having no distribution capability, to those that distribute files and programs, to those that carry distribution as far as it will go by spreading intelligent program execution on demand throughout a network.

Multitasking and Multiusing

Before we look at the different methodologies networks use to distribute processing, we should review the more conventional and historical notions of computer processing resource distribution: multitasking and multiuser systems.

First, there is the notion that one CPU should be able to multitask. The operating system slices up the CPU's execution cycles and apportions the slices to alternately execute processing tasks. The time slicing and apportionment is usually transparent to the user, but it is not without the cost of apparent retardation of each task. This is not only because more than one thing is being done at the same time, but also because the slicing process incurs an overhead.

Multitasking permits a single user to do multiple simultaneous tasks on a single dedicated DtC *and* it permits multiple users to each perform one or more tasks on a single CPU. When several users share a single CPU by remote terminals, it is known as a *multiuser* system. Each user perceives complete ownership of the computing system, when in fact the users alternately share the remote CPU through multitasking.

It is, of course, easier to perceive ownership when all resources are on your own desktop. Quick and intimate access to all computer resources, e.g, graphics, mass store, keyboard, mouse, and printer, are what make desktop computing an interactive and productive experience. When these resources are shared over long and low-speed communications channels, the feeling of ownership diminishes with each additional second the user must wait for a response from the remote CPU.

It is not uncommon for an EP workstation under Unix to support five to twenty database users. Through plug-in multiple serial interface boards, Unix can easily support a large number of serial interfaced dumb terminals. This configuration can be used for relatively closed and low user-interaction applications such as infrequent DBMS updates and canned report runs. This computing situation has the same limitation as mainframes connected to terminals have: low interactivity through bottlenecking serial interfaces.

Times change and computing environments improve. Stripped-down DtCs are competitively priced with dumb terminals so that we now have DtC servers that act like mainframe computers by concentrating data or processing capability while each user's terminal is a powerful desktop computer in its own right.

Networked client/server applications that use DtCs are a more integrated approach since it gives each user the double advantage of a personalized workstation and the ability to distribute applications to other DtCs on the network. All of this is combined with rugged and secure communications with other workstations at a reasonable price.

Levels of Distribution

Interactive DtCs can work together over networks to form synergistic computational systems. Let's look at different ways of sharing applications and programs on networks. We investigate four increasingly complex methodologies:

Level 0 – No distribution: Independent workstations with individual software programs and data is shared by trading floppy disks.

Level 1 – File distribution: Separate software products are operated, controlled, and viewed on each workstation. Data and program files may be stored and shared by way of a central server.

Level 2 – I/O distribution: Programs run on remote DtCs and can be viewed and controlled by the local DtC as if they were running on that DtC. Control includes using graphics screens and special I/O devices.

Level 3 – Process distribution: Multiple processors accomplish a task on the network automatically, with each workstation contributing to the process according to that workstation's individual capability.

Level 0 – No Distribution

Many users, particularly home users, are not LANed to friends and neighbors. Costs or security reasons keep DtCs operated as independent workstations. Since there is no network to mediate between file formats, data transfers must occur through external media such as:

- *Communications services* – Many users move files using commercial store and forward services.

- *Work computers* – Many of us are LANed internally within our work environments. Often these LANs incorporate an external dial-in capability. Through appropriate permissions, the LAN can be called from home over dial-in lines and files transferred through store and forward bulletin boards.

- *Bulletin boards* – For those requiring quick file transfers, a DtC is dedicated as a bulletin board. Autoanswer modems are incorporated and automatic bulletin board software is operated that permits store and forward file transfers with the dedicated DtC. Using electronic switches, available for around $100, the telephone line is automatically switched to the modem or the phone depending on whether the modem carrier signal is present. The bulletin board DtC shares the analog phone line.

- *Disk formats* – Without distribution capability, disk compatibility between users is essential. Special hardware and software are available to match disk formats between different platforms. Users of the same platform require the highest levels of communication, since they share data and executables.

- *Utility software* – Within a given platform category a variety of utilities can be used to simplify data transfers between remote DtCs. For example, entire subdirectory structures can be backed up to floppy disk for transfer to another DtC. Built-in file compression can often double the amount of data placed on the floppy. The utilities are easy to use and contain high reliability data checks on the transferred data.

- *Removable media* – Removable media hard disks offer a convenient means for moving large software systems between remote DtCs.

- *OCR* – If all else fails, you can always move data between two non-connected computers using optical character recognition. For ASCII files, just print the file in a recognizable font, hand carry it to the receiving computer, and scan it in with OCR software to recover the ASCII-character content. APA images can be printed and scanned back on the other end with appropriate aspect ratio corrections, but there will be a loss of resolution from the physical media conversions, going to printed paper and back.

The techniques listed above involve the exchange of DtC files either by floppies or over ordinary phone lines. Such communications are *loosely coupled*, since there is an explicit and obvious operational protocol required of the user to accomplish the transfers. Whether the protocol is a dial-in procedure or a floppy disk exchange, the result is the same. Files can be transferred, but the fact that remote files or programs are ultimately used in a local DtC is certainly not transparent to the user.

As we shall see next, there are higher levels of distribution that do become user transparent. Let's look at transparent file distribution over LANs.

Level 1 – File Distribution

Through file distribution, programs and data execute locally on your DtC but may be stored remotely on a network server. Programs and data that run through a network, but appear to users to be local, leads to many advantages, and also to some headaches. There are two ways of distributing files throughout a network. One, disk service, allows a DtC to treat remote disks as if they were local, while the other, file service, acts more intelligently at the file level.

Disk Service

The early networks allowed users to share mass storage disks or volumes. The networks featured disk service, meaning that the servers were extensions of the mass storage peripherals installed in attached workstations. Drives A:, B:, and C: might be resident volumes within a local DtC, while drives M: and N: could be network volumes linked into your DtC system at boot time by programs resident on the local DtC.

Each user could have additional hard disks and use them transparently, or with no software modifications other than specifying an N: rather than a C: drive. Transparency means that you can select an N: drive, move files between it and DtC memory and not care that the N: drive is not really in your office connected to your DtC, but rather is connected to a server in another room, building, or even country. The obvious benefit is that each user has access to remote drives, possibly larger than the local drive.

You could run a software base over the network, as though it were installed on your own local disk drive. For example, you could change to the N: drive, type 1-2-3, and *voila!*, 1-2-3 would be executing on your DtC. Note that 1-2-3 was loaded into DtC memory from the server over the network, but the fact that the 1-2-3 executable was remotely stored is transparent to you. DtC network drivers, in conjunction with hardware on the network interface, took care of the details of getting the 1-2-3 executable from the server, hauling it in from the network, loading it into your memory and executing it. Once in your memory, the 1-2-3 program behaves as though it had been loaded from your own local hard disk. You could also load data files transparently from the server. While executing 1-2-3, you might need access to a file named BOLTS located on the server. In the 1-2-3 menu, you simply enter N:/BOLTS instead of C:/BOLTS, and Lotus 1-2-3 will load the file BOLTS into DtC memory. The 1-2-3 program doesn't know that the BOLTS file is actually located on a remote hard disk. All of these details are handled by local network drivers. The only difference to the 1-2-3 program is a different volume specifier, the N: volume.

You can see from the DtC point of view, shown in Figure 86, that programs or data come into memory essentially the same way, whether from the network or the local hard disk. The enhanced network BIOS, usually provided as a resident program, performs more than the usual hard disk routines. Additionally, it redirects file inputs from network disk servers to travel over the network. Hardware on the network board take care of the details of getting the request across the network and the resulting file from the network through a sea of other requests and files. The returning file is passed by the network BIOS back through the operating system,

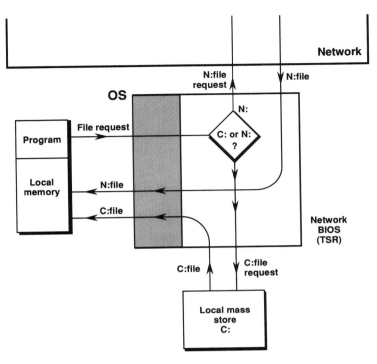

Figure 86. **Disk service methodologies:** A remote disk looks no different to applications software than the local hard disk.

which passes it on to memory. In both cases, the programs and data execute in your DtC's memory and the memory or the program that called the data does not care where the file or program data came from.

This notion of disk transparency is powerful because it means that you can run your existing software base unmodified, yet access programs and data that exist on mass storage devices connected to other DtCs in the network.

Disk service transparency can be problematic when multiple users need access to the same files *at the same time* over the network. Each DtC's network software and hardware provides access, usually on a first come, first served basis. The network software will simply process each request in turn, and deliver the data to each DtC as soon as possible. The problem is not with people reading programs or files at the same time over the network, but rather with multiple users trying to modify files concurrently on the network server without an underlying control methodology. The following is a specific example of a disk service problem. Two remote users access a disk server volume containing an inventory. User A links to the volume and a copy of the server volume's FAT is loaded in user A's local workstation memory.■

■ File allocation tables, stored on your mass storage device, keep track of your hard disk file logistics. Information such as file size, name and pointers to where clusters of data are located are stored in the FAT.

User A accesses a file called NUTS, which occupies areas 1-10 of the FAT, and adds a record to the file, expanding its size. The local operating system expands the file NUTS into the next free area on the disk, area 21.

Meanwhile, user B has linked to the volume for the purpose of adding to the file BOLTS, which occupies areas 11-20. At the time user B linked, the local copy of the server FAT shows that area 21 is available, and the file BOLTS is expanded into that region. User B has just overwritten the data written into area 21 by user A. User B finishes the work and unlinks, writing back the copy of the FAT to the server disk. The FAT, from user B's point of view, is accurately showing that the file BOLTS occupies areas 11-21.

Now user A unlinks, writing the copy of the FAT to the server, overwriting user B's copy. The server's FAT is corrupt because it indicates that part of the file NUTS is in area 21, which in fact has been permanently lost and replaced by the extension to file BOLTS. The file NUTS will contain an extension, but it will actually be the data from the file BOLTS in area 21 of the volume. The server FAT is not correct, and the volume will need to be repaired. Figure 87 shows how each file extends into area 21, causing the confusion.

File Service

At first glance, the disk service process appears to be identical to the techniques used in today's networks; however, the underlying mechanics of disk service technology don't provide for simultaneous updating of disks by multiple users. The inability of users to share data on disk volumes prompted Microsoft to incorporate network functions in Version 3.1 of MS-DOS, allowing a single copy of the FAT to be maintained completely on the server, and updated continuously in step with changes to the data written to the server. This type of network is a *file service* network. Most DtC networks in operation today incorporate file servers, which also double as print servers.

Through the use of the SHARE command, a server administrator can provide many different network users access to the same files in a controlled fashion. For

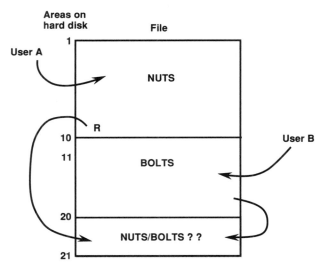

Figure 87. Disk access problems: In a disk access LAN, two or more users accessing the same file can cause trouble.

example, a file `N:\WP\WPDATA` resides on a file server `WPSERVER`. Figure 88 shows the network administrator allowing shared access to the `N:\WP\DATA` files on server `WPSERVER` by issuing on the server the command:

```
SHARE WPDATA N:\WP\DATA
```

This command assigns the sharename `WPDATA` to the `D:\WP\DATA` directory on the file server. The `SHARE` command is generic and can take several different forms depending upon the type of network software used. Network vendors usually assign a logical name as a pointer to a file server directory. This sharename can then be referenced in a link command to attach a remote workstation's disk designator to the directory on the server. The Microsoft standard link command has the format:

```
USE DRIVE:\\SERVERNAME\SHARENAME
```

where `DRIVE:` indicates the local workstation's drive designator (`A:` through `Z:`), `SERVERNAME` is the registered network name of the desired server, and `SHARENAME` is the pointer to the linked directory on the server. In order to link the directory shared in the previous example a user would issue the command:

```
USE C:\\WPSERVER\WPDATA
```

allowing the local drive `C:` to reference the `\WP\DATA` directory on the file server `WPSERVER`. Other workstations could link their local drive designators (`A:` through `Z:`) to the same sharename as shown in Figure 88.

Sharenames can be assigned various levels of privilege, including read only; read and write; and read, write, and create. On single tasking platforms such as MS-DOS, these privileges are global to the sharename, that is, all users of the sharename have the same level of access to files. This is not a limitation on multitasking systems, however, and individual users can be granted different levels of access to the same sharename. For instance, one primary user may be given permission to update records in a shared database while other users are permitted to only read the data.

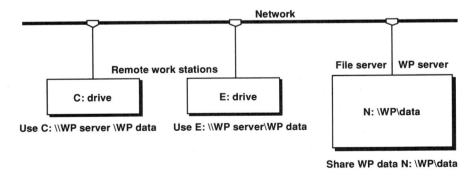

Figure 88. File service methodology: Two remote users link their `C:` and `E:` drives respectively to the `N:\WP\DATA` file on the file server.

Precise control over sharenames provides the security needed to guarantee the privacy and integrity of centrally-stored datasets.

Files servers can be standard desktop computers, specialized dedicated servers, minicomputers, or even large mainframe systems. Shared data and applications supporting file sharing are becoming commonplace now that the consistency and protection of the data can be enforced. Network versions of word processors, spreadsheets, scheduling packages, statistical programs, graphics applications, and other varieties of software abound throughout the industry. The advances of graphical user interfaces have contributed to the easy use of distributed resources on local and wide area networks. You can now select applications and data located on your workstation, or resources on servers located at varying distances from your location without having to remember complex linking commands. It takes only the swish and click of a mouse.

Peripheral Sharing

Sharing of resources is not limited to files. Printers, fax machines, modems, plotters, typesetting and imagesetting machines, and other equipment is being made available to the network, and consequently to all the users of a LAN. It is far less expensive and more efficient to share these peripherals on the network than to provide each user with a dedicated device. Many other specialized uses of network sharing are surfacing.

> **EXAMPLE**
>
> In a hospital, a LAN that links several buildings is used to keep tabs on critical care unit patients. One 80386-based DtC is dedicated as a monitoring station and implements special hardware interfaces to all of the CCU patients. This specialized station is connected to the LAN and operates remote network software that runs the monitoring equipment remotely from the network stations in the physician's office. Since the network may also have a dial-in feature, the CCU monitor may be accessed from a physician's home or from another hospital. The configuration provides a doctor with real time graphical information on a patient's condition, thereby decreasing the need for visits to the CCU.

Standardization of network protocols and network operating systems makes it possible to distribute data, applications, and peripherals on computing platforms suited to the size and nature of the resource. Small, localized programs or data can reside on microcomputer-based servers that are inexpensive and easily maintained. Larger datasets and applications can be put on mini or mainframe class machines that are more complex and more expensive, but provide the necessary processor power and storage capabilities. It would appear that networks have reached their goal in extending the individual desktop to include many useful and powerful resources that could not begin to fit into the confines of an independent workstation.

File Distribution Summary

The advantages of server-resident applications and data include:

- *Maintenance and upgrade* – Only the server copy needs to be installed or changed when upgrades are received. Technicians can resolve applications problems without having to go to each user's computer. Applications that are developed in-house can be centrally maintained without requiring redistribution when changes are made.

- **Back up** – All server resident programs and data can be backed up for better integrity of both shared and individual user information.

- **Large applications and data** – Can be housed on servers with larger mass storage devices, allowing less expensive configuration of netstations ranging from no mass storage at all on user's computers to medium-sized fixed disks.

- **Licensing** – Instead of purchasing copies for each user, an applications software package may be licensed more efficiently and often at less cost for several stations on a network.

- **Data sharing** – Data can be shared and maintained more easily for multiple users and can be transferred more efficiently between computers attached to the network.

- **Standardization of data structures** – Directory arrangements on the server will look the same to all users and changes made to those directories are immediately reflected across the user base. Menus can be provided to users who are less aware of the technical network access mechanisms allowing them to use server resources without having to become network gurus. Standardization is better for training and maintenance practices.

- **Access control** – Access to applications and data can be permitted or denied according to specific requirements on either a temporary or permanent basis.

- **Software piracy control** – Software can be more easily controlled since users do not have access to distribution disks and can be prohibited from downloading software from the server.

- **Standardization of applications** – Users will tend to learn and use supported server-resident programs rather than strike out on their own with non-supported software.

- **Access** – Access to mission-critical applications and data is not subject to the availability of any single workstation. If one workstation fails, the work can still continue on other stations unhampered by the temporary loss of one access point.

Advantages of local applications and data include:

- **No network downtime** – Your work is not at the mercy of the network.

- **No access denial** – Access to resources is not subject to priority usage of the server or network media and is only limited by local machine configuration and capabilities.

- **Data privilege** – Data is absolutely private. No one accesses data unless the owner personally delivers them by providing a diskette or by allowing access to the computer file.

- **Custom data structure** – Data can be structured according to personal preference. Resources on the mass storage device can be arranged in any order and may be easier to find and use by individual users.

- **More RAM** – More RAM will be available for use by local applications since no memory network drivers will be required to support the network interface.

Most installations rely upon a combination of local and network residency of applications and data. However, few individuals would disagree that the power of the desktop computer lies in its ability to communicate with and use resources outside itself. The standalone personal computer is rapidly being replaced by the netstation in all computing environments. Even home computer users are beginning to look at network solutions.

Level 2 – I/O Distribution (Client/Server)

With file service, all processing is accomplished on individual workstations. The file server does not process data and does not execute any applications. Instead, the server executes programs associated with distribution permission, and verification of resident data and various print services such as managing print queues and providing output to attached printers. The bulk of applications processing occurs on individual workstations. The separation between processor and storage media often requires frequent and inefficient transfer of data across the network. We next look at the client/server methodology, which offers a different form of transparency.

NOTE

The inefficiencies of file-service LAN configurations and restricted network bandwidth has led to the development of a less intensive and much more efficient network methodology called client/server applications. Applications of this type are written in two parts, one that executes on the server and the other that runs on the netstation. The two parts of the application communicate across the network by a protocol that identifies the particular client and synchronizes the client part with the server half of the program. The server part of the program executes and provides file and print services. However, these services are not usually associated with the client/server application, which operates independently.

The client/server approach allows the programs and data to reside on the same workstation server, while remote DtC clients are used simply to control and view the ongoing events.

File vs. I/O Distribution

To differentiate between file service and I/O client/server service, let's compare a typical database problem addressed by each technique.

File distribution: If the database application program is stored on a server, the workstation must download it. This could involve a transfer of 150K to 500K. When a dataset is chosen, one or more index files may be downloaded to the workstation. Depending upon the size and complexity of the databases and the amount of RAM resident on the workstation, the transfer may be quite large. Repeated transfers of large files during a session can tie up considerable resources. Each time a request is made for data, the workstation must pull sections of the database across the network to process the information locally. In the worst case of a non-indexed database, if the user requests the last record, the entire database must cycle across the network and through the local processor before the requester gains access to the desired data record. When sorting databases, the complete dataset travels across the network many times. While this inefficient use of communication resources is not a problem when users are few, the performance of both the network and the server deteriorates as the number of users increase.

I/O distribution: The client requires data. A request is sent to the server describing the data desired in as much detail as possible. The use of blind or wild-card requests are discouraged and limited by the client half of the application. When the server half of the application receives the request or query, the server processes the search and returns *only* the requested data to the client, in fact, only requests and requested data are transmitted across the network. The client provides the user interface and local buffering of the data, while the server containing the database provides the database engine and processes searches, additions, and deletions. It also indexes and performs other data-associated operations. Usually the server part of the application is written in such a manner that it can accommodate multiple concurrent requests from different clients and can process many queries simultaneously.

User Interfaces

Notice in Figure 89 that several clients, an MS-DOS computer, a Unix box, and a Macintosh, are communicating with a server that is operating a database engine and database. Each client is free to provide its user with that a particular interface. One DtC in the network, the database server, operates the appropriate network database server software such as Novell's SQL – a database engine tightly coupled with the Novell network.

> **NOTE**
>
> ### SQL (Structured Query Language)
> SQL is a powerful database query language. It originated on the mainframe and was ported to DtCs in the Oracle DBMS. The SQL command set is dedicated to extracting information from complex, multifile databases. In SQL there are few commands, but they are powerful. SQL on DtCs is an important trend for these reasons: 1) SQL queries support networked databases. 2) IBM's OS/2 operating system supports SQL. 3) Many DtC DBMS products already have SQL capability (dBASE, DataEase, Paradox, Oracle). Since the SQL language is robust and difficult to comprehend at the command level, many DtC DBMS products have SQL front ends, which permit English-like queries and convert them to appropriate SQL commands.

Several clients have a need for the data. A Mac client displays data obtained from the server in an Excel spreadsheet and associated pie chart generated by Excel. A Unix user gathers some data for complex numerical processing and a plot. An MS-DOS client needs to extract some information into a Paradox database system and respective bar chart. For each client there are special SQL link software hooks to the respective application to establish the SQL connection. The rest of the application, however, is operated with off-the-shelf heavy duty programs such as Paradox and Excel that interface with the data. Paradox and Excel don't care where the data is or how it is stored, and the server doesn't know how Paradox and Excel display data.

Indeed, the user interface can become quite customized. There is no reason why the received data should not be implemented in multiple applications on a single client in a Windows environment. Recall the example in which Microsoft Word and Excel applications were exchanging data by dynamic data exchange. The Excel spreadsheet might have been filled from a portion of a database on the server. A front end such as Windows Q&E would establish the SQL link with the server.

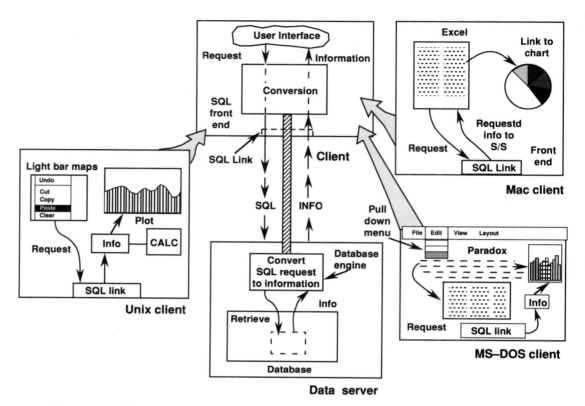

Figure 89. Client/server database application

Most of the details could be satisfied with Excel macros; the user simply points to a button on the screen that extracts the required server data and displays the final output in Excel. Notice what is going on in the example shown in Figure 89:

- *Familiar software* – Each client DtC user is operating familiar software and its appropriate user interface.
- *SQL queries* – The client DtCs send only SQL queries or SQL triggers over the network.
- *Query results sent* – The server DtC processes the query and sends only the query results, a subset of the database, over the network.◼

◼ The server DtC may have had to relay the query to other higher hierarchy DtCs or to a mainframe to fulfill the query if the requested information was not in fact on the local server.

┌─ NOTE ─────────────────────────────────────

The SQL Trigger

A complex SQL query could be replaced by an SQL trigger. Instead of a large SQL file, a smaller SQL trigger is sent to the server. In addition to the trigger, necessary parameters are transmitted, representing time of year, region, or other defining variables. Custom-developed SQL queries resident on the server are actuated by the incoming trigger and the parameters and the resident SQL finally gather the request data. SQL triggers relieve users and the local software from creating custom SQL requests and allow complex queries to be centrally developed and managed on the server DtC. Thus, a variety of different users and needs can be managed centrally and the query SQL can be developed by a single source with everyone's needs and efficiency in mind. All that travels through the network is the trigger and the defining parameters.

All exchanges between client and server occur with the client having no knowledge of the specific database structure on the server. The client need not be aware of indexes, data organization, or field names. Likewise, the server concentrates on the database maintenance operations without concern for the user interface.

Since the client manages the user interface, different versions of the client can run on different platforms. For instance, an application might feature Macintosh, MS-DOS computer, and Unix clients, all of which communicate with a common Unix server.

This architecture permits the client to take on characteristics of the native platform on which it executes. In fact, the client can assume the look and feel of the resident environment entirely, reducing training and maintenance requirements and encouraging wider use of the application, since users are more apt to use applications that they perceive as friendly and familiar.

A Specific Client/Server Example

A company maintains logs and references to company memoranda. Each department of the company maintains a separate numbering sequence. Accounts payable might use ACCP, year, number while personnel uses PERS, year, number. To log a new memo, a new sequential memo number is obtained from the server by the client issuing the request, including the department identity. The server looks up the last number in the department's log and passes the number back to the client. The server then increments the memo number by one and waits for the client to enter the new reference. The client displays a form prompting for author's name, subject, and other information. When the form is completed, the client formats the data, packages it into a request for service, and ships it off to the server.

To search for references in the memo database, the client (once more through a form) selects the type of search by number, by author, or by division. The server processes the search and returns the data to the client, which displays the information.

Multi-Tiered Data Distribution

Client/server systems often act over several hierarchies of data. In some SQL implementations the server can also assume the role of client in order to reference data from other servers. This architecture establishes a powerful capability for distributing data among several servers in a data hierarchy while confining queries to local servers.

Consider a hierarchical company-oriented data distribution method using a multi-level client/server/server/server architecture. Each small working group of users (10 to 30 individuals), primarily accesses a small OS/2-based workgroup server. This server contains only workgroup-specific data and manages all permissions for both resident data and for access to higher-level servers. When the workgroup server can not satisfy a request for data locally, it checks for proper access privileges and triggers a request to the division-level server, perhaps a medium-powered minicomputer. If the division server can not satisfy the request, it queries the company server, a high-powered mini or mainframe computer.

Since most work is accomplished at the workgroup level, a high percentage of network traffic can be isolated behind bridges, routers, or gateways. All user-access privileges could be managed at the workgroup level and could be confined to small subsets of the global user base. The three-tiered data structure would provide for the controlled distribution of company, division, and group level data as well as an orderly collection of data in the reverse direction. For instance, time card information could be collected on the workgroup server on a daily basis, then transferred and verified on the division server at the end of the pay period, then transferred to the payroll office on the company server.

Client and Server Role Reversal

There are client/server systems in which the roles of the client and server are reversed. The clients are in fact the remote computers that execute the applications. The servers are the local DtCs that view and control the remote applications. This arrangement is a hybrid approach to conventional remote applications executing on mainframe computers controlled by terminals, but the client/server approach is much more flexible and powerful. A specific example of this type of client/server approach is the X Windows system described later.

Level 3 – Process Distribution

Tasks may be shared across computing equipment. For more than a decade computer scientists have been advancing the idea that data processing could be improved by using an approach known as process distribution. Process distribution allows several CPUs, or more appropriately, application-specific processors, to participate in a given problem, each CPU specialized for its part. In a certain sense, modern DtCs are multi-processing units wherein the application is processed by a variety of specialized components; graphics by graphics controllers, math by math coprocessors, and communications by network coprocessors. Enhanced bus capabilities allow multiple CPUs to contribute to problem solving in a single DtC.

In a larger sense, however, current network technology does not permit such intense CPU resource sharing between desktop computers. The high rate of data sharing needed and the non-parallel nature of networks call for deeper levels of network protocol and technology than are currently available.

In the following possibilities for data distribution, one can see the network traffic rates going through the roof:

- *Peripheral communications* – A high resolution graphics controller's memory being directly manipulated by a remote CPU. A laser printer combining partial images from several workstations.

- *Intra-CPU communications* – Synchronization of parallel CPUs, or moving partial data from CPU to CPU sequentially or in parallel.

- *Communications between coprocessors* – One could imagine coprocessors such as math and graphics sharing data across the network as images are constructed from highly connected math and graphics processes.

- *Memory sharing* – Blocks of memory being shared across the network by blocks of data rather than by crude I/O files. Shared memory methodologies are already implemented within single DtCs. These methodologies will need to be extended to operate over networks.

- **Problem hierarchy** – Portions of problems and partial solutions distributed among participating workstations. Different portions of the problem would be submitted to appropriate computing units specializing in an appropriate area.

- **Problem results** – Results might have to be gathered from several computers. Often, the results occur first in CPU memory.

> **EXAMPLE**
>
> Figure 90 shows a group of DtCs working out a complex problem. One DtC handles the user interface and final graphics output display while other DtCs in the network operate on the problem according to their capabilities. Notice that two DtCs share the number crunching task in parallel.

All of this activity must be coordinated somewhere. Partial and final results must be compiled and gathered. Program development compilers and methodology will change radically with higher levels of integration and distribution. Recall the more complicated Windows and Macintosh software development as compared to straightforward MS-DOS programs. Likewise, great changes in methodology will be required to adjust to process distribution. There will be a need for protocols to coordinate program execution and considerable increases in network bandwidth to handle higher levels of communication.

Ultimately, we should be able to pose a problem to a system of DtCs, and let them worry about how to distribute the process. While each DtC may be performing individual work, they could also be collectively working on a large-scale problem whenever they are idle.

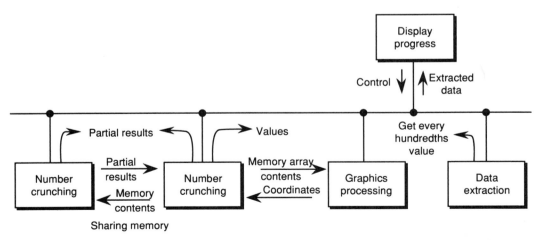

Figure 90. **Processing distribution:** To share execution at finer levels will require higher network traffic rates and standards in areas we can only imagine. In level 1 and 2 distribution, what traversed the network were programs, files, control packets, SQL, and subsets of data sets – *not* internalizations of the problem being solved.

Improved buses such as Futurebus+ and higher-performance local area network connections such as the fiber optic distributed data interface (FDDI) will be the key to this type of process distribution among DtC units.

Distributed Processing Summary

In a level 1 system, information is moved about in the network as files. Individual programs can operate as though their executable and data files were local, even though they may be stored elsewhere in the network. The workstation executing a given program also displays that program's output and controls that program's execution.

In level 2, more than just a program's final data output files are moved through the network; a program's commands – screen and keyboard I/O – are also moved. A program on one workstation can be displayed directly on another workstation and can be controlled directly from a third workstation. What flows in the network are graphics and control I/O representations in addition to ordinary data files. This requires considerably greater network data transfer speeds, by an order of magnitude, and places restrictions on the sequence of transmitted data packets.

In level 3, computing DtCs are like ants in a colony. The intelligence is distributed throughout the network at many levels. DtCs may share a problem at different levels, passing partial results and data throughout the network.

As we progress to higher levels of distributed processing, higher data transmission speeds are required. In level 1, we simply sent the program or data over the network, at that level it is executed locally. In level 2, a program's continuous graphics and control I/O are flowing through the network. In the level 3 network, more intimate connections between system memories and CPUs may exist, which calls for even higher data transmission rates.

Bit rates need to accommodate the different processing levels:

```
Level 1 - 100 Kbits/sec to 10 Mbits/sec
Level 2 - 10 Mbits/sec to 1000 Mbits/sec
Level 3 - 1000 Mbits/sec to 100 Gbits/sec
```

Current optical LAN technologies are pushing level 2 rates. Although there are data standards for level 1 file I/O, ASCII and PostScript, for example, standards for level 2 screen and keyboard I/O are newer. One such standard is the X Windows protocol, described next. Standards for level 3 are still in the laboratory.

X Windows

The X Windows system, widely used in the Unix environment, is an example of client/server architecture that does not require a database. It features the reverse assignment of client and server operations. In the X architecture, multiple clients can host specific applications that can be controlled and displayed by another server in the network.

Whenever you do a remote control operation, whether it be long-distance banking, flying a model aircraft, or executing remote applications programs, you want interactive control of the application as well as an inside view into what is going on during execution. X is a distributed, network transparent, device independent, multitasking, windowing, and graphics system. It runs an application on one machine, directs the output to the screen of another machine, *and* runs multiple applications in different windows on the same display. X Windows is the software that lets a single system's display, keyboard, and mouse be shared by several programs at the same time. A desktop publishing application may be running on a high performance workstation shared by the office, and a number-crunching statistical analysis may be running on the home office mainframe a thousand miles away. The output of both applications can be displayed concurrently on the same local screen.

The promise of X Windows is to provide the best of two worlds: 1) the ability to control an executing application on a remote computer, and 2) the intimate feel of running a dedicated application on one's own DtC. The system is highly portable. It runs on many different computers, and it is widely supported.

Alternatives to X Windows are NeWS (Network/extensible Windows System), marketed by Sun, and Display PostScript. Both of these products use Adobe's PostScript language internally.

How Does X Windows Work?

X Windows splits applications into two parts, server and client. The server can operate on any multitasking machine and multiple servers can reside on a single network. Applications execute on the client and communicate display, keyboard, and other I/O information to and from servers on the network in a standard X protocol format. It is important that transmissions of X protocol over networks be received in the order sent.

The X client portion usually resides with a remote computer that hosts the application while the X server portion resides on the user's netstation and manages the user's interface peripherals such as the display screen, keyboard, and mouse. X Windows fulfills the definition of a level 2 distributed system. While the database client/server network I/O is in the form of queries and datasets, the X Windows network traffic is in the form of application program control and display information.

Data for the client applications will also be found in the client portion of the client/server pair; local buffering of data is not provided by the X server portion. The X protocol, associated with servicing screen updates, mouse movements, and other user I/O operations, is used to transmit data across the network.

The client portion of the application is more intelligent than the server netstation, which is often little more than a simple X terminal.

NOTE

X terminals are inexpensive and limited platforms. The X terminal has a high resolution monitor, keyboard, and mouse, a fair amount of memory, as well as a specialized processor and Ethernet interface. No local disk or local processing capabilities are required beyond the network software. X server software is bootstrapped from the network or burned into ROM. X terminals provide the simple solution since they require little management by network and system administrators.

The client application describes output screen windows, icons, text, and widgets (buttons, scrollbars, etc.), and the X server window manager implements the functions on the end user's graphics screen. X Windows can provide a graphical link for MS-DOS DtCs to existing Unix networks to provide faster, easier to use, and more sophisticated network services. Figure 91 displays a few client applications running with two servers. As you study this figure, note the following:

- Client and server can reside in the same computer.
- Client applications usually execute in remote computers.
- The X protocol is what is transmitted between X clients and servers.
- The X server has hardware dependant functions.
- Multiple clients can be viewed on one server.
- More than one server can view the same client.

The server side of X Windows is written for and resides on the viewing workstation and translating X protocol command packets from the network to the hardware-dependent control and viewing I/O functions. Since the programs are not actually running on the server workstation, more memory is available to the user interface and to execute multiple tasks. Also, applications can reside on client machines that are more capable of handling large jobs without excessive delays.

The Evolution of X Windows

In the early days of computing, users communicated with their mainframe applications through dumb terminals at low speeds across slow communications lines. Local screen updates were slow and output data was limited to monochrome ASCII text. Intelligent terminals that were capable of displaying graphical data used proprietary formats and were inefficient for processing large quantities of information.

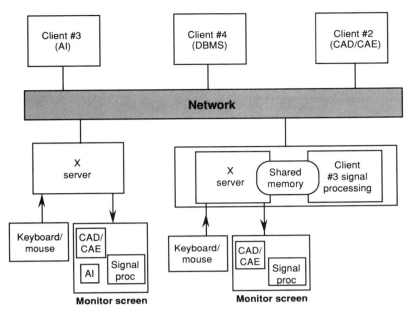

Figure 91. General X system: The clients actually run the applications software while the servers provide display and control functions.

ANSI Sequences – The Precursor to X Windows

The American National Standards Institute (ANSI) adopted a standard set of sequences that permitted remote applications to manipulate a local terminal screen so that a remote program could display something more than an ensemble of lines. The ANSI escape sequences provided a uniform way of controlling remote terminals more efficiently by allowing full screen cursor positioning, color switching codes, and other display functions such as clearing the screen or switching video modes. Still, there was no standardized support for graphics or of mixed text and graphical information.

The Introduction of DtCs

When low-cost DtCs were introduced, users could execute their own applications that performed crude graphic display operations locally. However, speed was inadequate and screen resolution was marginal. Large quantities of memory and disk space were required to handle the programs. DtCs have improved dramatically in recent years in display resolution, memory capacity, and CPU speed, but large graphical applications still require more resources than most DtCs have. The resource shortage is aggravated by the introduction of multitasking to the DtC world, making speed and memory allocation even more critical.

While many applications lend themselves well to DtCs, artificial intelligence inference engine and database engine programs scream for large memory capacities, high CPU capability, and high bus bandwidth in order to operate efficiently.

Today's DtCs have easy-to-use windowing interfaces that can display several local programs on the graphics display concurrently and mouse-driven command procedures that have finally given the DtC the appearance and feel of a well-managed desktop. While all of this bodes well for desktop computing, communication between DtCs and the more powerful computing hardware required for powerful applications has not progressed much beyond early terminal operations. True, DtCs can emulate several types of terminals, and network connections have accelerated the exchange of data, but programs that execute on large computers are still oriented toward terminal users and do not provide windowed displays.

We can run high-end applications and adequately control them with less than powerful DtCs if we can find a way to distribute the work equitably. Sharing the workload muscles up an underpowered workstation. In order to distribute the work meaningfully, we need a standard methodology, a versatile user interface for highly interactive remote control computing, and trouble-free communication over a robust network.

The Answer to Remote Control Computing

■ X Windows is endorsed by many companies including DEC, Hewlett-Packard, Sun Microsystems, and IBM.

X Windows provides a uniform, fully-windowed interface to multiple applications and operates across all major local area networks.■ Users of various workstations or DtCs can access and execute concurrent applications across the network and in graphical environments as if the applications were running on local equipment. X Windows also provides a hardware-independent development environment in which applications writers can produce programs without regard for display, keyboard, pointing device, or printer support.

X was developed at Massachusetts Institute of Technology, and was based on the earlier W windows system from Stanford University for the V operating system. Robert Scheifler was the primary developer. Work on X began in the summer of 1984, focusing on two projects that needed windowing systems. One was for debugging distributed multiprocess applications, and the other was for thousands of workstations with bit-mapped displays that needed a common windowing system. Since MIT was working with a mix of hardware from DEC, IBM, and other manufacturers, the system would have to be hardware independent. Moreover, the developers decided not to rely on any unique capabilities of the operating system. The design criteria include:

- *Applications transparency* – It must not be necessary to recompile or even relink an application for a new hardware display.

- *Multiple displays* – The system must support multiple applications displaying concurrently.

- *Variety of interfaces* – The system should be capable of supporting many different application and management interfaces. No single user interface is best and therefore the system should be capable of supporting a number of them.

- *Flexible windowing* – The system should support a hierarchy of resizeable windows, and an application should be able to use many windows at once. The system must support overlapping windows, including output to partially obscured windows. Arbitrary levels of nesting of windows is important. The system should provide high-performance, high quality support for text, 2-D synthetic graphics, and imaging.

- **System expandability** – The system should be extensible. Facilities not handled in the core system must be supportable as optional, transparent extensions.

- **Hardware independence** – The critical requirement for X is that it be hardware independent as well as independent of any particular operating system or network software. Client and server cannot be required to run on the same vendor's equipment, nor do they have to run under the same operating system. In fact, they do not need anything in common except the X protocol.

Inside X Windows

Let's separate X into its two main parts: the client side, or application; and the server side, which is control and display.

The X Client Side

The client application is connected to the outside world by X library functions, which are standardized, controlled, and distributed freely by the X consortium. The client does not care about hardware details of the various X servers that will be used to display the outputs of applications.

X Library Functions

In Figure 92 X library (lib) is called by the client application for transmitting display output or receiving keyboard or mouse input. It acts as a software interface between the client application and the X protocol that is needed to communicate with the outside world.

The X client runs on a remote host and uses the X lib functions. X lib is a set of C language functions that are called by applications for handling basic operations such as DRAW LINE, PRINT TEXT STRING, and CHECK MOUSE BUTTON status. The functions convert the C language, the only language currently supported on MIT tapes, to the X protocol. Requests from the X client are sent to the X server by X protocol on the network and on the server. The server then translates the requests into the hardware commands required to satisfy them. Properly implemented X servers can execute the X client without modifying the client. By using X lib, the X client remains device-independent. Device independence underpins the success of X. Once an X client is purchased, everyone with an X server can run it immediately. Multiple versions of software are not required.

The X lib functions can be implemented through a window manager and an X toolkit. The manager and toolkit permit developers to easily program icons, buttons, and menus, and then create the necessary X lib C code to implement them.

X Window Manager

The X window manager is at the highest software level. It controls the layout of the screen and the rules for switching between applications. The window manager provides bars, borders, and other window decorations for each application and provides a uniform means of moving and resizing windows. The window manager can modify the appearance and operation of the application itself. It is the window manager that provides the look and feel of the application, and many window managers are available, each with its own characteristics.

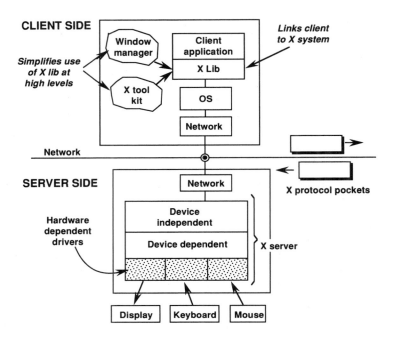

Figure 92. X software components: The client program sends packets of instructions to the server. The server contains the hardware-dependent drivers for the server workstation. An X server controls not only the screen, but also the keyboard and a pointing device with up to five buttons.

The more popular window managers are Motif from Open Software Foundation, MIT X Toolkit, and AT&T Open Look Toolkit (Unix International), Sun X View, and DEC X user interface.

The X Toolkit

The X toolkit provides the developer with pre-built user interface objects such as menus, scroll bars, command buttons and facilities that allow the developer to use existing widgets or create new ones.◼

■ Popular widget sets are: MIT's Athena Widgets, HP Widgets, and Sony Widgets

The toolkits use the lower-level X lib functions, but developers are free to think about the development problem at a higher level. Rather than build a control button through the lower-level X lib functions, the developer simply positions a pre-built control button on screen and the relevant X lib code is automatically constructed. Similar toolkits are available for programming in the Macintosh and MS-DOS Windows environments.

The X Server Side

The X server is the interface between the X protocol packets and the particular operating system and hardware specific drivers of the server. The X server runs on the local station and is the device-dependent portion of the X system. Using the X protocol, client applications send instructions to the X server over the network. These instructions can request a variety of actions to take place on the local display, including to:

- open or resize a window.
- update the contents of a window.
- overlay a window on another.

The X server implements the instructions for the specific system hardware. It controls the X devices (display, keyboard, and mouse) and implements the X protocol. The X server also interprets and sends back input device (mouse and keyboard) activity to the X client using the X protocol. Only the X server knows the hardware details of the local X server station. The X server is responsible for handling all device-specific requirements and for freeing the X client from having to respond to them. The client can then do whatever application it does best – database, graphics, and the like. The X server's primary job is to apportion server resources among the client applications that request them. The two primary resources are processor time for drawing and text manipulation and display screen space. The X server is actually composed of two parts:

1. One portion receives and sends X protocol packets. This portion is device independent.
2. The other portion, which is system specific, controls the hardware of the X-server by calls to device-specific drivers. This portion is device dependent.

When moving the X server to different platforms, only the device-dependant drivers need to be rewritten. The X server and protocol front end remain unchanged.

X Server Performance Requirements

In practice, X servers have been Unix-based workstations. However, as MS-DOS and Mac DtCs grow in power, they also grow in server popularity. MS-DOS DtCs need at least 80386 capability and VGA displays to be good X servers. Products such as PC-Xview from Graphics Software Systems, or DESQview X from Quarterdeck Software provide X server software for only a few hundred dollars, enabling a high-end DtC to become an X server.

Hardware X windowing involves installing a card that has X windowing software built into it. This allows the host DtC to have most of its CPU free for applications while the card takes care of the protocols and the displays. One example is X/PAC by Integrated Inference Machines.

Advantages of X Windows

With X Windows, duplication of applications on individual stations can be minimized and costs can be reduced considerably. The standardization of the user interface allows more consistent training procedures and less concern for standardized hardware and software products. Organizations can develop applications without fear of obsolescence and the programs can be shared across a wide variety of devices.

By running applications on remote hosts and displaying results locally, the X server allows you to access software and provides you with power that you might not have otherwise. You can do your work at a much higher level on the computing platform of your choice.

Client applications can be centrally developed and maintained without providing different versions for individual user environments. End-user environments are provided by the X server software that is now available for virtually any platform, including Macintosh and IBM DtC stations. Computers from Intel 286-based DtCs to RISC-based workstations can access, control, and view client applications running in their environments.

Problems with X Windows

To handle the increased I/O traffic generated by distributed applications, networks need to become faster and protocols have to work more efficiently. Users accustomed to the speed of local workstations won't tolerate a shift back to the time when coffee breaks were taken while waiting for program output. The management and load-balancing of X Windows servers requires knowledgeable support personnel and the end user must be familiar with the X environment.

Selecting X does not ensure a single look and feel. There are differences in the various window managers. For applications to be truly useful, they must be written specifically for X, not kludged after the fact. Even simple cut-and-paste functions may not work between applications not written for X. Currently the number of X applications is limited. This is changing as new and significant products are being delivered. There is even software for converting existing text-based software to X Windows operation.

X Windows Summary

Through X Windows, less powerful workstations can be augmented by the power and resources of other computers in the system. A DtC with at least moderate CPU and display capability can be the director with eyes on work going on elsewhere in the network. We see a merging of capabilities of MS-DOS, Unix, and Macintosh machines. With X Windows, the computerized desktop, electronic document transfer, and peer communications become realistic and affordable. For engineering and research personnel, X Windows provides capabilities on the workstation that previously required expensive mainframe resources and long turnaround times.

Network Software and Hardware

- Operating Systems
- Applications Programs
- Hardware
- Acquisition
- Administration
- Security

The advent of DtC LANs, and the popularity of server-oriented LANs in particular, have lead to the development of special software designed to manage LAN resources in a distributed environment.

Network Operating Systems

Having multiple elements resident in many devices makes network operating systems (NOS) unique among DtC software. As Figure 93 illustrates, the major component of the NOS is often file-server resident, while a small network driver or shell is located in each LAN-connected DtC. A multi-server LAN will normally run one more or less autonomous copy of the NOS in each server.

Each of the two NOS components serves a decidedly different purpose. The DtC-resident driver or shell places itself into execution during connection to the network. The component is usually a resident program that acts as a network shell for the workstation operating system. In the MS-DOS environment, for example, the shell sits between the user and DOS, intercepting commands that you or your applications programs issue to DOS. The commands are examined by the shell to determine whether DOS should handle them locally or whether they should be routed across the LAN to another DtC or to the file server.

Because the shell is memory resident, its size should be considered during LAN selection and acquisition. The combination of operating system software, the LAN

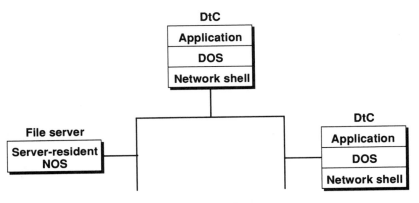

Figure 93.   Network operating system components

shell, and the largest application program must be less then the amount of RAM available on the DtC. A reasonable size for a LAN shell is 30K to 60K. A companion NetBIOS emulator, required to support many LAN applications, can consume an additional 20K to 30K, with much of this software loaded into upper memory.

When the term *network operating system* is used in casual discussion, it usually refers to the larger and more complex server-resident portion of the LAN software. In a server-oriented DtC LAN, the network operating system is the single most critical component. Its design can impact a broad range of DtC LAN characteristics, including:

- Ease of administration
- LAN security
- LAN throughput – how rapidly data and program files can be obtained from the server
- LAN reliability and robustness
- Ease of installation
- File sharing capabilities
- How many DtCs the LAN can effectively support
- The simplicity of the user interface

It is safe to say that with a server-oriented LAN, you don't know much about the LAN until you have acquired hands-on experience with the network operating system.

The distinction between workstation shell and server-resident NOS is blurred in a peer-to-peer LAN. Since workstations and servers can be one and the same, all networking software must be available for all devices. Whether a DtC is primarily a workstation, a server, or both, it may need to contain the necessary software to perform both the shell function and the server-oriented NOS function. You may configure network software to whatever level is necessary. Server-oriented LAN NOS types include IBM's PC LAN, DCA 10-NET, AppleShare, and most TCP/IP-based networks, which use no common NOS.

LAN Applications Programs

When you run your software on a LAN, you must consider everything from licensing agreements to network data error rates.

Many programs run by DtC LAN users are the same programs used in the standalone DtC environment – word processors, spreadsheets, and compilers. These applications are single-user by nature, and are not difficult to install on a DtC LAN. In some cases, software vendors allow the standalone version of their product to be used in a shared environment, providing that it is not used by more than one user at a time. Most vendors of popular DtC software provide a LAN version that has been modified to support the more complicated file management required in a multiuser environment. A user familiar with the standalone version of an application will see little or no difference in the user interface when they use the LAN version.

Important concerns arise when installing single-user programs on a DtC LAN. First, be absolutely sure the application that is to be moved is fully compatible with the chosen LAN. Support for a given application is one of the major criteria in selecting a particular DtC LAN. It is a good idea to get reciprocal agreements from both the LAN vendor and the application vendor, verifying the compatibility of each with the other's product. Second, be sure that the software licensing agreement will permit the product to be used on a LAN.

The network administrator must choose carefully which programs will be shared over a LAN. Vendor licensing requirements and copy protection schemes on the applications software will complicate the matter. It may be more advantageous to give each network user the software to execute locally from the mass store of the individual workstation. Most DtCs don't care where software or data is initially stored, as long as they know the drive letter.

Some LAN administrators choose to maintain applications on the LAN server to centralize and control the software. This guarantees that all users are running the same version appropriately written for data sharing. Standardizing a set of LAN applications for the user community is important, particularly if the LAN administrator must also provide user support for the software. Allowing users free reign to select LAN applications will guarantee that a wide range of applications and versions will require support and will reduce compatibility of data files between applications. This, of course, imposes an additional responsibility on the network administrator.

Programs stored on the server need not be squeaky clean as long as they are merely stored, and not executed. Once they execute in your remote, they become subject to your system hardware. Concerns about computer viruses have led some organizations to prohibit users from storing unauthorized software on the file server. A variety of vendors offer software that monitors a network for unauthorized applications and suspected viruses.

> **NOTE**
> The discussion above assumes the most common file server network configuration. Under more complex distributions of program execution networks, such as I/O and process distribution, users may not be aware of where programs are executing. In higher level networks, programs may be executing throughout a system of DtCs, and concerns about viruses and program integrity become considerably more complex.

The LAN usually moves binary and extended ASCII files in the same way that the operating system does, so you need not be concerned with any internal details. Error detection and correction is handled in most LAN interfaces, with error rates below one in 10^{13}. You can, then, remain comfortably unconcerned with data integrity.

Binary and extended ASCII data are transmitted between workstations by:

1. *Copying* – Files are copied between server and workstation as they might be copied between floppy disks or hard drives on the same system. For occasional copying, rates between systems are not critical.

2. *Executing* – Files are loaded from server to workstation memory for execution as though it had come from the workstation's floppy disk or hard drive. Here data rates become critical, particularly when many users are executing the server-stored programs and large amounts of program and program data overlaying are needed.

All of this overlay activity will take place over the network, degrading network performance.

NetBIOS and Compatibility

The most common applications program interface (API) for DtCs LANs is NetBIOS. NetBIOS is a standardized method for allowing applications programs to interact with the LAN. NetBIOS was originally developed for IBM by Sytek, and has become a standard supported by most DtC LAN vendors and applications developers. While NetBIOS provides a simple, well documented set of network services for the application, it does not support internetwork connections and is perceived to be slow and incomplete compared to other application-to-network interfaces. While having NetBIOS in common does not guarantee that a given program will run on a specific LAN, one is safe in assuming compatibility where NetBIOS or NetBIOS emulation is supported by both the LAN and the application.

Several LAN vendors provide alternate application interfaces to their systems, in addition to supporting NetBIOS. Novell, for example, uses a proprietary application interface called Transportation Layer Interface (TLI), that tends to provide better performance than Novell's NetBIOS emulation mode.

Many applications support NetBIOS along with several other vendor-proprietary application interfaces. Today, however, NetBIOS is the lowest common denominator application interface with the widest base of compatible products. IBM's announcement of Advanced Program-to-Program Communication (APPC) and LU 6.2 may provide a de facto application interface standard to support the internetworking capability lacking in NetBIOS. Acceptance of APPC has been slow, and is complicated by the introduction of Microsoft's Named Pipes remote application interface.

Multiuser Databases on LANs

One of the most difficult groups of applications to implement in a DtC LAN environment is multiuser database systems and the related applications, such as accounting and inventory systems, that use them. There are currently two groups of database products being used on DtC LANs. One type of database is the LAN version of DtC-oriented products, including R:Base, Advanced Revelation, Paradox, DataEase and dBASE X products, and clones. These products are reasonably priced and user friendly, but because they were originally designed to serve only a single user, they lack significant data security and integrity features. Also, support for database standards such as SQL remains inadequate.

The second group includes a growing number of database systems that are being ported from the mini environment to the DtC LAN. These products require high-end DtC hardware for satisfactory performance. This group includes Oracle and Informix, with others, such as Sybase, close behind. These products are streamlined versions of big system databases, with more comprehensive security features, and better adherence to standards than the DtC-oriented products. In addition, because these products were designed for the multiuser environment, they handle file and record sharing more efficiently. The disadvantages of these systems lie in their complex user interfaces, their healthy appetite for RAM, and their higher price tags. Their greater sophistication appeals to a smaller market.

File and Record Locking

The issue causing concern in the LAN database world is the lack of file and record locking standards. The problem stems from the fact that, unlike the mainframe or mini database, DtC LAN database systems must execute simultaneously in multiple machines. Queries and updates must be formulated in a workstation different from the file server that actually manages the data. The potential exists for two or more users to simultaneously perform conflicting database transactions.

The solution has been to lock a file or record to prevent more than one user at a time from modifying the data. Locking the entire file is both simple and foolproof. Unfortunately, locking the file while one user is entering a transaction limits access to the entire database by other users.

Locking individual records presents a different set of problems. MS-DOS was not designed to be a multiuser operating system and did not even support record locking before version 3. Version 3.x record locking is crude at best. MS-DOS is simply told by the database application to lock a certain physical portion of a file, which may in fact contain one or more logical records. MS-DOS-based network operating systems can use this facility to provide standardized but simplistic data-integrity management. Most database files are not sequential, so the MS-DOS approach is clumsy.

Network operating systems that are not MS-DOS based have more effective record locking approaches. Unfortunately, each product seems to have its own record locking procedures, making the possibility for a sophisticated record locking standard unlikely in the near future. This in turn has slowed the evolution of LAN-oriented database systems, which must currently be designed to accommodate a variety of file and record locking systems.

Server-oriented LAN database servers may soon have a significant impact on the multiuser database. The database server functions at the interface between the user and the file system; its presence may alleviate much of the file and record locking problem. In addition, the subsystems are optimized to handle database transactions formulated in the standard SQL, providing a database environment more powerful than those available on today's LANs.

Transaction Tracking

An addition or update to a database is commonly called a *transaction*. Transaction tracking is an accounting system that allows database transactions to be recorded in case of problems. One standard approach to transaction tracking is to capture the individual elements of a database transaction in a holding file. The transaction is later applied to the master database file. The transaction holding file may be preserved for some period of time, facilitating a companion process called transaction backout. Transaction backout permits an earlier version of the master database to be recreated by extracting transactions from the holding file in reverse order. This capability is required only where the database contains critical information, or where the entry of an erroneous transaction cause a problem.

Additional insurance against database corruption can be obtained through the use of fault tolerant systems, and a UPS and tape backup system.

LAN-Specific Applications

Several applications seem to fit well into the DtC LAN environment. The most obvious is electronic mail (E-Mail). A good E-Mail system is frequently specified as one of the goals of a LAN implementation. E-Mail applications permit you to send a message to any other user connected to the LAN, referencing the recipient of the message by a simple name, rather than by location or machine address. If the receiver is not currently connected to the network, the message may be queued in a server until that person logs in, at which time a `Check your mail` message appears on the DtC. These systems are indispensable in an office environment for employees who are often out or in meetings.

Some E-Mail applications are bundled with DtC LAN products, but most of the better packages are separately priced, frequently from third party developers. Third party E-Mail systems usually achieve their generic character by using NetBIOS as the underlying mail transmission mechanism. It should be obvious that the value of an E-mail system is directly proportional to the number of individuals who can be reached through that system. Standards for inter-vendor E-Mail systems are available from TCP/IP's Simple Mail Transfer Protocol and the ISO X.400 standards.

LAN utility packages make it easier to use, manage, and troubleshoot the DtC LAN. In this category are LAN monitors, LAN management software, and special applications. LAN monitors are usually DtC-based combinations of hardware (special NICs) and software that allow an administrator or technician to watch traffic for signs of overloading or conflicts. Monitor prices range from $10,000 to $30,000, making them too expensive for most offices, but perhaps cost effective for institutions that provide internal technical support for multiple networks.

LAN management software makes it easier for the LAN administrator to perform such tasks as adding and deleting user IDs, monitoring disk file space, managing directory structures, and controlling LAN security. As with E-Mail systems, many administrative packages are available from third party vendors who have recognized the need for comprehensive administrative tools in many DtC LAN products.

Standard LAN management protocols are beginning to emerge as well, facilitating the monitoring and control of a variety of network devices, including bridges, routers, NICs, and modems, from a central location. Simple Network Management Protocol (SNMP), a TCP/IP related standard that evolved in the Internet community, is currently positioned as the inter-vendor management protocol of choice. Network hardware and software products that support SNMP are available from over 100 vendors.

The special utilities category, often called office management software, augments E-Mail with simple applications that use the always on-line status of a DtC. DtC. Currently available are phone messaging ("while you were out") systems, locator programs that track employee whereabouts, meeting schedulers, and multiuser project management systems. The appropriate term for these LAN-based applications is *groupware*.

Some DtC LAN hardware is available that is not found in the standalone DtC environment and may be unfamiliar even to experienced DtC users.

Let us first examine LAN interfacing hardware, including LAN wiring, network interface boards, transceivers, multiple access units and active and passive hubs. Then let us consider two LAN support devices: uninterruptible power supplies and tape backup systems.

LAN Media – **Wiring the Network**

Three classes of cable media are widely used to carry data signals between devices in the DtC LAN environment. They are depicted in Figure 94. Several configurations of coaxial cable (coax) are frequently encountered. Coax is a cable that contains a single conductor surrounded by an insulator, with a braided shield and exterior plastic shell. It is similar to, or in some cases the same as, the media used in cable TV systems. Coax is capable of carrying a moderate amount of digital information – up to 300 Mbps in some broadband systems.

The most common example of a twisted pair conductor is telephone cable. It comes in several shielded and non-shielded forms. IBM's shielded twisted pair cable is considerably more expensive than plain telephone cable. The shielded cable is designed for 16 MHz data rates, whereas regular telephone cable, designed for voice communications, carries data at speeds in the 1 to 10 Mbps range. Recent advances promise 100 Mbps rates in both shielded and unshielded twisted pair before the mid-1990s. Many DtC LANs use twisted pair because newer buildings have extra twisted pair runs between telephone closets and offices, reducing media installation costs considerably. Twisted pair has traditionally been limited in the total amount of data that it can carry, and is susceptible to interference from sources of electrical noise.

The third and newest media is fiber optic cable. Fiber is more expensive than coax or twisted pair, but has three advantages that make it useful in certain environments.

1. It can carry a larger volume of information than coax or twisted pair.
2. It is narrower in diameter than other media, making it easier to install in the crowded cable conduits of older buildings.

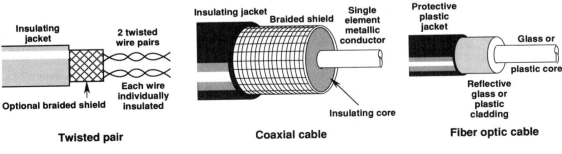

Twisted pair   **Coaxial cable**   **Fiber optic cable**

Figure 94.   LAN media

3. It is not susceptible to interference from electrical noise because fiber transmits light rather than electrical current.

Multimode (MM) fiber has traditionally been the media of choice for fiber optic LANs, but the greater bandwidth and distances supported by single-mode (SM) fiber, along with recent cost reductions, are making single-mode fiber grow in popularity for new fiber LANs. Table 32 on page 457 compares the characteristics of coax, twisted pair, and fiber.

Cable Character-istics	Twisted Pair	Coax	Fiber Optic
Cost	Low to Moderate	Moderate	Moderate
Connect Cost	Low to Moderate	Low	High
Bandwidth	Low to Moderate	Moderate	High
Maximum Cable Length	Short	Moderate	Long
Installation Difficulty	Easy	Moderate	Moderate to Difficult
Connectors	D-Plug or RJ-45	D-Plug or BNC	Special

Table 32.   Characteristics of various media

All types of cabling should be installed by a licensed electrical contractor with LAN cabling experience due to the special handling and routing requirements of LAN media. In addition, fire codes may dictate the type of cabling that may be used in ceilings and ventilation ducts. Broadband cabling systems require the services of an electrical engineering firm.

LAN Interfacing Hardware

Many special devices are used successfully to transmit and receive information over LAN media. Devices most likely to be encountered in the DtC LAN environment are discussed here.

The *network interface card* is a circuit board that provides the data path between the DtC internal bus and the LAN cable. The NIC must be designed to fit both the microcomputer and the LAN. NICs are usually half or full length boards, and are reasonably simple to install. Complications may arise if there are conflicts between the NIC and other DtC boards or applications, caused by contention for system hardware interrupts or memory (RAM or ROM). Memory conflicts between NICs and MS-DOS computer VGA and Super VGA graphics cards are particularly nasty, and common in systems configured for CAD or desktop publishing applications. The services of an experienced DtC technician may be required in order to configure the NIC to avoid such conflicts. NICs currently range in price from $200 to over $1000, depending upon the type of LAN.

A *transceiver* is a component that converts a DtC data signal to a signal appropriate for transmission on the LAN. In addition, certain transceivers manage the media access control protocol that maintains orderly data flow on the LAN. Most DtC LAN systems use a NIC containing an on-board transceiver. The only environment where one would likely encounter a separate transceiver is on a conventional Ethernet or IEEE 802.3 LAN. Ethernet transceivers cost about $300, in addition to the cost of the NIC. Cheapernet (thin Ethernet) NICs use an on-board transceiver. The type of Ethernet NIC can be determined by examination. The Cheapernet NIC has a cylindrical BNC connector. A conventional Ethernet NIC has a 15 pin "D" (DIX) connector. Ethernet NICs that have both types of connectors support both systems.

The 10BASET systems, transmitting Ethernet packets over twisted pair wire, use a special 10BASET transceiver that performs a function different from the conventional Ethernet transceiver. A conventional Ethernet NIC can be connected to a 10BASET system using a 10BASET transceiver in lieu of the conventional transceiver. Many NIC manufacturers also offer a 10BASET version of the Ethernet NIC, with the 10BASET transceiver built into the NIC. This feature adds about $100 to the price of the NIC, and is recommended over the external 10BASET transceiver when the option exists.

Multiple access units are used on token ring LANs to distribute data from the backbone to individual workstation drops. Because token ring has become an IEEE standard, the MAU and other token ring hardware is available from a variety of sources in addition to IBM. The MAU is usually placed in a phone closet, where it can be connected conveniently to unused twisted pairs, providing a ready-made wiring system for DtC LANs. With the use of phone lines, the range and speed of the connections will be only half that of the more expensive and difficult to install IBM shielded twisted pair. MAU power to energize a relay to connect to the ring is provided through the twisted pair cables, thus no AC connection is required.

The ARCNet system uses cable splitting devices called active and passive hubs. ARCNet is based on the distributed star topology, with an active hub at the center of each star. Either a passive hub or another active hub may be connected to the opposite end of an active hub connection. The AC-powered active hub functions as a signal repeater; the passive hub is a simple signal splitter that requires no power connection. Active hubs support 8-12 connections, passive hubs support a total of four. Neither hub provides any bridging or routing capability.

Nodems

No, not modems. A nodem is a free-standing LAN interface unit with its own power supply that can be configured in a variety of imaginative ways. The big difference between the nodem and LAN interface systems offered by IBM, Novell, and 3COM is that the nodem interface is an SCSI device. The nodem interfaces to a network, and DtCs wishing to participate in the LAN plug into the nodem by their SCSI interfaces. SCSI boards are available for MS-DOS computers, and some DtCs already have them, the Mac, for instance. Connecting to LANs by nodems will be relatively simple. As with modems, the nodem is system independent – it is not bus interfaced – so any DtC with an SCSI interface can plug into the nodem just as any DtC with a serial interface can plug into a modem.

LAN Support Devices

There are several other devices which should not be overlooked when designing a DtC LAN.

The *uninterruptible power supply* is a DtC-sized device that contains a substantial storage battery. The only effective type of UPS is the non-switched variety. The microcomputer device plugged into the non-switched UPS runs on battery power. The battery is simultaneously recharged by line current. The UPS is used to support critical devices; in the DtC LAN environment this means file servers. Even a momentary power failure or surge can corrupt the file management structures on a hard disk, rendering every LAN user's data temporarily or permanently inaccessible. A switched UPS, which monitors input current and switches over to the battery power as necessary, is sometimes too slow in the switching process to prevent the corruption of data.

Some network operating systems can accept a signal from the UPS indicating that a power failure has occurred. If the AC power is not restored after a few minutes, the NOS will shut down the file server rather than allow the battery to drain to the point where it would pose a risk to hardware and data. UPSs are rated in K volt amps. A 0.6 KVA UPS, costing under $1,000, is usually sufficient to protect an AT-style file server, unless a large amount of disk storage is used.

A device used in conjunction with the UPS in protecting shared data is the tape backup system. Although the disk files to be backed up are normally located on a server device, the tape backup system is usually connected to one of the LAN workstations. Accompanying software makes it easy to do comprehensive or selective file server backups. Some systems can be programmed to automatically back up selected files on multiple servers at fixed intervals.

Some tape backup software has been found to be incompatible with the data structures used in certain network operating systems. A new system should always be backed up and restored during installation, to verify full compatibility.

As mentioned before, network printers must be connected to a print server or file server device. The requirement for placing a printer at a remote location presents a problem, particularly if the printer needs a parallel port. Parallel connections are normally restricted to a distance of a few feet, effectively preventing a printer cable from being run from floor to floor or even from room to room. To overcome this problem, short-haul modems may be used. The print or file server parallel port is connected to the short-haul modem, which uses twisted pair to transmit the signal up to several thousand feet. A companion modem at the printer reconverts signal to the parallel format required by the printer. A more expensive, more flexible solution places the essential components of a LAN node in a small box, with a complement of serial and parallel ports. These specialized printer servers allow several shared network printers to be connected to the LAN at a convenient location, without the added cost of a workstation or file server to support them.

DtC LAN Acquisition and Management

Everything from the facility layout to secured cable runs to remote user support must be considered when selecting a LAN. The selection process is no less complex than the selection of applications software or the selection of your DtC. In the LAN selection process may well be more complex for an extensive network.

A DtC LAN represents a specific solution to what may be a general requirement. It is best, then, to begin by thinking in terms of what the system is required to do, rather than which products should be acquired. Develop a requirements specification by answering the following questions:

- How many and what types of users need to be supported?
- What is the user's technical level of sophistication, and what sort of user interface is required?
- If there are already workstations or terminals in place, what are they?
- What specific peripheral devices must be supported, especially printers?
- What capabilities need to be added to the office information system that currently do not exist, or are inadequately supported?
- What level of administrative support can be expected for the system? One person part time? Two people full time?
- What commercial and homegrown applications programs must be supported?
- How much shared disk space will be required initially and in the future?
- What level of system reliability and security will be required?
- What system response time will be required?
- What is the layout of the physical facility?
- Will remote users be supported?
- What central mainframe or minicomputers will need to be accessible, and what type of services will be required? Terminal emulation? File transfer?
- Will this system need to tie in to other networks now or in the near future?

The need for a requirements definition cannot be overemphasized. Many institutions have put the cart before the horse by selecting a specific DtC LAN product before developing a clear definition of what facilities the new system must provide. Organizations unsure about specifying such requirements should hire a consulting firm to conduct a site survey and make recommendations. After system requirements have been defined and proposals have been accepted, finalists should subject their proposed systems to the following tests:

- Demonstrate important applications programs in a true multiuser environment. For example, have three users try to update a database file simultaneously.
- Have an unsophisticated user try to log in to the LAN and retrieve a file.
- Get your most notorious hacker to try to access or delete a private file.
- Switch off a DtC while an applications program is processing a database file. Log back in and check the database for signs of problems.
- Pull the plug on the file server's UPS, check for file access problems after restarting the network.
- Log as many users in as possible and monitor system response time.
- Consult sources such as *PC Magazine,* and *LAN Reporter* for their recommendations.
- Check compatibility with the actual workstations being supported.
- Try to connect to other required computers or networks.
- Ask the vendor to do a full tape backup and restore to prove compatibility with the tape backup software.

In addition to the price quoted by the chosen vendor, other costs are built into the procurement and operation of a DtC LAN. One-time costs include user training, LAN administrator training, installation of the cable plant, purchase of new LAN versions of applications programs, conversion to new applications when the old ones won't run on the LAN, consulting fees, costs of interfacing special devices, and installation of new communications hardware and software in minis and mainframes that are to be connected to the LAN.■

■ Cable plant refers to the totality of cabling that interconnects a distributed computing system.

Ongoing costs include cable plant maintenance including runs to new offices and workstation relocation, salaries for LAN administrators, training of new employees, maintenance contracts, leasing fees for long-haul lines required to connect remote users or networks, upgrades of file server hardware, and new NOS releases.

Cable Plant Installation

Installation of the LAN media should be handled by an electrical contractor in all but the simplest of configurations. This requirement is often reinforced by a combination of local electrical and fire codes and by insurance requirements. In addition to being a licensed contractor, the cable installer should be certified by the LAN hardware manufacturer, particularly if a newer media like fiber optic cable is being used. The hazards of a poorly-installed cable plant are several. Most important, the wrong type of cable in an inappropriate location can act as a conduit for fire, carrying it above a suspended ceiling from one office or floor to the next. Some types of cables give off toxic fumes as they burn.

Less critical but potentially more irritating is that a cable damaged during careless installation may cause intermittent transmission problems that mimic failing network interface boards or bad software. Certain types of cable installed in close proximity to sources of electromagnetic radiation from fluorescent lights and transformers are subject to interference that may affect LAN throughput without blocking transmission entirely.

Cable technology is evolving rapidly, driven by the installation of traditional media, such as coaxial cable, becoming prohibitively expensive in a DtC-oriented office system. Most new approaches use existing building wiring in order to reduce cable plant installation costs. Many vendors provide Ethernet products that run on twisted pair, allowing the designer to connect LAN devices using the extra unshielded twisted pair telephone wiring that exists in most newer buildings. Standard Ethernet network interface cards can be used in conjunction with external or built-in 10BASET transceivers. Most 10BASET systems require new wiring only for the backbone, which connects cable concentrators on different floors. The trend is toward moving greater volumes of data across media formally considered to have insufficient bandwidth for use as LAN media.

Workstation and OS Standardization

The ability to accommodate a variety of workstations, operating systems, and even operating system versions varies widely from one DtC LAN product line to the next. At a minimum, most LANs support a single class of machines, for example, MS-DOS computers. The number of LAN vendors that support interconnection of unlike classes, MS-DOS computers to Apple Macintoshes or Unix DtCs, is increasing. Be sure to scrutinize the level of compatibility that a DtC LAN product promises. Can a DtC user really interact transparently with a Macintosh, or does compatibility simply mean that both can coexist on the same LAN?

Even within the class of MS-DOS machines, some LANs permit a range of MS-DOS versions to be used at different workstations, others require standardization on a single version. Try to stick with MS-DOS 3.1 or later – earlier versions lack necessary LAN support features.

The mixing of workstation operating systems will become more complex as OS/2, with its fuller set of LAN support features, enters the workplace. A good compromise between compatibility and user flexibility is to limit LAN support to a reasonable set of workstations and operating system versions, specified early enough in the process to prevent procurement of incompatible hardware. Be sure to identify which hardware and operating systems will need to be connected as part of the requirements specification effort.

Placement of LAN Hardware

Ideally, a file server should be located in an environmentally-controlled computer room, under the watchful eye of operations personnel. However, other practical accommodations are sufficient. The server should be placed away from heavy traffic areas to avoid bumping and tripping over cables, and it should be powered so that it cannot be inadvertently unplugged. If the server uses a console, it should be physically protected from tampering, perhaps by locating the console in the network administrator's office. Servers without consoles can simply be locked in a telephone or utility closet with reasonable ventilation for heat dissipation. Several network operating systems now provide a remote console facility that permits operation of the file server console from any authorized workstation on the network.

The specific location of LAN cables should be determined by the electrical contractor, with general cable plant design provided by the LAN vendor or consultant.

LAN Administration

Any DtC LAN, no matter how small, will require some ongoing administration. In the simplest of LANs, administration may be handled informally, but the task of keeping the LAN running smoothly should be assigned to one or more administrative staff members. In most environments, the administrator will have access to all data stored on the LAN, which places them in a trusted position. An effective LAN administrator needs the following skills:

- Familiarity with the applications that LAN users will be running and, in particular, with the workstation operating systems used.
- A general understanding of LAN technology.
- A detailed understanding of the security requirements of the site.
- Experience in working with printers and other LAN peripherals.
- Enough managerial authority to successfully enforce LAN security and procedural policies.

Familiarity with user requirements and a practical background in microcomputing are more important than a high level of technical knowledge. Most of the LAN-specific technical information required to manage the LAN can be obtained by reading the vendor's documentation.

DtC LANs should be configured to enforce a reasonable level of user validation. Usually, this means that to access LAN resources, you must enter a user ID and a password. Where no security is required, passwords may be optional, although it is a good idea to use them to provide a first line of defense against unauthorized use. The user ID is required in some DtC LAN systems because LAN services are administered based upon that user ID, rather than by workstation. User IDs should be assigned and managed by the administrator. User IDs should be eight characters or less, unique, and published for exchanging mail and sharing files.

In addition to user validation, most DtC LANs manage shared file access by users. LAN file access control is more sophisticated than that provided by single user microcomputer operating systems like MS-DOS. At minimum, the network operating system should provide the following levels of file access:

- Open and read only - single user
- Shared read only
- Read and write
- No privileges granted

Privileges may be assigned on a user or group basis, or may be attached to the files and directories. This type of security is only as good as the set of mechanisms that prevent an ordinary LAN user from entering administrator mode. A LAN administrator should use two user IDs, one while performing normal user operations, and a second, supervisory ID, for performing administrative procedures. The supervisory ID should *always* have an associated password, and the password should be changed frequently. An unprotected supervisory ID effectively defeats most of the LAN security mechanisms.

Dedicated and Nondedicated Servers

Many DtC LAN systems permit file, print, and communications servers to reside with user applications on a non-dedicated server. A non-dedicated server is simply a workstation that has been given the additional task of running server software. Such options should be viewed with a healthy skepticism, as they involve both compromises and risks.

The most practical problem of using a non-dedicated server is that the server process must provide more or less continuous services to all network users. Any machine that can be halted, whether by applications-software failure, user error, or even by being switched off, is a poor choice as a network server platform.

Assuming that the workstation will remain up and running dependably, the issue becomes more technical and the type of server becomes significant. Since print and communications servers require little of the CPU in the device that they occupy, a user application could run on a device that also supports a server running in background mode. However, conflicts may occur if special hardware must be supported. A typical asynchronous communications server, for example, will support 8 to 16 modems. A print server might use one serial and two parallel ports to support three printers. While such competition would not necessarily bog down the CPU, it might render a system ineffective as a practical workstation.

File servers present a different problem. The file server is the central device in many DtC LAN architectures and must operate with great efficiency when managing shared file resources. File servers require the service of a substantial CPU – at least an 80386 or 68030 – and may not provide adequate performance if required to share those resources with a user applications program. This depends, of course, upon how many network users the file server is supporting. In most cases, it makes good sense to dedicate one machine to file service.

Network Printer Management

Because DtC LAN technology permits printer sharing, a good quality high-speed laser printer can be made available to users for somewhat less than the cost of individual dot matrix printers. Laser printers use technology similar to that used in photocopy devices, and require roughly the same frequency and type of maintenance. Either the LAN administrator or some appointed user must take responsibility for keeping the printer loaded with paper and toner, switching it on in the morning, and calling the service company when it breaks down. While laser printers are reliable, it is a good idea to configure dot matrix printers for use as auxiliary network printers for draft printouts or for high speed line printers.

The sequential nature of network printers requires automated management that lets user applications transfer documents to the network printer, regardless of whether or not the printer is in use. This function is often handled with a spooling program that emulates a printer interface to the applications program, storing the printer-bound file temporarily on disk until the document reaches the front of the print queue.

The LAN administrator may be required to manage printer queues in a small LAN, and will usually have to support spooling software. The latter can be a tricky proposition since laser printer interfaces and drivers are non-standard. A spooling system that interfaces easily with one laser printer may be incompatible with another. The situation should improve as laser printer interfaces are standardized. For now, specify which make and model of laser printer must be supported in the LAN requirements specification, or purchase one of the laser printers supported by the LAN spooling software.

Legal Aspects of Shared Software

Applications vendors providing software specifically designed to be used on the LAN license their software in one of three ways. The first way is to site license, which permits software use on a per LAN basis. The software may be reproduced and used by multiple users within the context of a single LAN or physical site. LAN utilities and functionally single-user applications such as word processing are frequently licensed this way.

Another approach is to design the application to monitor the number of users simultaneously running the package. Because of their centralized design, many database systems can track the number of users. The application may be available for 5, 10, or 20 users, priced accordingly.

The third, and least-enlightened, approach is simply to not accommodate users wanting to run an application on a LAN. A few vendors have chosen to force LAN users to purchase one copy of the application for each user who might simultaneously use that program. This approach not only ignores the growing LAN applications market, but also encourages LAN users to illegally share the single-user version of an application.

Hopefully, a unified approach to DtC LAN software licensing will develop as more LAN-oriented application programs become available. In the meantime, metering utilities are available from third party vendors, which limit the number of users running an application to a configured number, preventing software license violations.

Fault Tolerant Systems

Other means exist for protecting critical data in a LAN environment. Already mentioned, but worth repeating, is the simple and effective tape backup system.

Tape backup combined with an uninterruptible power supply will protect most LANs nicely, with backups done on a daily or weekly basis, depending on transaction volume.

Organizations that cannot risk the loss of even one day of work may look to a class of systems called fault tolerant. These DtC LANs combine one or more of the following methods to effectively prevent the loss of LAN-based data.

1. Automatic write verify options check data after writing to disk, before the RAM-resident copy is discarded.
2. Disk mirroring maintains the same data two separate disk drives, making the risk of data loss from disk hardware failure unlikely.
3. Two redundant file servers may be placed at different physical locations, reducing the possibility of loss from fire or flooding, or dual cabling systems can be installed.

As with any other data protection scheme, the cost of the protection must be balanced against the value of the data being safeguarded.

LAN Security Considerations

DtC LANs present security risks above and beyond those found in the standalone DtC environment. Several mechanisms have been discussed that can enhance the basic security of the DtC LAN. They include passwords, file access control mechanisms, physical protection of LAN servers, fault tolerant design, tape backup systems, and uninterruptible power supplies. Used in combination, these systems are sufficient in a civilian government agency or commercial office environment. More comprehensive LAN security measures are required in environments where LAN-based data includes trade secrets, financial information, or where classified government and military information is being managed.

The LAN is fundamentally a *broadcast-oriented system*, that is, any message transmitted on the LAN is available to any network interface board connected to the LAN. While the typical user may be unaware of this characteristic, it is a simple matter to modify a NIC or to use a test device to monitor all LAN traffic. Measures must be taken to prevent unauthorized users from accessing LAN traffic when security is a concern.

Formal LAN security technology is in its infancy. The most comprehensive government document on network security is the National Security Administration's *Trusted Network Interpretation* (NCSC-TG-005), published in 1987. There are few formal standards to which government LAN administrators and contractors can turn. NSA has instituted an evaluation program that has thus far produced one NSA-evaluated secure LAN product: the Verdix VSLAN. The secure LAN architectures that result from certification programs will use a combination of encryption, physical access controls, security monitors, and formal security methodology to provide a high level of LAN security. These trusted networks will depend upon one or more trusted processes within the LAN to manage security.

Also under final development is a trusted security server technology called Kerberos.■ A Kerberos server is connected to the LAN, managing network security by issuing a timestamped ticket to a user wishing access to a network service. The ticket is used in place of a password, which prevents passwords from being trans-

■ Kerberos is the
Greek pronunciation of
Cerberus, the
mythological three-
headed dog that guards
the entrance to Hades.

mitted on the network and risking possible disclosure. The Kerberos server uses encryption so that both user and service is assured that the other is an authorized network entity and not someone masquerading as a user or service.

In the meantime, DtC LAN implementers should be aware of the open quality of LAN architectures and should provide as much physical security as is necessary to protect LAN data from disclosure or corruption. In particular, users in the government arena should refrain from using current DtC LAN technology to create systems that must support multilevel defense security classifications.

The Impact of Standards on LANs

The range of data communications standards that affect DtC LANs is a complex topic. Whether formal U.S. and international standards, or de facto vendor-specified standards, their impact on the LAN industry is substantial. Let us first define the term *protocol*. In data communications, a protocol is an agreement about the way in which devices will communicate. An analogy can be drawn between the way a set of protocols controls the behavior of devices on a LAN and the way that *Robert's Rules of Order* governs the conduct of a formal meeting.

A protocol may describe which device controls the network at any point in time, how other devices may gain the floor, the format of a message, the speed of transmission, the media used, or what action to take when an error occurs. Virtually any characteristic of inter-device communication is defined by one or more communication protocols. The standards being discussed here are simply protocols that have been formalized and adapted by a sponsoring vendor, institution, nation, or association of nations.

The ISO Model and Standards

In the late 1970s, the International Standards Organization (ISO) introduced the concept of using a model or framework to describe any set of communications protocols that might be used in a system. This now well-known model was named the Open Systems Interconnection (OSI) model. The OSI model defines seven layers of protocol functions for communicating between computers across a network. The OSI model is a framework for describing protocols, but it contains no actual protocol specifications. ISO has also been engaged, since the late 1970s, in working from layer one up to define specific protocol standards. These will eventually be endorsed by ISO as its international suite of communication protocol standards, the ISO Protocols.

The ISO Protocols will be formalized by the end of the decade, and will include various methods of interfacing computers, both in the LAN and WAN environments. Although the ISO Protocols are new and currently incomplete, the OSI Model has become the common framework for discussing the functions of data communications hardware and software components, whether those components use the ISO Protocols or one of the other sets of proprietary or standard protocols. Anyone who deals with LANs needs to possess a basic knowledge of what the seven layers of the OSI Model represent.

Layer	Name	Function	Standards
1	Physical	Defines how the electrical signal is transmitted between computers. Includes such things as connectors, pin assignments, voltage levels, and encoding schemes.	V.35, X.21, IEEE 802.3 (partial), and 802.5 (partial).
2	Link	Guarantees reliable data transfer between adjacent machines in a network, handles flow control, error detection, and retransmission.	HDLC (LAP-B), SDLC, BISYNC, IEEE 802.3 (partial), 802.5 (partial), and 802.2
3	Network	Establishes, maintains, and terminates communication between endpoints across a network. Permits upper layers to be unconcerned with transmission and switching methods.	X.25
4	Transport	Provides reliable data transfer between endpoints, including error detection and flow control. Makes lower layers transparent to applications.	DoD TCP, ISO TP4
5	Session	Provides logical communication between applications. Establishes, manages, terminates sessions between applications, facilitates checkpoint recovery after aborted session.	ISO Session, IBM NetBIOS, IBM APPC (LU 6.2)
6	Presenta-tion	Concerned with presentation of information to user, translates character sets, performs compression and encryption.	DoD Telnet Virtual Terminal Protocol, X Windows, and perhaps eventually OS/2 Presentation Manager or Apple Macintosh user interfaces.
7	Applica-tion	Includes network application support interfaces for access to network-based services.	DoD Simple Mail Transfer Protocol and File Transfer Protocol, ISO X.400 and X.500, Network Management Protocols

Table 33.   Layers of the OSI model

In the DtC LAN environment, we are most concerned with the first four layers. A recent federal standard called GOSIP (Government Open System Interconnection Profile) mandates that new communications network procurements use the ISO Protocols where possible. GOSIP, which became effective in 1990, requires vendor support for subsequent ISO Protocols in future federal procurements of computer networks. GOSIP is ambiguous with regard to LANs, leaving the option of using proprietary LAN protocols open to interpretation for the moment.

Ethernet is the earliest de facto LAN protocol standard. For several years during the early 1980s, Ethernet was the principle standard used in the LAN environment. A push to formalize Ethernet and other LAN protocols lead to the establishment of the IEEE 802 Committee. The 802 Committee initiated a process of bringing together LAN vendors and researchers for the purpose of formalizing LAN standards. The result was the following IEEE 802 standards for local area networks.

Version	Specifications	Comments
802.3	Coax bus or twisted pair cabling; uses CSMA/CD	Formal version of Ethernet. Official variations include standard Ethernet (10BASE5), thinner Cheapernet (10BASE2), STARLAN, and Ethernet on twisted pair (10BASET).
802.4	Token passing on coax bus.	Used mainly to support factory automation systems.
802.5	Token passing around a ring on twisted pair	Formal version of IBM's token ring.

Table 34. IEEE 802 LAN standards

All of the above standards define LAN protocols for layers one and part of layer two in the ISO model. Another IEEE standard, 802.2 defines a link-layer protocol, similar to HDLC, which can operate above any of the above 802 protocols in order to provide a uniform and more reliable interface to upper-layer protocols.

The IEEE standards have been adopted as the LAN interface component of the ISO Protocols.

IBM's Systems Network Architecture

An unofficial set of communications standards that have had considerable impact on the office environment is IBM's Systems Network Architecture. SNA predates the ISO standards, and is the de facto communications networking standard in many corporations and government agencies.

IBM has moved to enhance SNA support for LANs and for OS/2 by announcing Advanced Program-to-Program Communication (APPC). APPC will be added to the SNA by designating APPC a new SNA logical unit, in this case, LU 6.2. LU 6.2 may provide a set of communications oriented commands that programmers in both IBM DtC and mainframe environments can use to exchange information between applications running on dissimilar IBM machines. Because of IBM's dominance in the industry, other vendors will probably announce support for LU 6.2. It is possible that LU 6.2 will become, for the near term, the de facto intercomputer application-to-application interface standard, although competition in this arena is appearing in the form of an ISO conformant remote procedure call (RPC) standard that is being supported by Sun and Novell.

In addition to APPC and LU 6.2, several other IBM standards must be understood by LAN designers. IBM's token ring network has replaced IBM's earlier PC Network product. Token ring is here to stay and will be widely used in environments where connection to a larger IBM computer is a requirement.

NetBIOS is similar to but less comprehensive than LU 6.2. It is, however, currently supported by most DtC LAN vendors and applications developers, and is even used in the TCP/IP environment.

While SNA is broadly similar to the ISO standards, there are enough fundamental differences between the two systems to cause most institutions to select one or the other as their central communications network architecture. Today there is certainly much more SNA than ISO in use, but endorsements of the ISO protocols by most other vendors, as well as by the federal government, make the ultimate dominance of SNA by the ISO protocols a possibility. The move toward open systems, requiring the interconnection of many vendors' computers, will pressure IBM to provide support for the ISO standards. Clearly, both communications architectures will coexist to some degree into the future.

Support for IBM Synchronous Protocol on LANs

Traditionally, most IBM mainframe-based applications expect the 3270 synchronous protocol rather than LAN protocols. Because DtC LAN-to-mainframe applications in the mainframe environment tend to be supported using token ring, the DtC must be able to emulate a synchronous (327X) terminal across the token ring network.

IBM's 9370 minicomputer, which serves as the platform for what used to be synchronous applications, also supports the token ring interface. The problem is that DtCs on the LAN still have to run 3270 emulation software, which restricts the set of services available to the LAN-connected DtCs.

This problem should be solved shortly when APPC admits a direct interface between DtC-based applications and those resident in the larger IBM machines. It is likely that other LAN vendors will support APPC and LU 6.2, so that connection of DtC applications to IBM minicomputers and mainframes will not be limited to the token ring environment. Nevertheless, the token ring will be the LAN of choice for those types of interfacing problems.

You may not be concerned about this capability if you are running standalone DtC applications products such as Lotus 1-2-3 and WordPerfect. As your applications become distributed, however, these capabilities will become important considerations.

TCP/IP

Further complicating the picture, DoD adopted a third set of standards for the near term. Because of the large scale interoperability requirements of the Defense Data Network, there is a need to interconnect the variety of computers currently used by the various branches of the military. This need, in combination with substantial security requirements, promoted the adoption of Transmission Control Protocol/Internet Protocol (TCP/IP). TCP/IP and its companion protocols have been used for a decade in the ARPANET environment, and meet DoD's requirement for a protocol methodology that is substantially more mature than the relatively new and incomplete ISO standards.

TCP and IP work hand in hand to provide data transfer between different computers and networks. IP is a highly flexible layer-three protocol that sends and receives packets across dissimilar networks, and can be placed above IEEE 802.2 or even directly above 802.3 or 802.5. Because IP is inherently unreliable, TCP (a layer-four protocol) is usually implemented above IP to provide formal connections between computers and to guarantee reliability.

TCP/IP supports a set of ready-made network applications that include a file transfer protocol (FTP), terminal emulation protocol (Telnet), and a simple mail transfer protocol (SMTP), and a simple network management protocol (SNMP). Upper-layer protocols (ULPs), along with many other lesser TCP-based applications, provide a reasonable level of communication for military, academic, and research users who must operate within the DDN and Internet environments. TCP/IP is widely supported in academic and Unix environments, and is increasingly available for DtCs. RFC 1001 and 1002 are standards that provide a way to implement NetBIOS on top of TCP/IP, overcoming the NetBIOS prohibition of internetwork connections.

Other DtC LAN Protocol Standards

Several other unofficial DtC LAN standards exist. One of the most widely implemented DtC LAN standards is ARCNet. ARCNet is an inexpensive coax-based LAN configured as a distributed star. During the past few years it has been competing with Ethernet in the office LAN environment. ARCNet has the dual advantages over Ethernet of being more fault tolerant due to its non-linear topology and of exhibiting more graceful degradation under heavy loads; it is a token-based system.

One of the most widely used LAN protocol suites is provided by Apple through its AppleTalk Share products. AppleTalk is Apple's Macintosh LAN technology. AppleShare is the Macintosh file server protocol, which is installed on a dedicated Mac. AppleTalk runs faster across an Ethernet network. The NIC functionality required to run standard AppleTalk is built into the Mac. To run the Ethernet version, a Mac Ethernet NIC must be purchased separately. In addition, some other network operating systems permit Macintoshes to share files with DtC workstations on a common server. The Sun TOPS product and Novell NetWare support this capability currently, and MicroSoft has announced plans to support Macs under LAN Manager very soon.

More prevalent in the minicomputer environment is the DECnet architecture, which uses the XNS protocols developed by DEC, Intel, and Xerox. XNS is a complete set of protocols designed to support almost any service that could be accessed from an office LAN. Because DECnet uses Ethernet for its lowest layers, Ethernet DtC LANs can use existing DECNet media, either by using XNS to communicate with other DECNet devices such as VAX minicomputers or, more likely, by simply sharing the cable without intercommunicating.

The protocols used by Novell's NetWare are similar to but not fully compatible with XNS. The central Novell protocol is Novell's IPX, an internet protocol somewhat similar to IP. IPX is a layer-three protocol that supports a common interface to a variety of layer-two protocols. Thus, Novell's NetWare can operate on top of a variety of media including Ethernet, ARCNet, and token ring. Novell's domination of the DtC LAN market has made IPX a de facto standard. Thus far, Novell has maintained IPX as a proprietary protocol, effectively limiting third party products that could support it.

Recently Novell added a reliable proprietary transport-layer protocol called SPX (similar to TCP). Also, Novell announced plans to implement the TCP/IP and SNA protocols in NetWare 386.

Network Summary

Intercomputer LAN communications can be characterized as occurring at one of three levels:

Level 1 – File Distribution: Files and programs are moved between machines manually by users, but this is ineffective when files and programs must be shared by many users.

Level 2 – I/O Distribution: Programs and data may execute in a more distributed fashion, and what transverses the network are direct program I/O and control. Better control between users and data and a better match between applications and their appropriate platforms is attained. More administrative control, however, is required to set up such a system.

Level 3 – Process Distribution: Applications are distributed throughout the network at whatever level is required and optimal use of resources is attained. This requires extraordinary high network data rates as well as techniques and protocol standards not yet even understood. Level 3 is presumed to be the next evolutionary step in network applications development. Parallel processing can be supported.

The current state of DtC networking is primarily file distribution with increasing I/O distribution applications. But the next few years will see the evolution of truly distributed systems that function at the process distribution level, paving the way for even more effective and transparent usage of computing resources as well as ensuring high levels of data control and security. The individual nature of the workstation, the main attraction of DtC usage, will be preserved through multitasking. Office workers will thus enjoy the best of both worlds.

When choosing a LAN for your computing environment, remember that peer-to-peer LANs tend to work best in small informal settings while server-oriented LANs support larger groups of users better and are suited for centralized management. Keep in mind the recommendations for DtC LAN design and implementation:

- Provide a user interface appropriate for the LAN user. If necessary, implement several types of interfaces for various types of users.
- Remember that ultimately, the efficiency of the network operating system is more important than the efficiency of the underlying hardware.
- Implement the safeguards necessary to guarantee the level of data integrity required for your environment.

- Consider the security risks posed by a LAN's open architecture and specify appropriate means of countering those risks.
- Review the suggested criteria for selecting a LAN administrator, and avoid the temptation to leave this position to poorly qualified personnel.
- Consider carefully the future requirements for interconnection to other networks or computers.

The LAN is the ideal methodology to connect similar workstations performing similar tasks, where transparent communication at high data rates is essential. Presently there is no better way to connect DtCs. The ability to accomplish true distributed processing will require significant advances in DtC bus design, data transmission speeds, operating systems, and applications software. When this occurs, the entire nature of computing in large organizations will change markedly. Those who become involved in LAN development will experience many challenges as this exciting technology evolves.

Part V. Peripherals

*The modern DtC is a combination of a powerful system unit and its periph-
erals. Many of today's peripherals are more sophisticated and intelligent
than the DtCs to which they are connected and which they support. Some
peripherals embody processing power that rivals that of their DtC hosts.*

Today's DtC peripherals are as complex and computationally impressive as any DtC
unit. Many peripherals operate CPUs at considerably higher instruction rates than
that of the DtCs CPU. Each peripheral CPU will be highly specialized to a particular
function. For example, most laser printer CPUs are ASIC chips designed to produce
well-defined character fonts. The CPU of a modem will be a DSP (digital signal
processing) chip that packs substantial amounts of data on the low-bandwidth phone
lines. An additional RISC or CISC CPU may be at work in the modem for
producing faxes, compressing and encrypting data, as well as automating communications dialogs. Your video display controller is generally operated by an ASIC
type of CPU, highly specialized in controlling graphics functions. As for the network interface, again you will find ASIC processors, made for network protocol
management and processing. For the hard disk to participate fully in system activities, it will need its own dedicated CPU.

When observed from a distance, the DtC unit and peripherals comprise a powerful, distributed processing system, with all of the attendant processing management considerations. A weak interface, an incorrectly-configured printer, an
immature operating system, or a slow DtC CPU can significantly hamper a system's
performance. Hopefully, the DtC and its peripherals will operate harmoniously, but
this will depend on how well the peripherals are interfaced, integrated, and supported by the applications software base. Whenever possible, peripherals should be
allowed to do the type of processing they do best. The printer should scale fonts,
the modem compress data, the display interface draw objects, the network board
handle communication protocol, the hard disk CPU buffer data and correct errors.
When each peripheral does its part, the DtC CPU can do what it does best – manage
overall data flow. When any of the peripheral functions must burden the CPU of the
DtC, the DtC will falter in data management, and you will have a sluggish system.

Of course, your CPU isn't alone in its task of data management. Critical to
overall system performance is a mature operating system, a fast and flexible bus,
and well-integrated high-speed interfaces. Without this support, the peripheral will
never reach full speed. Today's HB DtCs are becoming integrated with their peripherals and their operating systems are supporting peripheral functions better than
ever. As this takes place, the distinction between HB and EP computers becomes
even fuzzier.

Peripherals complement DtCs and often each other in many important ways. The functions they perform, their configurability, and programmability must be evaluated to derive sensible guidelines for selection. Of particular interest are these items:

Mass storage: supplements the executable memory. Mass storage devices are of different types, each offering particular benefits, performance characteristics, and problems.

Video display and interface: is the portal through which you view most of your work. The wide variety of video displays that are available provide so many choices it is easy to fall into bewilderment. Careful selection of this peripheral is important to software compatibility and your productivity.

Input devices: offered on the market range from keyboards, to mice, to joysticks, to light pens, to optical character recognizers, to barcode readers. Your choice will be critical to ensuring your productivity.

Output devices: make data and information visible to the outside world. Many considerations are involved in choosing the output device that best showcases the information to be presented.

Special peripherals: match the diversity of microcomputers by providing capabilities beyond those offered by general-purpose DtCs.

Mass Storage

The single most important peripheral in your system is the mass storage device; it is the mechanical work-horse of the DtC. The device stores large quantities of data that must be loaded into executable memory to be accessed by the CPU. Moving temporary data, storing longer-term programs, and housing archives are all critical missions for the mass storage system, and will affect the DtC's overall performance.

Mass storage is an essential component of any workstation. Mass storage capability works in harmony with the CPU and memory to extend a DtC's computational reach. Mass storage size, speed type, and configuration are critical in determining the overall usefulness of a DtC. There are several popular forms of mass storage:

- *Hard disk* – The centerpiece of most mass storage systems, and the most direct supplement to a CPU's accessibility to executable memory and short term storage of programs and data that are likely to change over time. Most DtC systems include a hard disk.

- *Removable media and drives* – Removables supplement the permanent hard disk and provide distinct advantages in two forms: removable media and removable drives.

  1. *Removable media* – This form of removable includes floppy diskettes, disk cartridges, and Bernoulli cartridges. Removable diskettes and cartridges are convenient for backing up programs and files and for transporting programs and data between non-networked DtCs. Removable cartridges may be the media of choice for confidential and security classified data. Bernoulli cartridges, for instance, are good for that purpose as well as for archiving programs and datasets.
  2. *Removable hard drives* – This form of removable includes the recording media, the reading and recording heads, the drive mechanism, and the related electronics. Removable hard drive units have built-in connectors that engage when the assembly is pushed into its slot.

- *Optical disks* – Opticals come in different types: CD-ROM for inexpensive mass-produced data such as catalogs, reference books, and encyclopedias; WORM drives for convenient archiving of large databases and development activities with built-in audit trails; and erasable optical (EO) disks, which acts like a huge but slow hard disk.

- *Tape* – Cost per MB makes tape the least expensive storage medium, and since the data density – bits per square centimeter – is usually much lower than that of a hard disk platter, high reliability archiving is possible. Access times that can run up to several minutes preclude the active use of taped programs and data that is possible with removable hard disk and optical drives.

Before considering different mass storage systems and strategies, let's look at the factors that drive the need for ever-increasing volumes of the mass storage resource.

- *Multiple software products* – If you use more than a few software products, larger mass storage capacity will save you the trouble of having to remove one software package to make room for another. Software installation procedures can be complex, especially for copy-protected software; it often involves more than just copying diskettes onto a mass storage device. There are intricate procedures for driver installations and other custom software configurations.

- *Large programs* – Programs such as compilers, database managers, and scientific/engineering analysis programs seldom fit entirely in executable memory. Usually a program is brought in as needed using overlays. As executable memory prices drop and operating systems support larger amounts, more of a program will load into memory. Nevertheless, computing history has proved that programs will always expand to sizes greater than memory can support, making the shuffling between hard disk and memory a classic problem.

- *Data-intensive programs* – High-resolution graphics images, large databases, graphics-intensive documents, large spreadsheets, and large numerical databases increase the need for mass storage. Large bit-mapped images can take one full megabyte of storage – *each*. Desktop-published documents average 100K per page when graphics are included. CAD graphics and numeric databases can easily run ten megabytes for a single page with the print files, multiple fonts, and underlying information. Scientific analysis programs often require a megabyte just to store intermediate results. Databases with multiple indexes sometimes have individual indexes as large as the database itself.

- *LAN servers* – Storage of data and programs for multiple users will require tremendous capacity. LAN users always want more storage.

- *Larger operating systems* – Operating systems such as Unix and OS/2 require more than 10 MB just for utilities, drivers, fonts, and the like.

Figure 95 shows the data density vs. data rates for mass storage devices. The floppy disk has both the lowest storage capacity and the lowest data transfer rates, but the price per MB is reasonable and floppy reliability is good. A hard disk won't hesitate to crash at the worst possible time. Since most DtC users have both hard disks and floppy drives in their units, the floppy becomes an important back-up medium.

Hard disks span the widest range of data rates and storage capacities, and their initial cost is low compared to the EO disks that stand in line to replace them. Removable hard disk cartridges are usually slower than resident hard disks and the capacity of a single cartridge is smaller. There is a favorable overlap region in which a removable cartridge fits nicely with an application if the application is smaller than the cartridge size. Optical storage devices can provide the highest data capacity, but they are expensive and they can not compete with the better hard disk data transfer rates. Tape drives (not shown) with capacities from 50 MB to 50 gigabytes are available to round out anyone's archival activities. All of these devices fit into a broad spectrum of mass storage capability.

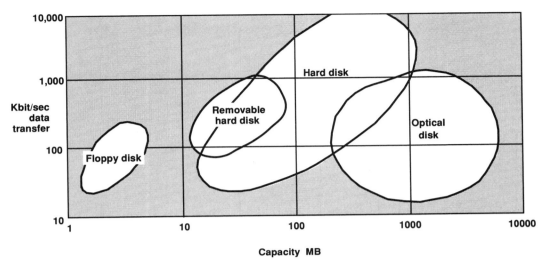

Figure 95. Capacity vs. data transfer rate

A system's main mass storage device, usually a hard disk, should be 20 to 50 times larger than the installed RAM and 20 to 50 times larger than the installed floppy drives. Removable hard disks charm you with the promise of enormous storage capacity, but you must be careful about the size of each removable disk. You need a disk at least as large as your largest programs or the modules in your modularized data bases.

Mass Storage Device Characteristics

Currently, the most popular recording media are floppy diskettes and various forms of hard disk. All disks except Bernoulli flexible disk cartridges are now recorded on both sides.

Several crucial parameters must be considered when choosing mass storage devices. You must know not only the number of programs and the quantity of data that can be stored on the medium of a device, but also if those amounts are sufficient for future requirements. How quickly programs or data can be loaded into CPU memory and the reliability of long-term storage can have enormous impact on office efficiency.

Platters, Tracks, Sectors, and Clusters

Most disk-type mass storage devices store data in concentric rings called tracks. Each disk is divided into pie-shaped sectors that divide tracks into segments (see Figure 98 on page 500).

The arc of a track within a pie-shaped sector of a disk is the smallest logical unit of storage known to the operating system. Most MS-DOS computers, for example, have a 17-sectors per track scheme; RLL recording methods have 26; while ESDI and SCSI drives have 34.

The number of tracks is determined by the disk drive manufacturer and is a function of media density and track positioning hardware. The number of sectors per track can be variable if the hard disk controller will support it. Sector size is not usually varied by the user, except for a RAMdisk, for which there are no physical media constraints. Sector sizes are established mostly at the BIOS level, while a larger data quantity, the *cluster*, is what an operating system might use for its minimum size logical data unit. An optimum size is chosen that matches the average user's file size. Too small a cluster size means that the operating system has to gather lots of clusters to build a large file. Too large a cluster number means that even tiny files will occupy the minimum cluster size on the hard disk and a lot of space will remain unused. Although some operating systems allow the user to modify cluster size, tampering with sizing can have disastrous effects if the adjustments are not accounted for at all levels of software operation.

Hard Disk Speed Parameters

Disk rotation rates, head access time, data transfer rates, interleaving, and read/write times are all related and have a profound effect on hard disk performance and how well it matches the capabilities of the CPU.

Data Transfer Rates

Typical HB hard disk transfer rates are around 500 K/second, while 5 to 10 MB per second is not uncommon on the EP computers. The removable hard disks run at the low end of the hard disk speed spectrum, usually less than 300K/second. Floppies are even slower. Although the read data times of the optical disk can compete with a hard disk's times, WORM and erasable optical write times can be markedly slower. Data transfer rate is heavily influenced by the type of mass storage interface between DtC and mass storage drive, file interleave factors, track densities, DtC CPU and DMA capability, and the ability of the applications software to absorb the data.

> **NOTE**
>
> There's no advantage to using a 5 MB/second hard drive if it is dedicated to a file-intensive applications program that absorbs data at only 100 K/second.

A hard disk has the best mass storage data transfer and access time performance, although optical and removable hard disk devices can be close seconds for many applications. The capacity of the latter becomes particularly apparent when active data files exceed 500 MB.

Interleaving

The disk controller has to keep up with the data being read as the disk spins. Following is the sequence of events:

1. A segment of data is read from the platter to a memory buffer.
2. The contents of the memory buffer is sent to CPU memory.
3. If the buffer is not empty when the heads are in position over the next sector, a pause will occur while the disk rotates to bring the desired sector back into position under the heads.

If data are stored in adjacent sectors, the buffer may not dump to the CPU fast enough. If data are stored in alternate sectors, there will be time enough to dump the buffer in the interval between the alternate sectors. If data are stored in alternate sectors, the interleave is 2; if every third, it is 3; and so on. With an interleave of 1, the controller picks up the data from sequential sectors as fast as they come around on the disk.

The data transfer rate of a hard disk is closely related to interleaving. Interleaving arranges data segments on a hard disk to ensure maximum data per unit time to and from the recording medium. Factors that determine the optimum interleaving scheme are the rotational rate of the disk, the sector sizes, the data transfer rates of the controller, DMA, and CPU, and the size of the hard disk controller cache.

Consider the typical MS-DOS computer hard disk running at 17 sectors per track with 512 bytes per sector spinning at 60 revolutions per second. 522,000 bytes per second are read at the heads. Since you can't slow the platter down, you'll need a fast hard disk cache to pass the data off or you'll need to use a different interleave sequence.

An interleave of 1 requires a good hard disk controller with cache memory to buffer the data, as well as a good DMA controller to get it quickly to the CPU. The CPU must then be able to cope with the data rate. Like a fire-fighting bucket brigade passes water down the line, the hard disk controller sweeps the data from the platter into its local cache memory and the memory is moved into CPU memory (shared or DMA) where the CPU tries to use it as fast as it comes. Usually the CPU and applications software are the bottlenecks.

If the interface cannot keep up with the data, you could disperse the data so that successive data are found in every third sector. This is an interleave of 3. Then the controller and the rest of the DtC would have time to take in data during the two sectors out of three that do not contain the next data. Most hard disk low-level formatting utilities give you a choice of interleave and some even test your hard disk to determine the optimum number.

Adjustments to hard disk interleaving are performed by special low-level formatting programs that maximize the data transfer rate to the hard drive for various CPU and hard disk types and rotation rates. Hard disk interleaving has considerable impact on hard drive performance and should be performed only by experienced personnel.

Access Time

Access time is quantified in two ways. One measure is how quickly the heads can move to the track and to the position on the track that carries the desired data. This is called *seek time*, and is nominally the time it takes to traverse half the distance across the recording medium. Seek times can range from 5 milliseconds for fast hard disks, to seconds on large optical disks, to minutes on large tape drives. Seek times can be reduced by partitioning the mass storage device into smaller drives and restricting a given application to one of the small drives.

The other measure of head speed it can move from one track to the next. This is called *track-to-track access time* and ranges from 1 millisecond to as long as a second for some optical drives.

Read and Write Times

Read time is usually governed by how fast the drive read electronics can pick up magnetic or reflective variations, and it establishes the mass storage read data transfer rate. In some situations, write times can be orders of magnitude longer. Long write times are mostly an optical disk phenomenon where writing to the media involves heating, melting, and changing crystalline structures. When this happens, processes take considerably longer on the write side than on the read side. The WORM drive's long write time is not too much of a problem since you suffer through it only once. For EO however, increased write times are a problem if you use the EO as a hard drive, with frequent rewrites to the media.

Data Transfer Rate vs. Access Time

The larger the file or program to be moved at one time, the greater the benefit of high data transfer rate. If the hard disk is moving large sequential datasets, data transfer rate will dominate access time. Operating several large programs in tandem involves moving large files. Programs that move small files will often benefit from fast access times. Creating indexes for a database involves shuffling small file portions of databases and indexes in and out of memory. Fragmentation of disk files, discussed later, requires more accessing and therefore data transfer rate is not the critical factor.

In-memory applications will only operate files that fit completely into executable memory, so their hard disk requirements relate to how much the in-memory program uses overlays. Since file-oriented programs operate on files larger than memory, they must shuffle both data and program overlays in and out of memory, which places a great load on the hard disk.

Conflicting requirements result in a tradeoff between access time, data transfer rate, and total capacity. Higher capacity, for example, means more tracks and therefore longer access time.

Head Positioning

Two types of head positioning mechanisms are used in rotating mass storage devices: *stepper motor* and *voice coil*.

The stepper motor is an electric motor with a shaft that moves a small portion of a circle every time a digital signal is applied to its windings. The drive heads are connected to the motor shaft through an arm mechanism. The heads are positioned one step at a time at fixed locations on the rotating disk radius or at different tracks. The positioning is independent of where the data actually are. Stepper systems are also known as open loop systems because information goes out to only the stepper motor, and is not fed back to the controlling electronics. Accurate positioning depends on motor and arm tolerances not drifting with time.

On an HB hard disk with track densities as high as 1000 tracks per inch of platter radius, only slight changes in head alignment can be tolerated. Problems of changes occurring between successive writes and reads of the same data are not as likely as the recorded data drifting from the original low-level format laid down when you first bought the hard disk. Programs such as SpinRite from Gibson Research can do a nondestructive low-level format of your hard disk *underneath* the data, to help account for aging of stepper systems.

In removable media systems that incorporate stepper motors, such as floppy disk drives used in HB computers, it is sometimes more reliable to format and write to diskettes on the same disk drives that will be reading them. The sensitivity problem becomes more serious as the number of tracks increase, and particularly if the device goes out of alignment. Finally, at track densities above 1000/inch, servo positioning, discussed later, becomes mandatory.

The voice coil method positions the heads by an analog signal connected to a coil through which the head positioning arm passes. Audio speakers work in a similar way. Rather than a one track per step system, the heads are positioned according to how strong the voice coil signal is; the stronger the signal, the farther the heads move. As with any analog control system, immediate positioning has the problem of overshoot and oscillation. Voice coil systems position from 2-5 times faster than stepper motor systems.

For numerous tracks, where accurate head positioning is critical, the more expensive servo voice coil positioning method is used. The position of the heads is determined by data amplitude under the head, or by a separate servo platter DSS (dedicated servo surface) that is followed by the heads. Position information is fed back to the controlling electronics, which adjusts the head position accordingly. The system is called a *servo* or *closed loop* system. Accurate head positioning is continuously monitored and controlled.

Servo systems are found in the higher capacity hard disks of one gigabyte and above and optical drives that support track densities as high as 40,000 tracks per inch. The hard disk found in the typical HB computer consists of 400-1000 tracks per inch, making stepper systems popular there. Lower density floppies also use the conventional stepper motors.

Rotational Speeds

Floppies rotate at 300 or 360 revolutions per minute, while a hard disk and removable hard disks rotate at 1800 or 3600 rpm. Surprisingly, inside of the removable Bernoulli cartridge you will find a 5¼" floppy disk rotating at 1800 rpm. This speed is possible because the heads do not touch the floppy but remain a set distance above it.

> **NOTE**
> The Bernoulli Principle states that a low pressure layer develops next to a surface moving rapidly in a fluid. The low pressure causes the surface to lift.

A hard disk is hermetically sealed to prevent head crashes caused by the high rotational rates and media data densities. Even a small dust particle can have devastating effects. Optical disks pack such high data densities that their rotational speeds are much slower, making them comparable to floppy drives. The exception is the analog video disk, which spins at 1800 rpm.

CLV/CAV

Removable hard and floppy disks usually rotate at a constant angular velocity (CAV), measured in rpm. Some optical disks and CD-ROM drives operate at a constant linear velocity (CLV), measured in inches per second past the recording heads. CAV drives pack higher densities toward the center of the drive, but the CLV drives make better use of overall storage density since data density does not change with distance from the center.

While most hard, removable, and floppy drives place their data on concentric tracks, with data sectors aligned as shown in Figure 98, some optical drives – CD-ROM and videodisk, for example – have spiral tracks with heads that track the data much like on a record player. Spiral tracks yield better data densities and are best for the larger sequential data sets where access time is not an issue.

1.3   Hard Disks

The magnetic hard disk is the mainstay of DtC mass storage systems, likely to be found in almost every DtC you encounter. The hard disk will contain the bootable operating system, most often used utilities, favorite applications programs, as well as frequently used data. Hard disk capacities begin at 5 MB and go up to several gigabytes. Popular sizes in HB computers range from 40 to 200 MB. For those requiring more capacity, the removable cartridge drives, or even optical storage are worthy supplements.

Sizes and Prices

For the higher-end EP DtCs, hard disks and interfaces are matched by the original equipment manufacturer. Capacities begin at around 400 MB and prices start in the thousands. HB computer hard drives, however, come in a variety of low-cost, installable packages from hundreds of manufacturers and thousands of dealers. Both 5¼" and 3½" drives are supported and typical capacities range from 5 to 600 MB with the popular sizes of 20, 40, 80, 100, and 200 MB. Today you can buy a 20 MB hard drive for around $150 and a 200 MB drive will cost around $600. You can see that the more MB you buy, the cheaper it is per MB. It is sometimes difficult to find the right balance between bargain price and adequate storage. Many people buying a hard disk underestimate their size needs by half, and some by much more than that. Remember that as you enter the HB DtC world, you may have only one or two applications in mind, not realizing how many things you will be able to do with your system. Your need for utility software and data storage will also be easy to underestimate.

Partitions

Often, the operating system will allow you to split up the hard disk into partitions in which different programs and even other operating systems may reside. MS-DOS versions earlier than 4.0 used a 16-bit addressing scheme to identify sectors in a given partition, which limited each partition to 32 MB. Sixteen bits defines 64K sectors. Multiplying 64K sectors by 512 bytes per sector equals 32 MB. Later DOS versions went to a 24-bit scheme that places maximum partition size at several gigabytes, adequate for most needs.

Low-Level Format

The low-level format converts a clean and random disk into an organized system for accepting data. Unique bytes identify sector addresses to synchronize timing, inter-sector gaps, and other information that cannot be recorded during ordinary data operations. The disk drive controller uses the low-level format to guide data into and out of the hard drive; the low-level formatting process is intimately related to the particular drive controller and hard disk BIOS. The higher-level operating system file-oriented processes are not even aware of the low-level format.

Hard disks and their interfaces are closely linked. Different hard disks require different interfaces, and low-level hard disk formats are usually not transportable. If a a hard disk is low-level formatted on a given interface controller, it will usually work only with that make of controller. If the hard disk is moved to another controller, it will require a new low-level format. Since low-level formatting will completely erase data, you'll have to back up the disk prior to the low-level format. Low-level format incompatibility should not concern those who purchase the hard disk and its interface as a pair, it should concern the mix and match crowd who put together parts purchased separately at computer shows.

Physical and Mechanical Considerations

Most hard drives come in 3½" or 5¼" sizes and fit into bays on the system unit. You'll need a conversion kit if you want to put a 3½" drive in a 5¼" bay. Be sure that a mounting kit with screws, bezels, size, adapters, rails, and front plates is included. Also check that drive cables match the interface and that you have an appropriate terminating resistor.

> **NOTE**
>
> Usually the last drive on a multiple drive cable must have a terminating resistor that absorbs data reflections on the cable. These resistors plug into sockets on the hard disk and floppies. Sometimes a permanently mounted terminator is enabled by a single jumper. It is important to identify which type of terminator you have and verify that only one is operative. Enabling more than one terminator will unduly load the controller's driver chip. Not enabling any will cause line reflections that can corrupt your data. In either case no physical damage is likely to occur.

Drives generally come in three sizes: full height, half height, and one-third height. Also, some drives can operate only in a vertical or only in a horizontal position.

Also, be sure that your power supply can support the hard disk and its interface. Remember that the drive's starting current exceeds its running current. Many disk drive interfaces also provide a connector for hard-disk LEDs that are located on the system's front panel, since an internal mounting might hide its own face plate LED. Be sure to plug in the panel LED.

Recording Technologies

Popular HB hard disks use one of these recording methods:

- *Frequency modulation* – In frequency modulation, the data 0s and 1s are interspersed with synchronizing data 1s. The 0s and 1s correspond to different orientations of the magnetized media. This method is not too efficient because there must be one sync pulse for every data bit.

- *Modified frequency modulation (MFM)* – In this method data replaces many of the synchronizing pulses so that they do not occur as often. Data recording density, bits per inch, is increased by approximately 100%.

- **Run length limited** – The run length limited schemes limit the minimum and maximum number of consecutive ones or zeros that can occur in the data stream through special encoding schemes. The magnetic medium favors particular flux transition scenarios, which allows for a higher recording density. In RLL 2,7 for example, the maximum number of consecutive zeros is two and the maximum number of consecutive ones is seven. RLL versions of the ST506/412 controller are available, but the higher recording density warrants that the hard disk be RLL certified.

Interface Types

Hard disk positioning and accessing parameters, as well as its interface to the DtC can affect its performance markedly. Next, we look at some of the popular hard disk interface types.

Storage Module Device (SMD)

Storage module device interfaces are the precursors to DtC hard drive interfaces and were popularized on minicomputers. SMD interfaces can read and write directly to the hard disk, although a controller is required to provide timing and other disk management duties. SMD is regarded as the first successful original equipment manufacturer's hard disk interface, offering a throughput four times that of the ESDI. Eight-inch platters store from 500 MB to several gigabytes. These units take 15 minutes to warm up and typify the performance orientation of the minicomputers.

ST506/412

The ST506/412, by Seagate Technology, is the oldest and most common MFM controller for HB computers. The early 5 to 40 MB MS-DOS computer hard drives used this interface, which was named after the first ST hard drive that contained it. Both MFM and RLL recording technologies are supported with a maximum disk size of 127 MB (200 MB RLL). The bit rate through the heads is 500K/sec, but the actual data transfer rate – once buffering, error correction, and data separation are accounted for – is around 100K/sec.

The ST506/412 is a low-cost, device-level interface based on a standardized disk controller chip that establishes the interface between serial disk data and the DtC parallel bus. Data bits are read as flux reversals (MFM, RLL bit patterns) from the disk and are transferred to the controller. There they are converted to data bits and separated from sector identification and synchronizing data bits. The data bits then go through serial to parallel conversion and are sent out to the system data bus. ST506/412 uses two cables: a wide control cable with 34 conductors and a smaller data cable with 20 conductors. The 34-line cable carries head and drive select controlling signals, position indexes, ready signals, step direction, and seek complete. The data cable has the MFM write and read data, grounds, and drive selected signals.

> **NOTE**
>
> *Device level* means that the interface connects directly to the specific peripheral, for example, the hard disk. The signals are specific signals that only a hard disk understands: serial data and head positioning. The hard disk merely provides signal conditioning electronics between the interface and the disk heads, positioners, write protect, and drive door sensors. Thus the device-level interface must be connected to its specific peripheral. The ST506/412 and ESDI are device-level interfaces,

whereas the IDE and SCSI are not. The SCSI controller is so general-purpose that it can control printers, hard disks, optical disks, and scanners.

Figure 96 shows the controller on the interface with the hard disk specific control and data cables connecting to the hard disk. When controlling two hard disks, which is the limit, separate data cables are used for each hard drive while the control cable connects both of the drives in parallel.

Integrated Drive Electronics

The integrated drive electronics (IDE) interface integrates both a hard disk and its controller in a single unit. This is unlike the device-level interface that also contains a disk drive controller. The IDE interface board is not much more than a device-independent I/O port. Parallel data captured by the IDE interface is sent to the disk drive unit where the data is converted to serial data and the necessary hard disk positioning functions by the controller on the hard disk. Integrating the hard disk with its controller results in a better match between hard disk unit functions and the controller. A similar match is found in speaker amplifiers where a particular speaker is matched with a particular amplifier in a single unit.

Notice in Figure 96 that a single 40 conductor cable carries the parallel data to the hard disk and the controller is located on the hard disk itself. In the

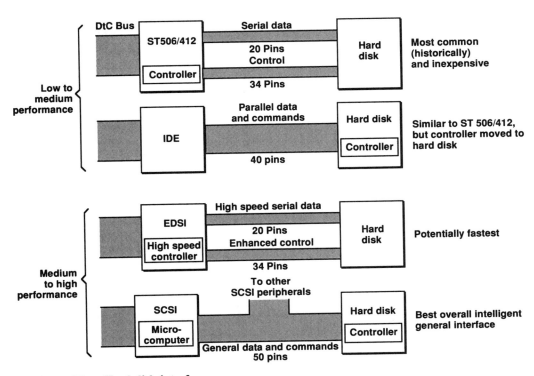

Figure 96. Hard disk interfaces

MS-DOS-compatible world, the IDE interface is called a poor man's ESDI interface.

Enhanced System Device Interface

The enhanced system device interface (ESDI) is an upgrade to the ST506/412, although it's still a device-level interface. As with the ST506/412, serial data travels between the interface and the drive on a separate data cable. ESDI signal transmitters and receivers are higher power and designed for the higher data rates. As with the IDE interface, the data is separated from timing and other information on the disk drive.

ESDIs can transfer data between drive and controller at the rate of 10 MB compared to the 500K maximum of ST506/412. As Figure 96 shows, the ESDI uses two cables to connect drive to controller, just like the ST506/412: one 34-pin cable for control and positioning and the other 20-pin cable for data. The pinouts, however, are not the same. The ESDI data cable implements additional controlling signals including cartridge changed, separate read/write clocks, seek complete, and drive selected.

The important difference between the ESDI, IDE, and ST506/412 is that the ESDI has sufficient control data width and signal lines to control a drive as large as 1 terabyte. ESDIs implement their own 8- or 16-bit microcomputers and can support streaming tape drives, optical disks, and even printers. ESDIs can handle up to seven devices; each device tells the ESDI controller its configuration through an 11-word command language that the DtC never sees. An exclusive recording scheme packs more data per track. The ESDI has higher data transfer rates and is more intelligent than the IDE or the ST506/412.

Small Computer System Interface (SCSI)

The SCSI is the most intelligent and general purpose of the interfaces. Due to its speed, the SCSI can be used to control the hard disk. For hard disk interfacing, disk addressing is not done by cylinder, head, and sector, but rather by device-independent, sequentially numbered data entities.

The SCSI scheme can support multiple DtC hosts or initiating peripherals that require service using an arbitration scheme to a theoretical maximum of 14,000 peripherals. The interface supports eight devices and eight logical drives; 256 logical subunits can be implemented within each device. With the SCSI adapter supporting up to eight peripherals, the number of required adapter cards in a given DtC is reduced. A single host interface can support multiple peripherals and multiple host computers can be attached to the same SCSI I/O bus to share the peripherals and data resources.

The SCSI is independent of the specific peripheral connected to it. Any compatible peripheral can be connected to the SCSI without hardware modifications. An intelligent command set allows the CPU to offload tasks to the SCSI. The SCSI supports such functions as automatic error detection, defect mapping, and self diagnostics.

SCSI devices frequently require large drivers, which eat up available executable memory. Memory consumption becomes a serious problem if you have several devices on SCSI controllers.

The SCSI is nothing less than a universal mass storage gateway. As SCSIs become standardized, the costly task of designing a new controller card each time a new disk drive comes to market will be eliminated. The SCSI has influenced the entire peripheral domain including such diverse devices as tape drives, printers, coprocessors, optical disks, LAN connections, and scanners. The SCSI is a complete bus specification, offering an extension to a computer motherboard. In contrast, the ST506/412 and ESDI are specifications that describe how a device will be connected to a bus. The SCSI allows daisy chaining, that is, connecting peripherals together on the same bus. The SCSI bus is a 50 conductor cable that can be up to 25 meters long. Current SCSI standards specify an 8-bit parallel path, and newer specifications include a 32-bit data width.

A SCSI peripheral can be performing its work without any DtC CPU intervention. For example, DtCs with bus mastering allow more than one CPU to share bus resources, so that a SCSI device can operate independently of the DtC CPU. A SCSI tape drive might be backing up the SCSI hard disk at the same time you are doing word processing.

The SCSI transfers data according to a block-oriented standard; it does not see data in disk sectors or clusters, but rather in device-independent blocks. Mandatory commands must be supported in every SCSI, and vendor-unique commands must be defined by the manufacturer.

Enhanced specifications that further increase SCSI capability are in the offing:

- **SCSI-2** – The SCSI-2 specification includes improved commands for magnetic and optical disk and tape, new support for optical scanners, and removable media optical jukeboxes. SCSI-2 provides for the expansion of the data path from 8 bits to 16 or even 32 bits.

- **SCSI-3** – Proposed enhancements include a single cable 16-bit option, more than 8 devices per cable, longer cable lengths, autoconfigure on the interfaced device, and addressing and operation on other physical layers such as fiber optics.

IPI-3

Intelligent peripheral level 3 (IPI-3) was defined by ANSI Standard's Committee X3T9.3 in 1980; however, the first products did not come to market until 1986. IPI-3 is based on the transfer of message packets that are independent of the transfer methodology. Independence simplifies the use of fiber optics instead of traditional cables as the transfer medium. One drawback of this interface is that it is more expensive than the SCSI.

Controllers and Floppy Disk Interfaces

Hard disk interfaces can also provide a floppy disk interface. Most units support two and some newer interfaces support four floppy disks. Floppy disk support on the hard disk interface can save you a bus slot.

Newer Magnetic Media Technologies

Advances in hard disk magnetic technology have resulted in storage densities for magnetic devices approaching those of optical storage devices.

- *Vertical recording* – Aligning magnetic domains at right angles to the recording medium rather than along its surface produces a tenfold increase in storage density.

- *Special media* – Special metal alloys and surface deposit technologies can yield an order of magnitude improvement in magnetic domain density. The hard disks found in the PCs of the early '80s stored 5 to 10 MB, while today 500 MB to 1 gigabyte drives are commonplace.

- *Improved read/write heads* – Early hard disks used a ferrite ring head that could distinguish 1000 bits per inch. High-performance drives now use thin film heads with electrical conductor particles deposited on a silicon substrate. These heads can distinguish more than 50 Kbits per inch.

- *Faster hard disk interfaces* – Today's SCSI is much faster than the early ST506/412.

- *Lower cost* – You can purchase a 200 MB hard drive for an HB computer for around $600; the price of a 5 MB drive ten years ago.

BIOS and Driver Support

Most operating systems accommodate a variety of hard disks by allowing BIOS ROMs or installed drivers to worry about the hard disk details, freeing the operating system to deal with file structures and relationships, as shown in Figure 97.

At the operating system level, concern is with file management; management of a particular mass storage device is handled at the BIOS and driver level. If applications programs deal with the mass storage through the operating system; then the operating system will shield the user completely from the details of the particular mass storage device. If applications attempt to control the mass storage device at the BIOS level, transportability of the software among different DtC systems with different mass storage configurations will not be assured. This intermediate software will be found in ROM or RAM depending upon usage.

- *ROM drivers* – Many hard drive interfaces provide their own BIOS routines. Most newer MS-DOS computers provide ROM support for popular hard disks in their built-in system BIOS. Interfaces with their own BIOS can be found in the earlier XT-style computers, or the later SCSIs. When you tell system BIOS that there is no hard disk, the operating system looks for ROM on the hard disk interface. It is fortunate that MS-DOS computers are so forgiving.

- *RAM drivers* – Customized drivers are required for hard disk supplements such as RAMdisks, Bernoulli drives, tape backup, and optical disk drives. Using special interfaces, SCSI drivers can be quite large. Usually these drivers are installed through system configuration files because they differ considerably from the system BIOS routines intended to support the stock hard drives.

The drivers allow software to operate transparently with different mass storage products; the added drives simply become additional drive letters in the mass storage repertoire. Mass storage with unique characteristics such as read-only optical, or tape drives cannot be so transparently installed because their features and software requirements are considerably different. Mass storage transparency is particularly important if the mass storage is located elsewhere in a network; say on a network server.

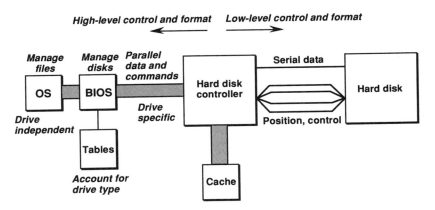

Figure 97.   Hard disk control hierarchy

Parking a Hard Drive

Most hard drives have a park position to which the heads are moved when power is turned off. Today's hard disks automatically park when you power down, but the early 1980s hard disks require software to park the head prior to power-down.

Parking is particularly important if you are going to move the DtC and subject it to shock. If the disk is damaged, certain tracks may not be available for use, or the entire hard disk mechanism may become inoperable. Your best bet is to back up the hard disk if you are going to move the DtC and you do not want to lose any hard disk data. Hard disks are becoming more resilient to shock, especially now that they are being used in laptop computers, which must provide for the inevitable bouncing and banging that the laptop will endure. It is always a good practice, however, to treat a drive carefully to promote reliable service and extend its useful life.

Hard Drive Security

Methods are available to disable the hard drive completely or make it read-only. Hard drive security methods fall into three general categories:

1. *Software* – Adjust the operating system drivers to disable the hard drives; make the drives impossible to write to by voiding software write functions; or make the operating system treat the drive as read-only.

2. *Breaking data paths* – Break data paths between the hard drive controller and the hard drive; or fool the hard drive controller into detecting faults in the hard disk hardware, rendering the controller – and therefore the hard drive – inoperative. The associated wiring will be activated with key switches to restrict access.

3. *Log-on hardware* – The software method for hard drive security can be defeated by simply booting a good operating system from a floppy disk. The hard drive can then be used. To prevent this, a special hardware add-on board that defeats the system's ordinary BIOS boot up procedures can force a logon procedure before the system will boot at all.

Security methods are complex and should not be attempted by the inexperienced user. Most large organizations will have established plans for handling security. A convenient security measure is storing secure data on removable disk. Removable disks can be easily locked up.

Hard Disk Software

The following are some of the more important software functions for tracking the performance of hard disks and ensuring their sound operation.

Performance Measurement

Software products are available that can compare the hard disk's relevant performance parameters against a reference. On MS-DOS computers this reference is the original XT's hard disk, which is considered to have a performance figure of 1. Higher-end performance compatibles can have performance factors exceeding 15.

Fragmentation Repair

As you place files on the hard disk, they accumulate from the outer tracks inward. When you delete and replace files, however, file fragmentation occurs, so that it is only a matter of time before any given file is scattered across the hard disk. Although the operating system is efficient at putting files together, when overlays and partial data files shuttle back and forth, fragmentation becomes a problem. Fragmentation slows your hard disk because the heads have to go to many different locations to pick up parts of the file. The fragmentation problem can usually be fixed in two ways:

1. **Fragmentation utilities** – Fragmentation utilities in the Norton, Mace, and the PCTools Utility toolkits will reorder files automatically. The process can take hours, making overnight a good time for such activities. Earlier fragmentation programs could cause headaches during a power loss catastrophe; today's utilities are bullet proof and perform the defragmentation in manageable and recoverable steps.

2. **Backup** – Perform a complete hard disk back up. Reformatting and reinstalling hard disk software will reorder all files. This method is drastic and time consuming, at best. It is not generally recommended.

File Recovery

In most operating systems, file erasure is a deletion in a directory somewhere, in which clusters are marked as unavailable. The file data remains somewhere else. Utilities can be used to recover erased files by appropriate repair in the directory or by searches in the scattered hard disk data. Recovery of a lost file by repairing the directory entry depends heavily on having had little or no disk activity following the erasure, which could scramble the otherwise useable data.

Low-Level Formatting

Although low-level formats are usually only performed upon disk installation, there are problems that can require another low-level format. Most hard disk vendors provide appropriate set-up and low-level formatting software on included floppy disks or on the hard disk itself. When installed, the hard disk will at least boot that software. You then copy it to a floppy for later use. Other hard drive manufacturers will place low-level format software in the controller ROM BIOS and give you instructions for executing it. The software will guide you through the delicate low-level format process. Most of this software will give you a choice of interleave; some even telling you which is optimum. For example, SpinRite from Gibson Research will operate on a data-loaded hard disk. It will tell you if your interleave is working, and if it is not, it will recommend a better one. Then, as if by magic, it will nondestructively reformat the disk at low level to the optimal interleave, underneath the existing data.

Hard Disk Backup

It is possible to lose hard disk data all at once by a variety of catastrophic problems. Partition table scrambles caused by a virus, misbehaved software that writes to the boot sector or partition tables, improperly configured hardware interfaces that conflict with the hard disk BIOS, scrambled CMOS memory configurations, or a jarred unparked hard drive can cause the hard disk to fail or lose critical data that governs its structure and setup. These problems are drastic compared to fragmentation problems and often require a low-level reformat that will sacrifice data. All of these potential data disasters make it important for you to find software that makes the chore of backing up a hard disk more straightforward.

Software such as Fifth Generation's Fastback Plus provides numerous features. These include backup by changed file, by date, and by exclusion or inclusion of files; data compression to save disks; error checking and correction; auto formatting; and creation of historical files to audit the backup. Standard 1.4 MB floppies can contain up to 3 MB per diskette depending on the extent of data compression. Backups can be to floppies, removable cartridges, tape drives, and even WORM or EO disks.

As stressed elsewhere, you must establish routine habits for backing up your hard disk. It is the hard disk that holds the most important system files: network configurations, operating system parameters, drivers, TSRs, command files, recent applications data, and most-used programs. Although the individual files may not be too hard to replace, getting the precise configuration restored can be troublesome.

RAMdisks and Cache Software

You can operate software products that reduce wear and tear on the hard drive. The software can supplement the hard drive for programs that are disk file intensive and that cannot use available memory properly, but instead must shuffle files to and from the hard disk. Memory that the software cannot execute can be used as a fake hard disk to reduce hard disk usage. This type of solution predominates in MS-DOS compatible DtCs with their historic problem of "fractured" memory support. Programs such as Windows, OS/2, and others provide improved memory and virtual memory support, which reduces the need for external RAMdisks and cache software.

Data Compression and Decompression Drivers

Software drivers are available that can link with the existing hard disk and its drivers to provide data compression and decompression on the fly. The process is transparent to the software and while it maximizes the hard disk capacity, it slows data transfer to the hard disk. Also, you can purchase hard disk interfaces that perform data compression and decompression on the interface hardware much quicker, and without additional software drivers. You will face a tradeoff between cost and efficiency.

Removable Media and Removable Drives

■ Soft removable media include floppies and Bernoulli cartridges.

Permanent hard disks come in hermetically-sealed cases that are attached by screws inside the DtC. Permanent drives are invariably supplemented by some form of removable media or by removable hard drives.■ Removable cartridges can be inserted, removed, and exchanged freely during DtC operation.

Removable Media

Among removables are diskettes, enclosed in flexible jackets, and the newer and smaller diskettes encased in rigid plastic cartridges. Supplementing these removables are the flexible disk cartridges known as Bernoullis. Removable diskettes and cartridges are convenient, economical, and otherwise desirable mass storage devices because they possess an infinitely large collective capacity. Not only can they function as large data backup and archival devices, they can also act like a hard disk. The only drawback is the need to label them for retrieval and to store them safely if you accumulate them in quantity.

Removable cartridges provide an attractive compromise between the convenience and portability of floppies and the speed and capacity of fixed hard disks. Given the number of applications now running on DtCs and the ever-increasing need for hard disk space, removables have become virtually indispensable. Uses for removables include:

- *Convenient but expensive data archiving* – Since the cost of cartridges is between $50 and $100, you may not want to use them for backup of large datasets. For smaller databases in which the data can be segregated by time or other category and volume is not large, the Bernoulli cartridge is appropriate.

- *Large, infrequently used software applications* – You could install an entire software system on one removable cartridge – a desktop publisher, or a drawing graphics program – together with all its related data. Although you'll want to install most often used programs on the permanent hard disk for speed, the convenience of keeping different software applications intact on removables could outweigh the speed advantage of the permanent hard disk for not-so-often used programs. Examples of applications for removable media could be game libraries, a huge Lispt compiler, or a database manager. Many corporate centralized help facilities store trial software applications on removable media. Software demonstrators also benefit from removables.

- *HB computer upgrades* – Many HB computer users who bought 40 to 120 MB drives couldn't imagine running out of disk space. There is rarely a space problem for a word processor, spreadsheet, and graphics program on a large drive. Add games, utility programs, a language compiler, and a vacation planner complete with digitized road maps, and suddenly the 120 MB drive doesn't seem quite so large. One solution is to install a removable media drive. Prices have fallen below $1000 for a single unit, which can be installed in a 5¼" drive slot. Those upgrading their hard disks should consider leaving the permanent hard drive in place and adding a removable hard disk drive. A large library of programs can be kept intact on removable media.

Removable Hard Drives

Removable hard drives, like the permanent hard drive, come as a complete assembly with the drive motor, read and write heads, recording media, and associated electronics. The entire assembly is physically removable from a DtC unit. Removable hard drives feature quick disconnect plugs, capacities of 40-100 MB, and shock resistance. These drives are used in the same way as fixed hard drives. While more expensive than fixed hard disks of the same capacity and they are more shock resistant. The main advantages are removability and speeds comparable to those of internal hard drives. Removable hard drives are particularly attractive for high security applications where hard disk speed and removability to secured storage are important.

Removable Brackets

A hard disk or floppy carrier can be mounted in a removable bracket for use with different DtC units. The entire assembly can be withdrawn from the system unit. A hard disk can then be mounted in a carrier frame that slides into a homing bracket in the DtC. The bracket incorporates a reliable interface-to-disk connector plug. When the bracket and disk are removed, the interface is disconnected from the disk. This enables a standard hard disk to be shared among many different units. For large numbers of non-networked DtCs, the bracket hard disk method is a good way to transfer data between DtCs.

Hard cards

Many vendors supply hard drives that are integrated into the hard drive interface; the entire unit plugs into a card slot. The units come in sizes from 10 MB to 120 MB. The advantages of these units are:

- *Easy installation* – Just plug in the board. The board does draw considerable power and you may have to replace the original power supply.
- *Saves bays* – Hard cards do not take up a bay in the DtC.

Potential disadvantages are:

- *Full slots* – The hard card takes up one full board slot, and sometimes two. Many of the newer interface boards for full-sized hard drives are short slot boards.
- *Power routing* – Power is usually routed to the hard cards by the bus edge rather than over separate cabling. Although add-on board power is typically supplied this way, the hard disk motor starting currents often exceed the carrying capacity of the thin bus traces. Hard disk motor power is better supplied over separate cables.
- *Hard card sectors* – Some hard cards vary sector per track density with track position to attain higher recording densities. This requires special operating system drivers and incurs occasional software incompatibility.

Silicon Hard Drives

Memory chips rather than rotating machinery are used in silicon hard drives. Recent chip technologies such as ferromagnetic memory and EAROM (electrically alterable read only memory) chips form the basis of silicon hard drives. The lower-cost DRAM memory can also be used as a silicon hard drive. A battery or large capacity capacitor within the silicon drive pack is used to power the DRAM memory when it is not connected to a DtC system. When it is connected, the battery or capacitor recharges. Silicon hard drives are faster and quieter than conventional hard drives, and could become cost effective as memory prices decline. Silicon hard drive applications are restricted to 10-20 MB systems, mostly used for flexible transportation of datasets and programs among many non-networked DtCs.

1.4 Floppy Disks

Floppy disks provide an inexpensive method for transporting data and programs between DtCs. The early HB DtCs relied on the floppy disks for loading the operating system, programs, and data files. Floppy drives now have a different focus:

- *Hard disk backup* – Using software designed for hard drive backup, you can back up an entire hard disk, or selected subdirectories and files using floppy disks.

- *Installation backup* – If you have insufficient hard disk space to save all of their programs or complete applications, floppies can provide a supplement. Separate software systems, usually set up in a subdirectory, can be backed to floppy using hard disk backup software. When you work again with the huge database system, restore the subdirectory from floppies. This area of software application backup is where the removable drives do well.

- *Program medium* – Floppies are how most HB and EE programs are initially distributed. This will change with the increasing use of local and wide area networks.

Sizes and Capacities

Current floppy disk sizes are 5¼" and 3½." Older disks were 8" and a newer 2" drive is in the making. Today, the 3½" size has become the universal floppy disk size, although many MS-DOS compatibles still use the 5¼" size popularized by IBM. Apple switched to 3½" early in its Apple II line; IBM followed much later in its PS/2 line. Popular MS-DOS computer floppy drive capacities are summarized in the next table. Apple's 3½" capacities are similar.

Size	Nomenclature	Tracks	Capacity
5¼	double density	40	360K
5¼	high density	80	1.2 MB*
3½	low density	80	720K
3½	high density	80	1.4 MB

Note: The capacity is more than twice that of the 40 track drives because of increased recording density as well as track density.

- *2.8 MB* – A new standard; a higher density 2.8 MB 3½" drive is supported by MS-DOS 5.0. The drive will be able to read the older 1.4 MB and 720K floppies, and is already available at computer stores and shows.

- *Servo-controlled floppies* – Vertical recording techniques and servo-controlled positioning promise floppies with 10 to 20 MB capacities using the same rigid jacket now popularized in the 3½" floppies. The problem with servo-controlled heads on floppies is that data errors can be accounted for, while errors in servo-control tracks cannot. Data channel errors are accounted for as with ordinary floppy disks. The controller performs CRC checks. The servo control track, however, is independent of the controller, and there is no mechanism to repair errors in the servo control track recording. Head positioning reliability, then, is at the mercy of the recording media.

- *Flopticals* – With an even higher capacity, the floptical disk consists of a magnetic medium to which an optical track with varying reflectivity is applied. Servo positioning of heads is maintained optically. The 5¼" flopticals are available with capacities rivalling optical disks. Reliability remains to be determined.

Options on MS-DOS Compatibles

The popularity and proliferation of MS-DOS compatibles has made a variety of inexpensive disk drive options possible:

- *XT-style compatibles* – Although XTs were initially outfitted with the lower-capacity 5¼" 360K drives, special floppy interface cards can easily provide support of any drive mix.

- *AT-style compatibles* – These DtCs provide adequate support of floppy drive mixes as an adjunct to their hard disk interfaces. The IDE interfaces support four disk drives. Separate floppy interfaces are available for both AT- and XT-style compatibles.

Often, software drivers are needed to supplement the operating system's understanding of what kind of floppies are running.

Hardware Considerations

If you are planning to add floppies to your DtC, be sure that the system unit box provides adequate drive bays. Some system unit boxes have up to eight 3½" and 5½" bays for add-on disk drives, removable media drives, optical drives, tape drives, and, of course, the hard disk. Make sure you get the right cables. Cables at interfaces generally have Berg connectors, while PC edge connectors are used in the older XT-style computers. MS-DOS floppy disk drive cables and some hard drive interface cables have a twist between first and second drives. A few of the wires are twisted to use identical drive select jumpers on the two disk drives.

Differences in Diskette Vendors

Floppy disk quality will vary with the vendor. Diskette quality can range from one bad disk per 10,000 to one bad disk per 10. Also, diskette performance depends on different makes of disk drive, environmental conditions, and handling. Once you have identified a good diskette brand for a particular system, use it consistently. The price of data is high compared to the price of the media.

Quality can vary in several ways:

- *Hub* – On 5¼" diskettes, this is where the floppy disk clutch holds the diskette. Most manufacturers reinforce this area with a teflon coating.
- *Jacket liner* – The type of liner within which the diskette rotates has an effect on wear. Liners need to be made of low-friction material; some liners even polish the diskette as it rotates.
- *Anti-static coating* – The coating absorbs static discharges to prevent data loss. The diskette jecket is electrically conductive so that a static charge will disburse throughout the jacket, rather than concentrating somewhere on the diskette material, which would erase the data.
- *Magnetic medium* – Type, density, consistency. The magnetic material on a floppy disk is oxide film. Less expensive film has less magnetic retension. The density and size consistency of the oxide particles will affect the data recording density and reliability. As usual, the more you pay, the better the quality control in the manufacturing process, and the more reliable the diskette.

The price and quality of floppy disks can vary considerably from vendor to vendor and there is no general rule to guide you. The best approach is to find a brand that works without data loss and stick with it.

Common Diskette Problems

Problems will occur, and when they do, you should first determine whether the problem is a defective diskette or a malfunction of the disk drive or DtC system. Problems can include:

- **Magnetic field damage** – Data may be lost if a floppy disk is left on or near a video display, power cable, or other source of a magnetic or electrostatic field. Perfectly good floppy disks can lose data by simple mishandling – touching the surface of the diskette with sweaty or soiled fingers or bending the jacket. Floppy disks cannot withstand temperatures above 140 degrees F.

  Data losses are known to occur from using magnetic paper clips to hold diskettes and by putting a desk phone on top a floppy.

- **Dirty disk drive heads** – Dirty heads can often write but not read data. "Data error during read" messages can be triggered by dirty heads. Excessive head cleaning can wear the heads; cleaning every few months should be adequate.

- **Software cockpit errors** – Errors can occur because of a wrong disk drive designator, misunderstandings about which drive is the default, formatting at the wrong density, and other conditions that make the data unavailable to programs. Some programs are sensitive to diskette exchange or diskette removal at particular times, and directories and file allocation tables can become garbled when directions are not followed.

- **High-low density confusion** – The drive will be confused by mismatched diskette densities. Factors involved in this class of error are:

  - Higher track density diskettes cannot be written, read, or formatted by lower density disk drives. This problem occurs with older 5¼" diskettes. On MS-DOS computers, 3½" disks can be used interchangeably in high and low drives. A 1.44 MB diskette, identified by a hole in its jacket, can be formatted as a 720K diskette if the hole is covered. Likewise, a 720K diskette can be formatted as a 1.44 disk if a hole is made in the jacket. The diskettes are interchangeable presumably because both the high and low density diskettes incorporate 80 track systems and often use the same diskette medium.
  - Lower density diskettes are usually readable by and often can be written to by the higher density drives.
  - Lower density diskettes should not be formatted by higher density drives. Problems may occur if you format a low density diskette as a low density disk on a high density drive. The high density drive treats the disk as low density, but low density drives frequently have problems reading the disks. If you accidentally format a low density disk as a high density disk on a high density drive, you are packing too much data into the less dense magnetic medium of the low density disk, and many errors will occur. Complicating the situation is the fact that the 5¼" diskettes are usually physically identical, except for their labeling, which sometimes falls off.

The occasional possibility of formatting or writing the lower density disks with higher density drives always causes confusion. The vendor may recommend against this, but many users find it successful. The problem is that the head structure of the higher density disk drive cannot generate a magnetic field strong enough to saturate the wider tracks of the lower density media, but it will generally have no problem reading those same tracks recorded on the wider heads of the lower density disk drives. Special operating system drivers that cause 80-track disk drives to write two 80-track cylinders per 40-track cylinder can alleviate the problem. Also, different write currents are used for high and low density disks.

The problems just mentioned may lead you to believe you have a bad diskette, when in fact the problem is more tricky. To determine the source of the problem, try the diskette on another disk drive on another system. The next step is to use another diskette known to be good on your system. Other sources of problems are:

- Differences in disk drive alignment can result in a particular diskette able to be read by only one particular drive.
- Differences in quality can cause a diskette to exhibit a problem in one disk drive, yet work well in another.
- Confusion about which disk was used where at what density while troubleshooting a complex problem. Intuition tells us that we shouldn't use lower density media in higher density disk drives. However, the inverse is also true; higher density media will exhibit problems when used in the lower density drives.

Bernoulli Flexible Disk Cartridges

The popular Bernoulli cartridge holds a special 5¼" flexible disk inside a rigid case. The disk spins at 1800 rpm. In comparison, the regular 5¼" floppy diskette spins at 300 to 360 rpm in a floppy disk drive. The high rotation rate of the Bernoulli disk provides faster data transfer rates, and is required for the mechanical operation of the device, developing a lift at the spinning surface that raises the disk toward the read/write head. The Bernoulli cannot experience a head crash because if power fails, the disk slows and bends away from the head.

Bernoulli cartridges come in 20, 44, and 90 MB capacities, and data transfer rates and access times are comparable to the slower to medium speed hard disks. The Bernoulli is not as reliable as the hermetically sealed, non-transported hard drive.

Bernoulli cartridges can be configured as if they were hard disks by using special boot ROMs on the Bernoulli drive interface and installing the operating system on the cartridge.

1.5   Optical Disks

Optical disk drives have undergone explosive growth in usage in recent years. As optical disk technology has penetrated into commercial applications with video disks and compact disk audio, the technology has become cheaper and more reliable. Computer applications ranging from electronic dictionaries to computer training with action video are now possible with optical disks.

For all but the EO drive, the main recording method consists of burning microscopic holes with a laser into a metallic coating laid on a polymer backing. A light beam passing over a track of holes will be reflected from points where metal remains and will not be reflected from the holes. Reflections of a light beam shining on the disk are sensed by an optical detector. Other recording techniques, such as modifying crystal patterns or thermal deformation, can be used, but the basic principle of reading laser light reflections are common to them all.

Analog vs. Digital Disks

Optical disks are currently used in two applications:

1. Analog audio/video playback systems
2. Digital computer data storage and retrieval systems

Although hybrid systems can perform both applications, most optical systems are dedicated to one or the other.

The analog optical disk systems are used for the playback of real time video or audio signals. Just prior to recording, the analog signals are converted to digital signals, and recorded on the optical medium. Upon playback, the digital signals are converted into their original analog form for display on a video monitor, or playback through stereo speakers.

In an analog system, the recorded data is nothing more than the digital representation of the live analog video data. For the video disk, the optical media rotates at 1800 rpm, and 30 frames of video are produced each second. The medium is a CAV spiral track system and is not particularly suited for the storage of computer data. This is because the media is intended to record and play back high speed analog data in real time as it is produced – 30 frames per second. All that is needed is to synchronize the rotational speed with the vertical scanning rate of the video display device. The usual CAV concentric track optical storage disks for computer data storage and retrieval devote considerable data space to a sector and position encoding scheme for more random access.

You may have heard of optical video disks being used to store digital computer data. It is possible, but it is not the primary design objective of the analog video disk. Computer data can be recorded within each analog video frame as a separate entity during the video retrace time. This data can be retrieved and used for still frame operation with sound.

Digital optical disks operate like a hard disk. Their purpose is to store computer data. Although the data could be graphics representations, or audio data; the data is not like analog video or audio data recorded on an analog video disk. There is no direct digital to analog conversion process to render real time audio or video from this data.

You could store a graphics image on a digital optical disk, but it would be in a particular data format, most likely compressed and stored as computer data. In a video disk, each spiral track carries the digital data that has been converted directly from analog video data as it occurred in real time in the video camera.

Figure 98 shows the important difference between analog and digital optical disks. The digital disk is usually organized into sectors of computer data. The data could be the type found on a hard disk: characters, numbers, spreadsheet files, or archived data. You might find compressed video and audio data stored on the digital disk that when appropriately processed by a digital video interactive (DVI) board in the DtC would result in audio or real time, or still frame video. A controller brings this data into the DtC as it would from any mass storage device. On the analog side of the same figure, a video disk is shown playing back real time video frame-by-frame. In the analog system, the main event is the real time video frames, although digital data can be recorded within each video frame during retrace time. The digital data could be interactive video programming or still frame audio.

NOTE

Still frame audio gives you 30 seconds of audio per video frame so that when you are displaying a single frame of video on a system you can have audio for that frame. Contrast this with a VCR that goes silent when it displays a single still frame. Audio is recorded within the video frames, but as an analog component of the video, which must be played back in real time with the real time video.

Optical Disk Classes

Digital optical systems can be divided into three distinct classes:

1. **CD-ROM (compact disk read-only memory)** – A read-only system.
2. **WORM (write once, read many)** – Data can be recorded by the user, but only once.
3. **EO (erasable optical)** – Data can be rewritten many times. It behaves like a slow hard disk.

Before discussing the different systems, let's look at their common attributes:

- **Long access times** – Access is slow because of the large number of tracks and high data density.
- **Long write times** – WORMs and EOs.
- **Data densities** – Optical disk data densities are up to 50 Mbits/cm^2, which is 5 times higher than the 10 Mbits/cm^2 possible on magnetic hard disks, which is 1000 times greater than today's floppy disks.
- **Good storage integrity** – Most optical disks are not susceptible to magnetic fields, and polymer coatings make them scratch resistant. Data longevity is said to be up to 100 years, but that statistic has yet to be proved.

CD-ROM

CD-ROM is a hybrid of sorts. While it is intended to store computer data, its origins are in the analog compact audio disk. CD-ROMs implement the CLV spiral track system and their record/playback head front ends are quite similar. A typical disk will contain 333,000 2K blocks of data, which is played back at 75 blocks per second. This amounts to a 150K/second data rate, more than adequate for both audio and CD-ROM applications.

Although CD-ROMs can be operated with most DtCs, MS-DOS is accepted as the standard operating system MS-DOS compatibles as the standard hardware. MS-DOS drivers are available for most CD-ROM drives. Software for CD-ROMs is still in infancy, but many useful applications are emerging. The strength of CD-ROM is its high data density and low initial cost. Hundreds of printed books or floppy disks can be packed into a single CD-ROM disk. The disks are damage resistant and possess high data integrity.

Predominant characteristics are:

- **Medium** – The platter is 120 mm, or about 5", in diameter. Data is represented by a track of pits and spaces on metal film that is deposited on a clear plastic substrate. CD-ROMs use a three-mile long CLV spiral track divided into sectors of

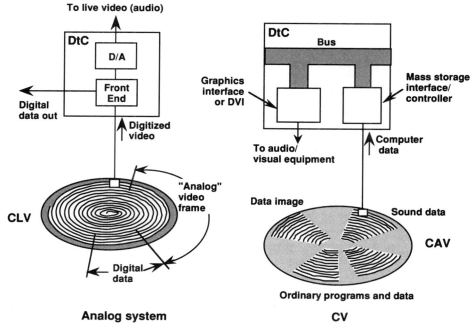

Figure 98. Analog vs. digital optical disks

equal length. Sectors are identified by a sector number in units of minutes and seconds derived from its audio history. Sector identifications provides random access of a particular sector, but access times are slow.

- **Software** – Most CD-ROM software comes in the form of operating system drivers that can make the CD-ROM appear as a huge read-only hard disk. You could make directories, copy files from it to the hard disk, and even execute the programs that are on it. More likely, however, a software shell will be provided that uses information indexes on the disk to access drive space. This data could be a passage in an encyclopedia or a map of a city. Hypercard systems pioneered by Apple can use a CD-ROM for highly interactive information systems with portions ROM data used for audio and even graphics sequences. The most common software, however, is the kind that helps organize the large quantities of information on the disk.

- **Read only** – You cannot write data to compact disks. They can, however, be recorded for you by firms specializing in CD-ROM recording. You send them a 9-track tape or other tape medium with the data and they record it. The first copy costs from $500 to $1000, and each additional disk costs about $5.

- **Seek time** – Average access times are approximately one second. The longer access time is not a problem, since the CD-ROM is storing large sequential data sets and software using them is oriented toward that data use.

- **Sequential data** – CD-ROMs were originally designed for the recording of sequential audio data. CLV spiral track is the recording method used.

- **Capacity** – CD-ROM capacity is around 700 MB. Each data sector contains a 2048 byte block with other bytes relegated to error correction, for a total of 2352 bytes per block. Multiply this by the 333,000 data blocks on the CD-ROM to yield the 700 MB capacity. The data is recorded on 90,000 tracks, which add up to approximately three miles.

- *Cost* – CD-ROM units cost around $600 while their disks run from $100-1000, depending on what type of data they supply.

CD-ROMs are widely used for storing text for on-screen retrieval and is an excellent medium for storing reference data that are not updated infrequently. Applications for the CD-ROM are blossoming. Manufacturing costs of CD-ROM drives have dropped to the $300 mark and associated software sold with the drives is maturing. The following are a few examples of CD-ROM disks currently available:

- *Microsoft's Bookshelf* – A variety of general-purpose references such as a dictionary, thesaurus, almanac, *Who's Who*, writing style guide, and other materials.

- *PC Magazine library* – Abstracts and indexes of articles from 40 leading DtC magazines and complete text versions of 10 of them.

- *Microsoft Programmer's Library* – An exhaustive reference for DtC applications programmers. The library contains 48 technical manuals, five published books, and indexed files of sample code for plugging into applications.

- *Public domain software libraries* – Hundreds of floppy disks of public domain software can be obtained on a single CD-ROM with periodic updates.

- *Library reference* – A variety of reference materials and book indexes are routinely placed on CD-ROMs.

- *Clip art* – Libraries of thousand of clip-art images.

- *Maps* – Digital maps and other geographic data.

CD-ROM users world wide are already networked to CD-ROM applications that give them access to valuable information resources.

Compact Disk Interactive

The interactive compact disk (CDI) is a combination CD-ROM, 68xxx microprocessor, and Unix-like operating system. With it, you can at one moment access an encyclopedia and at the next, listen to a Glenn Miller recording. Programs that run on the 68xxx are contained on the CD-ROM along with data, audio, and video still frames.

In the CDI, it is the mass storage device that drives the overall computer system design, not the computer system unit, as is the case with conventional DtCs. With CDI we have a DtC-like device with enormous program storage capability at very low cost. Initially dedicated to consumer markets, these devices may make the CD-ROM obsolete. CDIs can provide multiple levels of audio playback, still-frame video, database activity, and computer graphics.

WORM

Unlike the CD-ROM, which must be recorded at the factory, the WORM drive allows you to record your own disks. Once recorded, the data cannot be erased.

WORM drive applications include:

- **Archiving with audit trail** – The primary advantage of the WORM over CD-ROM is that you can write to it – *just once*. This limitation can be put to good use.

    Earlier data versions cannot be written over, as with EOs or magnetic media. When a new data version is created, the old directory entry is marked obsolete, and the entire updated file is written onto a physically different location on the WORM drive. As a result, you get a perfect audit trail. Using appropriate software, you can work backwards later and recover each updated data version in correct order. When the disk is filled, you go on to the next disk. Work involving large volumes of incoming data to be archived, engineering design files, image storage, financial records, data logs, incremental computer backups, database distribution records, audit trails, and microfiche libraries are some of the applications that benefit from the WORM's write-once capability.

- **File cabinets** – WORM disk drives are a central peripheral for the electronic file cabinets. The electronic file cabinet systems combine WORM drives with optical scanners and high resolution video displays for the storage of large document files and databases for instant retrieval and viewing according to indexes that you create during the recording process.

- **Storage of programs/data** – Ordinary DtC programs and unchanging data files can be operated from WORMS. DOS driver replacements that come with WORM drives allow the operating system to access WORMs as though they were a read-only hard drive.

The major characteristics of WORM drives are:

- **Operating system support** – Special software is required for WORM drives because you write only once to the media. Proper organization and indexing of data must be accomplished by the software for effective retrieval of information stored on the WORM drive. The data organization is important because of the long optical seek times and sequential nature of the medium.

    Read-data functions can be supported by the redirection of the usual operating system file management functions, through installable device drivers. In this configuration, the WORM drive can appear as a multiplicity of smaller read-only hard drives. Handling the write-once characteristics of the WORM optical drive is not as simple. You'll want to avoid fragmenting data sets on WORM, which could cause prohibitively long read times. Access times are rather slow on WORMs. To handle WORM drives, most applications programs using them provide their own custom support of drive functions. For example, you can buy a program that lets you put all of your software on a write once drive. The software comes with its own operating system that manages the write process as you upload floppy disks to the WORM drive. Once loaded, installable device drivers operate the programs as if they were located on a read-only hard disk.

- **Speed parameters** – The data transfer rate approaches that of the slower hard drives. Write times are slow, and seek time is on the order of seconds.

- **Capacity** – WORM disks store from 200 MB to 1 GB.

- **Interfaces** – Inexpensive interfaces will support the WORM drive. The SCSI is a popular WORM drive interface type.

- **Size** – Some WORM drives will fit into a 5¼" floppy disk drive bay.

- **Cost** – Between $1000-2000 and disks cost around $100.

Erasable Optical Media

A newer technology, the erasable optical (EO), allows erasing and rerecording of data. Optical storage should not be considered a replacement for a hard disk, but rather a supplement. Excessive write times and longer access times characteristic of any optical disk makes optical drives not too useful for active data sets. Active data sets still need a hard disk, or its alternatives.

Although the EO drive can be used for the applications described for CD-ROMs and WORMs, its erasability is an obvious benefit. When teamed up with a good hard disk, the EO provides the DtC with a combination of speed and huge volumes of mass storage space.

Clearly, the EO optical disk has the greatest potential for gaining widespread use. The EO's ability to be repeatedly written to is a clear advantage over the WORM, which is intended for archival and historical applications. The EO's disadvantage is its relatively slow access and write times compared to magnetic hard disk.

EO drives incorporate innovative technology for erasing and rewriting. Three recording methods are commonly used:

1. *Phase change* – First introduced by Matsushita Electric Industrial (Panasonic) in 1983. PCE Technology used the transition between crystalline and amorphous states of a recording layer that is deposited on a disk substrate. A blank disk is completely reflective by being in crystalline state. Writing to the disk causes the crystalline state to transform to a less reflective amorphous state.

2. *Dye polymer disks* – When writing, a high power laser thermally deforms the recording layer composed of organic-based dye bound to a polymer binder. Reading with the same laser under lower power detects the deformations as changes in the amplitude of the laser's reflected light. The same laser system, operating at low power, detects the light reflected from the deformations. Erasing occurs when a second laser, operated at a different wavelength from the primary laser, irradiates a second layer, which removes the thermal deformations. This method is least popular even though manufacturing costs are low and it exhibits high immunity from degradation due to oxidation. The problem with this method is its low cyclability of <1000 write/erase cycles.

3. *Magneto-optic* – The magneto-optic method writes using a strong magnetic field to modify the crystal pattern on the platter. The changes are detected as a change in the polarization of reflected light when reading with a low power laser. The magneto-optic method has the advantage of cyclability: there is no limit to the number of write/erase cycles. It has the longest research and development history and it is likely to become the method of choice for erasable optical disks.

Current material limitations give phase change erasable and dye polymer disks low writing recyclability, making them impractical for EO use. Almost all EO drives now use the newer magneto-optic technology, which has higher writing recyclability.

Erasables cost more than magnetic technology. They have a hard disk break-even point of around 1.5 gigabytes, the capacity of a couple of EO optical cartridges. As your total storage capacity requirement increases, optical disks become much cheaper than magnetic, rising almost vertically, as shown in Figure 99. If more than 1 gigabyte of storage is needed, magnetic hard disk technology becomes impractical. Then, the contest is between magnetic removable media and erasable optical. At around 2 gigabytes, erasable optical becomes cheaper than the removable magnetic media.

Optical drives are gaining popularity, but magnetic technologies have improved considerably. Higher density materials and vertical recording techniques have scored dramatic improvements in hard disk storage capacities and lower costs. Multiple platter 3½" drives are now available in 200 to 500 MB sizes. Optical disks, however, have the definite advantage of high capacity combined with removability and resistance to rough handling. Recorded data are protected by a plastic coating and only the laser beam ever touches the medium. Also, most optical disks are immune to magnetic fields. Sophisticated error correction methodologies and the space for redundant data have made unrecoverable data errors in optical systems practically unheard of at one error per 10^{18} bits. Laser disks continue to be plagued by standards problems and high seek and write times compared to magnetic technologies, so they continue to be limited to archival uses. We can expect considerable price drops in the next few years, from $5000 to perhaps $500 per unit. Presently, the EO benefits should be carefully weighed against its present inconsistency and high cost.

NOTE

Advanced Graphics Applications (AG) began shipping the DISCUS system in 1989. The system is a 650 MB erasable optical disk drive compatible with MS-DOS hardware and software interfaced through a 16-bit SCSI controller. Other vendors with similar systems are Sony, Verbatim, Maxtor, and Tandy Corporation. The NeXT computer uses a Sony EO.

ISO (International Standard Organization) standards are emerging for EOs. The standard specifies disk format, error correction, and SCSI standards. Standards will allow transportability so that a cartridge written on one make of drive may be used on another. The standard defined is for a 650 MB disk.

1.6   Tape Backup Systems

Tape backup systems provide you with a large storage volume, primarily for data archiving. You might use tape backup for the entire hard disk, or just for selective subdirectories and archiving large databases.

Files on the hard drive may be backed up or restored from the tape drive, but they cannot be invoked quickly for execution, as is the case with files on the permanent or removable media drives, or WORM and EO optical drives.

Tape is sequential, and it could take minutes to locate a file. Tape systems are therefore impractical for use with active programs and data, especially where reasonably fast turnarounds are desired.

The nine-track magnetic tapes still used on mainframes and minicomputers have enormous capacity, but the bulk of the media and the size of the player do not fit into the desktop setting. For desktop computers, there is an assortment of low-cost cartridge tape backup units to fit almost any need. These come in two types: the lower-cost, lower-capacity longitudinal and the higher-cost higher-capacity helical.

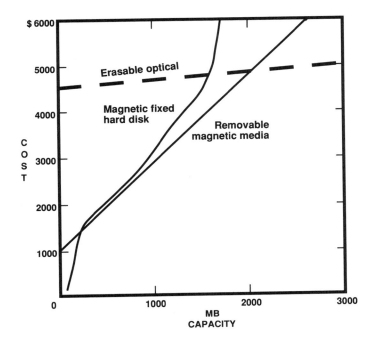

Figure 99.   Optical vs. magnetic disk costs:

Longitudinal Systems

Longitudinal tape systems are inexpensive and are used for moderate-sized backups of 50 to 200 MB. Standard digital tape casettes about the size of a VHS video tape are used. Stationary tape heads record data on digital tape at speeds of a few inches per second. Most systems include menu-driven software outside the domain of the operating system, which lets you perform selective hard disk backup and retrieval. Directories are stored on the tape, read in, and used to assist you in retrieving stored data. You can reach a particular subdirectory or even a particular file, if you wish. Most tape backup systems provide robust software support and directory management software that lets you to find a single file on the tape. Some tape drives can search for data headers at considerably faster rates than they read the data. Access times can be in the range of minutes because the records are sequential.

Characteristics of longitudinal tape backup systems:

- *Transfer rate* – Slower than floppy disks or around 5-20 K/second.
- *Capacity* – Common capacities are from 40-200 MB on a single digital cartridge.
- *Cost* – Less than $1000 for a drive and $20-$50 for digital cartridges.
- *Reliability* – Extremely high due to the relatively low data density of the tape.

Helical Scan Tape Systems

Helical scan tape backup systems are also appropriate for rarely-used archival backup, but have much greater capacity than do longitudinal systems. Helical scan systems are popular for backing up the hard disks of large local area network servers, CAD databases, document archives, or applications in which very large hard drives must be periodically backed up.

Helical scan technology is similar to that in a VCR. A drum rotating at 1800 rpm has heads mounted on its periphery. The tape is wrapped around 90 degrees of the drum and is slightly offset from the drum's axis of rotation. The tape speed around the rotating drum is approximately 1 inch per second, but the effective tape speed is high, 150 inches per second because the heads take diagonal swipes across the tape as it passes. This process yields a 1 MB per square inch recording density. Tape cassettes are similar in size and appearance to 8-mm VCR tapes.

Characteristics of helical tape backup systems:

- *Data transfer rate* – Similar to the slower hard disks at 100 Kbits/second.
- *Capacity* – 2-5 gigabytes per tape cassette.
- *Cost* – A few thousand dollars for the unit and $20-$50 per tape cassette or about a penny per MB.
- *Reliability* – Reliability is as good as longitudinal. Although the data density is higher, error rates are good because a large amount of redundant data can be recorded for use in error recovery.

The typical helical system uses 8-mm tape cassettes and stores 2 gigabytes of data in about two hours. The drive can fit into an internal 5¼" bay. The software provided enables you to access and deal with this enormous volume of data effectively. Helical tape drive capacity compares favorably with the older 12" 9-track tapes discussed previously; however, where a helical could take two hours to move 2 gigabytes, a 9-track system would take only a few minutes.

DOT

Digital optical tape (DOT) is a variation of WORM disk technology and involves burning holes into a tape rather than into a disk. The DOT costs about $250 per cartridge, 1/2 cent per MB. Each cartridge will store 50 gigabytes of data or 23,000 copies of War and Peace. The entire Library of Congress could be stored on 190 DOT cartridges. Data transfer rates and access times are comparable to helical scan magnetic systems.

Tape Backup vs. Removable Hard Disks

Purpose is the deciding factor between removable media drives and tape backup drives. The lower capacity removable media drives are useful for their operating system transparency, their ability to act like a hard drive for active data manipulation and for program execution. Some centralized support facilities use Bernoulli cartridges to store most of their evaluation software collection. For reliable backups of large >100 MB datasets, the tape backup units are best.

1.7   *Mass Storage Selection*

The hard disk is a vital part of a DtC. While it provides high speed program and data storage, it has limited capacity. Often the storage capacity of a hard drive needs to be supplemented by other media. When evaluating mass storage alternatives, reconcile the storage capacity of each medium, the access times, and read-only capability with the application it is intended to support.

Removable media cartridges provide a good overall supplement to the hard drive for the average user, where programs and data sizes are not exhorbitant. Floppies are indispensable for hard disk and data backup when the DtC is not connected to a LAN. Tape units are best for archiving large datasets, while the opticals provide both archival and hard disk-like execution capability. However, initial cost is high.

Table 35 summarizes the relevant information pertaining to the mass storage devices. The table is intended only as a guide. What should stand out are the differing speeds, purposes, and initial costs of the hardware.

Medium	Data Transfer	Access Time	Capacity	Purpose	Initial Cost
Hard disk	Fast	Fast	High	Central operations	Depends on size, low to high
Removable media HD	Medium	Medium	Medium	Small archive application, installations, HD backup	Medium
Floppy	Slow	Slow	Low	Transportation to HD, HD backup	Low
CD-ROM (optical)	Slow	Slow	High	Reference Material	Low
WORM (optical)	Medium	Medium	Medium	Revisions, audits, archiving	Medium to high
EO (eraseable optical)	Medium	Medium	High	Huge hard disk and archiving	High
Tape, longitudinal	Slow	Slow	Low	Ordinary HD backup, small archives	Low
Tape, helical	Medium	Slow	High	Large archive	Medium
DOT	Medium	Very slow	Very high	Huge archive	High

Table 35.   Mass storage comparisons

The most important mass storage selection criteria include:

- *Removability* – Do you need to remove media for security reasons, or just for huge storage capability?

- *Speed* – What are your performance requirements? If you are simply archiving programs and data, speed is less important than if you are using large programs and data files interactively.

- *Capacity* – What is the total installed size of your software and data system? For removable media drives, how do you want to segregate data and programs or what does the size of modules need to be? Breaking up a database into one month chunks might be fine on 90 MB Bernoulli cartridges, while larger systems might demand the increased capacity of tape or optical systems. Some databases could be archived on floppy disks.

- *Purpose* – Is the mass storage device primarily for program and data execution or for archival backup? If the latter, you may prefer erasable optical systems over

WORMs and tape backup systems, or the faster and more accessible removable hard disk systems if data capacities are not excessive. Of course, breaking up a system into smaller pieces may suffice, but you have to store the disks somewhere.

- **Reliability** – Different mass storage systems have different reliability levels. For example, tape backup systems are more reliable than Bernoulli removable cartridges, which are designed for fast access to data. If your data is precious, you should be willing to wait longer for it.

- **Compatibility** – Are the drivers and software that come with the mass storage device compatible with the operating system and applications program needs? Can the drivers be installed easily? How much memory do they require?

- **Physical size** – Will the mass storage device fit into your existing drive bays, or will you need an external unit that requires its own power supply and external cabled connections? Due to the popularity of 3½" and 5¼" floppies and hard disks, most alternative mass storage systems are designed to fit into the same bays.

- **Interface** – Is your mass storage device just one of many sophisticated peripherals? The high speed ESDI and SCSI are general purpose and are intended to work with a variety of peripherals. For low-cost HB installations, the ST506/412 or IDE interfaces may be adequate.

2.0   Video Display Systems

The video display is the window to the DtC computing world. Behind the display monitor is the memory, often a CPU, and complexity rivaling the DtC system unit itself. You may not realize the great effect the display system has on overall system performance.

The two primary components of a DtC video display system are its video display monitor and its video display interface, also known as a graphics display interface. The video display interface isolates the video display from DtC specifics, just as the serial interface isolates the modem or mouse. The video display interface provides memory for displayed character and graphics storage, and some provide intelligent graphics controllers to help the CPU produce complex images.

Figure 100 depicts the two major system components; on one side are possible video sources and on the other are the possible video displays. Video sources include a DtC, video disks, VCRs, and a video camera. Video displays include TV, composite, and RGB monitors. When setting up DtC systems, you must match the display interface capability with the monitor, considering many parameters. It is best to have help from a knowledgeable expert, but you still need to know the parameters and possibilities.

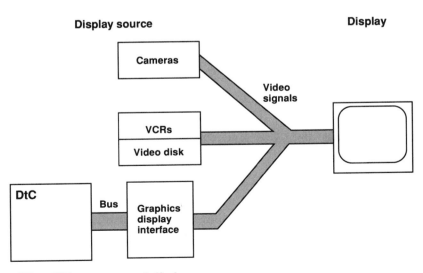

Figure 100.   Video sources and displays

You may want to consider how to display other than computer generated images on the video display; and you might want to display the images along with computer images on the same screen. Many video monitors will display video from a variety of sources, while others are special to a particular medium. DtC graphics display interfaces come in as many forms as there are DtC models.

2.1   Signals and Nomenclature

To better understand the different types of video sources and display units, we need to learn some video signals and related terminology. First, we will study the makeup of composite video, which is the main course of commercial video equipment, and is used by computer equipment. We will examine composite video as a low frequency baseband signal, and then observe how it can be shifted to RF (radio frequency) so as to be transmitted through the air. This will prepare us to look at sources of composite video and the display monitors that use it. Although most computer display outputs are different than composite video, often the DtC has to handle composite video for applications that require the combined use of composite video and the RGB analog outputs of most DtCs.

Composite Video

Composite video is actually several video signals put together to travel on a single wire. Figure 101 shows several different video sources, starting at the top with a television station. While many devices, such as VCRs or video disks, can store and reproduce composite video, its main source is the video camera. The video camera's output is a combination of brightness (luminance), color, and synchronization signals.

An image is formed through the camera lens on three different light sensitive devices behind red, green, and blue color filters. The sensors are scanned, and the red, green, and blue signals are produced, the intensity varying with each color. In older B/W cameras, a single light sensitive sensor was scanned without color filters.

Luminance Signal

In early B/W systems, only the total brightness, called luminance, of the scanned image was needed. The TV set had only one electron gun to display the image. Today's composite video monitors may use green or yellow (amber) phosphors, which many believe is easier on the eye than the earlier white on black monitors.

In a color system, the luminance signal represents the brightness of the three color signals combined, and is the equivalent of the luminance signal in a B/W system. The luminance signal, shown near the top of Figure 101, covers a frequency spectrum from 0 (DC) to 6 MHz. The smaller the granularity of the image being represented, the higher the frequency of the video signal; a dark or white screen with no granularity would be represented by 0 frequency and a granular display of a stadium crowd would be close to 6 MHz. If you were to look closely at the frequency spectrum of the luminance signal, you would find that it occurred at harmonics, or multiples, of the horizontal scanning frequency, which is 15,750 Hz in a NTSC (National Television Standards Committee) signal. This is because the number of brightness variations on screen at any time will repeat at a rate equal to the number of horizontal scans of the screen. If the screen had five brightness var-

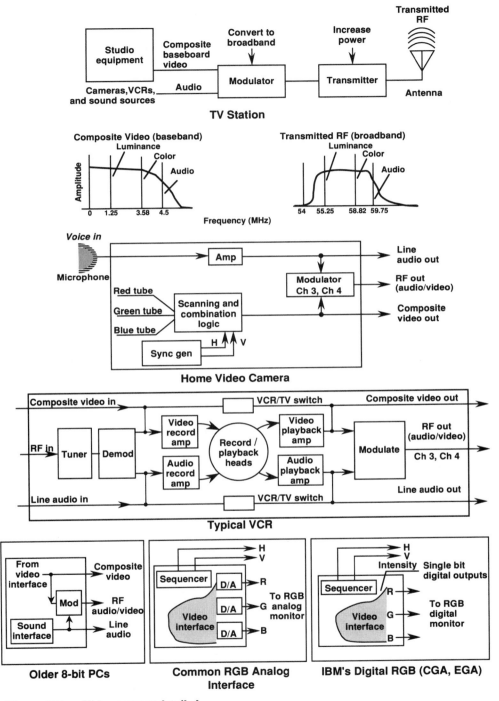

Figure 101.   Video sources detailed

iations from top to bottom (say five telephone poles), then the signal representing that would be five times the horizontal scanning rate. Likewise, if you had four telephone poles, the signal representing that would be four times the horizontal scanning rate.

Color Signal

The color or chrominance signal represents the difference between the intensity of the three color signals and the intensity of the total luminance signal. The chrominance signal is piggybacked on a phase-shifted 3.58 MHz carrier signal. The choice of 3.58 MHz for the chrominance carrier is derived from communication theory and is based on the fact that the resulting chrominance frequency spectrum conveniently intersperses itself between the luminance signal harmonics. Thus, both B/W and color information can coexist, without much interference in the video signal frequency spectrum.

Scanning or Synchronization Signals

The video source scanning electronics produce horizontal and vertical synchronization signals that allow the video display to scan its phosphors in synchronism with the video camera. The scanning beam sweeps horizontally across the camera's field 15,750 times per second, and travels vertically from the top to the bottom of the field 60 times per second. A pulse is generated for every horizontal scan line and every vertical retrace. These pulses, called H and V synchronization signals, are used by the TV scanning hardware to keep it in step with the video source.

Each vertical sweep covers alternate lines. One sweep covers even lines, the next sweep covers odd lines, giving a new picture 30 times per second. This is also known as interlace scanning and is part of the NTSC standard for commercial television. All lines could be scanned 30 times per second, but that method would create an annoying flicker. Some video displays scan all lines 60 times per second, which is called non-interlace. Non-interlace, however, costs more and the displays and interfaces are not compatible.

Color Composite vs. B/W Composite

The only difference between a color and a B/W composite signal is that the B/W composite does not have a chrominance signal. If a color composite signal is fed into a B/W composite monitor, the monitor ignores the color information. If a B/W composite signal is fed into a color monitor, it renders a B/W image. The color demodulator circuits becoming non-functional, sending a signal to all three guns that is proportional to the luminance signal.

The composite video signal contains a luminance signal that can be used for B/W displays, a chrominance signal that works with the luminance signal to produce color, and horizontal and vertical synchronizing signals. All of these are combined on a single wire. The composite video signal is a baseband signal because it starts at zero frequency. The color composite signal ranges in frequency from 0 to 6 MHz.

RF Signals

Although the baseband video signal is good for local transmission through coax cables, it is low frequency and doesn't propagate well. In order for a TV station to transmit it, the composite video signal must modulate a higher frequency and more powerful carrier signal.

The type of modulation used varies the amplitude of the higher frequency carrier at a rate corresponding to the amplitude changes of the composite video frequency. We now have a higher frequency signal with the low frequency composite video signal impressed upon it. The modulation process effectively shifts the entire spectrum of the baseband composite video signal to a higher transmittable RF frequency.

Figure 101 shows the baseband signal modulated up to the broadband signal channel 2 and it is now based from 54 to 60 MHz rather than 0 to 6 MHz. The broadband offers two advantages:

1. It creates a frequency that can be broadcast. The signal is brought back to the baseband at the TV for viewing.

2. It allows us to shift baseband signals to different portions of the radio spectrum. Each TV channel is separated by a discreet bandwidth of frequency. The shifted broadband TV signals can share the available broadcast spectrum with cable TV at the same time. Instead of time multiplexing, that is, slicing up baseband signals, all signals can be transmitted concurrently on different frequencies. This is known as *frequency multiplexing*.

For example, the other TV channel carriers separated by the 6 MHz bandwidth of their information content are:

Channel	Carrier Frequency
2	55.25
3	61.25
4	67.25

and so on. Add 6 MHz for each channel.

Then there are the UHF (ultra high frequency), cable TV frequencies, satellite frequencies and so on.

> **NOTE**
> Most LANs use baseband signals for transmission on cables. Multiple signals are handled by time multiplexing alternately transmitting packets. Some broadband LANs, however, use TV-like frequency multiplexing to allow simultaneous data transmissions. The broadband LANs can operate on the same cable as cable TV.

Audio Signals

Analog baseband audio signals occupy a frequency band from near zero to about 20 KHz. In composite video systems, the audio signals are moved on a separate *auxiliary*, or *line audio*, wire. For broadband transmission, the audio is frequency modulated on a carrier signal 4.5 MHz above the video carrier so that the audio occupies a small part of the video spectrum.

> **NOTE**
> Frequency modulation varies the frequency of the carrier. The resulting signal is more immune to noise than an amplitude-modulated signal because the interference signals tend to modulate the carrier in amplitude.

Figure 101 shows a video camera bringing out the audio once amplified on a separate line audio wire for local use or modulating it along with the composite video creating an RF signal that contains both audio and video on your choice of channel 3 or 4.

Raster vs. Vector Systems

Video systems that repeatedly sweep out a video image are called *raster* systems. Look closely at a DtC or TV video screen and you can see scan or *raster* lines. These lines repeatedly sweep across the display screen. Electron guns fire a stream of electrons with the video signal modulating the intensity. The beam paints the image on the video screen. The intensity of the electron beam turns the screen pixels on and off: high for on, low for off. The horizontal scanning electromagnetic coil or electrostatic plate is fed a repeating signal that looks like a ramp, and the beam goes from left to right as the ramp goes from its low to high value. When the ramp returns to zero, the beam returns to the left side. The vertical deflector is fed a lower frequency ramp. As the beam repeatedly goes across the screen, it slowly travels down the screen. The frequency of these ramps are synchronized with the video source ramps using the H and V signals described above.

Raster scanning does not occur in vector systems. Instead, the object is drawn on a high persistence phosphor screen by deflecting the electron beam to trace out the lines of the image. Vector systems are better for drawing line graphics, while raster systems are better for random images. Since most CAD applications involve placement of thousands of lines, vector systems are often more appropriate. Vector systems are found on some engineering workstations, and is another feature to distinguish EWs from the raster-oriented HB and EE DtCs.

Pixels vs. Phosphor Dots

A pixel is the smallest dot that a display interface can create on a video display screen. The size of the dot is limited by the density of the phosphor dot triads on the phosphor screen. Each triad contains a red, green, and blue phosphor.

The sweeping electron beam in the CRT does not know where the phosphor dot triads are. A shadow mask immediately ahead of the phosphor coating causes each color gun to focus on only its own color phosphor dots. The color phosphors are excited to the level of the intensity of their electron beams.

Individual display pixels do not correspond to individual phosphor dot triads, but rather to some local composite number of phosphor dots that are excited during a short time interval by the passing electron gun. To prove this, you can use BASIC, for example, to plot a single point on the screen. Look at the screen with a magnifying glass, and you will see that the single dot you created consists of several phosphor triads.

The density of sweep lines that a video interface can produce and the number of intensity variations per unit time determines the interface output resolution. No matter how good a display interface is, however, pixel density is limited to monitor dot pitch, that is, the density of phosphor triads. Video interface capability, the amount of video memory, scanning rates, and dot speeds, also limit the resolution of the displayed image.

Newer flat panel display technologies hard wire display phosphors to display pixels to create better images. In flat panel displays, there is no distant electron beam generator; display phosphors are semiconductors hard wired in a display matrix.

2.2   Video Displays

Video display units are usually called monitors. Figure 102 offers an overall perspective on different types of video displays.

Television Sets

The old 8-bit DtCs used TV sets to function as the video displays. As TV resolution improves, they will once again be used, this time integrated with tomorrow's DtCs.

How a TV Works

At the top of Figure 101 is a basic TV set. Its input is the RF signal transmitted from the TV studio or brought in by cable. A channel is selected using the tuner, which filters the selected channel from the many channels available. The signal is then shifted to an intermediate frequency for further amplification.

Next, the signal is demodulated and the audio separated. At this point the signal is in the form it was prior to modulation and transmission, a baseband composite video signal.

H and V syncs are separated and the composite signal continues on to a color demodulator or goes straight to the electron gun video amplifiers if the TV is B/W. The color demodulator separates the colors from the luminance and yields three color outputs, red, green, and blue, to be amplified and then fed to the red, green, and blue electron guns of a color TV set.

The three signals are swept at the same frequency as in the originating video camera by ramp generators in the TV that are synchronized by the H and V signals. Additional circuitry and hardware assist the three beams in focusing to a sharp point on the screen as they repeatedly sweep across the screen. On the screen are triads of phosphor dots each sensitive to one of the three primary colors. If the phosphor triads were all illuminated in a particular proportion to the luminance signal, the output would be B/W. The chrominance signal causes the three guns to vary according to the original scene colors, providing compatibility between the B/W and color systems.

Resolution Problems

When using a TV as a DtC computer display, several problems will result in poor resolution.

- **Band limiting** – In order to reconcile the chrominance and luminance signals, the color signal is band limited to occupy no more than 1.8 MHz in the video spectrum. This reduces color resolution but does not affect the luminance signal. Black and white information is more highly resolved than color information.

    This means that the smaller the object, the more difficult it it is to discern its color. Color data on the TV screen is not nearly as finely resolved as B/W information is. As you watch a color TV, you probably do not notice that the tiny figures in a stadium crowd are really being represented in black and white. On a DtC, however, color objects might be text or dots in a graph, and the overall result will be a blurring of text. The smaller the object, the more it will be black and white.

- **Dot pitch** – Most TVs implement a dot pitch, or phosphor diameter, of around 0.44 mm. This pitch is adequate for its purpose, which does not include presentation of

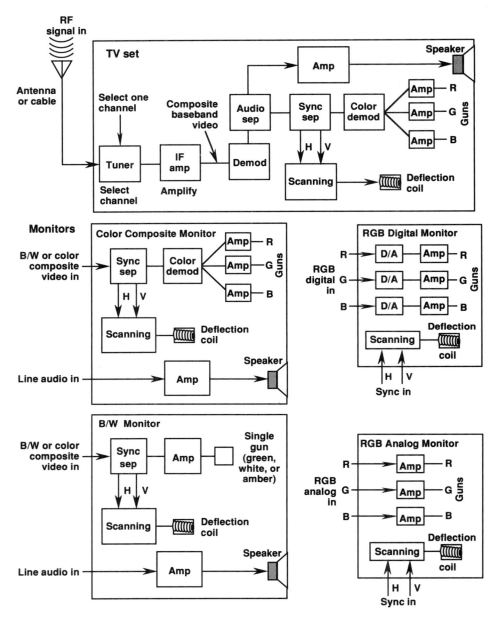

Figure 102. Video displays detailed

finely resolved text or graphics. The smaller the dot pitch, the higher the density of the phosphor triads. Phosphor densities on color TVs are not as high as on the color composite or RGB monitors.

- **RF noise** – A TV antenna is subject to broadband noise, which won't hurt the football game as much as it will hurt the word processor characters you try to read on the display.

- **Modulation/demodulation losses** – Resolution degrades incrementally as the RGB signal is converted to composite, is modulated, and then is demodulated in the TV.

- **Audio noise** – Although the audio signal occupies only a small portion of the video spectrum, it will cause some interference with the video signal. Watch someone on TV closely as they speak and you will see small wavy lines.

Resolving Capability

When used as a computer video display device, the average TV set can only display 40 columns by about 25 rows of text, or can support an APA resolution of around 250 by 350 pixels. This puts the TV on the low end of DtC graphics displays. High resolution television (HRTV) will double current TV resolution, and will be appropriate for DtCs.

Composite Video Monitors

Composite monitors are designed to display composite video directly. Since composite video is standardized, and provided by most video equipment and many low-end DtCs, the composite monitor is quite popular. It falls in the same price range as a TV set.

Color Composite Video Display

You should notice in Figure 102 that the color composite monitor is really just a cut down color TV missing the tuner, intermediate frequency amplifiers, demodulator, and audio separators. It remains expensive because additional care is taken in making the electron beam converging hardware shadow mask and converging electronics. Depending upon the quality of the composite monitor, the density of color phosphor triads in a composite monitor will be smaller than in a TV set.

■ To see what an RCA jack looks like, just look at your stereo's audio connectors.

Color composite monitors generally use RCA jacks for their composite video inputs.■ The video signal must be terminated with a 75 ohm resistor, and most composite video monitors provide a termination enabling switch. The switch is used when hooking up multiple composite monitors to a single signal because the last one should be terminated. Some composite monitors provide separate video input and output jacks, with the output signal reamplified so that a long line of composites can be daisy chained. And some composite monitors have line audio inputs and built-in amplifiers to provide sound output.

The composite monitor provides better resolution than a TV. This is due not only to better dot pitch, but also to better converging electronics and better shadow masks. You view a composite video signal directly. On a TV set, the existing composite signal is modulated to an RF signal, only to be demodulated to a composite signal before it can be viewed.

When making video tape copies, connecting the playing VCR composite video and line audio output to the recording VCR composite and line audio input will result in a better recording. When using a VCR as a TV tuner, connecting a composite monitor to a VCR composite video output rather than connecting a TV to its RF output will preclude an additional modulation and demodulation. A VCR TV/VCR switch passes the demodulated audio and video to the VCR composite video and line audio outputs for this purpose.

Although the problem of band-limited color signals is still present, color composites will display more characters than TV sets because there is no modulation and demodulation process. Text resolutions of 64 columns by 40 rows are no problem; and while 80 column rows are possible, the characters become blurry at this density.

The primary advantage of the composite monitors is that their composite video signal inputs are standardized NTSC and are carried on a single conductor with shielded cable. Therefore, there are no cable compatibility problems, and most commercial video equipment provide composite video compatibility. The following are typical uses for a composite video monitor:

- **Quality display of VCR output** – A VCR (see Figure 101) provides composite video output, the recorded video tape is baseband video. Connecting a composite monitor to a VCR composite video output avoids having to convert the signal from baseband to channel 3 or 4 and then tune and demodulate the signal in the TV back to baseband.

- **Display of video camera output** – A video camera also modulates its composite video output for use by standard TV sets. Hooking up a composite color monitor to the camera composite output will produce a better quality image than hooking up a regular television to the camera channel 3 and 4 output.

- **Display of DtC video** – Although most DtC display interfaces provide analog or digital RGB outputs not compatible with composite monitors, earlier units and some EE computers still provide composite video output. The color composite monitor is more than adequate for displaying arcade graphics and the type of applications operated on the low-end HB and EE computers.

B/W Composite Monitors

B/W composite monitors, sometimes called green screen monitors, can be picked up at computer shows for $20-50. B/W composite monitors have only one color phosphor (white, green, or amber), one electron gun, and no color demodulator. If a color composite signal is fed in, you will see a perfectly good white, green, or yellow image. You might connect a B/W composite to a low-end DtC graphics display interface, which provides composite video output. Since it lacks three color guns and has no convergence problems, the B/W composite monitor has a higher resolution character display than the color composite. B/W composite monitors can display 80 to 132 columns of 25 to 50 character rows with appropriate display interfaces and software drivers.

TV Composite Video Capability

Some TVs have composite video inputs that directly connect composite video signals. The inputs bypass the TV tuner, IF amplifiers, and demodulator. Additional audio amplifier line inputs are provided for DtC audio signals.

RGB Monitors

RGB monitors are the most popular display used in DtCs. While composite monitors are cut down TVs, RGB monitors are cut down composite monitors. There are two major types – analog and digital – and both forms can be purchased with multisync capability to provide display capability from a variety of different DtC display interfaces.

RGB Analog Monitor

The most popular RGB monitor is the RGB analog monitor. Most DtC video display interfaces provide the separate R, G, B and digital H and V signals required. As Figure 102 on page 516 shows, the RGB analog monitor is cut down even more than the composite monitor. The RGB analog monitor cost is tied up in lower dot pitches of 0.2 to 0.3 mm, high quality beam convergence, precision shadow masking, accurate color rendition, high stability, and high bandwidth video amplifiers to yield the higher resolutions possible with these monitors. RGB analog monitors resolutions can go well beyond 1024 by 1024 pixels, with the typical range being 640 by 480 to 1024 by 768. Since RGB inputs are analog, the number of displayable colors is infinite. The color rendering capability depends largely on the type of phosphors used in the CRT.

Some TVs provide for analog RGB inputs, bypassing most of the TV signal processing and allowing entry directly to the RGB gun amplifiers.

RGB Digital Monitor

The RGB digital monitor is mostly an MS-DOS computer phenomenon. In order to manufacture its early PCs cheaply, IBM made video display interfaces with only digital outputs. The interfaces supported only a few colors, and required less display memory. There was no need for expensive D/A converters in the display interface. The A/D converters convert groups of memory bits to represent multiple colors. On a digital monitor, each red, green, and blue color signal can be either on or off, which yields only 8 possible colors.

An additional intensity bit could turn on all guns at higher intensity, which would allow 16 colors. The RGB digital monitor is quite similar to an RGB analog monitor, except for input signal requirements. A TTL (transistor transistor logic) level signal is required for the digital monitor. Zero volts for the logic low and five volts for the logic high. This is quite different from the analog RGB inputs, which range from 0 to 1 volt and have infinite gradation. Some digital RGB monitors are back-fitted RGB analog monitors with built in D/A converters, as Figure 102 shows. This is an instance of paying more for less.

Special Conversions

- **Digital/analog converters** – Hardware is available that can convert the digital RGB output of an MS-DOS computer CGA or EGA display interface output to an RGB analog signal suitable for display on analog RGB monitors and analog RGB projection monitors. Due to an odd horizontal scan rate of 22 KHz the converted EGA output must be displayed on a multisync analog RGB monitor.

- **Scan converters** – Scan converters are complex electronic equipments that can take an image produced by a particular DtC, place it into an internal memory, and in real time reconstitute it in a fashion suitable for an otherwise incompatible graphics display. For example, IBM's digital EGA output can be converted to an analog signal, then scan converted to display on a standard RGB analog monitor. Scan converters cost thousands of dollars.

If you plan to display DtC video on large screen video displays be sure that the display is compatible to the DtC RGB output. If the monitor provides only composite video input, or if the monitor cannot synchronize to an odd scanning frequency, display will not be possible.

Projection Monitors

Projection monitors can be an internal screen or an external display type. Internal screen units use three-color focused light projected on an internal glass-bead screen, which can provide a large display without a large CRT. External displays are about the size of a small suitcase, and beam lenses protrude from the box. You supply the projection screen for display. Projection monitors, like DtC monitors, come in different designs. Multisync projection monitors can handle a large variety of DtC video outputs, or scan converters can be used to drive NTSC-compatible RGB analog monitors.

External screen projection monitors can be suspended from the ceiling and some are sufficiently portable to be hand carried and operated from a table top. A good external projector will cost above $5000, and even at that price their light outputs are not very strong. A relatively dark room, sharp focusing by the operator, and a reflective screen instead of a white wall are required for good viewing.

Large CRT Monitors

These video displays implement large CRTs of 37" to 40". The large CRT monitors perform considerably better than projection monitors of the same size, since the large CRTs do not have the convergence and focusing problems, or the narrow viewing angles of projection monitors.

Viewgraph Video Displays

A variety of video displays can be placed on top of an overhead projector, and technology improvements have finally resulted in sufficient colors and picture clarity for viewgraph displays to be an acceptable medium. Viewgraph display systems consist of variable transparency screens that modulate the light passing through the projector. Until recently, only two color systems were available. Newer systems can support higher resolutions up to 640 by 480 and up to 256 colors. Accompanying software allows you to match the reduced color capability to the software's higher color output.

Higher resolution multiple color systems may cost several thousand dollars. The interfaces to viewgraph displays are compatible with existing DtC video display interfaces, so you can plug the projector into the existing DtC video interface. The units weigh only a few pounds and are quite portable. Couple one with a laptop DtCs with external RGB connections, and you have a great demonstration system.

Video images provided by viewgraph displays are as bright as the light source in the viewgraph projector, but attaining sufficient contrast between colors, or black and white can be a problem. As with projection displays, low light and smaller rooms make for better viewing. Some viewgraph displays require a special display interface add-on board, the laptop DtC, then, may need to have an expansion slot.

Video Display Factors

Important considerations for choosing video displays are:

- **Dot pitch** – What is the size of your phosphor dot triads? A display monitor capable of 1024 by 768 resolution will require a dot pitch of no more than 0.28 mm. The size of phosphor triads must be small enough to handle the maximum dot resolution of the display interface.

  A normal retina is capable of resolving 2000 dots per inch. The maximum resolution of current monitor technologies is 150 dpi, caused by a combination of limitations in the video interface and video display and CRT phosphor densities and shadow mask technologies. This means that 13" diagonal video displays with viewing areas 10" by 8" are limited to resolutions of 1500 by 1200 dots. Of course, larger monitors can support higher resolutions, but you would have to view their screens from a greater distance.

- **Bandwidth** – The bandwidth of the display's video amplifiers will determine how high a dot frequency it can amplify without distortion. This places a limitation on its resolution regardless of other factors such as sweep rates, dot pitch, and video interface outputs. A TV's video bandwidth was described as being 6 MHz; a good RGB monitor will have a video bandwidth of 45 MHz and above. For a typical 640 by 480 dot resolution, the dot rate is 640 dots per line on 480 lines; all of this occurring 30 times a second, or 15 million dots per second.

- **Monitor type** – Analog RGB, digital RGB, and composite monitors do not connect to the same video interface outputs.

- **Color fidelity** – The more expensive and rare minerals produce higher fidelity colors. Chromaticity diagrams show great variations of colors with different types of color phosphors.

> **NOTE**
>
> Triangular chromaticity diagrams are used to define the total color capability, given the three primary phosphor wavelengths and purity levels. Each corner of the diagram represents the pure phosphor color. The area inside the triangle, how much the triangle bows out, contains the total representable colors. Distance toward the center of the triangle represents less saturated colors, and the center is white.

Different video displays vary greatly in their ability to render different color hues and intensities. This factor is sometimes a matter of personal preference, but you will probably be happier with the color performance of the more expensive monitors. Reading vendor ads and looking at color photographs of monitor displays is not enough when choosing a monitor. You must see an actual demonstration of the monitor and its companion video interface.

- **Color purity** – Here the concern is with overall color fidelity through the screen viewing area. Purity is best checked with an all red signal, which is the most sensitive to purity problems. Generate an all red signal and see if it is uniformly red throughout the screen. Color purity is particularly susceptible to magnetic fields.

- **Color or monochrome** – More software products are using color to improve friendliness, with messages in red, block marks in blue, and column markers in yellow. After you become accustomed to a color display, a monochrome display may seem dull and lifeless.

The higher-cost monochrome monitors will support higher resolution. They have only one electron gun and are superior for the demanding high resolution work of desktop publishing. Apple has a one page B/W portrait and two page B/W monochrome monitors that are excellent for DtP purposes. Monochromes are generally less expensive than color monitors with equivalent resolution.

- **Synchronization** – The polarity of H and V signals may be important. Some monitors provide switches to change the polarity. Also, some RGB monitors employ a single H+V sync line, while others use two separate connections for the H and V signals. Still others combine the sync signals with the green signal.

- **Multisync capability** – What is the range of horizontal and vertical frequencies to which the monitor will synchronize? How will it maintain an adequate screen size when it switches? When switching between different DtC video signals, will the monitor vertical and horizontal sweep circuits keep the picture the same size?

- **Interlace or non-interlace scan** – Does the interface provide non-interlace capability and can the monitor display it?

- **Controls** – Where are the important controls such as brightness and contrast on the video display? Can you vary horizontal width and vertical height? What about color hue? The better multisync monitors implement a microprocessor that controls these parameters and let you adjust them digitally with memory and other bells and whistles. Are they convenient? Do they exist at all? Do you have to take the monitor apart to get at them?

- **Persistence** – Screen persistence can affect flicker and smearing when changing screens. Low-persistence phosphors produce higher fidelity colors.

- **Relays** – Some multisync monitors use relays that have an annoying click when they change modes.

- **Video interface signal compatibility** – Although standards apply to video output signals, different video interfaces will output different contrast signal power levels and different hues of the same color. This combined with the different monitor response characteristics will make it difficult to compare monitors unless they are being driven from the same DtC video interface. Choose the optimal match between the monitor and video interface signal characteristics.

- **Focus** – Is the viewing area properly focused everywhere, or are characters on the edges fuzzy?

- **Dynamic convergence and pincushion effect** – Complicated beam compensation electronics and shadow mask technology help the three electron beams to converge on their color phosphors. The compensation is necessary due to the flatter screens, yet radial scanning beams. Good convergence throughout the viewing area is critical to crisp text and sharp graphics displays. Pincushion effect is a common malady in lower-priced monitors. The screen image bows along the right and left hand screen edges.

- **Static convergence** – How well is the electron beam focused throughout the viewing area? More expensive monitors will focus the beam at several radial positions and different focus potentials will be used for the different color beams.

- **Magnetic shielding** – Monitors vary widely in how well they are shielded from external magnetic fields that can distort the image and cause interference with other equipments. High-strength magnetic fields are produced by the monitor, and can prevent interference with other equipments. Monitors will interfere with one another if they are separated by less than three feet. Static magnetic fields from magnets can cause permanent damage to the monitor shadow mask. Also, most monitors have built-in degaussing coils to erase static magnetic fields built up on the monitor shadow mask or other internal magnetic materials. You should be particularly careful about placing floppy disks near the monitor because the magnetic fields it produces can erase the disk data. You should not operate fans or other appliances generating magnetic fields within two feet of the monitor.

An HB DtC RGB monitor will cost from \$200 to \$5000, depending on the characteristics discussed above and on screen resolution. Close inspection of the lower-cost Asian monitors will usually reveal defects in the above areas. Some of the commonly observed bargain monitor deficiencies include different hues of the same color at different points on the screen, curved edges pincushion, poor focus, poor dynamic conversion, lack of controls, and poor magnetic shielding. Sometimes a real bargain will come along, but quality is reflected in price.

2.3   DtC Video Display Interfaces

There are many different display interfaces. The most popular ones are known as the dumb video interfaces. The more powerful intelligent interfaces are discussed later when we look at the sprite generator, a type of video interface found in the early EE computers.

DtC display interfaces can be grouped in three categories:

1. Dumb interfaces found on most HB computers.
2. Intelligent interfaces found in EP computers.
3. Specialized interfaces found in EE computers.

The Dumb Display Interface

The dumb display interface continues to be the most popular interface found in the HB DtCs. Unlike the widely varying and complex intelligent graphics controllers, dumb interface operational characteristics are quite similar in the different DtC models. Software drivers for the different dumb interfaces have differences in resolution and color, but they do not have the significant differences in implementation schemes that the intelligent interfaces have. Also, the cost of the dumb interface is quite low.

Although the performance of the dumb video interface is minimal, it is adequate and appropriate for HB software. The low performance becomes a hindrance when HBs try to do engineering graphics and desktop publishing applications.

The dumb video display interface has only one responsibility – to periodically sweep the contents of video memory and transfer the patterns and colors to the display screen. The DtC CPU is responsible for creating and animating the image. As an image moves across a DtC screen, the CPU is rewriting the video memory for each new image. As character lines scroll, the CPU rewrites the entire screen for every new line presented.

CPU involvement is often justified for small images composed of randomly-lit pixels. Intelligent controllers excel at manipulating complex geometric systems. If you are just trying to display text or simple images, the increased overhead involved with commands and languages could be stifling. There is a tradeoff between the overhead of a high-level system, and the ease of performing simple tasks.

Display Memory

Since both the CPU and the display interface must access memory, display memory is found on the display interface. Display memory on dumb display interfaces is mapped into the CPU executable memory area and is directly accessible by the CPU. Indeed, you could execute programs there, but the space should be reserved for video images. Due to the rate at which display memory must be scanned, this memory is usually the more expensive and fast static memory found in the disk or instruction cache. The amount of display memory depends upon the number of pixels (APA mode) or characters (text mode) that are displayed and the number of colors.

MS-DOS computers permit only 128K in the 640K-1 MB upper memory block region to support dumb video interface memories. The higher resolution dumb interfaces requiring more memory will bank switch up to 2 MB of video memory using the 128K as a switching window. This is similar to the way MS-DOS computers implement their expanded memory. The 68xxx-based EWs and Apple Macintoshes do not place such harsh restrictions on display memory, permitting up to 2 MB of executable memory for this purpose. The more sophisticated intelligent video interfaces manage their own separate video memory areas up to 4 MB in size, however, MS-DOS computer interfaces will usually maintain a small CPU memory area for software compatibility with the lower EGA and VGA modes.

Text Mode Operation

Dumb video interfaces can sweep their display memory in two different modes: text (character) and APA (all points addressable) dot mode. The Figure 103 depicts a generalized dumb interface in text mode with APA mode inset.

In the text or character mapped mode, each byte of video memory represents a complete character. For example, the decimal values 66 and 67 shown stored in memory represent the ASCII codes for the characters B and C. A sequencer connected to video memory address lines scans memory periodically. Each video memory location corresponds to a specific character location on the video screen. In most text interfaces, characters located across a given row on the monitor are stored in sequential memory bytes. MS-DOS computer interfaces reserve alternate bytes for characters and character attributes including colors, blinking, and underline.

As the memory is scanned, the data output ASCII coding is used as addresses to a character ROM. The dot patterns that generate each character are stored in ROM. The sequencer sequences additional address lines on the character ROM to address each row of the character's dot matrix during the scanning process. As display memory is scanned, character ROM outputs each character's dot matrix as a stream of dots. The digital quantities representing dots pass through a lookup RAM color palette that permits value change and therefore color change on the way out of the interface. In analog systems, bit groups are finally converted to an analog signal for transmission to an RGB analog display.

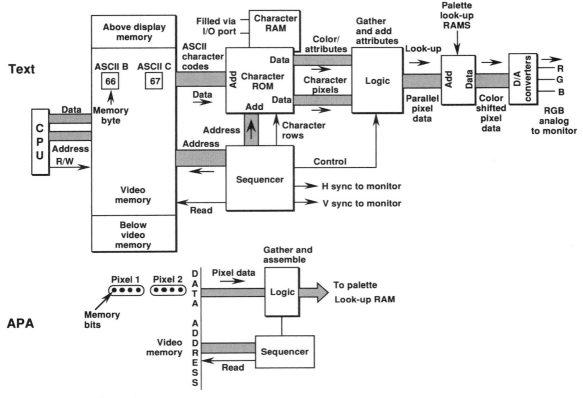

Figure 103. Dumb display interfaces – text vs. APA

In the text mode display interface, the number of displayable characters depends upon the number of display memory bytes. The resolutions of the displayed s character depends on the density of the character ROM and its appropriate scanning. Such attributes as character resolution and font are unknown to the display memory; these attributes are in the ROM character generator.

Text mode display interfaces may also have extended ASCII characters stored in their character ROMs. The upper 128 characters could be a special character set, a set of a different font, or text-graphics characters.

Some character-based display interfaces implement a character RAM that can be switched into the place of the character ROM and downloaded with different character sets. The display interface can support a variety of different fonts, but only one at a time.

The advantages of text mode are:

1. It requires less display memory. Since a single memory byte represents a character regardless of the size of the character matrix less display memory is required.

2. It is easier on the CPU. The CPU can generate characters on screen by sending a single ASCII coded byte to a display memory location. The display interface does the rest. Generating screens of text is a simple matter in text mode. Also, by

changing the contents of the RAM character generator, different fonts can be represented without adding to the CPU's burden.

Text mode video interfaces are a mixed blessing for MS-DOS computers. The early slow MS-DOS computer CPUs needed text mode for video display text scrolling speeds and screen rewrites. MS-DOS computers operate video display interfaces capable of text or APA modes, but text mode is often used for speed or compatibility since MS-DOS doesn't support APA graphics. The MS-DOS operating system and its software base was initially geared for text mode video displays and used extended ASCII characters to perform the limited graphics.

The disadvantages of text mode are:

1. You can display only one font at a time on screen. For those character generators using the upper 128 codes for another font, the number of displayable fonts would be two.

2. Variable sized characters are not possible on the screen at one time. Although the text mode scanning hardware can switch modes and generate different-sized characters, each mode applies to the entire screen. Therefore you can have a screen with 40 column, or 80 column, or 132 column character sizes, but not more than one of these at a time. A limitation also applies to number of lines and line spacing – only one for the entire page.

3. APA graphics are not possible. Since the mapping between display memory and screen is memory-byte oriented, the display screen is divided into character-matrix blocks; each with only 256 possibilities. The number of blocks depends on the specific interface but is usually from 80 by 25 to 132 by 50.
   Text graphics are possible, but the graphics are limited to whatever characters are represented by the upper ASCII codes. The box characters can at least permit you to draw boxes on screen, which are useful for creating menus, and highlighting information. Since the box character's color can be controlled, fairly good screen displays are created in this manner.

APA Dot Mode

In all points addressable mode (see Figure 103 inset) each pixel on the screen corresponds to an individual bit in display memory. Each pixel is turned on or off, corresponding to the memory bit being set to a 1 or 0. To represent more than two colors, groups of dots must be scanned. Some color display interfaces organize their display memory into separate planes for each of the primary colors. As the blue plane is scanned, for example, groups of blue plane bits will correspond to the intensity of the blue signal. At any given time, the three color groups will each have a digital value representing a particular color hue.

Prior to passing through its D/A converter, each color intensity digital value can be changed through a palette lookup RAM. The lookup occurs as each dot color digital quantity passes through. Finally the resulting digital quantity is converted to the required analog signal for each primary color: red, green, and blue.

A resolution figure of 640 by 480 means that the display interface puts out 640 dots across each horizontal scan line, and there are 480 of these lines from the top to the bottom of the active image area. The display monitor's requirements are closely related to these figures.

The advantage is that in APA mode, each display pixel is controlled independently. Therefore, any sized character, many different fonts, different line spacings, and any graphics image within the APA resolution can be constructed.

The disadvantage is that the CPU must perform the constructions and this places a heavy burden on it. Each character will need to be drawn dot by dot, and higher resolution characters will require more dots; in text mode, the CPU needs only a single ASCII code to draw an entire character. Also, more video memory is required since each display dot requires memory bits. In the character mode interface, a single memory byte can represent a complete and highly-resolved character.

Combined Text and APA Interfaces

MS-DOS computer display interfaces combine text and APA mode interfaces; text mode continuing to be used for many word processors, editors, DBMS packages, and other systems where the primary screen output is text. The presence of both modes is a neverending source of problems for software developers who must consider both modes when developing software and operating systems. Although earlier Apple II interfaces had dual mode interfaces, the Macintosh line abandoned text and went for the APA interface and software support. Windows and a growing APA software base increase the use of the APA portion of the MS-DOS computer display interfaces. It is expected that the text mode will eventually disappear.

Dumb Interface Summary

The dots or characters that you see driven from a dumb display interface correspond to bits or bytes of the display memory. For every scan of display memory, the video display sweeps out one frame or for interlaced systems, two alternate frames. Color is represented by attribute bytes in text mode and groups of bits in APA systems. Many DtCs have gone to APA interfaces for WYSIWYG display output. Text modes linger, however, as a throwback to a darker age when slow CPU speed was a critical problem.

Intelligent Display Interfaces

Intelligent controller display interfaces are necessary for the more advanced DtC graphics and CAD applications. Intelligent display interfaces are standard in the engineering workstations where graphics applications are heavily used. Often intelligent controllers are designed around the VLSI graphics chips made by the major chip manufacturers including Intel, Texas Instruments, and National Semiconductor. Built-in graphics chip functions include image panning, zooming, multiple screen images that can slide over one another, windowing, geometric transformations, text and font operations, 2-D and 3-D effects, and color dithering.

Intelligent graphics interfaces operate at a higher level than dumb video interfaces. As shown in Figure 104, the controller rather than the CPU manipulates the memory that is mapped to the video screen. Intelligent graphics controllers can support high graphics resolutions through their large dedicated video memories. A DtC CPU can not execute this memory, although shared memory is sometimes mapped into executable memory for display data transfer.

Intelligent Display Interface Software Support

Unlike the dumb display interfaces that simply sweep a CPU memory area, you will find wide variation in the way that intelligent display interfaces operate. Some

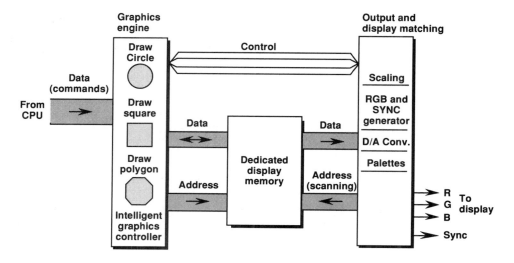

Figure 104. **Typical intelligent display interface**

operate internal programs and output graphics according to how their internal program execution paths are modified. Others present the developer with a command interface (draw circle, color area, rotate object). Others intercept graphics commands in the CPU instruction stream in the same way described for the Intel math coprocessors.

Developing software for intelligent controllers is very different than for the dumb APA display interfaces. Although the controller does remove drawing tedium from the CPU and the software developer, it is not as amenable to construction of application-independent software display interface drivers.

On HB computers, which mostly implement dumb display interfaces, applications software programs can be written independently of their display interfaces. Software drivers for each different dumb display interface convert applications program outputs, which pixel should be which color, into proper positioning in display memory. The conversion of relative pixels to absolute memory data is not complicated, nor is it very different for different dumb display interfaces. HB category software can be written with little knowledge of display hardware and finally matched by independently-constructed software drivers.

Intelligent display controllers are much more involved with the higher-order drawing functions and are closely married to applications. The applications software must be matched to a display interface.

The software development process is more demanding for intelligent interfaces than for dumb ones because the developer must understand clearly how the intelligent controller hardware operates. The developer cannot easily support a variety of different display interfaces by rewriting simple display drivers as can be done with dumb APA interfaces. Appropriately matching good software to intelligent hardware provides performance with low CPU overhead. You will pay more for your EW computer hardware as well as software. The display interface is more integrated with the rest of the DtC system, and the software is highly integrated with the display hardware. Performance will be the reward.

Intelligent Display Controllers in HB DtCs

Intelligent display controllers are only recent additions to lower cost HB computers. Operating system and applications software supported the dumb interfaces, but now the use of HB computers in desktop publishing and CAD applications have made the intelligent controllers a necessity rather than a curiosity. Although the intelligent controllers are not well integrated with the rest of the system hardware, as is the case with EP computers, performance improvements can still make it worth the investment. Both IBM and Apple have produced intelligent display systems for their computer lines, but much of the HB software base continues to use the dumb interfaces.

Compatibility Modes

On HB computers, intelligent display controllers may need to be software compatible with the popular dumb display interface. In this compatibility mode, the controller can emulate a dumb display interface and implement shared memory identical to the dumb interface display memory. You should determine if you will need this compatibility when purchasing the intelligent interfaces, and verify the level of compatibility by checking with those who use the system with the same programs you plan to run.

Remember, you will need special drivers to get your applications software to work with intelligent display interfaces. If you develop your own software, be sure your development system supports intelligent interfaces.

Dual Display Systems

You could buy a dual display system with the usual dumb interface and monitor for an HB software base and an intelligent display system for high graphics performance applications. Often, the high-performance graphics applications will make particularly good use of the dumb display interface for displaying commands, menus, and programs.

Today's graphics chips are more sophisticated than the current software base can use. Within the next few years, the software will catch up, providing spectacular graphics applications on DtCs. Already most HB DtC CAD software packages, AutoCAD for example, support video interfaces based on sophisticated graphics controller chips. The only barrier to a virtual graphics software explosion is the lack of graphics function standardization in the major chip manufacturer's VLSI graphics controller chips. Instead, we must rely on software industry support of less powerful, and often proprietary graphics devices provided by the major DtC manufacturers such as IBM's 8514/A. DVI systems will also enhance video display system performance through a variety of value added functions.

Sprite Generators

Video display interfaces vary widely. Figure 105 shows a generalization of a popular type of video display interface incorporated in some of the earlier EE DtCs. The interfaces are designed for animations effects at relatively low resolutions. Animation is achieved by custom hardware that manipulates low-resolution images, known as *sprites*, directly in display memory rather than making the DtC's CPU do it.

Sprite generators are great for translating, zooming, and coloring images for spectacular animated game effects. High-level languages on EE DtCs directly support this with sprite commands. Commodore and Atari video display interfaces have more complexity than the figure shows, implementing many of the higher-level functions ascribed to the intelligent graphics controllers.

Often the interfaces combine animation effects and sprite collision detection with geometry functions. Also, in the EE DtCs, the display interfaces are highly integrated with other specialized chips for audio, hard disk controller, and DMA controller, making effective use of other system components in conjunction with the video effects.

RGB vs. Composite and RF Video Interfaces

Figure 101 (bottom) shows the different outputs available from DtC video interfaces. Most of today's DtC interfaces provide direct RGB analog and sync outputs. Early IBM CGA and EGA interfaces provided RGB digital outputs and required special digital RGB monitors.

Early IBM CGA, the early Apple II, EE DtCs, and the popular dedicated entertainment systems such as Nintendo still provide composite video outputs. Some include internal modulators to provide RF channel 3 and 4 signals for connection to a TV set, or a plug with composite video, audio, and power connections for a modulator. TV viewing is generally restricted to lower resolution graphics. The RF outputs are about 320 by 240 with 256 colors and provide surprisingly good images for games and entertainment.

Display Interface Factors

Many factors should come into play when you choose a video display interface. As newer display interfaces offload more graphics functions from the CPU, interface performance must be considered when selecting system hardware. Also, the display interface will need to match the monitor. The more important parameters to be considered are discussed next.

Resolution

What is the required resolution and what does the video display interface provide? As resolution goes up, so does price. For MS-DOS applications be sure that the software base will support the higher-resolution modes of the display interface; if not, the added monitor resolution will be unusable.

Resolution is directly related to the interface dot frequency, which is related to how much and how often the interface scans memory. The larger the number of bits scanned, the higher will be the dot frequency. Non-interlaced interfaces of 60 complete frames per second will require twice the dot frequency of interlaced, 60 half frames per second, or 30 complete frames per second. Higher frequencies require more costly design and circuitry. The interface must scan video memory completely at least 30 times per second, putting interface scanning rates in the neighborhood of 100 MHz.

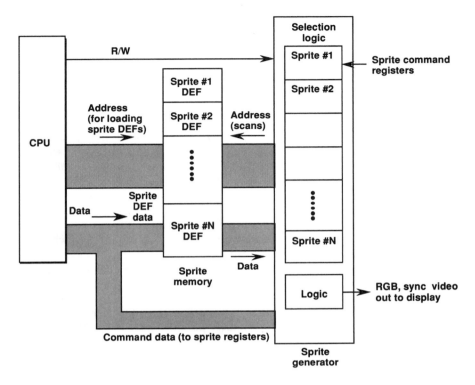

Figure 105. **Typical sprite display interface**

Colors

How many different colors can each screen pixel be at the same time on screen? It is said that 24-bit (16.8 million) color is essential to adequately render color objects and meet the eye's ability to distinguish colors. Many claim that 15-bit (32000) color is a reasonable compromise, and some insist that 8-bit (256) color will do for most graphics applications. Still others say that most text and some graphics applications are fine with 4-bit (16) color, and some even rationalize 2 color (monochrome). Color dithering can give you more colors with less memory. The increased interface memory, electronics, and higher scan rates of more colors per pixel up the price.

> **NOTE**
> **Color Dithering**
> Color dithering displays a large number of separate colors using groups of pixels rather than individual pixels to represent colors. Each pixel in a group is set to a different hue. The composite output represents one color, because at a distance, the eye resolves the groups of pixels into a single color. The image resolution, however, decreases proportionately, giving it a markedly grainy appearance. For displaying large areas in a single color, graininess can produce a desirable effect.

Scanning Parameters

Different interfaces will output different horizontal and vertical scanning rates. Most have interlaced scanning, but some output the higher quality non-interlaced scanning. Your monitor will need to handle the range and type of scanning.

Interface Memory

How much display memory is contained in the display interface? Each display pixel must correspond to at least one memory bit. If pixels are to be colored, n memory bits will be required for 2^n colors per pixel. In APA interfaces, there is a direct relationship between horizontal and vertical resolution numbers, the number of colors per pixel, and the size of the required video memory. For a 256-color interface this means 8 bits per pixel. Apple's 24 bit interface requires 3 bytes per pixel. On a 640 by 480 pixel display, 640 by 480 by 3 bytes or close to 2 MB of memory is required. MS-DOS computers only provide 128K of directly addressable memory for their display interfaces, and you'll need to check that other memories are not mapped into the 128K region. Larger amounts will need to be bank switched or idependently supported by an intelligent display interface.

For character-mapped interfaces, display memory size is dependent on the column by row number of characters that can be displayed on the screen and their possible attributes. For example, an 80 by 25 character display where one byte defines a character and another byte defines the character attributes will require 80 by 25 by 2 bytes or approximately 4K of display memory. You can see that text-based interfaces have much lower memory requirements than APA displays.

Palettes

Most display interfaces give you a specified number of colors from a much larger array of possible colors called a palette. The color palette determines the total number of different colors that can be displayed. When color numbers for video interfaces are specified, there are two numbers given: 1) simultaneously displayed colors and 2) total colors. The number of different colors that can be on the screen at one time is limited by the amount of display memory. Palette size, however, does not affect display memory size.

For example, IBM's VGA interface can display 16 colors at a time on screen, chosen from any of the 262,144 colors available on the palette. The color is determined through a lookup RAM as each colored pixel is output from the display interface. Additional display memory is not required for this large number because you are still displaying only 16 colors at one time.

Light Pens

Many video interfaces provide a connection for light pens. The light pen is synchronized with the interface scanning registers and can be used as a screen position sensing device. Light pen support will be found in most display adapter BIOS video function support as well as in many languages.

Outputs

A video interface may provide analog or digital outputs while some provide connectors for both. You might want to check if composite video capability is provided if you want to view outputs on the more conventional composite video monitors. Also, the availability of individual horizontal and vertical synchronization signals, rather than a combined H+V signal, or H+V combined with the green signal, may be important. This will depend upon the specific monitor that will connect to the interface.

Bus Width

How wide is the data connection between the interface and the host CPU? For example, when using AT-style MS-DOS computers, a 16-bit video interface will be more desirable from a performance standpoint. This 16-bit interface will not always be compatible with 8-bit XT-style systems. Some 16-bit cards can detect that they are in an 8-bit slot and can drop down to a single-byte transfer mode. There will need to be room for the remainder of the 16-bit connector that has nowhere to plug in. Newer HB DtCs, and the EP DtCs provide full 32-bit wide data paths with on-motherboard display interfaces, or interfaces using the improved NuBus, EISA, or MCA bus.

Display Memory Speed

How fast is the display memory on the video interface and what are the access mechanisms between memory and the host CPU? Is DMA permitted? Are wait states invoked?

Intelligent Interface Performance

For the intelligent display interfaces, consider the interface and CPU performance. What graphics functions are implemented? How efficiently? Although fast, are software drivers available for your software applications? Does the interface support a compatibility mode for HB applications?

Bus Type

The two MS-DOS computer bus types, ISA and Micro Channel, require different interfaces. Most IBM PS/2 computers and other vendors of MCA computers usually have built-in VGA interfaces, but more sophisticated interfaces will be bus plug-ins. Macs implement direct and NuBus slots. Be sure you know what type of slot you have.

2.4 HB Computer Interfaces and Monitors

Now that we have a general background in the various types of displays and display interfaces, we can look at some specific system hardware. We concentrate on the popular HB MS-DOS and Apple computers.

Figure 106 shows stock MS-DOS and Apple computer interfaces, which are well supported by the software base. Early MS-DOS computer CGA and EGA interfaces are on the low end, while VGA is higher on the scale. Apple's stock dumb interfaces have better color and resolution than IBM interfaces. Apple always emphasized good resolution and APA display interfaces with appropriately high-level operating system support. Both IBM and Apple computers can be outfitted with the higher performance and more specialized intelligent graphics controllers, although they are not well supported by software bases. In the EP category, systems routinely support the higher-end intelligent display controllers. The EE category interfaces, while specialized, provide good resolution and color capability.

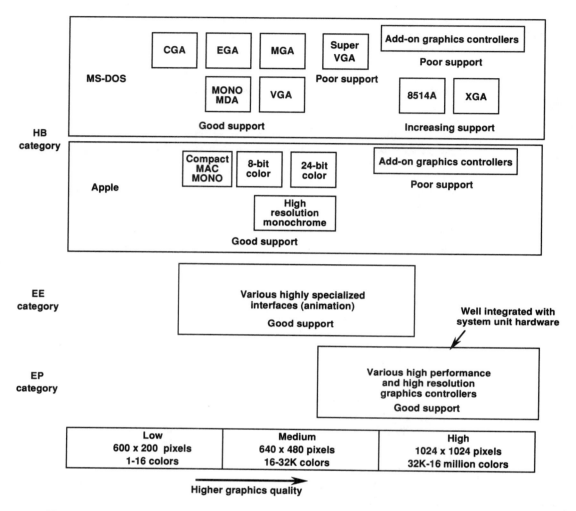

Figure 106. Display system comparisons

MS-DOS Computers

A review of the popular interfaces found in MS-DOS computers, starting with their early CGA and finishing with their latest XGA interface, is now in order. The IBM CGA, MDA, EGA, and VGA interfaces are considered stock IBM interfaces because they were initially designed by IBM and they have widespread software support. The software support for initialization and character mapped-mode is found in the MS-DOS computer motherboard BIOS ROMs for the CGA and MDA, and on interface ROM for EGA and VGA adapters. Most MS-DOS compatibles have reverse-engineered display interfaces at the BIOS level and some go all the way to the register level. To support higher-end graphics applications and to improve the stock video interface support, IBM has produced two graphics displays: the 8514/A and the newer XGA interface.

CGA

The CGA (color graphics adapter) was IBM's first graphics interface, found in the early IBM PC, XT, and AT computers. The interface is a combined character-mapped and APA mode interface with moderate text display capability and low graphics resolution. Its specifications are:

- *APA resolution* – 640 by 200 two colors or 320 by 200 four colors (palette of eight colors).
- *Character mapped* – 80 by 25 or 40 by 25 text mode (16 colors).
- *Outputs* – Digital RGB, intensity bit, and H,V sync on a 9-pin connector.

A special digital RGB monitor, manufactured initially by IBM but now widely cloned, is required. The vertical resolution of 200 is relatively poor, so text characters are grainy and graphics resolution is unacceptable to most users. The CGA video output can convert to an analog RGB signal to drive standard RGB analog monitors, mostly for large screen video, and the CGA interface has a composite video for driving composite monitors. You can connect a modulator to display the output on a TV set.

The CGA is not recommended for current DtC applications because of its poor resolution and potential for creating eyestrain. Composite video monitors can be driven from an RCA jack on the CGA interface. Asian vendors product CGA interfaces including parallel printer ports for as low as $20. Since you can purchase a cheap used composite monitor for $10, many MS-DOS compatible users start with the CGA/composite monitor combination for a very low-cost starter computer.

MDA Monochrome Adapter

The early monochrome adapter provided a special digital monochrome signal and the monochrome monitor was a special digital single color monitor. IBM's MDA interface to this monitor supports an 80 by 25 text mode with a denser than CGA character dot matrix. IBM's original monochrome video interface did not provide APA operation. Its purpose was to support fine character byte-mapped text mode for text-based applications.

Other display interface manufacturers, primarily Hercules, provide display interfaces with monochrome compatibility modes. More importantly, they provide a good 720 by 350 APA mode for IBM monochrome monitors. Each software application will need to supply the appropriate graphics software drivers because an APA monochrome mode was not provided in IBM's early BIOS ROMs.

The early Hercules APA interfaces saved early IBM PCs because IBM's CGA APA resolutions were inadequate for graphics applications. In fact, the Hercules graphics resolution exceeded that of IBM's next introduction, the EGA, albeit with only one color.

Since the newer IBM VGA monitors and interfaces are capable of supporting higher resolution characters and multiple gray scale monochrome modes, IBM's original MDA is practically extinct.

EGA

The EGA (enhanced graphics adapter) improved upon the CGA, but it is still inadequate for the higher-end graphics and desktop publishing applications. Its specifications are:

- **APA resolution** – 640 by 350, 16 colors from a palette of 64.
- **Character mapped** – 80 by 25, 80 by 43, and 132 column text modes.
- **Outputs** – Digital RGB, intensity, sync, on a 9-pin D connector.
- **RAM character generator** – The EGA has a downloadable RAM character generator that increases font flexibility in character-mapped mode.

Like the CGA, the EGA video display is a non-standard digital monitor and worse, it implements a non-standard horizontal scan rate. However, it did become popular, and many Asian manufacturers produce it for around $200. When converted to analog, EGA output is not compatible with standard video equipment, but special scan converters or multisync monitors can be used to display EGA outputs. Although the EGA resolution still lacks the capability for serious graphics applications, it is remarkably suitable for many business graphics, games, and other low-end graphics applications.

VGA

IBM introduced the VGA (video graphics array) display interface with its PS/2 line of DtCs. The VGA finally provided MS-DOS computers with an acceptable analog display interface. Although severely color limited, the APA resolution could support reasonable analog graphics applications. Still a dumb video interface, the VGA supports many different graphics and APA modes. A few of the more popular modes are described next. Its specifications are:

- **APA resolution** – 640 by 480, 16 colors or 320 by 200, 256 colors (palette of 262,144).

> **NOTE**
>
> The 320 by 200, 256 color mode, called MCGA mode, is intended to match the performance of a standard home TV.

- **Character mapped** – 80 by 25, 80 by 43, 80 by 50, and 132 column text modes.

- **Gray-Scale monochrome mode** – A 64-color monochrome mode provides pleasing performance on IBM's custom analog monochrome monitor, the 8503.

- **Outputs** – Analog RGB, and sync through a special 15-pin plug.

- **Compatibility mode** –The VGA can provide all previous IBM adapter modes including MCA, EGA and CGA.

You cannot, however, connect the digital CGA, EGA, or MCA monochrome monitors to the VGA adapter output. To do this, you will need a special adapter with a 15- to 9-pin A/D converter to connect the digital EGA monitor to the analog VGA interface output. IBM made the VGA display interface a part of its motherboard design on the new PS/2 line. However, it can be disabled to allow addition of improved video display systems.

Compatible Character-Mapped Modes

The CGA, EGA and VGA character-mapped modes are software compatible; they all support an 80 by 25 character mode, and video interface character ROMs, not software, accomodates differences in character resolution. These interfaces are initialized by separate BIOS initialization software that is transparent to the software base. The compatibility, however, does not apply when higher character densities of 132 by 50 are attempted on the lower character density interfaces.

Stock Interface Software Compatibility

When you purchase MS-DOS compatibles, display interface compatibility with IBM stock CGA, EGA, and VGA display interfaces will be an important consideration. Since most software supports documented IBM EGA and VGA display modes, your compatible's display interface should be compatible with those modes. There are two levels of compatibility to be considered:

- *Register compatibility* – To be register compatible, the MS-DOS compatible interface must be compatible at the register level. Several control registers in the display interface control such operations as display interface timing, vertical and horizontal scanning rates, dot resolutions, and number of colors. A host of different text and graphics resolutions are supported, and switching between display modes involves writing specific quantities to specific control registers. If software designed according to well-documented IBM specifications writes directly to your compatible's display interface registers, your display had better react in exactly the same way as intended for the IBM adapters, or you may be viewing wrong colors, or worse, a smeared display screen. Most software vendors will resist writing to the hardware and will use BIOS support.

- *BIOS compatibility* – To shield software developers from the details above, the MS-DOS computer BIOS provides functions through hardware-independent software routines, each matched to its display interface. At the BIOS level, you simply ask for display mode, by function number, and let the BIOS worry about the makeup of the interface control register, which will usually not be identical to IBM's. The display adapter BIOS will also take care of initializing the display adapter on power up.
  The BIOS-supported functions are less demanding than direct use of the interface at the register level, so BIOS compatibility is easier to get. When writing directly to display adapter control registers according to IBM specifications, software vendors risk limiting operation to only IBM computers. You will find such behavior, then, an oddity.

BIOS Pixel Graphics Support

IBM provides complete documentation on BIOS support of pixel-level APA graphics in the very popular EGA and VGA display adapter modes. Others have written entire books that discuss precisely how the functions work. Pixel support, however, is the lowest possible level of graphics support, giving you only the ability to draw individual pixels of a color. The functions are at least independent of the particular display interface and specify only relative pixel screen positions. The BIOS routines take care of the details of setting the appropriate bits in a given display adapter memory, and this BIOS will be found on the display interface board. You could write software that wrote directly to display memory, but it would then become specific to the particular way that a given display interface implemented its display memory. Since the IBM display adapters are original, and the best documented, vendors would only write directly to display memory according to the IBM specifications. They would do it for the sake of speed – it's faster to send data directly to memory than to send it indirectly through a BIOS routine – but this would limit their software base to operating on interfaces exactly the same as the IBM display interface.

MS-DOS graphics programs designed to operate on the many MS-DOS compatible display interfaces will have to use the pixel oriented BIOS functions to operate compatibly on the many MS-DOS compatible EGA and VGA interfaces. You could think of the BIOS pixel routine as a shield between the pixel-graphics needs of a program and the display interface.

Real Graphics Support

Although some might call pixel-level support *graphics* support, that would be an injustice to what you would find in the Macintosh BIOS, or the Windows and OS/2 environments. In these you'll find centralized support for graphics primitives (draw line, circle) and even higher-level functions such as draw an icon, or display a radio button. This relieves the software developer from having to write higher-level functions and provides a consistency in the software base. Don't forget, though, that aspiring to higher-level graphics support functions will require higher-performance CPUs, faster display interfaces, and a rewritten software base.

Super VGA

The Super VGA mode is a departure from the stock IBM CGA, EGA and VGA interfaces. Unhappy with limited resolutions and colors, other manufacturers have created oodles of different and improved VGA interfaces.

Since many vendors are supporting resolutions higher than VGA, some resolutions are becoming standardized. The more popular super VGA resolutions are:

Resolution	Palette
640 by 480	.... 256 colors
800 by 600	.... 16 or 256 colors
1024 by 768	.... 16 or 256 colors (called super-extended)

The memory required on a video interface to support these resolutions can range from 64K to 1 MB. Most VGA and extended VGA modes support a color palette of 262,144 colors.

Since they are not stock interfaces, super VGA display interfaces will bring a new set of problems:

- **Mode compatibility** – Does the interface support your application's mode of operation? In addition to the more popular CGA, EGA, and VGA modes, more than 100 different text and graphics modes are now supported in most super VGA interfaces. Which of these modes will your applications suite require?

- **Software drivers** – Up through the VGA modes the stock interfaces are universally supported. Many MS-DOS compatible display interfaces are reverse-engineered to the register level, and others maintain BIOS compatibility by performing their individual initializations through BIOS ROMs on the interface. Most CGA, EGA, and VGA programs work universally on the IBM and various compatible interfaces, with no need for additional software drivers. Super VGA interfaces, however, are so different – there never was an earlier IBM display interface to copy – that each requires a unique software driver. Be careful that the board you buy has drivers for your software. Also, as your software versions are updated, will the vendor continue to supply updated software drivers?

EXAMPLE

A particular vendor's super VGA board supplied video drivers for Windows Version 2.0. for operation in 800 by 600, 256 color mode. When Windows went to Version 3.0 the old drivers did not work. Worse yet, the display board manufacturer was out of business and the anticipated 3.0 drivers became vaporware.■

■ *Vaporware* refers to products that are announced but never actually make it to market.

IBM's 8514/A Adapter

The 8514/A is an IBM proprietary custom display controller that is offered despite the fact that major chip manufacturers produce incredibly powerful VLSI graphics controller chips for the general market.

The 8514/A comes as an add-on board for the PS/2 computers, supports resolutions of 1024 by 768, and requires an IBM 8514 or compatible multisync non-interlace scan monitor. Both VGA and 8514/A adapters from IBM can be used at the same time to support dual monitor systems, as can the other vendors reverse-engineered 8514/A boards. The 8514/A display interface is classed as a display controller, with the following features:

- *Character sets* – Advanced text and alphanumerics including different fonts and sizes.
- *BIT-BLT (Bit block transfer operations)* – This allows rectangular arrays of data to be moved at high speed.
- *Drawing* – Hardware-assisted line drawing.
- *Rectangular scissors* – Portions of the screen can be masked to allow faster updates of bit planes. This can involve the performance of pop-up menus and multiple screen windows
- *Mixing* – Logical manipulations between bit planes for special color and animation effects.

The 8514/A is oriented toward multiple bit operations; the XGA is a better interface for geometry-oriented CAD applications. Some say the 8514/A is a compromise between the earlier dumb video interfaces and those implemented with the full-fledged intelligent graphics coprocessor chips manufactured by TI, National Semiconductor, and Intel.

IBM's XGA Display Interface

Pushing for a new VESA (Video Equipment Standards Association) standard, IBM introduced its Extended Graphics Adapter (XGA) interface in early 1991. This interface supports 1024 by 768 non-interlace mode with a 15-bit (32,000) color capability and will support up to 24-bit color with appropriately installed display memory. Among the many features that make it comparable to interfaces implemented with the popular vendor's intelligent coprocessing chips include high-speed line drawing capability. The XGA is the first interface to be offered in IBM's PS/2 line that approximates an engineering workstation display interface. It is an important step toward the further blurring between HB and EP DtCs.

The higher resolution, more intelligent modes are becoming important for the higher-end CAD applications. Also, the modes are required when running GUI environments like Windows, in which several applications must display graphics APA output in restricted screen windows.

IBM Display Monitors

IBM monitors for the PS/2 line of computers include:

- **IBM 8503** – This 12" analog white on black monitor can display 256 shades of gray at 640 by 480 resolution. The 8503 can be used with PS/2- and MS-DOS-compatible models implementing an IBM-compatible VGA interface.

- **Color 8512** – This is an analog display monitor designed for the VGA's lower resolution MCGA 320 by 200, 256 color mode. When displaying MCGA output, the 8512 provides TV-like color images. The 8512's .41mm dot pitch is not adequate for serious graphics work or for use in higher than MCGA resolution VGA display mode.

- **Color 8513** – This 13" RGB analog monitor is intended for use with mode VGA adapters. It can display 640 by 480 resolution graphics, but will not operate multisync.

- **Color 8514** – This 14" RGB analog video display has better resolution than the 8513 and it can be used for CAD applications. It is intended to be driven by a high-resolution video interface such as IBM's 8514/A adapter. The 8514 can display 1024 by 768 in non-interlaced scan. Many other vendors produce its equivalent in their super VGA multisync monitors.

MS-DOS Compatible Monitors

If you would rather purchase a monitor from someone other than IBM, you'll have no problem finding a supplier. And you will enjoy a competitive price spread. Compatible monitors come in two main classes: the VGA compatibles, and super VGA monitors.

- **VGA Compatibles** – Many American, Japanese, and Asian makers are anxious to sell you a VGA-compatible monitor. These monitors are priced around $250 and provide adequate performance compared to IBM's 8513 monitor. Be careful: most VGA compatibles are not multisync monitors. Although many VGA interfaces do provide CGA- and EGA-compatible outputs, the VGA-compatible monitors are unable to display those outputs.

- **Super VGA** – Super VGA monitors have a wide range of display resolutions, and support most of the super VGA interface resolutions. They commonly support the VGA resolutions and some are flexible enough to display EGA and CGA resolutions if there is appropriate conversion of digital CGA/EGA signals. Most go up to 1024 by 768, a few go higher, and you can get non-interlace capability. Many are compatible with IBM's 8514/A monitor. This mode is quite popular for many higher-end graphics applications, so you may want the interface and monitor to be compatible with the 8514/A. Later, XGA compatibility will become important.

Full-Page Displays

Different manufacturers make full-page displays for MS-DOS compatibles for desktop publishing page layout applications. The displays feature a page aspect ratio and high resolution monochrome capability. Of course, you will have to match the display with an appropriate interface and software drivers.

Performance Costs

In all of the video display interfaces discussed, be aware of the performance penalty that comes with increased resolutions and colors. As resolution and color increase, the work involved in building a display image becomes more intensive for the CPU, which has to rewrite the increasing number of memory locations. A 1024 by 768 display with 256 colors involves several times as much memory as does a VGA display of 640 by 480 with 16 colors.

A new line of super VGA interfaces is now available implementing the TI, National Semiconductor, or Intel graphics coprocessors. These boards and software drivers are available for the higher-end CAD, desktop publisher, and windowing environments. Recent performance surveys show conflicting performance requirements. Depending upon the board maker and application, performance of the intelligent interfaces can vary from half the speed of the dumb interface to several times faster. They can run slower if an application program is simply setting a lot of individual pixels rather than taking advantage of a particular intelligent controller's command repertoire. When operating in compatibility modes, the intelligent systems can run slower than the original dumb interface.

Apple Displays and Adapters

Much of what was said about the MS-DOS compatible display interfaces and monitors is true also of the Apple. The primary difference between the two types is that Apple Computer has dedicated more effort to fewer, but more powerful APA video interfaces. Likewise, their software support has always favored APA mode.

The early Apple II had a 320 by 290 six-color display and interface. Display memory was located in a 16K region below their memory mapped I/O region at C000-CFFF hex. When you consider that BASIC occupied 12K, which included the operating system, and the ROM BIOS occupied 4K, only about 28K was left for programs. This extreme limitation forced programs to execute in display memory during text modes that didn't use all of the APA memory. The interface allowed you to operate text and APA modes on the same screen. On the lower portion of the screen, you could display a few lines of text-mode characters while the remainder of the screen was mapped as APA-mode graphics. Also, the entire screen could be APA or text. These flexible modes led to many useful applications and made efficient use of Apple's then only 8-bit CPU.

The compact Macintoshes first implemented a low-cost cost 512 by 340 B/W monitor, nicknamed their blue monitor since the white phosphor had a pleasing bluish tinge to it. The monitor was small and was built into the Mac unit, intertwined with its power supply. A dumb APA video interface was used, but because of the 68000's power, drawing speeds weren't bad compared to the text mode CGA and EGA interfaces of the MS-DOS compatibles that relied on 8088 CPUs to manage their screen pixels.

Most Macs today have the Mac 640 by 480 8-bit (256 color) or 24-bit (16.8 million color) display interfaces and monitors. Although the initial stock interfaces were dumb, Apple and many other makers also provide higher performance intelligent controllers at those resolutions and colors. The Mac also implements a very high resolution monochrome portrait and two page B/W monitor for desktop publishing.

Some of the MS-DOS compatible multisync monitors can be driven by the Mac interfaces and competition will drag prices lower.

Figure 106 shows the Macintosh stock monitors as considerably better than the MS-DOS compatible's stock EGA or VGA monitors, but the super VGA monitors are beginning to compete. Another advantage of the Mac interfaces and monitors is that they are well supported by the Mac software base. Their drivers are well integrated in ROM. In fact, they are so well integrated that you can operate seven monitors on a Macintosh and spread an image across all seven of them. You may not think there is much use for that, but many users operate 8-bit and 24-bit color interfaces when developing illustrations, sharing the image rendition load effectively between the two monitors.

2.5   Display System Summary

Display interfaces found in the HB computers have historically been low-cost dumb interfaces, catering toward text and low-performance graphics applications. Lately, an effort has been made to boost their capability by increasing resolution and colors and using the intelligent display controllers. The software base and operating system support is currently in a state of flux as they adjust to the higher performance.

Most EP systems, particularly the engineering workstations, do not implement their display interfaces as an afterthought, but integrate them into the rest of their system design. High performance and highly-customized design, in adding capability to display interfaces and monitors also makes them and their software base more expensive.

The EE display systems are competitive with the HB DtCs except for the special visual effects supported.

2.6   Special DtC Video Applications

If you look at Figure 101 on page 511, you'll see that there are other sources of video besides a DtC graphics display interface. First, a home video camera is a source of composite video. A line-audio signal is available as well as an RF-modulated combination of the two. A VCR and videodisk can provide a source of composite video.

Viewing Other Video Sources

For a variety of reasons, you might want to view TV stations, or outputs from video equipment on your DtC screen. Since most of today's DtCs display monitors require analog RGB inputs, this will be a problem. Technology comes to the rescue in the following ways:

- **Multisync monitor composite video input** – Some of the RGB analog monitors provide a composite video input that can be connected to a VCR. Using this input you can watch video movies on the DtC video display or even TV using a VCR tuner.

- **TV board in DtC** – Today you can buy a graphics display interface for an HB DtC that combines the usual video interface with a software controlled RF tuner, and color demodulator circuitry found in a TV set. Hook up an antenna to the add-on board and you can watch a TV station full screen or in one corner of the DtC video display. On MS-DOS computers, this capability requires VGA and above monitors.

Interactive Video

Interactive video promises to be the next major technological revolution. In short, interactive video is the combined use of a computer, its graphics and text outputs and those of live video sources such as VCRs, video cameras, and video disks.

Figure 107 shows the different levels of interactivity.

Level 1

The DtC acts as an intelligent controller selecting either its own output or the output of a VCR, videodisk, or camera, which is then output on a monitor. Control of the video source can be accomplished with DtC interfaces and the existing remote control capability of the VCR or video disk. At this level there is no synchronism between the computer-generated graphics and text and the live video image.

Level 2

Level 2 provides more interactivity, and adds the following capabilities:

- **Dual display** – Displays both computer-generated and live video on the same monitor screen. Level 2 systems require a special display interface that can generate synchronizing signals to the video equipment or be synchronized by the video equipment.

- **Signal combination** – The computer and live video signals are combined in the front-end electronics of the special display interface. There are serious limitations on the flexibility of combination systems as compared to level 3 systems. For example, you might be able to place the live video image in the upper left or right hand corner or the center, and you might have two or three choices for how large it will be. Imagine how nice it would be to work a spreadsheet while watching the news on one corner of the video screen.

> **NOTE**
> Some EE DtCs provide level 2 capability in their display interfaces. For MS-DOS compatibles, you'll have to buy an additional, special-purpose display interface.

Level 3

Level 3 integrates the computer and external video. To better combine with computer graphics capability, the analog video images are converted to digital data and are brought into display memory on a special display interface board. In addressable display memory, the video data is subject to processing by the DtC CPU or better yet, by special digital processors. When digital signal processing capability is added

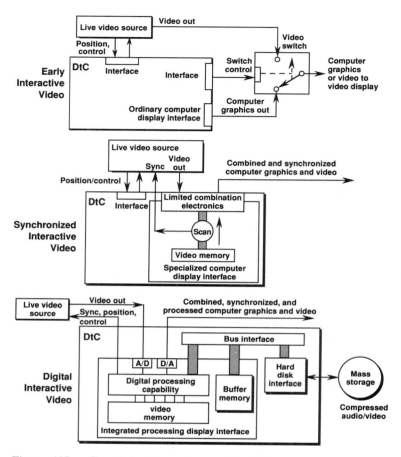

Figure 107. Combining live and computer video

to the third level, a metamorphosis occurs. The industry acronym DVI (Digital Video Interactive) only begins to convey the power of the combination. With DVI, a powerful processing element is added between the A/D/A converters and the video interface memory.

Intel's DVI system, for example, uses a custom-developed DVI digital processing engine with several MB of RAM for algorithms and video buffers. Intel's system not only performs complex image processing functions such as rotations, contours, and multiple images, it can also compress the video in real time by factors of as much as 160. Once compressed, the video can be stored on a hard disk. Complete systems including CD-ROMs are used in conjunction with high-powered development software to create educational and training scenarios. An impressive demonstration of the technology is a walking tour where you investigate various objects controlling movement with a joystick. You can look up, down, sideways, and even simulate walking about.

Up to ten minutes of full-motion video, several hours of high-quality stereo audio, or any combination of the two could be stored on a 100 MB hard disk using data compression. CD-ROM interfaces and software are available for practically unlimited storage of audio and video. Imagine going to a record store and listening to samples from any record in the store. DtC software could guide you to the record name and producer you want. Even digitized images of the record jackets could be provided as you listen to excerpts from each album.

When will DVI become popular? The processing requirements of DVI are extraordinary and current equipment costs are still quite high, in the range of thousands of dollars for the DVI hardware, and thousands more for the development software.

It is rumored that Intel will be devoting considerable acreage to DVI on their forthcoming 80786 CPU chip. Now operating systems such as Windows are including drivers and multimedia development software that can assist developers in using this fascinating technology.

Level 3 systems are considerably more expensive than level 2 video interfaces because of the high performance hardware A/D converters, memory management, and signal processing chips required to perform the real time conversion, processing and storage into memory.

Since level 3 systems can capture live video frames in real time and store the compressed data to mass storage, or process the data in video memory, the applications and special effects are limitless.

You can use languages and special windowing libraries to create spectacular video special effects. Better yet, you can use programmed interactive video software that provides functions for combining video and computer generated images. Such languages are usually bundled with DtC-based interactive video equipment.

Imagine this application: take document X and display it on the screen. Now take video sequence frames 400-1000 −a short film of you explaining the document − and display the video sequence in a window at the center of the screen. Next, slide the video image across the screen from location x to location y. Now, make the center of the video image transparent for a computer-generated chart to show through.

The image is in the computer's memory. Why not use a screen capture program to get this image of you, a document, and a data chart into a disk file? Load your favorite paint program, load the image, and see what you look like with a handlebar moustache.

Level 4

A level 4 can be defined that adds to level 3 capabilities within the video source that include programs and computing capability.

For example, an intelligent video player could control its own functionality by software included between video frames. Detailed controlling functions for slow motion, for displaying every third frame, or for accelerating motion can be offloaded to the video player. The capability of the microcontroller in the video player, combined with local DtC processing provides an enormous selection of possibilities.

3.0   Modems

The modem or MOdulator DEModulator is a DtC's gateway to the outside world. Today's modems include a variety of useful functions including the ability to send a fax.

3.1   Modem History

▣ The message, "What hath God wrought?", was sent from Washington, D.C. to Baltimore, Maryland.

In 1844 Samuel Morse and Alfred Vail performed the first telegraph transmission. ▣ The telegraph code was comprised of three states: off, on for short – dot, and on for long – dash. This dot-dash alphabet system became known as Morse code. In 1861, with the help of Congressional appropriation, the telegraph became the main United States long distance communications service.

Later, in the 1890s, a New Zealander named Donald Murray invented the teletype. This teletype produced a two-state code of on and off pulses for the representation of characters. Before the end of the 19th century, another transmission code was developed by the French telegrapher Emile Baudot. The code incorporated only five bits to represent 32 different characters. To increase the number of representable characters, two of the 32 keys could combine with any of the remaining 30.

At about the same time, the telephone was becoming popular and telegraph benefitted by the expansion of the telephone network. Now you could send telephone conversations and telegraph messages over the same wires. The voice conversations were transmitted in the bandwidth between 250-3400 Hz and telegraph pulses were sent in the bottom 20 Hz bandwidth. In the 1920s, vacuum tubes allowed multiple telephone conversations on one circuit by shifting the 250-3400 Hz band to the 4250-7650 Hz or the 8250-11,650 Hz band before transmission. Improved filtering and 600 Hz guard bands permitted up to 12 simultaneous conversations per telephone connection.

Remote Control Communication

The first demonstration of remote computer control is believed to have taken place in 1940 when George Stibitz, a mathematician, along with Samuel Williams, an engineer at Bell Labs, showed off their complex number calculator, one of the first digital computers. While delivering a paper about the machine at Dartmouth college, Stibitz submitted numerical problems posed by the audience to the machine over a makeshift terminal using Bell system's TWX Teletype Exchange. He used the ordinary teletype circuit from New Hampshire to connect to the computing machine in Manhattan. Williams had built a terminal using special Baudot code to encode each keystroke for transmission. A decoder in New York translated the signals into ones that the calculator could understand. This was the beginning of remote control computing.

The Modem

What was needed was a self-contained device and standards for converting between a computer's digital outputs and the type of signal required for transmission on the analog phone lines. Modems convert the computer's digital signals to analog signals that can be transmitted on the phone system's limited bandwidth analog lines. At the receiving computer, another modem reconverts the analog signal back to the digital signals required for the computer.

The early phone systems were analog throughout. Multiple conversations were carried on frequency shifted signals. When the analog voice signal reaches a switching station it is converted into digital signals, which are much easier to multiplex and process than analog signals. What happens to the computer's digital signal is this:

1. The modem converts a digital signal to an analog signal.
2. The phone system converts the analog signal to digital for processing.
3. The phone system converts digital back to analog for transmission on the phone lines.
4. The modem converts the analog back to digital for use in the computer.

It's a wonder that this system works at all. Except for the external lines between the phone and the switching centers, today's modern phone system is almost completely digital. Digital phone systems provide a much more straightforward path for communication between digital computers.

Initial Hurdles

Although the phone system's bandwidth is fine for voice transmission, modem designers had to develop complicated modulation techniques to squeeze high speed digital signals into the voice band. The limited bandwidth of the commercial phone's analog system is only one roadblock to reliable, high-speed communications. Echoes from different frequencies traveling at different speeds, noise on the lines, and bad connections spelled doom for the early modem-based communications systems. Although a little static or voice echo won't destroy a conversation, the problems are devastating to the complex digital/analog modulation techniques that modems use.

Cleaning Up the Phone Signal

In 1964, Robert W. Lucky of Bell Labs developed an automatic line equalizer that filters out echoes and line noise.

> **NOTE**
>
> Although the phone system does provide equalization, the equalization was designed for voice messages and the modem turns it off with a 2100 Hz tone. Some earlier phone systems (pre-1960) won't know how to turn their equalization off, which will cause problems.

Lucky's equalizer required a training period of one or two seconds. During the training period the originating modem sends sample pulses. The equalizer examines the sample pulses and measures the echoes, generating artificial echoes to negate the ones that caused distortion. The technique was later improved to counteract echoes continuously without a training period. Today the method is called *adaptive equalization.* Adaptive equalization coupled with new modulation techniques, improved error correction, and more reliable hardware have improved transmission rates over phone lines, making low-cost, reasonable speed modems a reality.

Acoustic Couplers

Another problem was the need to use acoustic couplers. Acoustic couplers are little more than a microphone and speaker in a cradle that accepts the standard phone handset. This couples the modem to the phone lines by sound through the air rather than by directly connecting to the phone system. The method is similar to recording a compact disk by placing a microphone in front of the audio speakers instead of just connecting the CD player directly to the recorder.

In 1968 the Carterfone Decision ended the prohibition that prevented the connection of foreign equipment directly to the telephone system. This reduced the modem's cost and improved reliability considerably, and today modem sales are booming.

How Fast Can It Go?

How high can modem data rates go? To answer this , first we must understand the difference between effective and actual data rate. The actual data rate is the number of data bits transmitted per unit of time, while effective data rate takes digital data compression into account. Compression ranges from simple methods that replace strings of 1's with special codes to those that replace repeating characters in the ASCII domain to more sophisticated systems that look for redundancies found in graphical, audio, or other data.

Compression will lessen the amount of data transmitted, but whether you compress or not, more data must be added to provide redundancy for error checking and correction at the other end of the transmission.

There are fractal techniques that compress images into recursive components to theoretically yield compression ratios for graphic images of higher than 10,000 to one. Such systems require enormous computational power for compression and less for reconstruction. The term *video modem* is already being used in the trade press. Using fractal compression techniques, the video modem could transmit compressed real time video over conventional analog phone circuits.

Currently, data compressions are between 1, which is no compression at all, to a ratio of 4 to 1 for program source and assembly language files. At that rate, every compressed byte sent would get as many as four bytes of real data back. The effective data rate of a modem transmitting at 9600 bits/second data that has been compressed by a factor of 4 to 1 is 4 by 9600, or 38,400. The following data compression table shows the ratios you can expect. The popular formats .arc and .zip can compress data prior to transmission or the modem can do the compression and decompression on the fly.

Item	Ratio
assembly language	3.5
pictures images	2.8

```
precompressed (.ARC files)  ....................... 1.3
random data  ................................................ 1.1
program source code  .................................. 3.3
spreadsheet data  ......................................... 2.8
ASCII text  .................................................... 3.2
```

The maximum possible transmission rates on analog systems is defined by *Shannon's Law*. According to the law, the limit occurs at 30,000 bps with a 30db signal to noise ratio. A perfect Shannon engine using a 4-1 data compression ratio yields 120,000 bps as the upper limit for an effective data rate.

Before resigning yourself to this limit, remember that people told the Wright Brothers they'd never fly. One way to increase the rate above the 120,000 bps would be to use enhanced data compression techniques, such as the fractal compression techniques discussed later. Another would be to use an anti-Shannon engine that would better understand the nature of the noise. Active research in noise modeling shows that some noise could be characterized by systems that are more deterministic than is currently supposed. The study of chaos and fractals is beginning to shed light in this area as systems previously thought to be random may indeed be deterministic, though chaotic. Such behavior can be accurately mathematically modeled so that, for example, non-random noise sources could be canceled.

Digital Phone Lines to the Rescue?

At first it was thought that the four-line DDS digital phone system would quickly surface as the global communications medium. Such systems can provide up to 1.5 Mbits/second transfer rates. Although an Integrated Service Digital Network (ISDN) standard is coming, it's hard to replace the low-cost phone lines in everyone's home. Availability of cost-effective modems, improved equalization circuits, and better modulation techniques, give modems reliable transmission rates up to 30,000 bps.

3.2   Modem Characteristics

Among the more important attributes of modems are speed, error correction and data compression capabilities, and programmable features.

Error Checking and Correction

Error checking and correction occur in three places:

1. ***RS-232 interface parity*** – Data passing through an RS-232 serial interface (external modems are connected this way) are subject to parity checks performed in the ACIA chip that implements the serial interface. The bit is calculated for each character passing through the ACIA. The parity bit is calculated such that the sum of bits including the parity bit come out as an odd or even number, called odd or even parity. The parity bit is sent as the highest-order bit of each transmitted character. The receiving computer's serial interface recalculates the parity bit and if it is not the same, an odd number of errors occurred.◼ As a result of the error, the ACIA chip will generate an interrupt. It is then up to the communications software to do something about the error; probably retransmit the block of data again.

◼ Usually one error occurs, and one is an odd number.

2. ***Software protocols*** – Rather than depend upon the serial interface hardware to detect errors, the data can be blocked and formatted prior to transmission and

logically redundant data added before the data is sent to the serial interface. On the receiving end, this data can be processed, and used not only for error detection, but also for error correction. Popular software protocols are Xmodem and Kermit. The software protocol places the error checking burden on the DtC CPU.

3. *Detection/correction in the modem* – In this case the modem itself implements the error checking algorithms and protocols. Most 2400 bps and above modems implement their own error checking.

> **NOTE**
>
> The complexity and number of extra bits that must be added to transmitted data for detecting and correcting errors on the other end depend on how many consecutive errors need to be detected and corrected. Since detection is easier than correction, a given system may be able to detect more consecutive errors than it is able to correct.

In the typical communications scenario, all three methods might be used.

Terms

The following terms are often used when discussing modems:

- *Baud* – This is the rate at which the carrier containing the transmitting signal changes. The more complex modulation techniques can encode several data bits into each signal change. A modulated carrier might be changing 600 times per second (600 baud), and each change could be further separated into a type of change. By encoding additional bits from the type of change encountered, a bit rate higher than the baud rate can be realized.

- *Bit rate* – The rate at which binary ones and zeros are transmitted over the communications interface.

- *Half and full duplex* – Half duplex can both transmit and receive, but not at the same time. Full duplex uses two signals, one for each direction of transmission. Full duplex requires more channel bandwidth and, as we shall see, is implemented in a variety of ingenious schemes.

- *Characters* – The transmitted characters originate in the DtC, pass through the RS-232 interface, and go on to the modem. The characters sent from the RS-232 serial interface are asynchronous and contain up to 11 bits per 8-bit character. The 11 bits include 7 for standard ASCII, or 8 if binary data is to be transmitted, 2 or 3 start and stop bits to indicate where one character ends and the next begins, and a few bits for a parity check.

External vs. Internal Modems

External modems accept a DtC's RS-232C serial interfaces signals and can therefore be used on almost any DtC that implements a serial interface. All you need is a proper cable between the DtC's serial connector and the external modem connector. The external modem usually implements LEDs with flashing that can help troubleshoot problems. The external modem has an advantage over the internal modem: when the external modem crashes, you can reset it by repowering. Internal modems connect more intimately with DtC data sources, often bypassing the RS-232C aspect of the data. Internal modems can be more intimately interfaced to DtC DMA, interrupts, and shared memory than external modems can. A more intimate connection can produce higher transmission rates with lower CPU involvement. Data buffering is improved and higher levels of communication are made possible by the more intimate contact a modem has with DtC internals. Internal modems, however, can operate only on a specific DtC due to the required bus connection. Some internal modems provide external RS-232 connections.

The CPU generally doesn't have the computing power to carry out the variety of modem functions. Just getting 9600 bps data to the modem over the serial interface can be a problem, which is why internal modems are often used. If it is internal, the modem can use DMA buffering, shared memory, and other more intimate DtC resources. If the modem is external, the DtC must first pump the data through the serial interface in standard RS-232 format. Other difficult functions for the DtC involve manipulation of modem-specific quantities, better done by the modem itself. The sophisticated error checking, correction, and modulation schemes described later involve hardware and special CPU capability that simply doesn't yet exist in a DtC.

Intelligent Modems

In addition to the powerful modulation, data compression, error checking, and noise suppression capabilities of a modem, most modems incorporate a suite of programmable functions that are useful for a variety of automated communications applications. The intelligent modem has a built-in microcomputer that gives it considerable functional power. The intelligent capabilities are used in conjunction with communication or other applications software operating on a DtC.

Intelligent modem functions include:

- *Character filtering* – The modem can filter out unwanted characters, which is useful for file checking and conversion on the fly.

- *Automatic session handling* – Through built-in scripting languages and automatic session handling, some modems can locally execute their own software that can control the scenario between the DtC and the system on the other end without any DtC intervention. For instance, you can automate a complex log-on procedure or you can create a script for calling different bulletin boards to selectively download software.

  Most DtC communications software programs have their own scripting capability, which is more functional and flexible than that found in a programmable modem. The choice of which to use is a trade-off between transparent modem operation and dedicating the DtC to control the scripting. Of course, the scripting could be performed as a background process.

- *Phone number storage* – Modems can store and manage phone numbers in their own local memory.

- *Asynchronous to synchronous* – Some modems can switch to synchronous communication modes once a connection is established after the initial handshake. Synchronous modes are compatible with some higher-level communication protocols and are more effective for error-free data transmissions.

- *Progress reporting* – Modems can report busy, no dial tone, or no answer conditions during automatic telephone dialing operations.

- *Volume* – Some modems have internal speakers so you can monitor the phone data or voice, and the sound level can be software adjustable.

- **Configuration** – Some modems save their configurations for answering modes, type of transmissions, and other internal characteristics in non-volatile RAM. The modem will report its configuration to the DtC when called for. Other modems contain configuration switches that control the on-board modem functions. When trouble arises in DtC modem communications, be sure to check the switch settings and the cabling between the modem and the DtC serial interface.

- **Dialing and answering support** – Most modems can dial out and answer an incoming telephone call after any number of rings. Dialing features include repeat dialing. Coupling dialing and answering support with robust communications software integrates phone capability with the DtC, as well as permits remote control applications.

Most intelligent functions are invoked by special function codes not ordinarily transmitted in a communications session.

You may be faced with deciding where to implement intelligent modem functions. It is best to perform the more general functions of character filtering and session handling in PC software, and there many powerful languages available on a DtC for this purpose. Modem-specific functions such as dialing and answering must necessarily be performed by the modem, which incorporates the requisite dialing and answering hardware. By sending commands to the modem, you can control dialing speed and the number of rings before the phone is answered. The Hayes standard, named after the popular Hayes modem company, has become the de facto standard that defines how the various intelligent features are implemented. Most intelligent modems incorporate this standard.

3.3   Modem Protocols

There are three main standards of modem protocol: transmission, error correction, and compression.

Transmission Standards

Modem transmissions standards will be classified as low, medium, and high speed. While the low-speed 300 bps modem is practically extinct, the 2400 bps modem is now popular, and soon 9600 and above modems will be standard fare. In the medium-speed modems, more complicated phase and amplitude modulation techniques are used to encode the digital data, allowing more bit patterns per carrier change. High-speed modems that approach Shannon's limit have particularly sophisticated schemes for squeezing high bit rates into the limited phone system bandwidth.

Table 36 lists the most popular transmission standards.

Perform-ance	Standard	Modulation Technique	Bit Rate	Baud Rate	Common Error Checking
Low	AT&T Bell 103	FSK	300	300	Software
Medium	AT&T Bell 212A	PSK	1200	600	Software, MNP
Medium	CCITT V.22 bis	QAM	2400	600	MNP
High	CCITT V.29	QAM	9600	600	MNP

Perform-ance	Standard	Modulation Technique	Bit Rate	Baud Rate	Common Error Checking
High	CCITT V.32	QAM Echo	9600	2400	CCITT V.42
High	CCITT V.32 bis	QAM Echo	14,500	2400	CCITT V.42

Table 36. Popular transmission standards: All of the standards listed are full duplex with the exception of the CCITT V.29.

AT&T Bell 103: The Bell 103 standard uses frequency shift keying (FSK) modulation. With FSK, a carrier frequency is shifted to one of two frequencies depending upon the transmitted one or zero. For duplex operation, four frequencies are required. The specification allows bit rates of 300. Error checking is performed with software such as Xmodem or Kermit or in the serial interface with parity checks.

AT&T Bell 212A: The Bell 212A achieves 1200 bps by encoding two digital bits per baud or carrier change. The modulation, known as quadrature phase modulation, produces four possible states of phase of the carrier (0, 90, 180, or 270) per baud. The baud rate, that is, the rate at which the carrier can be in one of the above four states, is 600. Each state represents one of the possible four combinations of two bits. The four states are encoded into two bits, which doubles the bit rate to 1200 bps. Most 1200 bps modems can sense 300 bps rates and will automatically drop back to 300 bps if line quality is bad.

CCITT V.22 bis: The CCITT (International Telegraph and Telephone Consultative Committee) V.22 bis is a modulation scheme that encodes 4 digital bits per 600 baud carrier change through quadrature amplitude modulation (QAM). Sixteen different modulation states, called a 16-point constellation, are provided per baud. Each state involves one of the possible 16 combinations of four digital bits. Thus, the bit rate is increased from 600 to 2400 bps. Most 2400 bps modems can sense 1200 bps transmissions and will automatically drop to 1200 bps transmissions and further down to 300 bps if line quality is bad. Universal compatibility on 2400 bps is guaranteed with V.22 bis.

CCITT V.32: The CCITT V.32 standard groups data into 4-byte nibbles similar to the V.22 bis, however, the carrier modulation rate is increased to 2400 baud and 9600 bps transmission rates are achieved. Increasing the modulation rate to 2400 uses up most of the 3000 Hz telephone channel bandwidth with half duplex operation (CCITT V.29), leaving room for only one 2400 baud data channel. To get around the problem, V.32 modems use *echo canceling* to achieve full duplex. Both modems transmit their data at the same time, but each one cancels out its own signal to be left with the signal received from the remote modem.

Although the signals overlap and interfere, the modem knows what it transmitted and is, at every instant, able to create scaled and inverted copies. The copies are added to the received data, and the modem cancels its own transmitted signal. The DSP digital signal processors in the modem operate at 20-30 MIPS, which is several times the power of the ordinary DtC. Processing is extremely complicated and expensive. Through *trellis encoding*, a fifth bit (32 modulation states) is created for error checking.

Alternatives to V.32

Several alternative schemes have been advanced for the expensive V.32 modems. These include:

- **Ping-pong** – Using buffers and the V.29 half-duplex standards the two modems automatically take turns transmitting, rapidly switching their carriers on and off.

- **Statistical duplexing** – This method adds a low-speed reverse channel outside the V.29 pass band that handles data at keyboard rates or 300 baud. The two modems watch the relative queue length of their I/O buffers for changes in the conversation, or for who is transmitting and receiving and at what rates. The modems exchange control information to know when to change the high/low speed channel assignments.

- **Data compression** – This method uses the less expensive 2400 baud modems with data compression, however, to reach 9600 bps, high levels of compression are required. Don't be overly impressed with the 9600 bps rate. This is an effective rate. Recall that 9600 bps actual data rate modems can transmit at an effective data rate of 38.4 Kbps, which is four times 9600 bps.

- **Spread spectrum** – This method spreads hundreds of individually slowly-modulated carrier tones across the telephone line bandwidth. The method recognizes and avoids bad spots in the telephone line, using carrier tones in those areas. The system self-adjusts its bit rate incrementally for maximum operating speed. The method is called packetized ensemble protocol (PEP). One advantage is that bit rate fallbacks occur in smaller steps than other techniques.

- **CCIT V.32 bis** – In 1989 the CCITT tried to extend V.32 to a 14,400 bps rate. The rate requires considerably better echo cancelers and much improved receiver quality over V.32.

These techniques have revolutionized the use of the commercial analog phone systems for digital communications. Prior to 1984, data rates above 2400 were possible only with four-wire leased digital telephone lines.

Error Correction Protocols

V.42 is the current error correction standard. When errors are detected, blocks of data are retransmitted. The retransmission requirement means that numerous errors will affect transmission efficiency. The V.42 standard uses an automatic repeat request (ARQ) when CRC errors are detected.

> **NOTE**
>
> Cycle redundance checking (CRC) adds redundant and logically related bits to data blocks. Upon reception, the process is reversed, and errors are detected. Depending upon how many bits are added and the encoding and decoding method used, some CRC systems can not only detect, but also correct bad data on the receiving end.

V.42 uses a special fifth bit for every 4-bit nibble transmitted. The fifth bit requires a 32-state trellis modulation to produce the five bits as compared to the 16-state quadrature signal described in the V.32 standard. The fifth bit is logically related to the 4-bit nibbles and acts as an error check similar to parity. The trellis method allows the modem to examine several consecutive received signals and look for known patterns before deciding the value of the signal. The V.42 is the most popular method used in the V.32 9600 bps modems.

MNP-4 (Microcom networking protocol) is a popular, less sophisticated error checking system which uses a CRC method.

Compression Protocols

When you buying a modem, look for one of the following compression protocols:

- **CCITT V.42 bis** – V.42 bis is the first official standard for data compression and decompression in modems. It is similar to the popular .arc and .zip compression techniques used in DtC file compression programs. Compression ratios of up to 4:1 can be realized, and it provides automatic real time compression and decompression on all data flowing between the modems, transparent to DtC operations. V.42 bis is popular on the V.32 modems. Depending upon the type of data being transmitted, effective data rates up to 38,400 bps can be reached.

- **MNP-5** – Referred to as a sequential and frequent character compression method; 2x compression ratios are possible. The format is older, less efficient, and not compatible with .42 bis. However, it is quite popular.

- **MNP-7** – This is similar to MNP-5, but includes look-ahead character recognition and 3- 4x compression.

- **MNP-9** – This is similar to MNP-7, but includes V.32 transmission compatibility.

3.4 Modem Applications

DtC as a Terminal

You can use a modem to communicate with remote mainframes or other DtCs over such diversified services as CompuServe for the general public, ARPANet for the armed services, and IBM's Prodigy, which is sold in computer stores nationwide for a variety of uses, including weather service, computer shopping, and even games. The computer that houses the data is referred to as the host.

> **NOTE**
> When two computers interact, it is common to think of one as the master and the other as the slave. The master is the host, allowing visiting slave computers to provide keyboard input and display output. The slaves ask to download data and files or ask the host to execute programs.

Often the computer you are communicating with will expect the DtC to look like a terminal. Terminal emulation by modem will be most successful when the necessary editing and data preparation can be done offline, reducing the cost of the phone connection.

The degree of modem success is often determined by how well the specific terminal characteristics expected by the host have been emulated. Most DtC communications software programs permit a wide flexibility of emulation characteristics, including:

- ***Full-screen support*** – Using ANSI keyboard sequences, full-screen operation is supported by many communications programs. Full screen means that the cursor may be placed randomly anywhere on the screen. In contrast, line by line entry has all characters appear line by line from the bottom of the screen.

- ***Function-key implementation*** – Does the keyboard provide the same special function keys that the emulated terminal does?

- ***Display size*** – 80 by 25 line systems are well supported, but you might have trouble if you have to display 132-column and greater than 25-row text displays. The ability will depend on the particular display interface and monitor.

- ***Graphics display capability*** – Only special modem support software can emulate the intelligent graphics terminals that might be expected by a mainframe host. The emulations are usually at substantially lower resolution than the emulated terminal. Hard copy at the DtC, however, may have higher resolution. Many information services such as IBM's Prodigy expect DtCs on the other end, so you may find it frustrating to try to use a terminal instead.

- ***Color support*** – Full-color emulation is not performed by most modem support packages. Some color support is available, but is usually limited to choice of colors to identify highlighted and normal text.

Remote Control Operation

Now available is communications software that is designed to allow two DtCs to interact over the serial interface connections and modems. Connected this way, DtCs can control one another and can act even in parallel. The DtC keyboard and screen drivers are rerouted to serial interface I/O routines; so that keyboard input and screen output from either DtC can go to either or both DtCs. This configuration can be useful for computer training.

The remote DtC can be made to execute programs, edit data, view its hard drive; responding to commands that arrive by its serial interface. The remote control setup is good for remote data acquisitions and processing. Devices connected to remote DtCs can be controlled over coast-to-coast distances.

Many set up their DtCs as bulletin boards or remote store and forward devices. Using auto-answer modems, DtCs can provide a convenient way station for a group's messages and question-answer information. Most of the public domain software base is distributed by bulletin boards. DtCs can even be connected like Nintendo game toys over phone lines for two players to play games interactively.

Special-Purpose Modems

- ***Short haul modems*** – This modem, sometimes called a port extender, connects by telephone wires through communicating equipment to another short haul modem that converts analog signals back to digital signals. Port extenders are good to distances of up to one or two thousand feet. Now you can locate a printer in another building by running a standard phone wire, and not tie into the phone system at all.

- ***AC power circuit modems*** – This modem plugs into AC power circuits from the DtC's serial interface allowing you to use the power circuits to communicate to other communicating equipment on the same power line.

- *Fax* – Special modems are now being used for facsimile transmissions. This applications area is described next.

3.5   *Fax Modems*

There is a new class of modems with fax capability. Unfortunately, protocols and standards for faxing are different than those for typical data communications. The standards look like this:

- *Group 1* – Popular in the 1960s. Transmits one page per minute with 100 dpi resolution and originates as an analog phone signal.

- *Group 2* – Appeared in the1970s. It transmits one page per three minutes at 100 dpi resolution, using the analog signal directly.

- *Group 3* – Became available in the1980s. Signals originate as digital signals similar to a computer's. The protocol includes data compression and transmits at a minimum of 2400 bps. A 9600 bps setup can transmit a page in 30-60 seconds, depending on compressibility. Group 3 supports resolution of 100 dpi standard or 200 dpi high. Not all Group 3 protocols are compatible and Group 3 is not compatible with the data transmission standards previously discussed for data modems.

- *Group 4* – Group 4 was recently developed for digital telephone networks. A 400 dpi page can be transmitted in five to ten seconds.

Most of today's fax machines use the Group 3 protocol and are not compatible with Groups 1 and 2. Group 4 is used only on dedicated digital phone lines.

Independent Fax vs. DtC Fax

With dedicated fax machines, the data source is paper that is scanned. A DtC fax can come from the scanner/digitizer, a disk file, a DtC's screen presentation, or other networked computer resources. Text or graphics can be converted directly to faxable form without the loss of resolution that occurs in the scanning process. Merging files for transmission is also simple. Remember that all fax transmissions are APA displays. This includes characters that might originate as ASCII, but are converted to graphics representations for faxing.

Most DtC fax software programs support the popular graphics formats, including:

- .cut – Dr. Halo
- .pcx – PC Paintbrush
- .img – GEM Paint
- .msp – Microsoft Paint
- .pic – Lotus

Use DtC resources to schedule fax transmissions, take advantage of time zone differences, and keep a log of transmitted items. Connect the fax system to your database and use the phone directory to broadcast to multiple receivers. The DtC clock can be used to time and date stamp the fax, and redial capabilities will retry the line if it is busy.

On dedicated fax machines, output is distributed as hard copy either on the tabletop or on the floor beneath the fax machine. Communication privacy is difficult for shared messages and restricted access. Fax messages can be forwarded by the

DtC through networks and bulletin boards. Mailing lists can reduce unwanted faxes. Modem functions will be integrated on fax boards to a greater degree.

Particular features to look for in a fax modem include send and receive, 9600 bps transmission, and background operation compatible with your DtC graphics applications. Look also at image quality, and see if the Group 3 high-resolution mode is supported. Other nice features include erasure after transmission, redirecting output from printer to fax, sending current screen to fax, and gray scale and dithering capability.

The disadvantages of DtC fax systems are that DtC overhead increases and you will need a scanner if you don't want to be limited to sending only DtC data files. Most DtC fax boards are slower than dedicated fax machines, and dedicated fax machines are easier to operate. Page formatting and page numbering will be a problem since DtC fax products typically do not pay attention to page breaks in your input file nor do they add page numbers.

DtC Fax Requirements

To implement a fax modem, you'll need the following hardware:

- *Fax board* – The fax board will take up a full slot in the DtC, however, a regular data modem is usually included on the same board.

- *Image scanner* – Some fax boards connect directly to a scanner. With others faxing is a two-step process where the image is first brought into the DtC using the ordinary scanning software and hardware, then sent using fax software and hardware. Some fax software systems include a graphics editor to create simple graphics, and some accept graphics files from a variety of graphics file formats.

- *Printers* – The Group 3 protocol is the current standard, and the printer should support 200 by 200 resolution. Most 24-pin dot matrix printers can support this, but a laser printer will generate faster output.

- *Video display system* – All of Apple's display systems are adequate; MS-DOS compatibles must have at least EGA capability.

- *Mass storage* – Graphics images can be 8.5 by 11 inches at 200 dpi and when uncompressed will need 1/2 MB each. Even compressed form will take up at least 50K per image. Often, you'll have to convert to hard copy to avoid hard disk overload.

- *CPU* – Early fax boards needed considerable CPU resources and operated only in the foreground. The newer boards use the DtC CPU only to check the fax activity log and retrieve fax messages from the hard disk. Since you will be using the fax in conjunction with graphics software, CPUs with at least moderate power are recommended.

Integrating Fax Capability with Modems

Group 3 fax transmits at 9600 bps, which is far above today's popular 2400 baud modems emerging as the norm in the DtC world. Also, Group 3 fax uses special compression and error correction techniques different from those used in modems. We can classify three levels of fax modems:

- *Low* – These fax modems receive and transmit 2400 bps data, but transmit only 4800 bps of fax.

- **Medium** – These fax modems send and receive 2400 bps of data and can send or receive 9600 bps of fax.

- **High** – These fax modems accept scanner input directly, and transmit and receive both data and fax at 9600 bps.

Fax modems are priced as low as $100 and can go as high as $1000.

LAN Fax Applications

Network users can install a single fax board on the server and share it over the network. Optical character recognition is often used to solve the problem of fax ownership, putting the fax text not in ASCII, but in APA representation. Some software systems can look for a particular receiver name using character recognition, although it is expensive to do so. Fax boards can recognize touch tones sent after the transmission to determine ownership. Some even support direct inward dialing like a PBX line. The individual directly dials a unique fax number for the network.

The CAS Protocol

Communications Applications Specification (CAS) is a protocol that simplifies DtC communications, including modem transfers. Using CAS, a DtC software program with appropriate drivers can fax documents from within the program. There is no need to store first, leave the program, and then execute the fax software. Instead, while you are still in a word processor or graphics program, you can press a key and out goes the fax. The transmitted fax document will be cleaner, clearer, and sharper than if you printed it out and send it over a standalone fax.

> **EXAMPLE**
>
> WordPerfect users can obtain WordPerfect fax drivers for their specific fax board and then transfer their WP files directly to fax.

CAS has been in use since 1989 when Intel's PCEO (Personal Computer Enhancement Operation) adopted it. With a 10 MHz Intel 80186 microprocessor and 256K of memory, high-speed background transfer of binary files, E-mail, and facsimile images were performed without interrupting the DtC's foreground jobs.

3.6 Digital Phone Systems

Although most of the foregoing discussion pertains to the use of analog phone lines for data and fax transmissions, lower-cost digital phone lines are just around the corner.

The ISDN (Integrated Services Digital Network) is an international telecommunications standard for simultaneous voice, video, and data communications. The technology provides increased bandwidth and line quality over the standard twisted phone lines and costs 20-60% more than a standard phone connection.

Two systems are available:

1. **Basic** – Two 64-Kbit (B) channels for voice and data and one 16-Kbit (D) channel for network signaling and control, known as 2B+D. A 48-Kbit channel is provided for miscellaneous transmissions.

2. **Primary** – Twenty-three 64-Kbit (B) channels and one 64-Kbit (D) channel, known as the 23B+D system. This one can support up to 1.544-Mbit bidirectional transmission rates, and is as good a rate as most enjoy on their LANs.

Some corporations operate their own internal digital phone systems, using the extra digital wires that are routed together with the analog phone lines. DtCs can use these digital wires through simple digital interfaces. The interfaces merely strengthen the existing RS-232 serial digital signals to the level of the RS-422 digital signal that can carry between buildings.

A central switching computer usually controls the overall digital phone system and more intelligent DtC to digital phone system interfaces can communicate with the central computer or with one another for such functions as managing and menuing phone numbers. The DtC to digital phone system interfaces can communicate with each other, but not with analog modems. Digital phone systems still incorporate analog dial-in modems for external communications, which are internally switched over to the digital phone system.

Internal digital phone systems can provide a low-cost alternative to local area networks, but they are not as flexible and sustain much lower data rates.

3.7   Modem Summary

The DtC modem of the future will be a fully-integrated fax modem with capabilities such as voice answering. It could have data rates rivaling those found in today's digital networks. The modem will be integrated into most popular software applications. Some modems can encrypt and decrypt data for security applications that do not have dedicated cryptographic devices and lines. Inasmuch as modems are including more sophisticated communications functions, they are becoming indispensable peripherals.

4.0   Input Devices

To limit the mode of DtC access solely to a keyboard is akin to restricting your mode of travel to snow shoes. Many innovative devices are now available that enable you to interact with a computer more comfortably and productively than the keyboard allows. Although you'll usually use the keyboard for text entry, the devices described next will make other functions such as menu selection a more pleasant experience.

There are many ways of getting information into a DtC. Although you are probably most familiar with the keyboard as an input device, it can be supplemented with other useful input devices. If you look around, you'll see mice, light pens, voice recognizers, and devices for the handicapped that can track eye movements, enabling paralyzed individuals to operate DtCs by looking at different areas of a display screen.

4.1   Keyboards

Don't underestimate the importance of a keyboard. It is the primary channel of communication between you and your DtC. The better the match between you and it, the more work you will accomplish on a DtC.

Keyboard Operation

Inside the keyboard, keys are connected to a cross-point matrix. Each key represents a connection between a specific row and a specific column. The matrices contain from seven to ten rows and columns; the actual number depends upon how many different keys are on the keyboard.

When you press a key, you connect a particular row to a particular column in the matrix. Contacts are generally sensed by metallic contacts, or moving plates that don't touch, their proximity detected by capacitive effects. Some keyboards implement magnetic reeds that touch when a magnet on the key plunger comes near. They maintain good contact since, being in a vacuum, the reeds do not oxidize.

Required Preprocessing

Before a software application ever sees a character, some functions should already have occurred. The functions to be described are usually carried out inside the keyboard. The older dumb keyboards passed this load to DtC software.

- *Scanning* – The cross-point matrix works in the following manner. Each row of wires in the cross-point matrix is connected to an output port, while each column wire is connected to an input port. Each row is successively enabled by outputting a digital 1 on that row. Following each row enable, the column wires are read until the 1 registers. The software knows which row was enabled at the time of the "hit," so it knows which key was pressed. The scanning process is quite intensive and is done in dedicated hardware on the keyboard

- **Debouncing** – When you press a key, the physical connection being made is usually not just a simple off to on transition, but a noisy on and off sequence as the contacts, magnetic reeds, or capacitive plates bounce between mechanical states. If the software reading the keyboard interpreted every bounce as a new key, it would read multiple key presses. Debouncing can be accomplished by dedicated hardware logic circuits as well as by software that reads the first contact; then remains insensitive for a settling period; then becomes active again for the next key press.

- **N-key rollover** – N-key rollover is how the keyboard reacts to overlapping keypresses, or pressing more than one key at the same time. Generally, the last key pressed should register, but different keyboards will respond differently depending on their design. Some can be custom programmed.

- **Typematic** – Typematic is how long the keyboard will wait after you hold down a key before it begins to repeat; and how fast the repetition will occur. Some keyboards can provide typematic that waits, with the repeats getting faster the longer you hold down the key.

Keyboard Types

There are essentially three types of DtC keyboards, they differ in internal processing capability and in the type of output they give to the DtC.

Matrix Output

The keyboard provides matrix ports and the DtC has to take it from there. DtC software needs to provide scanning, debounce, rollover, typematic, and any other desired characteristics. This is termed a DtC software-intensive solution since all keyboard functionality has to be provided by the operating system. The early Commodore 64 and Radio Shack TRS-80 computers used this method, which placed a heavy burden on software, but made for less expensive hardware.

The matrix output method provides the most flexible keyboard system. The scanning and interpreting software is controlled by the DtC, and within the control software you can handle the key encoding process any way you wish. You could for example, have a unique code for pressing down a particular combination of ten keys simultaneously.

Parallel ASCII Output

ASCII keyboards have a microprocessor that does row/column scanning, key debouncing, typematic functions, n-key rollover, and then outputs the ASCII code for the character that is pressed. The output is a parallel 7- or 8-bit byte and a strobe. The strobe tells the DtC input port that a character is available to be read. ASCII keyboards were quite popular on the early 8-bit CP/M computers and were also found on the Apple II. The advantage was very low DtC software overhead because most programs can take ASCII input directly.

Serial Output

Most of today's DtCs use this type of keyboard. The serial output keyboard also uses a microprocessor on the keyboard but converts each keypress into a serial signal. The conversion to a serial signal has two advantages:

1. *Less wiring* – Fewer wires are needed between the keyboard and DtC, and this is important for the portable keyboards. Some are even wireless, transmitting the serial codes on an infrared or RF link. The *chicklet* keyboard on IBM's PC Junior used an infrared link.

> **NOTE**
>
> The keyboard was so named because the keys look just like Chicklet gum squares; little square protrusions, difficult to find, and a trying typing experience for most.

2. *More special keys and characters* – Serial output was used to achieve greater functionality and to accommodate more special keys because serial operation permitted more codes than were possible in the byte-wide 7- or 8-bit ASCII keyboards.

Levels of Programming

Keyboards can be programmed at two levels, 1) the keyboard microprocessor, and 2) the operating system or applications software. Even a keyboard is an example of multiprocessing.

Keyboard Microprocessor Controller

At the lowest level, microprocessor key acquisition functions can be modified. Functions better implemented at the keyboard include typematic, n-key rollover, debouncing, and scanning. Some keyboards provide a programming path to the keyboard controller for changing these functions.

Operating System

At the higher level, the operating system or applications software can be enhanced to react to keys collected by the keyboard's microprocessor. There is almost no limit to how sophisticated a keyboard can become with appropriate software enhancements. Some examples of keyboard enhancements at the higher level are:

- *Command editors* – Give a keyboard the apparent capability of recalling past DOS commands for re-execution or editing.

- *Macros* – Define keys to mean much more than just a single character. For example, set a key equal to a data entry prompt; followed by a pause for real entry; followed by more prompting.

- *Remapping* – Change the meaning of keys; for example, exchange the meanings of ESC and ALT if you don't like their current placements.

- *Type-ahead buffers* – Provide system memory buffers for accumulated keypresses so that you can type faster than perhaps software can accept the keys. The early MS-DOS operating system provided a 16 key type-ahead RAM buffer, which was adequate for most. The faster typists, however, could increase the buffer size with the usual assortment of public domain utilities. In most situations, the type-ahead buffer is implemented in system RAM and not in the keyboard.

- *Cursor positioning* – It is often necessary to provide more enhanced typematic functions than possible through the keyboard controller. For example, a variable repeating function could affect cursor direction or position. Cursor positioning enhancements can make cursor positioning more bearable for those without a mouse.

Many keyboard enhancements appear to change a keyboard's operational characteristics, but they really modify the software's reaction to what is coming out of the keyboard.

Popular Keyboards

Keyboards differ in their key arrangements, numbers of keys, key touch, and how they perform. The keyboard available for MS-DOS computers has become a de facto standard.

The IBM Selectric

IBM set a standard for keyboard layouts with their IBM Selectric typewriter. The Selectric standard included not only the usual QWERTY placement of alphabetic and numeric keys, but also the placement and size of the shift and carriage return keys. The Selectric served as a standard for early computer terminals. The early IBM PC departed from the Selectric layout because so many new keys were required, including a numerics keypad with cursor control, programmable function keys, and a second code modifier, the ALT key.

Original IBM PC and XT Keyboards

The original IBM PC and XT keyboards have shift and carriage return keys that are smaller than the ones on the Selectric and in a different location. Some key label names are cryptic arrows. Another characteristic of the XT keyboard is that the cursor controls share the numeric keypad keys. A NUM LOCK key toggles between the two. CAPS LOCK functions somewhat like it does on the Selectric except that it toggles between the caps lock and non-caps lock modes with successive hits. In caps lock mode, shifted characters type in lowercase and non-shifted characters type in uppercase, much to the surprise of many. Also, the CAPS LOCK and the SHIFT keys function differently. Shifting changes numbers to symbols, but CAPS LOCK does not. The original XT keyboards did not provide on-keyboard indicators of toggle key states, which frustrated users endlessly. You had to remember the last toggle, or note your error after you typed several incorrect characters.

IBM's original keyboards incorporated the click and feel of a Selectric. Initial reaction to the keyboard from experienced touch typists was negative, but after a while many grew used to its idiosyncrasies. A variety of public domain software attempted to cure a few of its ailments. These included programs that set NUM LOCK and CAPS LOCK to a predetermined state upon DOS initialization. Also, there were utilities that could display their states on screen above the usual software output.

AT-Style Keyboards

The IBM PC/AT keyboard corrected many of the prominent shortcomings of the PC/XT keyboard. Larger ENTER and SHIFT keys and LEDS to indicate CAPS LOCK, NUM LOCK, and SCROLL LOCK conditions were provided on the keyboard. The sound and feel of the original IBM PC/XT keyboard were kept, along with the number and placement of programmable function keys.

IBM's Enhanced Keyboard

IBM's enhanced keyboard is a compromise between its PC and mainframe terminal keyboards. The enhanced keyboard was introduced with IBM's PS/2 line, and it is widely available for the AT-style compatibles. The keyboard features 12 function keys across the top; the original XT and AT keyboards had only 10 on the side. The 12 function keys are more compatible with IBM terminals that have 12 PF keys. The enhanced keyboard also has separate cursor control and numeric keypads. The new keyboard may need a BIOS upgrade when used with an original IBM AT or an older AT-style MS-DOS computer.

Incompatible IBM Keyboards

Although both XT and AT keyboards implement the same microprocessor controllers, the keyboards are not electrically compatible, and therefore, not interchangeable.

The primary operational difference is that the AT has a programmable controller interface 8042 microprocessor between the keyboard serial output and the AT parallel bus. The 8042 is located on the AT motherboard, is programmable, performs parity checks, can run diagnostics on itself, and creates the IBM scan codes. The XT keyboard creates the scan codes internally and the XT interface to its keyboard is a dumb, serial to parallel converter.

MS-DOS Computer Keyboards

Most DtC systems come packaged with a keyboard, and you have little choice about what you get. MS-DOS computers are an exception to this rule since they are produced around the world by thousands of different manufacturers. You will have an incredible array of different keyboards from which to choose, particularly if you put together your own MS-DOS computer.

Combined XT/AT-Style Keyboards

Most compatible keyboard producers will sell you keyboards with an XT/AT slide switch on its bottom for plugging into either XT- or AT-style MS-DOS computers.

Costs, Features, and Reliability

Several American companies, notably Keytronics and Northgate, and hundreds of Asian producers have developed a line of keyboards that are functionally interchangeable with the IBM PC keyboards, but which improve upon IBM's keyboard inadequacies. Improvements include enlarging certain keys, adding more descriptive legends, colors, and better keyboard layouts. The keyboards also underwent changes in touch and in such mechanical characteristics as key travel. Users acquired built-in control over the audible/tactile click to suit personal preference.

As with modems, printers, and video interfaces, there are occasional compatibility problems with MS-DOS computer keyboards. However, the larger problem is mechanical reliability. You can find keyboards for a few dollars at computer shows, probably missing a key cap or two, as low as $25 from Asian producers, and for around $100 from U.S. and Japanese vendors. Almost any feature can be found: key placements, number of function keys, built-in trackballs, audible key clicks, different key feels, and switchable NUM LOCK and CAPS LOCK functions. Beware that the less well-known keyboards suffer from ailments such as poorly constructed interconnecting cables and plugs, poor RF interference shielding, static transmission to the DtC unit, poor mechanical contacts, and poor tactile feedback.

Some keyboards mimic IBM's enhanced keyboard, but function keys are returned to the left side of the keyboard, where many users prefer them. Preference for having function keys on the left side stems from the fact that many software products use function keys together with SHIFT, ALT, or CTRL keys, which are also located on the left side of most keyboards. Many users learn how to press multiple keys with the same hand, which is not easy if the function keys are at the top of the keyboard.

Scan Code Compatibility

The IBM and compatible keyboards are the serial output type and generate what IBM calls scan codes. The scan codes are IBM-specific two-byte quantities, different from ordinary ASCII, that identify which key was pressed. Each key generates a code corresponding to its position on the keyboard, with modifiers for use in conjunction such as SHIFT, CTRL, and ALT. Ultimately, the scan codes are converted to ASCII for use by an application or the operating system.

Keyboards that are to be compatible with IBM's or compatible among themselves must communicate with the DtC electrically like IBM's keyboard, but also must generate the same scan codes.

To give you an idea of possible problems with scan codes consider the following example. Certain software applications use the scan codes generated by the + and – keys on the keyboard's numerical keypad as control functions. The keypad codes are different from the scan codes generated by the + and – keys on the top row next to the numbers. Similarly, the number keys on the numeric keypad generate scan codes different from the top row number keys, even though their final ASCII translation is identical. A compatible keyboard must provide exactly the same arrangement for generating all of the scan codes available including the scan codes generated by all of the special function keys, and by shift keys, individually or together. Many software products depend on rather unusual keypresses to invoke their special actions. For example, to invoke a particular Windows screen saver program, press CTRL SHIFT and S at the same time.■ A compatible keyboard will need to produce exactly the same scan codes if it is to be compatible with MS-DOS software.

■ Screen savers darken the monitor after a predetermined period of keyboard inactivity to save screen phosphors.

Keyboard Selection Guidelines

Keyboard selection is a highly personal one; however, there are some factors of importance to all:

- *Keyboard feel* – This is mostly a matter of personal preference. You should try different keyboards to see which fits your typing speed and style best.

- *Keyboard key layout* – Try to use the same keyboard wherever you might be; at work or home. Different function keys, ESC, CTRL, ALT, locations; different ENTER and SHIFT key sizes, and different locations for CAPSLOCK, NUMLOCK, and SCROLL LOCK can seriously interfere with data entry.

- **Keyboard compatibility** – Make sure your keyboard functions properly with all of your applications. Talk to others using your applications with the same keyboard, DtC unit, and software.

- **Static susceptibility** – Some keyboards can transmit static discharges directly to the system unit while others are designed to prevent this.

- **Reliability** – Many vendor's keyboards have unreliable key switches, occasionally missing keys, or even typing multiple characters or wrong characters. The problem can depend upon typing speed.

- **Keyboard size** – Be particularly careful about keyboard size and how well the keys fit your fingers. The compact Macs and notebook DtCs squeeze keyboards to fit a small footprint. In order to do this and maintain reasonable spaces between the important character keys, function keys must be arranged in an approximately square aspect ratio, which can be very frustrating. Also, the distances between the very important ASCII character keys may be squeezed, dropping typing reliability considerably, and adjacent keys may bind occasionally. The problem is particularly irksome if you are hopping between two keyboards, one on a laptop, the other on a desktop. When purchasing a notebook DtC, be sure to try the keyboard for comfort. Some notebook DtCs let you plug in alternative keyboards. This, of course, will reduce its portability, but carrying a familiar keyboard with you might be worthwhile.

The Best Keyboard

The best keyboard, it turns out, is the one that you are used to. Along these lines, when setting up systems for multiple users who will be sharing machines such as DtC training centers or a secretarial pool, it is important that all keyboards in the same facility be identical. All keyboards should have identical layout and identical feel. Otherwise, those who have developed proficiency with one type of keyboard, will become significantly less productive when faced with another, regardless of how minor the variations seem to be.

4.2   Mice

■ A planchette is a small, three legged pointer on a Ouija board, moved by the fingers to spell out occult messages.

The main alternative to the keyboard for controlling a DtC is the position-sensing mouse. A mouse is a palm sized planchette-like device.■ As a keyboard supplement, the mouse's main purpose is to assist the keyboard's limited pointing and selecting capability. Both the mouse and higher-resolution position digitizing devices are heavily used in graphics applications. Similar input devices include the trackball, light pen, joystick, and touch screen, but none are as popular as the mouse. Voice recognition is still developing as a means for selecting items from menus; but applications that can be calibrated to recognize specific commands are available now.

The market teems with DtC mice. Popular mouse manufacturers are Microsoft, Logitech, and Mouse Systems.

Serial and Parallel Mice

On most MS-DOS computers, mice interface to existing RS-232 ports. If you want an external modem, which also requires that port, you will need two RS-232 ports, or a two-way serial switch. The serial mouse has the definite advantage of being portable. It plugs into any DtC that has an RS-232 serial interface. The parallel bus version of the mouse has higher resolution and speed, but a custom parallel interface board is required. The parallel mouse needs a bused interrupt. Jumpers on the board allow you to select an available interrupt. MS-DOS computer users often select an interrupt that is already being used by one of the RS-232 serial ports, causing a conflict. The parallel interface is implemented by a PIA (Parallel Interface Adapter) chip and is quite reliable.

Some video interfaces include this parallel mouse interface, which has become standardized thereby saving that additional slot. The parallel mouse connector is a small DIN connector and is notably different from ordinary serial cables. The differing cable can be a definite advantage for those with a variety of similar looking serial cables dangling about their DtC. Some mice are interfaced by infrared or radio frequency links and more special interfaces for the handicapped.

Mechanical and Optical Mice

One of two methods is commonly used to sense mouse position, 1) a hard rubber ball (mechanical), and 2) LED (optical) transmission. The mechanical method senses motion when the rubber ball underneath the mouse rolls. The ball turns wheels that are offset by 90 degrees. As the ball revolves, the wheels rotate and break LED beams inside the mouse. The resulting pulses are interpreted as positional changes by mouse driver software.

The optical method senses motion by LED emission from the bottom of the mouse, which is reflected from a crosshatched surface on a mouse pad. The LED-emitting mice are said to produce repeatable positions better than the rubber ball mice, but they do require special pads. The hard ball mice can roll on almost any surface. Both types of mouse have proven reliability and both require occasional cleaning.

Different Mouse Forms

- *Pen type* – The mouse doesn't even look like a mouse, but rather like a pen with a small rolling ball in its tip.
- *Trackball type* – A trackball is rolled instead of the mouse. Selection switches are also on the unit.

Pen and trackball mice are available that are software compatible with the usual hard rubber ball and LED mice. Other mouse differences include the number of digital switches for selecting and entering data, switch positioning, and the physical size and feel of the mouse. When you type on a keyboard, your fingers move around, stretching out and pulling in. Mousing sessions can leave your hand in the same clutched position for hours on end, so a proper-fitting mouse is important. Try a few different makes before you commit to one.

Primary Mouse Applications

- *Pointing to menu items and selections* – As you move the mouse, a cursor, usually an arrow, moves on the screen. When the cursor goes on top of what you want, or enters a particular box or icon, a click of the mouse button selects the item.

- *Dragging items around the screen* – To select an area to be dragged, you click on one corner, drag a rubber-band like box that expands to the opposite diagonal corner and click again. The trapped material is moved by moving the mouse. After you have dragged the material to where you want it, click again to let it go. The dragging method is much friendlier than attempting a move with keyboard cursor keys.

- *Drawing* – Use the mouse to draw on screen. Although movement resolution is limited, roughing out perimeters, indicating diagonals of boxes, and other functions are not inhibited. For more precise drawing and pointing, a graphics tablet should be used.

Mouse Software Drivers

As with other HB peripherals, hundreds of manufacturers produce mice. The most popular mice – by Microsoft, Logitech, and Mouse Systems – are software compatible, and if not, come with their own software drivers. Be sure that your application supports your mouse. Many vendors bundle their mice with mouse-oriented painting and drawing software and some even include Windows. The particular bundled software will vary by mouse manufacturer.

Mouse Languages

Some mice come with a mouse language. What's powerful about the language is that its operation can be transparent to the operating software. This way, you can add mouse-driven capabilities to programs that were never intended to have them.

A typical use of a mouse language would be to present a context-sensitive pop-up menu on the monitor screen. The menu would depend upon the current software program displaying on the same screen.

The language works as a background TSR, periodically checking video memory. When a particular pattern is seen, the pop-up menu is presented in a screen window. You pull down the menu with the mouse to the desired selection and press a button on the mouse. Magically, a string of characters is transmitted through a redirected keyboard driver to the foreground applications software. The applications software responds as though you had typed the command from the keyboard. The mouse language can operate independently of an existing program since video memory locations and their mapping to the video screen are absolute quantities, independent of any internal program memory buffers or procedures. This is not an integrated solution, but it is effective if you want to use a mouse with a non-mouse program. Popular applications include after-the-fact menuing and typing assistance for the handicapped.

4.3   Graphics Tablets

Graphics tablets, also known as digitizing pads, are high-resolution devices designed for precise positional user inputs. Precision is necessary for accurate CAD systems. Digitizing pads are typically capable of 0.001 to 0.0005" input resolution. Most digitizing pads are interfaced by the DtC serial interface. Most software applications operate at 9600 bps to reach respectable positional update rates. The update rate, or the number of times per second that a new position is transmitted from pad to DtC, is programmable on most digitizing pads. A typical pad size is 16" by 16", and provides a square foot of work space. Digitizing pads cost between $400 and $1200. Input to the pad is with a pen-like stylus or a mouse-like puck. Buttons on both instruments are used to execute functions selected on the screen by the cursor.

Many CAD and drawing software packages allow you to define menu areas on the digitizing pad for selecting often-used functions. These menu areas usually surround the active drawing area. What is menu and what is active drawing area is programmable by the software – the pad knows none of this. Some programs, notably the AutoLisp programming language of the AutoCAD program, provide a programming environment in which hierarchical menus and sophisticated prompting screens can be created. When properly programmed, complicated drawing activities may be engineered to be practically automatic. As with any programmable system, however, casual users will probably not reach high enough levels of expertise to take advantage of these programmable features.

4.4   Trackballs

Trackballs are similar to hard rubber ball mice, except that a hard plastic ball protrudes from the top of the ball enclosure and you roll the ball with your fingers, instead of rolling the mouse over a surface. The ball is faster than the mouse because the cursor can be made to fly across the screen with a single flick of the fingers. In contrast, the mouse has to be moved, picked up, and moved again to cover the same distance. Applications for the trackball include games, and they are particularly convenient for moving rapidly about large spreadsheets and other large displayed information systems, and for the physically handicapped. For accurate positioning, the mouse may be better; for rapid, less accurate movement, you'll find the trackball more suitable.

Many mouse vendors now provide trackballs with compatible interfaces, software drivers, and selection switches. Trackballs are showing up more frequently built into keyboards, especially on laptop computers, where a separate mouse could interfere with portability.

4.5   Joysticks

Joysticks are similar to mice except that motions of a perpendicular stick are sensed within the unit and the motions are used through software to move objects on screen.

Joysticks are generally used for absolute analog proportional control. Most joysticks contain two analog position sensors mounted on two perpendicular positioning axes. The farther the stick is deflected from the center position along each axis, the greater the output signals. On the video display, the outputs are converted to up/down, right/left movements. The magnitude and direction of joystick deflection governs the position of the controlled object on screen in an absolute manner. As you push on the joystick, the screen object moves in exact proportion. Software applications may make use of analog control for drawing, or for directly controlling objects on screen. The effect is particularly useful in a variety of games. The analog joysticks require special game ports with built-in A/D converters as well as digital input capability for their selection switches.

Some joysticks provide only digital outputs corresponding to north, south, east, and west movements of the joystick. Once a particular joystick position is reached, the digital output value changes and remains constant until the stick is brought back. The position at which the value changes is usually adjustable. Software is used to translate the joystick digital output to some incremental stepping rate of the on-screen object as long as the joystick is deflected past the on condition. When you click the joystick north, the object steps up the screen. When you return to center position, the object stops. When you click the joystick to south position, the object starts stepping down the screen. Likewise east and west joystick motions cause the object to move across the screen.

Joystick features to look for include the ability to calibrate the center position and an automatic return to center. On some joysticks, the return to center can be adjusted with respect to north-south and east-west positions.

Most HB computers have both digital and analog inputs for joysticks and include joystick commands in their BASIC programming languages. Joysticks are so popular that the Turbo C and Pascal languages provide joystick commands for use in game and educational software. MS-DOS computers implement a game port consisting of a digital interface and a low-grade 6-bit analog interface, considered adequate for game purposes. Some of the MS-DOS computer serial and parallel and memory expansion add-ons contain the game port, rather than dedicate an entire slot to it. Joysticks often include additional digital switches on the unit or on top of the stick for such things as pulling triggers, launching rockets, and firing missiles.

Most joysticks are DtC system specific. Although there are no standards for connecting cables, interfaces, and the number and type of switches, it is sometimes possible to buy joystick adapter connectors.

4.6   Barcode Readers

Similar to those found in the supermarket, you can buy barcode readers that interface to a DtC by its serial or parallel printer interface. The device scans barcodes with a laser beam and some can use a DtC printer to print the codes. Included software permits use with unmodified DtC software that can receive its input from the scanner as though it were coming through the keyboard. Barcode readers are often used in inventory management applications. The more popular DBMS software programs have add-on software for barcode readers. Sometimes they use redirected keyboard drivers, and sometimes assembly language libraries support the reader. Using the libraries, a developer can integrate the barcode reader capability into the software application.

4.7   Touch Panels

Touch panels fit over the viewing area of a video display screen, and are designed to detect your finger as you point to an area on the screen. Infrared transmitters and receivers are mounted around the edges of the panel to detect the x,y position of your pointing finger when one of the beams is interrupted. Touch panel screens are often interfaced by the RS-232 serial port, although some require custom parallel bus interfaces. The panels typically have from 10 to 20 LEDs per side; the number governing the pointing resolution. Touch screens are used in conjunction with interactive video systems for store directories, interactive training, and other applications where space is limited, reliability is important, and close proximity between what you point to and what you see is important. The technology is expensive, and many would like to see it become more popular. Imagine, moving word processor text around your monitor screen by pointing your finger instead of moving a clunky mouse. Although you can purchase touch panels that mount in front of an ordinary video display, the better touch panels are integrated within their display monitors for repeatability and reliability.

4.8   Light Pen

A light pen is a light-sensitive device that reacts to the scanning lines of a video monitor screen and provides a computer input that determines where on the monitor screen the light pen is pointing. An optical lens focuses the monitor scanning trace on a light sensor inside the pen. Many DtC hobbyists have built light pens from gutted felt-tip pens, using optical sensors purchased at a local Radio Shack store. Homemade pens can cost less than $10.00 while those that come with professional graphics workstations can cost over $1000.00.

There are two types of light pens: synchronized and unsynchronized. The synchronized type of light pen is an integral part of video interface circuitry. The pen uses special registers built into the video interface that track the position of the monitor scanning trace as it moves across the screen. When the monitor trace triggers the light pen sensor, a pulse from the pen freezes the registers, which can then be read to pinpoint the position of the light pen. Some languages, Microsoft BASIC, for example, have a `PEN ()` command that is used to determine pen position.

Unsynchronized light pens are not integrated with the video interface, so you, as the programmer, will have to determine the pen's position on the monitor screen. This is done by successively flashing various portions of the screen, then reading the pen to determine which flash resulted in a pen output. The method requires clever programming to minimize annoying screen flicker. This type of pen can be used only for indicating a small number of menu blocks on the screen because it is impractical to flash large portions of the screen. Items smaller than a single character can seldom be found by this technique. Pixel-level pointing is more practical with the synchronized light pen, although it is not reliable on the HB DtCs.

Applications for light pens on DtCs are generally limited to menu selection – pointing to characters or small rectangular blocks that are highlighted by your application and selected by the pen when you make a menu choice. Some synchronized pens can operate at pixel level, and can be used for drawing. The pixel level pens, while expensive, have good optics and operate with monitor screens designed for that purpose. HB DtC light pens are not particularly reliable because of the different types of monitors, varying ambient light conditions, inaccuracies in sensor optics, and restrictive pointing conditions. On higher-priced graphics workstations, more attention is paid to optical quality and to special monitors that are designed to work with light pens. In such cases light pens have higher resolution and allow you to draw lines on-screen. For DtC workstations, mice and touch screen panels are more reliable for selecting options by pointing.

4.9   Voice Input

Considerable research is underway in the area of continuous recognition or the ability to recognize speech in context in real time. Practical devices on DtCs, however, are limited to vocabularies that seldom can exceed 50 words. Special add-on boards provide the necessary signal processing power to perform the recognition function.

Applications for voice include command inputs to software products, particularly on assembly lines, and for use by the handicapped whose only ability to contact the computer may be by voice.

Reliability through Recognition Hierarchy

Since DtC-based speech recognition devices are reliable only with relatively small vocabularies, hierarchical vocabularies are used. In this situation, the word set being recognized is changed, depending on the particular recognition category required at any particular time. This can result in larger effective vocabularies, but complex programs for changing these vocabularies are required and are difficult to program and set up.

Since the entire recognition burden will be on the recognition peripheral processors, DtC CPU capability is not always an issue. The need for rapid retrieval of recognition libraries and large memory buffers for their temporary storage drive system requirements toward faster hard drives. The need to manage large amounts of vocabulary buffers in future systems will demand the memory management capabilities of the high-end CPUs. Open architecture is necessary since speech recognition peripherals usually plug into the DtC bus.

Current speech recognition research includes neural network technology and OCR techniques being applied to the speech recognition problem. There are reliable speech recognition systems, but they require computing platforms beyond the HB DtC. These speech recognition units cost up to $100,000 and plug into EP class DtCs. Speech recognition systems may also take the form of dedicated computers of minicomputer size.

Keyboard Replacement

The ability to emulate the keyboard with other devices is a practical application. We would all prefer to talk to our computers than type on keyboards. Creative inputs include pupil tracking by a device that forms an image of the eyeball and recognizes the pupil orientation, joystick control by chin movement, and galvanic devices that connect to fingers. There are even devices that can be strapped to the head to pick up brain waves and convert them into usable cursor positioning signals.

Two approaches can be taken when using alternate keyboard inputs for the handicapped. The first is to patch the operating system with appropriate drivers that can operate the existing software base transparently, as if the inputs were coming from the keyboard, while the second involves custom software to accept special inputs.

Using Existing Software

There are applications in which you would like devices to replace your keyboard entirely and transparently to your applications software base. Special software drivers can replace an existing keyboard driver, which will allow applications programs to use voice or character recognizer input. Moreover, the inputs can be used transparently or in such a manner that the applications software thinks that the characters came from the keyboard. The transparent methodology can be particularly useful for providing access to the entire software base.

NOTE

There is also much activity in output devices for the blind. These include large character monitors and Braille printers. Special software drivers can let a blind person read the monitor screen by moving a selection box around the screen, seeking out desired areas. The drivers provide this capability transparently to the applications software base.

In order to be successful the applications software base must be available without modification. A variety of creative schemes are used. The most common is to menu available selections and keypresses in a window on the same screen that is displaying the usual output. In this window will be a menu of available characters or selections, which can be scanned. When the appropriate character is reached, the individual activates a switch, joystick, or eyelid switch and the character is entered into the keyboard entry buffer as though it came from the keyboard. With a proportional joystick, the individual can point to the desired characters directly. Unfortunately, the transparent solutions are not integrated with the software that is being used.

Writing Custom Software

The second approach is to develop software for special input devices. Most of the existing software base would have to be rewritten to effectively use the input devices. Software really needs to be designed in the first place to be integrated with special inputs.

NOTE

Being integrated means that the software was designed around the special input device. For example, eye tracker software might not be practical for inputting individual characters. Instead, the user could put together larger items such as menued phrases to form messages. The focus of the software would be reliable phrase selection and intelligent message construction. Using an existing word processor transparently might supplement such a process, but would not replace it. Pointing to a single character at a time can be extremely frustrating if it takes a minute per character.

Optical Character Recognition (OCR)

OCR peripherals recognize characters in a wide variety of fonts. Documents may be fed by sheet feeding apparatus, or mouse-like scanners may be passed over the written information. OCR peripherals are quite reliable when used with the fonts they were designed for. Many allow you to upgrade to more fonts and can learn to read new fonts.

On some systems, new fonts are not restricted to characters, but can be music notes, electronic schema, or other symbols. As with speech recognition peripherals, some OCRs come with installable device drivers that allow them to work transparently with existing software. By redirecting normal input from the keyboard to the recognition device, you could enter data directly from the OCR into a database or document. Internal database or document formats are not a problem because the data appears to come from the keyboard.

OCR systems can be found in three configurations, arranged here in the order of their cost:

- **Low cost** – These systems use the common, standalone image scanners to read in digitized images of characters and run DtC software to perform the recognition functions. Since the DtC runs the recognition software, heavy restrictions are placed on recognition reliability and performance.

- **Medium cost** – More expensive systems can use ordinary scanners, but special processing add-on boards are used to perform the character recognition functions. The add-on hardware contains the necessary intelligence to recognize characters from the digitized bit maps. This is a complex, dedicated processing task, so high-end Motorola 68xxx, RISC, or ASIC processors are used on the boards. The boards themselves have from 2 to 4 MB of memory for algorithms and for managing the bit maps. The boards often have more processing power than the host DtC and cost from $500 to $4000. More expensive, accurate, and repeatable scanners are used for higher-end OCR systems. If you buy a scanner with OCR in mind, be sure to choose one that can be integrated with an add-on processing board, or at least one that is supported by DtC OCR software.

- **High cost** – Higher-cost OCR systems integrate both the scanner and character recognition processing hardware inside the same box. Integrated systems are the most reliable because the scanner is specially designed for character recognition. The interface to the DtC might be as simple as a serial interface through which the recognized characters flow. Other systems are completely dedicated to such functions as reading books for the blind.

In the medium to high cost systems the DtC is relegated to providing higher than recognition-level functions. The functions include recognition font storage, running the user interface, converting applications software file formats to allow seamless integration with a given word processor, spreadsheet, or database program with the OCR function.

In addition to the usual ASCII outputs, current DtC-based OCR systems can output a variety of text, spreadsheet, database, and graphics formats, including many word processor, desktop publisher, and graphics program formats. Figure 108

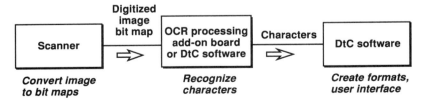

Figure 108.   OCR

shows the major components of a DtC-based OCR system, which includes the scanner, an OCR board, and the DtC. Each component plays a role in the character processing.

The choice of OCR systems depends on the type of image digitizing equipment you already have and the sophistication of character recognition required. OCRs that use low-cost image digitizers in conjunction with DtC add-on boards cost between $500 and $5000, while complete OCR peripherals, including an integrated image digitizer, can cost as much as $50,000, with commensurate performance capability. At the high end you can even get handwriting recognition.

Popular OCR methods include matrix matching, in which characters are fitted into defined matrices; omnifont, where certain symbol characteristics are matched; and neural networks. Many problems are associated with the character recognition process. They can fail to recognize kerning, proportional characters, letters joined in ligatures, broken characters (missing dots in the character matrix), underlined text, descenders, and skewed (italicized) characters.

OCR for forms is much easier than page-oriented systems because only certain entries are allowed in defined fields. Also, if the form and the entries are of a different color, the computer can be programmed to read only the entries.

More powerful and expensive OCRs can recognize handwriting under certain conditions. One such system lets you enter written data manually, using existing forms on special tablets. Included software allows custom forms to be used and accepts variable sized writing. Other systems being investigated at the National Archives recognize handwritten text from smudgy historical documents, including maps and other random images along with text.

4.10   Electronic Scratch Pads

The electronic scratch pad is a small computer that accepts handwriting as input. The advantage is that it can be small enough to carry to places where standard sized computers are too bulky. The scratch pad computer can hold many different forms. By storing just the entered data, the user need not carry any unnecessary forms. One particular system integrates a smaller than notebook sized MS-DOS computer with a magnetic touch screen; position is sensed by a pen's magnetic field.

Neural network technology is used to do the handwriting recognition and special developmental software is bundled with the system. The software is oriented toward developing data entry systems for handwriting input. Libraries include menuing, boxing, and appropriate dialogs for maximum throughput. Imagine your insurance agent giving you an estimate or your waiter getting your order on a electronic scratchpad. After entering your order, the waiter simply plugs the scratchpad unit into a desktop computer, which sends the order to the kitchen.

> **NOTE**
> As you might have guessed, some restaurants use desktop computers for proportioning ingredients, controlling ovens, and creating menus.

4.11   Image Input Devices

Images are entered by two different technologies, the video frame grabbers and the scanners.

Video Frame Grabbers

Video frame grabbers allow the DtC to capture a frame of live video information and convert the analog signal to digital form, which is then stored in video interface memory and subject to processing by the DtC CPU. The video image could be from a TV camera, a VCR, or a radar set. Frame grabbers can handle both monochromatic and color images. Through special-purpose on-board processors, a variety of image-processing capabilities are possible. Possibilities include edge enhancement, contrast adjustments, pixel management, mono/color conversions, dithering, and image compression and decompression.

Scanners

Scanners, also called hard copy digitizers, are photocopy-like devices that scan printed material. One of the more desirable special input peripherals, scanners are making the data entry process productive and hassle-free.

The matter that is scanned, textual or graphic, is first digitized into an APA image, and then stored on the DtC. Color scanners take multiple passes through different color filters, and their digital output is stored as multiple datasets. Resolutions range from 150 to 400 dpi.

Stationary bed scanning systems have moving scan heads that sweep across the paper, giving a more accurate scan than can the less expensive scanners that move the paper past a stationary head.

Hand-held scanners are becoming quite popular for convenience, but their images and repeatability are not as good. With time, more intelligent software will become available that can compensate for different scanning speeds and overlapping passes that occur in the hand scanning process. Some even have LEDs that verify skew between sweeps and tell you where and how fast to scan.

Low-cost scanners and image digitizers are available from Hewlett-Packard, Dest, Canon, Datacopy, IBM, Panasonic, and others. Scanners vary greatly in cost, depending on the type of processing that is built-in and the scanning resolution and repeatability. A good scanner to serve average needs can be acquired for around $300.

Scanner software can include functions for:

- *Vectorizing* – Some scanning software can convert the APA-type scanned images into vectorized or other formats so they can be exported to PC CAD and display graphics software packages accepting that form of data.

- *Area-sensitive processing* – Most scanning systems don't know the difference between characters or graphics images, although there are specialized systems that do, in fact, recognize text and provide area-sensitive processing of text vs. graphics images. This is necessary because different constraints apply to the reproduction of text and images.

- *Halftones* – Some systems can scan halftones rather than just off or on tone, and now color is available. Some systems can scan up to 16 shades of gray.

- *Graphics enhancement* – Some digitizers come with software for improving image quality; however, this software doesn't compete with the general drawing graphics software base.

Scanners with Drawing Programs

Most DtC drawing graphics programs will accept scanned-image formats. A variety of drawing graphics software from simple paint programs to full-power illustration and image enhancement software can be used to clean and dress up the scanned image. Capabilities as far ranging as adjusting individual pixels and image processing capability are available, and include contrast enhancement, color hues adjustments, aspect rations, and complex gray-scale toning. You can scan in a photograph, or even capture a video frame; and decorate it with your favorite drawing graphics program. Then you might include it in a document created by your desktop publisher through its graphic format import capability.

DtC System Requirements

The digitizing process is performed in the scanner, and what comes out is an APA type data stream. More expensive scanners that can recognize halftones, or provide area-sensitive processing will often, although not always, perform those functions internally. The extent to which DtC CPU resources are used for more complex operations will depend on higher performance CPUs.

Some OCR systems use common, standalone scanners for character input. Most will include a special processing add-on board for the DtC, others are software-only systems that use an existing image scanner and DtC software. If you buy a scanner with OCR in mind, be sure to choose one that can be integrated with an add-on processing board or that is supported by DtC OCR software. Those not using dedicated processing hardware will require high-end DtC CPUs because the character recognition burden is enormous.

Medium to high resolution video displays will be required if you want to view the scanned images interactively. Also, be advised that scanned images, particularly color and halftone images take up a good deal of space on a mass storage device, driving up its requirement. Lower-cost image scanners can simply plug into a serial interface, but scanned image data rates will be slow. Most scanners use custom interfaces to attain the necessary image data transfers to the DtC. Some scanners can interface directly to fax and OCR processing boards.

4.12   3-D Input Devices

There is increasing interest in the use of 3-D position inputs as a means for accurately reproducing the position of one's hand, or head. An applications area, known as virtual reality (VR), requires 3-D position inputs. There are two aspects to the virtual computing environment. The first is the generation and display of a 3-D environment. The second is the capability of a user to interact with data in 3-D using gestures to identify and alter the data. In a virtual reality system, you are presented with a three dimensional scene through which you can navigate and modify. Dedicated VR systems have been in existence for quite some time as flight trainers.

Researchers and inventors say that expanded computational techniques and input capabilities will permit new methods of working and playing in electronic fantasy worlds that will transform entertainment, education, engineering, and medicine. To achieve realistic interactions, input devices other than a keyboard or mouse are required.

The 3-D position sensors might be in a helmet, and eye movements might be used, to direct flight, for example. Future helmets might project 3-D images onto a screen inside the helmet rather than rely on a display monitor for creating scenes. Imaging helmets are already available in the home entertainment market.

The more popular hand-trackers measure hand position, movement, and articulation. The devices measure movements in a variety of ways:

- *Fiber optic cables* – Light transmission changes when cables are bent.

- *Flexible glove strips* – Flexible strips in a glove vary their resistivity when bending, tracking changes in hand orientation.

- *Ultrasound* – Ultrasound is beamed from two or three transmitters on the glove, and the sound is received on a few receivers juxtaposed on the display monitor. By measuring the difference in arrival times, position can be sensed. The ultrasound method is popular for Mattel's data glove used in Nintendo games.

- *Magnetic fields* – Measurement of yaw, roll, and pitch through movable and fixed magnetic fields through coils on the glove that move in relationship to fixed coils. The data glove concept can be extended into the data suit in which sensors are stitched to signal whole body movements. You can literally walk through an artificially generated scene. Although the computational requirements for usable systems are staggering, we can look forward to interesting adventures on future DtCs. Those who would say that there must be a limit to necessary CPU MIPs haven't yet left the ground.

5.0 Printers

Printer technologies have improved significantly in the last few years. They have become less expensive and more reliable. Every DtC workstation should have at least one. Hundreds of vendors are eager to supply you with almost any feature imaginable. Currently, the two most popular categories are dot matrix and laser printers.

At the outset, DtC printers can be divided into two sets of two categories. The first set categorizes by whether or not the printer supports graphics. The second set categorizes by impact and non-impact printers. The non-impact class members include thermal, thermal transfer, laser, electrostatic, and ink jet printers. They offer quieter operation and sometimes superior quality to dot matrix impact printers, but they do not allow the use of multipart forms and they often require special paper. Hard copy may be printed in a number of ways. Some important evaluation features are suggested in Table 37.

Feature	Thermal Dot Matrix	Impact Dot Matrix	Daisywheel	Laser	Band	Inkjet
Speed	Medium	Medium	Slow	Fast	Fast	Slow
Quality	Draft	Near-letter	Letter	Typeset	Draft	Draft
Graphics	Good	Good	Limited	Extensive	Limited	Good
No. copies	One	Several	Several	One	Several	One
Expendables	Paper	Paper ribbon	Paper ribbon	Paper toner	Paper ribbon	Ink
Cost	Low-Medium	Low-medium	Medium	High	High	Medium
Primary attribute	Color	Low-cost Draft	Low-cost letter quality	Text/graphics	Print speed	Color
Color	Yes	4-color ribbon	Yes	yes	Coming	Yes
Plots	Good	Good	Good	Excellent	Character only	Good

Table 37.   Printing methods

The table compares and contrasts the more important features of different types of printers. Each of these printer categories boasts a number of features that should be compared when matching your application to a printer. *PC Magazine* publishes an annual round-up of up to twenty features for at least a hundred different printers. The most recent comparison would be a good place to start when evaluating printers for your application.

5.1 Operational Modes

The following is provided as background together with explanations of some jargon that will be useful for subsequent discussions on different types of printers. Emphasis is on the newer technology.

Text Mode Characters

In text mode, characters are formed by the printer using an internal process that takes ASCII codes from the printer interface and maps them to the characters to be printed by a character-generating ROM. The principal characteristics of text mode are:

- *Applications software simplicity* – Applications software needs to send only ASCII character codes to the printer.

- *Limited font control* – The font of characters printed is not within DtC software control, but is contained within the printer's character ROM. Daisywheel printers could be stopped by a font change code, whereupon the operator could manually switch daisywheels and mount another typeface or set of special characters.

- *Minimal character height control* – Minimal vertical character size capability is due to an inability to control the printing algorithms also contained in ROM on the printer.

- *Minimal character width control* – Only a few horizontal character size and density controls not related to font are possible in text mode. These include compressed, 132 as compared with 80 characters per line; width, 40 characters per line; and a few modes that print more dots horizontally, slightly feed the paper between multiple head passes, and strike the paper harder. Combined use of these modes will improve the appearance of the characters, but will reduce the printing speed by a factor of as much as four.

- *Limited graphics* – Limited to the supported extended ASCII character set.

Downloadable Character Sets

An innovation in printers gave them the ability to implement additional font specifications that could be downloaded from the DtC to a RAM in the printer. This provided the same simplicity – one ASCII code transmitted from DtC to printer to get a character printed – but you could choose the particular font. To change the font, you simply downloaded a different font. With software available for DtCs, you can graphically design the desired character font specifications and then download the font to the printer. Public domain utilities are available that can download fonts as pop-up functions, transparent to the operating program.

Text/Graphics Mode Characters

In text/graphics mode, the printer operates much the same as in text mode except that its internal algorithms and character ROM can now handle character specifications for the 128 upper ASCII or extended codes between decimal 128 and 255. These codes specify special symbols including Greek characters, hearts, pointers, and box characters with permutations of horizontal and vertical lines sufficient for drawing fancy boxes. When properly printed, these characters provide a crude but often efficient graphics capability. The advantage of the text/graphics mode is that applications may still use the standard BIOS printer drivers, which generally map bytes to printed characters, yet go on to possess some graphics capability.

The major problem encountered when using the text/graphics mode is that different printers implement different characters for the upper codes. Worse yet, the DtC video drivers may not print the same characters for extended ASCII codes on the video screen. Therefore, when you do a screen dump that sends text on the screen to the printer, the resulting printout may not be the same as what is on the display screen. If the printer has downloadable font capability, you will be able to download the appropriate character set to match that of the DtC video driver.

Bit-Mapped Mode

Also called APA or graphics mode, this printer innovation is the ability to control printing in a way that disables the printer's internal font specification and allows independent control of each printed dot. The printer is placed in graphics mode with special control codes, and the data transmitted to the printer is no longer interpreted as character codes, but rather as individual dot printing codes. The following characteristics emerge:

- Graphics images may be printed.
- Data rates higher than in text mode are required between DtC and printer to print characters.
- There is much greater print flexibility than in text mode. Since printed dots are controlled individually, any size and font character may be printed.

Special Printer Drivers

The burden of printing special character fonts in the APA mode can be localized to a single software driver, which can replace the standard BIOS printer driver. The software application may still think of the printer as being in text mode, but ASCII characters transmitted to BIOS will be intercepted and appropriate APA sequences transmitted to the printer to generate the required characters. Pop-up menus offer you a variety of fonts, with more flexibility than the downloadable fonts. Greater flexibility comes about because the printer is operating in a graphics mode, rather than in the more constrained text mode.

Near Letter Quality Characters

Near letter quality (NLQ) is a particularly creative combination of a font specification and various print densities and sizes that produces fine printed characters. The dots can hardly be seen, and the printed characters look almost as if they were produced by laser printers. Near letter quality may be achieved in two ways:

1. The printer implements NLQ internally in what appears to software as a text mode. You simply send a single command to the printer indicating NLQ mode, or press a button on the printer's front panel to accomplish the same thing. Pressing a printer button has the advantage that mode selection is independent of the software

running. Different applications carry out special printer functions in different ways, and it is not easy to remember them all.

2. Modification of the DOS printer driver to print characters in the APA mode.

These modes are popular and a printer should be able to implement both.

Similarities to Video Interfaces

Printers are similar to video monitor interfaces. Both support character and bit-mapped or APA modes and downloadable character fonts. Because of the similarities it should be a simple matter to print output, which is often the display on a monitor screen. But this is seldom the case because the DtC video and printer interfaces are not integrated and standards, such as PostScript, have only recently been established for graphics and combined text/graphics operations. Images seen on the CRT are stored in the addressable memory of the DtC, while images sent to the printer may exist initially in applications programs memory and file areas. The disparity between video screen resolution and printer type, with little standardization in the area of commonly-used functions, compound the problem. Utilities that match video screen to printer can help resolve this difficulty.

5.2 Daisywheel Printers

Daisywheel printers print characters by the impact of a 'petal' on a 'daisywheel' through an inked ribbon onto paper. There are also other types of impact printers, including a 'thimble', other orientations of a daisywheel, a rotating drum, and the older Selectric ball. Daisywheel printers generally have a 15" carriage, although smaller ones can be found. All paper handling methods are supported.

Although some daisywheel print heads support individual pixel characters, and, when appropriately controlled, can print a graphics image, the process is complex, time consuming, supported by few applications, and therefore not recommended.

Some daisywheel printers have two heads, which lets you select characters from two different character sets. Different daisywheels are available for a variety of character types and styles, but they must be exchanged manually on the printer. Dot matrix and laser printers can download any number of different character styles under software control. The daisywheel printer became popular for a time, particularly with staff members accustomed to manual typewriters who wished to transition smoothly from manual to computer-driven printing. Because of the advantages of dot matrix and laser printers, daisywheels are not recommended for DtC use.

5.3 Dot Matrix Printer

Basic Design

Dot matrix printers have a print head that contains a number of wires that are fired electrically at the paper through an ink-soaked ribbon. As the print head moves across the paper, characters are formed. The width of these characters depends upon the printer mode selected and other software factors. When in text mode, character height is limited to the height of the print head and width to a few different dimensions selectable by escape sequences. These sequences are standardized in the dot matrix printer industry.

> **NOTE**
>
> The escape sequence is the escape character (ASCII 27) followed by other ASCII characters that will act as printer control characters.

Early Dot Matrix Printers

The earliest dot matrix printers passed a column of seven wires over the paper, primarily in a character-mapped text mode. This raised two major problems. First, the characters were not fully formed and betrayed their origin; they looked as if they came from a computer because the coarse dot pattern made by the wires was clearly visible. Secondly, there was insufficient resolution to place the descenders of the lower case p, q, g, and y below the baseline. These characters were written above the baseline and often with truncated descenders. Because of such deficiencies, outputs from these printers are not universally acceptable.

Until recently, dot matrix printers were inferior in text quality to daisywheels. Where daisywheel printers provided fully-formed characters, dot matrix text looked like a collection of dots that typified impersonal computer output.

Dot Matrix Improvements

Dot matrix printers greatly improved in the 1980s, adding such features as variable impact force, fine control of paper advance, multiple print head passes, graphics modes, multiple-color ribbon, and more wires in the print head for finer resolution. These printers now provide what many individuals consider true letter quality.

When these printers are in APA mode, a particular set of commands are used to control the print heads. When in text graphics mode, a specific set of extended ASCII codes specify special graphics characters. The specific combinations of wires that are used to form the various characters is determined by choice of font. Dot matrix printers can support up to a dozen built-in fonts, as well as the capability of downloading fonts from other sources. Many commercial and public domain utilities are available for downloading these special fonts.

When in bit-mapped mode, these printers generate characters of any size and typeface by software running on the DtC, and therefore the concept of downloaded character fonts does not apply.

NLQ Mode

Two advances enhanced the output quality of dot matrix printers: more print wires in the same space, and multiple pass techniques. These features improved the smoothness of the characters on the paper. The output became usable for business purposes, but it was still not as good as daisywheel or laser printer output. This type of output is called *correspondence quality* or *near letter quality*. The most recent dot matrix printers contain a 24-pin printhead, which is capable of producing NLQ in a single pass, and true letter quality in multiple passes.

Today, whether the output of high-density 24-pin printhead dot matrix printers is comparable to daisywheel impact print is debatable and a matter of personal preference. Dot matrix printers are faster than daisywheel printers.

Dot matrix printers have two standard platen widths: 10", which allows an 8.5" sheet of paper to be loaded in portrait, and 15", which allows portrait and landscape paper loading, as well as the use of standard data processing paper. Up to 132 characters can be printed per row on standard paper and up to 240 characters can be printed on data processing paper. If you operate large spreadsheets, for instance, you might want to choose the 15-inch platen. Dot matrix printers can be found to support all of the various types of paper-handling methods.

Epson Standard

IBM initially used Epson printers, which led to the development of the Epson/IBM Graphics Standard. This standard relates to the different control codes used by the printer for the various operational modes. Most software applications will support this standard first.

Summarizing important features of the Epson Standard:

- Epson/IBM graphics compatibility.
- NLQ mode by software or directly from the front panel.
- Downloadable font capability.
- Built-in IBM character set. This character set was not found in some of the early Epson MX and FX models.
- IBM or Epson graphics compatibility.
- Specific control codes for special printer functions.

5.4   Laser Printers

An exciting innovation for the DtC is the laser printer. Laser printers provide true letter quality, and full graphics, together with high speed and quiet operation.

Theory of Operation

A local microprocessor in the laser printer controls a rotating mirror that sweeps a laser beam across an electrostatically charged drum. The beam is turned off and on by a modulator. Wherever the drum is illuminated by the beam, the charge dissipates. The unexposed parts of the drum remain charged. After the laser beam has finished painting an image on the drum, an oppositely-charged powder, called *toner* is dusted on the drum. The toner sticks only to the charged portions of the drum. The powder image is then transferred electrostatically to paper, after which the paper passes under a hot wire that fuses the powder image permanently to the surface. This electrostatic process is the same as that used in xerographic machines. The only difference is the way in which the image is created. In one case a laser beam draws the image; in the other, focused light produces the image on the electrostatically charged drum.

The typical DtC laser printer provides resolutions of 300 by 300 dots per square inch and printing speeds of 8 to 10 sheets per minute. Prices range from $1500 to $6000. Resolution and on-board processing power are the major cost factors. Laser printers have an inherent bit-mapped mode and ability to create multiple fonts using plug-in cartridge fonts or laser printer software fonts. Laser printers sometimes have special interfaces to their printers, if integration between the DtC and the printer architecture is essential. Laser printers feed sheets of paper automatically, some can print duplex, on both sides of the paper, and some can even print envelopes.

Combination laser printer and copying machines are available. However, combination machines are not as robust and reliable as their individual counterparts. The Xerox 4045 laser printer is an example of a printer that also doubles as a copier. This printer/copier has a high price tag and is not compatible with HP laser printers.

The HP Standard

As with most DtC peripherals, there is a standard laser printer that applications packages support. For MS-DOS computers, this is the Hewlett-Packard LaserJet Series II and III printers. The LaserJet III printer is especially interesting because it modulates its dot size so that its 300 dpi capability becomes comparable to 600 dpi. You should be aware that laser printers have huge memory requirements. The higher the resolution and the greater the print area to be used for APA graphics, the larger the memory requirement. Different manufacturers offer several different memory expansion capabilities for the same laser printer.

Laser printers require a high level of integration between system, printer, and application. Your decision to get a laser printer should be based on the requirements of your specific application. Since the HP laser printers are supported by most MS-DOS software, only these printers, or carefully chosen compatible clones, are recommended. Laser printers produce excellent bit-mapped graphics, and many with special DtC software or built-in hardware can emulate IBM dot matrix graphics modes. This feature may be important if you are using pre-laser printer software.

Laser printers, like dot matrix printers, have many built-in capabilities. Having finer resolution and significantly greater internal processing capability, laser printers represent a much higher level of sophistication between DtC, user, system, and application. To minimize the complications of integrating applications with a printer, you should choose the specific printer that is supported by most of your applications. Compatibility concerns will become less important when standards evolve in text/graphics processing. The PostScript language appears to be such a standard.

PostScript

A special language called PostScript has been designed to define and draw complex combinations of text and graphics. Although PostScript is generally used in laser printers, PostScript video displays are available. Instead of controlling a laser printer or video display, dot by dot, using the DtC CPU, PostScript commands are sent. Inside the printer, a PostScript processor converts the commands for generating text and graphics into the necessary dot patterns. The higher-level command interface results in a better sharing of resources between DtC and printer as well as ensuring a standard methodology for creating and printing complex images.

PostScript is licensed by Adobe Systems. Many laser printers come with a PostScript processor. Other laser printers can be backfitted with such a processor by installing add-on boards. The cost of a PostScript upgrade is one to two thousand dollars when the upgrade is technically possible. PostScript can also be implemented through a print driver. In this case, the applications program sends PostScript commands first to the software driver, which generates the appropriate APA sequences for the printer. The processing that occurs places an enormous burden on the resources of the DtC CPU. It is better to implement the PostScript capability at the printer, where it can be integrated with printer capabilities.

What may become most important when you buy a laser printer is whether or not it supports PostScript.

Laser and Dot Matrix Compatibility Considerations

As mentioned earlier, dot matrix and laser printers provide for bit-mapped graphics modes to attain graphics capability. Programming this capability into applications software is difficult, so the range of supported printers for a given application is limited. The menu of supported printers for MS-DOS computer software, however, includes IBM graphics printers, IBM ProPrinters, and Epsons. Several public domain utility software packages can download printer fonts.

Text printing consists of straightforward rendition of ASCII character codes, but each printer may support one or more fonts. Font attributes include character set, the shape of each letter (style), character sizes, character spacing on the line (pitch), and so on. Font selection not only determines how the text looks, but also how much text can appear on each line. In certain types of printers, specifically laser printers, font choice will also determine whether text appears across the short dimension (portrait), or the long dimension (landscape) of the page. Another major issue is whether the printer supports the IBM extended character set. This set provides special characters in addition to the 128 ASCII characters. The selection of extended characters often differ from font to font, but usually include letters with diacritical marks that occur in foreign languages and special symbols. IBM's extended character set has a set of ruling characters including horizontal and vertical lines, cross-over connectors, and corners of boxes. Word processing programs developed for the IBM PC often use the IBM extended character set for drawing boxes, sometimes called *cursor draw*.

Color Printers

Three basic technologies are used for producing color graphics printouts, not including plotters. With the exception of electrostatic printers, all are variations on dot matrix techniques.

Ink Jet

The most intense colors are produced by an ink jet printer, which sprays droplets of ink on paper. Although any paper will work, the most vivid colors are generated when specially coated paper is used. Transparencies can be generated by this method, using special acetate, but the resulting colors are significantly less intense than art department quality viewgraphs.

Color Ribbon

Color ribbon dot matrix impact printers allow for printing color by multiple color ribbons. The colors appear washed out as compared to inkjet coloring. Special transparency paper is also available for these units.

Thermal Transfer Color

Using special colored ribbons, thermal transfer printers produce intense colors on special paper. Thermal printers support resolutions of up to 300 dpi. The medium is similar to crayon. The main problem is the difficulty of loading paper and the lack of automatic features.

When operated in black and white mode, most color printers emulate the respective IBM graphics printer models in text and graphics modes to varying degrees. Because of the enormous compatibility differences between these printers, be sure they support your applications software before you invest.

5.5   Plotters

Plotters draw lines and construct graphic images by moving pens and/or paper on two orthogonal axes, x and y. There are two versions. In one, the pen is moved in both x and y directions; in the other, a pen is moved in one direction and the paper or other medium in the other.

As with other peripherals, the selection of an appropriate plotter depends on the software to be used. The size of the user base should dictate plotter choice.

Application

Although printers can support some plotting functions and plotters may support some printing functions, applications most suited for plotters are precise, multicolored plots:

- Architectural drawings
- Chip layouts
- Flow diagrams
- Mechanical design layouts

These examples require precise superposition of multiple colored figures, and are best produced with plotters. A good test of plotter precision is to plot the same image twice on the same paper. If the paper control of the plotter is good, you will see only one plot on the paper.

Soon we will have color laser printers and electrostatic color plotters that compete in price with the better DtC plotters. However, due to current software support, the plotter continues to be the best output device available for drawings, layouts, and diagrams.

Plotters are seldom used to output bit-mapped graphics, but rather to draw complex sets of predefined lines, boxes, and arcs. More suitable for bit-mapped images are the laser and electrostatic printers. Dot matrix printers do well for simple applications.

Pricing

Plotters are grouped here into three price categories:

1. *Low* – Basic capabilities, only one paper size, four colors maximum, few features. Cost $100-$300. These plotters are generally suitable for home use.

2. *Medium* – HP7475A Plotter, more pen colors (six to eight), finer drawing resolution (0.001 inch), and repeatability. Better pens and pen handling. Price is $800 to $2000. These plotters are adequate for many data display applications, particularly business graphics and presentation graphics.

3. *High* – Houston Instruments DMP Series and Roland. Up to fourteen pens, practically any size paper, many programmable features such as plot speeds, special internal algorithms to enhance performance, higher repeatability and resolution,

front panel indicators, etc. Price is $5000 to $12000. These plotters are used for professional design.

Compatibility Concerns

Because they are usually interfaced serially, plotters can be made to operate on almost any DtC. Plotters, however, implement high-level plotting languages internally. These languages allow considerable functionality at relatively low baud rates between DtC and plotter, and offload the intricate details of plotting complex forms from the DtC CPU. Syntactic differences lead to incompatibilities between applications designed to use plotter languages and the plotter. The most popular language, HPGL (the Hewlett-Packard Graphics Language), stores plots in vector graphics format. It is implemented by most plotters, but due to different features, paper sizes, and plot speeds, incompatibilities arise. As with other peripherals, make sure the software you are using is in the software selection menu of the plotter you intend to use.

Spooling Buffers

Data rates between DtC and plotter are slow, so large files may take hours to plot. Therefore, it is advisable to use print spoolers between DtC and plotter. Though the plot will not be produced faster, the DtC will be freed for other work.

5.6   Electrostatic Color Printers

The electrostatic printer passes a chemically-treated paper through several different dyes. Prior to each dye pass, the paper is electrostatically charged with the color bit-map image. Following several passes, a composite color image is formed. By "dithering" bits – causing adjacent bits to be of varying colors – a wide spectrum of color hues and intensities is possible. These printers produce high quality color images, but don't compare with photographic film outputs. Prices vary from several thousand for DtC-based printers to nearly 100 thousand for large format, high quality systems. Print times are on the order of minutes. Electrostatic color printers occupy a middle ground between plotters and film image devices where complex multicolor images need to be printed.

Film Imaging Systems

Devices that will expose standard sheet film under computer control are available for DtCs. Two major modes are implemented. One type of film imager uses a video monitor signal to expose the monitor screen image on the film. This film imager can generate the equivalent of a high-quality screen dump of whatever is on the monitor screen, independently of the current applications software. The other type of film imager is controlled directly, a bit at a time, by a custom interface and custom software. The custom software is used to develop or obtain whatever image you desire. These devices produce exceptionally high quality output, and represent an alternative to manual film imaging systems.

Paper Handling Methods

The following is a summary of the different paper handling mechanisms of DtC printers.

Friction Feed

■ Small disks of paper punched out of tractor holes are called chad. The holes themselves are called chad-holes.

Single sheets of paper are moved through the printer mechanism by rubber rollers and a *platen*, much like the one on a typewriter.

Tractor Feed

Paper is fed through the printer by sprockets that engage holes punched along the edges of the paper.■ Tractor feed is required for preparing mailing labels to ensure sufficiently accurate positioning of the labels with respect to the print head. If you intend to print labels, be sure the printer you buy can accommodate the label stock you are going to use. There are two main types of tractor feed. One pulls the paper through the paper guides while the other pushes it through.

Sheet Feed

Mechanical devices feed individual sheets of paper, picked one by one from a stack, through the printer.

For DtC users who need only draft outputs, the tractor feed, and bulk tractor feed paper are often the most convenient. For those who need to generate professional-looking final documents, sheet feed capability is a must. Most laser printers and some dot matrix printers support automatic sheet feeding, but with limited capacity of 100 sheets or so before needing to reload.

Printer Sharing

Although it is possible to share printers on LANs through peripheral sharing techniques, each DtC user should have at least a low-cost dot matrix printer. The very nature of DtC applications software demands the immediate availability of printed output supporting the interactive and high-turnaround times of most DtC products.

As the price of laser printers drops, and becomes significantly less than the cost of the DtC system unit, more users will insist on having their own laser printers.

Printer Support Software

A variety of utility software can assist you in operating a printer. These packages include large print buffers (spoolers), and a variety of utilities to simplify interpretation and use of the many different printer control functions.

Evaluation Factors

Several important characteristics should be considered during printer evaluation for a particular application:

• Volume of output expected in the application.
• Types and volumes of output expected if several dissimilar applications are to be serviced.

- Compatibility with other components in the system.
- Document lengths: single page letters vs multiple page reports.
- Paper sizes: letter-size sheets vs. roll or fanfold paper.
- Printer output rate: characters per second, lines per minute, or pages per minute; rate of combined text/graphics.
- Output rate of computer.
- Spooling capability.
- Output quality desired.
- Printer character buffer size.
- Number and sizes of fonts, special characters required, etc.
- Graphics capability.
- Forms capability, with multiple copy considerations.
- Label and envelope handling.
- Archival storage considerations (e.g., thermal paper tends to age poorly).
- Office space and location available for printer.
- Printer noise control.
- Color capability, type of paper required.
- Repeatability for forms.
- NLQ mode support.

General Compatibility

Standards controlling signals, cable connections, and other mechanical parameters such as line widths and character sizes are not well defined. The following areas should be checked when purchasing a printer other than the one supported by your particular application. Supported means that a particular manufacturer's model number is found on the program's menu when setting up printer driver support.

- *Cables* – Different signals for printer handshake lines.
- *Control codes* – Use of different codes for changing character sizes, fonts, densities; different codes for graphics; different text/graphic characters.
- *Mechanical differences* – Different ribbon or toner cartridges, carriage sizes, paper feed mechanisms, paper requirements.
- *Different type of printer* – Trying to use a laser printer where a dot matrix printer is called for, or trying to use an ink jet printer where a dot matrix is called for.

Choosing a Printer

The choice of printer should be based on the type of outputs you will be generating. The following is a rough guideline for selecting a printer. As always, make popularity a guiding criterion.

- *Low-cost dot matrix printers* – Rough drafting, applications programming listings, relatively small spreadsheets and databases, and other applications requiring unstructured printout.

- *High-cost dot matrix printers* – Printout of very large files, and particularly labels, by tractor feed. Production of very complex forms requiring large numbers in rough environments. The need for wide-carriage printouts and carbon forms.

- *Laser printer* – High-volume printouts requiring professional letter quality and high repetition rates. Complex combinations of text and graphics as required by desktop publishing and other drawing systems. As the cost drops and better paper feed techniques emerge for the laser printer, it will continue to replace the dot matrix printer in all applications areas.

- *Daisywheel printer* – Continues to be used on some dedicated word processor systems where fine impact quality and reliable paper feed mechanisms are required.

6.0   Special-Purpose Peripherals

- Voice Synthesis
- Sound/Music
- Data Acquisition
- Computational Add-ons
- Process Control
- Development systems
- Test Equipment Add-ons

Just as a variety of software enriches the internal functionality of a DtC, special-purpose peripherals enrich the external scope of DtC applications.

To describe all of the specialized peripherals available for DtCs would require another book, so let's concentrate on the more popular and useful devices that will benefit DtC users.

6.1   Voice Synthesis

DtCs are now being used to integrate voice and data. There are many exciting applications for this technology, discussed next.

Applications for Voice Synthesis

As the number and variety of end user computing applications grow, and as processing power continues to move away from the central host computer to the individual desktop, a need is emerging for a device that integrates voice and data while communicating in multiple protocols with mainframes, minicomputers, and DtCs. Applications for voice output include:

IVD Systems

Because of its diverse capabilities, the integrated voice data (IVD) workstation is well suited for the role of a complete desktop workstation.

In its simplest form, the integrated voice and data workstation is a DtC with a telephone handset and keypad attached. To be effective, the IVD workstation must be able to switch between voice and data contexts simply and quickly. IVDs are particularly useful for stock brokers, reservation agents, and collection agencies because they allow the end users to perform data access and data entry while carrying on a voice conversation.

The IVD workstations function as voice messaging systems (VMS) through the use of special modems that allow for digitizing, storing, and playing back incoming speech. Some even recognize dial tones, which can be used, for example, to automate a mail order business.

IVD system software permits you to dial numbers on screen, as do most common communications software programs using conventional modems. Two phone lines are typically used: one for voice and the other for the computer data. Newer systems, however, can multiplex both over a single telephone circuit. ISDN phone networks with their greatly improved data speeds will play an important role in voice and data communications.

Speech for the Handicapped

Phonetic speech synthesis can create speech directly from input text. The DtC can be made to speak whatever is typed in. Many phonetic speech devices are used by the speech impaired; and some phonetic synthesizer hardware comes in both male and female voices. Apple and the EE computers can use hardware sound generators already in place to create phonetic speech. Many people find communicating through the phonetic speech preferable to signing, using pointing boards, or writing messages on paper. Portable units are available, and of course, many phonetic synthesizers synergistically combine with DtCs for increased capabilities such as message pull-down menus, and sentence constructors.

MS-DOS computers will usually need an add-on board containing the phonetic synthesizer. Some creative enthusiasts have even used the built-in low quality single digital bit speaker found in an MS-DOS computer to create speech by a software-intensive approach. The software uses phonemes stored as digital strings and then outputs the phonemes from converted text. The process involves special pulse-width modulation techniques to get maximum efficiency. The resulting sound is impressive, considering the limited audio capability of the MS-DOS computer speaker system, originally designed for clicking and beeping.

Creating person-specific speech with all of the contextual inflection through text to speech conversion is still in research; its processing and storage requirements are beyond current DtC technology. Contextual recognition of unlimited speech is an even more complex technological problem.

Voice Prompting and Annotation

Voice prompting can provide a friendly environment, particularly for child education. By storing digitized speech phrases and appropriately appending additional words when required, realistic conversational scenarios can be produced with familiar voices. Phonetic speech can be used for unlimited speech capability, but the robotic sound sometimes gets in the way.

Voice annotation in software applications can add a kick to otherwise inanimate data. On-screen documents would have special annotation markers. When the DtC user moves the video cursor to a marker, a prerecorded digitized voice segment plays. Digitized audio need not be restricted to human voice; it could include music and virtually unlimited sound effects.

Phone Answerers

Specialized modem boards can use a DtC as an intelligent phone answering service, playing back selected voice messages stored as your digitized speech. The playbacks can be related to dial tones that are recognizable. Also, with special software you can view the digitized waveforms, clean them up, compress dead space, and perform other useful functions.

Voice Messaging

In addition to the usual electronic mail sending text messages over the network, voice mail systems send digitized speech. Special data compression techniques that can cut down on the data requirements of digitized speech are particularly important.

Instead of reading a lifeless text message, the DtC user can selectively play voice mail messages at a workstation. Some DtC modems have speech processing capabilities that include LPC speech synthesis.

Dictation

Digitized voice is subject to the processing capabilities of the DtC or processor add-ons. DtC-driven speech dictation add-ons can provide a variety of useful functions through software and hardware signal processors. For example, you can speed up or slow down your voice without affecting its frequency – try that with a tape recorder dictation machine. The dictation sequences can be controlled right from the display monitor with time sequences and flexible pull-down menus.

Military Applications

Voice messages sent as phonetic speech require very low data rates and these can be transmitted very reliably over low-grade signal channels. Sending messages this way can reduce the possibility of noise interference.

Types of Voice Synthesis

Currently three methodologies may be used to generate voice output: phonetic, digitized, and LPC.

Phonetic Voice Synthesis

The voice is artificially duplicated by a VLSI device that synthesizes words from 50 to 200 phonetic sounds. Signals generated by internal algorithms stimulate a vocal tract model. In effect, an artificial throat is made to talk. Phonetic codes are transmitted to the VLSI device either directly or through text to phoneme translation software. The process is depicted in Figure 109. The translation software lets you send text strings to the phonetic device, which produces the corresponding utterance. The sound is totally synthetic. The device can utter any text string put in – without context – and the sound that is heard contains only rudimentary inflection. Questions, statements, exclamations, and so on are expressed with robotic intonation. Moreover, the voice heard does not belong to any particular person. The advantage of phonetic voice synthesis is that it has a very low data rate of approximately 70 bits per second, but can generate comprehensive speech.

Phonetic synthesizers take two forms:

1. **Add-on board** – The add-on board contains the hardware filter, shown in Figure 109, necessary to create the phonetic sounds. The DtC supplies the intensive text-to-speech processing software. Additional software drivers redirect a conventional line printer or video driver commands to output the phonemes through

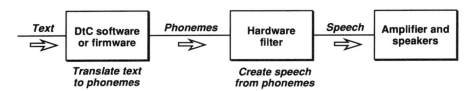

Figure 109. **Phonetic voice synthesis**

the board's sound interface. You can use the standard operating system capabilities for listing and printing text with the listings spoken through the add-on board.

2. ***A complete system*** – Some phonetic systems, the PSS (Professional Speech System) by Votrax Corporation, for example, perform the text to speech processing internally. It interfaces to the DtC by standard RS-232 or parallel printer ports and contains a microprocessor, phonetic synthesizer, ROM, and RAM. The PSS can perform the text to speech algorithms internally, or you can send it phoneme codes if you think you can beat its internal algorithms. In text mode, all you have to do is send the text you would like spoken over the interface port. Without any special software and using the existing printer, keyboard, video display drivers, and language commands, you can have a talking typewriter or talking printer.

Other capabilities include flexible inflection programming, programmable speech frequency, and exception processing such as replacing foul language with more acceptable words automatically. Also, the PSS couples a complex sound generator with the hardware phoneme generator for phonetic voice singing, whispering, and even crying.

The following BASIC program is all you need to have a talking typewriter with the available phonetic synthesizers:

```
LINE INPUT "Input what I should say"; A$
LPRINT A$
```

The program prompts you to input a line from the keyboard, and then prints the line to the line printer. The program works with either the add-on board or the external PSS system. With the add-on board, the PSS connects to the printer port; with the external PSS system, software drivers redirect the usual BASIC line printer output to the add-on hardware's phonetic synthesizer.

Digitized Voice Synthesis

Voice synthesis converts voice from analog to digital form in real time. The resulting digital data is placed on the hard drive. Figure 110 is a simplified block diagram of the steps involved in the process. One advantage of a digital synthesis is voice fidelity. Your favorite person's voice may be used. Another advantage is that no special hardware other than A/D and D/A devices are required for recording and playback of digitized voice. A disadvantage is the large memory required to store voice, around 50,000 bits per second, and therefore the impracticality of storing the entire English language for random recall.

One low-cost digital speech synthesizer comes in the form of a small box that plugs into the DtC's parallel printer port. Inside the box is the D/A converter and speaker amplifier. You plug a speaker into the box and your DtC acquires voice capability. To obtain recordings of your own voice, plug another low-cost speech digitizing board into a DtC bus slot. Using supplied menu-driven software you can plug in a microphone and make voice recordings. More sophisticated voice systems using LPC speech are described later.

Experimental text to speech digitized voice applications have been worked out. Here phonetic sounds rather than spoken words are voice recorded. Then, as with phonetic devices, text to speech software converts input text strings to invoke phonetic sounds. The speech created will sound like the human voice that produced the

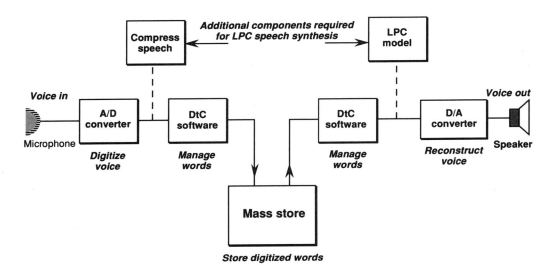

Figure 110.   Digitized and LPC speech

phonemes for the recording. Stringing these pre-recorded voiced phonemes together is quite a task and intonation within context is a problem just as it is with hardware phonetic devices.

LPC

The LPC (linear predictive coding) method is similar to digitized voice, except that the input voice is compressed prior to recording in memory, and then decompressed upon playback. LPC voice synthesizers depend on considerable on-board processing power to do voice compression and LPC model-driven expansion. Processing power is found on add-on boards that contain dedicated signal processors for voice compression and hardware filters that implement what could be considered vocal tract models. When the compressed voice signals excite the hardware filters, natural sounding voice results. The primary difference between this method and digitized speech is the data rate of 2000 to 3000 bits per second that is necessary to develop natural sounding speech.

Although natural sounding speech is not as true as digitized, it is fairly close, considering the drastic reduction in the required data rate. Figure 110 shows the additional components of real time voice compression and the LPC model that implement LPC speech.

IBM and other manufacturers have boards that contain voice components. IBM calls its board the VCO (Voice Communication Option). The VCO plugs into the DtC bus to perform LPC functions. The DtC is used as a host supplying power and user interfaces, managing voice files, and incorporating the files into software. Many DtC-based voice annotated software applications use this method.

DtC System Speech Synthesis Requirements

Most speech synthesizers provide additional hardware that manages the speech creation process, which makes the main consideration the mass storage requirements of the stored voice. Phonetic systems performing internal text to speech translation require medium-power CPUs. Digitized speech system's mass storage requirements depend upon the amount of speech being stored and the data compression scheme. The more sophisticated contextual speech synthesizers require considerable CPU power and are currently outside the range of today's DtCs. Most of the specialized systems described above require add-on hardware, and many integrate voice functionality through special-purpose built-in modems.

6.2   Sound/Music Peripherals

DtC add-on music synthesizers and complex sound interfaces can range from a $50 add-on sound generator to a $10,000 DtC-based Moog synthesizer. There are a variety of complex sound generator chips available that easily interface to microcomputer buses, are programmable, and can generate a variety of sound effects. Most DtC sound boards use these chips and, through additional software, allow you to access their power.

Many DtCs come already equipped with music and sound generation devices as part of the initial DtC design. MS-DOS computers provide only minimal on-board sound support by a small speaker controlled by a single digital bit.■

■ The IBM PC Jr. and some Radio Shack DtCs have built-in music chips.

The speaker is suited for simple prompting such as beeping and buzzing, although you can find innovative software that plays music and speech that sounds good in spite of speaker quality.

Types of Music and Sound Hardware

Serious music connoisseurs will likely require expensive special hardware. The devices possess a wide range of capabilities, but they tend to fall into two main categories:

Digitized Audio Playback

The playback systems are inexpensive and allow you to simply record and play digitized sound segments through an 8-bit A/D converter, usually placed in series with the parallel printer port. An additional board can be purchased for recording digitized sounds and voice. Also, software comes with a recording board to allow editing of the recorded signals, and data compression and decompression. What the system amounts to is a low-cost digital tape recorder, but its advantage is that the sounds are software controlled and can be integrated with software programs. Included software takes advantage of the hardware to add realistic sound effects to games, and music and voice to educational software. Compact audio disks are being used more and more with DtC audio effects and sound enhancements.

Sound Synthesizers

■ Sound hardware found in the Macintosh, Commodore, and Amiga computers provide a combination of the synthesizers and sequencers.

Sound and music synthesizers develop their own complex waveforms that can be added, modified, and stored. Sound synthesizers can recreate real instruments as well as instruments and sounds of your own design. To create the most lifelike duplication of existing instruments, the sequencing of digitally recorded data from the instrument is required and many sound synthesizer hardware units permit this. Synthesizers with sequencing capability repeatedly scan memory areas where the fundamental characteristic signals are stored. ■

The software included allows you to construct the waveform to be sequenced either by drawing it on-screen, or by using actual sample recordings. This provides the freedom to customize the sound in any manner you choose. Other systems synthesize the sounds completely in VLSI hardware. VLSI chips found on these boards have multiple tone and voice capability, and a variety of other special effects. A popular effect is known as ADSR (attack, decay, sustain, and release) control. ADSR control allows you to make the artificially created sounds seem realistic. For example, a gong has a quick attack and a slow exponential release. The gong is rich in dissonant harmonics, which can be synthesized artificially. Noise generators permit non-tonal sounds such as gunshots, propeller blades, rocket motors, surf, and explosions.

Many synthesizers use analog techniques and special oscillators to create sophisticated sounds and phasing effects that can not be created digitally. Such systems are very expensive and can be found in music studios. With a DtC's additional capabilities you can create, store, and manage multiple sound tracks to assemble your own simulated symphony orchestra.

One DtC system music synthesizer implemented a complete database management system to set up and manage the various sound effects. Each record in the database contained fifty different sound characteristics. Database records could be selected by criteria relating to the desired effects. Each record was created in a visual GUI system of sliders and buttons designed to allow the creator maximum flexibility to manipulate the sound waveform on screen.

Sound Portability

Apple, Commodore, and Atari computers build considerable sound capability into their motherboards, while the MS-DOS computers require add-on sound boards. The problem with add-on sound systems is software portability. Your friends with add-on sound systems will be able to enjoy your musical compositions only if your sound board is identical to theirs.

So far, vendors have been reluctant to support add-on sound devices since there is no guarantee that a particular add-on will become popular and be worth the developmental effort. Also, when the sound capability is part of the initial DtC design, it will be supported by the DtC's operating system, programming languages, or other preprogrammed software. Software support is abundant on the Apple, Atari, and Commodore DtCs with built-in capabilities, and it is quite scarce on the MS-DOS compatibles.

You will find a few standard MS-DOS sound systems emerging – synthesizers and digital recorders – that are becoming de facto standards. The Soundblaster is one such system.

Music Interfaces and Keyboards

There has been little standardization of sound-making device architecture or of operational characteristics. The MIDI is the only current standard, and it covers the control of music synthesizers and devices.

Using a plug-in MIDI, a cable, and supplied software, you can connect MIDI-capable music synthesizers to a DtC. Or you can buy an add-on synthesizer board, plug it into a DtC, connect an external MIDI keyboard, and connect the output or the music board to a stereo. With this rig you can create multichannel symphonies with special effects that would impress even Bach. Included are complete music development software systems with capabilities for creating a wide variety of special sound effects and unique musical instruments.

Of course there is also the complete range of standalone computer-controlled musical keyboards, Yamaha and Roland, for example, that you probably have seen at the local mall. These keyboards are more integrated with keyboard, sound generator, and waveform generator, but can still benefit from being DtC-controlled with a MIDI and appropriate software. Several magazines are devoted to the art of music synthesis and control and DtC add-ons and software are topics often covered.

6.3   DtC-Based Data Acquisition Peripherals

The DtC is an excellent platform for systems that can collect data from external sources. As shown in Figure 111, most data acquisition add-ons contain A/D and D/A converters, built in microprocessors, shared memory, and a variety of additional programmable capabilities. This built-in capability combined with a DtC's capabilities provides yet another synergistic combination.

Before continuing, let's take a brief look at the fundamental components of these peripherals: the A/D and D/A converters.

A/D Converter

An analog to digital converter can take as input a continuously variable signal, such as a voltage, with a value that depends on a temperature or water height. The analog signal is converted to a digital signal with a resolution that is based on the internal capability of the converter. The A/D converter periodically samples the analog quantity automatically or by your direction and the digital quantity waits in a parallel register. The register appears as any I/O port or memory address and can be read through conventional I/O or memory instructions.

For example, a sensor might output a voltage from 0 to 5 Volts as the sensor's temperature changes from –32 to 100 degrees Fahrenheit. Presume that an 8-bit A/D converter will take the 0 to 5V as input and convert this signal to 255 different discrete digital quantities ranging from 00000000 to 11111111 binary, or 0 to 255 decimal.

Since a temperature range of 132 degrees is represented by 256 quantities, each digital weight represents 256/132 or 0.52 degrees, and this becomes the digital resolution of the 8-bit system. If we read the A/D converter and get a value of 200 decimal, and apply the conversion weights and range, the resulting temperature must then be –32+(200 times 0.52) degrees or –32+104, which is a comfortable 72 degrees Fahrenheit.

A/D converters usually come in single chip versions, in a variety of speeds and conversion resolutions. Some can support multiple conversion channels that are software selectable.

D/A Converters

As you would expect, the digital to analog converter performs the inverse function of the A/D converter. Rather than being read, the D/A converter is written to. For

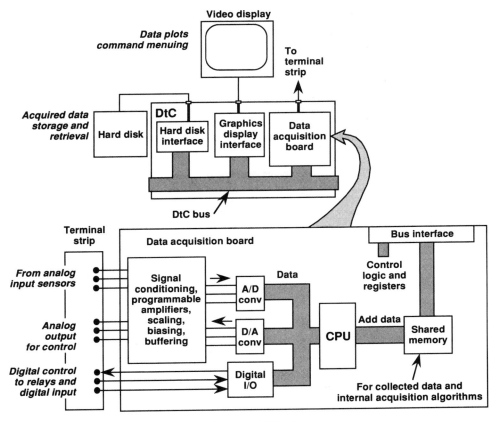

Figure 111. Data acquisition add-ons

example, an 8-bit D/A could convert a byte written to its register into an analog output signal. The 8-bit converter might have a conversion range of 0 to 5 Volts. Therefore the conversion resolution is 5 divided by 2^8 or 5/256, which corresponds to a 0.01953 volts/bit resolution. If a decimal 55 was written to the D/A converter, a 55 times 0.01953 = 1.07 volt signal would result. The 1.07 volt signal might be used as a proportional control signal on an x-y plotter, or to control a motor speed.

D/A converters are often used as function generators to create complex waveforms. A number of quantities representing the waveform's amplitude with time are stored in a sequential memory, which is repetitively sequenced, the values being sent to the D/A converter. The output creates a repeating waveform of any desired complexity depending upon the converting resolution and the amount of memory sequenced. Music sequencers use this principle to create their waveforms.

Primary Data Acquisition Board Components

Most data acquisition boards will contain the following components:

- *A/D converters* – To receive the incoming analog sensor data.
- *D/A converters* – To provide proportional control or waveform functions.
- *Microprocessor* – To control the various activities on the board.
- *ROM* – Contain dedicated routines for the data acquisition process.
- *Shared memory* – To buffer the acquired data from the on-board converters. Data acquisition boards contain from 64 to 256K of RAM memory. The memory is also used to store acquisition variables such as scaling factors and amplifier gains.
- *Programmable amplifiers* – Amplifier gains can be controlled by a DtC, so that simple scaling can be provided in real time without additional processing.
- *Digital ports* – I/O ports for digital signals are provided. These may be used for reading switches or controlling on/off functions such as thermostatic control systems, alarm indicators, and the like.
- *Terminal strips* – A terminal strip will usually plug into the back of the add-on card, which provides easy access to the special terminals and other signals that you will connect to your data acquisition system.
- *Software* – Included software is usually in the form of subroutine libraries custom-developed for the particular A/D/A board. There are considerable differences in software quality between the various data acquisition board vendors, and a board selection process should include analysis of the software and its documentation and technical support.

Figure 111 shows another combination of a DtC and a special peripheral. The DtC is responsible for storage and final processing of the data, and sometimes uses DSP boards or other processors. Graphic displays and the usual software can be used for managing and reporting on your acquired data. The boards take care of the low-level processing and data gathering functions while the DtC CPU operates on the data at a higher level.

6.4   Special Computational Add-ons

Most DtC CPUs are either RISC or CISC processors. While the CISC processors are general purpose, most of the RISC-based workstations have CPUs that specialize in graphics functions. To adequately supplement more specialized signal processing needs, you can purchase a wide variety of special-purpose processing boards.

Many DtCs do have built-in math coprocessors, but these chips are of a general nature and are useful for the ordinary math needs of most software products. Spreadsheet programs and CAD packages that use lots of math will benefit from a math coprocessor. To supplement the more specialized requirements of signal and computational processing, there are a variety of array processors, DSP chip boards, and even neural network and fuzzy logic boards. We shall look at the typical DSP board as an example of a computational add-on. Chips that specialize in the processing of converted analog data have become almost as popular as RISC CPUs.

DSP Architecture and Specialization

Digital signal processors specialize in the high speed signal processing that often involves skipping about large arrays of numerical data while performing relatively simple operations on the data. Billions of operations may be required for a single signal conversion. Such applications benefit by flexibility in addressing memory arrays, and by CPUs that can implement the simple math functions of addition, multiplication, and transcendentals quickly and in parallel. DSP chips are ideal for performing such repetitive functions as Fast Fourier Transforms, voice processing, and other complex signal conversions and processes.

NOTE

FFTs are used to convert digital time domain samples of data to their frequency content, also represented as digital data.

Interestingly, the NeXT, Apple, and lately, Commodore computers provide DSP chips right on their motherboards, so we can expect language and operating support of DSP functionality to improve on those units. Figure 112 shows a simplified DSP board plugged into a DtC. The DSP processor usually shares some memory with the DtC through a shared memory interface. Also, certain DSP operating parameters are controllable through additional logic.

DSP Data Inputs

On the DSP board there could be special I/O interfaces for outside voice, telephone, or video inputs. More often, the data will be acquired through other add-ons specialized in obtaining a particular form of data. For example, a video capture board might capture a video frame, or a data acquisition board might pick up a few MB of flight data. Let the other boards get the data and let the DSP board concentrate on its processing.

Parallel Processing Add-Ons

Parallel processing is useful for a specific class of problems and are not necessarily a boon for the typical user. Digital signal processing (FFTs), pattern recognition, and image processing problems are applications types suited for parallel processors. Parallel processing shines with problems that require lots of overlapping operations. As with other specialized devices, special software compilers will be required to get the maximum benefit from parallel processing architectures.

A variety of processor add-ons contain multiple parallel processors for increased throughput. Systems have been seen that provide overlapped memory and as many as thousands of processing elements, where data can be propagated through the system in different flexible modes. This type of processing is just not possible with the conventional Von Neuman serial architecture of today's DtCs.

Software Support

DtC language compilers are providing support for special computational systems through special compilers and subroutine libraries that know how to take advantage of the hardware capabilities provided. The software industry is lagging behind the capabilities found in the computational add-ons, and many DtC applications will have to wait until such systems become more popular. As with other special peripherals, standards in computational techniques are non-existent. There are, however, IEEE standards in the representation of numerical data, and most math coprocessors and computational add-ons use them.

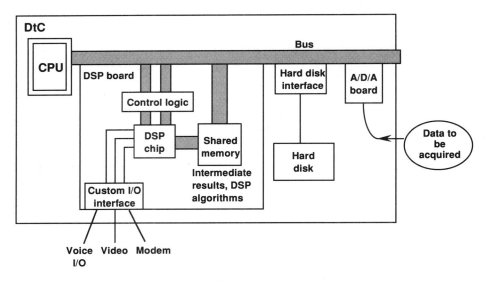

Figure 112. Digital signal processing board

6.5   Process and Environmental Control

Due to higher reliability and greater popularity, the DtC is now being used for manufacturing process control and environmental control applications. Remote locations can be monitored and controlled using the DtC as the central element, as shown in Figure 113. The figure shows the combination of a DtC with remotely located data acquisition and control systems. The remote control units are called multiplexers and are themselves custom microcomputers. The remote units have their own A/D/A capability through plug-in boards. Boards can be purchased for control of light or heavy equipment, acquisition of sensor data, digital alarm controls, and digital inputs for reading simple switches. Also, special plug-in boards are used to supply filtered power to the sensor units.

At the remote unit, all I/O signals are collated into single RS-232 channels for remote transmission to the main system controller, the DtC.

DtC-based environmental system control software can include the following:

- *Graphics* – Screen presentations can include floor plans showing sensors and flow diagrams. Flows and sensors can change color depending upon temperatures, humidities, and the like.
- *Alarms* – Alarms can be generated, displayed, and remotely printed through short haul modems.
- *Reports* – Sophisticated reports of alarming conditions; when and how they occurred, and other complex relationships.
- *Storage* – Sensor readings and alarms can be stored on mass storage systems for further analysis and after the fact reporting.
- *Database* – A sensor database contains the sensor-specific information including name and conversions that the system needs to know in order to process the incoming sensor data.

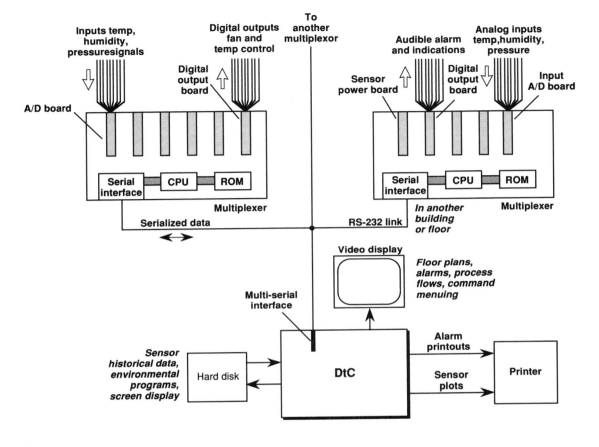

Figure 113.   Environmental DtC system

- ***Programming language*** – An internal programming language can permit you to link controlled processes to incoming sensor readings in many different ways.

Most industrial control systems use high-reliability microcomputers for the central computing agent where more than simple environmental functions are required. You probably wouldn't want to trust an MS-DOS computer to control a nuclear reactor or the heating and cooling of your office building. When DtCs become more reliable, they will be important components in such systems.

6.6   *Microcomputer Development Systems*

Historically, the building of a custom microcomputer has required an expensive microcomputer development system. Such systems, manufactured by companies like Hewlett-Packard and Tektronics, could plug directly into the microprocessor socket of a newly developing microcomputer system and emulate the functions of its base microprocessor in real time. This gave the developer considerable control over the hardware and software functions in the DtC.

Now DtCs can provide this emulation function through special add-on boards. Each board can represent a particular microprocessor and comes with associated software for cross-assembling and cross-compiling code that will operate on the target microcomputer. By using DtCs for the development process, engineers also have all of the other powerful tools such as editors, DBMS and spreadsheet software, and utilities that DtCs have to offer.

The power of a rich software base and low-cost peripherals make DtCs an attractive alternative to the expensive microcomputer development system. In deciding between conventional and DtC-based systems, you will need to perform a tradeoff analysis. The conventional microcomputer development systems are well-integrated with high levels of control possible between the development system and the developing microcomputer, while the DtC-based systems are not as well integrated. The tradeoff is integration for low cost and available auxiliary software.

Microprocessor Add-On Emulator Capabilities

Most of the popular process control-oriented microprocessors are supported by emulator add-on boards. Available boards have different microprocessors. With the switching logic on the emulator, you can use memory and I/O ports on the emulator board and control them directly from the DtC. Thus, the microprocessor can first execute in the very controlled environment of the emulator board, and then slowly be weaned to make use of resources on the custom microcomputer being developed. Figure 114 depicts this process.

Notice the cable coming from the emulator board, which plugs into the socket intended for the microprocessor of the target system. During the development process, this cord is plugged into the custom microcomputer, with the microprocessor of the custom microcomputer first located and controlled by the emulator board. Finally, when the development is complete, the cord is removed and the ROMs that have been developed and the original microprocessor plug into the custom microcomputer.

6.7 Test Equipment Add-Ons

A large assortment of add-on boards can make a DtC act like an oscilloscope, spectrum analyzer, digital voltmeter, or other piece of test equipment. Software graciously endowed with GUIs can make a DtC video screen look like a real control panel displaying the measured data. The test equipment industry is quick to replace such good user interfaces with their own built-in computers and displays, and we are witness to an interesting race. In many cases, the DtC video display is not adequate for the type of fast custom CRTs found in the test equipment. Also, speeds between memory, displays, and sensors require close integration with computing elements.

The tradeoff is between well-integrated test equipment and the software flexibility of the desktop computer. You can choose the well-integrated test equipment from such manufacturers as Tektronics and Hewlett-Packard, both of which have long and stable performance histories. Or you can choose from a large variety of

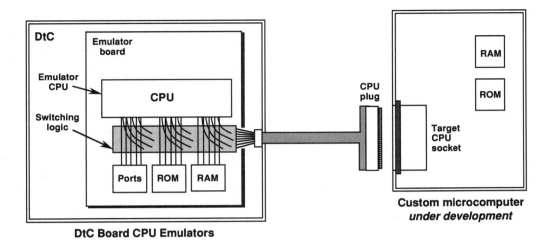

DtC Board CPU Emulators

Figure 114.   DtC-based CPU emulators

less-integrated signal processing add-ons that acquire the signals and then let the DtC process them using its array of flexible software.

6.8   Special-Peripheral Considerations

Many of the equipments mentioned above are designed as standalone units with highly specialized and integrated capabilities as well as add-on units with DtCs. The standalones will be better integrated with their environments, however, their programmability may be limited to whatever built-in capabilities they possess. Many times, the capabilities are limited to firmware, or limited programming languages, which are not as flexible as those found in the overall DtC software base.

On the other hand, software included in standalone units will often be customized for the job at hand. HP's BASIC, found in their test equipments, provides a variety of useful data acquisition and IEEE 488 interface-oriented commands.

The DtC can give special peripherals a new meaning, but you may have to give up some performance. In the add-on's favor, flexible DtC mass storage and video displays can offer much more control over data. The many different flexible and higher-level programming languages allow unlimited capability for processing data. Database management systems can help you find the data, spreadsheets can help you play numeric games, and graphics software can help you visualize the data. Automatic and other special control can be implemented thorough application-specific and object-oriented languages at levels previously thought to be impossible on the dedicated equipments.

Most of the special equipments described above will have special software support. You must be familiar not only with a processing board's programmable functions, but also with the technical method of using DtC hardware and associated software to complement the functions of a given add-on board. Usage and configuration with other common DtC interfaces such as LANs, hard disks, and video display interfaces will often lead to resource contention problems. Contending resources could include system memory, I/O channels, DMA channels, and interrupts.

Therefore, it is imperative to choose vendors that have a good reputation for technical support of their hardware in association with the particular DtC system you plan to use. Be sure that they can provide the necessary technical information for schematics and troubleshooting.

6.9   *Everyone Wins through Increased Productivity*

At this point you should be able to appreciate how the DtC can provide a powerful basis for integrating the functions of different add-on systems for data acquisition and processing. Peripherals are becoming quite intelligent as evidenced by today's laser printers, which can incorporate mass storage and have built-in PostScript capability as well as an armload of other special functions. Due to the popularity of the DtC and the competitiveness of the industry, we have many choices, and when the choices are made carefully, increased productivity is the payoff.

Subject Index

cut and paste
   data transfer method 362
   Windows feature 304
Cyrex FastMath 83D87
   compared with Intel
     80387 189
   performance 189

D

D/A converters
   (digital to analog converters)
   as function generators 601
   color manipulation 526
   operation 600
daisywheel printers
   compared to dot matrix
     printers 584
   features 583
   font selection 583
   operation 583
   two-headed 583
DARPA
   (Defense Advanced Research
     Projects Agency)
   ARPANET sponsor 406
data
   ASCII representation
     example 125
   integrated with voice 593
data acquisition
   add-ons
     figure 601
   board components 602
   mass storage
     requirements 113
   peripherals 600
data backup
   removable media 492
   software 491
   tape system 458
   UPS 458
data bus
   communication with address
     bus 244
data compatibility
   desktop publisher
     requirements 97
   engineering databases 111
   file transfer problems 97
   process control 113

   text editors 97
data compression
   add-on boards 54
   development trends 158
   drivers 491
   modems 554
   ratios 548
   ratios compared 549
   transmission protocols 555
data decompression
   drivers 491
data direction control
   read/write signals 235
data distribution
   enterprise oriented 437
   level 0 427
   multi-tiered 437
data elements
   context 118
data exchange
   between HP equipment and
     IBM PCs 271
   clipboards 302
   dynamic 363
data fetching
   CPU function 197
data files
   compressed format 121
   separation from programs 135
data formats
   application specific 120
   ASCII 118
   coding 118
   conversion 101
   conversion errors 125
   conversion programs 124
   data transfer 122
   DIF files 120
   encapsulated PostScript 121
   graphics images 106
   language considerations 128
   network software 117
   program specific
     figure 123
   recorded form 116
   summary 130
   types 118
Data General Eclipse
   early minicomputer 39
Data General Nova
   early minicomputer 39
data items
   hardware factors
     table 89

data lines
   buses 233
data locking
   LAN systems 453
data management
   mass storage devices 99
   mass storage requirements 99
data manipulation
   integrated software
     solution 362
data movement
   format representation 122
data processing
   mainframe vs. network 425
data rates
   actual of modems 548
   effective of modems 548
   factors affecting 18
   modem throughputs 548
data sharing
   character-based 360
   examples 360
   merging files 360
   methods 302
   Publish and Subscribe
     feature 386
   software requirements 362
   video memory 361, 362
data storage
   costs 10
   space requirements 476
   strategy 135
data transfer
   between programs 122
   by diskette 405
   by DMA controllers 249
   clipboards 362
   database managers 127
   DMA channels 185
   DMA signals 235
   LAN systems 406
   media independent 117
   over networks 405
   SCSI standard 487
   software requirements 362
   summary 130
   with DESQview 362
   with X Windows 362
data transfer methodology
   media access control 416
data transfer rates
   constraints on 9
   DMA controllers 184
   factors affecting 480

I

J

K

role in graphics input   110
scan code compatibility   566
selection factors   15, 566
serial output   563
types   562
Korn shell
Unix   319

L

M

music hardware
    types 598
music synthesizers
    MIDI 599
musical instrument digital interfaces
    See MIDIs
musical keyboards
    Roland 600
    Yamaha 600
musical sounds
    creation techniques 599

N

N-key rollover
    keyboards 562
Named Pipes
    introduced by Microsoft 452
NAND gate
    description 195
    operation 195
        figure 205
National Security Administration
    See NSA
National Television Standards
 Committee
    See NTSC
near letter quality
    See NLQ
NEC computers
    entertainment applications 85
NetBIOS
    APIs 452
    compatibility questions 452
    connectivity 452
    network services 452
    substitutes for 452
    support 452
NetWare protocol
    Novell 469
network bridges
    operation 422
    types 422
network interface boards
    compatibility problems 146
    contention problems 456
    functions 456
    interaction with
      transceivers 456
network layer
    communications protocols

      table 466
network management protocols
    standards
      table 466
network operating systems
    characteristics 450
    components 449
      figure 450
    LANs 449
    on file servers 449
    peer-to-peer
      configuration 450
    server-resident 450
    shells 449
network printers
    LAN connections 419
network security
    Kerberos 465
network systems
    client-server roles 438
    distributed processing 425
    peripheral sharing 432
    routing between 424
    shortcomings 421
    traffic control 438
    user interfaces 435
network topology
    distributed star
      figure 415
networking
    a revolution 405
    as seen in SAA 377
    current status 470
    future trends 157
    hardware 449
    modem communication 408
    multivendor systems 377
    need for maturation 151
    software 449
    with Unix 321
networking DtCs
    origins 77
networking software
    data flow control 117
    data formats 117
    MacAPPC 70
    MacWorkStation 71
networks
    CAD requirements 111
    graphics transfers 106
    group writing 97
    information management 101
    overview 403
    performance levels 92

    servers 417
    Sprint Telenet 406
    summary 470
    Tymnet 406
neural network technology
    handwriting recognition 576
New Technology
    See NT
NeWS
    (Network/extensible Windows
      System)
    alternative to X Windows 441
NewWave
    HP file manager 305
NIC
    (Network Interface Card)
    features 456
    functions 456
Nike net
    definition 405
Nintendo
    entertainment computers 85
NLQ
    (near letter quality)
    character formation 582
    dot matrix printers 584
nodems
    description 457
    functions 457
noise suppression
    telephone lines 547
notebook computers
    uses 63
Nova
    See Data General Nova
Novell
    IPX protocol 469
    NetWare protocol 469
NSA
    (National Security Adminis-
      tration)
    LAN security standards 464
NT
    (New Technology)
    evolution of Windows 388
NTSC
    (National Television Standards
      Committee)
    display standards 510
NuBus
    See Apple NuBus
null codes
    keyboard controls 120
null modems

Q

R

importance 442
X Windows 444
remote control
of digital computers 546
removable cartridges
overview 492
removable drives
overview 475
removable hard disks
compared to tape systems 506
removable media
comparisons
table 507
data backup 492
overview 475, 492
types compared 507
report utilities
memory usage 351
resolution
television screens 515
TV screens 517
resource ownership
multitasking environment 426
resource sharing
AppleEvents 387
retina
visual acuity 521
rewrite times
CPU deficiencies 8
DtP screens 7
RGB signals
converters 519
Richie, Dennis
Unix development 315
ring
LAN topology 413
RISC technology
speed factor 108
RISCs
(reduced instruction set computers)
advantages 174
characteristics 174
compiler needs 174
engineering software 107
features 175
maximizing benefits 174
production 175
vendors 174
RISC/6000
See IBM R/T6000
RLL
(Run Length Limited format)
hard drives 54

robotics
applications 107
Rockwell AIM 65
8-bit micrcomputer 34
Roland
musical keyboards 600
ROMs
(Read Only Memory)
configuration problems 202
EP computers 201
functions 9, 200
game cartridges 85
minicomputers 201
routines 201
support for 201
rotation rates
Bernoulli cartridges 481
floppy disks 481
hard disks 481
routers
addressing 423
compared to bridges 423
functions 423
LAN connections 423
networking support 424
operation 423
RS-232
(serial interface)
bit rates
table 261
characteristics 257, 258
table 271
conventions 263
detailed implementation
figure 260
for mice 251
for plotters 251
implementation 190
need for 258
operation 254
overview 259
peripherals support 261
pinouts 262
shared by peripherals 265
signal nomenclature
table 263
signals 262
transfer rates
figure 258
troubleshooting 265
used with logic level
converters 258
used with modem
figure 258

RS-232-C standard
problems with 263
R:Base
multiuser database
applications 452

S

SAA
(System Application Architecture)
announcement by IBM 369
communications role 377
networking role 377
principles 369
scanners
See also color scanners
digitizing process 578
drawing programs 578
hand held type 577
overview 577
software 577
stationary bed type 577
scanning signals
functions 512
interlaced 512
schedulers
office systems 454
Scheifler, Robert
V operating system development 444
scientific software
performance levels 93
scratch pads
See electronic scratch pads
screen dumps
to printers 332
screen resolutions
application requirements 19
Script
conversion to PostScript 96
manuscript preparation 96
scripting
communications software 551
computer operations 551
scroll bars
functions 301
scrolling
response times 7
time lags 8
SCSIs